Queensbury, NY 12804

DISCARDED

AFRICA YEARBOOK 2004

AUI Library
64th Bay Road
Queensbury, NY 12804

REFERENCE

AFRICA YEARBOOK 2004

EDITED BY

ANDREAS MEHLER

HENNING MELBER

KLAAS VAN WALRAVEN

BRILL
LEIDEN • BOSTON
2005

This book is printed on acid-free paper.

Library of Congress Cataloging-in-Publication Data

A C.I.P. record for this book is available from the Library of Congress.

ISSN 1871-2525
ISBN 90 04 14462 5

© 2005 by Koninklijke Brill NV, Leiden, The Netherlands

All rights reserved. No part of this publication may be reproduced, translated,
stored in a retrieval system, or transmitted in any form or by any means,
electronic, mechanical, photocopying, recording or otherwise, without
prior written permission from the publisher.

Authorization to photocopy items for internal or personal use is
granted by Brill provided that the appropriate fees are paid directly to
The Copyright Clearance Center, 222 Rosewood Drive,
Suite 910, Danvers, MA 01923, USA.
Fees are subject to change.

PRINTED IN THE NETHERLANDS

Contents

Preface

This *Africa Yearbook* is a joint undertaking by the African Studies Centre in Leiden (ASC), the Institute of African Affairs in Hamburg (IAK) and the Nordic Africa Institute in Uppsala (NAI). It has its origins in a German *Afrika Jahrbuch* that has been produced by IAK for the past 17 years. In May 2003, the Africa-Europe Group for Interdisciplinary Studies (AEGIS), a network of European academics working on Africa, encouraged the three centres to publish an *Africa Yearbook* with a wider international appeal. IAK, ASC and NAI – all very active AEGIS centres sharing similar profiles – accepted this challenge. The edition for the year 2004 is the first of what we hope will be a long series to come.

The country-specific articles cover domestic political developments, foreign policy and socioeconomic trends in sub-Saharan African states in the calendar year under review. The *Africa Yearbook* also contains articles on each of four sub-regions, focusing on major cross-border developments and sub-regional organisations. In addition, one article analyses continental developments while another addresses European-African relations. While the editors recognise the impossibility of finding a fully objective indicator of the comparative importance of each sub-Saharan state, the length of each country-specific article aims to reflect the approximate relative political, economic and/or demographic weight of each country.

While the *Yearbook* is based on scholarly work, it is oriented towards a wider target-readership, including students, politicians, diplomats, administrators, journalists, teachers, practitioners in the field of development aid as well as businesspeople. Thanks to the support of the three partner institutions, it can be offered at a price attractive to this broad readership. The volume is primarily concerned with providing factual (though not necessarily neutral) information. In contrast to other publications, each issue of the *Africa Yearbook*, in focusing on developments during a particular calendar year, will provide a completely fresh annual overview of events.

We wish to express our gratitude to all the contributors for their collaboration in this endeavour; to the partner institutions in AEGIS for encouraging us to embark on this ambitious project; to Peter Colenbrander for his meticulous language editing; to Sylvia Steege for her unfailing coordinating assistance; to Brill Publishers for taking such professional care of publishing matters; and last but not least to our three institutions for providing the necessary support and opportunities to allow us to turn this idea into a reality.

The Editors
(Hamburg, Leiden and Uppsala, June 2005)

List of Abbreviations

ABN	Autorité du Bassin du Niger (Niamey)
ACP	Africa, Caribbean, and Pacific Group of Countries (Lomé/Cotonou Agreement)
ADB	African Development Bank (Abidjan)
ADF	African Development Fund (Abidjan)
AFD	Agence Française de Développement (Paris)
AGOA	African Growth and Opportunity Act
APRM	African Peer Review Mechanism
AU	African Union (Addis Ababa)
BCEAO	Banque Centrale des Etats de l'Afrique de l'Ouest (Dakar)
BEAC	Banque des Etats de l'Afrique Centrale (Yaoundé)
CAR	Central African Republic
CBLT	Commission du Bassin du Lac Tchad (N'Djaména)
CEEAC	Communauté Economique des Etats de l'Afrique Centrale (Libreville) = ECCAS
CEMAC	Communauté Economique et Monétaire de l'Afrique Centrale
CEN-SAD	Community of Sahel-Saharan States (Tripoli)
CEPGL	Communauté Economique des Pays des Grands Lacs (Gisenyi/Rwanda)
CFAfr	Franc de la Communauté Financière Africaine (UEMOA; BEAC)
COMESA	Common Market for Eastern and Southern Africa (Lusaka)
CPLP	Comunidade dos Países de Língua Portuguesa
DAC	Development Assistance Committee (Paris)
DDR	Disarmament, Demobilisation and Reintegration
DRC	Democratic Republic of Congo
EAC	East African Community
ECA	United Nations Economic Commission for Africa (Addis Ababa)
ECCAS	Economic Community of Central African States (Libreville)
ECOWAS	Economic Community of West African States (Abuja)
ECOMOG	ECOWAS Ceasefire Monitoring Group
EDF	European Development Fund (Brussels)
EIB	European Investment Bank (Luxemburg)
ESAF	Enhanced Structural Adjustment Facility (IMF)
EU	European Union (Brussels)

FAO	Food and Agricultural Organisation of the United Nations (Rome)
FTA	Free Trade Area
GDP	Gross Domestic Product
HIPC	Heavily Indebted Poor Countries
IDA	International Development Association (Washington)
IDP	Internally Displaced Person
IFAD	International Fund for Agricultural Development (Rome)
IFC	International Finance Corporation (Washington)
IGAD	Intergovernmental Authority on Development (Djibouti)
ILO	International Labour Organisation (Geneva)
IMF	International Monetary Fund (Washington)
IOC	Indian Ocean Commission (Quatre Bornes)
IORARC	Indian Ocean Rim Association for Regional Cooperation (Port Louis)
MDGs	Millennium Development Goals
MRU	Mano River Union (Freetown)
NEPAD	New Partnership for Africa's Development
NGO	Non-Governmental Organisation
OECD	Organisation for Economic Cooperation and Development (Paris)
OIC	Organisation of the Islamic Conference (Jeddah)
OPEC	Organisation of Petroleum Exporting Countries (Vienna)
PALOP	Países Africanos de Lingua Oficial Portugesa
PRSP	Poverty Reduction Strategy Paper
PTA	Preferential Trade Area for Eastern and Southern African States (Lusaka)
SACU	Southern African Customs Union (Pretoria)
SADC	Southern African Development Community (Gaborone)
SAF	Structural Adjustment Facility (IMF)
SDR	Special Drawing Right (IMF)
STABEX	Stabilisation of export earnings from agricultural commodities (Lomé Agreement)
SYSMIN	Special financing facility for mining products (Lomé Agreement)
UAE	United Arab Emirates
UEMOA	Union Économique et Monétaire Ouest-Africaine (Ouagadougou)
UMA	Union du Maghreb Arabe
UMOA	Union Monétaire Ouest-Africaine (Dakar)
UN	United Nations (New York)
UNCTAD	United Nations Conference on Trade and Development (Geneva)
UNDP	United Nations Development Programme (New York)
UNEP	United Nations Environment Programme (Nairobi)
UNESCO	United Nations Educational, Scientific and Cultural Organisation (Paris)
UNHCR	United Nations High Commissioner for Refugees (Geneva)

UNICEF	United Nations Children's Fund (New York)
USAID	United States Agency for International Development (Washington)
WFP	World Food Programme (Rome)
WHO	World Health Organisation (Geneva)
WTO	World Trade Organisation (Geneva)

Factual Overview (as of 31 December 2004)

West Africa						
Country	Area (in sq km)	Population (in m)	Currency	HDI	Head of State	Prime Minister
Benin	112,622	6.7	CFA Franc	0.421	Mathieu Kérékou	
Burkina Faso	274,122	12.1	CFA Franc	0.302	Blaise Compaoré	Paramango Ernest Yonli
Cape Verde	4,033	0.5	Cape Verdean Escudo	0.717	Pedro Pires	José Maria Pereira Neves
Côte d'Ivoire	322,462	16.8	CFA Franc	0.399	Laurent Gbagbo	Seydou Diarra
Gambia	11,295	1.4	Dalasi	0.452	Yahya Jammeh	
Ghana	238,500	20.4	Cedi	0.568	John Agyekum Kufuor	
Guinea	245,857	7.9	Guinean Franc	0.425	Lansana Conté	Cellou Dalein Diallo
Guinea-Bissau	36,125	1.5	CFA Franc	0.350	Henrique Pereira Rosa	Carlos Gomes Júnior
Liberia	111,370	3.4	Liberian Dollar		Gyude Bryant	
Mali	1,240,000	11.7	CFA Franc	0.326	Amadou Toumani Touré	Ousmane Issoufi Maïga
Mauritania	1,030,700	2.7	Ouguiya	0.465	Maaouiya Ould Sid Ahmed Taya	Sghair Ould M'Bareck
Niger	1,267,000	11.8	CFA Franc	0.292	Mamadou Tandja	Hama Amadou
Nigeria	923,768	135.6	Naira	0.466	Olusegun Obasanjo	
Senegal	196,192	10.0	CFA Franc	0.437	Abdoulaye Wade	Macky Sall
Sierra Leone	71,740	5.3	Leone	0.273	Ahmad Tejan Kabbah	
Togo	56,785	4.9	CFA Franc	0.495	Gnassingbe Eyadéma	Koffi Sama

Central Africa

Country	Area (in sq km)	Population (in m)	Currency	HDI	Head of State	Prime Minister
Cameroon	475,442	16.1	CFA Franc	0.501	Paul Biya	Ephraim Inoni
Central African Republic	622,984	3.9	CFA Franc	0.361	François Bozizé	Célestine Le Roi Gaombalet
Chad	1,284,000	8.6	CFA Franc	0.379	Idriss Déby	Moussa Faki
Congo	342,000	3.8	CFA Franc	0.494	Denis Sassou-Nguesso	
DRC	2,344,855	53.2	Congolese Franc	0.365	Joseph Kabila	
Equatorial Guinea	28,051	0.5	CFA Franc	0.703	Teodoro Obiang Nguema Mbasogo	Miguel Abia Biteo Borico
Gabon	267,667	1.3	CFA Franc	0.648	El-Hadj Omar Bongo Ondimba	Jean-François Ntoutoume Émane
São Tomé and Príncipe	1,001	0.2	Dobra	0.645	Fradique de Menezes	Damião Vaz d'Almeida

Eastern Africa

Country	Area (in sq km)	Population (in m)	Currency	HDI	Head of State	Prime Minister
Burundi	27,834	7.2	Burundi Franc	0.339	Domitien Ndayizeye	
Comoros	2,166	0.6	Comoran Franc	0.530	Assoumani Azali	
Djibouti	21,783	0.7	Djiboutian Franc	0.454	Ismail Omar Guelleh	Dileita Mohamed Dileita
Eritrea	125,000	4.4	Nakfa	0.439	Isaias Afwerki	
Ethiopia	1,121,900	68.6	Birr	0.359	Girma Wolde-Giyorgis Lucha	Meles Zenawi
Kenya	582,646	31.9	Kenyan Shilling	0.488	Mwai Kibaki	
Rwanda	26,338	8.3	Rwandan Franc	0.431	Paul Kagame	Bernard Makuza
Seychelles	444	0.1	Seychelles Rupee	0.853	James Alix Michel	
Somalia	637,657	9.6	Somali Shilling	n.d.	Abdulahi Yusuf Ahmed (Somaliland: Dahir Riyale Kahin; Puntland: Mohamed Abdi Hashi)	Ali Muhammad Ghedi
Sudan	2,505,805	33.5	Sudanese Dinar	0.505	Omar Hassan Ahmad al-Bashir	
Tanzania	945,087	35.9	Tanzanian Shilling	0.407	Benjamin William Mkapa	Frederick Sumaye
Uganda	236,036	25.3	Ugandan Shilling	0.493	Yoweri Kaguta Museveni	Apolo Nsibambi

Southern Africa

Country	Area (in sq km)	Population (in m)	Currency	HDI	Head of State	Prime Minister
Angola	1,246,700	13.5	Kwanza	0.381	José Eduardo dos Santos	Fernando da Piedade Días dos Santos ("Nando")
Botswana	581,730	1.7	Pula	0.589	Festus Gontebanye Mogae	
Lesotho	30,355	1.8	Loti	0.493	King Letsie III	Pakalitha Mosisili
Madagascar	587,041	16.9	Malagasy Franc	0.469	Marc Ravalo-manana	Jacques Sylla
Malawi	118,484	11.0	Kwacha	0.388	Bingu wa Mutharika	
Mauritius	1,865	1.2	Mauritius Rupee	0.785	Sir Anerooth Jugnauth	Paul Raimond Bérenger
Mozambique	801,590	18.8	Métical	0.354	Joaquim Alberto Chissanó	Luisa Dias Diogo
Namibia	824,292	2.0	Namibian Dollar	0.607	Sam Shafishuna Nujoma	Theo Ben Gurirab
South Africa	1,121,038	45.3	Rand	0.666	Thabo Mvuyelwa Mbeki	
Swaziland	17,363	1.1	Lilangeni	0.519	King Mswati III	Absalom Themba Dlamini
Zambia	752,614	10.4	Kwacha	0.389	Levy Patrick Mwanawasa	
Zimbabwe	390,759	13.1	Zimbabwe Dollar	0.491	Robert Gabriel Mugabe	

I. Sub-Saharan Africa

During the year, a variety of local, sub-regional, continental and global events gave off different signals. At times, there were indications of measurable achievements in terms of advancing African interests, but there were, in contrast, also setbacks. Inadequate performance continued to be the hallmark of many African economies, while conflicts still raged in many sub-regions, notably Central and West Africa and Sudan's western province of Darfur. Sub-Saharan Africa remained overall the least developed and most impoverished region in the world, though initiatives to overcome the constraints and address the challenges were apparent.

African Union

The **African Union** (AU) continued to expand its institutional architecture, despite unresolved budgetary issues. This also cast a shadow over the growing peacekeeping role ascribed to the organisation and so desired by Western donors, the AU Commission and several of its member states. Thus, some bold decisions were taken to create new institutions or organs or to launch new policy initiatives. In some cases, these decisions were actually implemented, but without addressing the underlying financial implications. These were, furthermore, complicated by the perennial arrears in contributions from member states and the frequent failure of Western donors to make good on past financial pledges.

On 18 March, the **Pan-African Parliament** was formally inaugurated in the Ethiopian capital of Addis Ababa. This fulfilled a promise made back in the early 1990s and, for the first time, provided the continental organisation, with a permanent forum for voices outside the strictly (inter-)governmental sphere. In July, heads of state decided to establish the parliament's permanent headquarters in Cape Town, South Africa. With five MPs delegated by each national parliament, the 265-strong parliament was given only deliberative and consultative powers for the time being. It was, nevertheless, hoped that the parliament, chaired by Gertrude Mongella of Tanzania, would make the AU's government-dominated executive organs more accountable.

It was reported that the parliament's existence would add another $ 30 m to the AU's budget. This came on top of the price tags for other new institutions not yet up and running, such as the court of justice ($ 3 m) and the economic, social and cultural council ($ 9 m). While only $ 13 m of the 2004 budget had been received by the time of the summit of heads of state in Addis Ababa (6–8 July), with several countries facing the theoretical possibility of sanctions (i.e., loss of voting rights), the chairman of the commission, Alpha Oumar Konaré, nevertheless launched one of the most **ambitious programmes for the continental organisation** ever. This plan, intended to propel Africa into the 21st century, would cost some $ 1.7 bn to accomplish and involve a doubling of the organisation's headquarters staff, raising the commission's operating costs to approximately $ 130 m a year. Konaré pleaded for an annual budget of $ 600 m, much of which would go to finance the AU's projected collective security arrangement (see below). He suggested that member states reserve 0.5% of their national budgets to fund AU activities. In a style characteristic of African continental politics, the heads of state endorsed Konaré's plan but refused to commit themselves to its financial implications, referring the matter to the executive council, which later approved a **fourfold budget increase** for 2005 from $ 43 m to $ 158 m. While this did not remotely approach Konaré's requested $ 600 m, it was decided that $ 63 m of the budget would have to come from obligatory contributions by member states, the other $ 95 m to be requested from wealthy members such as Libya or Western donors. With $ 75 m of the 2005 budget projected for peace and security issues alone, the AU in effect confronted Western donors in particular with the financial implications of their much-favoured slogan, 'African solutions to African problems'.

The AU's official policies on defence and security appeared to take several steps forward when its Peace and Security Council (PSC), whose protocol came into force on 26 December 2003, was solemnly launched at a meeting in Addis Ababa on 25 May ('Africa Day'). Earlier in the year, on 20–21 January, African defence ministers adopted a plan for a common defence and security policy that would include an African peacekeeping force of 10,000 to 15,000 troops. This **African Standby Force** (ASF) was endorsed by the heads of state at a special meeting in the Libyan town of Sirte (27–28 February) and would comprise troops from several countries, including South Africa, Nigeria, Egypt and Kenya. Uganda also offered troops through an East African arrangement that would become part of the ASF, which would comprise four sub-regional brigades of 4,020 soldiers each. The standby force was to operate under the PSC, which, contrary to many reports, only has a mandate in 'peace support' operations (which presumably require the consent of the member state concerned). Decisions about more forceful military actions in cases of war crimes, crimes against humanity or genocide are reserved for the AU's Assembly.

The projected peacekeeping role was first put to the test with the unfolding disaster in **Darfur**. While the UN Security Council did not get beyond issuing verbal threats against the Sudanese government, the AU Assembly decided at its July meeting to send an armed protection force of 300 men to the troubled Sudanese region (African Union Mission in Sudan, AMIS). Its initial role would be to protect the 60 AU officials monitoring a ceasefire hammered out between the Sudanese government and two rebel movements rather than to shield the civilian population from attacks by armed groups. The size of the force was clearly insufficient to help restore stability to the huge Darfur region, and it took several months before the troops, from Rwanda and Nigeria, arrived on the scene. On 20 October, the PSC decided to enhance the force's mandate to include the protection of the civilian population. The force was expanded but by the end of the year still stood at less than a quarter of the projected total (3,000 to 4,000). While the Darfur operation was estimated to cost some $ 26 m, only $ 1.6 m had been paid into the AU's peace fund by July.

The deployment of troops was part of a wider AU concern with the crisis in Sudan, a concern that was given concrete expression in a ceasefire agreement brokered and signed at AU headquarters between the Sudanese government and the two rebel movements on 28 May. This was a follow-up to the ceasefire agreed between the Sudanese forces in N'Djaména on 8 April. The PSC concerned itself with this matter at several of its meetings, while Nigerian President Obasanjo, elected chairman of the AU's Assembly at its summit in July, convened talks between the belligerent forces in Abuja on 23 August, in the presence of Commission Chairman Konaré. These talks went on intermittently for the rest of the year, without a fundamental breakthrough being achieved regarding security on the ground. Thus, in the course of new talks held in Abuja from 10 to 21 December, Konaré expressed concern about the **deterioration of security** as a result of numerous ceasefire violations.

Other issues on the AU agenda concerned the continuing crisis in eastern DR Congo, Côte d'Ivoire, Burundi, Somalia and Zimbabwe, among others. Some of these problems were tackled more directly by other organisations or countries, such as the UN, ECOWAS and France. President Mbeki of South Africa, as AU representative, mediated in the Ivorian conflict with limited success.

The AU's summit in July also discussed the **rights of women**, pleading for a strategy to improve the situation of women, as well as AIDS-related issues and the social dimension of globalisation, among other subjects. The continent's aspiration for its own seat in the UN Security Council has so far proved divisive, with diplomatic wrangling between some of the AU's leading countries (South Africa, Nigeria, Egypt) as to who would be entitled to the seat in the event that such permanent African representation was achieved.

The New Partnership for Africa's Development (NEPAD)

During the year, NEPAD implemented the first steps of the **African Peer Review Mechanism** (APRM), which is considered an essential innovation and important tool for achieving more collective responsibility among African states. On 13 February, Rwanda's President Kagame hosted in Kigali the first summit of the committee of participating heads of state and government in the African Peer Review Mechanism (APR Forum). The heads of state from the Republic of Congo, Ethiopia, Gabon, Ghana, Mozambique, Nigeria, Rwanda, Senegal and South Africa attended this inaugural meeting. President Kagame expressed the view that the APRM would offer assistance in tackling the challenges of governance. Nigeria's President Obasanjo, as chairperson of the Heads of State and Government Implementation Committee (HSGIC) of NEPAD, was unanimously elected chairperson of the APR Forum. The forum endorsed the appointment of Marie-Angelique

Savané of Senegal as the chairperson of the **APR Panel** of Eminent Persons for a one-year-period. The panel has a further six members from Algeria (for North Africa), Cameroon (for Central Africa), Kenya (for East Africa), Mozambique (for Southern Africa), Nigeria (for West Africa) and South Africa (also for Southern Africa). It is tasked with facilitating the implementation of the APRM and ensuring the integrity of the process. With two representatives each from West and Southern Africa, the panel reflects in its composition the leading role played by the presidents of Nigeria, Senegal and South Africa in the establishment of NEPAD. The APRM is defined as "an instrument voluntarily acceded to by Member States of the African Union as an African self-monitoring mechanism." To facilitate the process, the APR Panel submitted a questionnaire for a country self-assessment for the APRM. Its four major sections correspond to the four areas identified as relevant to the APRM: 1) democracy and good political governance; 2) economic governance and management; 3) corporate governance; and 4) socioeconomic development. The APR Forum had – in line with the claim to African ownership of the process – at its inaugural meeting in Kigali approved a minimum contribution of $ 100,000 by each participating country towards the operationalisation of the APRM.

In a presentation to a NEPAD stakeholder dialogue in Johannesburg (22–23 October) on the occasion of the initiative's third anniversary, the NEPAD Executive Secretary Wiseman Nkuhlu (previously economic advisor to South Africa's President Thabo Mbeki) pointed out that 24 African countries (including North Africa) already had signed the APRM Memorandum of Understanding and thereby volunteered to be reviewed by their peers. During the year, the APRM was initiated with Ghana, Rwanda, Mauritius and Kenya. The first **APRM support missions** took place on 24 to 29 May (Ghana), in June (Rwanda and Mauritius), and on 26 and 27 July (Kenya). The second group to be reviewed in the near future consists of six countries, Algeria, Mali, Mozambique, Nigeria, Senegal and South Africa.

At the **third ordinary session** of the **AU Assembly** of heads of state and government in Addis Ababa (6 to 8 July), the chairperson of the 15-member HSIGC, Obasanjo, warned that "unfulfilled commitments" by rich nations could pose one of the greatest threats to the envisaged development of Africa through NEPAD. He called on wealthy countries to move beyond rhetoric and start taking action and warned of the "crippling capacity gaps" hampering NEPAD's planning and the implementation of its development programmes at all levels. A progress report indicated a new emphasis on the Regional Economic Communities (RECs) as a strategic shift towards closer collaboration with existing sub-regional bodies. Progress was noted in the implementation of **sectoral priorities** with sub-regional perspectives. Most prominent among these are the Comprehensive African Agriculture Development Programme (CAADP) and the Short Term Action Plan (STAP) for infrastructure, including telecommunications, transport routes, power supply schemes and shared river basins. Both initiatives managed to secure considerable external financing. The FAO funds medium-term investment programmes to fast-track the implementation of

CAADP, while the World Bank provided $ 500 m to the Multi-country Agricultural Productivity Programme (MAPP). The ADB approved financing for nine investment projects under STAP, amounting to $ 580 m, and the World Bank approved financing for STAP projects to a total of $ 570 m. However, as was noted in the communiqué issued at the end of the 10th summit of the HSGIC in Maputo (23 May), the total budget required from external resources to fund all NEPAD infrastructure projects would amount to $ 8.1 bn.

Support by the United Nations was reiterated in a report by the Secretary-General submitted to the 59th session of the UN General Assembly on 4 August (A/59/206). A 13-member advisory panel monitors international support to NEPAD through the UN system, including technical assistance for institutional development, capacity building, project development, resource mobilisation and advocacy. The UN Economic Commission for Africa (ECA) provides leadership for the regional consultation meetings of UN agencies with the aim of establishing thematic clusters for NEPAD priority areas. The report recommended more efforts towards coherence in the international community's support for Africa's development agenda, as well as an increase in donor funding. It stressed the need for a strengthened partnership in which African countries deepen their commitment to the priorities of NEPAD.

This could be read as a diplomatically phrased reservation, shared by critical observers both on the continent and outside, that NEPAD might not meet the original expectations had of it. NEPAD organs continued to abstain from critical comment or other forms of interference with regard to **Zimbabwe**. The deteriorating situation there was considered to be a litmus test for the notions of good governance stressed by NEPAD, combined with the emphasis on collective responsibility versus national sovereignty. Owing to the avoidance of a critical stand with regard to the Zimbabwean crisis, however, donors started to question the political will and determination of the NEPAD architects to honour the commitment expressed in the document. In the absence of subsequent actions, policy statements were increasingly seen as mere lip service to noble goals rather than as directives for serious initiatives. The visible shift in priorities towards material infrastructure projects over policy issues gave additional reason for questioning the determination to implement the original political agenda. As a result, external financial support for NEPAD failed to match original expectations. Senegal's President Wade expressed his frustration at the **NEPAD stakeholder dialogue** held on 22–23 October in Johannesburg by stating, "We are spending an enormous amount of time and money on conferences, but . . . we have not had one single (project) that has been realised."

Before the end of the year, the **12th HSGIC summit** met in Algiers, the capital of one of the five founding member states of the initiative (23 November). The heads of state of Algeria, Botswana, Republic of Congo, Egypt, Mali, Nigeria, Rwanda, South Africa and São Tomé and Príncipe attended. To accelerate the implementation of NEPAD, the summit identified the following goals: 1) increased development assistance; 2) debt cancellation; 3) increased access to markets of the North without insistence on reciprocity; 4) the pooling of resources provided by partners; 5) effective engagement with the UK Commission for Africa and in the implementation of the G8 Africa Action Plan; and 6) use of the 5th anniversary of the MDGs to achieve tangible results. The integration of NEPAD into AU structures and processes was mentioned separately in the final communiqué. One critical issue was the continued operation of the NEPAD secretariat out of offices based at the Development Bank of Southern Africa (DBSA) in Midrand (between Pretoria and Johannesburg). This contributed to reservations that the initiative was being too much driven and dominated by South Africa. Recommendations that NEPAD move physically to the AU underlined the continuance of suspicions within the family of African states that the initiative is being used to promote the particular interests of a minority of states who wish to pursue their own agendas within a continentally defined framework.

Africa and Globalities

In November, the World Bank issued a gloomy assessment of Africa's economic perfor-mance in 2004. While the continent reaped the benefit of booming commodity prices, the effect was more than offset by rising oil prices, from which, however, some African oil-pro-ducing countries benefited enormously. Although per capita incomes were expected to increase modestly, the increase was not enough to catch up with other parts of the world. The growth rate, which in November was estimated by the IMF at 4.5% for sub-Saharan Africa, would not be sufficient to meet Millennium Development Goals on poverty reduc-tion, health and education. Ineffective economic structures and inefficient government spending were still considered a fundamental problem.

As in other recent years, the world's leading industrial powers in the **Group of 8** (G8) discussed African issues. Six African countries (Algeria, Ghana, Nigeria, Senegal, South Africa and Uganda) were represented at the summit's African session, held at the US Sea Island resort in June. The results were widely viewed as disappointing since, despite British backing, the industrial countries refused to agree to a comprehensive write-off of multilat-eral debt owed by the Heavily Indebted Poor Countries (HIPC), most of which are in Africa. So far, only $ 30 bn of a total of $ 100 bn of multilateral debt had been forgiven, with even the IMF and World Bank admitting that the HIPC scheme had fallen short of expectations. The G8 agreed to expand funding for the existing HIPC scheme and to extend it until the end of 2006. As part of its Africa Outreach plan, the summit also vowed to create a global HIV/AIDS vaccine initiative, intended to help coordinate scientific research into finding an effective treatment for the disease. In the area of conflict, the G8 agreed to launch a multi-year scheme (until 2010) to train 50,000 to 75,000 African troops for peacekeeping missions on the continent. In part, this initiative was intended to coordinate existing training pro-grammes offered by the US, Britain and France. Nevertheless, world leaders did not dis-cuss such issues as Zimbabwe, while the bloodshed in Darfur merely triggered a call for the

UN to take the lead in stabilising the situation in Sudan, while the UN, in turn, left the matter to the African Union.

In contrast, the **WTO** made a more tangible step forward when one of its trade panels ruled that American **cotton subsidies** ($ 3 bn) distort international trade. These subsidies have been particularly detrimental to cotton producers in some poor West African countries. While the US appealed the decision, which is expected to be upheld by the WTO, a group of poor countries led by Rwanda struck a deal with the Americans in Geneva on 31 July to conduct separate negotiations on cotton subsidies and trade. By the same token, the WTO pressed the EU to cut its subsidies to sugar farmers further, a programme strongly defended by poor African, Caribbean and Pacific countries whose **sugar exports** are bought up by the EU at more than three times the world price.

United Nations and Peacekeeping

Despite its ineffectual stance on Darfur, **UN peacekeeping operations** commenced or continued in several countries, including Sierra Leone, Liberia, Côte d'Ivoire, Eritrea, Ethiopia, Burundi and Congo. From April to September, the UN Mission in Sierra Leone (UNAM-SIL) gradually handed over control of security to the country's police and army. Once the biggest UN peacekeeping operation in the world, UNAMSIL's size was reduced to some 8,000 men by autumn and was expected to drop to 3,500 by the end of the year. Although initially projected to be withdrawn from the country by the end of 2004, the Security Council extended the mission's mandate until July 2005 in view of security worries in Liberia and Guinea and doubts about the ability of the Sierra Leonean government to face up to potential external threats. The UN's Liberian operation, UNMIL (UN Mission in Liberia), some 10,000 to 15,000 men strong, was engaged in overseeing a protracted disarmament exercise as part of the country's attempts to achieve a return to peaceful politics, with elections scheduled for 2005. Little if any coordination in security matters occurred between the UN operations in Sierra Leone and Côte d'Ivoire, whose security problems frequently spilled across the forested international borders. The UN Mission in Côte d'Ivoire (UNOCI, 6,240 men), which ran in parallel with the UN-approved French presence and integrated former ECOWAS contingents, was approved by the Security Council on 27 February, with deployment beginning in April. The Security Council also imposed an arms embargo on the country (15 November) as a consequence of Ivorian government attacks on French peacekeepers on 4 November. By the end of the year, none of the international forces had managed to break the deadlock in the Ivorian conflict. The UN Observation Mission in Congo (MONUC) continued to experience serious difficulties. Although the Security Council agreed, on 1 October, to expand the peacekeeping force by over 5,000 men to a total of 11,000 and beef up its mandate, it was unable to put an end to the violence by various militias or the interference of neighbouring countries such as Rwanda. A sex-abuse scandal further tainted MONUC's standing, already impaired by its inability to protect the civilian population in the volatile eastern region. By the end of the year, in the wake of the emerging peace deal between the Sudan People's Liberation Army (SPLA) and the Sudanese government, a new UN force was projected to be installed in the south of the country. A special Security Council meeting in Nairobi on 19 November welcomed the signing by the Sudanese parties of further arrangements detailing their peace agreement. This was notwithstanding the UN's ineffectual stance on Darfur, which was partly the responsibility of China and Russia. Both countries have major economic interests in Sudan (arms exports and importation of Sudanese oil) and consequently opposed sanctions against Khartoum. The UN Mission to Ethiopia and Eritrea (UNMEE) continued to patrol the border region disputed by the two countries, with little progress towards genuine peace being achieved. Finally, on 21 May, the Security Council approved the deployment of 5,650 military personnel as part of the UN Operation in Burundi (UNOB). This was to take over from the under-funded AU African Mission in Burundi (AMIB), which consisted of 2,870 troops from Ethiopia, Mozambique and South Africa and was mandated to oversee the implementation of ceasefire agreements; support disarmament, demobilisation and the reintegration of combatants; and ensure favourable conditions for the establishment of the UN mission.

Peace and War

War continued to affect the lives of many African people. UNHCR provided support for about 3.1 m refugees (4.6 m in the previous year), primarily from Sudan, Burundi, Sudan, DR Congo, Somalia, Liberia and Angola. Tanzania remained the country with the highest number of refugees (approx. 690,000) on its soil. In West and Central Africa and in the Horn there were ongoing violent conflicts. Only the region of Southern Africa was untroubled by escalations. The complex cross-border conflict situation in the Great Lakes region was only seemingly pacified, with numerous small-scale violent incidents continuing. Most attention was attracted by the Darfur conflict. In Côte d'Ivoire, French troops were placed in an awkward position – as peacekeepers, saviours of French interests and as 'neo-colonial oppressors'.

The Great Lakes region once again had its share of armed violence: in DR Congo violence escalated again at the end of May in Bukavu (South Kivu), with fights between government and dissident army troops, the latter obviously supported by Rwanda. Congolese Tutsi fled the war-torn area across the border to Burundi. Their camp was attacked in August under mysterious circumstances and approximately 160 people were murdered. New fighting was reported in North Kivu in December. Ten thousand civilians fled until a ceasefire came into effect on 21 December.

One positive development was a basic agreement between the governments of DR Congo, Rwanda and Uganda during a meeting in Kampala that included the disarmament within a year of groups operating from their respective territories against neighbouring states. Nevertheless, Uganda and Rwanda deployed troops along their common border. A joint declaration of eleven heads of states aimed at ending the conflicts in the Great Lakes region was signed in Dar es Salaam (20 November). In addition, the peace process between northern and southern **Sudan** made significant progress. The core of the new relationship was an agreement on the allocation of benefits from natural resources that was signed in Naivasha, Kenya on 5 January. This should have meant the end of a conflict that had raged for at least 21 years. However, in January, new fighting broke out in the Darfur region in the west and escalated into a new war. In March, the so-called Janjaweed militias extended their assaults and plundered hundreds of villages, murdering their inhabitants. Given the situation of ongoing killing, US Secretary of State Colin Powell stated on 9 September that genocide had taken place in Darfur. According to the UN, half of Darfur's six million people were directly affected by the conflict. The death toll was variously estimated: while the lowest reliable number was 70,000, in December Caritas estimated the number of deaths to be 180,000.

Contradictory developments were reported from still unpacified **Somalia**. On the one hand, there were new local conflicts (the battle at Kismayo in September and fights between Somaliland and Puntland over a disputed border line in October). On the other hand, it was possible to establish a transition government in Kenya (22 August). Tensions remained high between Ethiopia and Eritrea, without however, any further escalation.

With the government's attacks on northern positions on 4 November, the 'frozen' civil war in **Côte d'Ivoire** escalated. At first, the UN peacekeeping force and the related French mission (4,000 troops) did not adequately counter the attack. On 6 November, the Ivorian air force bombed the town of Bouaké, the rebel stronghold, and launched an apparently targeted attack on a French military camp there. During the attack, nine French soldiers and one US citizen died. The African Union and the UN Security Council both discussed sanctions against members of the regime. The violent outbreak precipitated a new wave of refugees into Liberia, where the ceasefire agreement between government and the two rebel movements remained shaky.

Democracy and Elections

Eleven national elections (plus one constitutional referendum) were held. They could be interpreted in different ways – some were steps towards consolidating fragile democracies, others as evidence of a blockage in the transition process.

Parliamentary elections in **South Africa** (14 April) led to the consolidation of the ruling party, combined with decreasing voter participation. Instead of characterising the free multiparty election as proof of the further consolidation of democracy ten years after the ending of apartheid, some commentators stressed the perils of the overwhelming dominance of one party. Thabo Mbeki was re-elected as president for a second term. One more recent phenomenon has been increasing acceptance of **constitutional limitations** on the number of consecutive presidential terms (usually two terms). Presidential and parliamentary elections in **Malawi** (20 May) ended with a slight shift in power. In **Namibia**, too, (15–16 November), President Nujoma, in office since independence, was not allowed to participate. Parliamentary and presidential elections in **Mozambique** (1–2 December) proceeded along similar lines, though they were heavily criticised by international observers for the irregularities and intimidation. President Chissano was not allowed to stand a third time as a candidate. Low expectations accompanied elections in notorious authoritarian systems: unfree parliamentary elections in **Equatorial Guinea** (25 April) were boycotted by the main opposition parties. An election of a less exciting nature was also held in **Cameroon** (11 October), where only about half the citizens of voting age were enrolled on the lists.

No major changes occurred in the course of parliamentary elections in **Botswana** (30 October), perceived as one of the oldest democracies on the continent.

Two other elections were viewed as part of a transition process: Parliamentary elections were held on the **Comoros** (14 and 21 March, 18 and 25 April). The result was a 'cohabitation' situation, with president and government from different political families. As a result of parliamentary elections in **Guinea-Bissau** (28–30 March), the former ruling party made a strong return to the political stage by winning 45 of 100 seats, more than any of its rivals. The return to civilian government, however, would only be accomplished with the presidential elections to be held in March 2005. One positive development was the gradual consolidation of the crisis-ridden democracy in **Niger**, following two rounds of parliamentary and presidential elections (16 November, 4 December). As favourably viewed were parliamentary and presidential elections in **Ghana** (7 December).

Succession crises in authoritarian states in which the rulers had serious health problems became more apparent. The rules of succession were obviously not clear and had already led to public discussion in some cases (Guinea, Chad, Togo, Cameroon and potentially Burkina Faso or Gabon).

Overall, instead of a democratic breakthrough (such as in Kenya in 2003), there were no uniform developments in 2004: there were some encouraging trends towards democratic consolidation but there was also the consolidation of some authoritarian regimes.

Coup Attempts and the Struggle Against Terrorism

There were several new signs of the inherent weakness of several African states in 2004. Four attempted coups d'état were recorded. A coup attempt in Equatorial Guinea, in which approx. 80 mercenaries from all over the world (especially South Africa) and the son of former British Prime Minister Thatcher were involved, was the most spectacular. The plane carrying the mercenaries was stopped in Zimbabwe's capital Harare. In Guinea-Bissau, a mutiny ended with the murder of the joint chief of staff and with the mutineers' demands being met by the government. In **Chad**, an attempted military insurrection was reported in

May, but government was immediately able to bring it under control. In **Mauritania**, a putsch attempt in 2003 was followed by two further attempts in 2004 (August and September). As already noted, the question of succession in several authoritarian states on the continent became acute. The personalised nature of power meant that the illness of heads of state in Guinea, Togo, Chad and Cameroon represented a threat to stability, though in Guinea the matter became less acute when the president's health appeared to stabilise. Ongoing ethnic conflicts in the Niger Delta, with hundreds of deaths, were a sign of the weakness of the most populous state on the continent, Nigeria. In addition, numerous states were unable to administer their whole territories, for example, the north in Uganda, usually considered to be a strong state.

US African policy was strongly influenced by the terrorist theme. The Pan-Sahel-Initiative (PSI, later renamed the Trans-Sahara Counter-Terrorism Initiative), led by the US's European Command (EUCOM) in Stuttgart, Germany primarily consisted of training and instruction for troops from Algeria, Mali, Mauritania, Niger and Chad in hunting down 'terrorists'. Officially, the initiative also targeted smuggling activities and international crime. The general staffs of these countries and their counterparts from Morocco, Senegal and Tunisia participated in a EUCOM conference in Stuttgart on the worldwide 'fight against terrorism' (23–24 February). In March, 43 fighters from the Algerian (and supposedly al-Qaida-supported) 'Groupe Salafiste pour la Prédication et le Combat' (GSPC) were killed. At the end of March, GSPC leader Amari Saif ('el para') was captured by a Chadian rebel group and handed over to Algeria (June). Amari Saif was responsible for the kidnapping of European tourists in 2003. In addition, US General Charles Wald visited 11 African countries (Morocco, Algeria, Nigeria, Angola, South Africa, Namibia, Gabon, São Tomé and Príncipe, Ghana, Niger and Tunisia). A parallel initiative was run in the Horn of Africa. It led to the capture of several dozen persons in Ethiopia, Eritrea, Sudan, Kenya and Djibouti (April). But there were also genuine African initiatives. At a high AU-government level a second meeting was held in Algiers (13–14 October) dealing with the prevention and fight against terrorism in Africa. The terror discourse was still being exploited by several African governments to denounce legitimate opposition movements and parties.

HIV/AIDS and other Epidemics and Disasters

Sub-Saharan Africa has just over 10% of the world's population, but it is home to more than 60% of all people living with HIV. According to an **AIDS epidemic update** for 2004 released by the United Nations Programme on HIV/AIDS (UNAIDS), the number of HIV-infected people up to the age of 49 years was estimated at over 25 million, the majority of these being women between the ages of 15 and 49 (over 13 m). It was further estimated that during 2004 more than 3 million further adults and children were newly affected with HIV, and that during the year close to 2.5 million adults and children died from AIDS.

While the average HIV prevalence in sub-Saharan Africa among adults was estimated by UNAIDS at 7.4% in 2004, all the **most affected countries** are in Southern Africa, which has a considerably higher rate (see further details in the regional chapter). AIDS is considered to be the leading cause of death on the continent (ahead of even malaria). The **Commission on HIV/AIDS and Governance in Africa** (CHGA) was established as a UN system-wide initiative in February 2003. During the year, it held two meetings, in Maputo (23–25 March) and in Addis Ababa (13–14 October). It organised an interactive conference in Botswana on treatment scale-up and the prevention of mother to child transmission (26–27 July); another in Ethiopia on HIV/AIDS and its impact on rural livelihoods and food security (12 October); a third in Ghana entitled 'The World of Work, Legal Frameworks' (18–19 November); and a fourth in Cameroon on gender and HIV/AIDS orphans in Africa (13–14 December).

Successes in combating the pandemic to date have been rare, the most prominent being in Uganda, where the earlier escalation in infection rates has been halted and the trend reversed. During the year, the **World Bank** published an interim review of the Multi-Country HIV/AIDS Program (MAP) for Africa. It identified a number of shortcomings in practice. Its recommendations include making national HIV/AIDS frameworks more strategic; strengthening HIV/AIDS governance and civil society involvement; improving public sector responses; expediting the completion of national monitoring and evaluation systems; further harmonising and simplifying procedures; and enhancing performance incentives.

Treatment access remained low: the WHO estimated that during 2003 (latest available figure) only 3% of the 4.4 million people in need received antiretroviral therapy. The World Bank agreed to allocate $ 60 m through a new treatment acceleration programme to scale up treatment, with Burkina Faso, Ghana and Mozambique as pilot countries. Botswana and Senegal have made their own substantial progress in increasing access to treatment. The AIDS pandemic remained far from being solved and continued to pose the biggest single threat to the welfare of the population, in particular in Southern African societies. On the occasion of World AIDS Day (1 December), a former chief writer for UNAIDS from South Africa commented upon the dilemma that "part of the problem also lies in the failure to reconcile the schizoid aspects of AIDS – as a short-term emergency and a long-term crisis."

Southeast Asia, with its **tsunami** at year's end, found itself, in top position in the ranking of worldwide catastrophes, a place normally reserved for Africa. In comparison to the death toll in Asia, the destruction in Africa caused by the tsunami seemed negligible. This was the reason international media attention on this aspect of the disaster was so limited. However, Somalia was badly affected, with approximately 300 people dying along a 650–kilometre strip of coast. About 18,000 households were seriously damaged or destroyed. In Tanzania, ten people died, in Kenya one person. On the Seychelles, there was considerable loss of property, and water reservoirs, especially drinking-water reservoirs, were contaminated.

The **plague of locusts** in the western Sahel affected many more people, and approximately 3.5 m ha of agricultural land were at risk. This was the worst plague of locusts in 15 years. FAO anticipated damage amounting to $ 245 m for 2004 alone. Worst affected were Mauritania, Mali and Senegal. Niger, too, was badly hit, with food shortages expected in the coming year. Technical support mainly came from the North African countries, specifically Morocco, Algeria and Libya.

Cross-regional Forms of Cooperation

On 26–27 November, the tenth **Francophone summit** was held in the Burkinabè capital Ouagadougou, bringing together 15 heads of state and six prime ministers. The summit discussed a range of African and international issues, including, officially and unofficially, the Ivorian crisis, and demanded strict application of the Linas-Marcoussis and Accra III agreements (see the West Africa regional chapter). The 'Autorité du Basin du Niger' (ABN), a grouping of nine West and Central African states, held a conference in Paris (26–27 April) to discuss cooperation in the sharing of river resources and the protection of ecosystems, but with few tangible results. CEN-SAD, dominated by Libya, held its sixth conference of leaders and heads of state in Bamako on 15 May. Côte d'Ivoire, Guinea-Bissau and Liberia were accepted as new members, thereby increasing the number of member states to 21. Ghana participated as an observer.

Andreas Mehler, Henning Melber and Klaas van Walraven

II. African-European Relations

The year 2004 saw several changes within Europe and Africa with the potential to impact the relationship between the two continents. Africa was not at the core of EU external relations, but achieved growing prominence on the EU's agenda. For years, the neighbouring continent to the south has been losing importance and the Cotonou Agreement was not the showcase its predecessor Lomé had been. This was less because of the reduced engagement of the EU in Africa, but rather because of the increasing European profile in other parts of the world, e.g., the Balkans and Eastern Europe. However, new developments in Africa, not least the formation of AU and NEPAD, posed new challenges to African-European relations and to Europe's reactions to change in Africa.

A debate on the amount of aid spent in Africa started and seemed likely to continue through 2005, particularly in relation to the UK's G8 presidency and Prime Minister Blair's Commission for Africa. The EU's Monterrey pledges of 2002 on increasing aid and on evolving international discussions made it likely that the amount of aid would considerably increase in subsequent years. One strong advocate for an increase in aid was Jeffrey Sachs, director of the Earth Institute at Columbia University and special adviser to the UN Secretary-General on Millennium Development Goals. In May, he claimed that small amounts spent on promoting Africa's economy could save billions and make the West more secure. Sachs's article in 'The Economist' (20 May) had to be seen as an attempt to build political pressure for the G8 summit in Sea Island, USA on 8–10 June. At the same time, it illustrated an increasing linkage between development assistance and security issues and was likely to be discussed further.

Bilateral Relations between African and European States

Several African presidents visited various European countries. Most notable was the visit by Nigerian President **Olusegun Obasanjo**. He visited London (23 January) as new Commonwealth chairperson and Geneva on 31 January. There, he met with Paul Biya, Obasanjo's Cameroonian counterpart, and UN Secretary-General Kofi Annan to discuss the issue of border disputes in the oil-rich Bakassi peninsula between Nigeria and Cameroon. Bilateral relations between Nigeria and the EU were fostered by a ministerial meeting on 18 May.

The issue of peace in Central Africa was on the agenda of South African President **Thabo Mbeki's** visit to Europe (15–18 November). Besides his meetings with EU institutions – the European Parliament, the EU Commission and the EU foreign policy representative Javier Solana – Mbeki also held bilateral talks in Belgium (15–17 November) and the Netherlands (17–18 November). Belgium – the former colonial power in the Congo – continued its engagement for peace in the African Great Lakes region. Foreign Ministers **Louis Michel** (Belgium), **Bernard Bot** (Netherlands) and **Lydie Polfer** (Luxemburg) – agreed on a joint Benelux mission to Central Africa (1 March). Burundi, DR Congo and Sudan were seen as regions for particular Benelux cooperation. Belgium, South Africa and the transitional government of DR Congo under President Joseph Kabila signed an accord in December to set up and train integrated DR Congo military brigades. The first two such brigades were to be established in the southeastern Congolese town of Kamina and the main town in the northeast DR Congo, Kisangani.

Mbeki also tried to become a peace broker in West Africa after he had helped broker peace deals in the DR Congo and Burundi. Mbeki's diplomatic activities were consistent with the rationale of an increasing African weight in peacemaking on the continent and ultimately with the "African renaissance" Mbeki spoke of. After unsuccessful attempts by **France**, ECOWAS and the UN to mediate a solution of the conflict in Côte d'Ivoire, France left peace negotiations to the South African president. Subsequently, French President **Jacques Chirac** raised doubts about Mbeki's West African expertise, which provoked angry or ironic comments in the African press. The South African president was called in as a peacemaker by the AU after Ivorian President Laurent Gbagbo launched an abortive offensive to recapture the rebel-held north of **Côte d'Ivoire** (4 November), breaking an 18–months ceasefire. Originally, French troops under UN mandate ('Opération Licorne') had prevented rebel movements from seizing power and the civil war from escalating. France was becoming increasingly entangled in the civil war in Côte d'Ivoire. Officially because of a 'mistake', French soldiers near Bouaké were attacked in Ivorian government air strikes on 6 November. President Chirac retaliated by ordering the destruction of the Ivorian air force. The move was followed by a manhunt for French citizens in Côte d'Ivoire. After an urgent UN Security Council meeting, EU foreign policy coordinator Solana called on the Ivorian government to stop all military action (7 November). A few days later, Jacques Chirac addressed the 10th **summit of the Francophonie** in Ouagadougou (26 November). The crisis in Côte d'Ivoire featured prominently in discussions in Ouagadougou: in a resolution, the Francophonie heads of state condemned the offensive by Ivorian government troops against northern rebels – including the attacks on French forces operating under UN mandate – and emphasised the need for a peaceful resolution of the settlement. Ivorian President Laurent Gbagbo did not participate in the summit. The official main topic of the meeting was sustainable development. Major visits by French officials focused rather on North Africa and the Far East. Libya, for example, featured on the itineraries of all key European actors, including Prime Minister Blair (UK) and Chancellor Schröder (Germany).

The British Prime Minister Blair appointed a **Commission for Africa** in February in preparation for the UK's presidency of the G8 in 2005, and pledged to make Africa a priority of the presidency. The mandate of the commission was to present recommendations to the G8 about actions to support African development. It created expectations for a high profile UK engagement on Africa, but was also criticised for duplicating African initiatives such as NEPAD and the AU, despite Blair's pledges to cooperate closely with these institutions. So as to build **legitimacy for the commission**, consultation meetings were held in Senegal, Cameroon, Ghana, Algeria and Tanzania. A consultation document, outlining the key issues, was published on 11 November. Questions of governance and a proposal for a sharp increase in aid to Africa were among the issues highlighted. The commission has 17 members and was chaired by the prime minister. Nine commissioners came from outside the UK, including the president of Ethiopia, **Meles Zenawi**, **Benjamin Mkapa**, president of Tanzania and **Trevor Manuel**, finance minister of South Africa. The commission met twice (on 4 May in London and on 7–8 October in Addis Ababa): a third meeting of the commission was foreseen before the publication of the report in March 2005. On 6 October, Blair visited **Sudan**, addressing the situation in Darfur. The crisis in Darfur was high on the public agenda in Great Britain. Foreign Secretary **Jack Straw** had already visited Sudan on 24 August, less than a week before the UN deadline for the disarmament of the pro-government militia blamed for the atrocities against the population in Darfur. Development Secretary of State **Hilary Benn** also paid a visit to Khartoum in June: Benn's portfolio embraces humanitarian assistance. Additionally, the UK took particular interest in the peace process between northern and southern Sudan, which should end one of the longest civil wars in Africa.

The year saw a number of high-level visits from **Germany** to Africa, presumably not least because of German ambitions for a permanent seat in the UN Security Council. Chancellor **Gerhard Schröder** visited Ethiopia, Kenya, South Africa and Ghana (January). His visit was aimed at fostering African initiatives, in particular NEPAD. During his tour, he also paid a visit to the AU headquarters in Addis Ababa (19 January). In Ghana, Schröder inaugurated the Kofi Annan International Peacekeeping Centre. The outgoing German president, Johannes Rau, made a short trip to Africa in March, visiting Nigeria and Tanzania, while a planned stay in Djibouti was cancelled owing to terror warnings. The first state visit outside Europe of the new German president, **Horst Köhler**, was to African countries (6–16 December). Köhler, a former head of the IMF, signalled his special interest in Africa. During his visit, which took him to Sierra Leone, Benin, Ethiopia and Djibouti, Köhler, as the largely ceremonial head of state, called on Germany to meet its international obligations. German Minister for Economic Cooperation and Development **Heidemarie Wieczorek-Zeul** visited Namibia for the centenary of the Herero uprising in the then German colony of South West Africa (12–15 August). The German minister officially expressed sorrow for the genocide that followed the battle at Waterberg in 1904. In December 2004, 290 German military were still in action in the Horn of Africa within the framework of the US-led 'Enduring Freedom' anti-terror campaign. In addition, German officers accompanied the UN-mandated missions in Ethiopia and Eritrea as observers.

Portugal signed an agreement with its ex-colony **São Tomé and Príncipe** (5 February), pledging to assist in the modernisation of its armed forces. Reform of the army had been demanded by São Tomé President Fradique de Menezes after a short military coup in July 2003. The agreement was one of several involving the Portuguese in military reform in Africa: an agreement with **Angola** had been signed in December 2003. In late 2004, a delegation of the community of lusophone countries (PALOP) committed the organisation to supporting the restructuring of **Guinea-Bissau**'s military forces. The delegation consisted of military personnel from Cape Verde, Portugal and Brazil.

The **Nordic countries** conducted a high-level meeting in Dar es Salaam on 24–25 November, with participants from the five Nordic countries and 20 African countries. The seminar was understood as a contribution to the Doha Development Round and was meant to foster dialogue and understanding between developed and developing countries. Consisting of government officials, the seminar was in preparation for a ministerial meeting in January 2005 and was part of a **Nordic Africa Initiative** launched in 2003.

Institutional Development in the Regions – EU and AU

The year 2004 did still not see a full EU-Africa summit, something that had originally been planned for April 2003: disagreement about how to deal with the Zimbabwean regime of Robert Mugabe was divisive. Consultations, however, took place on a working level. The **EU and AU Commissions** (at the level of EU Commission President Prodi, Trade and Development Commissioners Lamy and Nielson and President of the AU Commission Alpha Oumar Konaré) held their first meeting in Brussels to discuss the emerging strategic partnership between the two continental institutions (26 March). Commissioners discussed ways of strengthening and deepening ties between the two institutions. On the agenda was an exchange of views on issues of common interest relating to the EU-Africa dialogue, including peace and security, regional integration, the ongoing negotiations for economic partnership agreements between the EU and African regions (see below) and cooperation issues such as water, energy and commodities. Discussions were also held on security issues. Javier Solana, senior EU representative for the **Common Foreign and Security Policy** (CFSP), met with Saïd Djinnit, commissioner for peace and security of the AU (30 March in Brussels and 23 October in Addis Ababa).

EU meetings with sub-regional organisations also took place, for instance the **EU-ECOWAS** ministerial troika in Dublin on 10 May. The main discussions at the meeting dealt with practical measures for advancing regional political and economic integration in the ECOWAS area. Another meeting between the EU and ECOWAS was held on 8 November in Accra.

EU Institutional Developments with Implications for Africa

The biggest single event in 2004 was **EU enlargement** (1 May). The establishment of programmes for development cooperation was among the standards to be met by a country before it joined the EU Even though still minor, these new donors were likely to gain weight in the mid- to long-term: their emphasis was traditionally not on Africa and was unlikely to shift soon. However, some new EU countries, such as Poland and the Czech Republic, were exploring possibilities to further engage in sub-Saharan Africa, in Angola, Ethiopia and Mozambique.

Ireland held the **EU presidency** in the first half of the year, with the Netherlands taking over in the second half. Both countries had written a joint presidency programme. Africa was not a perceptible priority and brokering an agreement on the European constitution was a priority the Irish inherited from the Italian EU presidency. The constitution was ultimately signed on 29 October in Rome. However, the Irish did organise an informal meeting of development ministers (1 June) to discuss a three-year strategic planning programme to be continued by the next five EU presidencies. The link between **security and development** ('human security') was also high on the Irish agenda (see below). The Dutch had discussions about the **development-migration nexus** on their agenda and the Commission issued a paper on migration and development on 4 June. In autumn, German Interior Minister Otto Schily sparked a debate about migration by suggesting refugee reception camps in North Africa rather than in Europe. He received divergent, mostly critical reactions from his European counterparts.

After an initial showdown with the European Parliament – newly elected in June – (on a disputed nominee as commissioner of justice and home affairs), Commission President Barroso had to change his team. The **new EU Commission** was agreed upon only in November. With regard to the administration of external relations, the Directorate-General for Development was maintained and the development portfolio retained its autonomy. However, the development commissioner was perceived as being weakened compared to the previous set-up. Development Commissioner Louis Michel, the former Belgian foreign minister, became responsible for development policy and humanitarian assistance and was largely restricted to Africa as his geographical area of activity. This corresponded to his expertise in the Great Lakes region in particular. One of his goals for was the revision of the 2000 joint development policy statement of the EU Council and the Commission. EuropeAid, the Commission's implementation agency, however, now fell fully within the portfolio of Commissioner for External Relations Benita Ferrero-Waldner, the former Austrian foreign minister. The new commissioner for trade was Peter Mandelson, a close political ally of British Prime Minister Blair, who has repeatedly emphasised the links between development and trade. Other members of the **external relations group of commissioners**, chaired by Commission President Barroso, were the commissioners for economic and monetary affairs (Joaquin Almunia), enlargement (Olli Rehn) and budget (Dalia Grybauskite). The group planned to meet once a month to ensure coherence, impact and visibility in the Commission's foreign activities. Its task was also to control the implementation agency EuropeAid, based on regular reports by Ms. Ferrero-Waldner. The policy on **fisheries**, of particular importance to a number of African countries, was not included in the external relations group. The Maltese former foreign minister, Joe Borg, became commissioner for maritime affairs, including the EU common fisheries policy.

In response to the AU summit of July, the EU declared that strengthening the institutional and operational development of African organisations and institutions would continue to be an important focus of the EU, and reaffirmed the importance of the EU-Africa dialogue and of the strategic partnership with Africa.

The Cotonou Partnership Framework

The negotiations on the **mid-term review** of Cotonou continued. The EU's country strategy papers and regional strategies were under revision and were subsequently discussed in ACP-EU meetings. The mid-term review was expected to be terminated in early 2005. Some ACP countries criticised the review as too early to produce meaningful statements and feared excessively negative results at this rather initial stage. The Cotonou Partnership agreement had been signed in 2000, but ratified only in April 2003. Issues in the debate over the review were the expected EU Commission demands for more flexibility in the management of funding, which was perceived by ACP states as a further erosion of the **partnership principle**: developing countries should be allowed to change at their own pace. The slow speed of EDF disbursements and the anticipated accelerated pace of liberalisation under the proposed EPAs would have to be synchronised, the EU Commission stated. This could also be seen as one of the reasons for the further rapid expansion of **budget support** by the EU to developing countries within the ACP group: 30% of funding was given as budget support. The corresponding figure in 1999 had been 7.9%, according to the Commission's 2004 annual report on external assistance.

During the mid-term review of the Cotonou Agreement, discussions on the introduction of new 'essential elements' in the Agreement arose (March). The EU wanted to introduce a clause on the rejection of **weapons of mass destruction (WMD)** as an essential element of the agreement. Violations of the essential elements can lead to the unilateral suspension of cooperation. Also discussed was an **anti-terrorism clause**, possibly as a 'fundamental element' of Cotonou, i.e., with a lower possibility of suspension of cooperation. The ACP countries criticised the provision for not being related to the development orientation of the

partnership and for not reflecting ACP priorities. ACP countries described the EU suggestion as inappropriate, particularly as ACP countries, unlike members of the EU, did not have
weapons of mass destruction.

The discussion on negative **conditionality in development assistance** in the form of
sanctions has not been very prominent in the last years, the focus rather being on reward-
ing 'good performers'. However, decisions under **Article 96** of the Cotonou Agreement –
ultimately leading to the suspension of cooperation – were taken against the Central
African Republic after a coup d'état. In March, the EU agreed for the third consecutive year
on sanctions against Zimbabwe, including a travel ban on regime members and freezing
their funds. **Political consultations** were also opened with **Togo** on 14 April on human
rights and fundamental freedoms (media). The consultations were meant to review the sanctions in force against Togo since 1998. The consultation with Togo reached a positive conclusion in April. Consultations were also held with **Guinea** (15 April), after the EU
expressed concern about issues of human rights and fundamental freedoms. **Guinea-Bissau**
concluded political consultations with the EU (14 June). The EU Council decided in June
that aid to **Equatorial Guinea** was to be made dependent on the willingness of that country's government to observe the principles of democracy. However, in light of the oil boom
in that small state in the Gulf of Guinea, it was increasingly debatable if it would need development aid.

Conflict and Security

The **linkage between security and development** has gained attention in discussions, not
least with regard to changes in EU foreign policy. Particularly the discussions about the
EU's mid-term financial planning have given rise to debates about the demarcation between
development and peace/security (see below). In October 2003, the EU had agreed on a
European Security Strategy, to be further brought into operation by member states and
the future European foreign minister. The topic also featured in African and EU discussions.
It was, for example, on the agenda of the joint ACP-EU parliamentary assembly when it met
in Addis Ababa (16–19 February).

The AU received funding via the **EU African Peace Facility** (APF), established for three
years out of unused development funds (31 March). African countries dedicated 1.5% of
their assistance from the EDF to the APF. The latter was endowed with € 250 m and arose
from a suggestion by the AU summit in Maputo in 2003. The major share of the funds
(€ 200 m) was dedicated to African-led peacekeeping operations, conducted by the AU or
sub-regional organisations with an AU mandate e.g., ECOMOG in West Africa. The APF
committed € 35 m for capacity building, i.e., support for policy planning and management
within African organisations. The **AU Peace and Security Council** was launched in
Addis Ababa on 25 May. In its funding, the council can draw on the € 250 m from the EU

financed by the APF. The request for funding from the AU will have to be endorsed by the EU Council: funding cannot be granted for ammunition, arms or military equipment.

The first time the funding was requested concerned the conflict in Darfur. In June, the EU decided to provide € 12 m in support of the **African Union observer mission to Darfur** for a period of 12 months (11 June). In October, the AU requested another € 6 m from the APF for its mission to Darfur (12 October) and the Commission reacted positively. As originally envisaged, the suggested observer mission would comprise up to 120 observers and a possible protection force of 270 military personnel. The AU summit of July ultimately agreed to send **300 AU troops to Darfur**. The observers were to support the implementation of the ceasefire agreement signed by the parties to the Darfur conflict in Addis Ababa on 28 May.

On 14 June, the EU Council of Ministers declared that it aimed to enable the **European Security and Defence Policy (ESDP)** to provide support to African organisations in the areas of Disarmament, Demobilisation and Reintegration (DDR) and security sector reform. These areas relate to **post-conflict stabilisation efforts in Africa**. The EU was also looking at ways in which ESDP might enable it to provide practical support to the AU and sub-regional organisations as they develop their conflict-prevention tools and peacekeeping capacities. The Council agreed on an action plan along these lines, aimed at supporting peace and security in Africa (22 November). **EU defence ministers** agreed on plans to create up to nine **rapid-reaction battle groups** that could be sent to international crises from 2007 (17 May). Under the scheme, each contingent would have 1,500 soldiers and could be deployed within two weeks. EU battle groups could thus react rapidly before handing over to regional or UN peacekeepers.

EU Development Assistance to Africa

EU development cooperation ministers discussed the follow-up to their **Monterrey commitments** of 2002 (27 April). The tabled report found that the EU was on track in meeting the commitment to increase average EU ODA to 0.39% of GNP by 2006, and all member states had committed themselves to raising their national level of aid to at least 0.33% of GNP by then. Improvements in coordination, however, remained an issue. Another issue was the **untying of EU aid**, promoted, for example, by the UK, Denmark and the Netherlands. The contested elements in the EU proposals concerned coverage of NGO funding, experts and reciprocity. Some NGOs feared that open tendering among NGOs would result in the loss of funding to them or to southern NGOs. The debate was expected to continue into the UK's EU presidency.

Discussions about including the **European Development Fund (EDF)** in the EU budget increased, in particular in the context of the discussion of the EU's overall financial planning for 2007–13, the so-called EU 'Financial Perspectives' (below). The debate started in the European Parliament (20 January) and in member states, after the Commission had tabled a proposal for **EDF budgetisation** at the end of 2003. EDF's inclusion in the budget would guarantee parliamentary oversight of EDF. However, it was feared that this would also subject the fund to EU's annual planning (as opposed to the current five-year programming), reduce the say of ACP partner countries and might consequently facilitate the siphoning off of funds from Africa to other regions. The European Parliament, favouring budgetisation, has suggested **'ring-fencing' the ACP funds** within the future budget. EDF budgetisation would also have potential fiscal implications, since some **EU member states** committed to pay less into the 9th EDF than their share of payments into the EU budget would suggest, while others have shouldered a greater share. France, for example, committed to pay 24% of the 9th EDF and would pay 16% if the EDF were budgetisted. The UK, on the other hand, paid 12%, but would have to contribute 17–18% if the EDF were included in the EU budget. No decision on the contentious issue of budgetisation was expected before agreement on the Financial Perspectives. However, initial planning on the 10th EDF started in late 2004.

The **Financial Perspectives** 2007–13 were the most important debate within the EU. Discussions on these have potential ramifications for Africa. The issues most contested are the overall **ceiling of the EU budget** at 1.24% GNP (as suggested by the Commission), or 1% GNP, as demanded by Germany, France, Britain, the Netherlands, Sweden and Austria. These six countries are 'net contributors' to the EU budget, i.e., they pay more than they get back via various EU programmes. The Commission pointed out that reducing the ceiling at a time when enlargement added funding needs could affect other policy areas, including external relations. The classification of expenditure was also a source of controversy. The Commission **proposed six financing instruments for external action**, establishing subheadings such as 'stability' (or peace and security) and 'economic cooperation and development'. It was feared the former would increase at the expense of the latter. However, this proposal would enable the Commission to allocate to the African Peace Facility in future funding. The cooperation and development grouping was criticised for blurring the focus on the development of poor countries. The debate on these subheadings was likely to continue throughout 2005. Currently, funding is mainly organised in regional programmes (the ACP being one of them) and a multitude of (relatively small) budget lines across regions.

On 29 March, the EU Council decided to create a **water facility**, initially endowed with € 250 m, for supporting the provision of clean water and sanitation to ACP countries. The decision was approved by the ACP-EU council of ministers in Gaborone (6–7 May). Of this amount, € 185 m was committed to support long-term development, € 24 m to cooperation and regional integration and € 41 m to fund the investment facility provided for in the Cotonou Agreement. It was foreseen that € 1 bn from unused EDF funds would later be transferred to the water facility. The facility was a follow-up on the **EU water initiative** that had been launched at the Johannesburg World Summit on Sustainable Development in August 2002.

Trade and Development

According to the Cotonou Partnership Agreement, which was ratified in April 2003 and replaced the Lomé Convention, the EU aimed at starting negotiations on EPAs with Cotonou partner countries in Africa, the Caribbean and the Pacific. After previous official launches, negotiations started in Central Africa (16 September), West Africa (20–21 September), Eastern and Southern Africa (20 October) and with SADC (7 December). According to the Cotonou Agreement, EPA negotiations will be concluded by 2008; and the agreements would then be phased in. EPA preparations embrace **impact assessment studies** and regional programmes, which fall within the all-ACP € 20 m facility for the preparations for EPA negotiations. African nations would need increased aid to become competitive in world markets, John Kufuor, Ghana's president, said on a visit to London (26 April). To help build the muscle, Africa needed aid as well as trade, he added.

EPAs are meant to replace the non-reciprocal trade preferences under the Lomé regime with reciprocal free-trade agreements between the EU and ACP sub-regions. Potentially, EPAs include trade in services, which might enable them to go beyond the 2001 **Everything-but-Arms (EBA)** initiative of the EU. EBA grants tariff- and quota-free market access to Least Developed Countries (LDCs) for all products but arms, with phased-out exceptions for rice, bananas and sugar (until 2008). Thirty-two countries in sub-Saharan Africa are classified by the UN as Least Developed. According to the World Bank classification, seven others are low income, but not least developed as defined by the UN: Côte d'Ivoire, Cameroon, Republic of Congo (Brazzaville), Ghana, Kenya, Nigeria and Zimbabwe. And eight countries are classified as middle-income countries: Botswana, Cape Verde, Gabon, Namibia, Mauritius, South Africa, Seychelles and Swaziland. All African sub-regions include LDCs and non-LDCs, i.e., the EBA provisions affect some countries within current negotiation regions, but not others.

Other than vastly differing levels of development, a number of other **problems with EPA negotiations** have been raised by critics. EPAs were only reluctantly initiated by some ACP countries and were opposed by a number of NGOs. The latter particularly question the developing countries' **capacity to negotiate meaningfully** with the well-oiled trade negotiation machinery of the EU. EU Trade Commissioner Pascal Lamy and his successor Peter Mandelson (since November) have both emphasised the developmental dimension of the agreements, i.e., their characteristics beyond mere free-trade agreements. The groupings of EPA partners were unclear and **overlapping membership** was an issue across the ACP. For instance, the EU negotiation with East and Southern Africa started in effect with COMESA. However, Egypt was also a member of COMESA, but was not an ACP country. In Southern Africa, the EU had a particular arrangement with South Africa, which was not part of the trade and aid provisions of the Cotonou Agreement. However, some Southern African countries (Botswana, Namibia, Lesotho and Swaziland) were closely linked to neighbouring South Africa via a customs union (SACU). Tanzania, Mozambique and others, on the other hand, were members of SADC but not part of SACU. Negotiations – not least in Southern Africa – were therefore likely to be complicated. It is very likely that, in consequence, **rules-of-origin** will be strict and/or complicated. Agricultural products will be difficult subjects in the negotiations. **Non-tariff barriers**, such as environmental standards or sanitary and phytosanitary provisions (EU consumer protection policy) are crucial issues in the negotiations. The Cotonou Agreement provides for the possibility of an **alternative to EPAs**, but no possible alternative scenario had emerged by the end of 2004 and the EU Commission made clear its preference for regional agreements.

During the ACP-EU council of ministers meeting in Botswana (4–7 May), several ministers expressed their shock at the **clause on the non-execution of EPAs** envisaged by the Europeans under the dispute resolution provisions arising from the implementation of the EPAs. Among EU's desiderata was the fact that this clause would come into force against all countries of a region if one of them violated the provisions of the EPA. A vast majority of ACP ministers felt that this 'collective punishment' was unacceptable.

The debate continued on the **reform of the EU sugar regime**, including the ACP-EU sugar protocol. This protocol was signed for an indefinite time, but was bound to be reformed by 2008. On 3 August, a WTO panel issued a preliminary ruling that the EU sugar market violated the WTO rule. The EU agriculture commissioner, Franz Fischler, stated his preference for reducing the price of white sugar by around 40% (from € 725 per tonne to approx. € 450). The Commission's scenarios for reform had been presented in September 2003 and identified several possibilities: the status quo, price reduction or liberalisation of the regime. Unsurprisingly, Fischler's statement sparked further debate but legislative proposals were not expected before early 2005.

Facing an equal prospect of reform was the **EU banana regime**. The European Commission adopted a proposal to open WTO negotiations to modify the import regime for bananas (early June). According to a Council of EU Ministers decision of 2001, the move to a tariff-only system is to be taken no later than 2006. The proposal foresaw that the Commission would negotiate the import tariff on bananas with the relevant producer countries. It pledged to maintain the same level of protection and preference for ACP countries as the existing regime provided, while fully respecting its obligations and commitments with respect to other trading partners, EU producers and EU consumers.

Throughout the year, discussions continued on how to restart the **WTO Doha negotiation round** on trade after the failed Cancún meeting. An African trade ministers' meeting in Kigali (27–28 May), issued a 'Kigali Consensus' on the WTO, in which they welcomed the emerging consensus to drop from the work programme the three Singapore issues of investment, competition and transparency in government procurement. EU pressure to keep the Singapore issues on the Cancún agenda had been held responsible for the failure of the Cancún meeting.

Sven Grimm

III. West Africa

The sub-region witnessed ups and downs on the political front. General elections were held successfully in Ghana, Guinea-Bissau and Niger, in addition to local elections in Mali, Nigeria, Sierra Leone and Cape Verde. On the negative side, there were two alleged coup attempts in Mauritania, a military mutiny in Guinea-Bissau and the occasional arrest of opposition leaders in Mauritania and Guinea. Political stalemate continued in Togo. The violence in Côte d'Ivoire, however, continued to be West Africa's biggest headache, with former Liberian rebels intervening in the conflict, persisting political tension between Côte d'Ivoire and Burkina Faso and economic dislocation from migrants fleeing from the war-torn country. Incidental benefits from trade diversion and capital flight to other West African countries hardly compensated for this situation. Violent exchanges between the Ivorian army and French peacekeepers led to a massive exodus of Europeans and the thorough isolation of the Ivorian government. Political instability by and large lessened in the forest region of the southwest, as Sierra Leone struggled to come to terms with its post-conflict situation, while Guinea-Bissau and Liberia continued their transition to normal civilian rule. Guinea witnessed, as a result of economic crisis and cross-border ties with Liberia, several violent uprisings, but with both government and the various opposition groups pulling back from the brink at the last moment. Partly as a result of the return to some degree of normality in Guinea-Bissau, the conflict in Senegal's Casamance region lost most of its intensity, leading to a peace agreement between the government and the secessionist movement in December. Violence in various forms (communal, criminal or involving militias) continued to characterise Nigerian politics and society, without apparent risk of complete state disintegration. Some Sahelian countries were troubled by the activity of the Algerian-based 'Groupement Salafiste pour la Prédication et le Combat' (GSPC), in addition to highway banditry and, in Niger, some rebellious actions by Tuaregs. GSPC activity encouraged further military intervention by the US in a range of countries (Mauritania, Mali, Niger as well as Chad), in the form of US military aid and training for these countries' armed forces. Finally, West Africa's economies were impacted by high oil prices and locust plagues in the Sahel. Growth rates ranged from a low 2.6% in Guinea to a high 6.5% in Burkina Faso, but in most cases this was not enough to offset the effects of high petrol prices or to keep pace with population growth.

Electoral Politics, Transitions and Threats of Coups

General elections took place in three countries, with **stabilising effects** for the political system in two of them, Ghana and Niger. The electoral contest in Ghana (7 December), while leading to victory for the incumbent New Patriotic Party (NPP) and the re-election of its leader, President Kufuor, was fairly balanced in its outcome. The main opposition party, the National Democratic Congress, won 94 seats in parliament against the NPP's 128, thus further consolidating a two-party system. Niger, too, maintained a degree of political (but not social) stability, with the successful staging of municipal as well as presidential and parliamentary elections. These were marked neither by the chaos of the previous elections nor by a serious deterioration of relations within the political class, such as the country experienced during the 1990s. In fact, the victory of incumbent President Tandja in two rounds (16 November and 4 December) represented the first renewal of government by truly democratic means in the country's post-colonial history. The success of legislative elections in Guinea-Bissau proved more contentious. As the first step in a two-year transition process following a bloodless coup on 14 September 2003, the parliamentary elections (28–30 March) saw some disturbances at polling stations and the **contestation of the results** by the second biggest of Guinea-Bissau's three main political parties. However, an ECOWAS delegation gave its approval to the way the polls were conducted and, after its intercession, all parties agreed to respect the outcome.

Cape Verde, Mali, Nigeria and Sierra Leone held **local elections**, in the last case as part of the transition process that began after the return, under UN administration, of peace in 2002. These polls proceeded peacefully, except in Nigeria, where local elections had to be postponed in some states because of strife and violence. Generally, these elections, which completed the election marathon begun in 2003, were marked by low turnouts, violence and fraud. While they confirmed the dominant position of President Obasanjo's People's Democratic Party, the legal battle over the outcome of the 2003 presidential contest continued throughout the year, with his challenger vainly asking for an annulment on the basis of vote rigging. Other countries in the sub-region went through **post-electoral periods** (Mauritania, Guinea) or faced the typical issues of a run-up to electoral contests (scheduled for 2005 or later), such as the revision of electoral codes (Burkina, as in Niger) or voter registers (Benin, but also Ghana) and the realignment of opposition parties (Gambia). Cabinet reshuffles, some of them more eventful than others, took place in Guinea, Mauritania, Nigeria, Senegal, Mali and Sierra Leone, while the governments of Burkina and Togo successfully played on divisions within the opposition. In the latter country, speculation about the presidential succession was encouraged by rumours of the ill health of the head of state, President Eyadéma, West Africa's longest incumbent ruler. However, similar concerns ceased to be an issue in Guinea, where the health of President Lansana Conté appeared to have stabilised.

As in Guinea-Bissau and Sierra Leone, politics in Togo could be said to be marked by some sort of transition process as the European Union negotiated a roadmap for democratisation with the government as a precondition for the resumption of aid, though with little sign of a genuine breakthrough by the end of the year. Liberia and Côte d'Ivoire also continued to be governed under **transitional arrangements** ahead of planned elections in 2005. In Liberia, this involved the inclusion – as a result of the peace agreement that ostensibly ended the civil war in 2003 – of members of all warring factions in the cabinet and ministries, leading to general dysfunction in government and the nomination of some 40 presidential contenders for the 2005 elections. Similar steps proved impossible in Côte d'Ivoire as a result of complete lack of agreement between the government of President Laurent Gbagbo and allied groups on the one hand and rebel groups in the north and west on the other over disarmament, reconquest by the government of national territory and constitutional reform that would enable Gbagbo's main rival, Alassane Ouattara, to stand for president.

Mauritania saw the partial renewal of its senate (9 April) through elections, but without discernible benefit for the political stability of the country. Twice the government announced it had foiled **coup attempts** (9 August and 28 September), claiming on the first occasion that the instigators were Mauritanian army officers based in Burkina Faso and, on the second, blaming the alleged ringleader of a failed coup attempt in 2003. Army officers were arrested, as were the members of opposition parties who were accused of collusion, leading to a mass trial of those accused of plotting the overthrow of the government. In

Guinea, opposition leaders were similarly arrested on a coup charge, followed by their release without further legal steps. No such events took place in other countries in the sub-region, although Guinea-Bissau witnessed a military mutiny leading to the **assassination** of the joint chief of staff (6 October) and what was seen as the government's capitulation to the mutineers' demands on a range of corporate issues. Burkina Faso saw the conviction of ringleaders accused of a coup attempt the previous year.

Violence, Conflicts and Security

Nigeria, rather than better publicised Côte d'Ivoire, was the sub-region's most violent country. Communal conflicts, fed by disputes over land and grazing rights and by ethnic and religious divisions, continued to fray the fabric of this complex, multicultural society, precariously held together by the centralising forces of the Nigerian federation, i.e., the armed forces and the distributive mechanisms for the country's expanding oil revenues. In addition to communal conflicts, the country was again struck by violent acts of armed militias, especially in the southeast. These began either as movements claiming to defend the birthright of an ethnic group – usually by demanding a bigger share of oil revenues and/or an end to oil pollution – or as vigilante groups fighting the combined effects of crime and inefficient policing. However, in recent years they have themselves degenerated into criminalised gangs, headed by veritable warlords trying to carve out personal empires. This development in turn has led to fighting among rival militia groups, in addition to their preying on civil society. These activities, together with high levels of gang violence and the violent practices of secret cults in the south, coastal piracy targeting the oil industry, highway banditry and, in the northeast, attacks by members of an Islamic sect, have contributed to the **general banality of violence**, with violence being used as an instrument to settle scores or 'resolve' conflicts. In this context, both police and the armed forces managed to maintain law and order only by employing the most brutal force themselves.

Thus, between February and July, Plateau State was struck by massive violence between farmers and nomads and, especially, between Muslims and Christians, which spilled over into the northern city of Kano, leading to the deaths of hundreds of people, the creation of tens of thousands of refugees and the declaration of a state of emergency in the state. In Adamawa State, similar clashes took place, leading to the displacement of 4,000 people. Nationwide, the federal authorities registered some **800,000 internally displaced persons**. Combined gang, militia and state violence in the oil-producing areas of the southeast had by mid-September claimed the lives of some 500 people. The maintenance of law and order took a heavy toll on the country's poorly paid, corrupt and inefficient police force, which itself allegedly killed more than 400 armed robbers between January and April alone. However, few if any manifestations of violence in West Africa's most populous state spilled over into neighbouring countries. Since they did not have sub-regional implications, they did not attract much international attention.

Conversely, the civil war in Côte d'Ivoire and the reluctance of its southern political class and northern-based rebel forces to fully implement the **Linas-Marcoussis** agreement of 2003 continued to draw in neighbouring, sub-regional and international actors (see below). While the rebel forces of the northern 'Forces nouvelles' were affected by a violent leadership conflict, the government of national reconciliation, which had come into being as a result of Linas-Marcoussis, failed to function as a result of a power struggle between President Laurent Gbagbo and (rebel representative) Prime Minister Seydou Diarra. In addition, the refusal of the rebels to disarm without a constitutional reform that would allow Ouattara's presidential candidacy, the desire by southern politicians to reconquer the north by violent means, the interference by armed militias in Abidjan, obstructiveness by the National Assembly and boycotts of government meetings by parties of the opposition made for **complete political deadlock**.

The first major crisis erupted on 25–26 March, when a **demonstration by opposition parties** was violently **repressed** by government forces and its allied militias, resulting in 120 fatalities, 274 people wounded and 20 disappearances, according to UNCHR estimates. This appalling government act was surpassed only by the decision of government forces to go on the offensive against the rebels in November. In the course of its attacks, French troops, interposed between government and rebel forces, came under fire from government planes, leading to several casualties. In reprisal, the French destroyed the entire – a couple of fighters plus helicopters – Ivorian air force, which led to a massive **witch-hunt** against French and white people generally by militias in Abidjan, which invaded homes, destroyed and looted property and raped several women. As a result, most French citizens (9,000, the largest French community in sub-Saharan Africa) were evacuated to Europe and Western embassies closed, leaving only 1,000 white people behind and an Ivorian leadership at rock bottom as a result of international censure and isolation.

By contrast, the **sub-region's biggest meddler**, Burkina Faso's President Blaise Compaoré, again remained untouched, despite his record of subversive support for rebellions in Liberia, Sierra Leone and Côte d'Ivoire. He even improved his diplomatic position (with Paris, if not others) by hosting the 10th Francophone summit (26–27 November).

While no violence, save that resulting from the rising crime rate, was recorded in **Sierra Leone**, unemployment among young ex-combatants remained a potential security threat. On the whole, however, the political process continued on its logical non-violent, post-peace agreement course. In **Liberia**, UN peacekeepers finalised the disarmament process of the former warring factions, although they were unable to prevent the sale of heavy weapons to parties in neighbouring countries, notably Côte d'Ivoire. Several hundreds of thousands of internally displaced persons and refugees continued to live in camps, waiting to return to their homes. While the training of a new Liberian police force was one further step in the transition to normal civilian government, evidence of mounting corruption in the political class did not point to a fundamental departure from past practice. **Guinea**, besides witnessing various popular uprisings in protest against rapidly deteriorating living conditions, was confronted with a sudden rise of youth gangs and militias in the capital. Potentially the most dangerous incidents from a sub-regional perspective, however, took place in the southeastern forest region, around the town of N'Zérékoré (17 June), where local ethnic communities with cross-border ties with kindred groups in Liberia engaged in fighting. This was halted by Guinean security forces, which arrested large numbers of people, including Liberian ex-combatants. The long-standing secessionist conflict in the **Casamance** area of southern Senegal came to a possible end with the signing of a peace agreement on 30 December between the Senegalese government and rebels of the MFDC ('Mouvement des Forces Démocratiques de la Casamance'), though not without some leaders of the movement distancing themselves from the deal. It was unclear whether local leaders of the MFDC, an extremely fragmented organisation, would support the agreement. Its true significance, therefore, remained unclear, although diminished support for the MFDC in Guinea-Bissau, itself halfway along an uncertain transition process marked by an unruly military, helped towards reducing the importance of this conflict.

Finally, the Sahelian countries, were faced with some **GSPC cross-border activity**. In terms of the frequency and intensity of the violent exchanges between GSPC fighters and the government forces of Mali, Niger and Chad, this was a conflict of marginal importance. However, because the Islamic fundamentalist agenda of the GSPC drew in the US, these conflicts developed a broader significance. US training of the Mauritanian, Malian, Nigérien and Chadian armies in counter-insurgency techniques and the provision of military materiel (all-terrain vehicles, desert warfare equipment) had the potential not only of raising the military capabilities of the region's national armies but also, as part of the same process, of **militarising relations** between states and non-state actors. Banditry in northern Mali and Niger proved ominous in this respect, especially in Niger, where it might be related to the dissatisfaction of some Tuaregs with their share in the country's political system.

Human Rights and the Rule of Law

In several countries, members of the **private media** were **harassed**. Even in Senegal, which markedly improved its stance on human rights by abolishing the death penalty, the editor of a newspaper writing about alleged corruption in the customs service and judiciary was arrested on charges of publishing confidential, false and politically sensitive information. The editor was released after a couple of weeks in jail, but his arrest led to a one-day strike by private newspapers (12 July). Although the Senegalese media continued to enjoy comparative press freedom, this case somewhat detracted from the human rights award presented by an American NGO to President Abdoulaye Wade for his former role as an opposition politician and his mediation of regional conflicts. The situation was much worse, however, in Gambia, where an **editor** was **assassinated** (16 December) after criticising a draconian new press law. Though the government condemned the murder and denied a link between it and tighter media regulations, journalists staged a one-week protest strike. A foreign journalist in Côte d'Ivoire was probably murdered after his **disappearance** on 16 April, this event following the murder of a French journalist the previous year. Similarly, in Togo an editor received death threats after publishing articles on an exiled opposition group and on Eyadéma's possible retirement – in spite of the introduction of a more liberal press code. In Burkina on 13 December thousands of people demonstrated as they had done every year, to protest the murder of a well-known journalist in 1998. The case, in which the president's brother and presidential guards were suspected of being implicated, again failed to come to trial. Less serious forms of harassment took place in Niger and Benin. Finally, in Nigeria, media harassment was more severe, with the government, irritated about foreign reporting, prohibiting local radio and television from relaying live transmission of news broadcasts from foreign stations. A magazine critical of the president faced the confiscation of its computers and copies of its publication, in addition to brief detentions of some of its journalists and the besieging of its offices by security agents.

Endemic **corruption** again elicited government campaigns throughout the sub-region, but generally without making headway in combating this widespread phenomenon. Nevertheless, Gambia, a small country, witnessed court cases against and dismissals of several high-ranking officials as part of a government-run campaign dubbed 'Operation No Compromise', though neither the president nor MPs were forced to testify in the courts. These cases went further than government action in Mali and Nigeria, for example. In the former, a case of embezzlement of ministerial funds worth CFAfr 2.6 bn led to few concrete moves, while in Nigeria – predictably, again judged by Transparency International to be one of the most corrupt countries in the world – not a single prominent figure was sentenced, despite 500 people being held in custody in various corruption cases. Racketeering by police in Benin led to a blockade in September by lorry drivers protesting against the extortions. As in Nigeria, judicial corruption presented special problems, leading to a court case against some 100 magistrates on charges of embezzlement. The judiciary in Benin was, moreover, embroiled in a dispute with the executive over the latter's interference in the judicial realm, a dispute that resulted in a magistrates' strike on 9–11 June.

Reports by the 'Fédération interationale des Droits de l'Homme', criticising the practices of the justice system in both Benin and Togo, were flatly rejected by both governments. In both cases, the charges involved the use of **torture and extra-judicial killings**, the latter phenomenon also being on the rise in Nigeria. In Togo, however, there was a slight improvement in the general human rights situation as a result of foreign pressure, with political prisoners (but also ordinary criminals) receiving a presidential pardon (17 August). In **Sierra Leone**, two of three major **trials** began in a special UN-assisted court against some of the perpetrators of the worst human rights violations during the civil war, including the former rebel RUF. The court also wished to try Charles Taylor, the former Liberian leader now living in exile in Nigeria, who was heavily involved in the Sierra Leonean war. However, the Liberian government did not back this initiative.

Cooperation and Conflict: Sub-Regional Dimensions

The principal issue in regional cooperation was the **war in Côte d'Ivoire**. The most important development from a sub-regional perspective was the decision by the UN Security
Council to deploy a peacekeeping force, UNOCI, totalling over 6,000 troops. While this
decision could be interpreted as flowing logically from the Linas-Marcoussis truce, to a considerable extent it symbolised the inability of sub-regional actors to end the deadlock in the
Ivorian conflict. UNOCI troops joined the separate French 'Licorne' force (4,000 men). The
troops provided by **ECOMICI** (ECOWAS Mission in Côte d'Ivoire) were integrated with
the UNOCI force. The ECOMICI force consisted of contingents from Senegal, Niger, Togo,
Benin, Mali and Ghana and initially totalled some 1,200 men who had been ordered to monitor the ceasefire. This mandate was later extended to ensure respect for the ceasefire and
protection of civilians. For this purpose, ECOWAS decided to provide an additional 2,000
men. With ECOMICI's integration into UNOCI, it was decided the force would be joined
by troops from Angola, Chad and Bangladesh.

Despite growing UN involvement, ECOWAS continued to try to resolve the crisis, with
the ECOWAS chairman, President John Kufuor of Ghana, vainly attempting on several
occasions to bring the warring sides closer together. Thus, a **mini-summit of ECOWAS
leaders** was convened in Abuja on 20 June at which heads of state from Nigeria, Ghana,
Togo and Niger, in addition to the president of Gabon, pressured President Gbagbo to work
towards a breakthrough. The talks were described 'frank', and Gbagbo agreed to get in
touch with his independent Prime Minister Seydou Diarra. The ECOWAS mediation and
security council, at its 12th ministerial meeting in the Ethiopian capital, Addis Ababa,
lauded the outcome of the mini-summit, even though it led to few concrete results. Then,
an extraordinary ECOWAS summit was convened in the Ghanaian capital Accra on 29–30
July, at which all Ivorian parties met with ECOWAS leaders, the UN Secretary-General
Kofi Annan and the presidents of Gabon and South Africa. The conference, dubbed **Accra
III**, confirmed the objectives of Linas-Marcoussis but again failed to achieve a breakthrough. On 4 November, President Obasanjo, chairman of the AU Assembly, convened an
emergency summit in Abuja in response to the **aerial bombardment of French troops**.
After Gbagbo's representative walking out in anger, West African leaders concurred with
a UN arms embargo, in effect underlining not only the isolation of the Ivorian regime but
also the inability of continental and sub-regional organisations to resolve the crisis.
Thousands of Ivorians, meanwhile, fled across the border into Liberia.

Although there was little coordination among existing peacekeeping missions in these
countries (including Sierra Leone), Ghana managed to secure a deal with Liberia and
UNHCR on the voluntary repatriation of 42,000 Liberian refugees. Guinea and Liberia also
improved their relations in the wake of the 2003 peace agreement in Liberia, despite the
fighting in N'Zérékoré, southeastern Guinea, involving Guinean security forces and,
among others, Liberian ex-combatants. Ties between Guinea and Sierra Leone also

improved, although here, too, security issues impinged on diplomatic relations. Guinean troops continued their occupation of the small border town of Yenga, inside Sierra Leone, not in order to press a claim but because of security considerations. The Yenga issue was discussed by Sierra Leone, Guinea and Liberia at the summit of the **Mano River Union** in Conakry (18–20 May), which also focused on wider issues of **border security** among the three neighbours. **Relations between Côte d'Ivoire and Burkina** continued to be hamstrung by the Ivorian conflict and by alleged Burkinabè involvement. In June-July, Burkina complained of the continued maltreatment of Burkinabè migrants in Côte d'Ivoire (350,000 of whom had returned home in the course of the civil war), in addition to alleged airspace violations by Ivorian aircraft. The latter charge was given little credence by European diplomats, but showed that relations between the two countries continued at an all-time low. Elsewhere in the sub-region, resolution of the dispute between Nigeria and Cameroon over sovereignty of the **Bakassi peninsula** (awarded by the International Court of Justice to Cameroon) made little progress. Although the Nigerians agreed to withdraw their troops, they backtracked at the last moment, asking for a postponement. With most Bakassi inhabitants in favour of union with Nigeria, Nigerian politicians opposed withdrawal, claiming that this required a change to the constitution and a UN-supervised referendum on the peninsula. This stood in marked contrast to the ease with which both countries had exchanged a couple of villages along their common border the previous year.

ECOWAS also mediated the political conflict in Guinea-Bissau in the wake of the parliamentary elections of 28–30 March. An **ECOWAS fact-finding mission**, involving among others the organisation's Executive Secretary Ibn Chambas, managed to persuade all political parties to abide by the electoral outcome, thus contributing vitally to the successful conclusion of the country's transition process.

General ECOWAS policy on defence and security went a step further with a one-day summit in January at which it was agreed to introduce a **peace fund** to meet the financial requirements of ECOWAS peacekeeping undertakings. Its initial seed money was $ 5 m. Ghana, Mali, Nigeria and Senegal made their contributions and other member states, as well as donors, were expected to follow suit. With some 1,400 troops in Côte d'Ivoire at the time and some 3,000 troops forming part of the UN peacekeeping mission in Liberia (UNMIL), the organisation searched for ways to put its military interventions on a more solid footing. The proliferation of small arms and light weapons again caught the organisation's attention, and a conference in Abuja (22–24 March) sought ways to reinforce the ECOWAS **Moratorium** on the Exportation, Importation and Manufacture of Light Weapons in West Africa (1999). The small arms unit inside the executive secretariat in Abuja was charged with coordinating initiatives on small arms with other international organisations, including the UN, SADC and several NGOs. So far, 13 of 15 member states have established national commissions to execute and monitor the moratorium's provisions. The UN Security Council pledged, at a special session held on 25 March, to support the organisation in its efforts to tackle the problems of arms trafficking, in addition to related issues such as child soldiers and mercenaries. A top-level meeting between ECOWAS and the United Nations Office for West Africa (UNOWA) was held in Abuja on 31 May in a bid to strengthen cooperation in the field of peace and security, and resulted in a memorandum of understanding to promote sub-regional democracy, good governance, peace and stability and improve ECOWAS capacities in conflict prevention. This was also the subject of a workshop in Ghana on early warning within the ECOWAS system, which recommended the improvement of communications equipment and analytical capacity in the organisation's four zonal bureaux for conflict prevention (in Banjul, Monrovia, Ouagadougou and Cotonou).

In more traditional vein, the ECOWAS defence and security commission sought to enhance the organisation's peacekeeping capacities by agreeing, at a meeting in Abuja on 17–18 June, to establish a standby unit of 6,500 highly trained and equipped soldiers as part of a **rapid reaction force**. The standby unit would comprise 1,500 soldiers to be known as the ECOWAS task force, to be possibly boosted by another 3,500 troops to form a brigade, with the remaining 1,500 constituting the reserve force. It was planned that the task force would be deployable within 30 days, while the brigade would be deployed and be self-sustaining within 90 days. The brigade would be made up of soldiers from pre-determined units. The ECOWAS executive secretariat would define funding needs, operational procedures and requirements, including for the logistics depots in Mali and Sierra Leone. This development was in conformity with the policy of the AU, which on 20–21 January adopted a plan for an African Standby Force (ASF; see the general chapter) made up of sub-regional brigades. However, it also followed on the decision of the ECOWAS defence and security commission to have member states pledge army units to constitute a permanent ECOMOG (ECOWAS Ceasefire Monitoring Group), as envisaged in the ECOWAS Protocol on the Mechanism for Conflict Prevention, Management, Resolution, Peacekeeping and Security. Since this decision had been taken back in July 2000, the current development also pointed to a lack of genuine progress in this area. Moreover, without financial and logistical support from Western donors, it would be difficult to get the sub-regional brigade up and running, this being quite apart from member states' caution about establishing sub-regional military bodies that could impinge on the security of their regimes. In this respect, the Canadian government pledged Canadian $ 4.5 m to ECOWAS for its peace fund, among other things.

Coordination of AU and ECOWAS policy was facilitated by the election of Nigeria's President **Obasanjo** as this year's **AU chairman**. Ghana's president and ECOWAS chairman John Kufuor has so far maintained good relations with his Nigerian colleague. However, in practice, Obasanjo devoted a lot of time to the Darfur crisis rather than purely West African issues.

Other forms of sub-regional cooperation included the signing of a general cooperation agreement between ECOWAS and the smaller Francophone 'Union Economique et Monétaire Ouest Africaine' (**UEMOA**) headquartered in Ougadougou. The agreement should help to prevent duplication of effort in relation to economic integration, an outcome made more desirable by plans by Nigeria, Ghana, Sierra Leone, Gambia and Guinea to establish a **second monetary zone** in West Africa, with a common currency to be called the 'eco', in addition to the West African CFA zone operating under the auspices of UEMOA.

Socioeconomic Developments

The decision to establish this second monetary zone in the sub-region had been taken in 2000. At a conference among Ghana, Gambia, Guinea, Nigeria and Sierra Leone held in Conakry on 3 September, it was observed that fulfilment of the required convergence criteria left much to be desired. While the summit agreed that the West African supervisory financial authority would be located in Nigeria and the monetary zone's secretariat in Guinea (with the interim precursor of the projected bank to work from Ghana), the stated objective to inaugurate the monetary union by July 2005 appeared **illusory**. In reality, it was UEMOA that was, according to the IMF, the furthest along the path to sub-regional integration, with its common currency tied to the euro and, since 2000, a customs union and a common external tariff. Thus, the two monetary unions, projected and real, pointed again to the **lack of economic integration at the level of ECOWAS** as a whole. Moreover, these organisational initiatives ignored the difficulties inherent in integrating non-complementary economies that are tied into an uneven dependency relationship with the global economy and disregarded the cross-border traffic taking place in the sub-region's substantial informal sectors. Thus, ECOWAS leaders in July – as a sign of lack of progress – again pledged their commitment to the ECOWAS trade liberalisation scheme, reaffirmed implementation of the programme on the free movement of goods, services and persons (the last issue made acute by the flight of economic migrants from Côte d'Ivoire) and promised to work towards the removal of all non-tariff barriers.

NEPAD, it was hoped, could make economic cooperation more tangible. On 20 March, ECOWAS leaders met with the president of the World Bank, James Wolfensohn, in Accra to review the integration process and the implementation of the NEPAD agenda. An **Accra Short-term Plan of Action** was adopted that would focus on three principal concerns, i.e., establishment of an ECOWAS-wide free trade area and customs zone by 2007, along with improved market access for West African exports; NEPAD-encouraged infrastructural projects in the areas of energy, transport and communication; and peace and security measures. The World Bank earmarked $ 450 m for such sub-regional projects, part of which would be spent in the ECOWAS sub-region. The bank also formed a joint task force with ECOWAS to monitor implementation of the plan of action.

Economic performance ranged widely across the sub-region. The highest real GDP change, according to the IMF, was registered in Sierra Leone (7.2%) and the lowest (1%) in Guinea-Bissau, with the sub-regional average around 4.5%. The rise in consumer prices reached an average of around 4.5%, but with Guinea (Conakry) and Nigeria into double digits and Ghana and Gambia still hovering around 6%. While one should be cautious about the reliability of these statistics, it is noteworthy that Côte d'Ivoire still achieved a GDP growth rate of 1.7%. With the government largely in control of the raw materials and the infrastructure generally intact, the country remained the main economy in the sub-region's CFA zone, even though the percentage of people living below the poverty datum line has increased in recent years from 38% to 44%. Guinea certainly performed worse than in previous years. Economic performance in neighbouring Guinea-Bissau remained very poor as well, with one out of three living under the poverty line, despite a relatively favourable climate and ecology. Nevertheless, this figure was again dwarfed by that of Sierra Leone, again last on the Human Development Index (HDI), with 70% of its people living in absolute poverty. By contrast, Senegal and Ghana had generally good years in socioeconomic terms, although the former was still rated 157 of 177 countries on the HDI. Its peasant population was hard lit by a **devastating locust plague**, which also descended on Mauritania (with nearly half its population under the poverty line, according to UNDP), Mali and Niger. In the last-mentioned country, the plague led to a record grain deficit that did not bode well for the coming year. Nigeria, the sub-region's economic superpower, still ranked 151 on the HDI, a rating that underscores the difficult living conditions faced by most Nigerians. High petrol prices, however, while hitting many countries in the sub-region hard, increased Nigeria's income and heightened expectations of a better future in several other (coastal) states where oil reserves have been found or anticipated (Mauritania, Côte d'Ivoire, Gambia, Liberia). Other good news came from **cotton**. The WTO rejected US subsidies to American cotton farmers as distorting international trade – a ruling whose effects on the sub-region's cotton producers (Mali, Côte d'Ivoire, Burkina and Benin, with a total of 10 million people dependent on the crop) was not immediately clear (see the general chapter).

HIV/AIDS, while marked by lower infection rates than in other sub-regions (3.5% to 4.5% of adults against a Sub-Saharan total of 7.4%, though on the basis of very tentative figures), continued its onward march. The fastest rise in absolute numbers occurred in Nigeria (5% adult prevalence in 13 states), while the highest adult prevalence in percentage terms was in Côte d'Ivoire, at 10.7%. Ivorian statistics on this tend to be more reliable than elsewhere and underscore the **relationship between conflict – often including sexual violence and exploitation – and HIV/AIDS infection rates**. Thus, in recent years the infection rate in the southwestern forest region has generally approached Southern African levels.

With rising fuel prices, **social conditions** were very difficult in many countries, making the planned achievement of Millenium Development Goals questionable. High petrol prices led to protests in Guinea and Nigeria. Strike action by workers and students protesting working conditions or access to educational facilities took place in Mali and Benin.

Klaas van Walraven

Benin

In 2004, one year after the parliamentary elections and two years before the presidential elections in 2006, no major political challenge faced Benin, even if the succession to President Mathieu Kérékou was still on the agenda. Relations between executive and judiciary, which gave rise to mutual criticism, were still very poor. Relations with Nigeria remained one of the main features of foreign affairs and socioeconomic developments. The government maintained macroeconomic stability, but public sector workers went on strike at the end of the year. This crisis illustrated that Beninese stability remained weak in some degree.

Domestic Politics

Political parties were to conform to the new '**charte des partis**' before 21 February. In 2003, the National Assembly passed this new charter, which increased the requirement for the number of founding members in a party from three to ten in each of the 12 departments. Only registered political parties with at least 10 MPs will receive financial support from the state. The amount of this support, which is determined by government, will not be less than CFAfr 5 m for each MP. Moreover, political parties are required to put up candidates for local and parliamentary elections. If a party does not take part to two successive parliamentary elections, it will lose its legal status. Of the 129 parties registered with the Home Office, 80 had complied with the charter before the deadline. However, the government postponed the deadline for three months to provide a further opportunity to the other parties to register.

On 17 March, the government decided to create a **permanent register of electors**, with the aim of guaranteeing reliable and fair elections. The next presidential election will be held in March 2006. A commission comprising politicians, members of civil society and the press will be charged with preparing this register. Until then, the electoral register will only be valid for one election and voters will have to re-register before each election. This process was severely criticised during the presidential election of 2001.

Two years before the end of Kérékou's presidency, Beninese politicians tried to prepare for his succession. According to the constitution, Kérékou may not stand in the next presidential election: he will be more than 70 and will have had two successive mandates (1996–2001 and 2001–06). A possible constitutional amendment would be advantageous for him and his predecessor, Nicéphore Soglo, current mayor of Cotonou, but no such amendment was proposed. On 15 September, 35 parties belonging to the president's majority and forming the '**Union du Bénin du Futur**' (UBF) – the main pro-Kérékou coalition in parliament – decided to put together a new party. But the struggle for leadership and presidential rivalries appeared to be the main obstacle to executing this project. Two days after the announcement, members of the parties supporting President Kérékou and his government announced their opposition to the creation of a single presidential party. In parliament, UBF and its allies have 53 seats (of 82).

During 2004, **relations between the executive and judiciary** were at their worst. On 10 May, magistrates decided on a boycott to protest the government's decision to transfer to Nigeria 12 Beninese who were accused of being part of a criminal network operating between Benin and Nigeria. These persons had been transferred to Nigeria on 3 May to be questioned by Nigerian magistrates. They were charged with being accomplices of Hamani Tidjani, a citizen of Niger who was responsible for many killings and who had recently been condemned in Nigeria. Beninese magistrates protested because they were not informed of this transfer. Many people in civil society and in parliament protested against this decision. The president of the 'Commission Béninoise des Droits de l'Homme' accused the government of transgressing the constitution and international law, and announced his intention to refer the matter to the constitutional court. The minister of justice, Dorothé Sossa, stated that the transfer was regular and did not interfere with the exercise of Beninese justice. The twelve persons came back to Cotonou on 22 May. On 9 June, magistrates went on strike for three days to protest against the executive's involvement in the judicial sphere. Finally, on 31 August, the constitutional court declared this transfer to be unconstitutional.

The 'Fédération Internationale des Ligues des Droits de l'Homme' (FIDH) published a **report on the judiciary** in Benin. The study was undertaken in February and the report published in July. It criticised the use of torture, the excessive prison population, discretionary imprisonment, prison conditions (especially for women and children), the workings of traditional law and judicial corruption. The minister of justice rejected these charges but announced the construction of a new prison in Akpro-Missérété in the near future. One thousand persons condemned to long-term imprisonment would be transferred to the new facility. The FIDH report also dealt with the case of the 11 former Togolese soldiers who had been charged with plotting a coup d'etat in Togo and put in jail. These men, who had been refugees in Benin for many years, alleged that they had been assaulted.

On 27 January, the celebrated '**trial of the judiciary**' opened in Cotonou. It concerned the most important judicial corruption scandal in Benin's history. About 100 magistrates and other judicial auxiliaries were brought to trial. They were accused of embezzling more than CFAfr 8 bn between 1996 and 2000. Of the 90 Beninese magistrates, 27 were prosecuted and only one tribunal (in Lokossa) was not involved in the trial. On 4 June, after a four-month trial, 37 defendants were sentenced to imprisonment (from 30 months to 5 years). The other defendants had their sentences remitted or were acquitted.

However, **corruption** did not affect only the judiciary. It remained a major issue in Benin and affected all sectors of the civil service. On 13 February, the government publicised a list of 214 cases of embezzlement from 1996 to 1999, involving the misappropriation of more than CFAfr 70 bn of public money. Proceedings were launched in 120 of these cases. Moreover, in addition to embezzlement, Beninese authorities estimated they lose more than CFAfr 60 bn each year through the corruption of the customs service and police. On 1 May, the former chief of staff of the Beninese army, Colonel Gandonou Kodja – who had lived in exile since his indictment for embezzlement in May 2000 – was arrested in Porto-Novo. He was accused of misappropriating the funds allowed to soldiers who served in ECOMOG (ECOWAS Ceasefire Monitoring Group), the ECOWAS peacekeeping forces in Liberia. On 6 September, more than 200 truck drivers blocked the main road connecting Cotonou to Porto-Novo and the Nigerian border, to protest against racketeering policemen. At the end of the year, on 30 December, President Kérékou announced the establishment of a new department to fight corruption, the 'Observatoire de lutte contre la corruption', which seems to duplicate the 'cellule de moralisation de la vie publique' that has tried to operate since 1996.

On 14 June, MPs adopted the new '**Code de la personne et de la famille**', an important bill that deals with questions related to marriage, family life and widowhood. The main provision is the prohibition of polygamy. A former version of this code, adopted by parliament in June 2002 – which gave monogamy and polygamy the same legal standing – had been thrown out by the constitutional court and its president, Conceptia Ouinsou, who objected to the code's unfairness to women. According to the new text, only monogamous marriage has legal effect. Moreover, a wife can keep her own name and is no longer forced to marry her brother-in-law after the death of her husband. Rosine Soglo, wife of the former president of the republic Nicéphore Soglo and current MP and leader of the parliamentary group of the main opposition party, the 'Renaissance du Bénin', fought over many months along with other women in parliament to have this bill passed.

For the first time since Kérékou's comeback in 1996, a journalist was jailed after being sentenced. On 16 March, Jean-Baptiste Hounkonnou, director of 'Le Nouvel Essor', the only daily paper published in north Benin, was sentenced to six months of imprisonment in Parakou after he was found guilty of defamation. In December 2003, he had published a newspaper article accusing a woman of adultery. Local NGOs and trade unions, such as the 'Observatoire de la déontologie et de l'éthique dans les médias' and the 'Union des journalistes de la presse privée du Bénin', protested against this sentence. According to the Paris-based NGO 'Reporters sans frontière', Benin always seems to be "the best pupil" in West Africa about **press freedom**. On 28 April, Hounkonnou was finally released. However, another journalist, Patrick Adjamonsi, director of the 'L'Aurore' newspaper, was arrested on 13 August and imprisoned in the Cotonou central police station. He was also charged with defamation.

For many years, Benin has been a very important crossroads in the **traffic in children**. In rural areas, parents usually entrust family members with their children so they can be educated in town. In fact, many children are sold to dealers who take them to Nigeria, Gabon, Cameroon or Côte d'Ivoire. There, they are reduced to slavery and work in cacao or sugarcane plantations or in quarries. According to the latest UNICEF report on the world's children, Benin is apparently one of the main providers of infant labour. Each year, many children are apprehended by police near the Togolese or Nigerian borders. Moreover, throughout 2004 hundreds of children were sent home from Nigeria. On 27 February, the government set up a national task force to combat the traffic in children and child labour. It included members of NGOs, of government and of the police and its aim is to establish new and more effective ways means to fight the growing traffic.

On 1 April, violence occurred on the main campus of Abomey-Calavi near Cotonou. Hundreds of students belonging to the 'Union nationale des scolaires et étudiants du Bénin' (UNSEB), one of the main student trade unions, tried to organise an 'assemblée générale', but police prevented them and used teargas Some students reacted violently: by erecting roadblocks and throwing stones at the police. At the end of the year, students were also mobilised to protest against university fee increases (see below).

Foreign Affairs

The **crisis in Côte d'Ivoire** continued to affect Benin, which sent more than 260 soldiers to that country as part of the West African peacekeeping force. Following the events of November – the attack by pro-Gbagbo pilots on a French camp and the killing of about 60 people in Abidjan – the Benin government proposed to voluntarily repatriate its citizens in Côte d'Ivoire. It entrusted the embassy in Abidjan with this task. By one estimate, about

350,000 Beninese lived in Côte d'Ivoire. On 26 November, the first group of returnees arrived in Benin, after a journey through Burkina Faso.

Relations with Nigeria improved. Security in the border region remained the main topic of discussion. Following the one-week closing of the border by Nigerian authorities to protest Beninese inaction over the growing insecurity, and the meeting between President Kérékou and Nigerian head of state Obasanjo in August 2003, police cooperation improved. Joint patrols were carried out in the border region and the Benin government collaborated with Nigerian justice authorities. From September to November, about ten policemen and gendarmes were killed while pursuing criminals fleeing to Nigeria. In addition, the two states attempted to adjust their 770 kilometre-long border. A joint commission was established in June and proposed an exchange of villages between the two countries.

Relations with Togo strengthened as a result of two joint projects for the production and distribution of energy. The main project was the upgrading of the Adjarala hydroelectric barrage on the Mono River, in the frontier zone between the two countries. The barrage had been built 40 years earlier and the total value of the current project is $ 162 m. For this purpose, international financial institutions were to be mobilised. The two countries depend on Ghana (especially the Akossombo barrage) for their electricity supplies. The second project is the north-south connection of the electricity grid within both countries: in Benin, as in Togo, the south has better electricity provision than the north.

In 2004, there were some important visitors to Benin to meet with President Kérékou. On 15 and 16 June, King **Mohammed VI** of Morocco paid his first visit since he mounted the throne in 1999. The king met with Kérékou and visited two buildings that Morocco had partly paid for (CFAfr 1.1 bn): he inaugurated one student residence, named after his father Hassan II, and visited the building site in Porto-Novo of the future supreme court. Ten days later, on 25 and 26 June, Benin received the Chinese vice-president, **Zeng Qinghong**. Relations between Benin and China had improved during the 1970s, when Benin was a Marxist country, particularly after Kérékou's coup d'etat of October 1972 and after Benin's politics became more revolutionary after 1974. The vice-president visited various buildings and signed financial and business agreements with the Benin government. President **Chissano** from Mozambique visited Benin from 23 to 25 July and South-African Vice-President **Jacob Zuma** on 7 August. The latter signed partnership agreements with the Benin government related to agriculture and trade. Exports from South Africa to Benin have increased. Finally, German President **Horst Köhler** visited Benin from 9 to 12 December. Along with President Kérékou, he inaugurated a new bridge in Cotonou (the so-called 'third bridge') connecting two parts of the city. This bridge was completely financed with German money (CFAfr 9.7 bn). The two presidents signed new cooperation agreements, especially regarding a new bridge in the north of Cotonou.

From 29 November to 10 December, **RECAMP IV** took place in Benin. 'Renforcement des Capacités Africaines de Maintien de la Paix' is a military peacekeeping exercise for West African soldiers initiated by France during the 1990s. This fourth exercise was jointly organised by Benin and France. The aim was to help African countries to manage their own peacekeeping operations on the continent. Thousands of West African soldiers trained together and with Western soldiers, especially from France. All the ECOWAS states sent troops, except Guinea and Liberia, because of their internal problems. Côte d'Ivoire sent just nine field officers, but the Ivorian chief of staff was observed talking with his French counterpart for the first time since November's events in Abidjan. Altogether, 14 countries took part in RECAMP IV. The EU, US and Japan contribute funds for this event. According to the chief of staff, General Fernand Amoussou, Benin was ready for greater participation in peacekeeping operations, and not only in Africa. Several years earlier, Beninese soldiers had participated in UN missions in Kosovo and Timor. In 2004, they were in Côte d'Ivoire and in DR Congo.

In September 2003, Benin was involved in a project on **cotton production** within the framework of the World Trade Organisation's (WTO) ministerial conference in Cancún. This specific initiative related to African cotton was proposed by Benin, Mali, Burkina Faso and Chad, and was aimed at protecting each nation's production. The four countries demanded the ending of the subvention policies of developed countries (especially the US, EU and China). Benin is one of West Africa's larger cotton producers, with 350,000 tonnes per year. After the conference's failure, a meeting was held in Cotonou on 22 March with the WTO's general manager, Supachai Panitchpakdi. Finally, in July, African countries and the EU worked out an agreement in Geneva, but this seemed to be disappointing for Benin.

Socioeconomic Developments

Benin's economy still was largely **dependent on Nigeria** and cross-border trading exchanges with this country were a key part of the economy, especially re-exports and smuggling. There is specialisation in re-exporting manufactured articles to Nigeria, after these goods are first imported into Benin. Goods coming from America, Europe, Asia and even Southern Africa, are unloaded at Cotonou's port and loaded on to trucks bound for Nigeria. One estimate is that about 75% of goods unloaded in Cotonou are exported to Nigeria. Consequently, Benin has profited from customs fees, which play a great part in the state's budget. However, since May 2003 Nigeria has forbidden the import of 46 articles – such as frozen chickens, orange juice, mineral water, clothes, shoes – with the aim of promoting local manufacture. Many of these products passed through Benin. The resultant drop in imports led to falling customs duties. However, on 28 November the Nigerians suspended the prohibition of imports of clothes and five others products: water, cotton seed, vegetable oil, palm nuts and palm seedlings.

At the beginning of December, Benin concluded an agreement with a Nigerian company, South Atlantic Petroleum (SAPETRO), concerning the exploration and operation of an

oilfield located in the border region. From 1986 to 1998, Benin had been engaged in the exploration of this oilfield.

In January, the **European Union** approved three main subsidies totalling € 109 m: € 55 m for poverty reduction, € 30 m for urban road works and sanitation improvements, and € 24 m for the rehabilitation of the road network. These subsidies were financed through the ninth EDF for 2004–06. Poverty reduction, construction work, road rehabilitation, rural development and drinking-water supplies benefited throughout 2004 from **African Development Bank** funds (about $ 130 m). ADF also gave $ 4 m for AIDS prevention and treatment. Moreover, the **World Bank** approved a credit of $ 50 m to improve the access of the poor to social and financial services.

Several projects for the production and distribution of **energy** were in progress. In October, the West African Development Bank of the 'Union Économique et Monétaire Ouest-Africaine' (UEMOA), approved a credit of CFAfr 4.5 bn for electricity connections between the northern and southern areas of Benin and Togo. The total value of this project is CFAfr 46 bn and work began in November. The aim is to improve the electricity supply from 10% to 30% in the areas concerned. As noted earlier, the two countries tried to mobilise funds for the improvement of the Adjarala hydroelectric barrage on the Mono River, which is a major project. Another great project is the 678-kilometre gas pipeline connecting Nigeria to Benin, Togo and Ghana. It will convey natural gas from Nigeria to the three neighbouring countries. On 24 November, the World Bank announced a $ 125 m guarantee for this project, the total value of which is $ 590 m and is part of NEPAD's agenda.

On 29 December, MPs passed the annual **budget** for 2005. It amounted to CFAfr 556 bn. Government spending was set to increase by 1.7% over the previous budget. Concerning revenue, the fiscal system will supply CFAfr 380 bn while CFAfr 176 bn will be financed through external funds. For 2005, GDP growth was estimated at 5.3%, inflation at 2% and the budget at 3.4% of Benin's GDP. On 4 October, government announced an increase in family allowances from CFAfr 1,500 to 2,000.

The end of 2004 witnessed a **social crisis** with strikes by public sector workers, especially in education, who demanded a pay increase, no more pay arrears, reduction of the rate of income tax, the re-grading of civil servants and the non-politicisation of the civil service. The 'Confédération générale des travailleurs du Bénin' (CGTB), one of the main trade unions, well represented in the education system and the civil service, called the first 72-hour general strike from 12 to 14 October: all of Cotonou's public schools were closed. Over the ensuing weeks, other 72-hour general strikes took place. The 'Confédération des syndicats autonomes du Bénin' (CSA-Bénin), which is represented in private companies, joined the CGTB for a larger strike from 19 to 21 October. All public companies closed, the national hospital and public broadcast services curtailed their activities, and service stations and banks were also affected. On 25 October, the government entered into negotiations led by the minister of public office, Boubacar Arouna. At the end of the negotiations, the CGTB called a new 72-hour general strike, with the support of the

'Centrale syndicale des travailleurs du Bénin' (CSTB) and, a week later, of the 'Confédération des organisations syndicales indépendantes du Bénin' (COSI). On 16 November, public schools, public companies and ministries were closed. New negotiations were opened with Bruno Amoussou, the state minister in charge of planning, prospecting and development, while the strikes continued.

At the same time, students protested against a considerable increase **in university fees**. On 3 September, the UEMOA ministers of university education decided to harmonise university fees. For Benin, this meant an increase from CFAfr 6,200 to CFAfr 25,000. When rectors of the two Beninese universities – Abomey-Calavi near Cotonou and Parakou in the north – implemented this decision, the students went on strike on 12 October. On 31 October, the minister of university education, Kémoko Bagnan, announced that university fees would only increase to CFAfr 15,000.

Cédric Mayrargue

Burkina Faso

The fundamental characteristics of the situation in Burkina Faso in 2004 were the preparations for the presidential election scheduled for November 2005 and the outcome of the Ivorian crisis, a matter of deep concern for Burkina Faso, since nearly two million Burkinabè people live and work in Côte d'Ivoire. More broadly, at the sub-regional and international level, Burkina Faso was allegedly involved in certain major political issues such as the abortive coup d'état in Mauritania. Nevertheless, Burkina appears to be a central though controversial actor in West Africa. In this respect, Ouagadougou also hosted the 10th Francophone summit in November, a fact that underlines President Compaoré's influence in 'Françafrique.'

Domestic Politics

The upcoming presidential election in 2005 was the crucial political issue in domestic politics. The central question was, would **Blaise Compaoré** run for a third seven-year term? The Burkinabè president took power in October 1987 after a bloody coup d'etat that resulted in the death of Captain Thomas Sankara, then head of the ruling 'Conseil National de la Révolution' (CNR). Multipartyism was proclaimed only in 1989 and the regime's liberalisation occurred at the beginning of the 1990s, owing to growing domestic and international pressures. Blaise Compaoré was legally elected president in 1991 and re-elected in 1998. At the same time, his party, the 'Congrès pour la Démocratie et le Progrès' (CDP), won a majority in the parliament and, thanks to its control over the major political and administrative levels, confirmed its hegemony. The opposition increased its influence over the years, mainly in parliament, where by 2004 it accounted for nearly half the deputies.

Apart from the question of whether Compaoré would be a candidate for a **third term**, the other central question raised by the presidential election in November 2005 was whether the opposition would be able to unite and present a real challenge to the president. As a consequence of the political crisis engendered by the murder on 13 December 1998 of Norbert Zongo, a well-known journalist and the director of the newspaper 'L'indépendant', the constitution was amended in 2000 and Article 37 was modified. This article stated that the maximum number of terms a president could have is limited to two. This meant, according to certain Burkinabè constitutionalists, that Compaoré, twice elected since 1991, was ineligible to run for a third term. This position corresponded to the stance of 14 opposition parties that announced at a meeting in Ougadougou on 15 May that they opposed a further term for the incumbent president. Other lawyers, however, argued that the constitutional amendment did not apply in his case as it had been made after his re-election in 1998. The other remaining point of suspense concerned the opposition's electoral strategy: would it boycott the election, as in 1991, on the grounds that Compaoré's candidature was unconstitutional? Or would it participate in the election and, if so, with how many candidates? While it was almost certain there would be no boycott, the rest of the electoral strategy remained unclear. By the end of the year, four candidates had emerged: Hermann Yaméogo, for the 'Union pour la Démocratie et le Développement' (UNDD), Gilbert Ouedraogo for the 'Alliance pour la Démocratie et le Développement-Rassemblement Démocratique Africain' (ADF-RDA), Nongma Ernest Ouedraogo for the 'Convention Panafricaine Sankariste' (CPS) and Norbert Michel Tiendrébéogo for the 'Front des Forces Sociales' (FFS), another political party laying claim to the heritage of the late President Sankara. A fifth candidate likely to run for the Sankarist movement was the very influential lawyer Bénéwendé Sankara, leader of the 'Union pour la Renaissance-Mouvement Sankariste' (UNIR-MS). In this context, it was difficult to imagine how the opposition would be able to unite behind a single candidate, a situation a well known Burkinabè academic, Laurent Bado, expressed in these words: "It is not the regime that is strong, it is the opposition that is weak." Significantly, in July the field of opposition parties was enlarged with the establishment of another political grouping by Jean Hubert Bazie, who also claimed to be in the Sankarist tradition.

The regime continued to play on the **opposition's internal cleavages**. Although the ADF-RDA was the most important party in the National Assembly, with 19 deputies, it became divided for reasons that are unclear. While only nine deputies remained faithful to Hermann Yaméogo, the party's 'historical' leader, and created the UNDD, the remaining ten followed Gilbert Ouedraogo under the name of ADF-RDA. Although this party claimed to be part of the opposition, by exacerbating the divisions within the opposition, its strategy was likely to favour Compaoré's re-election. The government did not hesitate to harass its opponents: this was the case on 28 September when Noël Yaméogo, one of the leaders of the UNDD, was arrested on his return from Abidjan and was accused of 'treason and of being a threat to national defence'. The opposition reacted by publishing a statement pointing to the fact that these accusations were false and were intended to weaken and frighten its candidates for the upcoming presidential election.

Despite some reforms that made it possible for the opposition to gain substantial representation in the National Assembly in the legislative elections of 2002, the presidential party, CDP, never really accepted the eventuality of having to relinquish power if the opposition won a majority. It, thus, introduced a **new electoral code** on 27 April 2004, which was passed in the Assembly on 29 April, although most opposition parties boycotted the vote. Voted on by 63 of the 111 MPs, the code included two major changes: the modification of the national independent electoral commission, which would now include state representatives, and the adoption of the proportional representation system (which existed before the reforms of 2002 but had been discarded to defuse political protests) aimed at conferring a crucial advantage on the big parties that are well organised throughout the country, such as CDP. The new electoral districts would be based on the provinces rather than the regions, thus increasing the districts from 15 to 45 and making it more difficult for poorly organised opposition parties to field candidates in each district. Called the '27 April new CDP code' by the opposition, this reform was obviously made to avoid unwelcome surprises in the forthcoming legislative and municipal elections and to ensure CDP a comfortable majority, a prospect that was described by Hermann Yaméogo as the "return of the single party." The country has enjoyed a certain institutional stability since 1987, but true democracy still seemed beyond reach, as no real alternative has been practicable. Instead, there was a continuing 'monarchisation' of power and its personification in Compaoré.

Yet, despite its unchallenged domination, the regime had to face two major problems in 2004: the **consequences of Zongo's murder** on the one hand, and the trial of the authors of the abortive coup d'etat of November 2003. On 13 December, as has been the case every year since 1998, thousands of people demonstrated in Ouagadougou, pledging themselves to pursue the truth and criticising the way justice officials had handled Zongo's case. It should be recalled that the president's brother, François, seemed to be directly involved, as well as soldiers from the Garde Présidentielle, Compaoré's protection force. Zongo's murder fuelled huge popular mobilisation but the truth concerning the murder was never clearly established and no real trial was ever organised. More than ten political parties, unions and human rights movements gathered into the 'Collectif contre l'impunité', headed by Halidou Ouedraogo, the president of the 'Mouvement Burkinabè des Droits de l'Homme et des Peuples' (MBDHP), and participated in this demonstration, while Zongo's widow claimed that she had asked for an international trial and feared that the witnesses of the murder might be 'eliminated'. While the trial of Zongo's murderers still had not happened nearly seven years after the event, the **trial of the 'plotters' of November 2003** took place on 6 April before a military court. According to the government, the coup involved 13 people, mainly military men who had close links with some of Burkina's neighbours, especially Togo and Côte d'Ivoire. Despite the fact that these links had not been clearly established and the reasons of the coup were not identified, seven of the conspirators were sentenced on 18 April to prison and six were acquitted. The alleged leader of the coup attempt, army Captain Luther Ouali Diapagri, was jailed for ten years, while opposition politician Norbert Michel Tiendrébéogo of the FFS, who was accused of complicity, was acquitted. Ouali confessed that he had considered organising a coup, but it appears that the soldiers had corporate grievances (such as pay) rather than political motives.

A major change in the composition of the government involved the replacement of the ministers of defence, environment and information early in the year, on 17 January. The head of Compaoré's cabinet, Yero Boli, became minister of defence. The new cabinet, however, was still composed of people close to the ruling CDP.

Foreign Affairs

The number and diversity of international events Burkina has hosted since the mid-1990s show how influential Compaoré has become. These events began in 1996 with the France-Afrique summit and included the OAU summit and, last but not least, the African football cup. The most recent event took place in Ouagadougou on 26–27 November 2004 in the form of the 10th **Francophone summit**, an opportunity for Burkina to prove to the world its ability to organise such huge events, despite its poverty and underdevelopment. However, there was substantial financial support from France and from Libya, which paid for the luxurious hotel built in 'Ouaga 2000', a large compound located a few miles outside the capital and including the new presidency, a congress centre and a large number of outstanding villas. Despite the fact that the major official theme of the summit was sustainable development, most of the discussions were centred on the Ivorian crisis, and the final declaration stressed the need for a true national dialogue to resolve it. There was a diplomatic incident between Burkina and Côte d'Ivoire at the time of the summit when the Ivorian delegation, headed by the Minister of Integration Théodore Mel Eg, decided to return to Abidjan after being frisked at Ouagadougou airport. Nevertheless, this summit was a real success for Compaoré and Burkinabè diplomacy, as there was no condemnation of their roles in Côte d'Ivoire and in West Africa in general.

Since the death of Félix Houphouët-Boigny in 1993, Compaoré appeared more and more to be seeking to become West Africa's 'big man'. His influence grew with the conflicts in which Burkina was involved: for example, in Liberia, where it supported Charles Taylor, and even in Angola, where Burkina was implicated by the US in major weapons traffic. The crisis in Côte d'Ivoire clearly revealed Compaoré's sub-regional ambitions, as it was obvi-

ous that Burkina was directly involved in the rebellion that resulted in the de facto partition of Côte d'Ivoire between north and south. The Marcoussis Agreement of January 2003,
negotiated under strong French pressure, was supposed to resolve the crisis and were
utilised by Compaoré as a means to reinforce Burkinabè nationalism and consolidate his
own legitimacy. By 2004, it was clear that this agreement was a failure and that **relations
between Burkina and Côte d'Ivoire** were far from good. In a statement in December to
the French newspaper 'Le Figaro', President Compaoré sharply criticised the 'current
power' in Abidjan and its lack of legitimacy. In other words, he considered that Laurent
Gbagbo, the Ivorian president, was not legitimate and that it was this situation that created
political instability in Côte d'Ivoire. In the same statement, Compaoré rejected all the accusations about Burkina's involvement in the rebellion, arguing that his country suffered dramatically from the xenophobia in Côte d'Ivoire, a result of the rhetoric of 'Ivoirité' that,
according to him, arose in 1999, i.e., before the campaign for the presidential election of
2000 that witnessed Gbagbo's election. What was clear, however, was that there was a personal dimension in the relations between Compaoré and Gbagbo. The latter admitted this
soon after Compaoré's statement that the Burkinabè president had efficiently supported him
when he was the only opponent to Félix Houphouët-Boigny – one reason Compaoré never
understood how Gbagbo could turn so 'anti-Burkinabè'. Another sign of poor relations
between the two countries concerned accusations by the government of Burkina that Côte
d'Ivoire violated its airspace with the illegal overflights of military aircraft, starting in
January, in the southwestern part of the country. While the government even hinted at shooting down these aircraft, the government of Côte d'Ivoire denied the allegations.

But the Ivorian crisis was not the only issue in which Compaoré's responsibility was
pointed to. There was also Mauritania, where in October 2004 President Ould Taya directly
accused Burkina and Libya of being involved in 'criminal plots' against his country by supporting and financing 'terrorist groups'. This was not the first time Compaoré's friendship
with Colonel Kadhafi was mentioned: both of them actively supported Charles Taylor and
it was reported in September 2004 that Compaoré and Paul Kagame, the Rwandan president, had begun to build an alliance with Thabo Mbeki, the South African head of state, in
order to counterbalance the rapprochement between Laurent Gbagbo and Angolan
President Jose Eduardo Dos Santos. But it was at the West African level that **Compaoré's
activism** raised most questions, as he frightened his major neighbours, even though his
country is one of the poorest in the world. According to President Gbagbo, Burkina trained
Central African mercenaries in the Burkinabè city of Pô, close to border with Côte d'Ivoire
and Ghana. They were intended to support the rebels who occupied the north of Côte
d'Ivoire. President Gnassingbé Eyadéma of Togo as well as President Lansana Conté of
Guinea often declared themselves to be suspicious of Burkina's support for their opponents.
Conversely, in September, Burkina accused Guinea of hosting a meeting of opponents of
Burkina's government with a view to destabilising the regime of Blaise Compaoré – a
charge Guinea denied.

Yet, despite his poor general record at the sub-regional and continental levels, Compaoré succeeded in making Burkina one of the closest and most influential partners of **France** in Africa south of the Sahara. Two major factors help to explain this success. The first was paradoxically related to the Ivorian crisis. For more than three decades, Côte d'Ivoire was perceived as the true Francophone 'success story', enjoying political stability and economic growth. But the Ivorian model collapsed at the end of the 1980s and the election of Gbagbo as president resulted in a divorce between France and its former West African 'protégé'. In this context, Paris had no choice but to support Compaoré in order to counterbalance this strategic situation. The second reason lay in the fact that Burkina has enjoyed uncommon political stability under Compaoré, which has made it another kind of those success stories that France needs to safeguard its remaining influence in Africa. As evidence of Compaoré's central position in the 'Françafrique' network, the Burkinabè president was awarded an honorary doctorate by the University Jean Moulin-Lyon 3 on 23 April. Initiated by Michel Guillou, the head of the private Institute for the Study of Francophonie and Globalisation, this ceremony was attended by academics and political leaders, with the notable exception of Gérard Collomb, mayor of Lyon and a good friend of Laurent Gbagbo.

Finally, Compaoré paid a very short official **visit to Germany** in March 2004. The first of its kind, it was aimed at enhancing bilateral cooperation in the fields of decentralisation, environment, agriculture and defence.

Socioeconomic Developments

One positive outcome of the Ivorian crisis for Burkina's economy was the commercialisation in Burkina and Mali of more than half the **cotton** produced in the north of Côte d'Ivoire in 2004. More than 220,000 of the 400,000 tonnes of cotton seeds were exported in this way to these two countries, which are both big cotton producers. Mali is the largest producer in Africa south of the Sahara and is second only to Egypt for the whole African continent. Prices in Mali and Burkina in 2004 were at least 20% higher than in Côte d'Ivoire. Moreover, there have been no official structures to collect cotton in northern Côte d'Ivoire since the abortive coup of September 2002 against Gbagbo's regime. This threat to Ivorian cotton production is not likely to improve as long as the de facto partition of Côte d'Ivoire continues. Thus, a consortium of European banks provided a new loan worth $ 78 m with which Burkina's parastatal cotton processing company 'Sofitex' hoped to increase local production by 20% with the help of fertilisers and pesticides. Cotton remained the country's largest source of foreign exchange.

As a result of the crisis in Côte d'Ivoire, the African Development Bank provided funds for a feasibility study for a new **railway link** between Burkina Faso and Ghana that would help remove obstacles in the country's export-import links.

The **water supply** has been a crucial problem in Burkina, and mainly in Ouagadougou, where the needs are proportionate to the capital's growing population. Recurring shortages have always existed, but it seemed that a decisive step towards a long-term solution was taken with the completion of the Ziga dam in July 2004. Located 50 kilometres from Ouagadougou, it has a capacity of 200 million m³ and should supply the capital with water until 2025. It cost CFAfr 150 bn (€ 228.5 m) and involved 12 international donors, among whom were the World Bank, the EU and many Arab and Islamic institutions. Until this dam was completed, water was supplied to Ouagadougou from the Loumbila dam and three smaller dams, with an overall capacity of roughly 36 million m³. In June, work was expected to begin on the Soum dam, some 150 kilometres west of the capital, with funds from the Islamic Development Bank worth € 8.75 m. This dam would help to boost irrigated agriculture and the production of vegetable produce.

A nation-wide survey investigating the results of 12-year long campaign against **female circumcision** showed encouraging results. In many areas, the practice had declined, possibly in part because of the penalties involved (imprisonment and fines).

The 2005 **national budget** was discussed and adopted by the government in September 2004. The country would need CFAfr 90 bn to complete it. The social sectors received 35% of the total budget while defence, foreign affairs and security represented 26%. The African Development Fund (ADF) approved a loan of $ 22.6 m to help the government with reforms under its Poverty Reduction Strategy Support Programme. The World Bank approved credits of $ 60 m for the government's fourth Poverty Reduction Programme and also provided a loan of $ 10 m to encourage statistical capacity building within the administration.

While economic growth was expected to reach 6.5%, people in the north of the country were confronted with potential food shortages due to a severe locust outbreak. As in Niger, the country saw the development of a gold mine that was expected to start production in 2005.

Bill Gates, the well known US billionaire, made a grant of $ 11.7 m in July 2004 to the University of Ouagadougou. Drawn from the Bill Gates Foundation, the grant aimed at developing a regional postgraduate course focused on 'health and population' in partnership with the University of Montreal. The first students to take the course would receive grants, but succeeding students would have to pay $ 10,000 for this training.

Bilateral relations between Burkina and the US seemed to enter a new phase by the end of the year, when President Bush decided to add Burkina to the list of African countries entitled to benefit from the **African Growth and Opportunity Act** (AGOA). Elaborated in 2000, this programme aims at providing African countries that accept the rules of liberalisation privileged access to the American market for certain products. This agreement was important from an economic point of view as well as from a political one, as Burkina had been excluded from AGOA because of its involvement in the Liberian civil war and its support for Charles Taylor.

This issue clearly underlined the fact that Burkina was strongly committed to **economic liberalism**, even if the country was still characterised by a wide-ranging public sector, including 17 state-owned companies whose annual financial results were fairly good. Yet the imposition of liberalism resulted in recurring organised demonstrations by the unions, traditionally active and powerful in the country. This was the case in December 2004 when several hundreds of **workers demonstrated** in Ouagadougou and other parts of the country in favour of higher wages and better living conditions. According to the unions, living conditions have deteriorated progressively since the devaluation of the CFAfr in 1994: fuel prices increased by 68% between 1994 and 2004, according to the unions, while sugar prices increased by 55% during the same period. They added that, "while prices increase, the men in power got richer and enjoy privileges." At the same time, corruption cost the country CFAfr 3 bn in 2003, according to a statement in September by the high authority charged with the coordination of the anti-corruption struggle. Given this situation, the economy was expected to be one of the major issues in the 2005 presidential election. In 1994, Blaise Compaoré launched an ambitious development programme called 'National Commitments', based on six objectives. Ten years after, while some of these were partly achieved, many still remained unfulfilled.

René Otayek

Cape Verde

Cape Verde has consolidated its position as a multiparty country with regular free and fair elections, a free press, high literacy rates, a vibrant civil society and three decades of political stability. On the economic front, Cape Verde has achieved a certain degree of macroeconomic stability, low levels of inflation and declining fiscal deficits. Despite a slight fall in its 2004 Human Development Index, the socioeconomic indicators are impressive as compared to other West African nations: life expectancy is above 70 years; primary and secondary school enrolment is almost 100% and 70% respectively and per capita income is rapidly approaching $ 1,500. These achievements have earned Cape Verde the dubious privilege of exiting the group of Least Developed Countries (LDC).

Domestic Politics

The highlight of domestic politics in 2004 was the fourth **local elections**, which testified to the country's high level of achievement in the area of local governance. In these elections, held on 21 March, the 'Movimento para a Democracia' (MpD), as well as independent groups supported by this party, made historic gains. MpD won 9 of the 17 councils at stake. For the first time, a woman candidate was elected as the mayor of a municipality, São

Vicente, an important commercial and cultural centre. In Sal Island, a traditional stronghold of the 'Partido Africano para a Independência de Cabo Verde' (PAICV), an independent candidate supported by MpD was able to unseat the PAICV-supported mayor, in power for the past 12 years. These gains gave MpD renewed hopes and strength for the legislative elections to be held in early 2006. While the ruling PAICV was able to retain the council in Praia, the largest municipality in the archipelago, the electoral results were interpreted as a warning to the government. Hence, on 3 April, the prime minister, Jose Maria Neves, reshuffled his cabinet, which led to the removal of four incumbent ministers and the inclusion of seven new members.

The efforts to reform the Cape Verdean electoral system were cemented in 1999 by the adoption of the **electoral code**. This code, which was aimed at harmonising elections-related legislation, revoked all previous laws. It equipped the country with a modern electoral system, and made it possible to organise the local elections in 2000. Thereafter, modifications were introduced into the code by 'Law 118/V/2000' of 24 April 2000, in order to remedy certain gaps in the system that had emerged through the application of the code at the time of these elections, and especially to reinforce the strictness and the transparency of the electoral acts. This modified code made it possible to organise and perfect the conduct of the local elections of 2004.

Although these elections proceeded without conflict, they are often the subject of legal disputes among the protagonists. It is worth mentioning that organising elections requires immense human and financial resources that the country often does not have. Modernisation of the electoral system was achieved by partly computerising the electoral system. The electoral files and unfolding results of the elections were placed on-line on the internet. In this way, most election results became available on the same night, with citizens on all islands being able to follow them at first-hand.

Following the loss of key municipalities during the local elections and an analysis of the situation, the PAICV-controlled government embarked on deep **structural reform** aimed at strengthening key sectors perceived as under-performing and liable to strong criticism. In this context, profound changes were introduced in foreign affairs, finance, economy, justice, internal affairs, labour and social solidarity, both at cabinet ministerial and senior director levels. Among other things, the government announced plans to create a constitutional court by 2005.

Security problems became much more pronounced during 2004 and were related to two major issues: (i) an increase in drug-related activities, Cape Verde being an important link in the traffic in drugs between the Americas and Europe; and (ii) petty crime related to an increase in both urban and rural poverty. An international meeting, supported by the UN Office on Drugs and Crime (UNODC), was held in October 2004 in Praia to help the government define a strategy and mobilise resources for drug and crime control.

Foreign Affairs

Cape Verde had a balanced approach to diplomacy and intended to make use of its prestige in this area to contribute to the preservation of stability in the West African sub-region. The Cape Verdean minister of foreign affairs chaired the contact group set up by the 'Comunidade dos Países de Língua Portuguesa' (CPLP) in July 1998 to provide mediation in the crisis in **Guinea-Bissau**. Cape Verdean authorities, following the events of October 2004 in Guinea-Bissau, were personally involved in the mediation of this conflict, and integrated the CPLP delegation. Membership in ECOWAS remained an important part of Cape Verde's foreign policy. Cape Verde armed forces took part for the first time in military exercises, named RECAMP IV, in Benin in December 2004.

Cape Verde sought to diversify external support in order to expand its traditional partners. South-African Vice-President Jacob Zuma visited Cape Verde in August 2004, while the Cape Verdean prime minister went on a visit to Beijing in the same month. In addition, the US showed a growing interest because of the strategic location of the archipelago and lobbied to obtain improved port and airport facilities. The privileged partnership with the Portuguese-speaking states of the South (Angola and Brazil, in particular) was maintained. The head of the Brazilian state, Lula da Silva, paid an official visit to Praia in July 2004, consolidating cooperation between the two countries. On the European front, **cooperation with Portugal** remained at a high level, as evidenced by the visit of Portuguese Prime Minister Santana Lopes in December 2004, which concluded with the signing of an Indicative Cooperation Programme (PIC) for the next three years, totalling € 54 m. Portugal has strongly supported Cape Verde's request for a special close status with the EU, and has been trying to mobilise other European countries in this cause.

Under the auspices of UN reform, the government was informed that the major agencies of the UN's country team had been selected, along with the UN system in the Maldives, to be a pilot for the implementation of the first-ever UN joint office. This initiative, effective from January 2006, would proceed under still to be negotiated modalities.

Socioeconomic Developments

Cape Verde experienced remarkable **growth** and development during the 1990s, having at times seen growth in excess of 7.5% annually. Although improvements in public health have ebbed in recent years, Cape Verde's social indicators remained among the highest in sub-Saharan Africa. This performance in human development, a result of the country's policy efforts to address poverty by fostering private sector development as well as promoting investments in human capital, contributed strongly to the decision to approve the removal of Cape Verde **from the group of Least Developed Countries**. This decision was made by the UN General Assembly in December 2004, based on the fact that Cape Verde had twice consecutively satisfied two of the three criteria, per capita income and human development indicators. As to the third requirement, economic vulnerability, Cape Verde remained one of the most vulnerable countries, making implementation of the UN's decision a special challenge. The UN also approved a strategy for a three-year phased transition in this process. Cape Verde's own strategy for this transition phase was supported by UNDP, the Special Programme on Least Developed Countries, the Small Islands Development States (SIDS) group and UNCTAD.

The **Poverty Profile** was formulated in 2004 upon publication of the results of the Household Income and Expenditure Survey (IRDF) carried out in 2001–02. Although there had been a measured economic growth in the previous three years, averaging 5%, it was found that relative poverty had increased significantly in Cape Verde over the previous decade. The poverty profile showed that: (i) 37% of the population was still considered poor, with most of them living in rural areas (62%), although poverty also increased in urban areas; (ii) of the total poor population, about 54% were considered very poor, which corresponded to 20% of the country's population; (iii) about 51% of the poor were women; (iv) poverty increased with family size; (v) education significantly affected poverty; (vi) the predominantly agricultural islands of Santo Antão and Fogo had most poverty; (vii) unemployment affected the poor more than the non-poor; and (viii) agriculture and fisheries workers were more likely to be poor than those in other sectors.

The current administration continued with its commitment to address the country's fiscal problems. The macroeconomic dialogue with the World Bank and the IMF, aimed at containing public spending and resolving external and domestic arrears, was maintained, with fairly good evaluations by both institutions. The government introduced the **Value Added Tax** (VAT) system in January 2004, with the resulting adjustment of customs duties and the abolition of other consumption taxes. These reforms were intended to address some anomalies resulting from a distorted fiscal structure. After a rocky start, several adjustments were made and the system seemed to be fairly well accepted by service providers and consumers.

Following several structural reforms that led government to align the domestic oil pricing mechanism with the international price and to adopt a system of scholarships for students in overseas universities, government sought and obtained support from the World Bank and UNDP to develop its '**Documento de Estratégia de Crescimento e Redução da Pobreza**' (DECRP), an initiative that is consistent with Cape Verde's IDA status. Government started negotiations with the World Bank aimed at obtaining concessionary credit under a Poverty Reduction Strategic Credit, to be implemented under the modality of budgetary aid. The Netherlands and the EU also made strong commitments to the government to provide future assistance under a budgetary aid mechanism. These new initiatives by the government were supported by a strong commitment from development partners to help put together stable and transparent budget control mechanisms.

The first **Millennium Development Goals** report was published. The studies that formed the basis for the publication of this report contributed significantly to the establishment of the DECRP indicators and demonstrated that Cape Verde was moving in the right direction in several areas, namely education, health and access to safe water. However, an additional effort was needed in poverty reduction if the established objectives were to be achieved in 2015. Cape Verde was also placed on the list of US beneficiaries under the newly created Millennium Challenge Account (MCA). This initiative benefits developing countries that have made commitments to and achieved results in economic growth and good governance, including respect for human rights. Negotiations were under way for the approval of an ambitious programme put forward by the government. The strategy adopted by government for the proposed MCA assistance programme was first discussed with civil society in May 2004 and placed emphasis on two areas: (i) developing the rural economy and (ii) increasing the competitiveness of the Cape Verdean economy in the global marketplace. The programme will address key bottlenecks that constrain economic performance and limit the nation's ability to end poverty. Targeted investment would support programmes that increase productivity, expand the rural economy and build a globally competitive economy that ensures sustainable growth while avoiding the creation of a dual society. A self-sustaining high growth economy is the ultimate goal.

Carlos Lopes

Côte d'Ivoire

Despite some apparent progress, 2004 was marked by the failure, yet again, of the process of reconciliation and repeated fiascos in the implementation of the resolutions of the Marcoussis Agreements. The situation took a tragic turn in November when the Gbagbo regime decided to break the ceasefire that had existed since May 2003. An open crisis with respect to the French army degenerated into looting and violence against French civilians and, more broadly, white people. As a consequence, the great majority of Europeans were evacuated and many enterprises ground to a halt or closed their doors, thereby jeopardising the fragile hopes of economic recovery. The country remained divided in two and ordinary people were taken hostage and were the main victims of this situation of violence, hate, insecurity, and dramatically increased poverty.

Domestic Politics

Five years after its first coup d'état, in December 1999, the country remained in turmoil. Since the further coup attempt instigated in September 2002 by 'rebel' forces, whose advance on Abidjan was halted by French troops based in the country, Côte d'Ivoire has been divided into the rebel-controlled north and the government-controlled south. A compromise agreement backed by the UN was signed in **Linas-Marcoussis** (France) on 23

January 2003, and the peace-keeping role of the French army (the 'Licorne' force) was recognised through a Security Council resolution.

What has since been at stake was the full application of this agreement, whose most critical terms were the "regrouping and subsequent disarming of all forces" and **the reform of Article 35 of the constitution concerning eligibility for the presidency**, currently limited to candidates whose father and mother are both of Ivorian origin. Throughout the year, the resolution of the crisis was marked by one step forward and two steps backward, and the very pessimistic outlook at the end of the year clearly called into question the holding of the next presidential elections in October 2005. The main protagonists stood firm and took every opportunity to reinforce their positions, because none of the parties was interested in making the first move: indeed, many of them continued to profit from the situation of neither war nor peace.

There were two main camps and two outsiders watching for the first opening. On one side stood **Laurent Gbagbo**, winner of the October 2000 presidential election, and his '**Front Populaire Ivoirien**' (FPI), backed by influential 'patriot' groups (so called by themselves and the media) such as Charles Blé Goudé's 'Congrès Panafricain des Jeunes Patriotes' (COJEP) or Eugène Djué's 'Union pour la Libération Totale de la Côte d'Ivoire' (UPLTCI). The Gbabo regime held to its two main goals: the reconquest of all the national territory, and the elimination of the main competitors for the next presidential contest, specifically his **bête noire**. **Alassane Ouattara** – leader of the 'Rassemblement des Républicains' (RDR), Houphouët-Boigny's former prime minister, and suspected of complicity in the rebellion. On the other side stood the rebel groups: 'Mouvement Patriotique de Côte d'Ivoire' (MPCI), 'Mouvement Patriotique du Grand Ouest' (MPIGO), and 'Mouvement pour la Justice et la Paix' (MJP), now renamed '**Forces Nouvelles**' (FN) within the national reconciliation government created by the Marcoussis Agreements. These groups sought constitutional reform before disarming (mainly the amendment of Article 35, which would allow Ouattara's candidacy). However, neither side is homogeneous and many rivalries exist. FPI has its hawks and its patronage networks; FN has experienced violent leadership conflict, as shown by the rivalry between FN political leader **Guillaume Soro's** camp and that of Ibrahim Coulibaly ('IB'), mastermind of the military rebellion, which spilled over into an open fight and a massacre in the northern city of Korhogo in 20–21 June. In this context the two outsider parties – the historic 'Parti Démocratique de Côte d'Ivoire' (PDCI) of dismissed President **Henri Konan Bédié**, and RDR – were not on the front line of the fight between FPI and FN, but played their own game from the perspective of the next presidential election, even if they were part of the various opportunistic alliances putting pressure on Gbagbo's regime.

All through the year, the national reconciliation government chaired by Prime Minister Seydou Diarra again faced great difficulties: lack of real authority because of obstacles placed in its way by the presidency and reluctance to transfer power; frequent suspensions of government meetings because of boycotts by the opposition; day to day interference by 'street' patriots and media; repeated meddling and obstruction by the National Assembly, etc. However, the year started well with the return on 6 January of the FN members, who had boycotted the council of the ministers since late September 2003. Many bills related to the Marcoussis agenda were adopted by government for submission to the National Assembly.

Unfortunately, the first major crisis occurred on 25–26 March, when a protest was repressed in Abidjan. The demonstration was against the rule of President Gbagbo and FPI after opposition parties accused them of obstructing the reform process. Attacks by the militias and security forces resulted in killings: a **commission of inquiry** appointed by the UN High Commissioner for Human Rights concluded (14 May) that "at least 120 people [were] killed, 274 wounded and 20 disappeared." Other sources gave higher figures. As a consequence, all opposition members decided to boycott the council of the ministers (PDCI's ministers were still on strike over the contract linked to the management of the port of Abidjan, see below), thereby stalling the reconciliation process once more. Soro did not hesitate to raise the **prospect of secession**.

April to June were months of high tension marked by continual verbal abuse in the press, threats and intimidation by militias, and the disappearance and probable assassination on 16 April of the French-Canadian journalist Guy-André Kieffer (following the assassination of Jean Hélène of Radio France Internationale in October 2003), who was investigating controversial issues in the shadows of Ivorian politics. In reaction to press leaks before the presentation of the results of the inquiry into the events of March, supporters of the regime protested in front of the UN building in Abidjan (13 May). Political tension again escalated in mid-May when Gbagbo fired three boycotting FN ministers from government without consulting the prime minister. In reaction, Prime Minister Diarra adjourned the weekly meetings of government, which tried to continue its work with the remaining ministers from FPI and the six representatives of four small allied parties. On 6–7 June, unknown forces attacked Gohitafla and Kounahiri (small towns in the mid-west) and were beaten back by the regular army – 'Forces Armées Nationales de Côte d'Ivoire' (**FANCI**) – and **French 'Licorne' forces**. In response, 'patriots' in Abidjan organised demonstrations and accused France of encouraging the attack and failing to protect civilians.

A lull occurred from late June with the end of the political round between the prime minister and the G7 (the opposition forces signatory to the Marcoussis Agreement). The final communiqué (21 June) requested the implementation of the Marcoussis programme and an ending of the obstacles in the way of the government's work. This step forward was consolidated by the international conference in Accra (29–30 July), which allowed the reconciliation process to start again by revalidating the Marcoussis agenda. The main result was agreement on a deadline (15 October) for the start of the disarmament process and the implementation of the DDR programme.

The next weeks were marked by renewed procrastination because of the preconditions put forward by each side. The extraordinary session of the National Assembly (16

August–28 September) did not result in significant progress for the reform process, and FN finally refused to disarm before Article 35 was amended. Thereafter the situation deteriorated sharply. Patriots exerted new pressure on the streets and in the media. On 17 October, former FPI Prime Minister Affi Nguessan (one of the signatories of the Marcoussis Agreement) demanded the resignation of Prime Minister Diarra and the formation of a government of 'national protection' instead of 'national reconciliation'. FN ministries were recalled to Bouaké (FN's headquarters). At that time, the hawks in the regime decided to change gear (4 November): the headquarters of RDR and PDCI and of some opposition's newspapers ('Le Patriote', close to RDR, and '24 Heures') were wrecked; protests and plundering broke out in Abidjan and other cities; and FANCI launched an **offensive against rebel troops** in a liberation war, with air strikes against some northern cities, without any response from UN intervention forces, followed by a ground attack on Bouaké, which was stopped by UN Moroccan troops. Simultaneously in Abidjan, foreign radio stations (RFI, BBC, Africa no. 1) were forbidden from broadcasting as the regime took direct control of 'Radio Télévision Ivoirienne'.

There was a further dramatic escalation on 6 November when **French troops** in Bouaké were attacked from the air and 9 soldiers died. France's President Chirac ordered an immediate reprisal and the destruction of the Ivorian airforce, based in Yamoussoukro and Abidjan (4 Sukhoi fighters and 5 Mi-24 helicopters). This in turn led to direct vengeance by the 'people', driven on by militias, against the French and, more broadly, white people, with physical violence (including rape, but no deaths), destruction of private assets (homes, businesses) and of all the symbols of the French presence, such as high schools. A confrontation between the crowd and French troops in front of the Hotel Ivoire, near the Gbagbo's residence in Abidjan, resulted in Ivorian civilian deaths (between 20 and 60 according to different sources). The result of this increasing chaos was the **evacuation of nearly 9,000 people** by French troops (increased from 4,000 to 5,200 in response to the crisis), while British and Dutch commandos took charge of the evacuation of some diplomatic delegations. At the end of the year, about 1,000 white people remained in the country.

This new round of violence led to unanimous condemnation by the international community. At that time, the Gbagbo regime offered goodwill tokens by accelerating discussion of the reforms by the National Assembly. Three bills were adopted on 17 December, including the amendment of Article 35, but the Gbagbo's insistence on the need for ratification through a referendum (which is correct from a constitutional standpoint) led to new dissent. Consequently, by the end of the year, the reconciliation process was again totally frozen in a context now marked by renewed violence in the mid-west (around Ouragahio) because of land conflicts. In short, the opposition sought constitutional reforms that require a referendum, which in turn implies territorial integrity, but FN refused to disarm without the reforms. It was a vicious circle.

This disastrous situation underscores the main Ivorian problem: the **absence of alternative leadership** and the inability of the political class to find an exit from the crisis. The

Ivorian drama is absolutely not the consequence of ethnic conflict, even if the 'Ivoirité' debate (based on who or what is Ivorian) is confusing. The country had faced a deep structural crisis, and the easiest solution in the context of the fight over the succession to Houphouët-Boigny was to discredit competitors using ethno-nationalistic rhetoric and to look for scapegoats. From that perspective, Gbagbo had played a **double game** from the beginnings of the crisis: an official neutrality or conciliatory role, to appear as the protector of the nation, while his nearest and dearest (Mamadou Koulibaly, FPI's president of National Assembly, and Simone Gbagbo, his wife and the Assembly's FPI head) and the hate media outdid each other in adding fuel to the fire.

Foreign Affairs

Due to its economic and political role in West Africa and the growing risks arising from the continued crisis, the country received constant attention from the international community, which expressed its commitment through greater and more direct UN involvement.

On 4 and 27 February, **the Security Council passed two resolutions** (1527 and 1528) and later decided to establish a UN operation in Côte d'Ivoire (**UNOCI**) to relieve the ECOWAS intervention forces. The mandate was for 12 months, starting on 4 April, and the French forces remained in order to support UNOCI. A total of 6,420 UNOCI troops were deployed between April and July – mainly from Bangladesh (50%), Morocco (15%), and West Africa (25%), partly including former ECOWAS forces – and joined the 4,000 French troops. This mandate aimed mainly at implementing the ceasefire agreement of May 2003, re-establishing trust between the Ivorian forces involved, starting the DDR process, protecting civilians and restoring authority. A further particular aim was monitoring borders, particularly the border with Liberia, which is one of the more sensitive both for the resolution of the Ivorian crisis and to halt its spread. **The aftermath of the civil wars in Sierra Leone and Liberia** continued to cast a heavy shadow over the Ivorian crisis. The situation in Liberia had repercussions for the Ivorian crisis. For instance, the rebels with the MPIGO were strongly supported by former Liberian President Charles Taylor, while the Gbagbo regime helped the Movement for Democracy in Liberia (MODEL), whose former fighters and weapons could now be found in some of the regime's militias, such as the 'Front pour la Libération du Grand Ouest' (FLGO).

The impasse in the Marcoussis process, the government's state of paralysis, the growing political stress, and sporadic violence and killings led the African heads of state to take the initiative. An **international conference involving** all the signatories of the Marcoussis Agreement was convened in **Accra** on 29–30 July by Ghanaian President John Kufuor (also the president of ECOWAS) and Olusegun Obasanjo, president of Nigeria and of the **AU**, and by Kofi Annan, UN Secretary-General. A dozen heads of state participated, indicating the high priority afforded the resolution of the Ivorian crisis. The conference, named Accra

III, was the sequel to the Marcoussis Agreement and confirmed all its objectives, but also set specific deadlines to strengthen the dynamic for reform and action.

The extent of the risks created by the November events led to a new and immediate response by the AU, which on 7 November gave a specific **mediation mandate** to South African President **Mbeki**. He travelled to Abidjan on 9 November, right in the middle of the crisis, met with President Gbagbo and saw a city under siege by both patriots and French troops. Soon after he returned to Pretoria, Mbeki made contact with the main protagonists in the Ivorian drama: Prime Minister Diarra, Alassane Ouattara, Alphonse Djédjé Mady (general secretary of PDCI), Guillaume Soro and Simone Gbagbo. An extraordinary African summit was called in Abuja on 14 November, where the FANCI attacks where universally condemned and immediate UN sanctions were requested. These **sanctions** were imposed on 15 November by UN Security Council **Resolution 1572**, which placed an **immediate embargo** on all weapons destined for Côte d'Ivoire, froze all the private assets of, and prohibited travel by leaders implicated in the spreading of violence (as from 15 December if there was no improvement).

In the following weeks, President Mbeki continued his mediation efforts to establish new guidelines. At the same time, Albert Tévoédjré, the special representative of the UN Secretary-General appointed shortly after Marcoussis in February 2003, decided to resign (6 December), noting the rupture of the ceasefire and the international fiasco in the resolution of the crisis.

By the end of the year, the **diplomatic isolation of the Gbagbo regime** was incontestable and the Ivorian president tried to reengage in dialogue with Paris, at the same time (20 December) seeking the condemnation of neighbouring countries, most pointedly Burkina Faso, that unofficially supported the rebellion. However, the provocation of the French troops and their riposte provided the Ivorian regime a new opportunity to focus on the 'bilateralisation – internationalisation' of the conflict to strengthen national cohesion and to again legitimise presidential power. Hence, for example, the patriot leader Blé Goudé, declared (15 November) that the crisis was now a "Franco-Ivorian crisis", while Mamadou Koulibaly spoke of a long-lasting war and claimed that "Côte d'Ivoire will be France's Vietnam" (7 November).

The civilian deaths caused by French troops deeply traumatised Ivorian opinion. It was easy for demagogic patriots to convey that what was at stake was the defence by the French government of French private companies and their profitable businesses. This discourse took shape around the idea of 'true independence for Côte d'Ivoire' after 40 years of neocolonialism. From this perspective, Côte d'Ivoire became for opinion in many African countries highly symbolic of the **fight against neo-colonialism** (well known in the former French colonies as 'Françafrique'). Some commentators drew comparisons with the Zimbabwean situation, with Gbabgo acting as a West-African Mugabe by facing international condemnation and drawing a line of defence against an international conspiracy.

Socioeconomic Developments

The strength of the economy continued to surprise many observers, given the division of the country and the state of war. With a GDP of around € 10 bn, Côte d'Ivoire was **still the main economy in the CFA zone**. Infrastructures were still intact (but not maintained), and the huge cocoa output (more than 1.3 m tonnes expected for 2003–04, around 40–45% of world production) offered substantial incomes to the state. The government still controlled most of the raw materials produced in the country: coffee, cocoa (around 40% of total exports), timber, and oil (whose production is promising) are in the south, often called the 'useful' Côte d'Ivoire. The economy of the northern part of the country under FN control (55% of the territory but less than 25% of the population and 15% of fiscal revenue) remains mainly based on cotton, production of which faced constant problems of supply and marketing, in spite of the gradual reopening of the railway to Abidjan and the development of substitute routes through Burkina Faso and Ghana. As a result, production was again expected to drop by about 30% to 250–300,000 tonnes of cottonseed.

However, Côte d'Ivoire has experienced **a four-year recession** since the 1999 coup (2001 was a year of a quasi-stagnation). The year 2004 should have witnessed an economic recovery, according to donor projections, but political events, endless instability and the climate of fear did not allow the private sector to regain its confidence. Above all, the disastrous events of November dispelled any lasting illusions. The cost of the destruction was estimated at CFAfr 150 bn (€ 22,5 m) and the impact on small and medium enterprises owned or headed by Europeans (about 500) was deep as many were obliged to cease activity when 130 foreign subsidiaries suspended their operations. As a consequence, about 30,000 redundancies arose and the state's fiscal revenue will probably collapse, given that these enterprises yielded about 60% of tax income.

The November crisis and its consequences could be the **final blow** for a country on the edge of the abyss. The average income per capita has halved over the last ten years of economic crisis and the **poverty rate** has increased from 38% to 44% of the total population in the last two years. No country in the world could withstand such a shock and it is not surprising that social cohesion and major values have collapsed in Côte d'Ivoire. This devastating situation, which offers no future for the large majority of the population, particularly the youth, leaves the door wide open to all sorts of political currents, and to the militias. And the 26% of the population of foreign origin (one of the highest percentages in the world) is hostage to this situation.

The accelerated **deterioration of governance** in the coffee and cocoa sector was symptomatic of the general climate to pursue money as a means for political power and personal enrichment. This sector, which has been at the heart of economic and political power in the country and intimately linked to state formation over the past 50 years, more and more resembled a mafia network and dramatically illustrated the failure of the liberalisation process in the context of the breakdown of the rule of law.

Since the dismantling of the publicly owned 'Caisse de Stabilisation' in 1999, new institutions under private control by the sector's economic agents – mainly producers – have been dedicated to the management of the export chain. There are five of them: 'Bourse du café-cacao' (BCC) and 'Fonds de régulation et de contrôle' (FRC) regulates exports and prices; 'Fonds de développement et de promotion des activités des producteurs de café-cacao' (FDPCC) is supposed to promote and modernise production; 'Fonds de garantie des coopératives café-cacao' (FGCCC), guarantees loans to cooperatives; and 'Autorité de régulation du café et du cacao' (ARCC), the only public organisation, approves exporter and trader activities. These institutions withhold specific taxes which, when added to the export tax, represent systematic exploitation of the sector. In 2004, the regulatory bodies of the sector plus the customs collected CFAfr 310 (€ 0.47) per kilo of cocoa exported, while producers were paid between CFAfr 200 and 250 per kg (the official price is CFAfr 280). Meanwhile, Ghanaian farmers received about CFAfr 600, and this disparity led to the smuggling of cocoa and coffee to neighbouring countries (now even Burkina Faso exports cocoa!).

All these bodies were often controlled by pseudo-producers with close ties to the regime and its different networks. Each institution exerted its own influence with the objective to have a share of the pie, and since 2001 major funds have been invested in very questionable operations (such as the repurchase of old assets of a bankrupt cocoa exporter, an old grinding mill in the US, a poultry farm, old plantations). In 2004, FRC and FGCCC repurchased DAFCI, an export company owned by the French group Bolloré (see below).

The **audit** of the financial flows of the coffee and cocoa sector, commissioned by the EU at the request of the Ivorian government in coordination with donors, in July 2003, was delivered by IDC consultant group and approved in September. The audit was under the supervision of the 'Comité interministériel des matières premières' (CIMP), chaired by the prime minister. Nevertheless, it was undertaken in very unfavourable circumstances, with limited or no cooperation from the different regulatory bodies in the sector. The audit confirmed the high degree of financial, technical and legal confusion in the management of the sector, including political interference in the nomination of boards and utilisation of funds, disregard of the rules, favouritism towards private companies close to the regime, interference with free competition, etc. Between October 2000 and June 2003, the total amount of tax collected from these bodies was at least CFAfr 300 bn (but probably nearer CFAfr 350 bn), but the fate of more than CFAfr 100 bn is unexplained. The global cost of these institutions monopolized by a few private clubs was CFAfr 18 bn, twice as much as the former 'Caisse de Stabilisation', which was unanimously denounced by all donors.

In this context of **extensive corruption**, farmers – partly manipulated by some of the regime's political networks – decided to mount a show of strength: they campaigned for an indefinite cocoa boycott from 18 October with the aim of protesting the tax burden and the misappropriation of funds. However, the events of November overtook the protest. At the same time, despite the existence of CIMP, the highest authority to define the sector's policy,

President Gbagbo created (22 October) a 'Comité de pilotage et de suivi de la réforme', under his direct control and with 75% of its members linked to his political network. This new committee clearly trespasses on the prime minister's sphere.

Two other facts made big news. In February, the French group **Bolloré** – which holds the main assets in the transport sector – won the contract to manage Vridi container terminal in Abidjan's port, the main port in West Africa. Intense controversy erupted, because of the lack of public tendering, and the contract was perceived by the opposition, specifically PDCI, as a goodwill gesture by President Gbagbo to President Chirac during his official visit to France. This approach was also denounced by the World Bank. At another level, the year was also marked by the replacement between 15 September and 31 December of CFAfr banknotes in all eight countries of the BCEAO zone ('Banque Centrale des Etats de l'Afrique de l'Ouest'). This process, unusual for its brevity given the scale of the under-taking, was of particular concern to Côte d'Ivoire, firstly because it holds 40% of the money supply, and secondly because the operation was mainly meant to stop the use and launder-ing of hundreds of millions of CFAfr robbed during the attack on BCEAO branches in Abidjan and in the north. It could also be seen as a way to destroy the rebels' war chest.

At the end of the year, the country faced a new fiscal crisis, which will escalate dramat-ically in light of the impact of November's events on private enterprises. The government experienced growing difficulty in paying the 90,000 civil servants' salaries. To address the fiscal shortfall, it asked foreign export companies for help: three medium-sized companies (Tropival, Amajaro and Outspan) agreed to pay one year's worth of anticipated export tax in exchange for a 10% discount!

Relations with donors deteriorated. Overdue payments to the World Bank resulted in the suspension of payments on 16 June, and was confirmed in November. The long-promised EU donation of € 300 m for the stabilisation of the cocoa sector remained sus-pended. On this point, the results of the audit were pointed out by the head of the European Commission, Romano Prodi, to Prime Minister Diarra when he went to Brussels in late September. Lastly, Côte d'Ivoire was removed from the 36-country list of the US AGOA in December.

Bruno Losch

Gambia

The year marked the tenth anniversary of the overthrow of Sir Dawda Jawara and his party, the Peoples Progressive Party (PPP) – which had been ruling the country since independence in 1965 – in a bloodless military coup on 22 July 1994. The celebration of this anniversary took place in a climate of economic crisis and fear. Economic instability, frequent changes in the composition of government and the top echelons of the civil service, and restrictions on press freedom were the most striking features of economic and political life. Although the rate of inflation fell from nearly 18% at the end of 2003 to less than 10% by the end of 2004, the depreciation of the Dalasi, the Gambian currency, placed strains on family budgets, since salaries and other forms of income remained low.

Domestic Politics

In October 2001, President Al Haji Yahya A.J.J. Jammeh, who led the Armed Forces Provisional Ruling Council (AFPRC) that ruled the country for two years following the coup of 22 July 1994 coup, was re-elected with a comfortable majority. As of 2002, when legislative elections were held, Jammeh's party, the Alliance for Patriotic Reorientation and Construction (APRC), controlled almost all the elected seats in the National Assembly, since the opposition parties had boycotted the polls. In April 2004, a **new political party** was added to Gambia's political life, called the Gambia Party for Democracy and Progress (GPDP). It was registered with the independent electoral commission, with Henry Gomez as its secretary-general.

During the year, both politicians who had been or were secretaries of state (ministers) as well as senior civil servants were required to testify before a commission of inquiry purposely established to investigate corrupt practices in government, the civil service and parastatal bodies. This was part of President Jammeh's **anti-corruption crusade**, dubbed 'Operation No Compromise.' The widely publicised hearings of this commission, which began on 19 July, reminiscent of the commissions of enquiry of the two years of the AFPRC (1994–96), were occasions for uncovering a multitude of corrupt practices. However, neither the president nor members of parliament were forced to testify. This year were also several cases of corruption before the high court, involving some high officials of the central bank and former ministers. As in previous years, several secretaries of state and senior civil servants were dismissed and replaced with others, making Gambia's Second Republic one of those in Africa with the highest turnover rates at these levels of the state. One of the senior officials dismissed, in December 2003, was a former close collaborator of Jammeh, **Yankuba Touray**, who was one of the leaders of the AFPRC, and had been a minister since he came to power.

Perhaps more illustrative of what appeared to be a shift in the domestic balance of power was the arrest, detention and **trial of Baba Jobe**, who used to be one of the strongest men in the ruling party. Until his arrest and detention in 2003, Jobe was Majority Leader in the National Assembly. His name was also on the list of people sanctioned by the UN, along with Charles Taylor of Liberia, for their roles in the conflicts and civil wars in West Africa, something against which the Gambian government vigorously protested. Later in 2004, he was sentenced to nine years and eight months, having been accused of a number of crimes, including the failure to settle bills with the Gambia Ports Authority. The trial was covered by the media and several senior officials were made to testify, including the governor of the central bank, Clarke Barjo, and the Secretary-General in the President's Office and Head of the Civil Service, Alieu Ngom.

Lamin Waa Juwara, leader of the opposition National Democratic Action Movement (NDAM) was freed on 25 June, after a six-month jail sentence was imposed on him in February. He had called on Gambians to demonstrate against the government's policies.

In the course of the year, the independent press and human rights organisations continued campaigning against **the draconian media laws** that came into force in December. A national media commission, a state-appointed committee, now had the right to force reporters to reveal their confidential sources and issue arrest warrants for journalists. Laws also made it a requirement for newspaper owners to deposit D (Dalasi) 500,000 (about $ 17,240) before being allowed to operate. The restrictions were strongly criticised by the Gambia Press Union, along with all major international human rights organisations and were subsequently amended to eliminate some of the most controversial provisions. Yet the legislation remained highly restrictive of press freedom. Thus, journalists could be sentenced to six months in prison for libellous articles and to three years if they had been convicted before.

Harassment of the independent media also continued. On 13 April, the printing presses of 'The Independent', the most important daily newspaper, were destroyed when six gunmen stormed its offices and poured petrol on the machines and set them on fire. The studios of Radio One FM, a private radio station, were subjected to an arson attack earlier on. The house of Ebrima Sillah, BBC correspondent and one of the leading journalists in the country, was also set on fire 15 August around 3 a.m. None of these cases was seriously investigated and eye witness reports carried by the local media linked the attacks to an obscure group called the Green Boys, a kind of militia that claimed to be defending the 22 July 1994 revolution. The most serious case, however, was the **assassination** on 16 December of Deyda Hydara, co-founder and editor of 'The Point', on the very night his paper was celebrating its 13th anniversary. Hydara was a veteran journalist and correspondent of Agence France Presse and Reporters Without Borders. He was once the president of the Gambia Press Union, and had made critical public statements on the media bill. In protest, hundreds of journalists marched through the capital, Banjul, and a one-week media strike was held, starting on 22 December. While the government also condemned the killing and denied any links between it and the tighter press laws, the president of the Press Union, Demba Jawo, called for an independent inquiry into this and other killings.

On the brighter side of things, civil society and opposition political parties showed signs of improvement in organisation and greater determination in their attempts to challenge government policies. The year was also marked by more serious efforts towards the formation of a **coalition of opposition parties**. Those efforts began to bear fruit when the leading opposition parties agreed to field a single candidate in two by-elections (including for the replacement of Baba Jobe as National Assembly member), which they subsequently won. A coalition of opposition parties, called the National Alliance for Democracy and Development (NADD), was subsequently formed with a view to approaching the October 2006 presidential elections and the legislative elections that would follow as a united force with an alternative political programme.

Foreign Affairs

A breakthrough in direct peace talks between the Senegalese government and representatives of the separatist movement of the Casamance, the 'Mouvement des Forces Démocratiques de la Casamance' (MFDC), appeared to augur well for peace in the subregion. It would mean fewer refugees fleeing into Gambia and consequently less tension with Senegal over the hosting of refugees from the Casamance. **Relations with Senegal**, with which Gambia at one time formed a short-lived confederation, had been tense since the Gambian government announced measures in December 2002 to dramatically increase the fee for residential permits for foreigners. The fee for ECOWAS citizens residing in the country was raised from D 55 to D 1,000 for each member of their families, and non-ECOWAS citizens were henceforth required to pay D 1,500 for each family member. Until then, Senegalese citizens residing in Gambia were not subjected to the same conditions as other foreigners. This time, the conditions were to be the same. This created fears among foreigners residing in the country, and several hundreds of people decided to leave the country in 2003 to go back to Senegal, Sierra Leone or other countries. Another occasion that year for tension between Gambia and Senegal was a football match played in Dakar that led to minor clashes between supporters of the two teams, the news of which led to attacks against Senegalese residents in The Gambia. In 2004, however, relations between the two countries improved as a result of the strong intervention of the authorities of the two countries, as well as religious leaders.

One of the most important issues that continued to be at the heart of relations between the two countries was **cross-border trade**, since Gambia imports large quantities of basic consumer goods such as sugar, rice, textiles and China green tea, with a view to re-exporting them to neighbouring countries, particularly Senegal, where trade tariffs were for a long time significantly higher. This has been seen in Senegal as an obstacle to efforts to build up local industries. Farmers on both sides of the border also purchase agricultural inputs and sell their produce on the side of the border where prices are more attractive. With the liberalisation and currency devaluation that took place in Senegal under structural adjustment, and tighter border controls, smuggling, as it is called in Senegal, has been substantially reduced. More generally, the Gambian state has continued to pose as a peace broker in the sub-region and cooperate in ECOWAS. The country's closest allies have been, however, an interesting mix, ranging from the US, through Iran, Saudi Arabia, Nigeria, the UK and France to Taiwan and Cuba. Gambia has been one of four countries in the world that offers emergency landing possibilities to American NASA space vessels.

Socioeconomic Developments

While the depreciation of the Dalasi in recent years and the inflation that ensued have been a major cause for concern, leading to a sharp decline in per capita GDP in real terms, the **inflation rate fell** by about half by the end of the year. Relatively high growth rates recorded in recent years provided some compensation. All hopes seemed to have been placed on the attempts to create a West African Monetary Zone (WAMZ), involving Gambia, Ghana, Nigeria, Sierra Leone and Guinea, with a view to adopting a single currency as the first step towards uniting all the ECOWAS member countries in a single currency zone. However, the time horizon for establishing WAMZ had to be postponed until 2006.

Gambia's foreign **debt burden** continued to be high, with the fiscal deficit increasing. By the end of 2003, total (external and domestic) debt stood at $ 666 m. The trade deficit also increased. In March 2004, the IMF issued a statement saying that its executive board had reached the conclusion that the fund had made two non-complying disbursements to the Gambian government in July and December 2001, each amounting to SDR 3,435 m (about $ 5.1 m), under the third annual Poverty Reduction and Growth Facility (PRGF) arrangement. The government was asked to repay those monies to the fund, with any accrued interest.

The marketing of groundnut produce continued to be rather haphazard after the dismantling of the Gambia Produce Marketing Board and the extreme weakening of the Gambia Cooperative Union. Positive news was sounded by the director of the National Agricultural Research Institute when he announced a new rice variety, called Nerica, and noted that it was expected to make the country self-sufficient in food by 2010. The African Development Bank approved a loan of $ 7.27 m to fund a project destined to help Gambians to better manage their agricultural resources. In his New Year message, President Jammeh announced the **discovery of large oil reserves** off the Gambian coast. An Australian company holds a licence for offshore exploration. Tourism contributed 12% to GDP, but **unemployment** and underemployment rates remained very high, particularly among the young, of whom 35,582 were unemployed, according to a national youth policy document, i.e., a high proportion of the workforce. Poverty continued to be a crucial problem, with the annual per capita income barely reaching £ 175. During the year the country's ranking on the Human Development Index dropped further to 155, compared with 149 in 2001.

Ebrima Sall

Ghana

The year was thoroughly dominated by the run-up to the **presidential and parliamentary elections** that were held on 7 December. Apart from the preparatory work carried out by the National Electoral Commission (NEC), most aspects of everyday policy and governance, including the budget, were interpreted in the light of the forthcoming polls. The proceedings of the National Reconciliation Commission (NRC) and the continuing fall-out from the murder of the Ya Na (king of Dagomba) and up to 40 of his retainers in 2002, were similarly highly charged. Even President Kufuor's attempts to mediate in the Ivorian crisis served as a heated debating point between the government and the National Democratic Congress (NDC). The electoral contest itself, which brought victory for the incumbent New Patriotic Party (NPP), was far more evenly matched than most observers expected, and confirmed the entrenchment of a two-party system.

Domestic Politics

At the start of 2004, the efforts on the part of NEC to resolve a number of looming problems in the election process proved contentious. One problem, which had become apparent during the 2000 polls, was that there was a large disparity in the size of constituencies. Moreover, the uneven rate of population increase threatened to create further distortions.

The chairman of NEC, Dr. Kwadwo Afari-Djan, justified the creation of **30 new constituencies** on the basis that they were the most appropriate way of resolving the anomalies. Although the opposition parties were suspicious – especially when NPP General Secretary Dan Botwe tactlessly stated that NPP should by rights win all the new constituencies that it had helped to create – the process did eventually win broad acceptance. In fact, far greater disagreement was caused by the creation of 28 new districts (whose boundaries cannot cross-cut constituencies) by virtue of the competition over the choice of new district capitals. In some cases, such as Adaklu-Anyigbe district (Volta region), this had a dramatic effect on the parliamentary campaign when what should have been an extremely safe NDC seat almost fell to an independent candidate. Another bone of contention was the **electoral register**, which most people agreed was grossly inflated in 2000. The NEC presided over the compilation of a new register and the issuing of photographic identification cards. The latter proved logistically difficult and many concerns were expressed about the likely disenfranchisement of large numbers of voters. However, the NEC, which remained in close contact with all the political parties, was able to resolve the problems to the satisfaction of most.

Kufuor and the NPP campaigned for re-election on the basis that the government had managed the economy successfully and had demonstrated its sincere commitment to 'zero tolerance' on corruption. On 8 September, Kufuor launched the NPP manifesto with a pledge to create an office of accountability within the presidency, if he was re-elected. The NPP also reminded Ghanaians of the poor standards of public accountability that had prevailed under the last NDC regime, as a result of which a number of ministers were incarcerated. The NPP also claimed that John Atta-Mills of NDC would not be his own man, but would be beholden to former President **Flight-Lieutenant Jerry Rawlings**, who played the key role in securing his renomination ahead of Dr. Kwesi Botchway (a respected former finance minister from the 1980s). The fact that Rawlings was so prominent on the campaign trail made this claim seem more credible. A recurrent theme in his rabble-rousing speeches was that Kufuor planned to rig the elections. In the run-up to the polls, the government claimed to have uncovered a coup plot, involving members of '64 Battallion'. Rawlings had created the latter as a counterweight to the army during the 1980s, but it had been disbanded during the return to democracy, while its commanding officer, Lt.-Colonel Larry Gbevlo-Lartey, had retrained as a lawyer. The authorities produced no credible evidence of a conspiracy and much of the independent press interpreted the announcement as a scare tactic. It also came against the backdrop of the **NRC hearings** in which Ghanaians were reminded of human rights abuses that had taken place under previous Rawlings administrations. The NRC, which borrowed from the model of the South African Truth and Reconciliation Commission, was extremely contentious from the start, with the NDC claiming that there was no need for such a body and that the NPP was seeking to carry out a witch-hunt. The allegation that **Kojo Tsikata** (a leading member of the former Provisional National Defence Council in the 1980s), and possibly Rawlings himself, had been complicit in the murder of three judges and a retired army officer in 1982 resurfaced at the hearings. The appearance of the two men before the NRC was itself seen as a victory of sorts by government sympathisers, although disappointment was expressed at how little was actually revealed. Though the NRC report had not appeared by the end of the year, sections were leaked to the press in the period before the elections in what appeared to be a blatant attempt to influence voter perceptions.

The NDC, on the other hand, insisted that Kufuor's economic programme hurt the poorest sections of society. The leadership disputed Kufuor's claim to have clean hands and pointed to a number of mini-scandals as merely the tip of the **corruption** iceberg. This included 'Bambagate', named after Alhaji Moctar Bamba, a deputy minister and deputy chief of staff in the office of the president, who was exposed for using official letterheads to secure loans for private companies he was involved in. When Bamba resigned, the information minister (Nana Akomea) hastily reassured Ghanaians that this did not preclude a criminal investigation. However, NDC claimed that corruption went much deeper and there was bound to be an official cover-up. The NDC could also refer to Ghana's 'Transparency International' ratings, which slipped from 51 to 73 out of 133 countries. However, NDC failed to come up with a big enough scoop to seriously tarnish the image of the Kufuor administration, even if some of the independent press (notably the 'Ghanaian Chronicle') began to make potentially serious allegations.

The NDC had more success with the government's mishandling of the **crisis in Dagbon**, with its press accusing the administration of being either complicit in the killing of the Ya Na or failing to protect him. The struggle over Dagomba kingship has been a recurrent theme since independence, with successive governments siding with either the Abudu or the Andani clan in a complex system of alliances. In 1987, the supreme court had confirmed the principle of rotation as well as the incumbency of Yakubu Andani II, something the Abudu militants never accepted. In March 2002, the government was aware of escalating tensions between the two factions. When violence threatened to break out in Yendi, a curfew was imposed but was subsequently rescinded. Thereafter, the palace was attacked, the Ya Na was beheaded and possibly as many as 40 members of his retinue were brutally killed. The government stood accused of failing to protect the Dagomba king because the police and soldiers posted to the crisis area unaccountably failed to intervene. All the most prominent Dagombas associated with the regime originated on the Abudu side, which is not surprising in view of their historic alignment with the Busia/Danquah tradition (Ghanaian leaders from the 1960s with which the NPP is associated). The list included **Vice-President Aliu Mahama**; the then minister of the interior and MP for Yendi, Alhaji Yakubu; Northern Regional Minister Imoro Andani; the national security advisor, General Joshua Hamidu; and the national security coordinator, Major Abukari Sulemana. This profile provided grounds for suspicion in itself, as did the revelation that the legal chambers of the then **attorney-general, Nana Akuffo-Addo**, had previously represented the Abudu faction. But even if there was no grand conspiracy, NDC partisans could argue that the government had adopted a very cavalier stance towards the safety of the Dagomba king, which would have been inconceivable if it had been the Asantehene (king of Ashanti) or the Okyenhene of Akyem whose life was in danger. The NDC expected to profit from a backlash in the northern region, and partly for this reason Atta-Mills chose a Dagomba MP, Muhammed Mumuni, as his running mate. The NDC press also exploited the concerns of non-Ashantis that the **Asantehene, Osei Tutu II**, was seeking to set himself up as the effective king of Ghana. Indeed, one newspaper claimed that Kufuor planned to change the constitution in order to turn the Asantehene into a constitutional monarch. This came on top of news of a substantial, and unprecedented, World Bank grant to the Asantehene to enable him to embark on a number of development initiatives.

Of the **smaller opposition parties**, most merely fielded a few parliamentary candidates. The exceptions were the Convention People's Party (CPP) and the People's National Convention (PNC), both of which claimed to be upholding the socialist ideals of Kwame Nkrumah, Ghana's first president. The CPP's former leader, George Hagan, bizarrely advised party supporters to vote for Kufuor rather than George Aggudey, who had succeeded him as the flag-bearer. Edward Mahama stood for president again, but on this occasion tried to forge a grand coalition between his PNC and Dan Lartey's Great Consolidated Popular Party (GCPP) and the Egle Party. When Mahama preferred Danny Ofori-Atta of the Egle Party as his running mate, Lartey walked out. The CPP and PNC both attacked NPP policies as being anti-poor, but they lacked the resources to carry their message to the Ghanaian people. Crucially, none of the newspapers championed their respective causes.

Although there was some violence around election time, most notably around Tamale (capital of the northern region) and around Kwamikrom (Volta region), the elections went ahead to the satisfaction of **independent observers** and most political parties, with the partial exception of NDC. Although the NPP won comfortably, it failed to achieve the total domination that it had confidently predicted. **Kufuor only narrowly avoided a run-off**, having secured just less than 52% of the vote to Atta-Mills's 45%. This was not a brilliant result for Kufuor, who had won 57% to Atta-Mills's 43% in the run-off four years earlier. In fact, Kufuor performed less well than his party did in the parliamentary elections (56% of seats). This was in spite of the fact that a number of rebels stood against official NPP candidates. Interestingly, while NPP made inroads into the regions that NDC had previously dominated (especially in the north, but also in Volta region), NDC reversed the pattern in some of the regions of NPP strength, including Ashanti. NPP received a particular shock in the **Greater Accra region**, where five new seats were created but the party ended up being one seat down. Remarkably, NDC gained six seats in the region. This highlighted the political volatility of the urban electorate, which began to complain of unfulfilled promises. Overall though, NPP gained a safe majority in parliament with 128 seats to 94 for NDC, four for PNC, three for CPP and a single independent. However, these results also underlined the fallacy of claims that had surrounded the hearings of the NRC to the effect that

Ghanaians associated NDC with a reign of terror carried out under Rawlings. It would be fair to conclude that memories were divided over what had transpired over the previous two decades. The Northern region remained the weak link in Ghanaian democracy and the authorities had good cause to worry about the ferrying of weapons from Côte d'Ivoire into Dagbon. The death of the CPP regional chairman while in military custody, in the immediate aftermath of the elections, merely compounded an already tense situation. The government promised a full enquiry into the circumstances of Alhaji Mobila's death, but the credibility of the Kufuor government in the north was at a low ebb.

Foreign Affairs

Foreign policy has never been President Kufuor's strong suit, and it was widely observed that he has been more or less anonymous on the continental stage since 2000. However, the president had a highly articulate minister in the shape of **Nana Akuffo-Addo**, who had been moved to the foreign affairs portfolio after the Dagbon imbroglio. It was hoped that Kufuor might make his mark on the continental stage when he assumed office as **ECOWAS** chairman in 2004. With fellow Ghanaians **Kofi Annan and Ibn Chambas** holding the key positions of UN Secretary-General and executive secretary of ECOWAS respectively, the stage could hardly have been more favourably set. While Kufuor's profile certainly increased, the results were mixed. The single most pressing challenge facing him was the ongoing crisis in Côte d'Ivoire in which he attempted to mediate on several occasions. In March, opposition parties in the south declared their intention to defy a government ban and to demonstrate in Abidjan against President Laurent Gbagbo, whom they accused of seeking to wreck the Linas-Marcoussis peace accord. Kufuor sought to use his good offices to deflect a stand-off. However, he was ultimately unsuccessful in preventing a government crackdown on 25 March, which left up to 120 opposition supporters dead. At the end of July, all the protagonists in the wider crisis were invited to Accra to participate in a fresh round of peace talks, which were also attended by Kofi Annan, Thabo Mbeki, Olusegun Obasanjo and nine other African heads of state. With considerable pressure being applied to all sides in the conflict, a fresh timetable for **implementation of the Linas-Marcoussis accord was announced** on 30 July. The signatories agreed that the political reforms would be implemented by the end of August and that the disarmament programme would commence on 15 October. While this was a successful conclusion, there were fresh outbreaks of fighting in November when Gbagbo chose to bomb cities in the rebel-held north. The lack of tangible results led opposition politicians in Ghana to claim that Kufuor did not enjoy the confidence of the parties to the Ivorian dispute. Indeed, Alban Bagbin, the minority leader in parliament, went on the radio to announce that both the Burkinabe and Ivorian presidents had confided their lack of confidence in Kufuor. Both later categorically denied that this was the case in official communiqués, which the pro-NPP press subsequently sought to use to cause the maximum embarrassment to Bagbin.

On Ghana's eastern border, relationships with the Eyadéma regime remained as harmonious as ever, by virtue of an established set of alliances which had previously pitted **Kufuor, Obasanjo and Eyadéma against Rawlings and Abacha**. Rawlings's poor relations with Eyadéma were partly rooted in his periodic support for Gilchrist Olympio, son of the first Togolese president (whom Eyadéma once claimed to have killed) who had repeatedly tried to stand for president himself. Immediately after the Ghanaian polls closed, Rawlings sought solace with his only remaining friend in a presidential office, namely **Dénis Sassou Nguesso of the Republic of Congo**. On the anniversary of the 1967 coup in Togo, the Kufuor regime dispatched a high-level delegation and a military band to celebrate the event. Many independent observers, including the Centre for Democratic Development in Accra, criticised this open fraternisation with the **Eyadéma dictatorship** as both distasteful and in fundamental conflict with Kufuor's claims to be a champion of democracy. The government, for its part, argued that, at a time when negotiations between the Togolese government and the opposition parties seemed to be making some headway, it was important to play a constructive role. The fertile rumour mill suggested that Eyadéma was providing Kufuor with access to the '*juju*-men' whose magical charms had kept him in power for four decades. Viewers in the Volta region even claimed to have seen evidence of this in Togolese television coverage of Kufuor's visits to Eyadéma's home area. When a cameraman from the Ghana Broadcasting Corporation made the mistake of photographing and tape-recording some of the proceedings and then leaking them to the NDC, he was dismissed, provoking an uproar in Ghana.

In recognition of Ghana's singular contribution to international peacekeeping duties (29 missions over 40 years), the UN Secretary-General opened the Kofi Annan International Peacekeeping Training Centre in Accra to offer courses on subjects such as **conflict management, elections monitoring and peacekeeping operations**. The largest single contributor to the funding of the centre was the German government (€ 3.1 m), and its inauguration was delayed to enable Chancellor Gerhard Schröder to be present. Britain, Italy, Canada and the Netherlands promised to further increase the funding base over subsequent years.

In his capacity as ECOWAS chairman, Kufuor also hosted a special summit in March to draw up a plan of action for the funding of the infrastructural side of sub-regional integration. The **president of the World Bank, James Wolfensohn**, attended in person and confirmed financial backing for various projects to the tune of $ 4.9 bn. The summit also discussed the **NEPAD** initiative and inevitably came back to the issue of sub-regional conflict management. The Ghana government's commitment has been symbolised in the operation of a separate Ministry of Regional Integration and NEPAD, with Dr. Kofi Apraku at its head. Within the sub-region, the Ghanaian authorities have been more inclined to implement ECOWAS agreements on the freedom of movement of people and goods than most of their neighbours. They have also been supportive of plans for launching a common West African currency, recognising the structural weakness of the cedi. However, progress on both fronts has been painfully slow.

Socioeconomic Developments

In his budget statement of 5 February, Minister of Finance Yaw Osafo-Maafo laid emphasis on consolidating the gains made over the previous year. In particular, the budget aimed at achieving a real GDP growth rate of 5.4%, a budget deficit of 1.7% of GDP and an inflation rate of below 10%. The regime continued to place its hopes on higher levels of inward private investment. In fulfilment of the NPP vision of a 'Golden Age of Business', Osafo-Maafo announced plans to reduce corporate income tax from 32.5% to 30%. Moreover, any new company that was listed on the Ghana stock exchange would qualify for a special reduced rate of 25%. The minister also made much of the fact that, having faithfully implemented the conditionalities under the **HIPC initiative** over the past three years, Ghana would benefit from substantial debt relief. Speaking publicly when the HIPC completion point was reached, Osafo-Maafo said that Ghana could expect to receive relief from $ 1.5 bn of bilateral and commercial debts and $ 100 m per year for 20 years from the multilateral agencies. The catch in HIPC was that the government was no longer free to borrow as before from the bilateral and multilateral agencies. Osafo-Maafo renewed the quest for financing from private sources, and not for the first time turned to companies whose business credentials seemed highly dubious. This provoked an uproar and the minister was forced to quietly withdraw from the proposed deal. In July, the limitations on ministerial power were underlined when Osafo-Maafo was forced to **rescind a promised salary increase** to public sector workers in response to IMF pressure. On 21 May, an agreement had been reached with the Ghana Civil Servants Association, the Ghana National Association of Teachers, the Ghana Registered Nurses Association and the Judicial Services Staff Association promising a 31% salary increase backdated to March. On 3 July, Osafo-Maafo was forced to write a letter to the managing director of the IMF outlining the background to the affair, his subsequent realisation that the increases would throw the budget out of balance and the decision to step away from the deal. The minister sought to create the impression of being transparent by releasing this letter to the press. However, it was more likely an attempt to demonstrate to union leaders, in what was after all an election year, that he had been prevented from carrying out his wishes by a power greater than himself.

The savings that were made under HIPC were expected to enable the government to channel greater resources into the fulfilment of its **Poverty Reduction Strategy Programme**. The government clearly sought to derive the maximum political effect from debt relief. Among the benefits of the HIPC initiative, for example, was the fact that the ministry of education was able to announce the upgrading of 31 secondary schools over the year. The HIPC brand was often placed on the buildings to drive home the point that government had been right all along. The government did not shy away from the need to mobilise more revenue internally, through new taxes and more efficient collection. Controversially, the NPP regime added 2.5% to value-added tax (raising the overall rate from 10 to 12.5%) in order to source the **Ghana Educational Trust Fund**, which was held to be the key to restoring the battered educational infrastructure of the country. The regime also launched a new White Paper, proposing significant reforms in the educational sector. The new set-up would consist of an eleven-year basic educational programme (between the ages of 4 and 15), to be followed by a four-year senior high school system. Students would be streamed according to their aptitude, to permit specialised training in vocational, technical, agricultural and general subjects, with apprenticeships held out as an alternative for those who did not enter the final cycle. The underlying rationale was that more Ghanaians would leave school with relevant practical qualifications.

In the health sector, the government insisted on the need for a properly resourced system, and tabled proposals for a **National Health Insurance Scheme** (NHIS) on 18 March. The idea here was that salaried employees would pay into the scheme at cedis 6,000 a month (the daily minimum wage being cedis 9,200 a day), while the districts would manage their own funds for non-wage earners. In his launch speech, President Kufuor expressed the view that it was unacceptable that 80% of cases of illness and death were easily preventable and pointed out that the NHIS would make it possible to address the main causes. However, treatment of **HIV/AIDS would be excluded** from the scheme, lest it overwhelm the budget. Apart from the cost of providing anti-retrovirals, a practical headache for the health authorities was the poaching of nurses by the British health service in particular, which the Blair government promised to address.

By the end of the year, the NPP regime was able to record some successes. The economy grew faster than projected, at 5.8%, even if inflation still stood at 11.8%. Although a slowing of foreign investment into Africa affected Ghana as well, there were some high-profile developments, most notably the **merger between Ashanti Goldfields and the South African giant, AngloGold**. This was expected to lead to larger investments in the gold mining sector. The government of Ghana, which had a stake of 17.2% in the old company, was to hold a stake of 3.4% in the new company, AngloGold Ashanti. Meanwhile, the mining lease at Obuasi in Ashanti region was to be extended to the year 2054. Another significant development was the merger between Guinness Ghana Ltd. and Ghana Breweries Ltd (owned by Heineken). Although the NPP regime was very keen to continue divesting the state of its stake in loss-making enterprises, it seriously considered buying out the bankrupt Kaiser Aluminium's 90% stake in the **Volta Aluminium Company** (VALCO). Ironically, this would also fulfil an earlier dream associated with Kwame Nkrumah – the nemesis of the Busia/Danquah tradition to which the NPP belongs – of owning the (shut-down) aluminium smelter. However, the development of the country's own bauxite resources remained as distant a prospect as ever. The **cocoa sector** continued to produce record export volumes, with an astonishingly high production figure of 700,000 metric tonnes being announced at the end of the season in July. NDC claimed that the government was reaping the fruits of their own agricultural policies, which was certainly true, given the time-lag between planting the trees and the first harvest. The cynics pointed out that the boom was also a sign of increased **smuggling** from Côte d'Ivoire. Indeed, Gbagbo himself complained that the Ghanaians were seeking to profit from the crisis in his country.

In the social sector, the year was dominated by blueprints rather than great success stories. However, the director of the **Ghana AIDS commission** noted that some headway had been made in the fight against HIV/AIDS. In 2004, the national rate of infection stood at 3.6%, with the eastern region (6.1%) being the worst and the northern region (2.1%) the least affected areas. Some 72,000 adults were estimated to have the AIDS virus. At the end of the year, it was suggested that Ghana would struggle to meet some of the Millennium Development Goals. In particular, it was questionable whether child mortality would fall to 78 lives per 100,000 live births and whether deaths from HIV/AIDS and malaria would start to decline in real terms. On a more positive note, primary school enrolment rates and the gender balance in education had both improved, as had access to potable water. Official statistics suggested a small dent was being made in the fight against poverty, but that there was a growing problem in the cities where **street children** have become a visible feature in recent years. What the authorities hoped to avoid was an influx of destitute refugees from across the border in Côte d'Ivoire.

Most Ghanaians considered that 2004 had been a good year. The country had mostly avoided the contagion of violence from the West African sub-region, had passed through a successful election process and even showed encouraging signs of economic progress. However, most Ghanaians were well aware that this could change if oil prices soared or if fighting in Côte d'Ivoire escalated.

Paul Nugent

Guinea

In 2004, Guinea continued to limp along, managing its internal tensions and a half-dozen small violent uprisings by the population without spinning out of control. The health of President Lansana Conté, long commented upon by diplomats and Guineans, ceased to be the key issue as he appeared to stabilise physically. Still, the general atmosphere of 'last days' prevailed, and by June it was common knowledge that the central bank had been completely emptied of foreign currency reserves. Massive inflation saw the price of rice more than double and fuel rise by two-thirds. A prime minister appointed in February lasted only two months before deciding to resign, because he was unable to institute any reforms, and the position remained empty for eight months until a replacement was named in December, promising significant reforms.

Domestic Politics

Guinea's politics were dominated by the dismal economic situation, which drove the population close to generalised rebellion. Several changes in the government did little to improve this state of affairs, and so the domestic political scene appeared somewhat frozen. The opposition parties were dealt a blow by the death of Siradiou Diallo, head of the 'Union pour le Progrès et le Renouveau' (UPR) party and a leading political figure in Guinea over the past four decades.

The year began with President Conté's 19 January inauguration for a third term. This term had been lengthened from five to seven years, as per changes to the constitution ratified in a 2003 referendum widely perceived to have been rigged by the government. The '**Front Républicain pour l'Alternance Démocratique**' (FRAD), which brings together all the major opposition parties, refused to acknowledge the result of the election, which they had boycotted.

On 23 February, President Conté **reshuffled his cabinet**. The new cabinet was a mixture of old and new, with five newcomers and the remainder being moved from one post to another. The major news in this round of appointments was the nomination of François Lonsény Fall to the position of prime minister. This position does not exist in the Guinean constitution, and thus is appointed at the pleasure of the president. In moving Fall from the role of minister of foreign affairs to prime minister, Conté's intention appeared to be to repair Guinea's relations with major international donors, from the EU to the World Bank and the IMF.

Conté carried out a second round of changes to his cabinet on 1 March. The highlight of these was the departure of the ministers of finance and trade and the president of the central bank, reflecting the dire economic situation. Additionally, former Interior Minister Moussa Solano, who had been shifted sideways to the ministry of employment on 23 February, was removed from the cabinet in the second phase of the reshuffle. Solano, the architect of Conté's re-election campaign, had been seen as responsible for causing the opposition to boycott the December elections. The leaders of FRAD expressed delight at his departure from the political scene but stated it was too early to say whether Conté might seek genuine dialogue with the opposition.

Siradiou Diallo died in Paris on 14 March and was buried on 25 March in his hometown, Labé. Diallo was former editor-in-chief at the pan-African weekly magazine 'Jeune Afrique'. With the advent of multiparty democracy in Guinea in the 1990s, he founded the 'Parti pour le Renouveau et le Progrès' (PRP). After an unsuccessful attempt at the presidency as the PRP's candidate in 1993, he formed the UPR, which he headed until his death. He had been a staunch opponent of Guinea's first president, Sékou Touré, and was one of the most significant opponents of President Lansana Conté.

Sidya Touré, the former Guinean prime minister and leader of the '**Union des Forces Republicains**' (UFR), and Ba Mamadou of the '**Union des Forces Democratiques en Guinée**' (UFDG) were barred from flying to Senegal in April. Shortly thereafter, senior officials of Touré's party were arrested for allegedly plotting a coup d'état. Speaking on state television late on 22 April, Security Minister Moussa Sampil said that three members of the UFR had been arrested and charged for organising a '**subversive dinner**' in Paris to discuss the assassination of the head of state and the dissolution of the state's institutions. FRAD dismissed the allegations as a sham. Touré was immediately questioned, but released without charge. Armed police, using truncheons, dispersed hundreds of Touré supporters gathered at the police station where he was being held for questioning.

In May, Touré was arrested on charges of plotting a coup. He and three members of his party were held until they were cleared on 22 July by an appeal court of plotting to overthrow the government. The authorities' decision to drop charges against Touré followed the start of fresh negotiations between the government and the European Commission on the release of a € 260 m package of EU aid for Guinea which had been held up since 2002.

The 29 April **resignation** of Prime Minister François Lonsény Fall brought an end to his attempts to introduce economic and political reforms in order to unlock millions of euros of aid. He resigned while in Paris and has since remained outside the country. His resignation was never publicly acknowledged by the government during the eight months that Guinea remained without a prime minister. In an interview, Fall noted that while he had demanded assurances that he would be able to institute significant changes in the political and economic status quo, especially as concerned the special privileges accorded certain businessmen close to the president, he soon realised that such change was impossible.

Ethnic unrest in the southeastern 'Région Forestière' (forest region) of the country broke out on 17 June. The area faced two days of fighting between Maninka (Malinke) and Kpelle (Guerzé) communities in N'Zérékoré. The fighting began when a Kpelle youth accidentally drove his bicycle into a Maninka elder emerging from prayers in one of the town's mosques. The ensuing tensions, leading to the deaths of two people, including the youth, rekindled memories of intercommunal violence in the same town in June 1991 that left 1,000 people dead in the space of 36 hours. After receiving a threatening anonymous letter, the UNHCR and WHO suspended their operations in N'Zérékoré for two days. Guinean security forces arrested a large number of people in the town, including Liberian ex-combatants, presumed to have been members of **Liberians United for Reconciliation and Democracy** (LURD), who had stockpiles of guns.

The year 2004 saw a sudden rise in the existence of **youth gangs and militias** in Conakry. While several militias had been cultivated for some time, especially by Conakry's governor, M'Bemba Bangoura, there was a sudden efflorescence of neighbourhood-based militias, several of which clashed in turf wars. Many of these gangs drew members from the 'young volunteers' who had participated in civil defence militias during the 2000 and 2001 attacks from Liberia and Sierra Leone sponsored by Charles Taylor and the Revolutionary United Front (RUF), but had never been properly disarmed or demobilised.

The second-half of the year was dominated by the growing desperation of the population as consumer prices rose precipitously, and violent uprisings in various parts of the country. In late June, there was a serious shortage of cooking gas, the price of rice rose to Guinean francs 58,000 (about $ 25), and rumours began to circulate about government increases in the state-regulated price of petrol. Groups of youths **pillaged four trucks** loaded with imported rice, throwing tree trunks across roads to stop the trucks and inviting entire neighbourhoods to come out and loot the rice.

On 6 July, President Conté suspended more than 100 elected officials in Conakry, accusing them of stealing subsidised rice meant to be sold cheaply though local government offices to the city's population. This did not quell popular anger, and on 8 July, gangs of angry youths again attacked food trucks in Conakry, causing police to shoot into the air to disperse the crowd. Hundreds of protesters pelted policemen with stones and bottles and chanted anti-government slogans. As news of the disturbances spread, youths in other parts of the city began holding up private vehicles, threatening to smash their windscreens unless the drivers paid them money. Two youths were reportedly killed by police during the disturbances. At this point, it looked as if the city might melt down in a state of general rebellion, but as has happened so often in Guinea, both government and the people pulled back from the brink.

Diffused uprisings continued, however, in other parts of the country. On 14 July, a demonstration in the town of **Télimélé** by **teachers protesting** the local authorities' failure to pay their salaries for two months degenerated into a violent protest by a cross-section of townspeople against the recently appointed *préfet*, Issiagah Marah. Government buildings were damaged during the protests, as security forces, who were unable to control the situation, withdrew from the scene. On 13–14 September, **student protests** took place over living conditions at the University of Kankan. The police and army were used to break up the protests in a heavy-handed manner. On 18 September, police halted an **opposition protest march** in Conakry after it had gone no further than 100 metres, and on 23 September police intervened to break up a labour union protest.

Police opened fire on 2 November on demonstrators who had gathered in the town of **Pita**, approximately 350 kilometres northeast of Conakry. The demonstrators complained of the price of electricity. The rioters also attacked the local police station. Police dispersed the crowd with gunfire, leaving one dead and three injured. On 15 November, residents of **Dabola** rioted against their **préfet**, Benjamin Camara, for having turned a blind eye towards armed robbers who targeted local shopkeepers. Local citizens accused him of colluding with these criminals, and of having been involved in the theft of rails from the Conakry-Kankan railway for resale as scrap metal. In the ensuing violence, his house was destroyed and one demonstrator was killed by security forces.

On 13 December, clashes took place between students of the University of Conakry and riot police following **demonstrations by students** protesting at the high cost of living and a decision by the minister for higher education, Sékou Décazy, to do away with student accommodation at the University, claiming that space was not available. In response to student complaints, the minister stated that the university was a well-known centre for prostitution and drug dealing.

On 9 December, the embattled president announced his choice to fill the vacant post of prime minister. **Cellou Dalein Diallo** was promoted from within the cabinet to assume the post. He had been a strong supporter of President Conté, serving in various capacities (minister of transport, communications and fisheries) over the preceding nine years. At the end of the year, much speculation surrounded President Conté's motives for naming Diallo as prime minister. Many surmised his intention was to weaken the hand of those ministers seen as constituting a strong ethnic clique around the president, including Minister of Security Moussa Sampil.

Foreign Affairs

Guinea's relations with other countries in 2004 were generally tense. Most European countries demanded significant political and economic reforms before releasing a blocked aid package; Guinea's relations with Sierra Leone were clouded by Guinean military incursions into Sierra Leonean territory, most notably around the village of **Yenga**; and worries about infiltrations by rebel fighters in and out of Liberia and Côte d'Ivoire caused significant tensions among those states, as well as for the civilian population of Guinea's southeastern forest region.

Early in the year, it was announced that the EU had frozen an aid package worth € 260 m meant for Guinea, and made the implementation of political reforms by the regime in Conakry the condition for the release of the new financial assistance. This pressure was instrumental to the naming of François Fall, and later Cellou Dalein Diallo – both reformers – as prime minister, as well as the release of opposition leader Sidya Touré from prison. Such **external influence on Guinea's internal politics** is almost unprecedented, and this indicates how bad the economic situation has become.

Guinea's relations with its **Mano River Union** neighbours, Sierra Leone and Liberia, remained cool during 2004. Guinean armed forces stationed along the border made incursions ranging from 50 metres to over a kilometre into Sierra Leonean territory in dozens of locations. The best known of these is the village of Yenga, which has become the subject of significant international discussion. Although the Guinean government publicly acknowledged that Yenga belongs to Sierra Leone, Guinean military personnel continued to occupy the area. Explanations offered for this behaviour ranged from the theory that the Guinean soldiers were mining diamonds in the river bank that borders Yenga to the idea that they wanted to control the strategic hill overlooking the village, close to the meeting point of the Guinea-Liberia-Sierra Leone frontiers, so as to be able to stop possible incursions by rebels from Liberia. Sierra Leone, which relied heavily on Guinean assistance in defeating RUF rebels during its civil war, was hesitant to speak out forcefully on this issue.

Relations with Liberia also remained awkward during the year. Conté's close personal relations with **Aisha Conneh**, leader of one faction of the LURD rebel group, threatened to draw Guinea into the increasingly chaotic internal divisions within LURD. On 22–23 May, the Conakry residence of **Sekou Conneh**, Aisha's estranged husband and chairman of LURD, was reportedly looted by men under Aisha's command. After arriving at the building, they allegedly requested some car keys and took away four vehicles. They also reportedly took $ 2 m and all valuable items from the house.

Towards June, there were many rumours in Liberia and Guinea centred on the recruitment by Mohammed Touré, son of Guinea's former President Sékou Touré, of Liberian ex-combatants for a possible incursion into Guinea. As time passed, it appeared that Touré had not in fact left Canada, where he lives, but that there was widespread recruitment of combatants in Monrovia to fight both for and against the Conté government in Guinea's forest region. Multiple sources indicated that there were fighters and weapons infiltrating 'Guinée Forestière' from northern Liberia. Aisha Conneh was said to be recruiting fighters from all of the Liberian combatant groups to defend the Conté government, while most indications pointed to former Charles Taylor associates in the recruitment of anti-Conté forces.

Although there were still no attacks in Guinean territory by the end of the year, many Guineans – both in the security forces and the civilian population – remained convinced that the possibility of a rebel attack remained high. On 23 July, it was reported that some Malians were arrested in the interior of Guinea in a vehicle loaded with arms. As a result of this development, troops in different parts of Guinea were put on alert to forestall any attack, including from Mali.

Despite these tensions, President Conté hosted a conference in Conakry in late May to reactivate the Mano River Union between Guinea, Sierra Leone and Liberia. The heads of state of Mali and Côte d'Ivoire were also invited. In a communiqué issued after the conference, the members of the Mano River Union and President Touré of Mali all pledged their support to President Gbagbo in the Ivorian conflict. They also agreed to take action on a number of common issues, including legislation to prevent the proliferation of small arms and light weapons in the sub-region, and engagement in efforts to promote joint border security. They also agreed to identify people who "used other countries in the sub-region to destabilise their neighbours." This was a reference to bringing former Liberian President Charles Taylor to trial.

The presence of refugees in Guinea remained a major aspect of the country's involvement in sub-regional affairs. On 3 May, UNHCR stated that the UN would end its assistance to the 6,000 Sierra Leonean refugees still in Guinea as of 30 June. Visiting refugee camps in Guinea, High Commissioner Ruud Lubbers said that the process of repatriating them was gathering speed.

The year 2004 also saw a continuing flow of returnees from unstable Côte d'Ivoire, which had been home to as many as 800,000 Guinean nationals. In June, hundreds of Guineans expelled from the diamond-mining area of northeastern Angola also began arriving home, complaining of poor treatment by the Angolan authorities as they were deported. A total of 461 Guineans arrived in Conakry aboard two planes and Guinean officials said about 1,000 more were expected. The government converted a former community youth centre in Conakry into a transit camp for the new arrivals.

In July-August, a refugee reverification exercise (that was greeted in several camps, especially those that had traditionally served as rear bases for armed factions such as LURD, with stone throwing, threats and verbal assaults) identified 78,318 refugees remaining in Guinea. This was down from some 500,000 throughout the 1990s and up to 2002. The large majority of these refugees were located in the Kuankan (22,960) and Laine (25,046) camps.

On 30 October, UNHCR began repatriating Liberian refugees, and by the end of the year, their numbers had shrunk to some 60,000.

Following the November conflagration in Côte d'Ivoire, Guinea reacted to allegations from the 'Forces Nouvelles' alleging that the Guinean government had sided with the Gbagbo government. In a statement issued by the foreign minister, Guinea denied that it was supporting President Gbagbo and declared that Guinea was only interested in seeing a swift return to peace so that the economy of the sub-region did not suffer. In November, the Guinean armed forces reinforced their positions on the Côte d'Ivoire border and effectively sealed it to prevent refugees entering Guinea.

Socioeconomic Developments

Guinea's economic situation in 2004 went from poor to catastrophic. On 13 August, **petrol prices** rose 67% from Guinean francs 1,500 per litre ($ 50) to Guinean francs 2,500 per litre ($ 80) and diesel prices from Guinean francs 1,350 to 2,300 per litre overnight. Shared taxis and 'magbana' shared minibuses more than doubled their fares. A 50-kilogram sack of rice rose to over Guinean francs 100,000, whereas prices normally hovered around Guinean francs 25,000–35,000. An average Guinean primary school teacher or policeman is paid about Guinean francs 25,000 ($ 34) per month and a doctor or university professor about Guinean francs 250,000 ($ 68) per month. Civil servants' salaries had not risen since 1996, and many Guineans saw their purchasing power cut in half or worse during 2004.

On the macroeconomic side, there was no good news. Economic growth did not keep pace with population growth, exports of bauxite (Guinea's main source of hard currency) decreased, and the country fell three places on the UN Human Development Index scale to 160 (of 177). Life expectancy was just under 49 years with an under-five mortality rate of 16.9%; literacy was 41%; and GDP per capita was $ 415. Over half the population did not have access to potable water. Net foreign investment and other private investment was zero. The IMF estimated that real GDP growth would reach a maximum of 2.6%, following on from 1.2% in 2003. Given population growth rates of 3%, this meant deepening impoverishment of the population.

In 2004, Guinea was '**off track**' in the estimation of both the World Bank and the IMF. The bank suspended loans in June until a $ 2.4 m arrears was paid. The IMF suspended its Heavily Indebted Poor Country (HIPC) assistance program in 2003, at the same time that the Paris Club and ADB suspended their activities in Guinea. Guinea's best chance of getting back 'on track' was to receive some € 260 m promised by the EU in 2002, but since blocked under Article 96 of the Cotonou accords, demanding economic and political reforms to establish better governance and genuine democracy before releasing the money. A Guinean contingent was expected in Brussels to discuss the status of governance reforms in April, but they never showed up for the meeting. Fresh negotiations on the release of the aid package took place in July, and as noted above, probably led to the release of opposition leader Sidya Touré. However, there was little substantive progress and the monies were not released.

Guinea maintained its expenditures of approximately 1.9% of GDP on education, and 1.9% on health, with 3% of GDP officially spent on defence, though off-budget expenditures probably pushed the real defence figure much higher. Some investments in infrastructure, including the road between Kankan, Guinea, and Bamako, Mali, and the enlargement of Conakry's autoroute, continued to move forward.

One bright spot was suggested by the news that a Japanese-backed company was reported to have signed an agreement with the government of Guinea to build a **major alumina refinery** in the northwestern mining town of Sangaredi. The estimated investment required for this plant, which would situate the refinery next to the biggest bauxite mining complex in the world, is $ 2 bn. Discussions continued throughout the year between the government and mining companies **BHP Billiton** and **Rio Tinto** about the exploitation of the iron reserves in the areas of Mount Nimba and Simandou. The deal remains blocked by Guinean demands that the companies construct a railway across the country, leading to the deep water port in Benty, to the south of Conakry. The companies would prefer to ship the ore out via Liberia, which already has a rail line leading from the Liberian side of Mount Nimba to the port in Buchanan. Ecological activists remained concerned that iron exploitation will destroy the environment in both areas, which are currently protected bioreserves.

Mike McGovern

Guinea-Bissau

Five years after the 1998–99 **conflict** between President Nino Vieira and the military junta led by Brigadier Ansumane Mane, Guinea-Bissau continued to be plagued by chronic political instability and persistent socioeconomic distress. In spite of convincing presidential and legislative victories in the 1999–2000 elections, the disastrous rule of President Kumba Yala and his ethnically-anchored 'Partido para a Renovação Social' (PRS) was marked by regular cabinet reshuffles, non-respect for the separation of powers and **widespread mismanagement** of public resources. Threatened by internal opposition both within his party and the National Assembly, Kumba Yala dismissed the legislative and executive bodies on 20 November 2002 and appointed a government of presidential initiative. Although limited both in mandate and duration, the interim government failed to organise legislative elections within the constitutionally provided time limits and prompted the virtual collapse of state-provided social services. Its lack of managerial capacity was made blatantly evident by its inability to pay civil service salaries during its ruinous 11-month rule.

On 14 September 2003, amid widespread discontent and growing fears of electoral fraud in the making, a self-proclaimed military committee for the restoration of constitutional order, led by General Verissimo Seabra, armed forces chief of staff, staged a bloodless coup that led to Kumba Yala's renunciation of power and the establishment of a new transitional framework. The transitional charter, signed by the military committee and 23 of the 24 legalised parties, established, *inter alia*, transitional governing structures and a two-stage electoral calendar for the return to a full constitutional order. A **new transitional president**, **Henrique Rosa**, was also appointed. **Legislative elections** were successfully held in **March 2004** and a democratically legitimised government was appointed by Rosa. Presidential elections in mid-2005 will bring the transition period to a conclusion.

Domestic Politics

The smooth execution of the elections of 28–30 March 2004 was marred by popular disturbances in and around polling stations in the nation's capital, compelling the national electoral commission to make an exception and allow for a second day of voting in 89 of Bissau's 510 polling stations. Although the election was deemed free and fair by international observers, the results were contested by the PRS. In consultation with other ECOWAS heads of state, Presidents Wade of Senegal, Obasanjo of Nigeria and Kufuor of Ghana dispatched a fact-finding mission to Bissau comprising Nana Akufo Addo (minister of foreign affairs of Ghana), Cheikh Tidiane Gadio (minister of state and foreign affairs of Senegal), Saidu Balarabe Samaila (vice-minister of foreign affairs of Nigeria) and Mohamed Ibn Chambas (ECOWAS executive secretary). The ECOWAS delegation was instrumental in brokering a **deal** whereby all parties undertook to resort to and respect the legally provided avenues for electoral disputes.

The confirmation of the **electoral results** by the nation's highest court marked the return of the 'Partido Africano da Independência da Guiné e Cabo Verde' (PAIGC) with 45 seats in the 100-seat chamber, followed by PRS and the 'Partido Unido Social Democrático' (PUSD) with 35 and 17 seats respectively. The remaining three seats were captured by the Electoral Union and the United Popular Alliance. In spite of assurances of non-exclusion, prime minister and PAIGC leader Carlos Gomes Júnior appointed a **cabinet** composed of party apparatchiks and technocrats close to the prime minister's personal sphere of influence. In the absence of an absolute majority in the National Assembly, PAIGC signed a **parliamentary pact** with PRS with the aim of securing legislative support for its governance programme.

The re-emergence of internal cleavages within PAIGC, namely between the oligarchy loyal to exiled former President Nino Vieira and rival factions, continued to elevate **internal party politics** to the national stage and diverted energy from the urgent national reform agenda. Similarly, the fragile alliance between PAIGC and PRS exposed governmental action to continual political bargaining between the two parliamentary groups. Notwithstanding a generalised predisposition to pursue politics over policy, the government of Carlos Gomes Júnior succeeded after taking office in having its programme and **budget approved**, thus promoting greater policy predictability and introducing greater rigour and discipline in public financial management.

Although seldom acknowledged publicly, the **ethnic card** has played an increasingly central role in Guinea-Bissau's politics. With no single group representing more than one-third of the overall population, and under the pretence of historically differentiated roles dating back to the liberation war and beyond, the political instrumentalisation of ethnic allegiances continued to be a driving force behind the Balante-based PRS. Through an appeal to a heightened sense of collective pride in the glorious conquests in the frontline of the liberation war and of the unequal division of the spoils of an independent state, the PRS has sought to assert itself as a bastion of the **Balante** and of segments of the rural underprivileged. Moreover, the over-representation of the Balante in the historically intrusive armed forces has remained a potentially destabilising factor.

Thus, the **military mutiny** of 6 October that resulted in the **assassination** of the joint chief of staff of the armed forces, General Verissimo Correia Seabra, and his spokesperson, as well as the overthrow of the army, navy and air force chiefs of staff, highlighted the fragility of the transitional process. The revolt, led by a group of captains representing the 650-strong battalion that had participated in UN peacekeeping operations in Liberia, alleged that their actions had been motivated by grievances over salaries, deplorable living conditions and generalised corruption within the **military hierarchy**.

In the presence of the presidency of the CPLP ('Comunidade dos Países de Língua Portuguesa'), represented by the minister of foreign affairs of São Tomé, Ovídio Pequeno, a memorandum of understanding was signed between the mutinous soldiers and the military leadership with the government acting as guarantor. As per the terms of the **agreement**, the demands of the mutinous soldiers were met in a move that was widely perceived as a capitulation on the part of the civilian authorities. After a month-long vacuum in the military leadership, President Henrique Rosa appointed the former inspector general of the armed forces, General Tagme Na Waie, as joint chief of staff. The agreement consolidated Balante hegemony over the armed forces and set in motion a contentious debate over blanket amnesties for all involved in military interventions since 1980.

Although delegated to the National Assembly, the **amnesty** debate was characterised by utter disregard for matters of impunity and justice towards victims, and could pave the way for, among other things, the return of exiled former President Nino Vieira. In the spirit of reconciliation within the armed forces, several high-ranking officers loyal to Nino Vieira were reintegrated and occupied mid-level positions under their former subordinates. The **'reconciliation' process** was not, however, extended to the military leadership that remained loyal to General Verissimo Seabra throughout the events of 6 October.

Preparations for the **2005 presidential elections**, the final leg in the transition period, were tainted by political tension, controversy over the electoral calendar and the legal implications of likely deviations from the originally stipulated framework. The possible return of Kumba Yala to active politics, as well as the eventual return of exiled Nino Vieira, could compel the supreme court to grapple with the eligibility of the two former presidents.

Poor preparedness on the part of the competent electoral bodies, generalised **lack of confidence** in the reliability of the voter registers and the associated difficulties in reaching a technical consensus on establishing a new voter registration process threatened to push the election date beyond the limits of the transitional charter. Faced with **international pressure** to adhere as closely as possible to the pre-established calendar, elections were scheduled for 19 June 2005, with a foreseeable second round in mid-July. Nonetheless, and in light of the inevitable delays in launching the electoral process, an amendment to the original transitional charter was required extending President Henrique Rosa's mandate beyond 7 May 2005, thus avoiding a potentially destabilising **power vacuum** in the nation's highest office.

Foreign Affairs

The **rehabilitation** of Guinea-Bissau's international image and the resumption of stable ties with its development partners has been the centre-piece of the country's foreign policy since the overthrow of Kumba Yala's disastrous rule and the flight of big donors, such as Sweden and the Netherlands. In this regard, President Henrique Rosa, an independent and respected businessman with no known political ambitions, took it upon himself to spread the word about Guinea-Bissau's plight to the highest international forums and throughout the sub-region. In light of the country's marginal importance on the international scene, the ECOSOC advisory group on countries emerging from conflict and the less formal Group of Friends of Guinea-Bissau tirelessly assisted the authorities in maintaining the small West African country on the international community's radar screen.

Capitalising on indisputable image gains by President Henrique Rosa and on observed improvements in economic and political governance, Prime Minister Carlos Gomes's foreign policy was driven by the need to strengthen and **diversify development cooperation** ties. Through membership in the Community of Portuguese Speaking Countries and ECOWAS, the authorities have sought to harness greater support to meet the country's immediate and long-term challenges.

Preparations for a round table conference of development partners, initially foreseen for November 2004 but postponed due to the events of 6 October, resumed in December 2004. The Portuguese government offered its support for rallying donor countries through a round table process in an effort to engage partners in a constructive **policy dialogue** over the country's development objectives and concomitant financing needs. The 22 expected development partners, including bilaterals, the EU, sub-regional organisations, the Bretton Woods institutions, the African Development Bank and the UN undertook to engage in support of Guinea-Bissau in the round table dialogue context, and subject to the successful holding of presidential elections in the first half of 2005.

In addition, government sought to strengthen relations with non-OECD/DAC partners. The prime minister visited **Cuba** in an attempt to revive cooperation with this historic partner, particularly in the health sector. Similarly, the **People's Republic of China** was promoting its interests in the country through large investments in infrastructural development and institution building.

Consultations with the IMF resumed and pointed towards the approval of a staff monitored programme in April 2005 that would pave the way for resumed EU and other bilateral budget support.

Socioeconomic Developments

The economic and social situation in Guinea-Bissau remained **fragile**, despite favourable resource endowments: climate and soil provide for excellent rain-fed agriculture and the territorial waters are among the richest in West Africa. Yet, one out of three people currently live under the **poverty line**. GDP per capita has declined some 25% since the early 1990s and was estimated at $ 200 owing to the combined impact of the 1998–99 conflict and poor governance.

Social indicators depicted an equally **gloomy picture** for the country's estimated 1.3 million inhabitants, the country ranking among the ten least developed countries on the Human Development Index. According to the report on progress towards the Millennium Development Goals launched in the last quarter of 2004, the expansion of the educational system towards universal coverage was the only goal likely to be achieved by 2015. The Poverty Reduction Strategy Paper, the central document at the upcoming round table, was finalised and sought to address the daunting challenges faced by the country.

The country's small industrial base had yet to recover from the **destruction** inflicted in 1998–99 and its **private sector** remained grossly undercapitalised. The economy, however, rebounded somewhat in 2004, thanks to an unusually favourable cashew harvest, the country's main export crop. In spite of significant gains both in the efficiency of **revenue collection** and **expenditure** control, government revenues were insufficient to allow for the normal functioning of the state. The wage bill alone accounted for 70% of expenditure. In 2004, the government succeeded in meeting its salary obligations due, on the one hand, to the improved **fiscal performance** and, on the other, to the budget support provided by the emergency economic management fund established and managed by the United Nations Development Programme.

Carlos Lopes with the help of Martim Faria e Maya

Liberia

This was intended to be the year that Liberia made major steps towards peace, stability and the rehabilitation of its government after 14 years or more of war. At the beginning of the year, the United Nations Mission in Liberia (UNMIL), established on 1 October 2003, was still building up to its full strength of some 14,785 soldiers, 215 military observers, 755 civilian police, 360 uniformed police units, 635 international staff, 798 national staff and 431 United Nations volunteers. The UN General Assembly had been asked to appropriate some $ 840 m for UNMIL for the 12 months beginning 1 August 2003, indicating the size of the budget required for the world's largest UN mission. UNMIL enjoyed a robust Chapter 7 mandate, with authority to disarm and reintegrate former fighters, to assist in the reconstruction of Liberia's national police force and to assist in reestablishing national authority throughout the country. The UN mission was empowered to work with the National Transitional Government of Liberia (NTGL), an interim administration established by the **Comprehensive Peace Agreement** (CPA) signed in Accra on 18 August 2003 between the former government of Liberia and the two main armed factions opposed to it. The Comprehensive Peace Agreement was intended to put a final stop to the war that had been fought in Liberia in fits and starts since the 1980s. It was made possible by the departure into exile of Liberia's elected president, Charles Taylor, on 11 August 2003 and his replacement by a government composed of members of the three armed factions that had been disputing control of the country, under a chairman of their choosing, the former business-man C. Gyude Bryant.

By the end of the year, both the National Transitional Government of Liberia under its chairman, Bryant, and UNMIL under special representative Jacques Paul Klein, an American diplomat and former air force general, were sticking to their **timetable** for organ-ising general and presidential elections in October 2005, prior to the inauguration of a new elected government in January 2006. However, many observers, including senior UNMIL officials, were concerned that Liberia's rehabilitation was being blown off course by an unduly compressed timetable, vast corruption in the Liberian government and mistakes by the UN administration. There was a notable loss of confidence among international donors, whose attention was diverted during the course of the year to other emergencies, pushing Liberia down the international priority list.

Domestic Politics

Liberia's **transitional government**, inaugurated on 14 October 2003, contains 21 cabinet ministers. These, plus a range of other senior government positions, are members or nom-inees of Liberia's former armed factions. One of the three such groups involved is the for-mer government of Liberia, previously led by ex-President Charles Taylor, itself originally formed from an armed faction active in the 1990s. The other two components of the interim government are Liberians United for Reconciliation and Democracy (LURD) and the Movement for Democracy in Liberia (MODEL). These two armed groups had inflicted a military defeat on Taylor's government in June–July 2003 with significant (although unavowed) backing from sub-regional powers, especially Guinea, and discreet support from the US government. The same three factions were also able to appoint members of Liberia's National Assembly, although this also contained representatives drawn from Liberian 'civil society.' However, some of the civil society representatives could more accurately be described as politicians not aligned with any of the three former armed factions.

As a consequence of these arrangements negotiated in Accra, the transitional government contained many familiar faces from the war, such as Defence Minister Daniel Chea, who had held the same position under President Taylor, or Labour Minister J. Laveli Supuwood, who had also been a senior member of Taylor's armed faction before joining LURD, or MODEL leader Thomas Yaya Nimely, appointed as foreign minister after discreet pressure from Côte d'Ivoire's President Laurent Gbagbo, a key backer of MODEL. UNMIL chief Jacques Klein was quoted as saying that "each of the warring factions got ministries which are then staffed top to bottom with their people." In fact, deputy and assistant ministers do not come from the same faction as the minister, and ministers and their deputies and assis-tants often disagreed with one another in consequence. This contributed to the general **dys-function** of government.

The nature of the transitional government had a notable impact on some of the key issues affecting reconstruction. Justice Minister Kabinah Janneh, a leading member of LURD, pronounced himself opposed to a war crimes court. Chairman Bryant, although not himself a member of any of the former armed factions, also publicly expressed opposition to the establishment of a truth commission or a war crimes court, although a truth commission was on the way to being constituted by year's end. Other ministers and senior officials too were opposed to prosecutions for crimes committed during the civil war. This was unsurprising inasmuch as some of Liberia's most notorious **warlords** held key posts and were to be seen driving around Monrovia with official escorts. In particular, the powerful speaker of the National Assembly, George Dweh, from the LURD faction, was widely known for his involvement in death-squad activities during the presidency of the late Samuel K. Doe (1980–90). Many senior UNMIL officials had served in other UN missions, notably in Bosnia: some expressed their amazement that the UN found itself playing a role in a situation where the leading instigators of a war continued to enjoy such immunity and were even able to use the transitional period to strengthen their positions.

Perhaps for related reasons, the government declined to petition the Nigerian government for the extradition to Sierra Leone of former President **Charles Taylor**, who has been indicted for war crimes by Sierra Leone's special court. At year's end, Taylor continued to live in Calabar, Nigeria, as a guest of the Nigerian government. Although he was reported to have curtailed his earlier communications with politicians and others in Liberia after warnings from his Nigerian hosts, Taylor's presence in the sub-region continued to cast a shadow over Liberian politics. Key associates of Taylor, including his wife, Jewel Howard Taylor, remain in Liberia.

Within some of the factions, even as they were officially transforming themselves into political parties, continuing **factional struggles** affected national security. Inside LURD there was a movement to unseat the movement's chairman, Sekou Conneh. The dissident group was led by military commanders who supported Conneh's estranged wife Aisha. Rival factions fought each other in the Bushrod area of Monrovia – a LURD fiefdom – in August. LURD was also prominent in attempts to replace Gyude Bryant as head of the transitional government, notably in a 26 January joint statement co-signed by the leader of MODEL. These efforts were unsuccessful, and Bryant finished the year in a relatively strong position. However, it is unlikely that he will emerge as a key figure in Liberia's future politics since according to the terms of the Comprehensive Peace Agreement, as chairman of the transitional administration he is disqualified from seeking election to the presidency in October 2005.

As evidence mounted of **corruption** among senior government officials, many observers concluded that members of the transitional institutions regarded the interim period as an opportunity to use their official positions to make money in the shortest possible time, since some of them were unlikely to be able to continue in government after the end of the year.

This may have been one factor contributing to the growing perception that the transitional government had little interest in tackling the problems needed to clear the way for an elected government that would restore Liberia to normality.

UNMIL's main concern during the year was **disarmament**. The disarmament exercise had started badly on 7 December 2003, when a first attempt had to be abandoned after administrative problems had led to violent disturbances by former fighters angry at being unable to hand in their weapons for cash. At least eight people were killed, causing UNMIL to suspend the disarmament process pending new arrangements. After the speedy termination of the first attempt at disarmament, a second phase began on 15 April. While the CPA had provided for the establishment of a 'National Commission for Disarmament, Demobilization, Rehabilitation and Reintegration', in practice much of the planning and implementation was the work of a 'Joint Implementation Unit', largely composed of civilian staff, that was under the immediate authority of the United Nations Development Programme (UNDP) rather than of UNMIL.

The disarmament exercise, substantially completed by 31 October 2004 but extended for a further three weeks in some remote areas, caused considerable **controversy**. This was mostly due to the very high numbers of people registering as ex-combatants and the comparatively small numbers of weapons or munitions that they surrendered. UNMIL had originally estimated that about 38,000 fighters would register for disarmament, becoming eligible for a $ 300 payment, and it planned further help with rehabilitation and reintegration. Other sources too had made estimates of a roughly comparable order. In regard to numbers of weapons, in February Jacques Klein estimated that there were around three weapons for each combatant in Liberia. However, at the completion of the programme, more than 102,000 people had registered as ex-combatants, handing in more than 27,000 guns and some 6.15 million rounds of ammunition. It was also notable that few heavy weapons were handed in, although the intensive bombardment of Monrovia in mid-2003 had revealed that the factions possessed quite a few heavy artillery pieces. Hence, at the end of the disarmament exercise in November, the UN had collected only one weapon for every three to four people reporting themselves as ex-combatants, and there had been more than twice as many people reporting at disarmament centres as anticipated.

The most likely **explanation** for these surprising figures was that the leaders of former combatant groups had sold many of their heaviest weapons in neighbouring countries, as intelligence sources suggested. Military commanders of armed factions also appeared to have distributed small amounts of ammunition and light weapons to non-combatants who could then deliver them in return for a cash payment of $ 300, which they were then required to share with the military commander who had provided the ammunition. In this way they were able to benefit from the conditions for registration introduced before the second phase of the disarmament exercise, opening on 15 April, which permitted anyone who produced 150 rounds of ammunition to qualify for processing as an ex-combatant, and not only people who handed over weapons. Some fighters had already experienced one or even two previous disarmament processes, in Liberia in 1997, but also in Sierra Leone, where some Liberians had also fought.

The fact that a substantially higher number of people were registered as ex-combatants than had been budgeted for left little money for the other leg of the disarmament and rein- tegration programme, namely provision for the **rehabilitation** of former combatants. By November, only some 11,000 ex-combatants were registered in various UNMIL training or work-creation projects, with almost 5,000 others registered as undergoing formal edu- cation, but with no guarantee that they would be able to pay school fees. Aid donors had also established some other job-creation schemes, most notably the US Agency for International Development (USAID), which ran a substantial infrastructure-repair pro- gramme that provided work for several thousand more ex-combatants, but this was a rather short-term solution. The risk in the longer term was that tens of thousands of ex-combat- ants who were unaccounted for after disarmament might turn to robbery or enlist as fighters in wars elsewhere in West Africa. In September, the transitional government and UNMIL circulated to donors a joint document pointing out the security threat posed by ex- fighters that had not received any further training or cash. Chairman Bryant repeatedly called for more money for the fund. UNICEF chief executive Carol Bellamy also criticised donors for failing to fund the resettlement and retraining of former combatants. She did mention, however, that 85% of the former child soldiers that had been associated with armed forces had returned to their families.

Other aspects of dealing with the massive problems of restoring stability to Liberia and establishing an efficient government caused further problems. In mid-year, the World Food Programme was feeding some 490,000 people, including **internally displaced persons** and newly returned **refugees**, as well as malnourished people. By the end of the year, there were still over 300,000 displaced persons, many of them living in camps, waiting to return to their homes, as well as hundreds of thousands of Liberian refugees living in neighbouring coun- tries. The exact population of Liberia is unknown as the last census was in 1984 and years of war have caused massive disruption, but is put by the US government at some 3.2 m.

On a more positive note, there was some progress in establishing a new Liberian **police** force to replace the old force that was largely untrained and unequipped, highly politicised and notoriously corrupt. On 13 July, UNMIL and the transitional government jointly launched a programme to recruit new police officers. The intention was to form a new force of some 3,500 people who would receive training from experts employed by the UN, as well as proper equipment. Progress in reorganising the armed forces was somewhat slower, but by year's end preparations were in hand for a new army to receive training from a US private security company that had previously worked for the UN in Bosnia.

Probably the most serious security concern during the year was the outbreak of **rioting** in a suburb of Monrovia on 28 October. Said to have been sparked off by a disagreement over sales pitches in a market, it soon mobilised ex-fighters of rival factions and took on a religious form, with attacks on mosques and businesses owned by members of the Mandingo ethnic group, who are generally known as Muslims and who were widely associated with support for the LURD faction. Subsequent reports suggested that the violence had been planned by some ex-Taylor commanders, and that the attacks on mosques were part of a wider strategy to provoke violence on religious grounds. At least 17 people were killed, with similar incidents being reported in other towns, including Kakata, Ganta and Buchanan. The gravity of the incident lay not just in the numbers of casualties and in the damage caused, but also in the indications that some key members of the old armed factions were reorganising and were developing strategies for the future, still based on the use of violence.

Nevertheless, there seemed little doubt that national elections would proceed in October 2005, with the UN and the main international donors strongly rejecting any arguments for postponement. Some 40 people declared themselves as **presidential candidates**, including the former world football star George Weah, who made his announcement on 23 November. Although Weah had almost no political experience, and no experience at all in government, it was generally agreed that this constituted part of his likely political appeal, as he was untainted by participation in Liberia's war, while his name was almost universally known. However, among the candidates who had declared themselves to be running for the presidency in October 2005, there were also plenty of experienced politicians and administrators.

Foreign Affairs

Since mid-2003, the Liberian peace process has received unprecedented outside support, from sub-regional powers and from major donors and the UN. This has occurred at a time when the UN has had major missions in neighbouring Sierra Leone and Côte d'Ivoire. But there was **little effective coordination** between the three missions in regard both to strategic issues and to tactical matters such as disarmament. For much of the year, for example, UNMIL was not deployed at key border crossings with neighbouring countries. This clearly raised questions concerning the possibility of armed groups manipulating the disarmament exercises.

The Liberian government, however, did make efforts to improve its relations with its **neighbours**. On 20 May, Chairman Bryant led a delegation to Guinea in an attempt to revive the Mano River Union. In regard to Sierra Leone in particular, one of the major obstacles was the question of former president Charles Taylor. The special court for Sierra Leone continued to press for his extradition from his home in Calabar, Nigeria. Officers of the special court for Sierra Leone and some US officials confirmed earlier media reports that Charles Taylor had cooperated with al-Qaida both before and after 11 September 2001 – although other US officials, including from leading intelligence agencies, could not confirm this allegation. A senior al-Qaida operative arrested in Pakistan on 25 July, Ahmed

Khalfan Ghailani, suspected of involvement in the 1998 bombing of US embassies in east Africa, was reported to have spent at least three years living in Liberia from the late 1990s.

In regard to the wider world, one of the most important changes in Liberia's foreign relations during the year was its recognition of the People's Republic of **China**. Previously, Liberia had been for some years one of several African countries that had alternated between recognition of the People's Republic of China and the Republic of China (Taiwan). This was generally a question of blatant financial interest: the Taylor government had secured extensive financial support from Taiwan, and Taylor was reported to have gone into exile on 11 August 2003 in possession of $ 3 m given by the Taiwanese government for disarmament. One of the interim government's first acts was to recognise China in place of Taiwan. In January, Beijing deployed 500 troops to the Liberian operation, its biggest-ever commitment to a UN mission. In general, China showed a marked interest in both Liberia and other African countries, most particularly in regard to purchases of minerals and other commodities.

Chairman Bryant travelled extensively during the year, including three visits to the US, during one of which he met US President George W. Bush. On 3 June he addressed the UN Security Council, pleading forcefully – but unsuccessfully – for the lifting of economic sanctions against Liberia (see below). Although the **US government** provided substantial financial help to UNMIL and was offering direct support for specific sectors, such as retraining the Liberian armed forces, US officials made clear that they did not envisage further major aid to Liberia after the termination of the transitional arrangements and the restoration of an elected government.

Socioeconomic Developments

On 5–6 February, a **donor's conference** on Liberian reconstruction was held in New York, co-chaired by Kofi Annan and Colin Powell. It pledged some $ 520 m, with the US pledging some $ 245 m for peacekeeping and $ 200 m for other purposes. However, at the end of the year, it remained unclear how much of this money was still earmarked for Liberia or whether it had been reallocated for other uses.

Both the transitional government and UNMIL continued to radiate optimism about an early **return to normality**, but there was growing evidence of problems. In Monrovia, one of the most contentious issues was the provision of mains electricity, which has not been available for years. Although some progress was made initially through rehabilitation of the national electricity corporation, the modest improvements in electricity supply were soon reversed due to corruption, as officials embezzled money or privately sold fuel and spare parts that were needed for the power supply. Similarly, government promises to reduce the prices of petroleum products and rice were not realised. One of the government's main policies was to centralise revenue collection, but there were consistent reports that much revenue never made its way to the central treasury.

A further example of how government disarray or corruption could have an impact on development concerned the export of a stockpile of hundreds of thousands of tonnes of **iron ore** that had lain on the quayside at Buchanan since the early 1990s. Various international business consortia expressed an interest in buying the stockpile, perhaps as part of a larger deal incorporating rehabilitation of the railway line from the iron ore mines at Yekepa to the port at Buchanan. A Chinese consortium negotiated to buy the Buchanan iron ore stockpile in rather unclear circumstances. Liberian political activists, learning that the iron ore was being loaded on board a Chinese ship, obtained an injunction from the supreme court preventing the sale of the ore. Nevertheless, loading continued in defiance of the court order and the Chinese ship sailed away fully loaded on 15 September. It is unclear precisely how much money was paid for the ore, or which officials received it.

International **sanctions** continued on various economic activities, including Liberia's diamond and timber trades. These were originally imposed by UN Security Council Resolution 1343 in May 2001 as a means of preventing then President Taylor's government from supporting the destabilisation of Sierra Leone, but international attention had gradually turned to using sanctions as a way of putting pressure on the Liberian government generally. The domination of the National Transitional Government of Liberia by nominees of the former armed factions threw doubt on the government's ability to inspire international confidence that it had eliminated the risk of abuse or smuggling in regard to timber and diamonds in particular. MODEL nominees had control of the FORESTRY DEVELOPMENT AUTHORITY AND THE BUREAU OF MARITIME AFFAIRS, enabling this former armed faction to continue profiting from national resources much as it did when it was still a rebel group. Largely for this reason, the UN had still not lifted its sanctions on Liberia by year's end. On 17 June, the Security Council adopted Resolution 1549, re-establishing a panel of experts, pursuant to Resolution 1521 of 2003, to conduct a report on the violations of sanctions. Three months earlier, on 12 March, the UN Security Council unanimously agreed to freeze Taylor's assets to prevent them from being used to destabilise the country. Timber and rubber are Liberia's main export items, with the country earning more than $ 78 m and more than $ 57 manualy from timber and rubber exports respectively. Liberia also has the world's second-largest ship registry, with more than 1,800 vessels registered, including 35% of the world's tanker fleet.

The scale of Liberia's economic problems is daunting. Its debt is generally estimated to be a little over $ 3 bn, and continues to accrue interest. This sum consists of debts to the World Bank, the International Monetary Fund and other multilateral institutions, plus Germany, France, Japan, the US and the African Development Bank. The transitional government, on the other hand, inherited a treasury containing just $ 2 m. In his annual state of the nation address on 26 January, Chairman Bryant recorded that government had revenue of $ 21.1 m – largely from its ship registry – and expenditure of $ 17 m. There was considerable improvement in this regard: during the year from 1 January, actual **revenue** collected amounted to $ 68.2 m, while expenditure was $ 67.8 m.

Liberia is often excluded from **statistical tables** due to the poor quality of its figures. However, it is reckoned that more than 80% of the population is formally unemployed, and 74% has no access to safe drinking water. Life expectancy is 48 years and infant mortality 157 deaths per 1,000 births.

West Africa continues to attract interest in the **oil** industry on account of the ongoing discoveries of important offshore reserves. In regard to Liberia too there was interest in offshore oil exploration. Liberia's offshore waters are currently divided into 17 blocks of unusually small size, an arrangement made by the Taylor government that was presumably intended to maximise the possible signature bonuses to be gained from contracts for exploration. One of the first actions of the new administration led by Chairman Bryant was to license the offshore oil-concession blocks.

Negotiations on oil exploration, and the controversy surrounding the export of iron ore from Buchanan, illustrated one of the main questions surrounding the functioning of a transitional government in the presence of a major UN mission: namely, whether the National Transitional Government of Liberia had the authority to sign concession agreements and enter into other long-term **contracts**. There was no resolution of this question by year's end.

Stephen Ellis

Mali

The general political picture was one of a calm, uneventful year, characterised by political consensus on the one hand and ecological problems on the other. Both the cabinet and the National Assembly were run on the basis of consensus rather than as an arena for opposing parties, although there was *pro forma* representation of the opposition in all cabinet councils. Though President Touré was able to keep the political parties united and relatively sidelined, the first signs of a political shift were apparent in 2004, as the parties began to position themselves for the 2007 elections, and some protests occurred. The major problems in the country were of an ecological nature, namely the locust plague and a poor rainy season.

Domestic Politics

Internal politics remained characterised by Mali's peculiar features: this is a multiparty state in which political parties play little or no role. The current president, Amadou Toumani Touré, usually called ATT, came into office without any party affiliation as a result of a popular multiparty 'Mouvement de Soutien' for his nomination in 2002. His prime minister, Ahmed Mohamed Ag Hamani, also had no party affiliation, but the cabinet was made up of representatives of the major parties, such as RPM ('Rassemblement Populaire du Mali') and Adema ('Parti Africain pour la Solidarité et la Justice', the party of the former president Konaré, now head of the AU Commission).

On 3 May, Touré appointed a **new cabinet**. Ousmane Issoufi Maïga, formerly minister of transport, became the new prime minister, many former ministers were reshuffled to new departments, while four new ministers were appointed, for a total of 28. The most important new appointments were Moctar Wanna, former career diplomat, to foreign affairs, Sadio Gassama, former army chief-of-staff, to interior security, and the economist Abubacar Traoré to finance. Culture, an important Malian export product, remained in the hands of movie director Cheick Oumar Sissoko, who is also president of the minority 'Parti pour la Solidarité Africaine'.

The overall impression was that Touré wanted more dynamism in his cabinet ("un gouvernement de terrain"). A more precise motive is difficult to pinpoint, though the old prime minister seemed to be ailing and had asked to be released. On the other hand, consensus politics in Mali, which had given Touré's government a long political honeymoon, seemed to be ending and some political parties started flexing their muscles for the 2007 elections. Positions crystallised and some **protests began**. Moreover, the non-partisan political movement that brought ATT to power was considering turning into a formal political party, but a sizeable number of politicians preferred to keep it a ground-swell movement. Indeed, in the past some of the parties had emerged in this way: Adema, for example, was originally a mass movement to remove Moussa Traoré in the early 1990s. Gradually, many of the 2002 election promises were seen to be failing and some changes were expected. However, throughout 2004 the political opposition was mute and even the trade unions decided not to take overt action, despite arrears in payments and lack of job opportunities. Union leaders declared that Mali was best served by unity in government and a high level of trust in the president.

Whatever the reasons for the cabinet reshuffle, if there were internal divisions within the cabinet, they remained **hidden**: the consensus culture of Mali's governance precluded publicity leaks. This was in keeping with the way ATT has continued Mali's policy since the advent of electoral democracy, in order to have stability and calm in the country. He also demands flexibility and modesty from leading officials. One major issue was the start of a major campaign against **corruption**, for which a 'Cellule d'Appui aux Structures de Controle de l'Administration' (CASCA) was inaugurated with the aim of being effective in 2005, plus the appointment on 1 April of a general national accountant (Sid Sosso Diara). One stimulus was the scandal over the embezzlement of CFAfr 2.6 bn (€ 4 m) in the departments of economy and finance. However, despite government rhetoric, actions were few and very slow, and it is debatable whether the government will have either the power or the stamina to fight this internal battle.

Some hitches in peace and stability proved to be minor ripples in the political pond. A persistent issue has been unrest among students at Mali's secondary and tertiary education institutions in Bamako. On 15 and 16 May, a general strike by teachers hit the country, but by the end of the year protests had become more focused. Irked by the commercialisation of education, non-payment of bursaries, infighting among faculty and inadequate educational facilities, and triggered by rivalries between students of different schools, **students** rose in a series of protests against school establishments, especially the faculty of economic and juridical sciences. On 30 November, this resulted in the death of one student (Mamadou Traoré, or 'Papou') that shook the country. His death was still under investigation at the end of the year, when nine students, three policemen and a government official were detained for questioning. The matter was aggravated by the later deaths of a girl and a boy. Though largely unrelated to the protest marches, they made for a nationwide scandal. Problems in **education** will probably remain on the political agenda in the next years of ATT's mandate, especially at the recently created, severely understaffed and under-equipped University of Bamako. Compared to the educational unrest, other protests had little effect. Protests by butchers (24 April) and journalists (28 August) proceeded more smoothly, as did one by Malian artists against illegal copying of their work (21 June). The freeing of the hostages from Qatar who had been in the hands of northern rebels was a boost for the government.

In February, the new election committee was appointed and installed and on 30 May **elections** were held in all 703 communes in Mali for the second time, and went quietly and well, with a record 43% voter turnout (5.6 m Malians voted). The winner was the former ruling party, Adema, with 28%, URD ('Union Rassemblement Democratique') trailing with 14% and RPM with 13%. Some alliances of smaller parties followed with 11% and a coalition of individuals with 9%. Other parties, historically important in the democratisation process, like the CNID ('Congrès National d'Initiative Démocratique') and BDIA ('Bloc pour la Démocratie et l'Intégration Africaine') fared less well. Observers were satisfied with the proceedings and generally concluded that democratisation processes in Mali were well under way. However, problems remained, such as the weak administration of justice and widespread and deeply rooted corruption.

The problems in the north of Mali have abated but seemed not to have been resolved, though the banditry in the empty north seemed to have no political overtones any longer. One incident occurred on 2 July, when a Malian Red Cross mission in the north was attacked and robbed of their vehicle by **bandits**. A more serious clash was between Arab and Kounta in eastern Mali, near Gao, resulting in 13 people being killed in September. Both groups have longstanding historical links to the area, having lived relatively peacefully under Kounta chieftaincy for centuries. However, decentralisation measures generated competition over access to the few resources of the region, both ecological – mainly waterholes – and political, namely control of the few trans-Saharan roads. In 2002 and 2003, there had already been clashes, but not on this scale. This clash seemed related to the Islamic fundamentalist group that kidnapped a party of European tourists in south Algeria in 2003, released them in August, and then sought refuge in the mountains of eastern Mali. As a consequence, the US sent military instructors to train the Malian army in anti-terrorist warfare techniques in Gao, providing them with all-terrain vehicles and desert warfare equipment, as part of the Pan-Sahel Initiative, now known as Trans Sahara Counter Terrorism Initiative (TSCTI). This issue was, of course, most vividly publicised when two stages of the Paris-Dakar rally, held from 1–16 January, were cancelled because of gang activity in northern Mali. French intelligence uncovered – and foiled – an Islamic militant plot to kidnap rally competitors.

Foreign Affairs

The largest external political problem for Mali was the **crisis in Côte d'Ivoire**. Since over a million Malians lived in Côte d'Ivoire, the ongoing conflict heavily impacted the Malian economy. At the end of March, the Ivorian army killed several civilians in the rebel-held north, which resulted in another wave of Malians living in that area returning to Mali. With them came an unspecified number of Ivorian 'rebels', who agreed, however, not to use Mali as a rallying point for the armed struggle. Several high-level conferences were held during 2004 (27 July in Bamako, 26 November in Ouagadougou and 15 December in Abuja) to address the issue. There were other international contacts, e.g., on 15–16 May at a conference in Bamako with the other countries in West Africa plus the Maghrib countries united under the CEN-SAD (Community of Sahel-Saharans States), namely Tunisia, Libya, Morocco, Gambia and Mauritania as well as Egypt, to address joint problems in the area, such as civil war, drought, AIDS, the world market for cotton and unemployment. On 26 and 27 April the countries bordering the Niger River conferred in Paris on the management of this crucial waterway and the development of inland fisheries on the river, just as they had done on the problems of cotton production and marketing on 19 February in Bamako.

Most external political efforts were directed at generating aid funds in various ways. Loans were obtained from the World Bank, the Islamic Bank, and the Bank of West Africa and the Sahel-Sudan Bank for various purposes, such as road construction, HIV/AIDS campaigns, security and water management. Deals with, among others, China, the US, the Netherlands, Belgium and Kuwait secured additional funds, plus the cancellation of some Mali debts (by China), and in the latter part of the year funds from various sources were secured to combat the locust plague.

Mali was visited by several foreign dignitaries, mostly from the sub-region, such as the representatives of the Francophone states (22 February); the president of Gambia (21–23 March); the premier of Morocco (11–12 April); the finance ministers of Kuwait (28 June) and of Canada (19 August); a Chinese delegation (15–17 November); and the premier of Haiti (28 November). President Touré himself was quite active in visiting other countries: Egypt (26–28 January); Libya (26–28 February and 18–21 August); Ghana (19–20 March); Guinea (20–21 May); Mozambique (23–24 May); Burkina Faso (21–22 June, 8–9 September, 26–27 November); China (15–19 July); Gambia (22–23 July); Libya (18–28 August); and Niger (11–12 October). On the international scene the former president

Konaré generated visibility for Mali as president of the AU; in October, he published an autobiography entitled "Alpha Oumar Konaré, an African from Mali."

Socioeconomic Developments

Just as in 1998, Mali was plagued by **locusts** in 2004. The previous two years had seen a moderate invasion of locusts, with a recrudescence in some places, especially the wetter spots in north and central Mali, the Mopti region. New swarms bred during the early months of 2004, on the border with Mauritania and Niger as well, and further east into Chad. The FAO at the start of 2004 tried mainly to preclude a locust migration from the northern Sahel into the northwest, to prevent further breeding in the Maghrib. However, this had limited success. Despite massive activity in the north (6 million hectares treated with insecticides), early spring saw several swarms mature and migrate towards Mali, where the wet season produced further swarms.

Estimates of **crop loss** ranged from one-third to (more probably) one-fifth of the national harvest (750,000 tonnes out of the expected roughly three million tonnes). However, later reports noted that the loss of the projected harvest was at least partly due to failing rains at the end of the season. President Touré, who toured the afflicted areas (the regions of Timbuktu, Mopti and Kayes in particular) assured the stricken population that famine was not expected and that all food would be shared ("as long as Sikasso has only one tuber of manioc, Mali will share it"). The reason for this assurance was that the main food producing area, the 'rice granary' of the Niger basin and the inner delta, were largely spared through joint international efforts, even though the southern part of the delta was affected. Algeria in particular, both through direct involvement and by leading the other Maghrib countries, spearheaded actual help in money, equipment and insecticides. More international aid followed from the EU and the US. The efficacy of **locust extermination** was, however, hampered by lack of equipment on the ground, outdated chemicals, lack of spraying aeroplanes and insufficient knowledge about locust extermination among both cadres and the local population. Also, the long-term risk of the chemicals for the environment and the immediate risk of the reuse of empty chemical vats by locals called for a sustained campaign. An early warning system was also re-established.

At year's end, the Asian tsunami diverted international attention from the locust plague, but also produced a wave of solidarity in the country, uniting expatriate Malians (estimated at 25% of the population) in helping their kin. Other countries were affected as well, such as Mauritania, but Mali produces 80% of what it consumes while Mauritania relies much more on imported food. Food distribution began to get under way in November 2004. At least 10% of all villages were severely afflicted and needed aid, and **distribution** was monopolised by the presidential office, which distributed the free food handouts. This was interpreted by some as a way to boost the president's standing among the grassroots and to position himself for the new elections, but it also reflected genuine concern in the central office (in August the president handed over one month's salary to the anti-locust campaign and urged his ministers to do the same) and did not seem to have harmed the efficiency of the distributions. If some areas remained outside the distribution programmes, as seemed the case, this was not different from earlier distributions.

A perennial ecological problem manifested itself earlier than usual, due to the locust plague. The hard hit north sent its cattle south sooner than usual. The usual arrangement is that cattle return south when the rice and millet harvest is well under way, with the major crossing of the Niger by the herds usually well orchestrated. In 2004, the transhumance areas were depleted well before that date, and the herds had to search for food south of the Niger before the harvest. This resulted in tensions with resident farmers, which in some places erupted into open conflict, though without casualties. The usual exodus of seasonal labour from the stricken areas also started earlier this year and more young people moved to the cities in search of gainful employment. There, they were thwarted by the loss of the Ivorian labour market, and more young farmers from the Niger bend moved into Bamako, south Mali and the cities of Ghana.

Despite the major attention on the locust plague, **drought** also remained on the political agenda. In August, government imposed a general ban on tree felling throughout Mali, and announced some initiatives for tree planting. The 10% of tree cover is under pressure from commercial logging and charcoal production. Given the status of the water and forests department, however, it is debatable whether this measure will have the effect intended. The department is seen by the majority of the rural population as a police force that penalises locals for any use of wood. Thus, the law on rural sales of wood, issued at the start of 2004, which aims at a more balanced use of fuel and construction wood and tries to regulate commercial wood extraction, probably will not have the effect intended. At the very beginning of the year, in January, the government promised to install 9,600 new village pumps during the next decade.

Mali in 2004 continued to suffer from its usual socioeconomic problems, but some improvement was discernible. Illiteracy declined slowly, to 71% (73% in 2002, 77% in 1997 and 81% in 1990). School enrolment rose to 61% in 2000 (41% in 1995, 25% in 1985). The national debt showed some reduction – $ 2,803 m in 2002 against $ 2,903 m in 1993 – though in 2002, 73% of the population still had less than $ 1 per day in income.

There were severe **health-related** problems. Average life expectancy declined from 45 years (1990) to 41 years in 2002. Infant mortality stands at 152 per 1,000, child mortality at 231 per 1,000, and maternal mortality at 630 per 100,000. The rising HIV infection rate – still severely underreported in 2001 at 1.7% – the rising incidence of malaria (still the largest killer in Mali) and an outbreak of cholera underscored the health vulnerability of the Malian population. Mali participated in a Chinese project to field-test their new Amonquinoline anti-malaria drug, and the results seemed promising. World demand for this new drug rose exponentially in 2004 and the Chinese will probably not be able to keep up with demand. Furthermore, the drug is still quite expensive for Mali. Cholera resulted in over 100 deaths at the end of 2003 and broke out again in the western part of the country in February and March 2004. In May, the region of Tla, 350 kilometres north of Bamako, reported 21 cholera victims. After the onset of the rainy season, no new cases were reported, but it is unlikely that the epidemic was fully over. Mali participated in a general West African vaccination campaign against poliomyelitis, which started at 8 October.

The government initiated a campaign against female **circumcision**, still a reality for the overwhelming majority of Malian women. In announcing the campaign, the government stressed that the practice was not Islamic: it argued that the custom was strongest where Islam was weakest. However, the incidence (91%!) that seems to hold for most parts of Mali. Of course, as has been stressed extensively in Islamic discourse, the observation that circumcision is not Quranic is correct. Indeed, the campaign would appear to be a soft sell to spare the evident sensibilities on the issue. It seemed more a donor issue than an internal Malian problem and the upcoming elections will probably force the government to soft-pedal this issue. Yet Mali did aim to play a major role in African Islam, and held a large conference on Sufism in Bamako (17–22 December).

Tourism was on the rise in 2004, as it was during the last decades. In the previous two decades, at least according to government statistics, the number of tourists rose from 35,000 to 150,000 per year. The government, together with several private partners, stimulated a widening of the tourist appeal. Though the Dogon country remained the main attraction, the implications of this tourist situation were increasingly realised. Government, the travel industry and travel agents, both international and Malian, became concerned about the impact of tourism on the Dogon area, realising that authenticity and mass tourism are not compatible. Measures to broaden the attraction of Mali tourism were discussed. The region of Timbuktu was singled out as a tourist development area; both the visits by the Aga Khan and Chirac at the end of 2003 and the new airports in Mopti (developed for the 'Coupe Afrique des Nations', the continental football championship) and Timbuktu were a stimulus. The latter airport featured as a projected direct air link between the US and Timbuktu, which authorities thought would not only increase tourism to that desert city, but also to the rest of Mali. The American fascination with Timbuktu has a long history, just as the city is the symbol for the ultimate foreign experience, but in this case a military interest was assumed by many commentators. The struggle against international terrorism has brought the Sahara region into focus as a zone of terrorist recruitment, and, as mentioned above, American military advisers assist Malian regular troops in desert tactics and anti-terrorist campaigns.

Malian tourism received additional international recognition in 2004. UNESCO put various buildings of Malian culture on the World Cultural Heritage list, such as the Askia tomb in Gao (15th century), and several objects in **Timbuktu**, for example, the mosques of Djingarey-Ber, Sidi Yéhya and Sankoré. These, together with the famous tourist destinations of Djenné and the Dogon country, which were put on this list in 1986, means that Mali is high on the world cultural agenda. The specific singling out of Timbuktu and Gao might help to develop a tourist infrastructure in the desert fringes. Also, Timbuktu saw a large store of manuscripts unearthed in August, a major find in the study of the history of Mali. The intellectuals of Mali, together with the diaspora Malians, united in their efforts to promote the safekeeping of their cultural heritage. The government restored the mosque of Shehu Amadou at Hamdallaye, the now deserted capital of the former Macina emirate, and inaugurated the building, which had to be rebuilt from scratch, on 11 June 2004.

Malian culture was exported in 2004 as well: several troupes of musicians, mask dancers, **griots** and artisans toured Europe and America. However, the high point of Mali's culture was the qualification of its football team for the Olympic games in Athens, and the fact that the team made it all the way to the quarter finals, where it was eliminated by Italy.

Walter E.A. van Beek & Moussa Fofana

Mauritania

In 2004 the political stability of Mauritania remained fragile. The main cause for concern were two alleged coup d'états that were thwarted and growing political and religious opposition to the regime. A currency crisis and increasing consumer prices were used by the president as a pretext to reshuffle the government. Social stability remained precarious, as the repression of the opposition continued.

Domestic Politics

President Maaouiya Ould Sid Ahmed Taya maintained his political dominance after winning the disputed 7 November 2003 presidential election. **Ethnic tensions** tore at the fabric of society. The light-skinned Bidan Moors of Nouakchott's small middle class were overjoyed by the re-election of Ould Taya. These Bidan form the backbone of Mauritania's ruling elite and are major beneficiaries of government in the form of jobs and patronage. Among Mauritania's **Harratin black Moors**, who comprise the majority of the population, there was silent resignation. The Harratin had formerly served as slaves to the Bidan. They have a high birth rate, are well educated and want access to power. Like the Harratin, the black population that live along the Senegal River valley are effectively excluded from power, even though they compromise about 30% of the population.

In mid-January, the constitutional council **rejected an appeal** by Ould Haidallah, main challenger to Ould Taya in the presidential election, that the results be annulled. In January, **Mohamed Jemil Ould Mansour** was arrested as he arrived by plane in Nouakchott. He was released on 19 January. Mansour is vice-president of the – not recognised – 'Forum Mauritanien pour la Réforme et la Démocratie' and secretary-general of the National Alliance Against Zionist Infiltration and the Defence of Palestine and Iraq. He was arrested in early 2003 during a government crackdown on politicians and religious leaders and escaped from prison during the confusion surrounding an attempted coup in June. Ould Mansour fled to neighbouring Senegal and then to Belgium, where he received political asylum.

On 7 April, a group of prominent Mauritanians who backed Ould Haidallah filed papers for the registration of **a new political party 'Parti pour la Convergence Démocratique'** (PCD). A few days later, the party's president, Cheikh Ould Horma, announced that the government had refused the application on the grounds that the party's leadership comprised Islamic radicals, a number of individuals being sought by the courts and others who had received suspended prison sentences. Ould Mansour is the party's vice-president. The leadership also includes black Mauritanians from the south. The Arabic initials of the party read 'El Hamd', which means 'praise to God', an obvious indication of the party's implicit **sympathy for Islam**.

On 9 April, the **partial senate elections** began in order to renew section B (one-third) of the 56–seat senate. Thirty-one lists representing seven political parties were involved in the contest for the sixteen affected constituencies. Outside Nouakchott, Ould Taya's 'Parti Républicain Démocratique et Social' (PRDS) suffered from the discontent of representatives of certain communities. PRDS won 14 seats. For the first time, the opposition 'l'Alliance Populaire Progressiste' obtained legislative representation with two seats. The 'Rassemblement pour la Démocratie et l'Unité' came third with one seat. The second round took place on 16 April and was won by PRDS.

On 20 April, the supreme court upheld a **verdict that Ould Haidallah was guilty of planning a coup** in 2003. A **libel suit** against the editors of four independent weekly newspapers 'L'Eveil Hebdo', 'L'Authentique', 'Le Journal' and 'Al Moujtamaa', brought by ex-finance minister Ould Houmeid was settled out of court. In May **a new political party** emerged called 'El Sawab', meaning 'the correct'. It was formed by politicians close to Ould Haidallah and advocated economic and social reform. Meanwhile two Mauritanian human rights groups 'SOS-Esclaves' and 'l'Association Mauritanienne de Défense des Droits de l'Homme' (AMDH) **criticised the treatment of detainees** involved in the coup attempt of June 2003.

On 25 July, Ould Taya **reshuffled his cabinet** in order to replace nine ministers (among them finance, economic affairs and trade), following a sharp rise in consumer prices and a decline in the value of the national currency. The ministry of interior **licensed the 29th political party El Sawab**. The party's bodies are composed of a central council headed by

Mohamed Mahmud Ould Guelma and an executive bureau by Cheikh Sidi Ould Hanenna. Messaoud Ould Boulkheir, former leader of 'Action pour le Changement', dissolved in January 2002, was elected president of 'l'Alliance Populaire Progressiste' (APP) on 1 August.

On 9 August, the government claimed that security forces had discovered **a plot to overthrow** Ould Taya. The 31 persons arrested were mostly officers from Ould Hanenna's Aoulad Nasr clan, light-skinned Bidan Moors from the Ayoun el-Atrous region. The army high command is dominated by officers who, like Ould Taya, are Bidan Moors from northeastern Mauritania. Ould Mansour was also detained briefly. The chief of staff of the national gendarmerie announced on state radio that the coup attempt was organised by Ould Hanenna and Mohamed Cheikhna, who lived at that time in Burkina Faso. They were said to have masterminded the coup attempt in June 2003. According to 'l'Observatoire Mauritanien des Droits de l'Homme' (OMDH), the August coup attempt did not actually take place. It suggested the attempt was fictitious so the government would have an excuse to take action against certain tribes behind the 2003 coup attempt. The government claimed the instigators were linked to the Al Zarqaoui terrorist group, close to al-Qaida and opposed to Mauritania's ties with Israel. The government announced that 131 military officers were to be tried in connection with the 2003 coup and breaching national security.

On 28 September, the authorities announced they had **foiled a second coup attempt** and seized a large quantity of weapons. Among those arrested was Captain Ould Mini, alleged ringleader of the 2003 coup. Three opposition members were charged with providing financial aid to the 'Cavaliers du Changement'. Its leader, **Ould Hanenna, was arrested** on 9 October and was suspected of playing a decisive role in the September coup attempt. Ould Haidallah, Ahmed Ould Daddah and Cheikh Ould Horma were also arrested. Ten of the arrested soldiers and civilians were released on 17 October and a further 20 were released during the following week. Most of those released are from Ould Hannena's Aoulad Nasr clan.

On 10 October, security forces arrested Ould Mansour as reports spread that Islamist elements were involved in the coup attempt. According to the **'Mouvement Islamiste'**, another unrecognised political party, Hacene Ould Dead and Moctar Ould Mohamed Moussa were also seized. They were released by 16 October and rearrested on 2 November. In November, **the mass trial commenced of 181 people** accused of plotting a series of attempts to overthrow the government. Government prosecutors alleged that the 170 military men and 11 civilians, including Ould Haidallah, were involved in three separate attempts to stage a coup against Ould Taya's 20-year reign.

Foreign Affairs

In mid-January, US deputy assistant secretary for African affairs, Pamela Bridgewater, announced that **military assistance** would be provided to Mauritania under the Trans-

Sahara Counter Terrorism Initiative (TSCTI), formerly known as the Pan-Sahel Initiative. This $ 100 m project provides military training, materials and logistical support aimed at countering trans-border terrorism in Mauritania, Mali, Niger and Chad. A training programme by US soldiers took place from January till March. During February, the London-based newspaper 'Al-Sharq al-Awsat' reported that special **anti-terrorism police units** stormed a residential compound in Nouakchott and arrested five individuals, among them an Algerian, a Tunisian and a Moroccan.

As part of the Mediterranean Dialogue that binds Mauritania with NATO, a Spanish and a Greek NATO vessel arrived in Mauritanian waters on 10 May. Talks were held between senior NATO military officials and the Mauritanian military. NATO gained information on arms, drugs, people trafficking and the proliferation of terrorism within the sub-region. President Ould Taya met NATO's deputy secretary-general, Minuto Rizzo. The Dialogue complements TSCTI. Strong ties with the former colonial power France weakened owing to US influence.

Mauritania's **relations with Israel** undermined Ould Taya's domestic support. Since 1995, the government has had full diplomatic and political relations with Israel and is pro-Western, while the majority of the population is against the government's stance and opposed the US-led military intervention in Iraq in 2003. Israel's assassination of Hamas-leader Al-Rantissi and Sheikh Ahmed Yassin in March/April led to anti-Israel protests. Relations between Libya and Mauritania have worsened since Mauritania resumed diplomatic ties with Israel and shifted support from former Iraqi President Saddam Hussein to the United States.

In March, Ould Taya visited Morocco's King Mohammed VI. During the year Mauritania received visits from the Spanish foreign affairs minister, UN officials and Sahrawi ministers representing the Western Sahara government-in-exile. Mauritania reiterated its position on finding a solution for the conflict in Western Sahara while respecting international law.

Mauritania accused **Burkina Faso** and **Libya** of involvement in the coup attempts. Burkina Faso denied this on 27 August and Libya challenged Mauritania to produce evidence. Both countries agreed with the request that the AU investigate the matter. In trying to drum up sub-regional support for his government's stance against Libya and Burkina Faso, the Mauritanian defence minister met with the presidents of Niger, Côte d'Ivoire and Guinea, while Ould Taya's advisor met the Togolese president.

On 10 July Mauritanian intellectuals living in Senegal and France created **'l'Alliance Patriotique'**, which advocated violent opposition to the current government. The alliance embraced the aims of the 'Cavaliers du Changement'. In reaction, the Europe-based members of Mauritania's ruling PRDS strongly warned against attempts to destabilise the country.

Socioeconomic Developments

The standard of living was affected by **deteriorating economic** and **social infrastructure** and falling agricultural production. According to a UNDP report, 46% of Mauritanians live below the poverty line. The illiteracy rate was 42% and the unemployment rate declined from 26% to 19%. The number of households with access to water was 37% and with access to sanitation facilities was 33%. Mauritania is the 152nd poorest country in the world out of 174.

Economic policies for reducing poverty were supported by the World Bank and the IMF. The approval of a new $ 8.8 m three-year Poverty Reduction and Growth Facility (PRGF) in July 2003 signalled IMF's resolve to continue funding and providing advice on the government's structural initiatives. The PRGF agreement stressed the need to improve budget management, reinforce banking supervision and establish a code of ethics in the civil service in order to strengthen good governance.

In April 2004, the World Bank granted $ 45 m for a project **to support decentralisation** and poverty-reduction initiatives. It also approved a $ 15 m loan for the education sector. In July, First Quantum Minerals of Canada announced that the Mauritanian government had approved its involvement in the development of the copper and gold deposits at Akjoujt. A new company was to be formed, 80% owned by First Quantum and 20% by 'Guelb Moghrein'. Mauritania signed **an agreement with Saudi Arabia** for $ 10 m to support the pumping of safe drinking water to Nouakchott from the Senegal River. The overall funding is estimated at $ 270 m. Mauritania has been sourcing funds from several international financial institutions, including the Kuwaiti Fund, Arab Fund for Economic and Social Development, the Islamic Development Bank and Japan ($ 2.6 m loan).

Mauritanian society used to be 95% nomadic but has experienced a significant change with **urbanisation** and increased settlement by nomads over the last thirty years. Of the total population, 60% lives in urban communities. Big towns like Nouakchott and Nouadhibou are expanding at a phenomenal pace, and this has propelled the building sector without any real relationship to the country's economic growth.

A system of family solidarity means that one working Mauritanian provides for several dozen people. The minimum wage before 2004 was $ 20 per month, a soldier's pay was $ 100 per month. In January, **minimum wages were raised** but this increase was almost completely absorbed by the renewed rise in inflation at the end of 2003. The country's national currency, the ouguiya, lost much of its value in relation to the euro, given the sliding dollar, the resumption of import demand and failures in the banking system. Inflation in 2004 was around 9%. The **budget deficit** continued, reaching ouguiyas 6.7 bn excluding grants, which is equivalent to 4.2% of GDP, but ouguiyas 700 m if grants are included. By the end of the year, Ould Taya announced another pay rise of $ 31 per month for all civil servants. This would boost the salary of the lowest paid government employees by a third.

Real GDP increase was forecast to slow to 3% as a result of poor agricultural growth. This was partly offset by continued growth in services, donor-funded infrastructure projects and some oil-related activity. The country is very vulnerable to external shock as it depends on foreign aid, the price of raw materials and agriculture. Its main resources are iron ore (13% of GDP and 61.6% of exports in 2002) and fishing (37.7% of exports in 2001).

Food prices increased as a result of the impact of a **locust invasion** on the agricultural sector. The authorities estimated that 1 m hectares had been infested, with up to 80 m locusts per km^2 by mid-August, when the country had completed most of its planting for the year. The swarms were rapidly devouring the sparse desert pasture on which herders depended and attacked farmers' crops in southern Mauritania, threatening large areas with famine. Some $ 3.5 m was provided to Mauritania to purchase 250,300 litres of pesticide. World Food Programme officials noted that over 200,000 subsistence farmers living on poor arid land in the south still relied on food aid, despite the good rains of 2003. Japan granted $ 2 m in food aid.

The **balance of trade deteriorated** in 2003 following the increase in the cost of oil, falling prices for iron ore and the decline of the ouguiya. The deficit exceeded $ 200 m. The national industrial and mining company, 'Société Nationale Industrielle et Minière' (SNIM), has been experiencing difficulty in exporting its iron. Fishing income fell by 11% because of lower prices and catches. The 470-km new road from Nouadhibou to Nouakchott, part of the trans-Sahara highway linking Morocco to Senegal, opened in 2004 and was expected to improve prospects for tourism and external trade.

The Mauritanian **economy remained vulnerable** because of its dependence on the mining and fisheries sectors, both of which were affected by changes in world market prices. Attempts to diversify the economy were limited. Exploration for minerals and diamonds was ongoing. **Oil production** provided **limited economic diversification** and employment opportunities. In 2002, a consortium led by the Australian company Woodside Petroleum struck oil offshore. In January 2004, it was announced that the offshore Chinguetti field was commercial. The reserves are approximately 100 m barrels. In April, the council of ministers adopted a draft bill proposing a simplified tax system for oil producers. In May, the Australian Hardman oil and gas exploration company successfully drilled off Mauritania. In July, Woodside Petroleum announced the employment of 1,000 Mauritanians and the investment of $ 600 m in the field. The total discovered volume of offshore oil exceeds 800 m barrels, making Mauritania a significant oil producer. The August coup attempt stopped oilfield development for seven days.

The Mauritanian private sector has developed considerably since the 1990s. The authorities have reduced the taxation of companies and early on liberalised nearly all areas, except the country's biggest employer, SNIM. The electricity company 'Société Mauritanienne d'Électricité' (SOMELEC) was to be transferred to private ownership but because of the lack of interested parties this did not work out. There have been discussions about the possible privatisation of SNIM.

Nicolien Zuijdgeest

Niger

In 2004 Niger maintained a fair degree of political stability. The multiparty democratic system was further consolidated by successful presidential, parliamentary and municipal elections. Cause for concern was a series of attacks by armed Tuaregs on civilians and army personnel in the north, and the activities of the 'Groupement Salafiste pour la Prédication et le Combat' (GSPC) in the country's frontier zones. The government maintained macroeconomic stability as a result of tight fiscal policies, a robust growth rate estimate and the financial assistance of the donor community. Agricultural output, however, declined as a result of poor harvests. Social stability remained precarious, while occasional government action against journalists underlined the limits of press freedom.

Domestic Politics

Niger's political landscape became more complicated when Cheiffou Amadou, a former prime minister, established a new political party, the **'Rassemblement Social Démocrate'** (RSD) in January. This was the culmination of a lingering two-year crisis in the second party of Niger's ruling coalition, the 'Convention Démocratique et Sociale' (CDS). Cheiffou Amadou and the CDS leader, Mahamane Ousmane, president of Niger between 1993 and 1995, struggled with each other for supremacy in the party. Amadou broke with the CDS in December 2003, and aligned his new party with the opposition. The main effect of this was that the principal party in the ruling coalition, the 'Mouvement National pour la Société du Développement' (MNSD) of President Mamadou Tandja, strengthened its position.

Municipal elections, first projected for 27 March and then postponed to 29 May and, again, to 24 July, were to be followed by presidential and parliamentary elections on 16 November and 4 December. The biggest challenge for Niger was to hold these plebiscites in the first place, neither marred by the chaos that marked the 1999 elections nor leading to a serious deterioration of relations within the political class. This, by and large, was achieved, with international observers concluding the polls were democratic, free and transparent. An important aspect of this success was the desire of political parties to maintain a degree of **consensus** and reduce confrontational politics.

Thus, on 15–20 January they met for discussions on the coming elections and the exercise of political power generally. They agreed on a number of general issues, such as deferral of the municipal elections for organisational reasons and the establishment of an all-party commission to discuss the prospective increase in the number of MPs, the redrawing of constituency boundaries and a change to the voting system. After the January forum, the government established a **'Conseil National de Dialogue Politique'** (CNDP) as a permanent body for the prevention and resolution of political conflicts and the promotion of consensus on national issues and democratic government.

On 26 March the national assembly adopted a number of amendments to the **electoral code** intended to simplify the registration of candidates for the municipal elections. The number of MPs was increased from the current 83 to 113 and agreement was reached on the redrawing of constituency boundaries. No agreement was reached on a change to Niger's system of proportional representation, in which seats are allocated on the basis of the 'highest averages' method that benefits the larger parties. The 'Commission Electorale Nationale Indépendante' updated the electoral register.

Both the MNSD and the main opposition party – 'Parti Nigérien pour la Démocratie et le Socialisme' (PNDS) of Mahamadou Issoufou – were expected to do well in the local elections, since they had sufficient resources to put up candidates in all 265 communes (municipalities). However, the other two members of the coalition government helped the MNSD to retain control of local councils: the CDS, the or 'Alliance Nigérienne pour la Démocratie et le Progrès' (ANDP) of Adamou Moumouni Djermakoye, together with the MNSD managed to secure 62% of all council seats. Although Mahamane Ousmane registered as presidential candidate for the CDS, his party allied itself officially with the MNSD in the municipal polls. This built on an earlier understanding between President Tandja and Ousmane, chairman of the national assembly, that delivered Tandja the presidency in the second round during the elections of 1999 and left the main opposition candidate, Mahamadou Issoufou of the PNDS, out in the cold. This state of affairs, in combination with the voting system, proved detrimental to the country's numerous smaller parties and thus encouraged an **aggregation of political forces**.

It also set the stage for the presidential and parliamentary elections, with the CDS, as the country's third largest party and weakened by the defection of Cheiffou Amadou, throwing in its lot with the MNSD. In the election campaign, the opposition parties focused on alleged government mismanagement, its attacks on press freedom and the poor state of Niger's education and health facilities. Tandja's major opponent, the 'socialist' PNDS candidate Mahamadou Issoufou, appealed to the young and unemployed, a logical strategy in a country where 70% of the population is under 25, recruitment to the public service has remained frozen for seven years and many university graduates are unemployed. By contrast, President Tandja enjoyed **support among subsistence farmers** for his rural development policies that have aimed at delivering new classrooms and health centres. He, therefore, concentrated on questions of stability, promising to increase surveillance of the western border where herders sometimes clash with cattle rustlers.

In the first round of the presidential elections, held on 16 November, President Tandja secured 40.7% of the votes, followed by Issoufou with 24.6% and the CDS leader Mahamane Ousmane with 17.4%. Compared to the first round in 1999, Tandja improved his tally by eight points, as did Issoufou, who won three points more than in 1999. However, since Tandja did not get an absolute majority, a run-off between him and Issoufou was necessary, and was held concurrently with the parliamentary elections on 4 December. With four of his adversaries from the first round rallying to his cause, victory could not elude **Tandja**, who **won the presidency** with 65.5% of the votes. Yet, Issoufou, with his stronghold in the central town of Tahoua, still did better than expected, increasing his share by ten points and taking more than one-third of the tally (34.5%). In the parliamentary elections, however, the ruling MNSD and CDS retained their majority, even though it was slightly reduced (69 out of 113). As a reward for CDS support for Tandja, Mahamane Ousmane was re-elected as chairman of the national assembly. The **PNDS**, which boycotted the election procedure, remained the **strongest party in opposition**, while more than a dozen parties did not get more than one or two seats, if they won any seat at all.

Undoubtedly, the most crucial aspect of the polls was the **peaceful re-election** of President Tandja, who thus not only became the first president since 1974 to complete a full first democratic term without being deposed in a coup but, indeed, also headed the first government in Niger's history ever to be renewed by truly democratic means. Yet while this pointed to the consolidation of the multiparty system, the stability is not without its limits. There is a general mistrust of the political class, who are perceived as corrupt and keen on defending its self-interests. The turn-out rates, which have traditionally been low in Niger's largely rural society, did not reach the 50% mark (48.2% for round one and 45% for round two). Occasional strike action by some of the country's unions also pointed to dissatisfaction with the way politicians have handled socioeconomic issues.

One political development had the potential to upset Niger's newly found stability. On 13 February, President Tandja fired his minister for tourism, **Rhissa Ag Boula**, for alleged involvement in the murder of a 26-year-old MNSD militant. Ag Boula, a Tuareg from

Agadez, formerly led the 'Front de Libération de l'Aïr et de l'Azawagh' (FLAA) during the Tuareg rebellion in the 1990s. As minister, he was popular in his own community for his active promotion of tourism. At the time, the effect of his dismissal on the peace settlement with the Tuareg community was downplayed, since Ag Boula was only one faction leader among many and Tandja quickly appointed another Tuareg, Mohamed Anako, to his cabinet in order to maintain the government's ethnic balance.

Nevertheless, Niger saw a recurrence of various **violent incidents**, in some of which **Tuaregs** were implicated. Thus, in May there were rumours about a new Tuareg rebellion following the desertion of former FLAA rebels who had been integrated into the army. On 2 June, some ex-FLAA members claimed to have resurrected their movement and called on former members to join up, while accusing the government of having failed to decentralise authority and reintegrate former rebels into society, and having diverted donor funds that were intended for this purpose. On 5 June, vehicles were attacked on the road between Agadez and Arlit, the country's uranium mining centre, and between Agadez and the eastern city of Zinder, with two people being injured.

The government denied there were mass desertions from the army and claimed the incidents involved highway banditry rather than the start of a politically motivated rebellion. Most observers did not believe that the incidents foreshadowed a revolt, pointing to a meeting on 10 June of the 'Haut Commissariat à la Restauration de la Paix', during which commanders of the former Tuareg and Toubou rebel movements reaffirmed their commitment to peace. Yet on 10 August, armed men travelling in four-wheel-drive vehicles laid three **ambushes** on buses on the road between Agadez and Arlit. They killed three people and wounded several others, robbing the passengers and kidnapping two policemen. In a radio telephone interview, the brother of Rhissa Ag Boula, Mohamed, claimed responsibility for the attacks, as he did for an ambush on government troops on 1 October. In this engagement in the Aïr mountains, five people died, four soldiers were injured and two went missing. Mohamed Ag Boula claimed to lead a 200-strong rebel group that was defending the rights of the Tuareg, Toubou and other nomadic communities. He accused the government of reneging on the implementation of the 1995 peace accords and demanded the release of former rebels. The government, while continuing to talk about 'bandit' and denying "so-called political demands", admitted that the same people who were involved in the previous attacks were involved in the latest ones.

While these incidents probably did not portend the onset of a new Tuareg rebellion, they showed that security remained a problem, with the United Nations introducing tighter restrictions on staff movements in the north. Moreover, tourism, which benefited from a re-opening of the airport of Agadez, could suffer from these developments, especially as groups of the **GSPC** attacked a convoy of French tourists in the course of infiltrating into Niger between 2 February and 5 March. Driven out by Algerian forces, the GSPC fighters also clashed with Niger government troops both in northwestern and eastern Niger, near the Chad border. In the latter case, the government claimed, in a joint operation with Chadian forces, to have killed 43 GSPC fighters and to have captured five, including one Nigérien national. During November–December, government troops assisted by US special forces again clashed with GSPC fighters, killing several of them, in operations near the Algerian border. GSPC is a guerrilla group that seceded from the 'Groupe Islam Armée' (GIA) and aspires to an Islamic state in Algeria. It was involved in kidnappings of Western tourists in southern Algeria in 2003. According to Western sources, it claims allegiance to al-Qaida. Others dispute this, arguing West African governments exaggerate this issue in order to receive Western military aid.

These intermittent cases of violence show that security in Niger remained precarious, notably in the porous frontier zones, but also elsewhere. Simmering social tensions can easily lead to violence, as happened on 19 November when herders and farmers clashed near the city of Gaya in southwestern Niger, leaving at least 11 people dead, crops damaged, cattle killed and graneries destroyed. This was one of the worst incidents of its kind since 1991, when more than 200 people died in a grazing dispute in the east of Niger. Thus, despite the efforts of its elites to contain the unsettling effects of political competition, Niger's political stability remained incomplete. This was underlined by certain government actions against the **private press**. Mamane Abou, director of 'Le Républicain', was arrested in 2003 for criminal defamation, but released on 6 January pending a second case against him. While this case led to a national and international outcry, on 12 August the director of an independent radio station was arrested over a radio telephone interview with Mohamed Ag Boula and held incommunicado, in violation of Nigérien law. He would be charged with complicity in connection with the ambushes north of Agadez on 10 August but was released after four days. Again, on 20 December, police seized the issue of 'Le Témoin', which contained photographs of four soldiers and gendarmes taken hostage by armed Tuaregs. As early as 2 October, President Tandja criticised the private media about their news coverage of the Tuareg issue.

Foreign Affairs

While the crucial dimension of Niger's foreign affairs is its dependence on external donors, the country has a certain strategic significance that has drawn in Western powers. For instance, Niger's uranium mines are the principal source for France's nuclear 'force de frappe', while the growing activity of the GSPC has reinforced French interest in its former colony, as it has that of the **United States**. Consequently, the close relations with **France**, Niger's principal bilateral donor, continued and benefited from the strengthening of relations in the wake of Chirac's visit in 2003. The fifth Francophone Games to be held in Niger in 2005 will reinforce this situation. Security agreements were signed with the United States in mid-April 2004. The IMF and World Bank approved of the government's reform record, while the European Union will provide € 350 m worth of grants from the European Development Fund in the period up to 2007.

The **'Autorité du Basin du Niger'** (ABN), a grouping of nine West and Central African states and chaired this year by Tandja, held a conference in Paris on 26–27 April and discussed cooperation in the sharing of river resources and the protection of eco-systems, an endeavour for which they received financial support from Western donors. Niger also tried to increase security cooperation with its neighbours, Mali and Chad, as a result of the problems in its poorly policed frontier zones. On 19 March, it agreed with other Sahelian and Saharan countries on a mechanism promoting 'conflict prevention' and cooperation along the lines of ECOWAS. **Relations with Nigeria** also continued to be strong, fed by ties between the Hausa-speaking communities north and south of the common border and Nigeria's status as Niger's principal trading partner, ahead of France. The Nigeria-Niger Joint Commission was transformed into an organ that could deal with issues other than border security. However, mutual security concerns between Niger and Nigeria retained importance, since some members of an Islamic sect, the Muharijun, fled to Niger after clashing with Nigerian government forces on 31 December 2003. Although there is not much support in Niger for Muslim fundamentalist ideas and its politics are marked by a secularist tradition, the activity of the Algerian GSPC did cause some concern. The French supported Niger's security forces by, among other things, monitoring cross-border traffic with satellites, especially in the border regions with Algeria and Mali.

During August and September, US marines provided training to around 130 Nigérien soldiers who are to form a rapid intervention force that can combat arms trafficking, smuggling, clandestine migration, banditry and 'terrorist' activities. Such aid is disbursed within the framework of the American **Trans-Sahara Counter Terrorism Initiative** (TSCTI), formerly known as Pan-Sahel Initiative, which was begun in November 2003. It takes the form of a $ 6.25 m project focusing on the southern borders of Algeria, which is seen as a breeding ground for Islamic fundamentalist groups. The United States intends to spend millions of dollars over the next several years through the TSCTI, which involves eight Sahelian and Saharan countries. By November–December, US special forces were assisting Niger's government troops in an operation on the Algero-Nigérien border. Seven **GSPC** fighters were killed, as were two of the 150 Niger army soldiers involved.

While these initiatives make life more difficult for the GSPC – its infiltrations into Mali, Niger and Chad stemmed in large part from the Algerian government offensive against it – they carry the risk of **militarising issues** that at bottom have other, specifically social, economic or political roots. Moreover, the desire to rein in the GSPC leads to the reinforcement of Niger's military apparatus, which could also be used against other groups or other forms of dissidence, leading to a military approach to Niger's nomadic communities.

Socioeconomic Developments

With several macroeconomic performance indicators having been met, the final disbursement was authorised on 30 June of the three-year Poverty Reduction and Growth Facility

(PRGF) of the IMF. In order to facilitate donor aid, the government hoped to sign a new PRGF programme, which would also focus on macroeconomic stability and poverty reduction. Earlier in the year, in April, Niger reached the 'completion point' under the Heavily Indebted Poor Countries (HIPC) initiative, so that it could receive aid with which to maintain a sustainable **debt-export ratio**, estimated at 150%. This would amount to a total of $ 1.2 bn (nominal terms). While the Paris Club of bilateral creditors agreed to write off a substantial part of Niger's debt ($ 230.9 m in 2002), the room for government manoeuvre remained limited in view of its dependence on agriculture and uranium exports. New loans would push up the debt-export ratio. The extension of value added tax to other consumer products was postponed until after the elections. The draft budget for 2005 amounted to CFAfr 401.9 bn in expenditure, which involved a drop of 1.14% as compared to the 2004 financial year.

Throughout the year, real GDP growth was estimated at between 4% and 5%, an estimate that will probably fall as a result of **disappointing harvests**. Though this is the lowest growth rate in West Africa, inflation also continued to be low, in part because of a slight fall in food prices caused by the bumper harvest of 2003, the third in a row, thanks to regular rainfall and government-distributed fertilisers. Yet, despite a cereal crop harvest of 3.6 m tonnes in 2003, the country still had to import cereals to cope with a structural deficit. Poor rains in 2004 and a severe **locust outbreak** worsened this situation. Consequently, for 2004 Niger registered a record grain deficit of 223,487 tonnes. The total crop harvest stalled at 2.6 m tonnes, forcing people in the Maradi region to abandon their villages.

The price of **uranium**, the export which accounted for 30% of total exports in 2003, remained stable. In addition, production began at the Samira Hill **gold mine** near the Burkina border, the first such mine in the country. The government has a 20% share in the production consortium, and estimated export earnings will CFAfr 15 bn. New prospecting agreements were signed in the autumn, while the Malaysian state oil company Petronas began drilling exploratory wells in the east of the country, where large oil reserves are believed to exist. Plans have also been made to boost the production of cotton, of which Niger is currently a small producer compared to neighbouring countries, from 8,000 to 100,000 tonnes in 2005.

The World Bank approved a credit of $ 14.8 m for technical assistance to improve the efficiency of the country's **financial sector**, with regard to which the government has embarked on a four-year restructuring project. The rehabilitation of the road network has benefited from European Union funds while construction work undertaken for the 2005 Francophone Games is expected to boost economic growth.

Niger continues to be one of the poorest countries in the world, occupying the penultimate place on the UN Human Development Index (figures 2003). Industrialisation is minimal, with 86% of the active population employed in agriculture, which accounts for 43% of GDP. Sixty-three per cent of the population lives under the poverty datum line, while 41% has no access to clean drinking water, with some regions falling well below this mark.

Just over 40% of children are enrolled in primacy school, which admittedly represents an increase of 7% over the last four years. These figures need to be set against the **high population growth**. A study by the government and World Bank showed that the population, now at approximately 11.5 m, rises 3.1% a year. On average, a Nigérien woman has eight children, more than anywhere else in the world. The study linked this growth to poverty and cultural and religious values. This demographic trend could lead to the collapse of the education and health system, already under threat in a society with one of the youngest age structures in the world (70% of the population being under 25).

Frequent student strikes calling for better conditions pointed to the continuing crisis in the education system, largely neglected during the 1990s. On 23 January gendarmes stormed the university campus in Niamey, dispersing students who called for an end to arrears in bursaries. This social crisis extends, however, beyond the education system, as shown by the **strikes** of public sector workers protesting pay arrears, retirement schemes and redundancies on 4–7 April and again at the end of May. Ministerial employees, workers for the privatised telecommunications company, as well as customs officials protesting stringent inspections participated in these protests. Although the 'Union des Syndicats des Travailleurs du Niger' (USTN) was weakened by a split in 2000, these strikes still represented a threat to the country's newly found stability.

Klaas van Walraven

Nigeria

In 2004, Nigeria experienced a wave of hitherto unknown political violence, ethnic and religious conflict and organised crime, affecting almost all the 36 states and Abuja. The conflicts sometimes reached a level that threatened the political system and endangered the still infant democratisation process. While the shariah issue lost political momentum in the world's biggest Christian-Islamic country, infighting for resource and financial control, especially at state and council level, reached new heights. Several local militias were able to increase their political influence and some even successfully turned themselves into local and regional powerbrokers. The federal government responded by pursuing a strategy of political dialogue and force, depending on the perceived relevance of the issue for the central government. In conjunction with the intensity and variety of conflicts, this policy revealed the weakness of the modern institutions and caused widespread frustration with the political and very limited economic progress. Against this background, President Olusegun Obasanjo and his government started a new economic and social reform programme and scheduled a national conference for early 2005 to create at least some legacy of 'democracy dividend' and economic progress.

Domestic Politics

The long-overdue **elections for the 774 local councils** took place in most of the 36 federal states and the Federal Capital Territory (FCT) on 27 March, and were aimed at completing the election marathon begun in 2003. In Sokoto and Niger states the electorate went to the polls in January, while voting for various councils in some states had to be postponed due to civil strife and violence. In one state, voting had to be cancelled. The ruling People's Democratic Party (PDP) of President Obasanjo, which already controlled most state governments and both chambers (senate and house of representatives) of the National Assembly confirmed its dominant position. The northern-based main opposition All Nigeria People's Party (ANPP) and the southwest based Alliance for Democracy (AD) only just retained their strongholds in states such as Zamfara and Lagos respectively. Voter turnout was extremely low, and the elections were largely marred by widespread fraud, violence and rather flagrant ballot rigging. According to the local transition monitoring group, the ballot could not be considered to reflect the will of the people.

A **constitutional crisis** developed over statutory allocations to local councils from the Federation Account. The 1999 constitution listed 768 local governments and 6 area councils within the FCT. But some state assemblies created additional councils. Lagos state, for example, the only state the Yoruba AD party ruled, established 37 new councils in addition to the listed 20. Consequently, the federal government denied those local governments funding allocations until the states reverted to the number enshrined in the constitution.

In April, the Lagos state government took the case to the **supreme court**, which declared in December that the president had no constitutional powers to withhold statutory funds to any tier of government. Nevertheless, the federal government continued withholding the funds and asked the supreme court for clarification of the verdict against the background of the first schedule, part I, section 3 of the constitution that lists the states of the federation, the local government areas and the area councils of the FCT, Abuja.

The legal battle over the outcome of the presidential elections of 2003 went on throughout the year. The defeated ANPP presidential candidate, former junta chairman Maj. Gen. Muhammadu Buhari (retd), challenged the re-election of President Obasanjo, himself a former junta chairman and retired four star general, in the court of appeal that had been mandated to act as the **presidential election tribunal**. He asked the court to annul the 2003 elections because of substantial rigging in at least 16 states and maintained that Obasanjo was not qualified to stand. On 20 December, the court in a three-to-one verdict generally rejected Buhari's petition. It confirmed vote rigging in some areas, including Obasanjo's home state, Ogun, where Buhari got just 680 votes as against 1,360,170 in favour of the incumbent. However, it found no evidence that this had tipped the overall result. The tribunal thus annulled the election in Ogun state on the basis of serious infractions there, ranging from violence and official intimidation to falsification of results.

At the beginning of the year, a power struggle within PDP between Anambra state Governor Chris Ngige and his closest former ally and sponsor Chris Uba caused a serious political and constitutional crisis in the state that even **endangered national security and stability**. On 2 January the Enugu high court ordered the inspector general of police, Tafa Balogun, to remove Ngige from office. The order was based on a lawsuit instituted by the suspended member of the Anambra state house of assembly, Nelson Achukwu, on the grounds that the governor had resigned in July the previous year. Another order from the Awka high court restrained the inspector general of police from executing the order. On 12 January, the court of appeal upheld this order, and on 27 January the Awka high court voided Ngige's purported resignation in 2003, after which he was temporarily arrested by special police forces on 10 July 2004 when he denied having resigned and refused to leave government house. On 30 November, however, the court of appeal finally set aside the decision by the Enugu high court, pointing out that it had no jurisdiction over the Anambra state government.

Between 10 and 12 November, supporters of the governor and Chris Uba clashed several times and the postponed council elections were put on hold indefinitely. The state-owned television and radio stations in the capital Awka, in Onitsha, in Enugu-Ukwu and a building of the Independent National Electoral Commission (INEC) in the capital were torched and some vehicles burnt. The federal government sent police reinforcements to Anambra state to quell the riots and there were conflicting reports about several people being killed. In an open letter on 6 December, Innocent Audu Ogbeh, the national chairman of the PDP, sharply criticised President Obasanjo and his government for the way the crisis had been handled. In a quick response Obasanjo blamed Ogbeh for shirking his responsibility as party chairman to attempt to resolve it. Then, Obasanjo urged the PDP leadership to force Governor Ngige to resign, and an emergency meeting of the executive committee was set for early January 2005.

Plateau state and its border area with Taraba state in the Middle Belt region became another serious conflict area. Here **deep ethnic and religious divisions** as well as competition between farmers and nomads over control of land, grazing rights and the allocation of funds fuelled political tensions. On 13 February, at least 11 people died in the Muslim-dominated village of Mavo (Wase local government) after being attacked by ethnic Tarok militias. The majority of Tarok are Christian. Around Tunga village on 19 February, four patrolling policemen were killed by assailants suspected of being ethnic Fulani. A week later, military and police forces were deployed to Yelwa town (Shendam local government) after Fulani herdsman killed some 100 people, allegedly including 48 seeking shelter in a church. In another attack around the same time by Christian militias in Garkawa, at least 40 Hausa-Fulani and Fulani of the Muslim faith were killed. And on the eve of the local government elections in Wase, at least 20 Muslims died after a raid by Christian militiamen.

Despite the peace initiative committee on Plateau state, inaugurated by President Obasanjo and comprising eminent people and stakeholders from the greater Plateau area under the chairmanship of the Emir of Zaria, Shehu Idris, the killings continued. In mid-April, Tarok militia attacked three villages near the town of Ibi on the Taraba state side, killing seven people and razing many houses. In Barkin Chiyawa (Qua'an Pan local government) more than 30 Muslims died when Christian militia raided the village. At the end of April, half a dozen villages along the Plateau-Taraba border reported at least 120 victims. After another attack on Muslims in the central market in Yelwa on 2 May, leaving 200–300 people dead, the government of Plateau state imposed a **dusk-to dawn-curfew** on 5 May and ordered policemen to shoot troublemakers on sight.

The Yelwa incident even spilled over into the ancient city of Kano where Muslim youths went on the rampage, killing dozens of Christians and driving several thousand people from their homes. The Christian Association of Nigeria (CAN), Kano branch, put the number of victims at almost 600, much higher than police estimates. A week-long dusk-to-dawn curfew was imposed on 11 May.

However, on 18 May, President Obasanjo declared a **state of emergency over Plateau state** because, according to him, national security was at stake. He suspended Governor Joshua Dariye and the State Assembly and appointed a former military governor of Plateau state and army chief of staff, Maj. Gen. Chris Alli (retd) as sole administrator. Within 48 hours, as stipulated by the constitution, both houses of the National Assembly confirmed the state of emergency in Plateau with the required two-thirds majority. The state of emergency was renewable after six months. On 1 June, parliament passed the new law, with eight regulations, sought by the president to enforce the emergency rule he had invoked in Plateau with the appointment of the administrator.

Apart from the ongoing killing that lasted until late June, more than 50,000 people, mostly Muslim, took refuge in neighbouring Nasarawa and Bauchi states. According to the Plateau state committee on the census of displaced persons, some 250,000 were displaced in Plateau state alone and had to live in camps. The national commission for refugees put the number living in relief camps nationwide at some **800,000 internally displaced persons**. On 16 November, the state of emergency was lifted, Joshua Dariye was reinstated as governor and the State Assembly reinstituted as parliament. This move was followed by an anti-corruption campaign against Dariye aimed at ensuring he was deposed. The federal government cited Dariye's involvement in a money-laundering enterprise under investigation in Britain. In late November, the state parliament declined to probe the governor, and in December courts in Abuja and Kaduna ruled in favour of the governor's constitutional immunity from civil or criminal prosecution while in office.

The oil and gas producing Niger Delta and its major cities Port Harcourt and Warri continued to be extremely volatile, despite the presence of some 5,000 troops. Violence caused by armed robbers, kidnappers, pirates, oil thieves, militias, militant youths and state security operations directly affected oil production by the major companies Shell, ExxonMobil, ChevronTexaco and Nigerian National Petroleum Corporation (NNPC). In addition, an internal power struggle between two ethnic Ijaw warlords in Rivers state,

Mujahid Dokubo-Asari and Ateke Tom, to a large extent mirrored the proxy war between rival factions in PDP. Moreover, a struggle over the control of stolen crude oil aggravated the volatile situation still further. It was estimated that between at least 50,000 and 100,000 barrels of oil were stolen per day. However, both warlords were offspring of the rigged 2003 elections in favour of Governor Odili and President Obasanjo because both played a vital role in intimidating opponents of the PDP. On the other hand, civil strife between ethnic Ijaw and Itsekiri in greater Warri area in Delta state had its roots in the longstanding struggle for political and financial control of resources at local level.

The Niger Delta People's Volunteer Force (NDPVF) led by Mujahid Dokubo-Asari and the Niger Delta Vigilante Group (NDVG), led by Ateke Tom, clashed on 1 February in Bugama near Port Harcourt over the right to collect compensation from Shell over an oil spill in the community. Bugama in Kalabari kingdom was the stronghold of Dokubo-Asari, where at least two-dozen people were reported killed. In early June, troops descended on Bugama, killing 20. Soon after, Dokubo-Asari, supported by 2,000 armed men, claimed to control three local governments in Rivers state. In mid-July, military forces, supported by the NDVG of Ateke Tom, killed 11 members of the NDPVF in the Amadi-Ama district of Port Harcourt. At the end of the month, gunmen opened fire in a bar in the oil city and shot several people. On 15 August, a longstanding dispute over a chieftancy title in the village of Ataba (Rivers state) culminated in the shooting of 13 people. By mid-September, an estimated **500 people had been reported killed in Port Harcourt** and its surrounding creeks.

On 27 September, Dokubo-Asari issued a communiqué, 'Operation Locust Feast', to wage war against foreign oil companies on Independence Day, 1 October, to highlight the will of the Ijaw people for self-determination. However, after the federal government agreed to peace talks with both **warlords** in Abuja, the attack was suspended. Having met the president, Dokubo-Asari and Ateke Tom agreed to a ceasefire and signed a disarmament and amnesty deal on 1 October. They promised to disband and totally disarm all militias and militant groups before the end of the year when the presidential amnesty expired. By the end of October, Dokubo-Asari's faction started handing over weapons to the government allegedly in return for cash. By mid-November, Dokubo-Asari stopped further disarmament, claiming that his rival was not abiding by the disarmament agreement. But the ceasefire held, and on 7 December Dokubo-Asari resumed the peace process.

On 17–18 January, Itsekiri militias invaded four Okpe communities in Sapele local government (Delta state) and killed 17 indigenes. Some seven people died after clashes between **Ijaw and Itsekiri militia** groups in Ogbeh Ijoh and Ode Itsekiri on the outskirts of Warri one week later. In April, a new peace initiative by the Delta state government set up a 14-member committee of leading local politicians representing both ethnic groups. On 23 June, a peace accord was signed, but later, three Ijaw signatories retracted their agreement, among them the well-known Chief Edwin Clark.

On 23 April, **pirates killed two US oil workers**, two local boatmen and three navy troopers on the Benin River in Warri North. The US citizens were working for ChevronTexaco, which indefinitely suspended oil production in the area, a loss of 140,000 b/d. On 2 February, militant Itsekiri kidnapped local oil workers of Shell in Sapele (Delta) and killed a naval officer. The hostages were released a few days later. On 20 November, about 80 youths from the Ijaw village of Ojobo (Delta state) occupied a Shell oilrig for almost four days. Soldiers of the 'Operation Restore Hope' joint task force came to disperse them and used their guns, wounding more than a dozen protesters. Ojobo community leaders, however, claimed that seven demonstrators had been killed. The military and Shell's new managing director, Basil Omiyi, denied the accusation. Towards the end of the year, the situation escalated when on 5 December unarmed protesters from the Ijaw village of Kula (Rivers state) near the Bonny oil terminal seized two oil platforms operated by Shell and one operated by ChevronTexaco, cutting off oil flows and demanding talks on jobs and development. The occupation ended two days later but Shell agreed not to restart production until the dispute had been resolved. This forced both companies to suspend oil exports of 134,000 b/d.

In the northeastern states of Borno and Yobe, a **radical Islamic sect** called Muhajirun or Hijrah and inspired by the Afghan Taliban movement attacked police stations in Damaturu, Kanamma and Geidam area (Yobe state) in early January, killing two policemen. The core of the sect was made up of students and young graduates. In September, they attacked Bama and Gwoza (Borno state), where three policemen and some civilians lost their lives. And in October, in another attack in the same state at Kala-Balge near the Cameroon border, they killed three people and took half a dozen hostages. The military and police forces launched several counterattacks, killing some 50 members, and five sect members were arrested in Cameroon by local security forces.

In Numan in neighbouring Adamawa state, Christian Bachama clashed with Hausa and Fulani Muslims in early June over the reconstruction of a mosque overlooking the palace walls of the local traditional Bachama chief. Some 130 people died, almost 4,000 were displaced and many houses were destroyed. On 11 June, a dusk-to-dawn curfew was imposed and extended to the capital Yola, where displaced Muslims from Numan were seeking refuge. Moreover, the state government deposed the chief because of his complicity in the violence.

The institutions of higher learning continued to be volatile places where for years **cult and gang violence**, especially in the southern parts of the country, had claimed hundreds of lives. At the Lagos State University and the Ambrose Ali University in Edo state, widespread cult violence resulted in the death of at least three students. After two students were killed at the Olabisi Onabanjo University (Ogun state) in early June, more than 80 were expelled on 21 June for alleged murder and secret cult activities. At about the same time, three students were killed at the country's oldest university in Ibadan (Oyo state). In March, a magistrate's court in Ahaoda (Rivers state) sentenced seven suspected cult members to various terms of imprisonment. And in November, a high court in Owerri (Imo state) sentenced to death a man who had killed his wife to sell her organs to ritualists. In early August, the Nigerian public was shocked when the police uncovered **fetish shrines** in Okija in Ihiala local government (Anambra state) filled with dozens of mutilated corpses, skeletons and skulls. Forensic tests proved that some of these victims were killed and their organs used to worship traditional gods. The police arrested some 20 people, most of them priests at the shrines, and charged them with murder.

Some well-known people were assassinated and several policemen and ordinary persons were victims of armed robbers, mainly operating along highways. A chieftain of the PDP in Delta state, Aminosoari Kalu Dikibo, was assassinated on 6 February. In early March, a local politician and an INEC commissioner in Kogi state, Luke Shigaba and Phillip Olorunnipa, and the former managing director of Nigerian Airways, Andrew Agom, were gunned down. Eshu Egbola, a close aide of the governor of Cross River, was murdered in his home state in August. In Kwara state, state civil servant Michael Agboola was murdered on 15 October, and Jerry Agbeyegbe, a captain and leading member of the Nigerian aviation safety initiative was killed in Lagos on 12 October.

Some 50 policemen lost their lives while on duty, most of them in Edo state. In Kwara, four were killed in July during a failed attack on an armoured van carrying money. In neighbouring Kogi state, armed robbers gunned down another four officers and a soldier in December. In October, two policemen attached to the governor of Delta state died after being attacked on the Asaba-Benin road. Prior to this, in April, the police claimed to have shot more than 400 armed robbers within three months.

A shake-up in the police force took place in early May, and several state police commissioners were redeployed, while 13 deputies were promoted to the rank of commissioner. Despite the loss of many lives and the poor salaries, the 300,000-strong police force retained its reputation for extortion, corruption and abetting crime, even though hundreds of policemen were dismissed and dozens arrested. To curb abuses against citizens, the Nigerian police set up a human rights service in July and launched a sophisticated nationwide PR media campaign.

In October, Transparency International listed Nigeria as the world's third most corrupt country. This was a clear indication that Obasanjo's anti-corruption campaign had so far largely failed. Although 500 suspects were in custody, neither the Independent Corrupt Practice Commission (ICPC) nor the Economic and Financial Crimes Commission (EFCC) were able to produce convincing evidence to bring a single prominent figure to book. Even the new **Money Laundering Bill**, introduced in March, has not yet yielded results. For example, the federal government withdrew the $ 214 m national identity card fraud case in June, after one suspect, former minister Sunday Afolabi, passed away. However, ICPC filed new charges against the suspects, among them two other former ministers, Hussaini Akwanga and Mohammed Shata. The biggest fraud trial so far, concerning the defrauding a Brazilian bank of $ 242 m, was pending in the Ikeja high court (Lagos state). In November, a trial of three rear admirals (Babatunde Samuel Kolawole, Francis Agbiti, Anthonio Ibinabo Bob-Manuel), charged with conspiracy and serious fraud, began in a

military court. Allegedly, they were implicated in the disappearance of an impounded Russian oil tanker, whose crude oil was siphoned off to a Nigerian oil tanker and replaced with water. The Russian crew was tried in a criminal court in Lagos for oil theft. Even the efforts to recover funds allegedly looted by the late dictator Sani Abacha were put on hold by the Kaduna federal high court on 24 September. In its judgment, the court voided the government's move to retrieve the funds from Abacha's cronies. The federal government accordingly took the case to the court of appeal.

The five-year trial of five imprisoned high-ranking officers and close allies of Abacha (Hamza al-Mustapha, Ishaya Bamaiyi, James Danbaba, Bala Jibrin Yakubu and Rabo Lawal) dragged on without a verdict. They were charged with the attempted murder of the 'Guardian' (Lagos) publisher Alex Ibru in 1995. In another trial in Ibadan (Oyo state), the main suspect, Iyiola Omisore, accused of murdering Minister of Justice Bola Ige in 2001, was acquitted in June. The other 11 suspects were later discharged because of lack of evidence. The case made headlines for more than a year because Omisore became a senator on the PDP platform while in detention. Another trial in Lagos in October caused serious concerns about the loyalty of the security forces. In April, local print media speculated about a **possible coup d'état**. However, the chief of defence staff, General Alexander Ogomudia, struck a panel to investigate the issue. Prominent among the suspects in the alleged coup attempt was Hamza al-Mustapha, already on trial for attempted murder. He was accused of holding secret meetings in Lagos's Kirikiri maximum security prison with military officers. Finally, he, along with two military officers, one of them on the run, and one civilian were charged with treasonable felony because they had planned to overthrow the president.

The **shariah** issue lost momentum despite the fact that shariah courts in northern Nigeria kept on handing down death sentences by **stoning** and other penalties such as amputation and flogging. However, nobody has been 'lawfully' stoned to death since 12 states introduced the shariah law in 2000 and 2001. The death sentences were either overturned on appeal or appeals were still pending. Nevertheless, on 5 January, a shariah court in Alkaleri (Bauchi state) sentenced Umar Tori to death by stoning for incest. In two other areas (Tafawa Balewa and Ningi) in the same state, two women, Hajara Ibrahim and Daso Adamu, were given the same sentences in September and October for having sex out of wedlock, but the verdicts were overruled in shariah courts of appeal. The same was true in March of a death sentence passed in 2003 against Jibrin Babaji for sodomy. In Niger state, the death sentence against Fatima Usman and her former lover Ahmadu Ibrahim, passed in 2001, was still pending. However, at the end of the year a shariah court in Gwarzo (Kano state) sentenced Danliti Rabiu to death by stoning for sodomy.

A minor **cabinet reshuffle** took place in June when two ministers of state (foreign and internal affairs) swapped portfolios. After a long battle in the senate, the president swore in the former minister of education, Professor Babaloba Borishade, as minister of state for power and steel. However, more importantly, on 30 April President Obasanjo appointed his special economic adviser, Charles Saludo, as the new governor of the Central Bank of Nigeria, thereby replacing Joseph Sanusi. For the first time, a woman, Wahir Mshelia, assumed a leading position by becoming deputy governor. Jacob Buba Jang became the new comptroller general of the Nigerian customs service.

Against the background of the poor security situation the record on **human and civil rights deteriorated**. Irritated about critical reports in the United States, Europe and at home, the federal government put pressure on local and foreign media. On 1 April, the national broadcasting commission banned local broadcasters from taking over live transmission of news broadcasts from foreign stations. The scripts of foreign news and related programmes were to be rewritten and voiced locally before being broadcast. This decision directly affected stations like the BBC, CNN, VOA and Deutsche Welle. On 4 September, the State Security Service (SSS) confiscated 15,000 copies of the magazine 'Insider Weekly', known for its strong criticism of President Obasanjo. Three staff members were briefly detained and computers confiscated. However, the magazine was back on the newsstands on 20 September, although security agents besieged the office. In February, the freelance reporter of the 'Economist', Silvia Sansoni, was deported. The federal government justified its decision on the basis of her disregard of immigration laws and abuse of accreditation terms. In November, Stephan Faris of the US magazine 'Time' was refused entry at Lagos airport by the SSS, even though he had a valid visa.

For years, poor prison conditions remained unaddressed. Some 26,000 of the 40,000 prison inmates nationwide were still on remand without being convicted. More than 400 were waiting in death row, some for years. In Kaduna, civil rights activists accused police of **extra-judicial killings**, a practice that was on the rise. In October, 12 people were shot, and police claimed they had killed suspected armed robbers trying to break out of jail. In June, a vigilante mob, indirectly protected by the police, lynched at least a dozen suspected armed robbers in the city of Ughelli (Delta state). In June and September, a dozen members of the banned militant Movement for the Actualisation of the Sovereign State of Biafra (MOSSOB) were arrested for holding illegal assemblies. In May, the federal government had already foreclosed the release of the official report of the human rights violations investigation commission, better known as the Oputa Panel Report on human rights abuses by past governments. The decision was based on the supreme court judgment that annulled the probe of the panel because of its unconstitutionality. The report had been submitted to the federal government as far back as May 2002.

The judiciary, embedded in a highly complicated legal system, technically called **legal pluralism**, still suffered from many years of military dictatorship. Moreover, the already overburdened courts were confronted with widespread corruption at every level that made it difficult to pass sentence and almost impossible to maintain independence. However, the highest courts are highly politicised and the vast majority of their verdicts were aimed at stabilising the political system, explicitly demonstrated in suits concerning the results of the elections in 2003.

Foreign Affairs

Nigeria's foreign policy focused on maintaining good relations with the US, enforcing its interests in the Bakassi conflict with neighbouring Cameroon and mediating in the Darfur conflict. Nigeria also tried to intensify its relations with Asian countries, especially China.

In February the US appointed career diplomat John Campbell as ambassador to Nigeria and removed Nigeria from a list of countries (in October) whose ports did not comply with US security standards. These decisions underlined the interests of both parties to keep close relations. The US increased its efforts to assist the Nigerian government in the Niger Delta by donating navy patrol ships and training Nigerian crews. Moreover, in July General Charles Wald, deputy commander of European Command (EUCOM), which also covers Africa, visited Nigeria. In August, General Robert Foglesong, commander of the US Air Force in Europe and Senator Chuck Hagel followed suit. Soon afterwards, it was agreed to hold **joint military training** in the Niger Delta. The first exercises took place in September as part of Joint-Combined Exchange Training (JCET). In addition, the US pledged to the military a modern medical laboratory, and in October US military transport planes flew Nigerian soldiers to Darfur. President Obasanjo met President Bush in Washington on 2 December, and the latter voiced strong support for Nigeria's efforts to help settle the conflicts in Darfur and Côte d'Ivoire. Serious legal problems arose towards the end of the year when the US refused Nigeria's new national carrier, Virgin Nigeria Airlines, to operate direct flights, due to begin in early 2005, into the US. In February, 115 Nigerians were deported for a variety of reasons ranging from overstaying to drug trafficking.

Through President Obasanjo's chairmanship of the AU, Nigeria was directly involved in the **Darfur crisis in Sudan**. In July, he sent the former junta leader Gen. Abdulsalami Abubakar (retd) to Sudan and Chad for talks on Darfur, which he viewed as a problem to be resolved by the AU. On 1 August, Obasanjo met his counterpart al-Bashir in Khartoum and shortly afterwards Nigeria sent a battalion of peacekeeping troops as part of an AU force to the war-torn area. Towards the end of August, peace talks between the two warring factions and the Sudan government began in Abuja under AU auspices. Despite Nigerian mediation, peace talks broke down several times and at year's end no real solution was in sight. In November, the AU named the former career diplomat and well-known politician Baba Gana Kingibe as its special envoy in Sudan.

The handover of the potentially oil-rich **Bakassi** peninsula by Nigeria to Cameroon, originally scheduled for May, did not take place during the year. The International Court of Justice (ICJ) in The Hague had ruled in 2002 that Bakassi belonged to Cameroon and redrew parts of the 1,600-kilometre land border stretching from Lake Chad to the Gulf of Guinea. Despite a meeting between Obasanjo and President Biya of Cameroon in Geneva at the end of January, initiated by UN Secretary-General Annan, and several further rounds of talks within the joint commission between February and November, Nigeria deliberately delayed the talks. On the domestic front the government was under political pressure to ignore the ICJ ruling, but within diplomatic circles it confirmed its alleged commitment to abide by it. At the same time, together with its counterpart, Nigeria used diplomatic channels to get the international community to financially support the demanding logistical exercise. An estimated $ 12 m was required, and the UN set up a trust fund. Both countries had already paid in $ 2.5 m, the EU contributed $ 500,000 and Britain $ 1.8 m. However, both heads of state met again in Yaounde on 29 July and agreed that all Nigerian troops would be out of Bakassi by 15 September at the latest. Despite the delay, two villages were exchanged on 13 July. Cameroon handed over Ndabuka to Nigeria and assumed sovereignty over Narki. Two days before the deadline, **Nigeria postponed the withdrawal of its forces** and a statement by Nigerian Foreign Minister Oluyemi Adeniji that a referendum would be the best way of deciding Bakassi's future put the whole issue on hold. Thus, the 13th meeting of the joint commission, scheduled for 7 December, was postponed to February 2005.

Nigeria continued to play a modest role in tackling the **Côte d'Ivoire conflict**, although President Obasanjo, AU chairman and head of the newly established Peace and Security Council, called several meetings to resolve the crisis. On 20 June, Obasanjo invited the Ivorian President Laurent Gbagbo, Ghanaian Head of State John Kufuor, Togo's President Gnassingbé Eyadéma and the executive secretary of ECOWAS, Mohammed Ibn Chambas for talks. In an emergency meeting on 14 November in Abuja, Obasanjo, Kufuor and Eyadéma were joined by Senegal's President Abdoulaye Wade, Blaise Campaoré of Burkina Faso, Gabon's President Omar Bongo and Alpha Konaré, chairman of the AU commission. They called for an immediate arms embargo on the government and rebel groups. Shortly thereafter, the UN Security Council voted unanimously for an arms embargo. On the eve of the meeting of francophone nations in Ouagadougou, Obasanjo discussed the Ivorian crisis with French President Chirac, whom he had already met at the 'Autorité du Basin du Niger' summit in Paris in April.

Nigeria continued its **peacekeeping activities** with military and police forces as part of the UN Mission in Liberia (UNMIL). Nevertheless, the exiled former Liberian President Charles Taylor, granted residence in Nigeria in 2003, began to haunt the government. The special court for Sierra Leone, mandated by the UN, had indicted Taylor for war crimes and in June a court in Abuja allowed a request by the Nigerian Coalition on the International Criminal Court (NCICC) for Taylor's repatriation to Sierra Leone to face war crimes charges. In September, the Nigerian government urged the court to strike the suit on the grounds that Nigeria granted residence to Taylor on humanitarian grounds and partly to resolve the Liberian crisis. The court upheld the objection and dismissed the suit. In October, UNHCR began repatriating some 1,000 Liberian refugees who had volunteered to return home.

The **joint offshore fields in the Gulf of Guinea** determined Nigeria's relationship with São Tomé and Príncipe. President Obasanjo and his counterpart Menezes met on 26 June and signed a joint declaration on transparency and governance in the Joint Development Zone (JDZ). Nigeria owned 60% and São Tomé and Príncipe 40% of the JDZ, which was divided into nine potentially lucrative oil exploration blocks. Under the agreement, all payments for exploration licences in the JDZ would be made public, the income audited and the accounts of a joint supervisory authority published. All nine oil blocks were first tendered in 2003, but only one was taken up. In November, five blocks were again put up for tender in Abuja, and 26 oil companies, including indigenous ones, submitted bids. In July, Nigeria granted São Tomé and Príncipe a loan of $ 5 m after an emergency request. In a similar move, Nigeria gave Ghana a loan of $ 40 m that was supposed to finance Ghana's share in the West African gas pipeline project.

Nigeria's **orientation towards Asia** first yielded results when NNPC entered into a service contract agreement with the state China Petroleum and Chemical (Petrochemical) Corporation (SINOPEC) for the development of two shallow water oil blocks in April. In May, NNPC's top manager Funsho Kupolokun signed an agreement with the China International United Petroleum and Chemical Company (UNIPEC) for the supply of 50,000 b/d crude oil. In September, a delegation from the Chinese National Petroleum Development Corporation (CNPC) held talks in Nigeria and signed a memorandum of understanding on cooperation in the oil and gas sectors. Around the same time, the Nigeria-China business investment forum took place in Shanghai. This was followed by the inauguration of a technical committee one month later to work out details of how to effectively execute a joint venture investment agreement. On 6 November, the chairman of the standing committee of the National People's Congress, Wu Bangguo, visited Nigeria, and both sides signed a cooperation accord on oil, technology and telecommunication. The accord included a grant of $ 2.2 m to Nigeria. As a political gesture, President Obasanjo ordered the closure of the Taiwanese commercial office in the capital, but it was permitted to relocate to Lagos state. Last but not least, the Nigerian Defence Minister Rabiu Kwankwaso officially visited China in June.

President Obasanjo and his ministers Oluyemi Adeniji (foreign affairs), Mrs. Ngozi Okonjo-Iweala (finance) and Adamu Idris Waziri (commerce) took part in an international development conference in Tokyo in early November. This Asian-African conference was part of a Japanese initiative to boost Africa's development. According to Prime Minister Junichiro Koizumi, Japan wanted Nigerian development to be a model for surrounding African countries. After the conference, the Nigerian president and his delegation proceeded to India. On 2 November, they held talks with the newly elected Prime Minister Manmohan Singh and had a session with the Indian Chambers of Commerce and Industry. In October, the Indian Oil Corporation signed a term contract for 40,000 b/d crude oil from Nigeria. Nevertheless, Nigeria tried to intensify the longstanding **military relationship with India's neighbour Pakistan**. The five-day visit to Nigeria (1–5 March) of the chairman of Pakistan's joint chiefs of staff committee, General Mohammed Aziz Khan, was aimed at increasing military cooperation in the fields of equipment and training.

Since the Iraq war, the relationship with the former colonial power Britain has cooled. Nevertheless, Hilary Benn, secretary of state for international development announced during his three-day visit in September that the British government through the department for international development would double its development assistance to Nigeria from £ 35 m in 2003–04 to £ 70 m in 2005–06. This was in line with the Country Assistance Plan (CAP) for 2004–07. In November, the president went on an official visit to Britain. Both governments agreed to step up the **fight against trafficking in people**. The bilateral accord targeted improved cross-border cooperation and tougher prosecution of traffickers. The agreement was signed by Britain's Solicitor-General Harriet Harman and Nigeria's Attorney-General Akinlolu Olujinmi. Against this background, Obasanjo undertook some important trips to London in his capacity as chairman of the **Commonwealth**.

Since it was revealed that **Swiss banks** harboured $ 700 m looted by the late military dictator Sani Abacha, the elected Nigerian government used legal and diplomatic means fairly successfully to get the money back. Some $ 500 m was still frozen when in August the Swiss government ordered its return to Nigeria. The Abacha family appealed this decision in the highest court of Switzerland, and the case was still pending at year's end. On 9 December, Abba Abacha, son of the late dictator, was arrested in Germany, after Swiss authorities issued an arrest warrant, but extradition to Switzerland was still pending.

Against the background of possible reform of the UN, President Obasanjo declared in his address to the General Assembly on 23 September that "Nigeria was qualified to be a permanent member of the **UN Security Council**." The 48th annual conference of the International Atomic Energy Agency elected Nigeria on to the board of governors, just before it put its first nuclear research reactor, at Ahmadu Bello University in Zaria, into operation on 30 September. Earlier, the UN honoured Nigeria's active role in Africa, particularly West Africa, when the Security Council visited Abuja on 26 June as part of its West Africa tour. Shortly before, President Obasanjo attended the G8 summit in the US, and in March he took part in a special meeting of ECOWAS and the World Bank in Accra and received the bank's president, James Wolfensohn, during his three-day visit to Nigeria.

In early August, the new managing director of the **IMF**, Rodrigo de Rato, started his first trip to Africa with a two-day visit to Nigeria. He underlined the IMF's rather positive attitude towards the critical role Nigeria had assumed as political and economic leader and its commitment to the new home-grown economic and social reform programme, the National Economic Empowerment and Development Strategy (NEEDS). Moreover, de Rato offered every assistance to repatriate Nigerian funds stashed in foreign countries by corrupt leaders and government officials. The visit followed the Article IV consultations between Nigeria and the IMF executive board on 16 July.

Socioeconomic Developments

Socioeconomic development was dominated by soaring oil prices, the boom in the mobile phone sector, the slowed privatisation programme and a political and legal battle between the federal government and the Nigerian Labour Congress (NLC) over new fuel prices.

Living conditions for most Nigerians, however, did not really improve, as indicated by an HDI of 0.466 (HDR 2004) that put Nigeria 151st of 177 countries.

Rising oil prices on the international market also inflated the annual budget. In addition, much bargaining between the presidency, the senate and the house of representatives to harmonise the bill, seriously delayed the naira 1.3 trillion ($ 9.6 bn) budget for 2004, which came into force on 21 April. The budget was related to the benchmark of $ 25 per barrel of crude oil and an exchange rate of naira 136 to the dollar. Nigeria produced some 2.3 m b/d, despite turmoil in the Niger Delta. The price of benchmark Brent North Sea crude went up from some $ 30 in January to $ 45 in August, to more than $ 50 in October and fell just below $ 40 in December. Thus, Nigeria's foreign reserves doubled from $ 8.2 bn at the beginning of the year to $ 16.1 bn at the end of it. Nevertheless, **external debts** increased and stood at $ 34 bn, because Nigeria pinned its debt service at $ 1 bn for the Paris Club, which it owed almost $ 28 bn, far below its obligation of almost $ 3 bn, thereby significantly increasing arrears. However, GDP increased by 5.5% and average inflation rate fell to 15%.

Throughout the year, NLC and the federal government confronted each other, using political and legal means over the sensitive fuel price issue. Fuel subsidies had been partly removed after an elected government took power in 1999, but fuel was still highly subsidised at the rate of $ 1.8 bn per annum, as most Nigerians considered cheap fuel a birthright. The introduction of a fuel tax of naira 1.50 per litre on petrol, diesel and kerosene, which came into force on 1 January, had to be suspended. NLC called off a **nationwide strike** on 21 January only a few hours after a court had ordered that both the strike and the intended tax collection be suspended pending a ruling on that issue. In early May, fuel marketers slightly increased the price to almost naira 43 and by the end of the month to naira 50 to 55. This was in line with a modest deregulation policy that allowed private marketers to import fuel and fix prices. NLC responded by calling a nationwide strike on 9 June, but it suspended the action on 11 June after filling stations slashed the petrol price.

After failed negotiations with the federal government in early October, NLC launched a four-day strike on 11 October to get the 20% price hike reversed. Only two days before, NLC leader Adams Oshimole was briefly detained by the SSS. NLC threatened to call another nationwide strike on 16 November, but on the eve of the strike suspended it after the federal government backed down and reduced the price of fuel and, more importantly, kerosene, which most Nigerians use for cooking. However, the court of appeal ruled on 16 December that NLC could not call a nationwide strike because of the fuel tax.

Shell was also hit by strike action by its staff. The two oil workers' unions, National Union of Petrol and National Gas and Petroleum and Natural Gas Senior Staff Association of Nigeria called a two-day warning strike in June and another in October to protest a planned cut of 1,000 jobs. Just before Christmas in a silent move, NNPC sacked 2,355 staff. The National Association of Resident Doctors (NARD) called a two-day warning strike in

November to press for the payment of salary arrears, and in mid-December NARD began an open-ended strike.

The **privatisation programme** slowed down again despite the ambitious five-year reform programme (NEEDS), launched in March. In November, Obasanjo ruled out privatising the nation's four refineries for the foreseeable future, after 13 companies were given federal government approval in October to commence construction of private refineries. In addition, the Aluminium Smelter Company of Nigeria (ALSCON), Ajaokuta Steel Company and Nigerian Telecommunication Limited (NITEL) were all causing serious problems. In August, Nigeria terminated the contract with the US company Solgas Energy. Instead, it signed a ten-year accord with an Indian company to complete and manage Ajaokuta. At the end of the year, Solgas Energy took the federal government before an arbitration panel of the International Chamber of Commerce for breach of contract. In July, a core investor from the US, the BFI Group Corporation, failed to acquire a majority stake in ALSCON. The federal government disqualified the company's bid because it had allegedly missed the deadline to pay the required 10% deposit.

Nigeria belongs to Africa's fastest growing **mobile phone market.** In recent years, $ 4 bn have been invested, mainly by private companies like MTN, M-Tel, Globacom and V-Mobile. According to the Nigerian Communication Commission some 5 m mobile and 1 m landlines were available in July and it expected to hit the 10 m benchmark within a year. But the heavily loss-making, state-run NITEL failed again (as in 2002) to find a strategic investor to acquire a 51% share. The Dutch consultancy company Pentascope International, contracted in 2003 to manage NITEL, admitted in November that it was overwhelmed by the company's problems and could not even meet 20% of the projected number of lines for the first year.

After overcoming all the legal issues concerning the liquidation of the national carrier Nigeria Airways, in February the federal government appointed South African Airways as strategic investor and technical partner to launch the new national carrier Nigerian Eagle Airline by the end of the year. However, subsequent negotiations broke down and the federal government chose the British airline Virgin Atlantic as its new partner in the creation of the new **Virgin Nigeria Airlines**.

The **power situation** went from bad to worse, since the National Electric Power Authority was able to generate just 3,000 megawatts per day, while estimated national demand was 6,000 megawatts. The launch of a second, small independent power supply project in Lagos state in August to some extent eased the industry's dire circumstances in the state and served as a potential model for further private investment in the power sector.

The **World Bank** approved a $ 120 m credit to improve urban water supplies, a $ 140 m credit to support the economic reform and governance programme, another $ 120 m credit for sustainable management of mineral resources, and it finally administered a $ 900,000 Japanese grant for the preparation of the Nigerian Urban Youth and Empowerment Project.

Africa's biggest industrial project, **Nigeria Liquefied Natural Gas**, was expanded again after the joint venture partners decided in July to invest a further $ 1.25 bn to build the sixth production train. Soon afterwards, NNPC and a subsidiary of ExxonMobil signed the financing documents for the more than $ 1 bn liquid natural gas expansion project.

Nigeria became the epicentre and source of the latest and fastest-**growing polio outbreak** and accounted for 80% of the world's polio cases. The international vaccine programme, targeted at 35 million children, met stiff opposition in some Muslim-dominated states, especially Kano and Zamfara. Radical Islamic clerics claimed that the US-made vaccine was manipulated to cause infertility. After a long political battle with the federal government, the international community and some influential Muslim moderates, the radicals capitulated, and in October WHO and UNICEF carried the campaign to the north.

The **spread of HIV/AIDS continued**, and in terms of absolute numbers Nigeria was second only to South Africa. About 3.8 m people were infected, most of them living in Lagos, and at least 13 states had prevalence rates of more than the critical benchmark of 5%.

Heinrich Bergstresser

Senegal

In 2004, general discontent with the president's policies continued, which was reflected in a proliferation of critical publications and counter-publications. It was also, again, a year of government reshuffles. On the positive side, were two important events: the abolition of the death penalty and the signing of a peace agreement between the government and the separatist movement in the Casamance. Continuing its economic liberalisation policy, Senegal made satisfactory macroeconomic progress and was eligible for important debt relief, but the majority of the population continued to live under the poverty line.

Domestic Politics

Since **Abdoulaye Wade** acceded to the presidency in March 2000, he has persistently been the subject of critical publications. During the past four years, at least seven books have appeared with Wade as their main subject. Almost all these books were a commercial success, ran into several reprints and resulted in animated debates in the national press. The book that kicked up the most dust was published in July 2003 and had a lasting effect into 2004. In his book 'Wade, un Opposant au Pouvoir: l'Alternance Piégée' ('Wade, a Member of the Opposition in Power: a Trapped Alternation'), the Senegalese journalist Abdou Latif Coulibaly painted a rather nasty picture of the president as a megalomaniac ruler, quick-tempered and excessively self-assured. It is said the book contributed to the dismissal, in April 2004, of Prime Minister Idrissa Seck, considered to be its initiator. Actually, the discharge of Seck was the outcome of intensified political tensions between the president and his prime minister. Seck was considered a serious rival to Wade because of his extensive network of strategic individuals within the state apparatus and the PDS ('Parti Démocratique Sénégalais'). There were also problems with regard to public expenditures, not only in the city of Thiès, Seck's political base (where he also holds the office of mayor), but also in some state enterprises and local communities where Seck had placed his men. In April, Macky Sall, hitherto minister of the interior and local communities, replaced Seck and became the fourth prime minister since the political changes in 2000. He immediately undertook a **reshuffle of the government**. The announced dismissal of two ministers, Modou Diagne Fada, of environment, and Aliou Sow, of youth affairs, gave rise to violent protests by student and youth movements and both ministers eventually retained their positions. Consequently, the new government, the sixth under Wade's presidency, did not bring much change: Cheikh Adibou Fall was accorded the post of minister of the interior and two new ministries were created, the ministry of local communities and decentralisation with Aminata Tall as minister of state, and the ministry of the maritime economy with Djibo Ka as minister of state. Further modest cabinet reshuffles took place in July, August and November, in which many of the important positions remained unchanged. On 2 November, Cheikh Adibou Fall was replaced as minister of the interior by Ousmane Ngom. The team of ministers (39 in total, instead of the more limited team of 20 ministers to which Wade had committed himself during his election campaign, in order to reduce costs) was made up of members of the PDS and 'Sopi' (which means 'change' in Wolof, the dominant local language in Senegal) coalition that brought Wade to power, and includes one opposition minister. All were chosen for their unswerving loyalty to the president.

This practice of the president to surround himself with admirers and yes-men was also criticised by Coulibaly, and he specifically mentioned the president's family: his son Karim and daughter Syndiély were both officially nominated as his advisors, but his wife and the daughter of his sister were also blamed for having too much influence on the president.

Accusations of bad governance by Coulibaly even led to the creation of a parliamentary commission to examine the various claims made in his book. Wade was greatly affected by the book but instead of responding to the allegations himself, he encouraged a team of nine members, directed by the vice-president of the parliament, Iba Der Thiam, to formulate a reaction. Even before the parliamentary inquiry and the work of his 'club of friends' was complete, Wade and his cabinet mounted a counteroffensive of sorts by publishing a White Paper in which he proclaimed the accomplishments of his regime over the past four years. Fifty thousand copies of the White Paper, entitled 'Le Changement, Preuves en Main' ('The Changes, Evidence in Hand'), were printed, as were 250,000 copies of an accompanying illustrated pamphlet. The paper and pamphlet were presented to a crowd of almost one million people gathered in Dakar for the fourth anniversary of Wade's mandate on 19 March. On that occasion, several political parties that had supported Wade in 2000 and had ministerial representatives in government refused to participate in the celebrations, thus demonstrating their dissatisfaction with Wade's policy. On 28 August, Iba Der Thiam and his team presented their attempted refutation of Coulibaly's allegations (without mentioning his name), also in the form of a published book: 'Un Procès d'Intention à l'Epreuve de la Vérité' ('The Truth as Evidence of Alleged Intentions').

The fact that such an intense and occasionally heated public debate about the president and his politics was possible, showed that Senegal was living up to its reputation as a country where freedom of expression is respected. But during the year, the limits of tolerance towards the press also became apparent. In July, privately owned newspapers decided on a **'day without the press'**. On that day (12 July), their newspapers were not published and private radio stations replaced their news bulletins with music as part of the strike. This was to protest the arrest of the editor of 'Le Quotidien', Madiambal Diagne. His paper wrote of alleged corruption in the customs service and interference in the judiciary, and Diagne was charged with publishing confidential reports and correspondence, false information and news 'which could cause serious political problems'. Although he was released within three weeks, the private press considered his arrest to be part of a government campaign to muzzle it, and editors of other newspapers feared that they would be next. They especially criticised President Wade for his slowness or unwillingness to 'clean up' the Penal Code and the Code of Penal Procedure in order to adapt them to the democratisation process in the country, especially as he was himself – when still in opposition – several times the victim of the much decried Article 80 of the Penal Code, which allowed for the arrest of journalists who publish news 'which could cause serious political problems'. At the end of the year, the president promised to decriminalise press offences.

However, the imbroglio involving the president and the press was no obstacle to the International League for Human Rights, an American NGO, which granted Abdoulaye Wade the **international award for human rights** not only for his perseverance during his years in opposition (from 1974 till 2000) against the hegemonic power of the Socialist Party, but also because of his role in the resolution of conflicts in Africa (Madagascar, Darfur, Côte d'Ivoire, Guinea-Bissau). Many Senegalese journalists and personalities (including the well-known musician Youssou Ndour), as well as a number of African heads of state and Kofi Annan, attended the ceremony on 22 September. Previous award winners included Nelson Mandela, Jimmy Carter and Andrei Sakharov.

Although the constitution prohibits the creation of political parties on the basis of religion, on 20 February Modou Kara announced **the creation of a new party** 'le Parti de la Vérité pour le Développement' (PVD). Modou Kara's full name is Cheikh Modou Kara Mbacké Noreyni, and he is a descendant of the founder of Senegal's most influentia brotherhood, the Mourides. The Mourides and other Islamic brotherhoods claim the allegiance of more than 90% of the population. Kara is very popular among young people and as the leader of an Islamic mass movement 'le Mouvement Mondial pour l'Unicité de Dieu' (MMUD), established in 1995, he claimed to have 500,000 followers or 'taalibe'. His announcement resulted in passionate debates in the press. In June, the 'marabout des jeunes' presented his new party at a press conference, stressing his intention to innovate the relationship between Islam and politics and to defend the interests of the pauperised urban youth, disappointed by the promised 'sopi' under the regime of Wade. In his speeches, he presented himself, however, not as a marabout, but as a citizen and his followers as citizens, taalibe.

Islamic influence also manifested itself in other ways. Firstly, it was apparent in the revival of the public debate on the reform of the 'Code de la Famille' (Family Law) of 1972, which was last revised in 1984. Muslim fundamentalists again advocated the adoption of the shariah. In March, a collective of 17 Islamic associations called for the prohibition in Senegal of 'Sexe d'Allah', a book written by a French female journalist who ventured that, through the centuries, Muslims always cultivated love and sensual pleasures.

Towards the end of the year, two major events occurred. On 10 December – the international day celebrating the adoption of the Universal Declaration of Human Rights in 1948 – the Senegalese National Assembly voted for the **abolition of the death penalty**, thus joining the 12 other African countries that had already made this 'choice of civilisation', as it was portrayed in the national press.

On the threshold of the new year, 30 December, Interior Minister Ousmane Ngom and the leader of the 'Mouvement des Forces Démocratiques de la Casamance' (MFDC), Father Diamecoune Senghor, **signed a peace pact** aimed at ending one of West Africa's longest-running insurgencies. The secessionist struggle in the **Casamance** had started in 1982, and was fuelled by complaints among the Diola, who form the majority in the Casamance, that their region was being marginalised by the government in Dakar. However, the MFDC was also obsessed with historical arguments and claimed that colonial France did not include the Casamance in Senegal and always granted it special status. As early as 1993 France had denied this. This protracted, low-intensity war between the Senegalese forces and MFDC resulted in the killing of several thousand people, including many civilians, and the forced displacement, internal and external, of tens of thousands of people. Spill-over effects were felt in the neighbouring countries, The Gambia and Guinea-Bissau. From the late 1980s, many attempts were made to negotiate an agreement (ceasefire agreements were signed in 1991, 1993 and 2001), but the serious fragmentation of the independence movement was one of the main obstacles to achieving a definitive settlement of the conflict. In July 2004, the National Assembly voted in a law providing an amnesty for all MFDC combatants, and in September, MFDC, in collaboration with national and international human rights movements, organised a large reconciliation forum in the main city of the Casamance, Ziguinchor, to lay the foundations for further negotiations. This forum was, however, not attended by officials from the government. The signing of the peace deal on 30 December could be the beginning of the end – at least that was what most ordinary Casamançais who had suffered through the conflict for many years were hoping. At the time of the signing it was still unclear which factions of the MFDC supported Diamecoune. Hints of division within MFDC were confirmed on the eve of the signing ceremony. The head of the external wing of the MFDC in Paris, Mamadou Nkrumah Sané, wrote an open letter to Diamacoune, in which he labelled the peace agreement as nothing more than "une déclaration de guerre contre notre pays, la Casamance" ("a declaration of war against our country, the Casamance"). And Magne Dieme, the self-promoted head of the 'Front Nord' of MDFC, also openly distanced himself from the peace agreement. For President Wade, who made peace with the Casamance a priority when he came to power, the agreement of 30 December could be claimed as a success for his policy. However, he still had to convince the international donor community that it constituted a real ending of the troubles in the Casamance in order to gain full access to the promised aid money necessary for the recovery programme and mine-clearing operations in the region.

Foreign Affairs

In foreign affairs, 2004 could be labelled the year of **French-American competition, with** Senegal wanting to show it was no longer under the heavy influence of France by mounting a charm offensive on the United States.

Since Wade's coming to power, **Franco-Senegalese relationships** have become very unstable. Abdoulaye Wade still felt a kind of resentment against 'Paris' because of French diplomacy's dismissive treatment of him when he was Senegal's main opposition leader, and the public friendship between Jacques Chirac and his predecessor, Abdou Diouf (of whose youngest daughter Chirac is godfather). Besides these personal considerations, there were other reasons for the deterioration in the relationship between Senegal and its former colonial power. In general, the Senegalese blamed France for the difficulties Senegalese encountered in obtaining visas to study or work in France. And in 2003, there had been serious confrontations between Senegal and France over the massive expulsion of Senegalese immigrants from France, their humiliating treatment by French customs officers and Senegal's response in expelling not only a French journalist but also some French people staying in Senegal without proper documents. From the French side, Abdoulaye Wade was accused of becoming too close to George W. Bush: "Bush is a friend and we understood each other from the beginning. He even telephones me just to know if I am fine," Wade declared in the French newspaper 'Le Figaro' in February 2004. A more specific example of Senegal's good relationships with the US is the agreement, signed in 2003, that neither country would extradite the other's nationals to the International Criminal Court in The Hague.

In an attempt to thaw Franco-Senegalese relationships, Abdoulaye Wade had a private lunch at the Élysée with his counterpart Chirac on 19 February, with the result that Chirac promised to make an official visit to Senegal during the year (it was later postponed to 2005). Chirac's last official visit to Senegal dated back to 1995, whereas Bush had honoured

Senegal by making a very short visit there on 7 July 2003. In the course of 2004, both countries took measures to resolve the problem of clandestine immigration by air, and France facilitated the issuing of special visas for Senegalese students.

The warming of Franco-Senegalese relationships was confirmed on 6 December in a message from Jacques Chirac, delivered by the French ambassador to the US at a gala dinner in Washington hosted by the National Democratic Institute, a non-profit-making organisation close to the American Democratic Party, in which he congratulated his friend Abdoulaye Wade ('Monsieur le Président et cher ami') for winning the W. Averell Harriman Democracy Award for 2004. During the afternoon of the same day, Wade had **a working session at the White House** with President Bush to discuss economic collaboration between the US and Senegal; investments in the context of the Millenium Challenge Account; Iraq, Darfur, the Ukraine, and Côte d'Ivoire; the war against terrorism; and Franco-American relationships. According to one of the confidants of Wade, the latter advised the American president that it was now opportune to improve his personal relationships with Jacques Chirac.

The king of **Morocco**, Mohammed VI, visited Senegal on 29 June where, in the presence of Abdoulaye Wade, he laid the foundation stone of the 'Université du futur africain' (to be named after his father, Hassan II) in Sebikotane, about 40 kilometres from Dakar. Morocco and Senegal have long had good relationships, not only because the Tidjani brotherhood – the most important one in terms of members in Senegal – was founded in Morocco, but also because the joint venture between Royal Air Maroc and Air Sénégal International, established in 2001, had proven by 2004 to be a real commercial success.

Relations with neighbouring countries, more particularly with The Gambia, Guinea-Bissau and Mauritania, were considerably improved in 2004. Senegal's relations with both **The Gambia and Guinea-Bissau** were long dominated by the conflict in the southern Casamance region. Both countries not only hosted several meetings between the government of Senegal and MFDC, but were also a refuge for large numbers of displaced persons. Moreover, during the conflict Guinea-Bissau was often accused of allowing MFDC members to train on its territory. Since his election, President Abdoulaye Wade's main strategy has been to make direct contact with the different factions within MFDC, without intermediaries: Guinea-Bissau and The Gambia were excluded from the peace process. The signing of the peace agreement in December may contribute to an improvement of relations with these countries. With regard to **Mauritania**, relations have improved progressively since the serious crisis between the two countries in 1989. An indication of improved relations was the decision by Mauritania's government to award 270 temporary fishing licences to Senegalese fishermen in June.

Finally, Abdoulaye Wade continued to intensify his **diplomatic influence** in West Africa and across the continent, not only in the context of NEPAD, but also by contributing to peacekeeping activities: Senegalese troops played an important role in the UN operation in Côte d'Ivoire that started in April.

Socioeconomic Developments

In general, Senegal made satisfactory economic progress, with an estimated **growth rate** of more than 6% (President Wade mentioned a growth rate of 6.7% in his state of the nation address). The major sources of foreign exchange remained tourism, fishing and phosphates. Senegal received about 900,000 tourists in 2004, the majority (60%) from France. Since many tourist activities take place in the Casamance region, it is expected that the return of security after the peace settlement might increase the development of this sector in coming years. Although Senegal's contribution to the international fish market is relatively small, the fishing sector, including processing, contributed more than 30% to the export of (semi-) processed products: small-scale fishing accounted for about 45% of fish exports. In this sector also, the return of security in the Casamance, the main fishing area, might have a positive influence. In the mining sector, the extraction of phosphates remained the dominant economic activity, contributing about 3% of world exports of phosphates. Gold has been discovered in the southeast at Sabodala. In October, the Senegalese authorities awarded gold exploration permits to Australia's Mineral Deposits Limited (MDL) and a Canadian-Saudi entity, Euro Mines.

However, the economic success could also be partly attributed to the ongoing crisis in Côte d'Ivoire, resulting in the diversion of more **foreign investments** to Dakar (direct foreign investment has doubled over the last three years). Meanwhile, the Senegalese government continued the process of economic reform and liberalisation by improving the business environment and adapting the relevant legislation. In February, a new 'Code des Investissements' (Investment Code) and 'Code Général des Impôts' (taxation law) were adopted to replace the previous laws, whereas a totally new legal instrument was introduced in June, when the 'Law on BOT (Build, Operate and Transfer)' was adopted. This law, whose official name is in English, is meant to boost investment in public infrastructure by stimulating public-private partnerships. In order to coordinate activities in this field, various structures were created, such as APIX, 'Agence de Promotion des Investissements et des Grands Travaux' (Agency to Promote Investments and Public Works) and CPI, 'Conseil Présidential sur l'Investissement' (Presidential Council for Investments). The intended long-term projects, to start from 2005, included the construction of a new international airport about 40 kilometres from Dakar, a toll highway between Dakar and Thiès (about 70 kilometres) and new railway projects. Attempts to privatise public sectors such as electricity (Sénélec, 'Société d'Électricité du Sénégal') and groundnut-oil production (Sonacos, 'Société nationale de commercialisation des oléaginaux du Sénégal') were unsuccessful in 2004, probably because of the ever-increasing debts of these parastatals.

In the **agricultural sector**, Senegal, like other West African countries, faced one of the most damaging locust outbreaks in 15 years. On 3 September, an emergency meeting with ministers from 12 affected countries in the sub-region took place in Dakar. Senegal decided to use its national armed forces to help combat the spread of desert locusts in West Africa.

The locust crisis, combined with deficient rainfall, resulted in disappointing yields of cereals and cotton (which declined 22% and 9% respectively). However, and in spite of the adverse natural circumstances, the production of groundnuts, sesame and cassava rose (28%, 56% and 121% respectively). On 25 May, the National Assembly adopted new agricultural reform measures, 'La loi d'Orientation Agro-Sylvo-Pastoral', aimed at a better agricultural production system. A first draft bill was released in 2003 on the initiative and under the supervision of the president himself. This 'Projet de Loi d'Orientation Agricole' was submitted for comment to representatives of the agricultural sector. They particularly criticised the top-down approach during the preparation phase and the fact that consultation about the draft bill was limited to experts, thus excluding the real stakeholders in rural development. After many workshops and information sessions at the local level, organised by the agricultural sector representatives, extensive and elaborate suggestions for improving the draft bill were sent to the president and the minister of agriculture, and most of them were subsequently integrated into the final law. As the revised title indicates, the act no longer focused only on agriculture, but also on forestry and cattle breeding. The most salient feature of the new act was its integrated vision of rural economic development, aiming at diversifying rural production (including rural tourism) and placed in the context of poverty reduction. In this respect, attention was given to the equal treatment of the men, women and youth working in the rural economic sector, including the development of a system of rural social security, the importance afforded professional training, modernisation of local and regional markets and development of public services in rural areas. But as a 'loi d'orientation', the act was mainly a framework for future government politics and most of the proposed measures would be implemented from two to ten years of the date of its promulgation. One of the most challenging provisions in the act was Article 23, which stated that "A new land tenure policy shall be elaborated and a land reform act submitted to the National Assembly within two years of the date of promulgation of this law." The planned land reform act would include specific provision for animal husbandry and pastoral activities. Finally, the act provided for the creation of a 'Conseil Supérieur d'Orientation Agro-Sylvo-Pastorale', chaired by the president, to monitor its implementation. This council was also commissioned to organise a yearly agricultural conference, bringing together all stakeholders in the rural development sector, and particularly representatives of professional organisations, civil society and development partners (Article 77).

In past years, Senegal had realised full internet connectivity, thereby creating a mini-boom in **information and technology-based services**. Dakar became an eldorado of call centres and e-business, creating thousands of new job opportunities. In Johannesburg in September, a Senegalese enterprise in this sector, Manobi, was declared 'Top ICT Company 2004' and granted the 'Award for the Most Innovative African Company'. The company provides local farmers and traders with up-to-the-minute market prices for their crops through their mobile telephones, and provides fishermen with information about weather conditions. Pastoralists can track their cattle herds using cell phones and Global Positioning Systems.

The motor of Senegal's economy, however, was heavily based on **migration**. Since many Senegalese migrants are illegal and a great number of the remittances are made through informal transactions, exact figures are unavailable. However, it is estimated that the Senegalese diaspora, amounting to about one to three million, contributed between 5% and 10% to the gross national product.

In the course of the year, Senegal became eligible for **debt relief** on several occasions. In February, Senegal reached its completion point under the enhanced Heavily Indebted Poor Countries (HIPC) initiative, and as a consequence IMF and the World Bank supported $ 850 m. in debt service relief. In June, an additional debt relief of $ 430 m was provided by the Paris Club creditors. Finally, in November, Senegal received relief for its entire debt with France, i.e., CFAfr 185.5 bn. On that occasion, the national press proclaimed triumphantly: "Le pays ne doit plus un centime d'Euro à la France" ("Our country does not owe one eurocent to France"), adding that the US only forgave part of Senegal's debt. Dakar committed itself to allocating the resources made available by debt relief to pro-poor expenditure programmes, as outlined in its Poverty Reduction Strategy Paper (PRSP), which has four strategic pillars: (1) wealth creation through economic reform and private sector development; (2) capacity building and development of social services; (3) improvements in the living conditions of the poor; and (4) implementation of the strategy and monitoring its outcomes. In order to meet these objectives, Senegal created a 'Comité National de Politique Economique'.

In spite of this economic success story, the daily living conditions for the majority of the poor people in Senegal hardly improved. According to the Human Development Index, Senegal, ranking 157 out of 177, still belonged to the category of countries with low human development. About 65% of the population was still living under the poverty line and life expectancy at birth was just above 52. On the other hand, the percentage of people infected with HIV/AIDS, estimated at 1.5%, was remarkably low in comparison with other African countries. Another success in the health sector was the vaccination rate of 99% of children against poliomyelitis. However, at the end of the year a million people living in bad hygienic conditions in Dakar were struck by cholera. The country faced deep-seated urban and rural problems of chronic unemployment (unemployment figures were estimated at 40–50%). The price increases of certain daily products such as bread, kerosene and fuel created some social unrest.

Gerti Hesseling

Sierra Leone

On 4 February, the president of Sierra Leone officially dismantled the National Commission for Disarmament, Demobilisation and Reintegration (NCDDR). This marked the official closure of a five-year programme that reintegrated 72,490 ex-combatants, including 6,845 ex-child combatants. These fighters had taken part in the decade-long Sierra Leonean conflict (March 1991–February 2002).

The year was characterised by a continuing recovery in the post-war socioeconomic situation. With a 6.5% rise in the GDP, economic growth was considerable. The country experienced a calm year on the domestic political front, with local council elections in May 2004 as the main political event. It saw its foreign relations further consolidated through a series of high-level state visits. In 2004, the United Nations Mission in Sierra Leone (UNAMSIL) maintained its presence on the ground but further reduced its numbers, as did numerous relief organisations that had provided aid to this war-torn country during and immediately after the war.

Domestic Politics

The president of Sierra Leone, Ahmad Tejan Kabbah, was still running the country with **broad support**. On 14 May 2002, Kabbah had won the most recent presidential elections with 70.6% of the total vote in what were labelled as a fair and peaceful election by international observers. The next elections are scheduled for May 2007.

In 2004 several **new ministers** were appointed by President Kabbah and approved by the house of representatives, such as Attorney-General and Minister of Justice Frederick Max Carew, who took office on 3 August. The new minister of health and sanitation, Mrs Abator M. Thomas, and the new deputy minister of agriculture, John A. Karim-Sesay took their oaths of office a week later. In contrast to the previous cabinet, the cabinet appointed by the president after the 2002 elections did not make room for Kabbah's political opponents or for former Revolutionary United Front (RUF) supporters.

The political landscape in Sierra Leone was dominated by the Sierra Leone Peoples Party (SLPP), which won the May 2002 parliamentary elections with 83 seats, and the All Peoples Congress (APC) (27 seats). The Peace and Liberation Party (PLP-PDA) of former junta leader Johnny Paul Koroma won two seats, but due to prolonged absence the two MPs, J.P. Koroma and Hassan Kamara, **lost their seats in** early 2004 and were replaced by Dr. Kandeh B. Konteh and Mohamed Idriss. The Revolutionary United Front Party (RUFP) – which under the 1999 Lomé peace accord had been created out of the rebel RUF – did not receive enough votes (2.3%) to obtain any seats.

On 22 May, **local council elections** were held as part of the further decentralisation of government. However, there was general concern that the impact of these decentralisation efforts was being restricted by inadequate resources, infrastructure and qualified personnel. Of about 15 political parties only four were able to register themselves with the National Electoral Commission (NEC). These were the SLPP, RUFP, PLP and the APC. In addition, some independent candidates registered. A remarkable feature was APC's victory in Freetown, where it won the majority of the seats. As a consequence, **the new Freetown mayor was the APC loyalist** Winston Bankole Johnson, who had previously been a businessman and banker. Upon his installation, he promised to create 3,000 jobs for Freetown residents in two years, a difficult but much needed task in a capital where 80% of the population is unemployed. In the east of the country, SLPP won nearly all the seats. In the south – a SLPP stronghold as well – the SLPP victory was not as total: independent candidates gained several seats. In the north of Sierra Leone – an APC stronghold – the APC indeed won most of the seats. In Makeni, the headquarters of the Northern province, APC won all the seats, despite President Kabbah's threats to withhold funds from councils that fell to the opposition.

Widespread corruption in Sierra Leone is considered as a major brake on economic development. Integral to the new good-governance strategy was the office of the ombudsman, but critics stated that incumbent Francis Gabbidon was more a government spokesman than an ombudsman. As part of the country's campaign to fight corruption, on 12 January Mrs. Neneh Daboh, the director of prevention and sensitisation in the Anti-Corruption Commission (ACC), in existence since 2000, presented the ACC's five-year strategic plan to the president. Part of this plan was to decentralise ACC's activities and by so doing increase its efficiency and effectiveness. On 15 October, ACC opened its first provincial office in the Southern Region headquarters town of Bo. A major case for the ACC concerned the Bank of Sierra Leone, where senior staff was accused of 'recycling' government cheques worth at least $ 643,000. No judge has yet been assigned to the case. No wonder media rights monitors stated that some subjects remained taboo in Sierra Leone, in particular cases of high-level corruption. However, the mostly privately run newspapers, such as the 'Standard Times', the 'Concord Times' and the 'Democrat' were often critical of government.

The **1999 Lomé Peace Agreement** stated that:

> To consolidate the peace and promote the cause of national reconciliation, the Government of Sierra Leone shall ensure that no official or judicial action is taken against any member of the RUF, ex-AFRC (Armed Forces Revolutionary Council), ex-SLA or CDF (Civil Defence Forces) in respect of anything done by them in pursuit of their objectives as members of those organisations, since March 1991, up to the time of the signing of the present Agreement.

However, on 16 January 2002 an agreement was signed between the UN and the government of Sierra Leone to establish a **special court** to bring to court those "who bear the greatest responsibility" in the country's past conflict. Of a total of 13 people who have been indicted by the court, only nine are standing trial. Rebel leader Foday Sankoh and the RUF's second-in-command, Sam Bockarie, have died. The former leader of the AFRC and MP Johnny Paul Koroma has been on the run since he was indicted by the special court, but is now presumed dead. Former Liberian leader and RUF supporter, Charles Taylor was granted exile in Nigeria. In August 2004, the special court's prosecutor, David Crane, indicated that the Libyan leader, **Colonel Muammar Kadhafi**, might also be indicted.

On 10 March, the ultra-modern courthouse at the special court's complex in Freetown was opened. The nine people standing trial in groups of three represented the pro-government CDF, the RUF and the (AFRC). The **CDF trial** started on 3 June, and included Samuel Hinga Norman (its former national coordinator, as well as deputy defence minister and former minister of the interior under the Kabbah government), Moinina Fofana (CDF's former national director of war) and Allieu Kondewa (CDF's former high priest). In particular, the indictment of Hinga Norman was controversial, since he is considered by most Sierra Leoneans as a war-hero. The **RUF trial**, that is the joint trial of Issa Sesay (the RUF's interim leader in 2001 and 2002), Morris Kallon (RUF's battle group commander from 2000 onwards) and Augustine Gbao (RUF's head of security from 2000 onwards), began on 5 July. The **AFRC trail** had not started by year's end.

Also mandated by the Lomé Peace Agreement was the **Truth and Reconciliation Commission** (TRC), which presented its final report to President Kabbah on 5 October, after previous deadlines of October 2003 and March 2004 were missed. The report contained 1,500 pages plus another 3,500 pages of testimony. The report concluded that "it was

years of bad governance, endemic corruption and the denial of basic human rights that created the deplorable conditions that made conflict inevitable," and that "the war was only
partly to do with diamonds, which fuelled rather than caused the crisis." About the current
post-war situation, the report stated that "corruption remains rampant and no culture of tolerance or inclusion in political discourse has yet emerged." According to the 2000 Truth and
Reconciliation Act, the government was required to take onboard the TRC's recommendations. Some of the **'imperative' recommendations** included measures to increase the
transparency of the mining industry, steps to improve the accountability of state officials,
judicial reforms and the abolition of the death penalty. In addition, President Kabbah's
claims that he was unaware of the atrocities perpetrated by CDF have been debunked in the
TRC report.

Sierra Leone has not witnessed significant violent upheaval, let alone conflict, since the
end of the war in 2002. Consequently, and because of the UN presence, the country's military expenditures have been low (in 2003 they were 1.5% of the country's GDP). However,
because the Sierra Leone economy was not strong enough to create significant employment
opportunities, particularly for young Sierra Leoneans, **a potential security threat
remained**. According the TRC report: "Many ex-combatants testified that the conditions
that caused them to join the conflict persist in the country and, if given the opportunity, they
would fight again."

From being one of the safest African capitals immediately after the war, the crime rate
(in particular **armed robbery**) increased, although exact figures for 2004 have not been
reported. Crime figures for 2003 showed that for most crime categories, at least 50% took
place in the Western Area, that is the Freetown peninsular. Armed robbers could count on
little mercy from the police, with the police commander of the Western Area, Santigie I.S.
Koroma, stating that "if they [the armed robbers] venture out their death will be categorised
as death by misadventure."

Another source of concern in 2004 was the return of Sierra Leonean combatants who had
fought in the conflict in Liberia, particular those combatants who had not been able to
benefit from Liberian Disarmament, Demobilisation and Reintegration (DDR) support.

Foreign Affairs

In April 2004 the UNAMSIL began handing over control of security in the interior to the
police and national army. This process was completed on 22 September with the handing
over of control in the Western Area. The strength of UNAMSIL on 31 December was 4,274
uniformed personnel, including 4,061 troops, 138 military observers and 75 civilian police
supported by 274 international civilian personnel and 511 local civilian staff. UNAMSIL
began on 22 October 1999 and increased its strength in several steps to an authorised maximum of 17,500 military personnel. From 2003 onwards, UNAMSIL reduced its strength
in light of the further stabilisation of the situation in the country.

The Security Council authorised an extension of UNAMSIL's mandate with a reduced presence until 30 June 2005. The budget of $ 301.9 m (gross) for 1 July 2004 to 30 June 2005 has been approved. In this last phase, the mission will remain under the leadership of the Special Representative of the Secretary-General (SRSG), Ambassador Daudi N. Mwakawago of Tanzania. While the UNAMSIL mission reduced its numbers, the United Nations Mission in Liberia (UNMIL) increased its strength in an attempt to stabilise the country that remained the greatest threat to Sierra Leone's peace.

The UK-dominated International Military Advisory and Training Team (IMATT) continued to support the Sierra Leone police and the Republic of Sierra Leone Armed Forces (RSLAF) in 2004. Furthermore, the UK stated in August that it would pay for a private security firm to provide intelligence training and advice to Sierra Leone. According to security analysts, among the possible bidders will be Aegis Defence Services of Colonel Tim Spicer, formerly of Sandline International, which had tried to smuggle arms to the pro-government forces in Sierra Leone in 1998, while the country was under an arms embargo.

Under the Trans-Sahara Counter Terrorism Initiative (TSCTI), part of the global war on terrorism, the US government, in conjunction with the Sierra Leone government and RSLAF, initiated training and logistical operations at the Murray Town logistics facility in Freetown for soldiers from Sierra Leone, Mauritania, Mali, Niger and Chad.

A one-day summit of heads of state of the **Mano River Union**, aimed at reactivating the union, was held in the Guinean capital, Conakry. The three leaders of the Mano River Union states, Lansana Conté of Guinea, Ahmad Tejan Kabbah and Gyude Bryant of Liberia expressed their commitment to supporting initiatives to promote confidence-building measures and security in the sub-region in order to strengthen cooperation among member countries and speed their integration and sustainable development. In October 1973, Sierra Leone and Liberia concluded the Mano River Union, aimed at establishing local free trade areas and joint industrial development projects. Seven years later, Guinea became a member. However, in 1986 all the union's training institutions were turned over to the national governments.

On 3 September, a joint communiqué was signed by President Conté of Guinea and President Kabbah on the issue of the Guinea-Sierra Leone border along the Makona-Moa rivers. The two presidents agreed and gave the mutual assurance that there would never be conflict between the two countries and that **the disputed village of Yenga**, occupied by Guinean troops in 1999 to fight the RUF inside Sierra Leone and to stop their cross-border raids into Guinea, belongs to Sierra Leone.

A series of **high-level state visits** took place in 2004. Vice-President Solomon E. Berewa visited the United Kingdom during the second half of January at the head of a high-level delegation to further cement relations between the two countries. President Kabbah left Freetown on 19 January to witness the inauguration of President Lansana Conté of Guinea and went on to visit to Nigeria and Libya. During the second half of November, the president paid another visit to Libya, as well as to Algeria. On 16 April, President Kabbah had a meeting with a group of senior officials of the European Commission (EC) in Brussels where he outlined some "outstanding issues that are critical to Sierra Leone's reconstruction programme." On 6 May, Commonwealth Secretary-General Don McKinnon visited President Kabbah and discussed a wide range of issues related to the Commonwealth.

Together with more than 50 heads of state, President Kabbah attended the summit of the African Union in July in Ethiopia. Later that month he participated in the Africa-wide launch of the UNDP Human Development Report for 2004 in Nigeria and made a brief stopover in Monrovia. This preceded a two-day visit by the chairman of the national transitional government of Liberia, Gyude Bryant to Sierra Leone the following month, with another one-day working visit on 15 October. During the first visit the presidents talked about measures to strengthen security along the mutual border to **prevent "infiltration** of subversive elements into each territory" and to continue exploring ways and means to revive the Mano River Union. From 30 September to 3 October, President Kabbah paid a state visit to Laurent Gbagbo, president of Côte d'Ivoire. On 6 December, the president of Germany, Dr. Horst Köhler, arrived at Sierra Leone for a three-day state visit.

Socioeconomic Developments

On 15 October the Sierra Leonean rice-breeding expert Dr. Monty Jones became the first African to receive the World Food Prize for his work on the 'Nerica' rice variety, developed in 1994 by crossing African and Asian rice species. Japan provided $ 923,010 in funds through the UN Trust Fund for Human Security, partly aimed at promoting the distribution of the 'Nerica' variety. In his address at the beginning of his second term in office, President Kabbah mentioned 2007 as the date to achieve **food security** in the country. Nearly 70% of the population still depended on (semi)subsistence agriculture. During the 2000–03 period, agricultural production grew on average by about 9%. In particular, after the first two post-Lomé years (2000 and 2001) agricultural production started to increase due to the resettlement of the rural population.

Some deforestation took place, the result of slash-and-burn farming methods and the harvesting of timber. However, no large and/or international timber companies have started operating in Sierra Leone since the war. **Overfishing** of Sierra Leone's territorial waters was a larger problem, particularly as it involved illegal activities by high-capacity foreign fishing boats.

In 2004 a nationwide population and housing census was carried out, but results remained provisional at year's end. According to other sources, the current population was 5,883,889 (July 2004 est.). The total fertility rate was 5.8 children born per woman, giving a population growth rate of 2.3%. With a median age of 17.5 years, Sierra Leone was a demographically young country. In all parts of the country **schools reopened** and primary school enrolment has increased by 70% since 2002. In 2004, Sierra Leone **again ranked**

last among the 177 countries on the United Nations Human Development Index. Seventy per cent of the population was below the poverty level with expenditures of less than $ 1 a day. Life expectancy at birth has increased over the last few years but was still shockingly low at 42.7 years (the UN Development Report 2004 stated an average life expectancy of 34 years). Infant mortality rates were 145.2 deaths per 1,000 live births. Latest HIV/AIDS figures dated from 2001 and indicated that 7% of the population was HIV/AIDS positive. In the absence of a strong prevention programme, this figure was likely to have risen considerably. Nutritional studies from 2003 revealed that 46.5% of deaths were associated with malnutrition. In August, an outbreak of cholera affected the border region between Sierra Leone and Guinea.

The United Nations High Commissioner for Refugees (UNHCR) completed the repatriation of Sierra Leonean refugees from within the sub-region in September 2004, bringing the total number of Sierra Leonean refugees who have been repatriated under the UNHCR programme to about 178,000 (270,000 according to other sources). In 2004, Sierra Leone was still hosting about 67,000 **refugees from Liberia**, over 80% of whom were accommodated in eight refugee camps. Repatriation was directly linked to the further consolidation of peace in Liberia. Migration of Sierra Leoneans to neighbouring countries or further afield is limited. However, close to 15,000 **Sierra Leonean war-related refugees** have opted to stay and integrate into the host countries within the sub-region.

In 2004, the country witnessed further rapid growth in the number of **cellular phones** (67,000 in 2002) with all major towns in Sierra Leone now connected to the mobile network. This has had a major socioeconomic impact in a country where physical infrastructure is still in such a bad condition. In 2004, Sierra Leone counted 277 internet hosts; internet cafes have become part of the urban landscape especially in Freetown, but increasingly in the country's two second-largest towns, Bo and Kenema. As to physical infrastructure, in April/May the EU granted – 17.8 m to improve the road between Rogberi (about 100 kilometres from Freetown) and the Guinean border.

After completion of the fifth review under Sierra Leone's Poverty Reduction and Growth Facility (PRGF) arrangement, the IMF approved a $ 21 m. disbursement. In May 2004, the **World Bank** approved five IBRD (International Bank of Reconstruction and Development) loans and 40 IDA (International Development Association) credits and grants for Sierra Leone, totalling approximately $ 686 m. The commitment value of eight ongoing World Bank operations was approximately $ 184 m. Much of the post-war recovery and development of Sierra Leone was channelled through the National Commission for Social Action (NaCSA), in existence now for two years. NaCSA was funded by the World Bank, the African Development Bank, the Islamic Development Bank and the government of Sierra Leone. The commission has three main programmes; the Community-Driven Programme (CDP), the Public Works Programme (PWP) and the Micro-Finance Programme (MFP). NaCSA has already implemented 1,084 projects in agriculture, education, health, governance and community infrastructure.

The **United Nations Transitional Appeal for Relief and Recovery** in Sierra Leone requested $ 60,030,200 for 2004, but received (or was pledged) only $ 6 m by mid-year. As a result, many UN agencies were forced to work within limited budgets, running the risk of losing what is perceived as momentum in the post-war reconstruction of Sierra Leone.

Sierra Leone's GDP in 2004 was $ 3.1 bn, a growth of 6.5% compared to the previous year. The country's debt was $ 1.5 bn in 2002. Inflation became an increasing problem in 2004 due to high oil prices, delays in aid disbursements and inadequate fiscal adjustment.

Sierra Leone has been well known for its **diamonds**, considered 'blood diamonds' during the war, since they provided revenues to the various warring factions. Smuggling remained a major problem, but partly due to the Kimberley process (which instituted a diamond certification requirement), the official registered output of diamonds in 2003 expanded by 44% over 2002 and reached just over $ 70 m. This was from alluvial sources, which, however, were increasingly reported to be drying up. In 2004, the country's diamond exports were likely to have reached $ 120 m. The Koidu Holding Company (owned by DiamondWorks Ltd.) implemented a $ 60 m kimberlite mining project in Kono district, which started producing during the first quarter of 2004. The company has also been awarded the exclusive licence for prospecting and mining the Tongo diamond fields, after Kono the largest in the country. Also during the first quarter of 2004, African Diamonds was awarded a mining licence in Kono, covering tailings of the former National Diamond Mining Corporation. Other major players were Mano River Resources Inc. and Sierra Leone Diamond Company, both of which acquired some large-scale prospecting and exploration licences.

A quarter of the 3% export tax on diamonds went into the diamond area community development fund to provide 'chiefdom development committees' with funds. However, because of mismanagement of these funds (an accumulated $ 840,000), payments to these committees have not been made since June 2003.

For as long as the country's **rutile production**, which accounted for about 25% of world supply before production ceased in 1995, and bauxite production is not in full swing, diamond production will account for most of the country's dollar value of registered merchandise: in 2003 some 85%. However, rutile production was scheduled to restart by the end of 2005 under the US-based titanium-minerals producer WGI Heavy Minerals Inc. The previous owners, a group of investors, had already spent over $ 110 m on this rehabilitation. While the smuggling of diamonds received much attention, experts estimated that close to three tonnes of **gold** were smuggled in 2003, with only seven kilograms of gold being formerly recorded.

In March, the Italian engineering contractors 'Salini Costruttori' (SALCOST) resumed work, after a seven-year lull, on the long-stalled **Bumbuna hydroelectric project** in the northern district of Tonkolili. This will, when completed, reduce the capital's dependency on fossil fuels for electricity generation. Indications were that the project might be commissioned by the end of 2005.

Krijn Peters

Togo

The roadmap for democratisation and economic liberalisation, negotiated with the EU as a precondition for resuming aid, dominated foreign and domestic politics. Opposition parties entered the new national dialogue on reconciliation only reluctantly in view of the authoritarian attitudes of the government. Rumours about the deteriorating health of the head of state, Gnassingbé Eyadéma, fuelled speculation about his succession. At the end of the year, he announced the dissolution of parliament and early elections in the first half of the next year. Socioeconomic development continued to suffer from the ongoing political crisis.

Domestic Politics

The **roadmap for democratisation**, negotiated with the EU on 14 April, served as the guideline for domestic policy throughout the year. Given the lasting stalemate between government and opposition, the motivation for meaningful and honest inter-party dialogue was clearly donor-driven. The economic crisis and the ensuing desperate need to come to terms with major donors, who had suspended aid since 1993 because of gross human rights violations and bad governance, placed additional pressure on the Eyadéma regime to make concessions to the opposition. On 8 January, the EU reopened consultations in terms of

Article 96 of the ACP Cotonou Convention of June 2000. The EU ambassador in Ghana, the German Stefan Frowein, was recognised by Lomé as mediator, albeit reluctantly, since the German government was accused of anti-government sentiments. Paris, the most ardent promoter of the normalisation of political ties, had difficulty in the EU in convincing more critical member states, like Germany, the UK and Spain, to reach consensus on the conditions for the resumption of aid: this was finally achieved on 22 March. On 14 April, Prime Minister Koffi Sama opened formal negotiations in Brussels, which resulted in a **22 point commitment** to democratisation, with serious implications for domestic policies. The major pledges by the government, to be implemented within six weeks to twelve months, included full respect for basic democratic and human rights principles, reopening a credible dialogue with the opposition, revising the electoral and press codes in accordance with international standards, and new free, fair and credible parliamentary and local elections, to be supervised by international observers.

The opposition welcomed these commitments but was eager to participate in shaping the agenda for future inter-party talks to ensure that government would honour its pledges. However, Eyadéma resumed his tactic of dividing the opposition, which was facilitated by **rifts within and between opposition parties**. Thus, in February, the youth leader of the largest party, 'Union des Forces du Changement' (UFC), Daniel Koffi Aganon, attacked the allegedly autocratic leadership of his party, which, according to him, was treated as the personal fiefdom of its leader Gilchrist Olympio. Apparently, the UFC party congress had never been organised according to democratic principles. The same month, a controversy within the 'Comité d'Action pour le Renouveau' (CAR) resulted in the departure of 54 members, who accused the leader, Yawovi Agboyibo, of secret negotiations with Eyadéma to the detriment of the party's interests. The government split the opposition further by its differential treatment of so-called 'radical', 'traditional' and 'democratic' opposition parties. This was expressed, *inter alia*, by delaying the return of the passports of outspoken Eyadéma critics, such as the former president of the National Assembly, Dahukun Péré, and major opposition leaders such as Yaovi Agboyibo and Gilchrist Olympio. The latter was thus barred from entering the country. The UFC leader lived in exile most of the time because of several assassination attempts by security forces. The most serious attempt on his life, presumably orchestrated by Colonel Ernest Gnassingbé, one of the president's sons, happened on 5 May 1992 during the election campaign in the northern part of the country, when Olympio was badly injured and only just survived. When Olympio tried to enter the country in April 2003 to oppose Eyadéma in the presidential elections, his passport was confiscated. For these and other reasons, the 'traditional' opposition, comprising three major opposition parties – Olympio's UFC; CAR, represented by Yawovi Agboyibo; and the 'Convention des Peuples Africaines' (CDPA) led by Léopold Gnininvi – boycotted the opening on 27 May of the **national dialogue** by the government. However, smaller opposition parties like the 'Parti pour la Démocratie et le Renouveau' (PDR), 'Parti Socialiste Panafricain' (PSP) and 'Convergence patriotique panafricaine' (CPP) participated. To overcome the **deadlock**, Prime Minister Sama met delegates from all parties, including UFC, on 10 June, and the Togolese authorities issued a temporary travel permit to Olympio on 28 July. The inter-party talks, attended by all major players, resumed on 26 August, but were hampered by the domineering attitude of government and the lack of meaningful guarantees for the opposition that would permit fair discussions and balanced settlements of enduring conflicts. Finally, the 'national dialogue' was limited to a **'coalition of the willing'**, formed of the government, the ruling party, 'Rassemblement du Peuple Togolais' (RPT), the CPP of Edem Kodjo, Zarifou Ayeva's PDR, as well as some smaller Eyadéma-dependent opposition parties. Until 14 October, this coalition drafted a revised electoral code, the hotly disputed centrepiece of the debate from the beginning, and this was adopted by the government on 27 October. In early November it passed in parliament, where RPT had enjoyed a comfortable majority since the rigged elections of 2002.

Even before this, Lomé had tried to fulfil other parts of it pledges. On 24 August, parliament replaced the draconian press code of 2002 with a more liberal version. The 2002 code had threatened critical journalist with harsh penalties and imprisonment, and had also allowed for the arbitrary seizure of newspapers. In theory, press freedom was significantly improved by the new code, notably through the abolition of custodial sentences for defamation of the head of state but also through a law, passed on 30 September, reorganising the office for press regulation, 'Haute Autorité de l'Audiovisuel et de la Communication' (HAAC). The opposition as well as independent observers cautioned against undue optimism, in view of their past bad experiences, the continuance of politically motivated oppression and the regime's record of not being prevented by laws from violating fundamental human rights, where these laws ran contrary to its interest. In September, for example, Jean-Baptiste Dzilan, editor of the independent weekly, 'Forum de la Semaine', received anonymous death threats after publishing reports on the exiled opposition movement 'Mouvement Patriotique du 5 Octobre' (MO5) and on the possible retirement of the president. On 17 August, the president pardoned some 500 detainees, among them political prisoners whose existence government had constantly denied, on the grounds that they were considered to be ordinary criminals. However, the chances diminished that the government would get Brussels's approval of the **upcoming elections**. The traditional opposition made it clear beyond doubt that, under prevailing conditions, it would participate in the ballot only if the consensual 2000 electoral code, unilaterally amended by the RPT majority in favour of the ruling party in 2002 and 2003, was restored. Even so, on 22 December, Eyadéma announced in another surprising move the dissolution of the state assembly and new elections for the first half of 2005.

Apparently well-founded and oft-repeated rumours about the **poor health of Eyadéma** at the beginning of the year, first spread by the opposition in August 2003 because of his medical treatment in Italy but vigorously denied by government, continued to fuel speculation about the presidential **succession**. It was an open secret that the president favoured a dynastic succession by Faure, one of his sons, aged 38. The latter had already been installed as minister of public works, mines and telecommunications in June 2003. In addition, he had the backing of important generals in the military, who, like himself and his family, were of Kabyé origin. Later, he was put in charge of the family's private financial interests through, for example, the exercise to privatise parastatals such as the Bénin breweries, Wacem (cement), and the management of the phosphate mines. Even more importantly, his candidacy had already been enabled well beforehand by the revision of Article 62 of the constitution on the minimum age of presidential candidates, as part of the constitutional coup d'état of 30 December 2002. The principal aim of the latter was to guarantee the continuity of the Eyadéma dynasty by allowing a third term for the incumbent president, and at the same time disallowing exiled opponents of the Eyadéma regime who had not resident in the country for at least one year prior to the elections to stand as candidates for the presidency.

Whereas Togo profited in various ways from trade diversion and capital flight from Abidjan, the **Ivorian crisis** also had negative political impacts. The most dangerous of these was the apparent destabilising effects of the politics of exclusion in the political domain. The politics of xenophobia put into effect by vested interests in the Gbagbo regime under the rubric of 'Ivoirité' had spread effects. An early example of a comparable policy of **'Togolité'** was the constitutional revision of December 2002, mentioned above, that excluded exiled opponents as candidates for the presidency on the grounds that they were 'foreigners.' Another example was the government-sponsored policy of ethnic differentiation along the 'fault-line' of 'authentic', 'original' or 'true' Togolese. The latter were opposed to 'southern immigrants', 'stateless vagrants' and 'traitors', and the president's northern Kabiyé ethnic group (about 14% of total population) enjoyed a premium in terms of political and administrative representation, government expenditure and development aid. Thus, 70% of the **military** was of Kabiyé origin. According to the only credible data on the 'Forces Armées Togolaises' (FAT), provided by the 1991 National Conference, 17 of the 26 units of FAT were commanded by Kabiyé officers, among them ten commanders, including relatives of the Gnassingbé family, from Pya, the home village of Eyadéma. This was one reason why the army was nicknamed the 'army of cousins' by the population. This politically constructed ethnic divide was used to legitimate continued rule by RPT and the Eyadéma regime, who were portrayed as the sole political and military force capable of preventing warlordism or even civil war in the event of a power vacuum created by a potential regime change. However, the opposition repeatedly maintained that it was not ethnic antagonism that was the issue, but the illegitimate perpetuation in power of the Eyadéma dynastic clan, which occupied strategic posts not only in the military and security services but also in the economy.

The flawed **human rights** situation, one of the major reasons of the suspension of aid since 1993, improved slightly under the combined pressure of foreign donors and the opposition. The government sharply rejected as unfounded critical human rights reports by the US state department and the internationally renowned NGO, 'Fédération Internationale des

Droits de l'Homme' (FIDH), which published, 'Togo: Arbitrariness as Norm, and 37 Years of Dictatorship' on 9 June in Paris. The FIDH report accused the Eyadéma regime of serious human rights violations, including rigged elections, excessive use of force, torture, extra-legal execution and immunity, and pointed in sum to the great risk the country faced of being plunged into a cycle of violence and generalised chaos. The report was based on a fact-finding mission conducted by FIDH in collaboration with the independent local human rights organisation, 'Ligue Togolais des Droits de l'Homme' (LTDH) in February. Although the report referred mainly to past years, it major findings were still valid. Thus, PANA (Pan-African News Agency) reported on 12 May the imprisonment of ten UFC members, with jail terms ranging from one to seven years, for allegedly distributing anti-government pamphlets, criminal conspiracy and inciting violence. However, some human rights abuses were certainly due to the poor training and management of the security forces or the deficiencies in the corrupt judicial and law enforcement systems, such as poor prison conditions and the poor handling of demonstrations. The following incidents illustrate these circumstances. After the announcement of the gradual resumption of EU aid on 15 September, RPT organised a pro-government mass rally in Lomé, which grew out of hand when the crowd, as usual attracted by the prospect of a cash distribution to participants, rushed to the presidential palace, trampling 13 people to death and injuring over 200 others. In a similar incident one month before, during a football match between Mali and Togo in Lomé, four people were trampled to death.

Foreign Affairs

Following the recommendation of the African, Caribbean and Pacific countries (**ACP**) to resume aid to Togo during the sixth session of the EU-ACP parliament in November 2003, ACP sent a fact-finding mission, comprising ACP ambassadors, to Lomé in mid-March, which underscored this recommendation. Shortly after, the ACP initiative was matched by a high-powered **EU fact-finding mission**, comprising Anna Silvia Piergrossi (Italy), Arend Biesebroek (Netherlands), Stefan Frowein (head of the EU delegation in Ghana and Togo) and Klaus Grohmann (German ambassador to Togo, also representing Ireland on this mission). During its four-day discussions (1 to 5 June) with representatives of the government, relevant parties and civil society organisations, the EU team tried to assess the progress towards meeting the 22 commitments for democratic reform agreed to in Brussels on 14 April. In summarising its evaluation at the end of the mission, Piergrossi, the team's leader, expressed her hope that the government would do more, although it had "shown willingness and good faith to carry out some of the major reforms." The judgment of the European Commission, delivered at the end of the **three month consultation** period that started in April in accordance with the Cotonou Agreement of 2000, which regulated trade and development arrangements between the EU and ACP, was disappointing for Lomé. Brussels considered the failure to reach agreement with the traditional opposition on major issues such as the revision of the electoral code as a major constraint on the roadmap for democratisation and the normalisation of external relations with the donor community. Earlier, the EU had promised the resumption of aid, notably funding under the current 9th European Development Fund (EDF, worth € 40 m), on condition that free, fair and credible parliamentary elections would be held. As this was by no means guaranteed, Brussels considered the immediate release of only the outstanding funds from the 6th and 7th EDFs (1985–95), as well as expired STABEX funds (1990 to 1994), estimated to have a combined value of some € 12 m, to finance ongoing social sector projects and as motivation for the better implementation of the government's democratisation pledge. Notwithstanding this setback, continued close monitoring of the democratisation process over the next year was agreed upon, including formal reviews every six months.

However, in view of continuing political pressure from Paris, the EU decided on 15 November, much to the delight of the government in Lomé, to resume its cooperation, taking into account that at least some of the promised reforms had been implemented. Other EU member countries such as Germany, Great Britain and Spain had taken a less favourable view of the progress being made. Notably the German representatives were criticised by Eyadéma for their allegedly haughty attitude as 'proconsuls'. Berlin had been accused in government statements in September of favouring a partisan approach that was strongly influenced by the UFC, thus inciting the traditional opposition to radicalise its position. It was an open secret that the vested interests of the old friends of Togo within the 'messieurs Afrique' network, notably the personal friendship between French head of state Jacques Chirac and Eyadéma, contributed to the **growing dissonance between Paris and Berlin** over Togo. Even though as late as 31 August, the European Commission had adopted the roadmap with several built-in checks for the coming 24 months, it finally bowed to French 'pragmatic' reasoning and acknowledged the alleged merits of the Eyadéma regime regarding Togo's internal stability and its contribution to sub-regional conflict-prevention.

Well before the April negotiations in Brussels, Eyadéma had been welcomed to **Paris** for a nine-day friendly working visit, ending on 7 March. This included talks with Chirac. This visit took place after the extraordinary summit of heads of state of the African Union in Sirte, Libya. Strained relations with Burkina Faso prevented Eyadéma, who complained of the constant meddling of his Burkinabè counterpart in Togo's internal affairs, from taking part in the 10th Francophonie summit in Ouagadougou on 26 November. Apparently Paris did not consider his absence to reflect a lack of dedication to Francophone interests, as it once again praised the progress towards democratisation in Togo on 24 December in light of Eyadéma's earlier announcement (22 December) of the dissolution of parliament and early elections. The US state department, by contrast, remained critical, given past broken promises, notably on human rights issues.

In the **Ivorian crisis**, Togo continued to play an ambiguous role. The Togolese army contributed a large contingent to the ECOWAS peacekeeping force of some 1,300 troops, which were integrated into the UN-supervised peacekeeping force UNOCI in April for at least a year. Notwithstanding his dubious reputation as lifetime dictator, Eyadéma was shown respect as an elder statesman not only by the Ivorian head of state, his ally Laurent Gbagbo, but also the rebels of the north. The leader of the 'New Forces', Guillaume Soro, visited Togo for talks several times, and he was even in Lomé when the Ivorian government forces started their attack on the northern rebel strongholds. However, Franco-Togolese relations soured temporarily when it became known that Lomé was apparently used as port of transit for illegal arms to Abidjan. On 17 October, three weeks before the bombardment of French positions in Bouaké by the Ivorian air force, two Byelorussian MI-8 assault helicopters and two Mig 23 jets had been airlifted to Lomé airport, evidently the port of entry for arms to the Gbagbo regime. Lomé denied this accusation and assured the French ambassador, Alain Holleville, in mid-November that the combat aircraft would not be used to replace the Ivorian aircraft destroyed during the French counter-attack. Otherwise, Togo benefited from the Ivorian crisis both economically and politically. In the aftermath of the renewed civil war in Côte d'Ivoire, many refugees of French origin fled to Togo and were either evacuated via Lomé airport or tried to transfer their businesses from Abidjan to Lomé, thereby re-consolidating the close relationship with France. Moreover, the harbour and transport business in Lomé profited greatly from trade diversions caused by the Ivorian crisis.

The **Chinese** vice-president, Zeng Qinghong, was welcomed on 24 June by Eyadéma in Kara. This northern provincial capital, the president's stronghold and hometown, proudly displayed several prestigious projects such as the airport, the hospital and a large conference hall. All had been built with Chinese aid, and China also financed the new presidential palace, currently under construction in Lomé, and due for completion by the end of 2005. The Chinese leader signed a number of economic and technological cooperation agreements, including a preferential loan for the Adjarala hydroelectric project. On 16 September, **Japan** announced the cancellation of debts worth CFAfr 8.6 bn (about $ 14 m).

Bilateral relations with **Ghana** improved further, given the close personal ties between the two head of states, John Kufuor and Eyadéma. In February, Ghana agreed to keep the major border crossing to Lomé at Alafo permanently open. The same month, Kufuor refused to reissue a Ghanaian passport to Gilchrist Olympio, originally granted under the Rawlings government. Since the assassination of the first post-independence head of state of Togo, Sylvanus Olympio, by Eyadéma in 1963, the Olympio family has had asylum in Ghana and was entitled to Ghanaian passports, especially as the wife of Sylvanus had been Ghanaian. Thus, the collaboration between Accra and Lomé in depriving the opposition leader of his travelling documents to enter Togo was remarkable, especially in view of the fact that his original passport had already been confiscated by the Togolese authorities in 2003.

Socioeconomic Developments

Economic performance, with an estimated 3% **growth** of GDP, remained disappointing for several reasons. The continuing suspension of development cooperation by major donors for political reasons hampered important investment in infrastructure. Additional external effects, like the rise in oil and energy prices, also had a negative impact on consumption and investment. Moreover, labour disputes over delays in wage payments, which had started at the end of 2003, continued in the first month and impacted production, notably in the phosphate industry. Phosphate production decreased by about a quarter in the first five months to 466,000 tonnes. However, exports increased by 47% compared with the previous year due to a reduction in stockpiles. Although the EU decision of 15 November to resume aid was linked to political and economic conditions, the government hoped the EU would release € 12 m of EDFs immediately. These, in turn, could trigger the renegotiation of additional external debt relief as well as funding for the Poverty Reduction and Growth Facilities (PRGF) of the IMF. On 10 November, the council of ministers adopted the draft **budget** for 2005, proposing a slight increase in government expenditure of 1.5% to CFAfr 202.8 bn, based on the doubtful assumption that capital projects could be co-financed through a significant input of external aid. Most **UEMOA** convergence criteria and targets remained beyond the reach of government. Poor compliance was largely due to the decline in domestic revenue and unrealistic assumptions about external aid. Most affected were secondary convergence targets such as the fiscal revenue/GDP ratio and the wage/revenue ratio. The public wage bill was expected to grow to 39% of domestic revenue and public debt was estimated to remain at over 100% of GDP. Privatisation of remaining parastatals, notably phosphate mining (International Fertiliser Group, IFG-Togo), several banks and Togo Telecom, remained slow, not least because of the partisan interests of the political barons of the Eyadéma regime. According to a World Bank report on the global business climate entitled, "Doing Business in 2005" and published in October, Togo was one of the worst performers worldwide. Nevertheless, there was still room for prestigious projects like the foundation of a second university in Eyadéma's stronghold, Kara, on 23 January, with an initial enrolment of 1,000 students.

Another negative impact of the Ivorian crisis concerned the economics of health. Road traffic grew considerably because of traffic diversions, adding to the already high level of overland traffic in a country that is the traditional transit corridor for its landlocked Sahel neighbours and the neighbouring growth poles, Nigeria and Ghana. One side-effect of growing traffic was the spread of **AIDS**. Infection rates were 6%, among the highest in West Africa. According to UNDP research results, this rate is linked to the growing prostitution business with lorry drivers, who contribute to the rapid spread of the virus.

Dirk Kohnert

IV. Central Africa

The sub-region continued to undergo various crises, given the spill over from the Darfur conflict into neighbouring Chad and the Central African Republic (CAR) and the ongoing conflicts in eastern DR Congo and Burundi. Violent attempts to topple the regimes in Chad and Equatorial Guinea failed before they really unfolded. The simultaneous double-digit growth in the same two CEMAC countries was the most positive news. However, achieving the Millennium Development Goals by 2015 remained beyond the reach of all the countries in the sub-region. Once again, a particular concern in the region was the protection of the environment, more especially the forests of the Congo Basin. No particular progress was recorded in the area of democratisation.

Democracy

The few elections held in the sub-region did not lead to any changes. Presidential elections in **Cameroon** (11 October) resulted in a landslide victory for 71-year-old President Biya, at that time already 22 years in office. Faced with an opposition that was once again disunited, he succeeded in winning another seven-year term of office. Parliamentary elections in **Equatorial Guinea** (25 April) resulted in continued strong domination by the ruling 'Partido Democrático de Representantes del Pueblo' (PDGE). In alliance with seven smaller parties, PDGE gained 98 seats (of 100).

A constitutional referendum was held in the **Central African Republic** on 5 December, after one postponement. Some 87% of the voters approved the draft, which differed little from the suspended constitution of 1995, except that the prerogatives of the prime minister were augmented compared to the earlier document. The referendum allowed for a return to legal government after the violent overthrow of Ange-Félix Patassé in March 2003. In **Burundi**, the constitutional referendum was set for 14 December, but had to be postponed to 28 February 2005. The text of the consociational draft had earlier been adopted by parliament: it provided several mechanisms for minority (Tutsi) protection.

However, the biggest challenge in the realm of democratisation in the sub-region – namely, holding elections in the **DR Congo** in 2005 – was already a hotly debated subject. Would the elections be premature? Would they trigger further violence and exclusionary politics in the whole Great Lakes sub-region? Faced with continuing local armed conflicts and a largely absent state in most parts of the country, it was difficult to imagine how to guarantee sound preparations for the election.

The most democratic regime, São Tomé and Príncipe, was still recovering from last year's coup attempt. It remained the only country of the sub-region rated 'free' in the Freedom House survey. Six countries received the 'not free' label (Cameroon, Central African Republic, Chad, DR Congo, Rwanda and Equatorial Guinea – the last rated worst) and three 'partly free' (Congo, Gabon, Burundi). Only one country changed its ratings: CAR, which deteriorated with respect to political rights. In sum, the sub-region lagged behind the democratic achievements of other sub-regions in sub-Saharan Africa.

Human Rights

Only one country – **São Tomé and Príncipe** – got a more or less positive human rights rating by the US State Department in its yearly country reports on human rights practices. In those countries touched by civil war and its aftermath (Burundi, CAR and DR Congo, in particular), numerous human rights violations by different parties were recorded, but could be fairly easily explained. Background conditions were different in other cases. While the record was worse several years ago, **Cameroon** was still not free from severe human rights violations, e.g., the violent breaking up of protest marches by an opposition grouping demanding electoral reform. Moreover, a local official of the major opposition party was murdered, probably by request, by the guards of a traditional chief and MP. The country's prisons remained overcrowded and very poorly administered. Policemen were responsible for numerous exactions. The head of the national police in **Congo** was arrested during a private visit to France on grounds of severe human rights abuses before being set free, apparently after diplomatic interventions and pressure. The International Court of Justice (ICJ) gave the government until year's end to provide more persuasive arguments in the case of 359 persons who had disappeared after they returned from DR Congo in 1999.

The federation of Chadian unions claimed that security forces killed five labour union members during the coup attempt of 16 May, but this allegation was not confirmed by any other source. However, in light of numerous other reports of severe violations, **Chad** remained one of the countries with the worst human rights record in the sub-region.

Spectacular trials revealed further human rights problems in two countries of the sub-region. In **Equatorial Guinea**, the proceedings against alleged coup plotters of mostly foreign origin attracted international attention. Accepted standards were not respected, some statements were obviously obtained under torture and interpreters for non-native defendants were not available. One suspected coup plotter, a German citizen, died while in Black Beach Prison in Malabo. **Rwanda**'s former president, Pasteur Bizimungu, was sentenced to 15 years in prison after a trial that fell short of international standards of fairness, according to international NGOs like Amnesty International and Human Rights Watch.

War and Peace

The subregional context remained important in conflict-related developments in the Great Lakes region. The largest country in terms of population and territory, **DR Congo**, continued to experience widespread violence, despite the formation of a government of national unity. In the eastern part of the country, new fights between government troops and dissidents in May showed how fragile the peace process was and how difficult it would be to maintain peace both on a national level and between local armed groups fighting for local objectives. Rwandan support for dissident troops in South Kivu was further proof of the complicated nature of this conflict, with its transboundary dynamics. This was also underlined by a massacre of Congolese Tutsi refugees in **Burundi** in August (about 160 people were murdered), which sent shockwaves throughout the region. Constant fears of a renewed outbreak of major regional war persisted till the end of the reporting year, after bloody new fighting was recorded in North Kivu as well. Burundi was touched by this escalation, but had earlier witnessed another episode of increasing home-grown violence. Owing to combat between government troops and Hutu rebels from the 'Forces Nationales de Libération' (FNL) a further 10,000 people were internally displaced. On 5 June, a meeting of heads of state and government of the Great Lakes region took place in Dar es Salaam, and participants appealed to FNL to join the peace process in Burundi and asked for strict compliance with the Arusha Agreement. Significantly, the African (peacekeeping) Mission in Burundi (AMIB) was transformed into a UN peacekeeping mission (UNOB), following authorisation by the UN Security Council (21 May). This step was necessary for financial and logistical reasons. One hope for a peaceful future was the (admittedly difficult) continuation of the transition process in Burundi. By the end of the year, a programme to demobilise 55,000 fighters had begun. This development has to be seen in a broader context: on 25 October the governments of DR Congo, Rwanda and Uganda concluded a basic agreement, in terms of which each agreed to disarm groups operating from its respective territory against neighbouring states within a year. Doubts as to the political will of all three parties persisted, particularly since Uganda and Rwanda continued to deploy troops along their common border.

A major **international conference on the Great Lakes region** was a still more ambitious development. Requested by the OAU council of ministers as early as 1995 and supported since 2000 by the UN Security Council, the initial preparatory conference was held in June 2003 in Nairobi and was attended by national coordinators appointed by their respective heads of state. In the following months, bilateral consultations were held. The special representative of the UN Secretary General for the Great Lakes region, Ibrahima Fall, was seen as the main architect of this multifaceted process, while some of the approximately 30 donor countries and organisations involved, known as the 'Group of Friends' (co-chaired by Canada and the Netherlands) lost patience. The AU Commission finally set up a liaison office with the UN coordinating office in Nairobi in spring. Together, they formed the conference secretariat. The objective of the international conference held on 19–20 November in Dar es Salaam was to establish a regional framework for adopting a stability, security and development pact centred on four main areas: peace and security, democracy and good governance, economic development and humanitarian issues. The broadening of subjects beyond security issues was the main product of the long consultation process. Preparatory meetings took place in Bujumbura (September), Kinshasa (October) and Kampala (November). Additionally, ad hoc thematic meetings were held with the participation of representatives of women, young people and NGOs. In the course of this process, the number of core members increased from seven to 11 (Burundi, DR Congo, Kenya, Rwanda, Uganda, Tanzania and Zambia were the original group, with Angola, CAR, Congo and Sudan being added only in September). While nobody denied that past crises had major impacts on Angola, CAR and Congo (less so on Sudan), an outside observer may wonder why South Africa, a major player in the region, particularly in the Burundi peace process, was not involved. UN-Secretary General Kofi Annan, current AU Chairman Olusegun Obasanjo and AU Chairperson Alpha Oumar Konaré took part in the conference. A joint declaration of the 11 heads of state, aimed at ending the conflicts in the sub-region, was signed in Dar es Salaam on 20 November. As this was the first time that all the heads of state had officially met on these issues, the 13-page declaration was inevitably a compromise text, sidestepping the most delicate issues, including some of the root causes of the enduring conflict. However, the declaration contained many promises. Peace and security priorities included refraining from any acts, statements or attitudes likely to negatively impact national peace processes; fighting genocide in the Great Lakes region; and promoting common policies to end the proliferation of illicit small arms and light weapons. In the area of democracy and good governance, it was agreed to fight all discriminatory ideologies, policies and practices; promote policies of national unity based on multiculturalism, tolerance and the culture of peace and dialogue; and adopt deliberate policies and mechanisms for promoting gender equality at all levels and in all sectors. Regarding economic development and regional integration, the declaration contained a joint commitment to build a unified economic zone for enhanced economic efficiency and for the eradication of poverty; and to engage the international community to support the countries of the region in declaring the Great Lakes region a specific reconstruction and development area with a special fund for reconstruction. Finally, in the area of humanitarian and social issues, the declaration committed leaders to, *inter alia*, prohibit recruitment of children into the armed forces; establish a regional early warning and rapid response mechanism for natural and man-made disasters; and strictly comply with the obligations and principles of the Universal Declaration of Human Rights. An inter-ministerial committee was set up after the summit to develop a programme of action and work on protocols for implementing the Dar es Salaam declaration.

The prominence of this conference pushed the activities of the UN standing advisory committee on security questions in Central Africa into the background. In 2003, CEEAC/ECCAS states had asked for the establishment of a permanent UN structure in the region, while the UN Secretary-General had preferred the use of a special representative. On 24 June, the 21st ministerial meeting of the advisory committee met in Malabo for a routine meeting.

The Darfur crisis in Sudan had a major impact on Chad (further details of this crisis can be found in the chapter on Eastern Africa), which was felt from January onward. The ethnic background of one Darfur rebel movement represented the initial link: President Déby is from a sub-group of the Zaghawa community that can be found on both sides of the border. Déby's failed mediation efforts and his lukewarm support for the rebellion were believed to feature among the motives of the coup plotters who tried to topple his regime in May. The massive influx of refugees into Chad had even more marked effects, in particular on the eastern part of the country. CAR was touched to some extent as well, although news from the sparsely populated east rarely made its way to the capital Bangui.

UNHCR published a report on 'protracted refugee situations' (10 June), in which the total number of refugees in both the Great Lakes and Central African areas was estimated at about one million people (end of 2003), of whom 33% were not receiving assistance.

Socioeconomic Development

As noted by the IMF, per capita GDP growth was particularly strong in countries where oil production increased sharply: in Central Africa this meant Chad (+30.5%) and Equatorial Guinea (+34.2%, figures according to IMF's World Economic Outlook). Other countries were also above the 5.1% Africa average: DR Congo (6.8%), São Tomé and Príncipe (6%) and Burundi (5.5%), while Cameroon (4.3%), Congo and Rwanda (4% each), Gabon (1.9%) and CAR (0.9%) were well below that level. Oil was clearly the export commodity that attracted most attention during the year owing to the high price on the world market and the pronounced interest of US and Chinese firms in African oil. Intense exploration activity for new oil deposits was noted. **Gabon**, in particular, tried to compensate for its relative decline in oil production through new offshore development drillings.

At the same time, efforts to control income from oil business were accelerated. The **São Tomé and Príncipe-Nigeria Joint Development Zone** (JDZ) was brought under the Extractive Industries' Transparency Initiative (EITI) in June. **EITI** arrangements provide that companies and governments publish what they pay in order to check corruption and mismanagement. A revenue management law was developed by the government of São Tomé in collaboration with the World Bank and other international partners. The decision to remove the Republic of Congo from the **Kimberley Process Certification Scheme** (KPCS, an international certification scheme launched in 2003 and aimed at preventing trade in conflict diamonds) made headlines in July. This decision was based on the findings of a review mission, which assessed compliance with the certification scheme in May. The review mission to the Republic of Congo had the consent of the government in Brazzaville, and comprised experts from governments, NGOs and industry under South African coordination. The mission found that the government's system of controls was inadequate, poorly enforced and was therefore unable to prevent conflict diamonds (mainly of DR Congo origin) from entering the legitimate diamond trade. The move was interpreted as an indication of a zero tolerance approach to violations of the Kimberley code. Of the five countries of the sub-region listed in the 2004 **Corruption Perception Index** of Transparency International, four received bad ratings, with Chad the fourth most corrupt country in the world (followed closely by DR Congo, Cameroon and Congo), and with only Gabon achieving a more or less respectable ranking (74).

Consumer price inflation in the CEMAC countries remained satisfactory in the eyes of BEAC, which noted an annual inflation rate of 1.3% and only 0.3% at year's end (compared to an average 2.6% for the UEMOA area in West Africa, also based on the CFAfr). Only in Equatorial Guinea was a substantial increase in consumer prices noted, especially for transportation. The inflation rate in DR Congo, over 500% in 2000, was down to an estimated 6% in the reporting year.

The size of the informal economy was difficult to estimate. As a result of prolonged phases of violent conflict in about half the countries of the sub-region, war economies have developed and spread across boundaries, and involved trafficking in precious resources such as diamonds, gold, coltan and timber. An OECD Initiative for Central Africa (INICA) was established on 3 February "as a platform for discussion and action around people and groups active in cross-border initiatives" in Central Africa, and involved civil society, the private sector, churches, universities, NGOs, local and national authorities, regional institutions and donors. It held its first consultation meeting on 29 and 30 September in Paris. In July, INICA presented the work of French geographer Roland Pourtier on cross-border regions in Central Africa. The particular interest of this work was its highlighting of the parallel challenges and opportunities arising from the numerous cross-border dynamics in the sub-region.

HIV infection rates were still on the rise. Official figures provided by UNAIDS (for 2003) should be used with caution, but show significant differences between the hardest-hit country in the sub-region, CAR (13.5%), the middle reaches occupied by Gabon (8.1%), Cameroon (6.9%) and Burundi (6%), and relatively better-off countries such as Rwanda (5.1%), Congo (4.9%), Chad (4.8%) and DR Congo (4.2%). No data were available for São Tomé and Príncipe or for Equatorial Guinea. In fact, only Gabon and CAR were above the African average of 7.4 %, but this was hardly reason for satisfaction. Other **MDG**-relevant data demonstrated further difficulties. In Cameroon, a country with a relative abundance of natural water resources, only 63% of the population enjoyed access to an improved water source (2003 data). In the DR Congo, the incidence of tuberculosis was steadily climbing and stood at a staggering 368.8 per 100,000 inhabitants in 2003. This country, the largest in the sub-region and the most populous (53.2 m), also recorded most of the worst results against relevant poverty indicators. Only Burundi had a lower GNI per capita, at about $ 90 (DR Congo, $ 100). Among the poorer countries of the region, CAR received the least aid per capita, at only $ 12.8 (compared to $ 239.40 for São Tomé and Príncipe).

In December, the FAO published its report on the state of food insecurity in the world, and noted that Central Africa had the highest proportion of undernourished people (2000–02) of all sub-regions in the world, with 55% of the total population falling into this category, up from 53% in 1995–97. The DR Congo, with 71% of its population in this category, was the second most severely affected country in the world (after Eritrea). CAR (with 43%), Congo (37%), Chad (34%) and even Cameroon (25%) also still had poor records, but had improved compared to 1995–97.

Ecology

Second only to the Amazon region, Central Africa is the largest area of tropical forest on earth (670,000 km^2, but with a recorded decline of almost 1% yearly). An extraordinary meeting of COMIFAC ('Commission des Ministres en Charge des Forêts en Afrique Centrale' at that time, later renamed 'Commission des Forêts d'Afrique Centrale') was held in Yaoundé from 26–29 May, and asked the new executive secretariat to draft the text for an international convention. A second extraordinary meeting was held in Libreville on 30 September and adopted the text of a 'Traité sur la Commission des Forêts d'Afrique Centrale', which was to be submitted to a heads of state summit scheduled for January 2005. The donor coordination body, the Congo Basin Forest Partnership (CBFP), met in Brazzaville from 24–26 June to discuss funding and implementing COMIFAC's 'Plan de Convergence', including debt-for-nature swaps and trust funds. The EU continued to support the Programme for Conservation and Rational Utilisation of Forest Ecosystems in Central Africa, ECOFAC ('Ecosystèmes Forestiers d'Afrique Centrale'), by earmarking – 33 m for the 2005–08 period. ECOFAC was used in the past to draw up resource inventories, which showed the distribution of specific species, as the basis for further action. On 14 January, the European parliament requested that the programme be used more actively in relation to the poaching of wild animals and for the adoption of dissuasive measures and judicial sanctions against illegal trafficking in bush meat.

Sub-regional Organisations

The yearly **CEEAC/ECCAS** summit was held in Brazzaville (26–27 January) with presidents Sassou Nguesso, Bongo, Bozizé, Fradique de Menezes and Kabila attending, while the vice-president of Burundi, the prime ministers of Angola, Equatorial Guinea and Chad, the foreign minister of Rwanda as well as the president of the 'Conseil Economique et Social' of Cameroon represented their countries The agenda was once again dominated by questions of peace and security. The conference noted progress towards stability in most of the hardest-hit member countries in 2003 (São Tomé and Príncipe, Angola, Burundi, CAR, DR Congo and Rwanda). Four declarations were adopted (on the implementation of the NEPAD programme in Central Africa, the planned establishment of a free trade zone in 2007, HIV/AIDS and on the equality of men and women). The heads of state decided, upon request, to assist São Tomé and Príncipe in the field of defence and security.

A first workshop on the implementation of **NEPAD** in the sub-region was held on 14–15 October in Libreville (Gabon). Besides representatives of governments, parliaments, civil society and the private sectors of all the member countries, key development partners (World Bank, EU, UNDP, ADB etc.) were present. Wiseman Nkuhlu, chairman of the NEPAD steering committee, addressed the workshop. In comparison to other sub-regions, the ECCAS zone seemed to lag behind in the NEPAD process. The event provided the opportunity to review the main NEPAD programmes. Sectoral presentations were also given. It is noteworthy to recall in this context that the preceding ECCAS summit had mandated the ECCAS secretariat to serve as the focal point for implementing NEPAD in the region. This implied that the secretariat took precedence over the CEMAC framework, which nevertheless appeared more functional, particularly with regard to economic cooperation (e.g., existence of the franc zone and strong common institutions) and peacekeeping (e.g., FOMUC: 'Force multinationale de la CEMAC' in CAR). A key and telling work-shop recommendation was that member states move from dialogue to action in imple-menting NEPAD reforms.

As a consequence of the expulsion of Congo from the Kimberley process, the mines min-isters (or their representatives) of Angola, CAR, Congo, DR Congo and Gabon met in Brazzaville on 13–14 December. They adopted a Brazzaville Declaration, which recom-mended the creation of a sub-regional diamond control organisation as a 'specialised organ' of ECCAS. It was intended to be the first step towards the creation of a so-called 'Organisation Africaine du Diamant'. The ministers vowed to better track the circulation of diamonds and their control at frontiers and to fight against corruption and embezzlement in the sector. They stressed the need for better cooperation between their countries in imple-menting the Kimberley process. The Angolan minister of mines claimed that with an esti-mated annual production of 6 m carats, his country would lose about $ 1 m per day as a result of illegal trafficking.

On 17–18 December, a meeting of ECCAS defence and security ministers in Brazzaville agreed that each country would contribute € 122,000 to finance joint military manoeuvres. These would be the first manoeuvres of their type and were to be held in Chad in 2005. This decision flowed from an earlier decision to create a regional high command and a standby regional brigade of about 2,400 troops.

CEMAC leaders met in Brazzaville immediately after the ECCAS summit (28 January). Bongo, Bozizé, Obiang Nguema and the host Sassou Nguesso attended in person, but the Chadian head of state was represented by his prime minister, while the Cameroonian head of state was represented by the president of the economic and social council. The president of São Tomé and Príncipe participated as an observer. The major decisions concerned the adoption of a non-aggression, solidarity and mutual assistance pact, an extradition agree-ment, and an agreement on judicial cooperation between member states. A convention on the future parliament of the community was adopted. One important subject of debate was the envisaged sub-regional air transport company (**Air CEMAC**). The leaders decided to launch the issuance of the Community's passport, which had already been approved in 2002. Sample passports had been distributed to CEMAC heads of state in 2003, attesting to the rather slow pace of implementation. The competent CEMAC ministers met before year's end (4 December) and accepted, with some modifications, a Royal Air Maroc (RAM) proposal to be the strategic partner for the Community's airline. The ministers adopted a calendar for the negotiations with RAM.

Déby, Sassou Nguesso, Bozizé, Evuma Owono Asagono (special minister in Equatorial Guinea's president's office) and Ngoubeyou (foreign minister of Cameroon) took part in a second (this time extraordinary) summit in Libreville on 1 June. The summit was convened in the wake of the coup plots in Equatorial Guinea and Chad. The CEMAC leaders urged the international community to act against mercenary activities, which they described as a form of terrorism. Cameroon, Congo, Gabon and Equatorial Guinea were urged, and agreed to give financial support of CFAfr 2 bn to Chad in order to help the population living in the zone bordering on Sudan's Darfur province. Fears were expressed about the consequences of the Darfur crisis for Chad and CAR. The CEMAC leaders also noted progress in the evolution of the transition processes in CAR and in the DR Congo, a non-member country.

On 16 July, a roadmap for the negotiations on the Economic Partnership Agreement (EPA) between Central Africa – defined here as CEMAC plus São Tomé and Príncipe – and the EU was signed in Brussels by Gabonese Trade Minister Biyoghe Mba and European Commissioner Danuta Hübner. The whole Great Lakes region was apparently no longer considered to be part of Central Africa. Before 2003, the bigger ECCAS grouping was generally seen as the right framework for the negotiations. It was now decided that the Central African negotiation team would be presided over by the secretary-general of CEMAC, with the deputy secretary-general of ECCAS serving as only the co-presiding officer. Outside interference (by the EU) in the overlapping architecture of Africa's sub-regional organisations was plain to see. An indicative timetable and a work programme was annexed to the roadmap. The first technical meeting took place in Douala on 16 September to determine the working procedures, examine the preliminary studies and discuss priority issues. A senior officials' meeting took place in December. Discussions focused on the creation of a regional market (the Central African Free Trade Area, CAFTA), while critical onlookers feared this would facilitate the development of imports rather than the development of regional production capacity.

Andreas Mehler

Cameroon

In 2004, Cameroon maintained a remarkable degree of political stability, in spite of its stark ethnic and regional cleavages. One of the most significant events was the re-election of the incumbent Paul Biya as president. This will most probably result in the continuation of the national and international policies pursued since his assumption of office in 1982. A major setback for Cameroon's socioeconomic development was the government's failure to successfully implement the three-year poverty-reduction and growth programme prescribed by the Bretton Woods institutions and Western donors.

Domestic Politics

The major event on the political scene in 2004 was undoubtedly the **presidential election**. It was not until 11 September that a presidential decree announced the exact date of the election, namely 11 October. Presidential candidates had to deposit their files with the ministry of territorial administration and decentralisation (MINATD) for approval before 16 September. It was only then that the 'natural candidate' of the ruling 'Rassemblement Démocratique du Peuple Camerounais' (RDPC), the incumbent Paul Biya, in power since 1982, declared his candidature. In a television and radio message, the 71-year-old Biya justified his decision to run for another seven-year term on the basis of the popular appeals by internal and external groups, which he interpreted as a mark of trust. The 'Union Nationale pour la Démocratie et le Progrès' (UNDP) of Bella Bouba Maigari and the 'Union des Populations du Cameroun' (UPC) faction of Augustin Frédéric Kodock supported Biya's candidature, and together with the RDPC formed the so-called presidential majority.

The main **opposition alliance**, the 'Coalition pour la Reconstruction et la Réconciliation Nationale' (CRRN) was then also obliged to decide on its presidential candidate. The CRRN was formed in November 2003 following high-level negotiations between Cameroon's two largest opposition parties, the Social Democratic Front (SDF) and the 'Union Démocratique du Cameroun' (UDC). The coalition agreed to put forward a common candidate in the 2004 presidential poll and succeeded in attracting several smaller parties into its membership. During the course of 2004, it organised several protest marches for electoral reform, especially the computerisation of the electoral register, but it continued to postpone the selection of the 'unity' candidate for the presidential election until the last moment. On 15 September, a CRRN selection committee agreed upon the candidature of UDC leader Adamou Ndam Nyoya, whose electoral base scarcely extends beyond his home region, Bamoun. The SDF then withdrew from the coalition and fielded its own candidate, its chairman John Fru Ndi, who is the most prominent leader in anglophone politics and arguably the most significant opposition politician in Cameroon. The degree of division among the entire opposition was also visible in the number of candidates that submitted their files to MINATD before 16 September: 46, of whom 16 finally remained. Most prominent among those who were refused admission to the presidential race was Chief Pierre Mila Assoute, the former leader of the reformist wing within the RDPC, the so-called modernists. The reason given for his rejection was confusion over his party affiliation. Disappointed with the lack of support within the RDPC, Assoute resigned from the party before the presidential election and declared his candidacy for the presidency on a reform platform.

As was generally expected, the RDPC candidate Paul Biya proved overwhelmingly victorious in the 11 October election. On 25 October, the constitutional council proclaimed the **definitive results**. Biya was declared elected with 70.9% of the votes, followed by the SDF candidate Fru Ndi (17.4%), the CRRN candidate Ndam Njoya (4.4%) and the 'Alliance pour la Démocratie et le Développement' (ADD) candidate Garga Haman Adji (3.7%). The results were strongly contested by the opposition candidates, who insisted that the election was marred by massive fraud. The SDF claimed its candidate had won the election with 45% of the vote, against Biya's 43%. As in the 1992 presidential election, Fru Ndi accused Biya of "theft of his victory" and threatened to form a government of his own. Massive troop numbers were subsequently deployed to Bamenda, Fru Ndi's fief, to crack down on any demonstrations against the election results. On 3 November, Biya was sworn in as new president.

Election observers appeared to be divided on the conduct of the presidential poll. Some former US congress members and the delegation from the Francophonie described the election as free, fair and without hitches "huge enough to influence the outcome of the poll." Their view was supported by François-Xavier Mbouyom, the president of the national election inspectorate, the 'Observatoire National des Élections' (ONEL), and Rev. Joseph Mfochivé, president of the 'Féderation des Églises et Missions Évangélique du Cameroun' (FEMEC). Other observers, like the 'Féderation Internationale des Droits de l'Homme' (FIDH) and the 'Parti Socialiste' (PS) of France firmly condemned the conduct of the election, pointing to 'numerous irregularities'. In its report, the Commonwealth observer team stressed that "in a number of key areas the election process lacked the necessary credibility." It, nevertheless, claimed that the election results broadly reflected the wishes of those who had been able to vote. The leaders of the Roman Catholic church made contradictory declarations on the poll. In an interview with 'Radio France Internationale' (RFI), Christian Cardinal Tumi, archbishop of Douala, who is a noted critic of the regime, condemned the election as badly flawed due to disenfranchisement of voters (only half the country's estimated eight million eligible voters were on the electoral roll), multiple voting, stuffing of ballot boxes and intimidation of opposition representatives in the polling stations. Victor Tonye Bakot, archbishop of Yaoundé and president of the episcopal conference, by contrast hailed the election as a major step towards the consolidation of Cameroon's democracy (31 October).

There was a minor **cabinet reshuffle** on 23 April, when Biya sacked four ministers. The changes were clearly aimed at assuaging public opinion because they targeted ministries whose difficulties had sapped the government's popularity and credibility. Following the presidential election, on 8 December, another major cabinet reshuffle took place with a view to realising the newly elected president's proclaimed 'great ambitions'. The president not only increased the number of ministries from 32 to 36 but also appointed 60 ministers and secretaries of state – a record in Cameroonian history. Prime Minister Peter Mafany Musonge, who had been in office since August 1996, was replaced by Ephraim Inoni, the former deputy secretary general in the presidency. Both of them are Bakweri – an ethnic group in the South West Province of anglophone Cameroon. Some long serving ministers, like Joseph Owona, Hamadjoda Adjoudji and Meva'a M'Eboutou were sacked. The cabinet reshuffle clearly restored the Beti-Grand North hegemony: 20 members of the new cabinet are Beti, the president's ethnic group, and 17 members originate from the Grand North. Anglophone Cameroon appeared to be the big loser. No less than five anglophone ministers were dismissed. Besides the prime minister, there was only one full minister from anglophone Cameroon in the new cabinet. The North West Province of anglophone Cameroon, the stronghold of John Fru Ndi's SDF, was not given any ministerial position. Remarkably, the cabinet reshuffle re-created the super ministry of economy and finance in an effort to better coordinate the IMF-World Bank poverty-reduction and growth programme within the framework of the Heavily Indebted Poor Countries (HIPC) initiative (see below).

Under heavy pressure from international donors, the government began implementing some long-awaited **institutional reforms** to comply with the 1996 constitution. In its June-

July session, the national assembly passed legislation that set up a constitutional council, introduced a limited form of decentralisation in the country, and empowered the National Commission on Human Rights and Freedoms (NCHRF). The NCHRF, created by the Biya government in 1990, was to receive financial autonomy and freedom to publish annual reports by itself.

The **Anglophone problem** continued to worry the regime. In his new year's message, the chairman of the Anglophone secession movement, the Southern Cameroons National Council (SCNC), Chief Ayamba Ette Otun, called for an anglophone boycott of the presidential poll. On 2 January, he and another SCNC activist, James Sabun, were arrested in Mutengene. Again, on 1 October, a number of SCNC activists and paper sellers in the Tiko-Mutengene area were detained, and were charged with distributing tracts that called for a boycott of the poll. The split within the SCNC, already evidenced by the existence of some six factions, was aggravated when a newly formed faction led by Thomas Nwanchan had talks with the minister of justice, Laurent Esso, on 21–23 January and allegedly was promised a huge sum of money should it agree to abandon the struggle. In January, Boniface Forbin, the publisher of 'The Herald', a private English-language newspaper, launched a new political party, the Justice and Development Party (JDP), whose main aim was to fight for the rights of anglophone Cameroonians. Standing as a candidate in the presidential election, he enjoyed little support in anglophone Cameroon. A great loss to the anglophone cause was the death on 12 July of Albert Mukong, a renowned opponent of the Ahidjo and Biya regimes, SDF founding father, ex-SCNC leader and retired human rights activist (former director of the Human Rights Defence Group).

After having been classified in two succeeding years, 1998 and 1999, as first on the list of **most corrupt countries** in the world, Cameroon has since somewhat improved its position. It moved up from ninth position last year to sixteenth position in the October 2004 report of Transparency International. While this may please the regime, the ordinary Cameroonian hardly noticed any amelioration in the widespread corruption.

Cameroon's **human rights record** has improved in recent years but remains flawed. National and international human rights organisations have reported renewed instances of violations of civil and political rights as well as of torture, and they continued to condemn the poor prison conditions in 2004. There was an increase in the number of incidents of repression and harassment against members of the opposition in advance of the presidential election. The CRRN's protest marches for electoral reform were mostly violently broken up. The chief of Balikumbat in North West Province, who is a RDPC parliamentarian and notorious for his ruthless behaviour towards political opponents, was held responsible by the SDF for the murder in August of John Kohtem, a local journalist and SDF district chairman. The SDF organised protest marches in Bamenda calling for a full investigation of the incident. Later on, 11 suspects were arrested, but the chief, who continued to deny any involvement, was not among them. Human rights activists have pointed out that the Kohtem murder follows the pattern of traditional chiefs' intimidating, torturing and detaining opponents of the RDPC while the authorities turn a blind eye. Another serious civil rights violation occurred during the presidential poll, when Ndi Richard Tanto, an election observer on behalf of the 'Service Oecuménique pour la Paix' was brutally beaten up by the police when he expressed his disapproval of their obstructive behaviour at a Bamenda polling station.

The minister of communication, Fame Ndongo, made various attempts to control **the media** in the run-up to the presidential election. In January, he closed twelve independent radio and television stations in the southwest of the country suspected of supporting the opposition. In the wake of a widespread rumour in early June that President Biya had died, a rumour that caused great panic among the population for fear of imminent ethno-regional unrest and a violent succession struggle, he formed a special unit within his ministry to monitor internet sites and track media coverage of events in Cameroon. In September, he ordered private radio and television stations not to broadcast any propaganda campaigns by presidential candidates. Following the presidential election, he blamed the RFI for partiality in its coverage of the election.

Foreign Affairs

The relations between Cameroon and **Nigeria** continued to be determined largely by their border adjustments in the wake of the October 2002 International Court of Justice (ICJ) verdict. Some progress was made on 13 July when there was an exchange of three border villages in the Lake Chad area. Nigeria acquired the villages of Bourba-Wango and Ndabakura and Cameroon took ownership of the nearby village of Narka. This latest border adjustment followed Nigeria's return of 33 villages near Lake Chad in December 2003. On that occasion, Nigeria received one Cameroonian village in return. However, the most delicate part of the ICJ verdict, the transfer of the oil-rich Bakassi peninsula to Cameroon, has still to be implemented. Under a working plan drawn up in 2003 and approved by the UN Secretary-General Kofi Annan and the heads of state of both countries during a tripartite meeting in Geneva on 31 January – the third of its kind – Nigeria was to withdraw its forces from Bakassi by the end of May. But at the 11 February session of the Cameroon-Nigeria Mixed Commission – a body set up by the UN to implement the ICJ verdict and chaired by UN Special Representative for West Africa Ahmedou Ould-Abdallah – Nigerian members requested a revision of the ambitious timetable, and a deadline of 15 September for the transfer of sovereignty over the peninsula to Cameroon was agreed upon. Nonetheless, Nigeria failed to respect the new deadline, citing technical problems. Nigerian authorities referred particularly to the vehement resistance by the majority Nigerian population on Bakassi to Cameroonian rule. On 25 September, the Nigerian House of Representatives called for a UN-organised plebiscite on Bakassi to decide upon an eventual transfer to Cameroon. Although the presidents of both countries pledged their commitment to a peaceful solution to the problem at their meeting in Yaoundé on 28 July, Cameroon and the

UN began to express their impatience with Nigeria's foot-dragging over withdrawal from the disputed peninsula during the October session of the mixed commission in Abuja.

Relations between Cameroon and **Equatorial Guinea** sunk to an all-time low at the beginning of March following the expulsion of over 1,500 Cameroonians from Equatorial Guinean territory in the aftermath of an attempted coup. The government of Equatorial Guinea tried to justify its action by alleging that the mercenaries involved in the coup attempt had a training camp in Cameroon. Reports of the ill-treatment of expelled Cameroonians caused a public outcry in Cameroon, prompting President Biya to recall Cameroon's ambassador to Equatorial Guinea on 16 March. Following visits by the Equatorial Guinean minister of foreign affairs, Pastor Miche Ondo Bilé, and President Obiang to Cameroon on 23 March and 11 April respectively, calm was restored between the two countries. Relations between both countries have also been strained by Equatorial Guinea's apparent support for Nigeria in the border dispute with Cameroon.

The inauguration of the **Chad-Cameroon pipeline** in Kribi on 12 June was hailed by the Cameroonian authorities as a manifestation not only of growing cooperation between Cameroon and Chad, but also of regional integration. Present at the occasion were the following presidents: Biya (Cameroon), Déby (Chad), Obiang (Equatorial Guinea), Bozizé (Central African Republic) and, unexpectedly, Compaoré (Burkina Faso). There was also a delegation from Congo-Brazzaville. Conspicuously absent was President Bongo from Gabon, undoubtedly due to the longstanding rivalry between the two neighbours.

The official visit of King Mohamed VI of **Morocco** at the end of June was aimed at strengthening relations between the two countries. Other points of discussion were the Western Sahara question and the wish of Morocco to reintegrate into the continental organisation.

Cameroon's relations with **Western countries**, the major donors to its development programmes, are generally good. Despite regular allegations of corruption, human rights abuses and stalled political reforms, most Western donors believe that they can exert a positive influence through cooperation. France remains Cameroon's foremost ally in the West, while Britain and the US regard President Biya as an increasingly valuable asset as the 'war on terror' takes on a West and Central African dimension. There was a temporary cooling of the usually excellent relationship between President Biya and French President Chirac on the eve of the Iraq war, when the Cameroonian president visited the White House on 20–21 March 2003. Chirac was inclined to interpret this visit as a manifestation of Cameroon's support for America's pro-war policy and its shift from the French sphere of influence to the Anglo-Saxon world. This interpretation appeared to be confirmed when Biya made an official visit to London on 24–25 February 2004. Subsequently, Biya kept trying to no avail to mend fences with Chirac. Chirac refused him an audience during the two-day Niger Basin Authority summit in Paris in April. Nevertheless, there are signs that Chirac intends to be reconciled with Biya. The French president rushed to congratulate Biya after his victory in the October presidential elections, even before the official proclamation of the results. In his congratulatory message, Chirac expressed the wish that Cameroon and France would strengthen the bonds of friendship and cooperation that have existed between both countries over the years.

In **Asia**, China and Japan remained the principal partners in Cameroon's development efforts. Japan made a major contribution to educational expansion in Cameroon, and China laid the first stone in the construction of a sports palace (6 August).

What is difficult to understand is the almost complete absence of any active Cameroonian diplomacy at the **sub-regional and continental level in Africa**. Since 1996, the year that he was elected head of the OAU in Yaoundé, President Biya has not attended any summit of the pan-African organisation. In July, he lived up to his reputation when he failed to attend the third summit of the African Union in Addis Ababa. Biya was also absent when Cameroon and the other five members of the CEMAC signed a non-aggression and solidarity pact in Brazzaville in January. The treaty, which included a mutual assistance clause, was intended to make CEMAC a more effective body for preventing conflict and maintaining peace and security in the sub-region, committing its signatories to contribute to an intervention force when the need arose. Biya's practice of sending subordinates to represent him at meetings of sub-regional and continental organisations was said to irritate his peers.

Socioeconomic Developments

The Cameroonian **economy** was marked by steady growth (5.1% in 2004) and a stable inflation rate (1–2%). Constant annual growth rates, however, are not yet reflected in a noticeable improvement in employment creation and poverty reduction. In fact, economists appear now to be less optimistic about the possibility of sustainable development than a few years ago. This is mainly due to the fact that Cameroon has failed to successfully implement the fiscal and structural adjustment programme prescribed by the Bretton Woods institutions and Western donors. On 30 August, Cameroon was declared 'off-track' by the IMF for its repeated failure to reach the 'point of achievement' of a three-year Poverty Reduction and Growth Facility (PRGF) within the framework of the Heavily Indebted Poor Countries (HIPC) initiative, which was due to expire in December 2004. The immediate consequences were that the donor agencies could no longer open lines of credit to the government and that a substantial external-debt relief, amounting to $ 2.3 bn (of an estimated total external debt of more than $ 6 bn) could not be granted. Henceforth, a substantial proportion of the annual budgets must be used for external-debt service (28% in 2005). As a result of these developments, relations between the IMF and the Cameroonian government deteriorated to a point where the resident representative of the IMF returned to Washington unceremoniously. Following a meeting between the director of the African department of the IMF,

Abdoulaye Bio-Tchane, and Prime Minister Peter Mafany Musonge on 29 October, both parties declared themselves ready to resume talks. On this occasion, the IMF director made it clear that before a new PRGF could be negotiated, the government would be required to demonstrate its commitment to fiscal discipline, to expanding its non-oil revenue base and to structural reform – the main aims of the now-lapsed PRGF – by pursuing a staff-monitored reference programme for six months. An IMF mission was in the country from 3 to 18 December to assess the state of the economy and to discuss the modalities and content of a reference programme for 2005.

In its IMF-inspired **budget for 2005**, amounting to CFAfr 1,721 bn and approved by the national assembly on 17 December, the government made a determined attempt to raise its non-oil revenues by introducing new taxes and augmenting existing ones, including an increase in the value-added tax from 17 to 17.5%. Additional revenues thus acquired will be used for investment in priority sectors, notably health, education, infrastructure and rural development, as well as for servicing internal debts. Oil revenues, however, continue to contribute more than a quarter of the budget. The steady decline in crude oil production (from 35 m barrels in 2003 to 32 m barrels in 2004) was more than compensated for by high world market prices. Cameroon was also fortunate that in 2004 there was not only an increase in output but also favourable prices on the world market for its other main export commodities – timber, cocoa, cotton, aluminium and coffee.

One of the reasons for the IMF's growing discontent with the government's performance was the slow pace of the **privatisation process**. Privatisation, however, created a number of technical and sociopolitical problems, which were largely responsible for the lack of progress in this field. The Cameroon Development Corporation (CDC), a huge agro-industrial parastatal in anglophone Cameroon, was a case in point. The privatisation of CDC has been regularly postponed because of fierce resistance from the Bakweri ethnic group in the Fako division, who claim ownership of the CDC lands. The so-called Bakweri Land Claims Committee (BLCC) has brought up the matter with the African Commission on Human and People's Rights, and in May this commission urged President Paul Biya to cause the suspension of "the alleged detrimental alienation of the disputed CDC lands in Fako pending a decision on the matter by the African Commission." The CDC used to have four sectors: banana, rubber, palm oil and tea. So far it has been able to sell only its tea estates, to a South African holding company, Brobon Finex Pty in October 2002. The new company, the Cameroon Tea Estates (CTE), is also experiencing a variety of problems. On 15 January, the CTE management laid off 585 workers "in a bid to reduce the company's cost of production which has soared to an unbearable level." On 18 June, its first general manager, John Niba Ngu, who was soon fired by the company's board of directors for unilaterally sacking 23 top management staff appointed by Brobon Finex, instituted legal proceedings against CTE and the Cameroonian state in the International Court of Arbitration in Paris for his alleged entitlement to 5% of the company's shares, claiming CFAfr 7.8 bn as damage.

The American company, AES-Sirocco Corporation, which took over the 'Société Nationale d'Électricité' (SONEL) in 2001 for $ 69 m, failed to keep its promise to guarantee an uninterrupted electricity supply in 2004. Various parts of the country suffered regular power cuts, leading to a reduction in economic output and various hardships to consumers. As a result, the American general manager, Helen Tarnoy, was replaced in March by a Cameroonian, Jean-David Bilé, the former assistant general manager. In July and August there were protests in Bamenda organised by the SDF against the 'excessive price' of electricity supplied by the company.

The Cameroonian government was happy when it finalised one of the most complex privatisations in 2004. On 28 June, the container terminal of the autonomous port of Douala was taken over at a price of about CFAfr 15 bn by a consortium consisting of Maersk (31%), Bolloré (28%) and certain Cameroonian enterprises.

Transport between anglophone and francophone Cameroon was seriously affected when a fuel tanker crashed on the Mungo bridge on 1 July, leading to the dramatic collapse of the historic crossing point between the two Cameroons and severe economic losses. It was not until 31 August that Prime Minister Peter Mafany Musonge officially opened a temporary bridge across the Mungo.

Long-standing problems at the **Postal Savings Bank** caused it to become insolvent in January. The bank could not pay its depositors, who were said to have CFAfr 45 bn with the bank. Although the bank controls only a small fraction of total deposits in the country, its difficulties affect many small savers, especially in the rural areas where there are few commercial banks. The government's rescue package for the bank involved the creation of the Cameroon Postal Company to take over the bank's operations and run it along with the national postal system, and the setting up of a special treasury account of CFAfr 60 bn to improve postal services and cover the bank's liability to depositors.

Following political liberalisation in the early 1990s, a large number of autonomous **teachers' trade unions** have emerged in the country and have been displaying a high degree of militancy. On 12 May, these trade unions and their federations decided to form a common front. The newly formed National Coordination of Teachers' Trade Unions in Cameroon is expected to tackle the enormous problems facing the educational sector, to fight for a substantial improvement in its members' deplorable living and working conditions and to force the government to adopt trade union legislation that conforms with international norms. One day after World Teachers' Day, on 6 October, the national coordination body initiated a series of intermittent strikes to bring pressure to bear on the government to increase the teachers' various allowances and to finally sign the texts bringing into effect the special teachers' statutes. On various occasions, **university students**, too, have protested against their increasingly precarious living and working conditions.

Western NGOs have become increasingly concerned about **environmental problems** in Cameroon. A major contribution towards responsible forest management was made at the end of April when the World Wide Fund for Nature coerced two foreign logging companies, Vedeka and Decolvenaere, to sign an agreement ensuring that timber in Cameroon is exploited and sold with strict regard for the forestry law. In a report published by Global Witness in July, the level of over-exploitation by companies active in the forest sector was exposed.

Piet Konings

Central African Republic

Insecurity in large parts of the country and its containment was the main feature of domestic and foreign affairs and of socioeconomic developments. In its face, management of the transition after the coup of 2003 proved particularly difficult. A constitutional referendum and preparations for elections necessitated massive outside support.

Domestic Politics

The spread of zones of insecurity in the countryside, attributed not only to the so-called 'Zaraguina' highway robbers (or 'road-blockers') but also to **former 'liberators'**, became a major source of concern. The latter group was comprised of the combatants who helped General François Bozizé seize power in 2003. These frequently undisciplined troops, most of Chadian origin, became racketeers among Bangui's residents. The episcopal conference on 13 January condemned numerous acts of violence perpetrated by "armed men in uniforms". Businessman Sani Yalo, linked to several financial scandals, and his brother Colonel Danzoumi Yalo, former security advisor to Bozizé and close to the liberators, were accused of preparing a coup d'état and transferred to a military camp: they were set free by court order in March. An exchange of gunfire between ex-liberators and government soldiers occurred on 17 April leaving eight to ten people dead. Individual houses in two Bangui neighbourhoods were looted in the ensuing days. After difficult negotiations, and with the help of the Chadian ambassador, about 200 ex-liberators agreed to be accompanied to the border with Chad, and others to integrate into civilian life after being paid undisclosed additional allowances (probably CFAfr 300,000 each). The government had started a $ 13 m Disarmament, Demobilization and Reintegration (DDR) programme with UNDP and World Bank support in February to integrate up to 7,565 former combatants.

Significantly, Bozizé met with Danzoumi Yalo during the crisis in April. In July, there were reports of some success in combating bandits on the northern border after the government deployed about 200 French-trained soldiers. An attack on Birao (northeast) on 20 November, with 21 deaths, was attributed to combatants of the Sudan People's Liberation Army. The **climate of fear** was reinforced by the regime itself, which alluded to the existence of mysterious coup plots. The Human Rights League, 'Ligue Centrafricaine des Droits de l'Homme' (LCDH) alleged that Bozizé exploited these rumours to reinforce his power. Even the army's high command was suspected of plotting a coup: the home of vice-inspector general Mazi was searched for weapons on 23 November.

In February, the provisional legislative body **'Conseil National de Transition'** (CNT) condemned the Bozizé government for malpractices, after it was not consulted on an important budgetary ordinance. This marked the end of the period of broad public endorsement. The CNT was gradually transformed into an openly oppositional body, with its president, Nicolas Tiangaye, the former leader of the LCDH, emerging as a strong defender of democratic principles. However, Bozizé's behaviour increasingly showed that he would stick to his position. Pro-regime demonstrations (on 19 June with 5–10,000 participants) prepared the way for the announcement of his candidacy for the upcoming elections.

Preparations for the elections started late. The installation of a mixed, independent electoral commission on 24 May was not initially on the government's agenda but was fought for by CNT: 10 representatives each from political parties, civil society and the administration were to make up the body. A compromise was necessary on the 10 disputed party seats: three seats for the 'Coordination des Partis Politiques de l'Opposition' (CPPO) platform, two for the 'Union des partis politiques pour la reconstruction nationale' (Uparena), one for the 'centrists' and four for individual parties. The registration of voters started only in October. Initially, the government wanted to submit its own draft text for the referendum. After protests, Bozizé agreed to submit a compromise text closer to the CNT's wishes. Both drafts were based on the suspended 1995 Constitution and the conclusions of last year's national dialogue. The most important changes concerned the shorter presidential term of five years (instead of six) and extended the prerogatives of the prime minister and his responsibility to the national assembly. All major political parties appealed for a yes vote in the **referendum**, which was postponed briefly from 28 November to 5 December. The text was approved by 87.2% of the voters – according to corrected figures provided by the newly appointed transitional constitutional court, after the invalidation of some results – and the participation rate was 77.4%. Technical problems were widespread.

Bozizé announced another postponement of **presidential and legislative elections** from 30 January to 13 February 2005. Besides Bozizé, ex-Presidents André Kolingba and Ange-Félix Patassé, Vice-President Abel Goumba, ex-Prime Ministers Jean Paul Ngoupande and Martin Ziguélé, ex-Defence Minister Jean Jacques Demafouth and others announced their intention to participate. Patassé and Demafouth both had actions pending against them at year's end and were expected to be excluded from the race by court order. Surprisingly, on 30 December the transitional constitutional court rejected most applications on mainly formalistic grounds, and only Bozizé, Kolingba, Goumba, the lawyer Henri Pouzère and ex-minister Auguste Boukanga were allowed to stand. This led to immediate angry reactions by those excluded: they asked Bozizé to annul the decision and dissolve the court.

A major **cabinet shuffle** occurred on 2 September after Finance Minister Jean-Pierre Lebouder, a former IMF official appointed in December 2003, had resigned in August (see below). The main change was the reduction of the number of ministries (from 28 to 24), while Lebouder was replaced by his deputy, Daniel N'ditifeï-Boysembé. Bozizé's outspoken information minister and former key ally, Parfait M'bay, was transferred to the agriculture ministry. Prime Minister Gaombalet retained his post.

Debates within the former governing party **'Mouvement pour la Libération du Peuple Centrafricain'** (MLPC) were intense and divisions became visible. With some important members under house arrest or in exile, resentment against the government rose. At the same time, an 'original trend' ('courant original') was formed and clearly supported Bozizé. From his exile in Togo, deposed President Patassé managed to be selected as an official candidate for the MLPC on 20 November. The ambitious former speaker of parliament and MLPC vice-president, Luc Apollinaire Dondon Konamabaye, who had himself boycotted this general assembly, expelled ten members of the party for "disrespect", "treason" and other misdeeds at year's end. Among those expelled were former speaker of parliament Hugues Dobozéndi and Désiré Péndémou, two initiators of the 'courant original'. Patassé's chances of winning another election were limited. His original power base was far bigger than his Sara-Kaba ethnic group, but he now suffered important defections. Bozizé, himself once a Patassé supporter, set about persuading the important electorate of the Gbaya ethnic group, who had voted massively for MLPC in the past.

The government continued to harass the **independent press**. The editor-in-chief of the weekly 'L'Hirondelle', Judes Zosse, was sentenced to six months imprisonment and fined for insulting the head of state (12 March), while the director of 'Le Citoyen', Maka Gbossokotto, was arrested on 8 July for allegedly defaming a former director of a parastatal company. Strike action by all the independent media and condemnation by several political parties followed; Gbossokotto was given a suspended prison sentence of one year.

Finally, on 26 November, the CNT passed an ordinance on the freedom of the press suppressing all imprisonment penalties for press crimes.

Foreign Affairs

Two constant aims shaped the foreign policy of the government: the search for recognition and fresh money and freedom from outside destabilisation. Bozizé travelled to **Libya** (26 June) to rebuild confidence, since Libya had sided with Patassé during the violent 2001–03 era, including by sending military aircraft. A visit to **Sudan** (25 July) was chiefly motivated by the impact of the civil war in the neighbouring country. The Sudanese press reported that President Omar al-Bashir offered his counterpart a free-trade zone on the Red Sea during their meeting in Khartoum. The Birao incident (see above) shed light on the potential dangers emanating from Darfur.

On 8 January, the **UN Secretary-General** was quoted as being "gravely concerned by the re-emergence of acts of rape, hold-ups and violations of the right to life," and two weeks later the UN Security Council urged the authorities to carry out reforms that would allow elections to take place according to the agreed timetable. The Security Council later welcomed the secretary general's intention to renew the mandate of the UN Peace-Building Office (BONUCA) until 31 December 2005.

The **CEMAC** peacekeepers – about 380 from Gabon, Congo and Chad – remained in the country. Bozizé attended the CEMAC summits in Brazzaville (28 January) and Libreville (1 June), as well as the CEN-SAD summit in Bamako on 15 and 16 May. Here, the heads of state, "convinced of the irreversible character of the process of restoring democracy and the rule of law," requested the authorities of the AU to allow the participation of the CAR "at an appropriate level" in the forthcoming statutory meetings. AU's president, Alpha Oumar Konaré, visited Bangui (9 March) and advised Bozizé not to stand for election in 2005. The head of state thereafter openly accused Konaré of interference. In an interview with 'Radio Centrafrique', Konaré noted that the AU would be prepared to open an office in Bangui after a successful transition process. African foreign ministers, meeting ahead of the 3rd AU summit in Addis Ababa, recommended against readmitting the Bozizé government pending the restitution of constitutional legality (the AU had excluded Bangui from participation after the coup in March 2003, in accordance with its Constitutive Act).

CAR's main European partner, **France**, reinforced her presence. Vice-Admiral Giraud, director of military and defence cooperation in the French foreign office, visited the army's barracks and was received by Bozizé on 14 January. He handed over 46 vehicles, plus equipment worth $ 3.2 m. Military trainers and support for the CEMAC troops would continue – meaning that about 200–300 French troops would stay in the country. Additionally, Sudan, Morocco and China engaged in military training. Bozizé took part in the celebrations marking the sixtieth anniversary of France's liberation in 1944. Bozizé thereafter visited China (19–23 August) and was praised for his 'One China policy' by the official media.

Previous CAR governments had frequently switched sides between China and Taiwan. The main subjects discussed were the export of timber and diamonds, budget support and military cooperation, including sale of weapons. On his way back home, Bozizé stopped in N'Djaména (**Chad**) where he had a short meeting with President Déby. A government delegation left for N'Djaména on 24 April to discuss matters related to the talks between the authorities and the former liberators. Moreover, about 27,000 **refugees** from CAR lived in southern Chad. On the other hand, some 37,000 refugees in CAR were set to return to Sudan. Refugees from the Yakoma ethnic group who fled after the bloody coup attempt in 2001 to Congo Brazzaville returned in March. There were still thought to be refugees from this episode in the Democratic Republic of Congo (DRC). About 10,000 Congolese refugees in CAR were set to be repatriated by end of the year.

Haiti's President **Jean-Bertrand Aristide** (plus his wife and his brother) were expelled to Bangui in a joint action by US and French intelligence services. Bozizé only agreed to accept Aristide when the plane was already on its way. He was granted asylum by the authorities on 1 March at the request by Gabon's President Bongo, who had earlier refused to host Aristide. The latter soon gave interviews that were adjudged to be problematic by the authorities, since he claimed to be the victim of a coup d'état and a modern version of kidnap. Part of the Central African Republic's elite wanted Aristide to leave quickly, while the government hoped to win material favour from important donors by keeping him for a longer period. Speculation that Pretoria would be his final destination was fuelled by the visit of South Africa's deputy foreign minister, Aziz Pahad, on 10 March. Eventually, Aristide left for Jamaica on 14 March. It is unclear whether the various demands of the CAR government were met by the US administration. In January, Washington took CAR off the list of eligible countries for the African Growth and Opportunity Act (AGOA), because of lack of progress towards free trade and poverty reduction. This step was interpreted as strong disapproval of the military takeover in March 2003.

Socioeconomic Developments

For many years the salary arrears for civil servants had been accumulating. The government announced that it would not be able to pay **civil service wages** in early January, a week later it transferred the October 2003 salary and on 31 May the equivalent of about two months of salaries. A joint IMF and World Bank mission in January led to the identification of priority actions. Better fiscal control and tight customs control of road links to Cameroon were called for, and customs exemptions not prescribed in the CEMAC framework were to be removed. Also recommended was a general suspension of recruitment into the civil service (with the exception of the health and education sector). A major gain in transparency was expected from the publication of all applications for exploitation permits in the timber and mining sectors. A new mining code was adopted on 4 February, but did not meet all the IMF's expectations. The new law gave government the right to be directly involved in buying and export activities. Soon after, government decided to cut the salaries of senior civil servants by 30%. This was a highly unpopular move, since extended families live on these salaries. The CPPO as well as major trade unions rejected the decision. School-teachers went on strike and asked for the payment of the last three months of their salaries. University students protested violently against the non-payment of their allowances and their bad working conditions. An agreement between government and the major unions was reached in mid-April when government committed itself to pay salaries regularly and to be transparent about state revenues.

On 3 May the government proclaimed a series of **austerity measures** within the framework of the 2004 budget that expected lower revenues (−12%) and lower expenses (−11%). Among the particular measures to fill state coffers were sanctions against companies refusing to pay taxes and the introduction of VAT for diplomats and NGOs.

After concluding its Article IV consultation in April, painting a very sobering picture of the economy (GDP shrinkage by 7% in 2003, fiscal revenue decline by 30%, etc.), the IMF approved a credit of SDR 5.57 m in **emergency post-conflict assistance** to stabilise the macroeconomic situation, support the ongoing reform process and catalyse external assistance. A rather optimistic assessment of the current reform trend led to this decision. It hinged on the authorities' plans to strengthen public expenditure management and to maintain strict control on non-priority spending. When Finance Minister Lebouder resigned in late August, a shock wave struck the relevant departments in the international finance institutions. According to the IMF, the country has not been servicing its external debt for almost two years (external debt servicing amounted to CFAfr 563 bn). The CAR has not qualified for debt relief under the HIPC initiative due to persistent instability. In addition to arrears to internal suppliers (CFAfr 93 bn), the state's debt to the national banking system was CFAfr 35.1 bn by the end of March. One of the possible reasons for the dropping of Lebouder was corruption at the apex of the hierarchy, where even the new authorities were believed to be involved in diamond smuggling.

The **European Union** lifted its suspension of development assistance imposed after the coup in 2003. EDF assistance worth CFAfr 9.5 bn was earmarked essentially for the payment of salaries, the mixed electoral commission and for the reimbursement of debts to the European Investment Bank.

Productivity remained low due to insecurity. Agro-pastoral producers still hid in the bush or in semi-urban areas, only returning to their fields after carefully assessing the risk of attacks. Cotton production was particularly affected. The distribution of goods was made virtually impossible. There were fears that farmers could lose a third consecutive planting season due to displacement. In June, the UN estimated that 200,000 internally displaced persons (IDPs) were scattered all over the country. The absence of IDP camps made it hard to establish accurate figures. Latest figures from the UN rated 73% of the population as living below the poverty line.

Andreas Mehler

Chad

During 2004, political stability of Chad was undermined by the Darfur crisis in neighbouring Sudan, and continued uncertainty about the revenues from oil exploitation. Both issues were said to lie at the origin of an attempted coup d'état in May. Rumours about the poor health of President Idriss Déby fuelled concerns about political stability. An amendment to the constitution that cleared the way for President Déby to stand for re-election after his second term was accepted in parliament. Foreign support for the current regime, mainly from France and the US, was still strong, since Déby seemed to be the only guarantee of political stability, the opposition being in disarray. The exploitation of oil is said to have increased GDP by more than 30%. Despite oil revenues, Chad still ranked as one of the poorest countries in the world, with 80% of the population living on less than $ 1 a day. The rainy season finished early and harvests were far below (30%) the levels of last year. Furthermore, the transhumance of livestock keepers to the south started as early as September instead of December, increasing tensions between nomadic herders and farmers. The damage done by locust plagues was relatively modest. However, there are indications that Chad is heading for a food crisis in 2005.

Domestic Politics

The Chadian government faced a formidable political challenge in 2004 in the form of the **Darfur crisis** and the spill-over of this conflict into Chad. President Déby took a neutral position towards the conflict, despite the fact that his fellow Zaghawa clansmen on the Sudanese side of the border were among the people butchered by the Janjaweed militia in Darfur. Relatives of Déby were also prominent members of the rebel groups in the area, such as the founder and president of JEM (Justice and Equality Movement), Khalil Ibrahim. The military and civilian leadership was mostly from the Zaghawa tribe and many blamed Déby for not doing enough to help the Sudanese Zaghawa in Darfur.

Opposition was also fuelled by President Déby's bid for a **third presidential term**. Though there was resistance from opposition parties, the Chadian parliament approved a constitutional amendment in May, which allowed him to seek more than the two presidential terms currently allowed. This constitutional amendment still has to be approved by the population in a referendum in June 2005. Though the official political opposition has long been divided and was unable to mobilise the population, internal opposition did gradually mount. A large number of opposition parties took a united stand in this political conflict and Chad's ambassador to the US, Ahmat Hassaballah Soubiane, stepped down and associated himself with opposition movements in the Sudan.

The beginning of oil production and oil exports – started in June this year through the World Bank-financed Cameroon-Chad pipeline – is said to have fuelled the **power struggle** in N'Djaména. Revenues from Chad's Doba oil fields were to be primarily channelled towards fighting poverty and improving infrastructure in accordance with deals struck with the World Bank. However, the armed forces, traditionally powerful in Chad, were allocated few of the extra revenues from the new export commodity. As oil revenues began to reach the country's fiscal authorities, army officials became increasingly disgruntled about the poor conditions in army barracks. Furthermore, opponents of Déby argued that he was too inclined to take direction from international donors and did too little for his own people.

Dissatisfaction with Déby's handling of the Darfur crisis, the constitutional change he proposed, and the management of oil revenues informed discontent within the president's closest circles. The expulsion of two Darfur rebel sympathisers from N'Djaména and support for Sudanese politics in the Darfur crisis triggered the **attempted coup d'état** against the Déby regime on 16 May. The coup did not succeed, but it took days of intense negotiations between insurgents and forces loyal to Déby to end the confrontation. However, the changes in high places that he made after the conflict indicated that the danger was coming from very close to him. Tom Herdimi, advisor to Déby and his cousin (both belong to the Bideyat clan) was removed from his post as coordinator of the oil project and replaced by the former Prime Minister Haroun Kabadi in June. Herdimi's twin brother, Timane, was removed from his post as president of the executive board of the important parastatal 'Société Cotonnière du Tchad' (Cotontchad). Above all, senior officers in the army and the secret police were replaced by people loyal to Déby. However, all these newcomers were also from the Zaghawa ethnic group. Moussa Faki Mahamat remained in his post as prime minister, though there was growing friction between him and President Déby.

These measures did little to end the tense situation, despite the fact that Déby took a harder position on the Darfur conflict. After this incident, the armed forces carried out several operations against suspected coup plotters. Security measures around the president were stepped up and it was reported that Déby look-alikes, surrounded by bodyguards, were spotted travelling on government planes in an apparent attempt to sow confusion about his whereabouts.

As his hold over the country seemed more threatened, Déby spent more and more time in the town of Abéché in the east of Chad, where the security situation deteriorated in 2004 as a consequence of the Darfur crisis. In June, 180,000 **refugees** were registered, in August, the number increased to 200,000 and refugees were still arriving in December. Eleven camps were created by December along the Chad-Sudan border. An additional problem was that, along with the refugees, an estimated 2.5 m head of livestock had spilled over the border. There was increasing concern that the dynamics of the Darfur conflict between nomadic herders and sedentary farmers would also spread to Chad, where inter-group relations were already tense following violent conflicts between nomadic pastoralists, who for decades have moved from north to south, and sedentary farmers over damaged fields and the management of wells and pasture lands.

In the south, **clashes** took place between groups of various ethnic and religious backgrounds (Muslim and non-Muslim) and destabilised the political situation. In March, Arab Missirie raided a village of the local Sara population in Mandoul department and seized large numbers of livestock, leaving 21 people dead and 28 wounded. In November 2004, ethnic fighting occurred between rival mobs of Muslim and non-Muslim residents of the south Chadian town of Bebedjia (35 kilometres from the oil-producing area of Doba), leaving 12 people dead and 16 injured. This incident started as a dispute between a trader and a customer. Similar eruptions of violence were regularly reported from other regions as well.

Foreign Affairs

The **Darfur conflict** dominated foreign affairs. Initially Chad took a neutral stance and opted for a role as intermediary in the conflict, supposedly, in part to please France and the US. Idriss Déby had already hosted peace negotiations in 2003 and again in April. However, the ceasefire agreements proved to be not worth the paper on which they were written. Over time, the position of Déby had become very difficult: he had to maintain a precarious balance between his fellow Zaghawa, who live on both sides of the border, and the Arabs, who are also strongly represented in both countries. On the one hand, for lack of military capacity, Déby could not afford a dispute with Sudan over Darfur. On the other hand, he lacked support among the Chadian population to fight for Zaghawa interests on both sides of the border after the group became increasingly unpopular. A further complicating aspect was that it was the current president of Sudan, Omar Hassan al-Bashir, who helped Déby come to power 14 years earlier by allowing him to organise his rebellion against former President Hissein Habré in 1990 on Sudanese soil.

However, cross-border incursions by Sudanese Janjaweed with Chadian allies (and opponents of the Déby regime) grew more frequent. Chadian Zaghawa were reported to be making cross-border raids to take revenge for attacks on their Sudanese brothers. According to senior government sources, this situation had the potential to degenerate into **a regional interethnic war** between a coalition of Arab groups and an alliance of other ethnic groups. There were also unconfirmed reports that Chadian opposition movements that had been silent for some years were rebuilding their bases in Sudan (in Kutum), and were obviously being tolerated by the Sudanese government. At the same time, there was great confusion about the organisation of and support for both opposition movements in Darfur, the SLA (Sudanese Liberation Army) and the JEM (related to the fundamentalist movement headed by Hassan al-Tourabi). The Sudanese government accused Eritrea of supporting these groups. However, it was highly improbable that they could maintain their presence in the field and seemingly even gain strength without logistical and military support from the Chadian side. The NGO International Crisis Group (ICG) claimed to have documented arms deliveries from Chad to SLA and JEM rebels in Darfur in August. On the other hand, the government of Chad also supplied troops to the Sudanese army in Darfur, according to UN sources. Khartoum, therefore, maintained positive diplomatic relations with N'Djaména.

Chad became the lifeline for humanitarian aid to the estimated 2 million Darfuris displaced by the conflict in western Sudan. Most **humanitarian operations** into Darfur commenced in eastern Chad. Consequently, stability in Chad was a major concern for the international community as a whole. The major foreign powers, France and the US, seemingly had placed their bets on the regime of Idriss Déby, because there was no viable alternative, with the divided opposition and no strong individual candidate to oppose the regime. For the **US**, Chad was also an important component of its mid-term strategy to secure the supply of African crude oil to the US and to become less dependent on the Middle East.

With the increasing threat of destabilisation in the eastern region, in August the **French government** decided to deploy 200 of its troops based in Chad ('forces pré-positionnées') to the country's eastern border to help prevent incursions by Janjaweed militia groups from Sudan's troubled Darfur region. It also made military transport planes and helicopters available to fly relief supplies to Sudanese refugee camps in eastern Chad, which were not accessible by road following heavy rains. France and the US were also strongly opposed to the spread of Sudanese influence in the region: France in order to counter Anglophone influence in what it regarded as the Francophone sphere of influence, and the US to try to counter fundamentalist Islam, which they feared would spill over from Sudan into Chad and other countries.

So-called 'liberators', the combatants who helped General François Bozizé seize power in Central African Republic (**CAR**) in 2003 – some of them of Chadian origin – posed security problems in Bangui (April). President Déby, the most important supporter of the new regime, and the Chadian ambassador in Bangui helped negotiate an agreement that included the transfer of some 200 ex-liberators to the common border. The Chadian contingent of 120 men formed the backbone of the CEMAC peacekeeping troops in CAR. Additionally, some 27,000 refugees from CAR lived in southern Chad.

Chad also became part of the **war against terrorism** initiative sponsored by the US administration. Within the framework of the Pan Sahel Initiative, re-baptised Trans-Sahara Counter Terrorism Initiative (TSCTI), a large military counter-insurgency operation, instigated by the Americans, was executed against a Salafist group ('Groupe Salafiste pour la Prédication et le Combat'/GSPC) led by Amari Saifi in the north of the country. In March, this group was chased out of northern Mali into northeastern Niger and into the Tibesti regions of northern Chad. There, as many as 43 GSPC militants were killed. Their leader escaped but was captured in October by a Chadian rebel group ('Mouvement pour la Démocratie et la Justice au Tchad'/MDJT).

Socioeconomic Developments

GDP for 2004 was estimated at $ 4.177 bn at current prices, $ 506 per capita and $ 1,627 at purchasing power parity. However, the distribution of income was extremely unequal, with 7 million people living of less than $ 1 a day. As a result of the oil project, Chad experienced an economic boom. Economic growth has been quite high over the past years (up to 9% and 9.7% in 2003) following large-scale investments in oil exploitation in the Doba basin (the fields of Bolobo, Komé and Miandoun) by a consortium of three oil companies, Esso Exploration and Production Chad (EEPCI) comprising ExxonMobil (40%), Chevron (25%) and the Malaysian group Petronas (35%). Estimated economic growth over 2004 was between 30% and 40% (+30.8% according to IMF) with moderate and sometimes even negative inflation (-5% in 2004, according to IMF), because of the start of oil exports. Over the second half of the year, almost $ 62 m were transferred to Chad. Per capita income was expected to double by 2005 as compared to the pre-oil situation. Yearly revenues from the three oilfields, estimated at 900 m barrels, were projected to amount to $ 200 m annually in the future at a production rate of 225,000–250,000 barrels per day (the estimated revenues per barrel of oil were only $ 2.5).

In August, the World Bank's portfolio amounted to $ 330.9 m spread over nine active projects, with 33% in social sectors, 56% in infrastructure, energy and environment capacity building, 6% in agriculture and 5% in capacity building for the management of the oil economy. In May, the consortium of foreign oil companies indicated promising developments in its search for additional oil resources in the area. In June, members of the consortium were awarded four new exploration permits in the Chari, Doseo and Salamat basins. They planned to start exploitation of three new oil fields in southern Chad by 2005 and 2006. A fourth oil field, Sedigi, north of Lake Chad, was still not exploited. It was planned to exploit this field and build a refinery in N'Djaména to provide fuel for the electricity supply of the capital. However, following the assassination of the main investor in the project in October 2003, these plans came to a standstill, despite the fact that a contract had been signed between the Chadian government and BID ('Banque Islamique de Développment') for a loan of € 23 m for the construction of an electric power plant of 25 megawatts in Farcha.

However, the management of oil revenues still posed many problems. Despite the influx of oil money, the government still had difficulties meeting its obligations. Payments to several international development projects were postponed. Salaries to civil servants were barely paid on time, leading to tensions between the president and the prime minister, his nephew Moussa Faki Mahamat. A large operation was launched to clean up the civil service and get rid of ghost civil servants, namely those who had long ceased working or had died and were still being paid. A similar operation was started in the armed forces, leading to considerable resentment, which may have contributed to the attempted coup d'état (see above).

World Bank programmes to build Chadian government capacity to manage the oil revenues for development have lagged far behind the speed with which the oil project has been executed. The result was that the government has remained unprepared, whereas the World Bank had justified its involvement in the project based on its capacity to transform Chad's economy. Chadian authorities have announced a new three-year programme to enhance economic growth and reduce poverty. Good governance and increased transparency were to be emphasised in the new oil producing country. There was quite some urgency required here, because international donors were growing impatient with the Chadian government. Following a mission to Chad, the IMF voiced severe criticisms in February and June of financial management and the transparency of the Chadian budget. It also imposed stiff conditions that would have to be met by government concerning financial management and macroeconomic policies before it would approve a new loan to restructure the state apparatus. By the end of the year, no decision to approve the loan had been taken.

An important question is whether macroeconomic policies imposed by IMF and financial reforms will have any positive effect for the large majority (80%) of the population who inhabit the countryside. For the rural poor 2004 was a difficult year. After a good start, the rainy season ended prematurely, leading to large production losses. Chadian officials and FAO estimated the cereal harvest at around 1 m tonnes, about one-third lower than in 2003. Production of the most important cereal crops, millet and sorghum, may have declined by

40%. Up to the rainy season (June-August), cereal prices remained stable, though high, at the four major cereal markets. However, by the end of the rainy season in October prices started to rise at the markets of Sarh, Abéché, N'Djaména and Moundou compared to the preceding five years, because of low harvest expectations. In Moundou and Sarh, prices rose by 60% and 76%. An important additional cause for this price rise was the higher on-farm price of cotton, which encouraged farmers to grow more cotton and fewer cereals. By November, it was clear that a food emergency was imminent, predominantly in Kanem, Batha, and the east and north, which were chronic deficit areas, but also in better endowed areas such as Guera, and Chari-Baguirmi.

The Chadian medical infrastructure remained poor, with only one medical doctor for every 29,000 inhabitants. In 2004, major infectious diseases raged through the country. Cholera outbreaks in June in and around N'Djaména and in N'Djaména and Mongo in October infected more than 2,000 people, with many casualties, though an exact figure could not be established, statistics being very poor.

The influx of refugees from Darfur over 16 months affected every aspect of the local population's livelihood base in the east of Chad. Initially, even in Abéché, the capital of the east, food prices did not rise despite the large influx. Apparently, refugees were fed from stocks at village level in the absence of food aid in the first months of their arrival. A nutrition survey conducted in May and June found Global Acute Malnutrition (GAM) rates as high as 29% among the host population and Severe Acute Malnutrition (SAM) was also reported, but these were not unusual phenomena in the Chadian countryside. More than 200,000 refugees were registered in overcrowded camps and already in June alarming malnutrition and health problems were reported. The provision of water was a pressing problem, with water availability per capita being below international standards, even in the refugee camps. Poor rains, rapidly rising staple food prices owing to increased demand and the early depletion of last year's stocks, which local households had shared with refugees, led to increased competition for local resources, including water, firewood and wild foods. The disruption of trade with Sudan also had severe consequences for the east and the whole north of Chad. With the below-average harvest, the host population was becoming less tolerant of the perceived and real stresses created by the refugee population. Moreover, not all refugees in eastern Chad were in camps, and competed directly with the local populace for bush products.

The price of sheep dropped, so that the exchange rate with cereals for livestock keepers declined. The supply of livestock at the main markets was quite high after the rainy season because of the early cessation of the rains and the damage done by desert locusts in Kanem and Batha, though this damage was less than anticipated. Dry conditions this year have limited water and pasture availability. This, along with an increase in livestock diseases (reportedly transferred from Sudanese animals to host livestock) put households' most important assets, their livestock, in danger. The transhumance movement towards the south had already started in September in some areas, as compared to December in better years. It was feared that this could lead to problems later in the season because of resource competition with local populations.

Mirjam de Bruijn & Han van Dijk

Republic of Congo

The 1997 armed conflicts that resulted in the fall of Pascal Lissouba continued to serve as the landmark around which the Republic of Congo (RoC) regime organised itself formally and ideologically. The end of the five-year transition period, proclaimed in August 2002, led to the establishment of new institutions, with Denis Sassou Nguesso as head of state. Yet in many respects, 2004 in the Congo was still largely dominated by the political and economic structures that had resulted from a series of armed conflicts.

Domestic Politics

As dissension between the leaders came to a head at the beginning of the year, the **'Forces Démocratiques Unies'** (FDU), the alliance that supported President Sassou Nguesso, entered a deep crisis. The tensions between reformers and conservatives intensified and became official. The conservatives represented the regime's leaders who had mobilised the most militiamen and had contributed to the 1997 victory. They continued to exert a strong influence on the army and pleaded in favour of the status quo. By contrast, the reformers, gathered mainly around members of the president's own family, tried to distance themselves from the FDU. However, at year's end the conflicts between the two wings had not yet culminated in the government reshuffle that had been expected since August 2004.

An event dating back several years continued to exacerbate tensions in the relations between the government and civil society on the one hand, and its international supporters on the other. This event was known as **'Beach Case'**, and referred to the disappearance in May 1999 of 353 refugees who were returning home from the neighbouring Democratic Republic of Congo (DR Congo). International human rights organisations and an association of relatives of the disappeared had asked for justice and had filed a lawsuit against the Congolese leadership for a 'crime against humanity'. In May 2001, an investigation was launched in the high court in Meaux, east of Paris. On 1 April, the head of the RoC national police, Jean-François Ndengué, was arrested during a private visit to France before being set free as a result of political pressures. The prosecutor of the French republic transferred the case to the Paris high court, which had to deliberate on its admissibility. The RoC government then decided to conduct local investigations: a court was convened and four officers were prosecuted on 7 July.

The **military** remained an important factor in the power game. On 12 August, 21 officers were promoted to the rank of general by presidential decree. The official explanation was that most of them had taken part in the operation to "blockade and cleanse the southern districts of Brazzaville and in the Pool, Bouenza, Niari and Lekoumou regions from 1998 to 1999." These promotions could be interpreted in at least two ways. First, many of these officers were close to retirement: the promotions would guarantee them a good pension and allay their grievances. Second, the present chief of staff, 'général de division' Charles-Richard Mondjo, had just been appointed the head of the army, although he was only a colonel. Thus, he had achieved his new position directly without ever holding the rank of 'général de brigade'. This promotion aimed at imposing Mondjo as head of the army and inevitably created tensions among the higher ranks of the military and police.

In the face of the FDU alliance, supported by the state's military apparatus, the **opposition** grew weaker and weaker. It comprised three poles: the old dominant parties of the 'democratic transition' era (their leaders living in exile); the two coalitions operating in RoC (Codesa, 'Code A') and the Nsilulu Movement; and, still perceived as the main opposition parties, UPADS ('Union Panafricaine pour la Démocratie Sociale'), MCDDI ('Mouvement Congolais pour la Démocratie et le Développement Intégral') and RDD ('Rassemblement pour la Démocratie et le Développement'), founded respectively by the former president of the republic, Pascal Lissouba, the former mayor of the capital, Bernard Kolélas, and the former prime minister, Jacques Yombhi Opangault. Since these leaders had been in exile from 1997 and relied on outside networks, their parties could no longer organise themselves as credible forces. The prolonged exile of their founders might have caused their parties to break up, and the RoC government clearly stated that it did not favour their return. While MCDDI lay in a shambles, UPADS appeared to regain a certain public audience through Joseph Kignoumbi Kia Mboungou, defeated UPADS presidential candidate in the 2002 elections, but elected MP and faction leader. He used his position in parliament to strongly criticise the government. Codesa ('Convention pour la Démocratie et le Salut'), a coalition of opposition parties, first appeared during the course of the 2002 elections. In this coalition, the 'Union pour la Démocratie et la République' (UDR)-Mwinda seemed to be the most powerful party. Its leader, André Milongo, was the prime minister during the transition period in 1991–92, and the speaker of the National Assembly. In 2004, however, it looked as if the party had distanced itself from the coalition. On the one hand, Codesa gradually lost credibility after it failed to alter the militarist stance of the government. On the other hand, UDR-Mwinda chose to profit from the crisis in MCDDI, whose original basis was in the Pool region where Milongo's party also received most of its votes. In sum, disconnection from the lethargic Codesa was a strategy to renew UDR-Mwinda's image.

The 'Coordination de l'opposition pour une alternance démocratique', nicknamed 'Code A', was a platform comprising 13 parties and political associations, which was officially created in August. For a six-month period after its creation, 'Code A' was co-ordinated by the lawyer Hervé Ambroise Malonga, and its spokesman was the MP Jacques Mouanda Mpassi. 'Code A' brought together various smaller parties and lesser personalities, and concluded strategic and non-binding alliances with MCDDI and RDD. These two parties took part in one official event. On 6 November, some 300–400 people attended a political rally organised by 'Code A' in Brazzaville. In their speeches, some orators virulently addressed sensitive issues such as insecurity, the violation of peace agreements, the return of exiles, embezzlement of oil revenues, the Beach Case, and notably the 'mockery of a trial' the government was keen to set up to deal with this affair. The official media boycotted the event.

However, the impact of these coalitions on public opinion, although not negligible, remained relatively weak, mainly because of their largely marginal presence among the population. Nevertheless, 'Code A' appeared to be the most active coalition opposed to the government.

The third coalition, the Nsilulu Movement, brought together militiamen close to Frédéric Binsangou, alias Pastor Ntoumi, the head of a neo-Pentecostal Church. Nsilulu became famous during the resistance to the 1998–99 'cleansing and blockade' operations in the Pool region (see above). Pastor Ntoumi had negotiated an end to the conflict when he was chairman of the 'Conseil National de Résistance' (CNR). A situation of 'armed peace' continued in the region, leading from time to time to confrontations between government forces and Nsilulu.

On the social front, civil society was still in a lethargic state and government used civil law associations to its own advantage. Many NGOs were, in fact, outgrowths of the state, and the subordination of the media to the regime only served to contribute to this lethargy. Even though 'independent' newspapers were allowed to express their opinions more or less freely, certain of them were either directly or indirectly manipulated by political leaders, with the exception of 'La Semaine africaine'.

There was, during the period under review, no public debate on major issues such as decentralisation, structural adjustment, poverty reduction or the intended reform of the education sector. **Corruption** appeared to be the only tolerated topic of public discussion, because it did not interfere with the political and economic interests of the leadership: on the contrary, it facilitated them. In March, two 'open letters' were released on the subject. The first was signed by retired General Emmanuel Ngouélondélé and the second by five leaders of FDU-affiliated parties. Both letters pointed to the decline of the army and lamented the declining notion of public service among civil servants, the lack of authority of the state, racketeering and corruption, fraud, widespread impunity and the selling-off of public assets. At the same time, government declared the fight against corruption a priority. Roger Rigobert Andély, minister of finance, and Simon Mfoutou, minister in charge of state control, initiated a few measures to combat corruption. In June-July, 93 economic operations suspected of mismanaging public assets were placed under state control. Most of these firms were run by people in the president's immediate entourage. Consequently, they were not much at risk and the whole initiative was instituted and controlled by the leadership. Andély and Mfoutou were dismissed during the government reshuffle. Little is needed to establish a link between their dismissal and their attempted steps against certain privileges of the 'Nomenklatura'.

Foreign Affairs

Foreign affairs were dominated by international agreements aimed at tackling the consequences of recent armed conflicts through operations to demobilise the militia and through the ratification of agreements with neighbouring countries intended to pacify the region.

France remained RoC's main partner in the fields of military cooperation and security. It continued to be in charge of reorganising the 'gendarmerie nationale' and training the main police units. This intervention in RoC's internal repressive apparatus was mainly aimed at restoring the security tools essential for the return of peace and the maintenance of order in the post-conflict era.

The **reintegration of ex-combatants** into society was governed by the National Programme of Disarmament, Demobilisation and Reintegration of ex-combatants (NPDDR), which was established with the assistance of the United Nations after the peace agreements at the end of 1999. According to official statistics, by July some 5,622 micro-projects had been financed, 11,997 light weapons had been collected and destroyed and 17,330 veterans had been reintegrated. The programme planned to integrate 42,000 former militiamen between 2004 and 2006, thereby defusing a potentially explosive situation. More than 16,000 demobilised militiamen have been awaiting reintegration since 2000 (not including the reintegration programme supported by the World Bank). Among them were 8,500 Nsilulu militiamen and 6,000 foreign soldiers who had taken refuge in RoC. In addition, NPDDR was planning to take care of 5,500 Congolese militiamen and military who were refugees in other countries of the sub-region, mainly Gabon and DR Congo.

A security agreement signed between RoC and **DR Congo** allowed for the return of militiamen and soldiers to their respective countries, the securing of borders and a mutual commitment not to give military or political support to belligerent forces in the sub-region. However, implementation of this agreement was not successful. While the militiamen and soldiers from Brazzaville who were refugees in the DR Congo have yet to return, the media were announcing the return of military and militiamen to the DR Congo and Rwanda. A certain number of military belonging to the 'Forces Armées Zaïroises' (FAZ) were incorporated into the 'Forces Armées Congolaises' (FAC). Relations between the two Congos were still very tense. The DR Congo government announced that the coup d'état that was foiled in Kinshasa on 24 March had been plotted in Brazzaville. The RoC government viewed DR Congo as a potential enemy, capable of launching an operation of military destabilisation. In fact, RoC leaders preferred Jean-Pierre Bemba, one of DR Congo's vice-presidents, to President Joseph Kabila.

On 25 April, RoC signed an anti-extradition treaty with the **United States**. On 15 July, RoC was excluded from the **'Kimberley Process'**, established in 2003 to detect the sources of 'blood diamonds'. The authorities declared the production of about 50,000 carats while export figures stood at about 5 m carats. Hence, the government was suspected of surreptitiously channelling parts of DR Congo and CAR diamond production on to the world market. This was a serious blow to the credibility of the government.

As to economic agreements, RoC's refusal to open its books regarding its management of oil revenues had put an end to one of the programmes supervised by the **IMF**. In 2004, the finance minister finally agreed to be transparent in order to discuss a Poverty Reduction and Growth Facility (PRGF) scheme and the reduction of Congo's $ 6 bn foreign debt as part of the Heavily Indebted Poor Countries (HIPC) Programme. This transparency operation echoed the anti-corruption initiative launched by the government. On 6 December, the IMF fulfilled RoC's wishes by approving a PRGF of $ 84 m over three years. This permitted the re-establishment of warmer relations with different donors. On 14 December in Tunis, the ADB announced the relief of part of the debt arrears and a new start in assistance operations for the country. Additionally, on 16 December, the Paris Club of creditors accepted the rescheduling of the bilateral public debts.

Socioeconomic Developments

In 2004, Congo's GDP increased by an estimated 0.8%. The budget deficit represented 12% of GDP and 30% of budget revenues. The foreign public debt reached $ 5,152 m and debt service amounted to more than one-third of budget revenues. Roughly 70% of the population lived below poverty level (€ 0.9 a day).

The European Union and Asia remained the RoC's main suppliers, and Asia and the United States its major clients. The **Chinese presence** is becoming more and more visible. By 2004, the Chinese were involved in retail trade in various areas of Brazzaville. More noticeably, they took the initiative to conclude agreements with leaders of the local oil company, 'Société nationale des pétroles du Congo' (SNPC).

As the country's primary source of wealth, **oil** accounted for 80% of export resources and 60% of annual fiscal revenues. Oil also remained at the centre of internal conflicts and external criticisms. Lack of transparency in oil management was the rule. This was highlighted both by IMF experts in February 2004 and by the NGO Global Witness in its March 2004 report. Nonetheless, at the end of the first quarter, the RoC government paved the way for an agreement with the IMF when it agreed to more transparency in its oil revenues by publishing an audit of SNPC.

The government continued two of the announced **grand development projects** of Sassou Nguesso's seven-year term: the construction of a hydroelectric dam (inaugurated on 23 September) and a road rehabilitation programme (which was to be officially launched in February 2004). It is worth noting that the country's capital relied heavily on the latter programme, which has not yet started, for its food supplies. The slowing down of this project can be explained by the political strategy of 'regional balancing' that was pursued unofficially by RoC's leaders. Indeed, a very strong majority of powerful leaders were from the northern regions. This fundamental aspect of Congolese political dynamics largely explains the project to divide the present Cuvette region in the north of the country in order to create a new region, Alima, whose main town Oyo happens to be the president's birthplace. This may also explain the decision to install modern infrastructure in the area, such as an international airport in Ollombo, a radio and television building in Oyo and various road projects around that city.

Rémy Bazenguissa-Ganga

Democratic Republic of Congo

The various political factions represented in the power-sharing government, inaugurated in June 2003, preserved an uneasy coexistence. The prospect of holding elections in June 2005, scheduled to end the transition period, appeared increasingly remote by year's end. None of the political challenges facing the country was even close to being met, including the disarmament and reintegration of combatants, the creation of a new integrated national army and the drawing up of legislation essential to an orderly wrapping-up of the transition. The transition from war to peace in the country tottered on the verge of collapse throughout the year due to renewed clashes in the country's Kivu provinces, the massacre of Banyamulenge refugees in Burundi, the (temporary) withdrawal of Vice-President Ruberwa from the transitional government, the continued presence of Rwandan Hutu rebels in Eastern Congo and the repeated threats of a new military intervention by Rwanda.

Domestic Politics

On 28 March several military bases in and around Kinshasa were attacked by a small group of unknown armed elements. Government forces finally defeated the attackers and captured 17 of them. A spokesman for President Joseph Kabila unconvincingly claimed that the assailants were Brazzaville-based former members of Mobutu's 'Division Spéciale

Présidentielle' (DSP) who had fled to the neighbouring Republic of Congo after the 'Alliance des Forces Démocratiques pour la Libération du Congo' (AFDL) insurgents of the late Laurent Kabila had invaded Kinshasa in May 1997.

On 11 June, an **apparent coup d'état** was staged by some 40 members of the presidential guard, led by Major Eric Lenge. The mutineers took control of the national radio station and declared the overthrow of the transitional government. Following attacks by loyalist troops, the mutineers withdrew first to Kinshasa's Tshatshi military base before fleeing to Bas Congo province. At year's end, Lenge and his group were at large and no investigation had been undertaken into the incident. As with the alleged DSP attack in March, the opaqueness of the event fuelled widespread rumours that the mutineers had acted on behalf of elements in Kabila's inner circle of Katangan hardliners, hoping to sabotage the transition, possibly by declaring a permanent state of emergency. On 18 June, Kabila fired the army chief of staff and the head of his 'Maison Militaire', the president's security cabinet that directs his praetorian guard.

President Kabila conducted a minor **cabinet reshuffle** on 12 July. The minister of treasury, Joseph Mudumbi of the former rebel movement 'Rassemblement Congolais pour la Démocratie' (RCD) moved to the ministry of higher education. Athenase Matenda Kyelu, the national president of the 'Fédération des Entreprises Congolaises', was appointed minister of the civil service. He took that position on behalf of 'civil society', which forms one part of the transitional government (together with the various belligerents, including the former Kabila government, and the political opposition parties). Vital Kamerhe left the ministry of information to become the secretary general of Kabila's 'Parti pour la Reconstruction et le Développement' (PPRD). He was replaced by Henri Mova Sakanyi, who had previously served as deputy foreign minister. Another change in government took place on 22 July when Foreign Minister Antoine Ghonda was sacked by his political formation, the former rebel group 'Mouvement pour la Libération du Congo' (MLC) led by Jean-Pierre Bemba. Ghonda's removal allegedly followed a demand by Ugandan President Yoweri Museveni, the former key ally of the MLC, after a series of disputes between the two men. Mobutu's former ambassador to France, Raymond Ramazani (MLC), took over the ministry of foreign affairs.

A major restructuring occurred in November when Kabila suspended six ministers – and ten executives of state-owned companies – in response to a parliamentary inquiry into government corruption (25 November). Those suspended were the ministers of energy (Kalema Losona), higher education (Joseph Mudumbi), mines (Eugène Diomi Ndongala), public works (José Endundo Bononge) and transport (Joseph Olenghankoy). It was alleged that Kabila took the step in agreement with his four vice-presidents.

The single most important crisis for the already ailing transition was precipitated by **upheavals in Bukavu**, where severe tensions between the political and military authorities erupted into violent conflict in May and June. In February, the newly appointed commander of South Kivu's 10th military region, General Nabyolwa (of the former government component) had discovered arms caches in the homes of RCD officials such as Governor Chiribanya and Major Kasongo. Nabyolwa arrested Kasongo and transferred him to Kinshasa (21 February). In retaliation, Nabyolwa's deputy, Colonel Jules Mutebusi (RCD) attacked Nabyolwa's compound, killing several soldiers and forcing the commander into hiding (24 February). Meanwhile, Kasongo's arrest prompted the RCD to threaten its withdrawal from the transition. To prevent this, the United Nations peacekeeping mission in the DR Congo (MONUC) and the 'Comité International d'Accompagnement de la Transition' (CIAT), an international body with representatives from 15 countries (including France, the US, UK, Belgium) aiming at assisting with the implementation of the 2002 peace accords, allegedly pressured Kabila to return Kasongo to Bukavu. In what appeared as a victory for the RCD, Nabyolwa was finally replaced by General Mbuza Mabe. Although Colonel Mutebusi was suspended from his duties, de facto he remained in charge of Bukavu. However, tensions persisted and on 26 May fighting between the troops of Mabe and Mutebusi resumed, leaving at least 30 people dead. According to Human Rights Watch, half of these were civilians from the Banyamulenge ethnic minority group, some of whom were apparently targeted by government soldiers because they were of the same ethnic group as Mutebusi. As a result, an estimated 3,000 Banyamulenge fled to the neighbouring Rwandan town of Cyangugu. Under the pretext of preventing genocide, Laurent Nkunda, a Congolese Tutsi and brigadier general in the RCD who, in 2003, had refused to integrate into the new national army – 'Forces Armées de la République Démocratique du Congo' (FARDC) – moved several thousand soldiers, many of whom were believed to be part of the North-Kivu-based 10th military region of the Congolese army, from Goma to South Kivu. After driving Mabe's forces out of Bukavu (2 June), Nkunda's troops resorted to widespread sexual violence and looting. Mediation attempts by MONUC's Bukavu-based contingent and Belgian foreign minister Louis Michel resulted in the pull-out of Nkunda's troops from the city (6 June) and loyalist forces under the command of Mabe took control of Bukavu. Following a series of minor skirmishes, Nkunda withdrew northwards to Minova (North Kivu). By September, his troops had returned to their units in the 10th military region in North Kivu. Mutebusi, on the other hand, crossed into Rwanda (8 June) where he and around 300 of his soldiers – after a short return to Congo – were installed in a military camp. Due to the fighting in South Kivu, several hundred people lost their lives and around 30,000 Congolese fled to neighbouring Burundi and Rwanda.

In political terms, the Bukavu crisis underlined that a politically and militarily coherent government had yet to materialise as the various factions – despite their putative cooperation within transitional institutions – warily sought to stick to the power bases they had built up during the war. The flare-up of tensions and conflict in South Kivu was a result of Kabila's attempt to wrest the province from the control of the RCD, notably by appointing a political governor to the province (from the political opposition) whom the RCD regarded as a puppet of Kabila (14 May). That this appointment shortly preceded the renewed eruption of violence in Bukavu (26 May) was no coincidence: members of the RCD were apparently seeking to retain their power in the Kivus (see below).

Further repercussions of the Bukavu crisis surfaced on 13 August, when a transit centre housing 1,767 displaced Burundians and Congolese refugees at **Gatumba** (Bujumbura Rurale) in Burundi was attacked by 100 to 300 armed elements. Of the 152 refugees who were slaughtered during the carnage, 147 were Banyamulenge who had found shelter in Gatumba in the wake of the May-June events in South Kivu. Responsibility for the killings was immediately claimed by the Burundian 'Forces Nationales de Libération' (FNL), the only rebel group still boycotting the Burundi peace process. Given that the attack was clearly directed at the Banyamulenge refugees, RCD-President Ruberwa, himself a Munyamulenge, who had visited the camp only hours prior to the attack, declared the massacre an act of genocide committed by Burundian, Rwandan and Congolese extremists, the latter possibly hailing from the Congolese army and Mai Mai elements integrated into it. An investigation by the United Nations was unable to firmly identify the authors of the crime but deemed it unlikely that FNL had acted on its own. Ruberwa declared the transitional process to have broken down and demanded a reassessment of the problems underlying this impasse. Back in the RCD's headquarters in Goma, he announced its suspension from the transitional institutions (23 August). Following strong international pressure and mediation efforts by South African President Mbeki, Ruberwa lifted the suspension and, together with other RCD ministers and members of parliament, resumed work in the capital on 28 August.

The Bukavu crisis not only rocked the transitional government as a whole, but also confirmed the existence of long-standing **cracks in the former RCD insurgency** movement. For a start, it laid open the fault lines between Ruberwa and the RCD elites in the Kivus. This group comprised individuals who were either deeply sceptical of the transitional arrangement or rejected it outright, such as North Kivu Governor Serufuli, South Kivu Governor Chiribanya and military commanders Nkunda, Kasongo and Mutebusi. Supported by Rwanda, this group distanced itself from Ruberwa and operated largely autonomously to undermine the transition process or, at least, to retain its foothold in the Kivus to the detriment of the Kinshasa government. The manoeuvres of this faction, consisting mainly of Rwandophones, placed Ruberwa, himself a Munyamulenge, in an uneasy position, particularly after the Gatumba massacre. On one hand, Ruberwa was probably unwilling to derail the transition process; on the other, failure to react strongly to the targeting of the Banyamulenge community in South Kivu and Burundi put him at risk of alienating his constituencies and losing his local power base to the 'peace spoilers' (Nkunda, Serufuli), who cast themselves as protectors of Kivus' Rwandophone communities. Both his criticism of Nkunda and Mutebusi and his temporary retreat from the transitional government reflected Ruberwa's dilemma. His balancing act, however, stirred further discontent within the RCD. For example, Ruberwa's decision to suspend the RCD's participation in transitional institutions was immediately contested by some RCD politicians in Kinshasa, who continued to exercise their functions. The opposite position had been taken by Bizima Karaha and eight other RCD members of parliament on 9 July. In an open letter to Ruberwa, the group's members (all Rwandophones from the Kivus) expressed their dissatisfaction with the course of the transition and suspended their participation in it. However, Ruberwa and the RCD's council of founders opposed the move and replaced the dissidents with new members of parliament.

North Kivu province, where spill-over effects of the Bukavu events heightened political and ethnic tensions throughout the year, entered a severe crisis in November. Following Rwanda's alleged military intervention in North Kivu (see below, Foreign affairs), President Kabila ordered the redeployment of up to 10,000 troops to the RCD-controlled parts of North Kivu (Masisi, Walikale) on 26 November. Given the precedent in South Kivu earlier in the year, when the arrival of FARDC units had driven Rwandophone communities into mass flight, the announcement was met with outright hostility among North Kivu's Banyarwanda, who make up an estimated 50% of the local population. Soldiers from the largely Banyarwanda-dominated 8th military region in North Kivu prevented aircraft carrying government troops from landing in Goma. Moving instead southward from Beni, the FARDC soldiers were defeated by former RCD troops in **Kanyabayonga**. Two weeks of fighting resulted in the displacement of 100,000 civilians in the area. Meanwhile, MONUC had established a buffer zone to keep the warring factions apart (22 December). Clearly, the Rwandan-backed remnants of the RCD had foiled Kabila's attempt to make inroads into North Kivu and – after the fall of South Kivu – retained control over its last bastion. Unsurprisingly, the crisis triggered local tensions between North Kivu's Rwandophone communities and so-called indigenous groups amid credible reports that local authorities under the leadership of Governor Serufuli distributed arms to Masisi's Rwandophone population.

In a highly symbolic move intended to signal the unification of the country, President Kabila travelled to Kisangani in October. On his first visit to Eastern Congo since becoming president in January 2001, Kabila received a warm welcome from the population. By contrast, his popularity plummeted in **Katanga**, which threatened to become another source of political instability in the country. Kabila's appointment of Kisula Ngoy – a member of the PPRD who took the post on behalf of the Mai Mai component – as the governor of Katanga sparked 3 days of violent unrest in the provincial capital of Lubumbashi (16 May). Singing secessionist songs and defaming Kabila as a 'Tutsi', the demonstrators were mobilised by former governor Gabriel Kyungu wa Kumwanza, who threatened to make the province 'ungovernable' unless a member of the Lubakat be allotted the governor's office. In an apparently unrelated incident, six members of an obscure group, the 'Mouvement Révolutionnaire pour la Libération du Katanga', briefly seized the town of Kilwa in southern Katanga (13–14 October). The group declared itself to be fighting for Katanga's independence, thus stoking further anxieties about possible secessionist attempts in the province. The political branch of the 'Front de Libération Nationale Congolais' (the so-called 'Katangan Tigers') denied any involvement in the incident. On 15 October, FARDC units retook Kilwa, in the process looting the town and killing over 70 people (13–15 October).

The Bukavu crisis severely tarnished the already poor image of the **United Nations Mission in the DR Congo (MONUC)**. Although the mission quickly increased its strength in the area from 450 troops to 1,004 troops by 1 June in response to the violent flare-ups, and provided shelter to several thousand civilians, its interventions were ineffective. Ignoring its Chapter 7 mandate in the Kivus (and Ituri), MONUC's indecisiveness allowed the warring factions to ransack Bukavu and commit severe human rights abuses. Rather than negotiating with warring factions and attempting to erect buffer zones, critics argued that MONUC should have taken sides with government forces to fight the renegades, given its mandate to support the transitional government. With the crisis in full swing, violent demonstrators took to the streets in Kinshasa and other cities to air their frustration at MONUC's inability to avert the fall of Bukavu as well as at the performance of the transitional government in general. The looting of United Nations premises across the country resulted in large-scale destruction of equipment and property. In Kinshasa, three demonstrators were killed by MONUC troops when they infiltrated a compound.

As a result of MONUC's inability to handle the Bukavu crisis, the Security Council extended the mandate of the mission only until 1 October, pending a report by Secretary-General Kofi Annan on MONUC's discharge of its mandate (Resolution 1555, 29 July). Submitted on 16 August, the report noted a significant shortfall in the mission's capacity to fulfil all the tasks laid upon it, notably by Resolution 1493 (2003), which asked MONUC to 1) protect United Nations personnel and installations; 2) ensure the security and freedom of movement of MONUC personnel; 3) protect civilians and humanitarian workers under imminent threat; 4) contribute to the improvement of the security situation in which humanitarian aid is provided; and 5) monitor the arms embargo imposed on Ituri and the Kivus in the same resolution. Furthermore, the resolution had mandated MONUC to, *inter alia*, provide assistance for security sector reform, the establishment of the rule of law and state authority and the preparation and holding of elections.

Annan mapped out a modified structure for MONUC, which entailed the increase of the mission's strength from 10,800 to 23,900 men and the expansion of its logistical capacities (attack helicopters, transport, air- and waterborne surveillance), thereby giving MONUC the military superiority to deter armed groups from sabotaging the peace process. Operationally, the concept proposed that MONUC should play a more active role in restoring a minimum of security and order; more effectively monitor the arms embargo; deploy more troops to sensitive areas (Kinshasa, the Kivus, Katanga, Kasaï); and speed up the disarmament of the estimated 8,000 to 10,000 Rwandan Hutu rebels of the 'Forces Démocratiques pour la Libération du Rwanda' (FDLR).

On 30 September, the Security Council adopted Resolution 1565, which extended the mandate of MONUC until 31 March 2005. By authorising the deployment of an additional 5,900 personnel to the mission, the Security Council lifted MONUC's troop ceiling to 16,700. Although this fell well below the figures recommended by Annan (23,900), MONUC became the largest United Nations-authorised peacekeeping force. By the end of the year, 13,950 personal were deployed to the DR Congo.

Allegations of **sexual abuse** and exploitation dealt a further blow to MONUC, resulting in a number of suspensions of MONUC personnel. A civilian member of staff was removed on allegations of rape, sexual aggression and corruption of female minors. MONUC and the United Nations department of peacekeeping operations launched a number of investigations, with reports expected in early 2005.

To some extent, the Bukavu crisis and its reverberations was a wake-up call for the international community, which came to realise the dysfunctional nature of the transitional government and the resultant need for sustained international pressure to prevent slippage in the transition timetable, if not the outright collapse of the peace process. In addition to strengthening MONUC, the Security Council called on the mission to reinforce its assistance to the Congolese government in three crucial areas (elections, security sector reform, essential legislation) in order to overcome the stand-still in the political transition process. To that end, Resolution 1565 mandated MONUC to establish three joint commissions in conjunction with government bodies.

Chaired by MONUC, the joint commission on **essential legislation** will "provide advice on the elaboration and implementation of key legislation," including the constitution, laws on decentralisation, voter registration, referendums and an electoral code. This was in response to the fact that only three pieces of crucial legislation were enacted in the course of the year. The first was the statute establishing the independent electoral commission (CEI), a 21–member body formed in June to prepare for and organise the elections to be held in 2005. The second law related to the organisation of the armed forces. According to this legislation, passed in July, presidential decisions regarding important issues such as a declaration of war must be confirmed by the National Assembly and the senate. Finally, a hotly debated new **nationality law** was adopted by parliament to address, *inter alia*, the citizenship of Rwandophone communities in the east (25 September). By granting citizenship to members of an ethnic group present on Congolese soil at the time of independence, the law will confer Congolese nationality on the overwhelming majority of Rwandophones in the Kivus. However, the fact that the Mai Mai members of the National Assembly boycotted the vote demonstrated that the law itself would not be enough to bring about local reconciliation in the Kivus. The laws on nationality and on the armed forces were finally promulgated on 12 November.

As regards the elections, the MONUC-sponsored electoral technical committee, established in 2003, was integrated into a newly created joint commission composed of

MONUC, the CEI and international election experts. The commission will provide counsel on managerial, financial and logistical issues. Even so, and notwithstanding the political turmoil in the east, the delays caused by slow legislative processes and the belated formation of the electoral commission will probably be significant. By year's end, the objective of holding local, parliamentary and presidential **elections** in mid-2005 was unlikely to be met. Electoral commission estimates put the cost of the elections at $ 285 m. In late 2004, donor pledges of about $ 167 m, including $ 106 m by the European Union, fell short of these requirements. The funds will be needed to set up some 10,000 voter registration centres and 40,000 polling stations and to recruit and train 40,000 registration officers and 200,000 polling officers. The probable postponement of the ballot angered the 'Union pour la Démocratie et le Progrès Social' (UDPS) of veteran opposition politician Etienne Tshisekedi. An opinion survey conducted in late November (limited to Kinshasa) gave Tshisekedi and his party a clear lead in both presidential (46%) and parliamentary (42%) elections over the closest competitor, i.e., President Kabila (18%) and his PPRD party (29%). Tshisekedi's exclusion from the transition process proved to be politically beneficial, in light of popular discontent with the participants in the government of national unity.

The creation of a joint commission on **security sector reform**, comprising Western donors, MONUC, Angola and South Africa, was in response to the scant advances made over the year in unifying the various armed forces into a new national army, as well as in such related issues as disarmament and demobilisation. Perhaps symptomatic was the fate of a training programme for 285 Congolese officers in Belgium. Shortly after their arrival, 16 Congolese deserted. While it remained unclear how many of the Congolese were actual officers (as opposed to would-be emigrants), the programme was immediately cancelled and the rest of the group returned to the DR Congo. It was only on 24 July that the government presented its national programme on Disarmament, Demobilisation and Reintegration (DDR) regarding an estimated 200,000 combatants from the various belligerent camps who will not be integrated into the new 100,000-strong national army. Yet virtually no steps were taken in the following months to commence implementation. By the same token, and except for the Belgian-trained army brigade in Kisangani, the formation of 'integrated' army units made little progress. Receiving neither pay nor rewards in the guise of demobilisation programmes, most combatants had to fend for themselves. As a result, the crime rate was thought to have increased significantly across the country. On 13 December, Belgium and South Africa agreed with the government to implement a joint security sector project in order to harmonise the various small, disparate and ineffective support programmes run by a wide range of donors (South Africa, France, Belgium, EU, etc.). However, both countries offered only technical assistance and the necessary financial help (estimated at $ 29 m) was not forthcoming. The contingency plan aimed at speeding up the DDR process and at forming and training six brigades before the elections in 2005 by setting up dozens of orientation and training centres throughout the country.

Similarly, little progress was made in the DDR process that targeted foreign combatants, in particular the Rwandan Hutu rebels from the **FDLR**. By the end of the year, MONUC had repatriated a mere 11,300 Burundians, Rwandans and Ugandans and only half of them were thought to be fighters. In August, MONUC conceded that continued voluntary repatriation would "not succeed in resolving the problem within an acceptable time period" and sought a more proactive approach in closer collaboration with the FARDC. However, the first attempt to implement this new policy in Walungu (South Kivu) yielded no tangible results (8 November), given that the FARDC units were seriously hampered by a lack of discipline, training and resources. Furthermore, several sources, including the UN, alleged that the repatriation programme was undermined by the continuing "wilful cohabitation" and "mutual assistance" between FARDC troops and FDLR units. However, it remained unclear whether this situation arose from localised arrangements or at the instigation of state elites in Kinshasa, or both.

Despite the creation of the **Ituri** brigade by MONUC and its deployment (since November 2003) to several positions outside Bunia, the security situation in Ituri district remained extremely volatile and, beginning in September, deteriorated sharply. Between 1 September and 15 December, MONUC troops came under fire from armed militias on some 40 occasions. The conflict between Hema and Lendu appeared to have subsided and gave way to factional fighting across the board, partly driven by economic interests. Thus killings, looting and rape by the various armed groups continued more or less unabated in the vast areas where MONUC was not present. Both the transitional government and the Ituri interim administration had little if any influence over the district. This discomforting status quo was underscored by the fact that Ituri's militias were not party to the national peace and transition process. Negotiating efforts to include seven of them politically resulted in an Act of Engagement (10–14 May), which yielded few concrete results and had become a dead letter by July. On 1 September, MONUC and UNDP launched a demobilisation and reintegration programme targeting an estimated 15,000 combatants from the various armed groups. However, keen to maintain their armed forces and autonomy, militia leaders obstructed the process. By mid-December some 900 former combatants, most of them children, had been registered. In December, a delegation of the **International Criminal Court** (ICC) visited the DR Congo. Earlier in the year, ICC prosecutor Luis Moreno Ocampo had announced that the massacres that had taken place in Ituri since 2002 would be the first to be investigated by the ICC.

Outside the combat areas, violations of **human and political rights** were pervasive. There were numerous reports of unidentified men in uniform forcibly entering private homes to loot them or kill citizens. In the vast majority of cases, no actions or investigations were launched to bring the perpetrators to justice. Arbitrary arrests were frequent. According to MONUC, only 20% of the country's prison population had been brought to trial. **Freedom of the press** was severely restricted. Often under the pretext of defamation charges, some 30 members of the media were detained, beaten and threatened over the year. For example, the director of the daily 'Le Potentiel' was temporarily arrested at the behest of Vice-President Z'Ahidi Ngoma after the newspaper had reported that he had taken illegal possession of a plot of land (13 September).

Foreign Affairs

Notwithstanding the formal resumption of diplomatic relations through the appointment of a Rwandan ambassador to Kinshasa (4 March), **Rwandan-Congolese relations** were extremely tense throughout the year. In April, the Rwandan government was reported to have repelled an armed incursion by Hutu rebels in the Gisenyi area. On 24 April, a MONUC patrol allegedly encountered Rwandan troops in North Kivu, sparking protests by officials in Kinshasa. As on later occasions, Kigali denied that Rwandan soldiers had entered the DR Congo. Kabila, in turn, accused Rwanda of supporting the mutiny of Nkunda in South Kivu. Numerous countries were involved in attempts to normalise relations between Kigali and Kinshasa (UK, Belgium, South Africa, US) before Presidents Kagame and Kabila held talks in Abuja, facilitated by Nigerian head of state Olusegun Obasanjo (25 June). Celebrated as a breakthrough, the Abuja talks resulted in an agreement to create a **Joint Verification Mechanism** (JVM) to examine allegations about Rwanda's military presence in the Kivus and to monitor the activities of Rwandan Hutu rebels in the DR Congo. UN Secretary-General Annan convened another meeting on the sidelines of the African Union summit in Addis Ababa (6–8 July). MONUC prepared the terms of reference of the JVM and these were subsequently adopted by Rwanda and the DR Congo (22 September). On 29 November, both countries finally endorsed the operational concept of the mechanism and the setting up of joint verification teams, which will be composed of representatives from Rwanda, the DR Congo, MONUC and the African Union. Additional diplomatic initiatives, including **Uganda**, were undertaken by the US government. Under its auspices, a series of meetings between the foreign ministers of Rwanda, Uganda and the DR Congo were organised. On 25 October, they resulted in an agreement to neutralise armed groups in the region and to create a tripartite commission to address regional security issues. However, its first meeting was cancelled after the Congolese delegation failed to travel to Kigali (10 December).

Organised by Annan's special envoy, Ibrahima Fall, the first summit of the **International Conference on Peace, Security, Democracy and Development in the Great Lakes Region** took place in Dar es Salaam (19–20 November). The 11 heads of government, including Kabila, Kagame and Museveni, adopted a declaration containing guiding principles to promote peace, stability, democracy and development in the region. They agreed to establish an inter-ministerial committee tasked with developing a plan of action to be adopted at a second summit scheduled for 2005. However, hopes for regional peace were almost immediately dashed when President Kagame informed the United Nations that he might send his soldiers back to the Congo (25 November). In the following days, he even hinted that Rwandan troops might already operate in the Kivus.

Probably not coincidentally, Kagame's threats coincided with the visit of the **Security Council mission** to the Great Lakes region (21–25 November). In its fifth visit in as many years to Central Africa, the mission held talks with Presidents Paul Kagame, Domitien Ndayizeye, Yoweri Museveni, Joseph Kabila and Congo's four vice-presidents. Although the ambassadors condemned Kagame's belligerence, the Rwandan president reconfirmed his willingness to take matters into his own hands. The crisis was exacerbated in December when Rwanda refused to rule out military intervention amid numerous reports that Rwandan troops had crossed into the Congo to conduct a short 'surgical strike' against FDLR rebels. Despite stepping up air patrols and stating its conviction that 'foreign troops' had entered the DR Congo, MONUC was unable to confirm a Rwandan presence in the Kivus. On 20 December, apparently due to pressure by donor countries, Rwanda declared that it would henceforth refrain from issuing threats of military intervention.

Crisis diplomacy continued to dominate Belgian and South African engagement in the DR Congo. Spearheading these efforts was President Thabo Mbeki of **South Africa**, who visited the DR Congo twice in the course of the year (14–15 January; 30–31 August). For his visit in January, Mbeki led a delegation of business people and ministers to Kinshasa. Various accords on political, economic and military cooperation were signed worth some $ 10 bn. As in previous years, Congo's former colonial power **Belgium** was an active player trying to defuse tensions and support the transition. Belgium's prime minister as well as the ministers of co-operation, defence and foreign affairs travelled to the Congo repeatedly. Most notably, Foreign Minister Louis Michel travelled to South Kivu at the height of the Bukavu crisis (6 June). On 11 June, he convened a meeting of his colleagues from Burundi, Rwanda and the DR Congo to discuss the relaunching of the largely defunct 'Communauté Economique pour la Région des Grands Lacs' (CEPGL). The Netherlands and the European Union signalled their readiness to assist the process. However, a diplomatic row between the Belgian and Congolese authorities erupted in October. Following his visit of the region (DR Congo, Rwanda), the new Belgian Foreign Minister Karel de Gucht harshly criticised Congo's transition and its leaders, publicly declaring that few of them had left him "with a convincing impression" and that the country had no "real government". In response, Kinshasa temporarily recalled its ambassador from Brussels.

Following Resolution 1533 (12 March), the United Nations set up a **group of experts** to monitor the arms embargo imposed on Eastern Congo by Security Council Resolution 1493 (2003). In its first report, the group provided evidence that Kigali had repeatedly violated the sanctions and had been actively involved in recruiting troops in Rwanda for Nkunda (15 July). In terms of Resolution 1552 (27 July), the Security Council re-established the group of experts until 31 January 2005 to monitor the embargo, examine the steps taken by states in the region to implement it and to provide evidence on activities and actors in violation of it.

Socioeconomic Developments

The humanitarian situation in the country remained extremely grim. According to a **mortality** survey by the International Rescue Committee, more than 31,000 people continued to die every month as a direct or indirect result of the war. The organisation put the total of war-related deaths since 1998 at 3.8 m, making the Congo conflict the deadliest since the Second World War. Even before the flare-up in Kanyabayonga in December, some 2.1 m Congolese were still displaced in their country. An estimated 80% of the population lived on less than $ 1 per day.

Despite the persistence of Congo's humanitarian disaster and the ongoing political chaos, bilateral and multilateral donors generally applauded the government's efforts to establish economic stability and conditions for recovery. Thanks to prudent monetary and fiscal policies and incremental reform efforts, **real GDP growth** was estimated to be 7% (2003: 6.3%). On 12 July, the **IMF** completed the fourth semi-annual review of three-year Poverty Reduction and Growth Facility (PRGF) and made a favourable assessment of the government's economic recovery programme. It approved the disbursement of another tranche of $ 40 m, bringing the PRGF-related amount of aid received by the DR Congo since 2002 to about $ 700 m. In November, an IMF mission arrived in Kinshasa to conduct the fifth review of PRGF. Results had not been announced by year's end. Due to the broad satisfaction with government's performance, the IMF extended debt service relief under the Heavily Indebted Poor Countries Initiative (HIPC) until July 2005. As a consequence, Congo's debt service fell by-two thirds in 2004 to $ 90 m, nominally enabling the government to allocate more resources for poverty reduction. Even so, donors have criticised the government's failure to shift more resources for this purpose and expected this to occur with the completion of a full poverty reduction strategy paper in August 2005. Provided there is solid economic performance, the IMF expects the DR Congo to reach the HIPC completion point in 2006, by which time the vast bulk of the country's external debt should be eliminated (2003: $ 10.5 bn).

Favourable assessments of the government's macroeconomic performance increased the generosity and confidence of donors. In the first five months of the year, $ 548 m was disbursed (of total pledges amounting to $ 1 bn for 2004) and further funds were approved over the course of the year. On 26 February, the **World Bank** approved a $ 200 m credit to finance economic recovery, capacity building (customs services), the building of infrastructure and balance of payments support. The bank also approved grants worth some $ 200 m to finance an HIV/AIDS programme (1 April) and an emergency demobilisation and reintegration programme (25 May). Finally, on 26 August, it approved a $ 60 m emergency social action grant to mitigate the ongoing socioeconomic crisis in the country. More pledges came forth on 11 November when the Paris Club of donors promised further $ 5.7 bn for the 2005–07 period in response to a new economic recovery plan by the government. On 19 May, the ADB approved a soft loan of $ 36 m to finance a programme in support of agricultural and rural development.

On 24 April, the National Assembly created a **commission of inquiry** to examine economic contracts, signed since 1996 during the course of the recent wars, between the government and foreign partners deemed to be at odds with the interests of the Congolese people (24 April). The creation of the commission marked a potentially significant attempt to rein in ongoing resource exploitation, pillage and corruption in the country. Given the shady business deals between the government and Zimbabwe that had previously been uncovered by a United Nations panel of experts examining illegal resource exploitation in the DR Congo, it was small wonder that Kabila's PPRD (unsuccessfully) voted in parliament against the creation of the commission. Another setback for Kabila occurred in June when a Belgian judge ordered an international arrest warrant for Jean-Charles Okoto, the national secretary of propaganda of the PPRD, who was accused of money-laundering, embezzlement and kidnapping.

A major bone of contention was the damning report in the so-called strategic audit of the DR Congo's **parastatals** that had been requested by the IMF as part of the PRGF programme (18 October). As expected, the parliamentary debate barely touched on the reforms to be undertaken to revive the largely defunct state-owned electricity, water, communications and transport companies (among others) and instead centred on their distribution among the factions directing the transitional government. In order to avoid the sharing-out of parastatals hitherto controlled by Kabila, his PPRD and the allied Mai Mai advocated an allocation based on competence, while all the other factions called for respect for the principles of the transition, that is, a distribution along party lines. At year's end, the conflict was not solved and threatened to further destabilise the transition process.

In late October, the draft budget for 2005 was unveiled. It projected revenues of FC 699.5 bn ($ 1.6 bn), 57.7% of which were presumed to be provided by donors. Expenditure was estimated at FC 861.4 bn. ($ 161.9 bn) while real GDP growth was expected to reach 7%. For 2005, the government targeted an average inflation rate of 5%.

Although the IMF declared that the DR Congo had advanced from the "stabilisation to the reconstruction stage", it remained doubtful whether significant reconstruction would be undertaken by either the government or private investors. The bloated transitional institutions appeared to consume much of the funds provided by donors and their political bickering hampered the creation of an economically favourable environment. On 1 November, however, Vice-President Bemba announced a $ 27.5 m reconstruction programme for North Kivu, parts of which were allocated to building roads linking Beni to Kisangani and Mbuji-Mayi to Bukavu. Furthermore, foreign investors remained reticent and President Kabila's two-week tour to Western Europe (Belgium, France, Germany, UK) elicited little response by foreign firms wary of the pervasive insecurity in the country. A major exception was South Africa's keenness to foster economic and business ties with the DR Congo and it was widely believed that preferential access for South African companies to the Congolese market was a 'peace dividend' in return for President Mbeki's sustained diplomatic engagement in the country. In late October, for example, a consortium led by South Africa's energy parastatal, Eskom, was awarded a $ 5 bn contract to rehabilitate and upgrade the hydroelectric Inga plant on the Congo River.

Denis M. Tull

Equatorial Guinea

The fall-out from the alleged mercenary plot uncovered in March dominated the political and diplomatic scene, and even overshadowed the parliamentary elections and a cabinet reshuffle. The ongoing border dispute with Gabon was at the centre of regional foreign policies. Relations with the United States were strained due to a report by the US senate that brought details of grand corruption and of the appropriation of oil wealth by the tiny ruling elite into the open for public scrutiny. Meanwhile, the economy continued to benefit from rising oil production and high international oil prices, but without having much positive impact on the impoverished majority of the population.

Domestic Politics

Continued rumours and paranoia, constant conspiracy allegations and real or imagined coup attempts with subsequent waves of arrests have been a constant since 1979. All have been skilfully mastered by the president and have mainly served to control the ruling clan and the larger political scene. The **alleged mercenary plot** uncovered on 6 March was no exception but continued to dominate the political scene in Equatorial Guinea for the rest of the year.

Events began to unfold when on 6 March the security forces started rounding up foreign nationals, mainly from Cameroon, who were rapidly deported. Later that night, some 67 mercenaries allegedly on their way to Malabo and led by Simon Mann, who had founded the well-known private military companies Executive Outcome and Sandline International in the 1990s, were arrested at the airport in Harare, Zimbabwe, and charged with the illegal purchase of weapons. These events were followed the next day by the arrest of 15 mercenaries led by Nick du Toit, former commander of South Africa's 32 Battalion, in Malabo. On 8 March, Agustin Nzé Nfumu, the minister of information, announced that the government, helped mainly by South Africa and Zimbabwe, had just prevented a coup attempt in which a group of mercenaries supported by foreign national and commercial interests had planned to take over and to install Severo Moto, the opposition leader in exile in Spain, as the new president.

Although President Obiang assured a press conference on 17 March that the crisis was over, the alleged coup attempt overshadowed the parliamentary elections and a subsequent cabinet reshuffle. As a result of the **parliamentary elections** on 25 April, the ruling 'Partido Democrático de Represenantes del Pueblo' (PDGE) maintained its grip on power in the 'Cámara de Representants del Pueblo' that had been expanded from 80 to 100 seats. Together with its seven allied parties, the PDGE gained 98 seats, while the main opposition party, the 'Convergencia para la Democracia Social' (CPDS) won the remaining two seats. The municipal elections held in parallel gave the PDGE and its allies 237 seats on local councils with the CPDS capturing the remaining seven. The CPDS, repeatedly the target of repressive actions by the government, denounced both elections as "an electoral coup d'état". Spanish elections observers spoke of "important irregularities".

In the wake of the elections, the long expected **government reshuffle** on 16 June brought a number of surprises. The prime minister, Candido Muatetema Rivas, was replaced by the former senior minister in charge of relations with parliament and legal affairs at the president's office, Miguel Abia Biteo Borico, who had served in the ministry of mines and energy and in the ministry of finance prior to his new assignment. He was seen as the main architect of Equatorial Guinea's oil policy. The new prime minister quickly announced his plans for reform mainly intended to improve the quality of public administration. The reshuffle added to the contested **succession issue** as well. Teodorín Nguema Obiang Mangue, the president's son and heir apparent, who is, however, fiercely opposed by many in the country's political elite, lost the lucrative ministry of infrastructure but remained a cabinet minister in charge of the equally lucrative forestry portfolio. President Obiang's other son and Teodorín's junior half-brother, Gabriel Mbegha Obiang Lima, was promoted from secretary of state to deputy minister for mines and hydrocarbons. As President Obiang's expert on the oil industry, the reshuffle added to Gabriel's status as a main challenger to Teodorín's ambitions. All in all, the new government remained firmly in the hands of the extended family with half of the 50 cabinet ministers being relatives of the president. But it also reflected a move towards more technocratic expertise by bringing in a total of 23 new and mainly younger appointees. There was a more pronounced, if partial, willingness to deal more effectively and efficiently with international companies and the challenges of managing the oil wealth.

After months of delay, the **trial** of the alleged mercenaries began on 23 August. Although intended to demonstrate the government's supposed openness and adherence to international standards through its invitation to international observers and the foreign media to attend, all reports from the trial were a disaster for the government. Amnesty International and the International Bar Association criticised the trial for flagrant breaches of international standards, and media coverage highlighted the excesses of the ruling elite as well as the controversial behaviour of the authorities prior to and during the trial. Allegations of statements made under torture, missing interpreters for the defendants, dubious evidence and a case built solely on a confession later denied by the alleged leader of the operation in Malabo, added to the many doubts expressed. After an adjournment of three months, the trial reopened on 16 November and on 26 November 19 alleged plotters were convicted in Malabo. All of the 14 foreign defendants are of Armenian and South African nationality – a German had died in prison allegedly of cerebral malaria 8 days after the initial arrests – and were sentenced to long prison terms. The five defendants from Equatorial Guinea who had worked for a company partly owned by the president's brother and director of national security, Armengol Ondo Nguema, came away with short sentences or were even released, while Severo Moto was sentenced *in absentia* to 63 years in prison for masterminding the coup attempt.

Foreign Affairs

In his press conference on 17 March, President Obiang publicly thanked South Africa, Zimbabwe and Angola for helping to avert the coup. In contrast, officials accused **Spain**, the former colonial power, other unnamed countries in the region, the United States, United Kingdom and various multinational companies either of involvement in the conspiracy or of having turned a blind eye. The escalating paranoia after the alleged coup attempt came to the fore when a Norwegian research ship working under a mandate from the UN World Food Programme was hit by several bullets on 26 June. The captain was detained overnight by coast guards. The Norwegian foreign minister lodged an official protest. The incident came only two weeks after Equatorial Guinea had accused Spain of sending a warship to stage yet another coup. In July, Equatorial Guinea recalled its ambassador to Madrid as a sign of protest at Spain's refusal to extradite Severo Moto. Tensions subsided, however, when a Spanish delegation visited Malabo in early August and the Equatorial Guinean ambassador returned to Madrid.

In the wake of the alleged coup attempt, foreign **relations with the United Kingdom** suffered. A perceived lack of cooperation on the part of the British government during the investigations, together with revelations that the British foreign minister, Jack Straw, knew of the coup plot as early as January 2004 might well lead to negative commercial repercussions for UK firms. Equatorial Guinea and the alleged plot made international headlines mainly because of the arrest of Mark Thatcher, son of former British prime minister, Margaret Thatcher, in South Africa on 25 August. As one of the alleged financial backers of the planned coup in Malabo, he was accused of violating the South African law banning the activities of mercenaries in the country.

The **maritime border dispute with Gabon** over Mbane, a tiny island south of Corisco island in Corisco bay off the southern coast of the mainland, dated back to 1972 and has prevented oil companies from carrying out full exploration of the area. Gabon and Equatorial Guinea officially accepted UN mediation on 25 January. Despite a series of meetings and the signing of a 'memorandum of understanding' by the two heads of state at the meeting of the African Union in Addis in July, no real progress emerged in the first year after the agreement. A resolution might be years away, since the two countries were not ready for the necessary concessions along the lines of the joint development agreements now in operation since 2001 with Nigeria and São Tomé and Príncipe. Spain claimed to have proof that the contested island was part of Equatorial Guinea, but this only helped to improve the tense relations between Malabo and Madrid. The other **border dispute, with Cameroon**, did not draw closer to a settlement either. Resolution of this dispute was certainly not helped by the expulsion of about 1,500 Cameroonians after the alleged coup attempt in March. As a consequence of this forced exodus, the Cameroonian ambassador to Equatorial Guinea was recalled to Yaoundé.

Relations with the United States received a blow, but less because of the alleged involvement of US companies in the coup plot. A report released on 15 July by the US senate's permanent subcommittee on investigations found corrupt payments and money-laundering activities linked to the Washington-based Riggs Bank and to top officials and relatives of President Obiang. The report also exposed the dubious practices of the three major US oil companies operating in Equatorial Guinea, i.e., ExxonMobil, Marathon Oil and Amerada Hess. The report referred to over 60 private accounts and 'certificates of deposit' (CDs) held by government officials at Riggs Bank with total balances that had reached between $ 400 to 700 m at times. Spanish satellite broadcasters immediately carried all the details of the report to an audience in Equatorial Guinea that had known about the appropriation of the oil wealth by a tiny elite for years but was eager to learn who had had how much money in what sort of accounts. It became obvious for everyone to see how an extended family had run the country's oil wealth as a family business. However, all charges were quickly denied by a government spokesperson on state television on 18 July. President Obiang denounced all accusations as unfounded and solely inspired by the country's many political enemies in his speech on 3 August, marking the 25th anniversary of the coup that had brought him to power.

Socioeconomic Developments

With respect to almost all available **macroeconomic and financial data**, Equatorial Guinea continued to be a rare exception in sub-Saharan Africa. The country remained one of the fastest growing economies of the continent due to growing oil production and high international oil prices, leading to ongoing associated booms in the country's service and construction sectors. **GDP growth rates** reached 24%, after 13.6% last year. The **current account** showed a surplus for the first time in years, **foreign exchange reserves** continued to rise and reached $ 759 m in October according to IMF data, the budget surplus exceeded 10%, and along with Angola, Equatorial Guinea was the largest recipient of **foreign direct investment** in sub-Saharan Africa, receiving $ 1.4 bn. **Inflation** was largely under control and down to 4% from 13.6% the previous year, but likely to pick up again because of the pressure from the oil industry. Low inflation was mainly due to the strong value of the CFAfr, which benefited from a fixed peg with the euro, thereby helping to contain imported inflation. On the downside, almost all other economic sectors have been rapidly marginalised, with oil now accounting for 89% of GDP, 87% of state revenue and 92% of total exports. And although hard data on **income distribution or poverty indicators** remained hard to come by, it was the tiny elite that benefited from the oil boom while the majority of the population continued impoverished. The prominent dubbing of Equatorial Guinea as the Kuwait of Africa continued, therefore, to be misleading. Meanwhile, public expenditure on health, education and essential road infrastructure was up but had produced few tangible results for those left out of the oil boom. Many of the projects were classified as 'work in progress' and were concentrated on the three cities of Malabo, Luba and Bata, whereas the smaller towns and rural areas were essentially left out. There was no country in the world where the figures for per capita income, in which the country scored high, and human development, in which the country ranked close to the bottom, were as far apart as in Equatorial Guinea.

New **data from the oil sector** revealed that oil production, currently estimated at 424,000 barrels per day, including condensates and liquefied natural gas, will continue to expand but might peak as early as 2007 unless new explorations turn out to be viable. On 1 November, the Petroleum Oil and Gas Corporation of South Africa (PetroSA), the national oil company of South Africa, signed a production-sharing contract with its Equatorial Guinean counterpart, 'Guinea Equatorial Petrol' (GEPetrol). The contract was interpreted as a reward for South Africa's role in stopping the alleged coup in March. Financially desperate Zimbabwe also benefited from an agreement signed in November that provided for the supply of oil from Equatorial Guinea. This was also seen as a reward for Zimbabwe's cooperation in preventing the mercenaries and alleged plotters from landing in Malabo in March.

Cord Jakobeit

Gabon

Omar Bongo 'Ondimba' (b. 1935) was Africa's second-longest serving head of state, and after 37 years in power showed no interest in stepping down. His family members held key government posts and his ruling 'Parti Démocratique Gabonais' (PDG) held 72% of the seats in the National Assembly. With unusually high oil prices supporting his economy, he spent the year preparing for upcoming presidential elections.

Domestic Politics

The focus of democratic resistance has been shifting away from political parties towards strikes and other forms of 'direct action', particularly in the education sector. On 7 January, the largest high school in the country, the **Omar Bongo National High School**, was shut down by special police forces, who fired teargas at **machete-wielding students**, after one student death, eleven injuries, seven damaged buses, and a general climate of violent disorder brought students from the national high school into fights with students from another college, over access to school buses. Most of the school buses in the capital of Libreville had broken down. Bongo's government claimed it could not afford to fix them.

From 1 January to 15 March, his namesake **Omar Bongo University** was also shut down, because of violent **student riots** that included barricades, a teacher strike and vocal public demands for the university rector, Jean-Emile Mbot, to resign. On 7 May, three student activists, Raoul Ovono Abessolo, Roland Mbadinga Koumba and Guy-Roger Ngogho-Ngogho, published a letter calling for an 'intifada' against the university. They were promptly arrested and thrown into prison.

On 6 September, Bongo responded with a conventional **cabinet reshuffle**. He left his two most prominent PDG notables – the current Prime Minister Jean-François Ntoutoume Emane (b. 1939), and his son-in-law, the current Finance Minister Paul Toungi – in place, as a sign of confidence. But he moved his maternal nephew General Idriss Ngari (b. 1946) from the interior ministry to the ministry of public works. Ngari keeps close personal ties with all the Téké officers who dominate Gabon's defence and security. Bongo's former brother-in-law and former national police chief, Jean-Boniface Assélé (b. 1939) was named minister of labour. The biggest loser was the ex-education minister, Daniel Ona Ondo, removed because of the spring student riots and summer's **catastrophic 'baccalauréat' results** (final secondary-school examinations). In the first round in July, only 35.1% of all students passed. In the second round in September, under the new education minister, François Owono, only 25.1% passed! Paulette Missambo, now ex-transportation minister, was removed from her post after a public investigation revealed that poor government standards for aircraft maintenance were responsible for the deadly **Gabon Express** plane **crash** in the summer. Bongo kept his son, Ali Bongo (b. 1959), as minister of national defence. Ali Bongo heads a progressive faction of ruling PDG called the **'Reformers'**, who want to create political change by reforming the ruling party. He was considered one possible successor for the presidency.

There were **no credible opposition** candidates inside Gabon with enough charisma, money or national standing to defeat his father in the next presidential elections. On 23 April 2004, former Catholic priest and Fang opposition leader, Paul Mba-Abessole (b. 1939) of the second-largest political party, 'Rassemblement Pour le Gabon' (RPG), who has for more than a decade called upon Bongo to step down from power, changed his position, calling upon his supporters to vote for the presidential majority in parliament and to support Omar Bongo's re-election. He is now third deputy prime minister. Another former opposition leader, Pierre-Claver Maganga-Moussavou (b. 1952), who represents the 'Parti Social Démocratique' (PSD) in the National Assembly, also yielded to temptation and officially joined the presidential majority in mid-June. He was named minister of state responsible for economic missions and structural reforms.

Still, some opponents kept their virtue by the end of this largely disappointing year, such as Pierre-Louis Agondkjo Okawé (b. 1936) and Pierre Mamboundou (b. 1946) of the **'Union du Peuple Gabonais' (UPG)**, who actually opposed Bongo's 2003 constitutional amendments removing his term limits, which allow him to run for re-election in 2005. Mamboundou is reported to have held discussions in 2004 with disgruntled PDG insider, Zacharie Myboto (b. 1938), a powerful Nzébi leader in the ruling Téké-Nzébi ethnic inner circle, who is independently wealthy and using his money politically.

Myboto financed a newspaper he called '**L'Autre Journal**', or 'The Other Paper', (referring to the government-run 'L'Union', the only daily newspaper still in circulation). In an act of state censorship, the 'Conseil National de la Communication' closed down his press for, it said, "attacking the dignity of the institutions of the Republic." The death of its editor-in-chief, Marc Boukoukou Boussaga, a few days after the police raided his offices and seized his computers and files, was still under investigation at year's end. In 2004, Gabon's **press freedom** rankings fell from 'Partly Free' to 'Not Free' on the annual Freedom House index. Gabon ranked 125 of 193 countries, a low ranking explained by the regime's "continued crackdown" on the private press, its persistent habit of "de-licensing" private news organisations and an "overall countrywide worsening" of the free speech environment.

As the year came to a close, the Bongo regime used low-intensity, selective government repression to inhibit the rise of any kind of opposition. On 15 November, Hervé Opianga, leading a peaceful march for the legalisation of his political party, was arrested by the police and thrown into prison. On 20 November, five days later, Abbé Ngwa Nguema, editor-in-chief of 'Radio Télévision Nazareth', was arrested for "irresponsible reporting" of the news, and an "illegal existence" outside the framework of national audiovisual laws.

Foreign Affairs

After decades of pro-French stability, Gabon's international relations showed signs of change in the direction of trade from the West to the East. Chinese workers finished construction of a new National Assembly building in 2004, and should complete a new senate building by the end of 2005. Chinese President **Hu Jintao** visited Gabon's capital, Libreville, in February – the first ever visit by a Chinese head of state – and said he would provide more aid to Gabon, including a $ 6 m interest-free loan "without political strings". Bongo declared after his meeting with Hu that he preferred this aspect of Chinese cooperation. On 29 May, China signed three new **oil agreements** with Gabon. President Bongo in turn visited China. He spent 8–13 September in Beijing, diplomatically courting the Chinese Communist Party leadership (men of his generation) to establish new, more remunerative foreign relations than those Gabon has traditionally conducted with Western powers.

Preparations for this trip were made in August by Foreign Minister **Jean Ping** – who is half-Chinese – and who, on 11 July, had become the first Gabonese **president** of the **UN General Assembly**. Using his largely symbolic office, he defended fellow African, UN Secretary-General Kofi Annan, facing criticism for corruption, by leading a standing ovation in the General Assembly on 9 December.

At the regional level, the **Gulf of Guinea Commission**, an international body comprising the heads of state of Nigeria, Angola, Cameroon, Republic of Congo, DR Congo, Gabon, Equatorial Guinea and São Tomé and Príncipe, provided Bongo with a multilateral mechanism to conduct personal diplomacy with other regional heads of state. For example, the controversy over oil-rich Corisco bay, located between northern Gabon and the southern **Equatorial Guinea** littoral, long a source of discontent between these neighbours (analogous to the controversy between Nigeria and Cameroon over the Bakassi peninsula) moved towards resolution in 2004 because of personal talks between the heads of state. Equatorial Guinea has long claimed sovereignty over its islands – **Mbane, Cocotiers and Congas** – based on Spanish colonial assertions. Bongo has also claimed the islands for Gabon, and even sent troops to occupy them. Gabon and Equatorial Guinea accepted the principle of UN mediation on 25 January. On 5 July, presidents Bongo and Obiang finally and formally agreed to let a **UN mediator** settle the territorial dispute. Following the model of the Bakassi case (decided by the International Court of Justice) the two men signed a **memorandum of understanding** – in the presence of Kofi Annan – promising future joint exploration of Corisco while they waited for the court to make its decision.

In other **regional diplomacy**, Bongo received General François Bozizé, president of the Central African Republic, on 28 April, and on 23 October he hosted a mini-summit for the Côte d'Ivoire, gathering the loyalists and the opponents of president Laurent Gbagbo. Since the Accra III summit, Bongo had been the main facilitator in that crisis and was invited to the Elysée on 28 October to discuss it with long-time personal friend Jacques Chirac.

Socioeconomic Developments

Gabon is considered a rich country by African standards. Gabon's high per capita income of $ 5,500 ppp (purchasing power parity) was four times that of most African nations. Moreover, its GDP nearly doubled in four years – thanks to high oil prices – from $ 4.9 bn (2000) to $ 9.1 bn (2004). However, a child born in Gabon in 2004 had a life expectancy of 56 years. The literacy rate was only 63.2%, with schools closed for months at a time. It is an economy where 21% of all working-age people are unemployed and over 60% of the active labour force works in the primary sector, earning 8% of the national income. Basic infrastructure was so poor that there were only 838 kilometres of paved roads for 257,667 km² of territory. Add to this a debt burden, and you have a **portrait of poverty** rather than riches.

Paris Club members – who have lent Gabon an estimated $ 2.46 bn – continue to take more than a third of all Gabonese government revenues every year. This heavy debt burden is only made worse by Gabon's high per capita income figures. "Presently we are the only country in the higher layer of **intermediate revenue**," complained Bongo in an interview, "So we don't benefit from debt forgiveness, much less any annulment."

Bongo convinced the **IMF** on 28 May to grant him $ 102 m in debt assistance, (equivalent to 4.1% of the total debt) accompanied by IMF approval, a prerequisite for debt rescheduling by the Paris Club. "The accord signed with the IMF arrived at after very long negotiations, and is a ray of hope for Gabon," boasted Bongo. "It is no secret to anyone that the economic and financial crisis has imposed a therapy of austerity," he said, "but the results of this **financial Ramadan** are reassuring." IMF interim general director Anne Kruger said she was pleased with the country's adoption of an **austerity budget**, and rated as 'satisfactory' its overall execution. Since mid-2002, she said, "Gabon has engaged in a vigorous policy of responding to the principle challenges facing the country," including finalisation of a new **Poverty Reduction Strategy (PRS),** which will define budgetary priorities in the future.

On 11 June – once the IMF had 'certified' Gabon – the **Paris Club** agreed to consolidate some € **717 m** of its debt, reducing € 456 m of arrears and € 261 m of maturities falling due through 2005. This rescheduling was expected to reduce debt services to creditors over the period from € 953 m to € 270 m.

Gender inequality remained a developmental problem, especially in rural zones where, for example, illiteracy reached 25% among men 15 years or older, but 48% among women. Only 10% of Gabonese businesswomen manage companies in the country. Women account for less than 5% of chief executive officers in companies in Gabon, and less than 1% of those who sit on the boards of directors. Although genital mutilation is not practised in Gabon, **polygamy** was still legal in 2004.

In October UNAIDS conservatively estimated the number of adults and children in Gabon living with the **HIV** virus at 48,000 in 2004 (estimates ranged between 24,000 and 91,000). The infection rate for adults 15–49 years of age was conservatively estimated at **8.1%** (range 4.1%–15.3%). Some 3,000 Gabonese died in 2003 as a result of **AIDS**, creating 14,000 new AIDS-related orphans between the ages of 0–17 in 2004.

Gabon was sub-Saharan Africa's fifth-largest oil producer in 2004. The high average price of crude oil in 2004, $ 39.3 per barrel, was good news for the short term. **Oil production declined** from an average of 266,900 in 2003 to 264,900 barrels per day in 2004. The largest oil producing company in Gabon was Total Gabon (formerly Elf), at 100,000 barrels per day. The second largest was Shell Gabon with 70,000 barrels per day, but which runs the largest producing oilfield in the country, Rabi Kounga. On 13 July, PanOcean and Vaalco oil companies announced they had made a new 6,600-barrel-per-day discovery at their offshore oilrig near the Etame field. The discovery should increase the field's daily crude oil production from 15,000 to 21,600 barrels a day, and is part of a long-term trend in the Gabonese petroleum industry: New discoveries are made all the time, not large enough, however, to stop reserve depletion. In addition to its drilling at Etame field, Vaalco expects to find more oil reserves offshore in the unexplored part of the richly yielding Gamba sandstone off southern Gabon. It is also interested in Corisco bay (see above). Shell Gabon and PanOcean made a new oil discovery on their Awoun concession. On 18 November, Shell Gabon announced that, after a period of rapid decline, production was expected to stabilise and perhaps even grow. "The reasonable growth that I am hoping for will depend on our success in exploration," explained Shell's Franck Denelle. "Even if we do not recover the levels we used to produce in the past," he observed, "Gabon still has some oil left." In 2004, proven crude oil reserves stood at 2,450,000,000 barrels.

In an effort to diversify the economy, the government announced that it would start exploring the possibility of developing commercial **gas** fields in the country. (Until now this gas has been flared.) On 14 July, it also announced that it would begin a new project to promote **fisheries** resources, with a $ 270,000 grant from FAO.

Forestry was largely stable, with a decline of 28% in the logging of okoumé, traditionally Gabon's premier wood, but total export of all other species of **wood** actually **increased 13%**. This increase in overall volume has been attributed to China. Jobs in the forestry sector rose 15% in 2004. Under pressure from the IMF, the government is forced to improve its rainforest management, including greater transparency, fair public auctions for tracts of virgin forestland and determination of all existing forestry permits. On 9 August, Bongo decreed a **temporary moratorium** on the allocation of new forestry permits until this could be done, and the IMF gave its approval. One IMF condition was that a map of concessions would be finalised before the end of 2004. This resulted in the preparation of a list of all forest **concessions**.

The publication of this list on 2 September created a political **scandal**. Information about who owns forest concessions (in hectares) was disclosed: Omar Bongo (200,000 ha), Ali Bongo (200,000 ha), Idriss Ngari (110,100 ha), and Paul Toungui (56,000 ha), and other members of the regime, holding in total millions of hectares. However, on 20 October, Transparency International (TI), in its annual corruption index, ranked Gabon only as the **74th most corrupt country** in the world.

Douglas Yates

São Tomé and Príncipe

This small country was again affected by political crisis and corruption scandals. A national forum to reconcile the various political groups in the interests of the country's development did not end the political instability. The emerging oil sector dominated economic development and attracted increasing international attention. Delays in the awarding of the first oil blocks, submitted to a bidding round in 2003, postponed the expected payment of signature bonuses to 2005.

Domestic Politics

In January, the submission of the Audit Office's ('Tribunal de Contas') first report on public accounts embarrassed the government. The 36-page document criticised anomalies in the management of public funds, including contracting for public works without the necessary public tendering and the arbitrary granting of housing subsidies to government members. Moreover, the auditors denounced the deficient management of state property, the lack of any inventory for this property and the inadequate archiving of documentation. Those blamed for these irregularities rejected the allegations as unfounded.

In late February, another **political crisis** broke out when Prime Minister Maria das Neves ('Movimento de Libertação de São Tomé e Príncipe'/'Partido Social Democrata' –

MLSTP/PSD) demanded the dismissal of ministers Tomé Vera Cruz (natural resources) and Mateus 'Nando' Rita (foreign affairs), both belonging to President Menezes's 'Movimento Democrático Força da Mudança' (MDFM) party, on the grounds that they had concluded government business without her consent. Vera Cruz had signed a controversial oil agreement with the Energem Petroleum Company that she rejected as detrimental to national interests. Rita had travelled to Luanda to sign a commercial air transport agreement with the Angolan government. Both ministers affirmed that Das Neves had been aware of their actions. In protest against the accusations, on 5 March all four ministers of the MDFM, including the health and justice ministers, left the coalition, depriving the government of a parliamentary majority. After the 'Partido de Convergência Democrática' (PCD) had declined the MLSTP/PSD's proposal to replace the MDFM, the four-party alliance Uê Kedadji (four seats) agreed to join a coalition comprising MLSTP/PSD (24 seats) and 'Acção Democrática Independente' (ADI) (four seats). Vilfredo Santana Gil (Uê Kedadji), Arlindo de Ceita Carvalho (ADI) and Ovídio Pequeno (independent) were appointed respectively as new ministers of health, natural resources and foreign affairs. The former secretary of state for public administration, Elsa Pinto (MLSTP/PSD), received the justice portfolio.

In April and May, two parties elected new leaders at their respective congresses. The opposition PCD elected the economist Leonel Mário d'Alva, prime minister of the transitional government (1974–75) and speaker of parliament (1991–94), as new chairperson. The position had been vacant since October 2002 after his predecessor resigned because of internal party disputes. The ADI, without an elected leader since the resignation of the former secretary-general in late 2001, elected Patrice Trovoada, son of ex-president Trovoada (1991–2001) and President Menezes's special oil advisor, as secretary-general.

After several delays, on 16 June the **National Forum for Reconciliation**, an assembly of political parties and civil society to debate the country's problems, stipulated by the memorandum of understanding of 23 July 2003 that had ended a one-week coup, held its inaugural session, which was presided over by President Menezes. In his speech, the president blamed politicians' self-enrichment and political intrigue to the detriment of constructive cooperation as a principal cause of the failure of development. After the inaugural session, the forum held local meetings all over the country to hear local concerns and expectations. At the closing ceremony of the forum, on 12 July, a long list of recommendations on and conclusions about political, social and economic issues was presented.

The national harmony exhibited at the forum did not prevent a further government crisis. In August, an audit report on the accounts of the food aid organisation 'Gabinete de Gestão da Ajuda' (GGA), a government department that administers the counterpart funds in local currency, stemming from the sale of foreign food aid, revealed a series of irregularities, including the illicit granting of credits to dozens of prominent people, payment for fictitious services without contracting, and illegal payments to the ministries of economy and finance. The report also disclosed that Prime Minister Maria das Neves had received various illegal payments from GGA accounts. After being informed of the investigation by the attorney-general, on 14 September President Menezes **dismissed the prime minister** for her alleged involvement in the GGA scandal. In turn, Das Neves accused Menezes of dismissing her without a trial or conviction.

On 18 September, Damião Vaz de Almeida (MLSTP/PSD), the labour minister in the previous government, was appointed prime minister of a new coalition government including his own party and ADI. Only six ministers from the former executive were reappointed, including the ministers of foreign affairs, defence, natural resources, youth and education. Four of the new ministers had no previous government experience.

While the political crisis provoked by the corruption scandal was brought to an end, the investigations troubled other politicians. On 2 November the attorney general, Adelino Pereira, filed an arrest warrant for the deputy and ex-prime minister Posser da Costa (MLSTP/PSD) for attempting to attack him in his office following reports that he was being investigated in the GGA corruption scandal. The National Assembly turned down the warrant on the grounds that Posser da Costa enjoyed parliamentary immunity, but subsequently allowed his questioning in the assault case. Later that month, displaying unusual harmony the National Assembly declined the attorney-general's request to lift the parliamentary immunity of four deputies, namely Posser da Costa, ex-prime minister Maria das Neves, and the ex-ministers Arzemiro dos Prazeres (PCD) and Basílio Diogo (MDFM), in connection with the GGA scandal.

Meanwhile, a number of relevant developments occurred in the oil sector. In October, a newly created 15-member National Petroleum Council (CNP) replaced the former National Oil Commission. At the same time, a National Petroleum Agency (ANP) was established to execute CNP's instructions and regulate the oil industry.

In November, the National Assembly approved the **Oil Revenue Management Law** that was largely based on the drafts of two teams of US experts, one headed by former Alaska governor Steve Cowper and the other a team from Columbia University in New York. The law provided for the transparent and accountable management of future oil revenues and regular audits of the oil accounts. The IMF had made future debt forgiveness conditional on the approval of this anti-corruption law.

Foreign Affairs

São Tomé and Príncipe's future oil wealth and strategic position in the Gulf of Guinea continued to attract **US interest** and cooperation. In February, the US Trade and Development Agency (USTDA) announced a grant of $ 800,000 to finance feasibility studies for the creation of a deep-sea port and the modernisation of the country's international airport. In March, at the request of the US European Command (EUCOM) in Stuttgart, a private US security company sent a defence consultant to the country to develop US military cooperation projects, including supplies for the coast guard.

In August, President Menezes and Defence Minister Óscar Sousa visited EUCOM. Later that month, US General Charles Wald, deputy commander of EUCOM, and Chuck Hagel, a Republican senator from Nebraska and member of the senate's foreign affairs and intelligence committees paid a visit to the country, during which they stressed its strategic importance for US interests in Africa.

In the same month, with the support of US military experts the armed forces destroyed their obsolete arms, most of them supplied by the former Soviet Union in the late 1970s at the request of the MLSTP regime. On this occasion, US ambassador Kenneth Moorefield declared his country was available to replace the destroyed material with adequate supplies of sophisticated modern armaments.

On 30 September, the US government's Millenium Challenge Corporation (MCC) announced that São Tomé and Príncipe was among the first seven countries to receive development assistance as part of the Millenium Challenge Account (MCA) on the grounds of the archipelago's commitment to political reform in favour of democratisation and economic liberalisation. The promised aid was part of a threshold programme, whose successful implementation is a prerequisite for future multi-year MCA assistance.

On 27 May, a majority of parliamentarians of the opposition MDFM/PCD and its coalition partner Uê Kedadji rejected a bilateral fishing agreement signed with Angola in January 2003 on the basis that Angola would benefit disproportionally from the deal. Despite the disapproval of the agreement, in July the Angolan ambassador in São Tomé, Pedro Fernando Mavunza, considered the diplomatic and political relations of his country with São Tomé and Príncipe to be excellent.

However, through its bilateral cooperation in the oil sector, Nigeria continued to be the more important regional partner. In June, President Menezes and Nigerian President Obasanjo signed the nine-point **Abuja Joint Declaration** on transparency in payments, expenditures and other dealings in the transactions concerning the two countries' Joint Development Zone (JDZ) established in 2001.

From 26–27 July, the 5th biennial **summit** of heads of state and governments of the eight-member 'Comunidade dos Países de Língua Portuguesa' (CPLP) took place in São Tomé, the largest international event ever held in the country. The meeting was also attended by Equatorial Guinea's President Obiang, who, despite his record of human rights violations and excessive corruption, had been invited personally by President Menezes as guest of honour. At the summit the Brazilian president, Luiz Inácio 'Lula' da Silva, passed on the CPLP's rotating presidency for the next two years to Menezes.

Socioeconomic Developments

In February the National Assembly approved the 2004 **national budget** of about $ 65 m, of which capital investment accounted for $ 42 m. The budget was $ 10 m higher than in the previous year and included $ 13 m from future signature bonuses to be paid by oil companies. Foreign donors financed some 80% of the budget. Education and health represented 18% and 17% of the expenditures respectively, while defence and security were also given priority.

On 18 February, the Canadian company DiamondWorks announced the signing of a memorandum of understanding with the government by its subsidiary, the Energem Petroleum Corporation, which included the establishment of a joint venture for trading in crude oil allocated to São Tomé and Príncipe by other African oil states and the commercial exploitation of hydrocarbon products extracted from the country's Exclusive Economic Zone (EEZ). Under the agreement, Energem would get 70% of the profits derived from the sale of crude, while 30% would accrue to the government. This transaction provoked the political crisis discussed above and was declared null and void by the council of ministers on 4 March.

Another controversial government deal failed in September, when the attorney-general declared null and void a telecom agreement signed in June between the infrastructure minister and the Greek company, Ronda Communications International, on the grounds that it violated the country's telecommunication law enacted in February. Under this law, the 'Companhia Santomense de Telecomunicações' (CST), set up in 1989, maintained the monopoly to run the country's telecommunications services until December 2005.

As part of the licensing of nine oil blocks in the JDZ initiated in 2003, in February and April respectively ExxonMobil and the controversial Houston-based Nigerian company Environmental Remediation Holding Corporation (ERHC) exercised their **preferential rights** under special agreements with the country within the JDZ. ExxonMobil exercised its pre-emptive rights to 40% in Block 1, for which ChevronTexaco had bid $ 123 m during the licensing round in 2003, but declined to exercise its 25% options in two other blocks, since it was unwilling to cooperate with ERHC, which had preferential rights in six blocks. In April, ERHC took four signature bonus-free stakes and another two stakes, for which signature bonuses were payable, in these six blocks.

Then unexpectedly, on 24 April, the Nigeria-São Tomé and Príncipe Joint Ministerial Council (JMC), awarded only **Block 1** to ChevronTexaco (51%), ExxonMobil (40%) and the Norwegian-Nigerian Equity Energy Resources (9%) and postponed the announcement of the successful bids on the other blocks to a later date. However, in October JMC declared the first licensing round closed, arguing that the bids for the other blocks had been unsatisfactory. In November, the Joint Development Authority (JDA) organised another bidding round for five blocks in the JDZ: these attracted 26 bids, which were dominated by Nigerian companies without deepwater expertise.

Meanwhile, the country's anticipated oil wealth attracted investments in the financial, tourism and energy sectors. On 13 March, President Menezes inaugurated the 'Banco Equador' to replace the 'Banco Comercial do Equador' declared bankrupt in 2002. The majority shareholders in the bank (with a capital of $ 3 m) were the Angolan groups Monbaka and António 'Mosquito' Mbakassi, each with a 40% stake. A week later, Menezes opened the National Investment Bank, owned by the private Portuguese airline Air Luxor (90%) and its subsidiaries in São Tomé and Príncipe and Cape Verde (5% each). The bank, with capital of $ 2.5 m, intended to increase this amount to $ 50 m within five years.

In May, the Portuguese hotel group Pestana signed an agreement with the government to build a five-star 100-room hotel and casino worth $ 30 m in São Tomé. At the same time, the government granted Pestana an exclusive 30-year concession over gambling in the country. In October, Pestana announced that from February 2005 it would take over the management of the Rolas Island resort owned by another Portuguese company.

In July, the London-based Synergies Investments and the government signed a contract for the construction of a 25-gigawatt hydroelectric plant on the Yô Grande River in São Tomé and the repair of the Contador and two other smaller hydroelectric plants. Under the agreement, which entailed investments of $ 50 m, the company was granted a 45-year concession to run the Yô Grande plant and a 35-year concession to exploit the Contador River plant.

Gerhard Seibert

V. Eastern Africa

In 2004, this part of the continent displayed some generally hopeful signs of the possible ending of several long-lasting conflicts, but also attracted major new international attention as a result of the brutal intensification of the Darfur conflict in Sudan. Political conditions in all the countries of the sub-region remained practically unchanged throughout the year, with no major elections and no unforeseen government downfalls. The main regional organisations, the Intergovernmental Authority on Development (IGAD) and East African Community (EAC) were able to boast some positive achievements. Economic performance was quite uneven but relatively solid in most of the larger countries, with evidence of continued dependency on weather conditions (negative impact of partial drought in some countries, good recovery after earlier drought in others). The countries in or bordering the Indian Ocean (Seychelles and Somalia, in particular) were also affected, albeit in a minor way, by the devastating Southeast Asian tsunami on 26 December.

Political Developments

The notorious case of **Somalia,** which had been without a central government or regular state structures since 1991, did give cause for guarded optimism after many years of despair and frustration, with the election of a president and the appointment of a prime minister of a new transitional government after lengthy discussions in Kenya by representatives of all the Somali clans under the aegis of IGAD. The compromise agreement was, however, still extremely precarious: even the physical return to Somalia of the new institutions remained uncertain as discussions got under way on the deployment of African military peacekeepers (under the authority of either AU or IGAD) to prevent a renewed outbreak of violence. Moreover, the self-declared, but still not internationally recognised state of **Somaliland** was completely left out of this new attempt to recreate Somali statehood. In neighbouring **Djibouti**, the president was fully in control ahead of the presidential elections scheduled for early 2005 in view of serious splits among the generally weak opposition groups.

In **Ethiopia**, the government also maintained a firm grip on all domestic developments, with only limited room for the political opposition in the run-up to the crucial parliamentary elections to be held in May 2005, despite some continuing local conflicts in different parts of this heterogeneous country. **Eritrea** remained under the draconian control of its authoritarian regime, with the long-promised national elections nowhere in sight, while various exiled opposition groups stepped up terrorist activities in the country and were being pressured to agree on more coordinated positions.

Developments in **Sudan** received by far the most international attention during the year, in respect of both positive and negative evolving scenarios. For years, peace negotiations to find a compromise formula for ending the civil war in southern Sudan between the Khartoum government and the Sudan People's Liberation Movement/Army (SPLM/A) had been pursued in Kenya, without noticeable progress, under the umbrella of IGAD and with international support: at long last a fundamental breakthrough was achieved, with formal signature imminent at year's end. This signalled the end of the longest armed conflict in Africa (ongoing since 1983), and the prospect of the establishment of a new semi-autonomous state administration in southern Sudan and a government of national unity in Khartoum. Partly because of the fear of being left out of the reconciliation process and of a share of resources (income from oil), the insurrection in Western Darfur province against continuing marginalisation by the central government escalated dramatically into full-blown armed conflict, with an alarming level of civilian suffering. Despite great international concern and substantial humanitarian relief operations, no workable solution to the Darfur nightmare was in prospect by year's end. The Khartoum government remained largely untouched by both external and internal pressures.

In East Africa, the year was by and large relatively quiet and uneventful in **Tanzania**, with the next national elections still one year away, but in the semi-autonomous island territory of **Zanzibar** noticeable political tensions persisted, as they had done for years. In

Kenya, the new coalition government that had come into power at the end of 2002, amid great expectations of reform, encountered serious internal disagreements and power struggles and lost much of its initial repute. Nevertheless, it was able to exercise undisputed control over the political affairs of the country. **Uganda** witnessed several important new developments, which, however, did not seriously challenge the dominance of the long-serving president and his unique 'movement' system. There was both some hesitant progress towards the expected return of a conventional multiparty political system and towards an end to the long, violent conflict in the north, but in neither case had anything definite been concluded by year's end.

The domestic scene in **Rwanda** was marked by quiet stability, the main development being the consolidation of the new political institutions after the crucial 2003 elections, the first since the 1994 genocide and the subsequent complete reversal of political power relations. Political discussion remained relatively subdued under the undisputed dominance of the inner power circle around the president. Neighbouring **Burundi** made some further slow progress towards national reconciliation and the introduction of new political institutions after years of armed conflict and political distrust, albeit with constant delays and the need to extend the originally agreed transition period. While a new power-sharing formula was agreed by all political players (except one), the holding of a referendum on the new constitution and of the crucial national elections had to be postponed to 2005.

The tiny island state of **Seychelles** saw the voluntary hand-over of leadership by the long-serving president (in power almost 27 years) to his anointed successor without new elections or any lessening of the dominance of the ruling party. In the **Comoros**, parliamentary elections were held after a two-year delay, thus finally completing the installation of the new institutions required to inaugurate the country's complicated new federal structure (with a union government and three semi-autonomous island authorities). This was a considerable achievement after years of dissension and the threatened disintegration of the country, although deep-seated mistrust remained almost unabated.

Transnational Relations and Conflict Configurations

The sub-regions of the **Horn of Africa** and of the **Great Lakes region** (encompassing parts of both Eastern and Central Africa) continued to be plagued by several highly intricate conflicts that cut across national boundaries and have implications for several countries in the region.

The long and tortuous process of establishing a new transitional government in **Somalia**, the most conspicuous case of a failed state in Africa, took place in Kenya under the mandate of IGAD and with considerable material and diplomatic support from the international community (mainly the EU and US). While Kenyan mediators played the most active role, Uganda, as IGAD chair since 2003, had also become involved. Many Somali groups, however, had strong reservations about attempts by Ethiopia to exert influence over the new dispensation, based on the recollection of much Ethiopian meddling in Somali affairs in the past. Ever since the collapse of the Barre regime in 1991, Somalia has not been represented in international and regional forums, although the practically inoperative transitional national government created in 2000 claimed to do so, with active support from Djibouti. What remained completely undecided was the future of Somaliland, which had declared its independence in 1991 and had managed to sustain a credible political structure, but without gaining any formal international diplomatic recognition. Practical cooperation with and support by Djibouti, however, greatly helped Somaliland to survive and to overcome the disadvantages of diplomatic isolation.

Djibouti, on the other hand, continued to be strengthened through its role as the key focal point in the entire sub-region (covering even Yemen) for the international war on terrorism. The US military base established in early 2003 – the only such base in Africa – was further strengthened and consolidated, while the continuance of the traditional French military base was also secured for the medium term, giving rise to some rivalry between Paris and Washington regarding influence in the area. Moreover, German navy units remained stationed in Djibouti as part of 'Operation Enduring Freedom', albeit on a reduced scale.

Tensions between **Eritrea** and **Ethiopia** remained high in the aftermath of the brutal 1998–2000 war, with its huge human losses. The Ethiopian government was clear that it was not willing to accept the 2002 boundary ruling of an international court of arbitration and insisted on a revision. There were intermittent rumours of a possible new outbreak of war, but given various international diplomatic pressures, no such outbreak in fact occurred. A UN peacekeeping mission continued to monitor the truce along the disputed border. The strengthening of triangular cooperation among Ethiopia, Sudan and Yemen also served to further isolate Eritrea in the sub-region.

Regarding **Sudan**, the peace negotiations that had dragged on for several years in Kenya, with frequent interruptions and setbacks, to end the long-running conflict in southern Sudan had many similarities with reconciliation for Somalia. Also under a mandate of IGAD, Kenyan mediators played the most active role, but with full diplomatic and financial support from a wide range of international governments and organisations, in particular the EU, major European countries and the US. At one stage, it was even foreseen that the official signing ceremony for the peace agreement could be in Washington. However, this did not transpire, because of delays and increased attention to the intensification of the parallel Darfur conflict, as a result of which the very intricate symbiotic nexus between the two conflicts became more apparent. While most international actors wished to conclude the peace deal for southern Sudan without being distracted by other problems, this very perception only fuelled the views of other marginalised groups in the country (not only in Darfur) about being left out and strengthened their resistance. At the same time, the central government was worried about a possible break-up of the entire national territory and, therefore, retaliated massively by instigating vicious local warfare between different ethnic groups against the background of traditional rivalries over increasingly scarce natural

resources (water, agricultural and grazing land). The horrendous plight of the civilian victims attracted a great deal of international attention, led to the mobilisation of large humanitarian relief operations; and also led to a heavy influx of refugees into neighbouring Chad.
Despite public concern and outrage in Western countries, the international community
proved practically helpless to stop the continued violence on the ground and to rein in the
Sudanese government. Divergent national interests of the member states of the UN Security
Council led to endless debates and prevented agreement being reached on strong sanctions
or punitive action against the government, while the eventual Security Council resolutions
did not convey any sense of strength and resolve. The AU sponsored several rounds of
(inconclusive) peace talks between the warring Sudanese adversaries in Nigeria and – in a
positive break with the OAU past – mustered a military monitoring force in Darfur. This
helped to improve the security situation in some areas marginally, but the force remained
hopelessly understaffed and was too poorly equipped to have a noticeable impact in
enforcing peace.

Bilateral relations between **Sudan** and **Uganda** showed further strong improvement,
given the imminent peace agreement in southern Sudan and the new role for the SPLM/A
as the dominant party in a future semi-autonomous administration. Uganda no longer
needed to give clandestine support to the SPLA, while the Lord's Resistance Army (LRA)
that had terrorised large parts of northern Uganda since the late 1980s no longer enjoyed
relative safety when retreating across the border into Sudanese territory. The LRA was thus
considerably weakened during the year, but was by no means completely eliminated.

In the region of the African **Great Lakes**, several conflicts continued to be closely intertwined, imparting to them a sub-regional dimension with an intimate linkage to events in
the DR Congo and other parts of Central Africa. Burundi, Rwanda and Uganda were still
in one way or the other closely affected by the fragile Congolese reconciliation process and
by the ongoing instability and violence in the eastern part of the DR Congo. Of these countries, **Uganda** had become relatively less directly involved since the withdrawal of its last
troops from the Ituri region of the DR Congo in April 2003, but it was still concerned about
the continued presence of different dissident and rebel groups on Congolese territory, which
served as a convenient and relatively secure rear base. During the year, bilateral relations
with the Kinshasa government improved noticeably and – with the inclusion of Rwanda –
tripartite agreements were reached even on the disarmament of all rebel and militia groups
in the eastern DR Congo, albeit with minimal practical consequences. **Rwanda** had, in fact,
even stronger reason to deplore the continued presence of its armed adversaries close to its
borders with the DR Congo. These adversaries were the remnants of the old pre-1994 Hutu
majority government and were seen as a threat to national security. Rwanda, however, also
still exerted a great deal of concrete influence in the Kivu provinces through its support of
local proxy forces, and at one stage, in November, even threatened to send troops back into
the DR Congo to disarm dangerous groups unilaterally. For a short while, the outbreak of
a new war seemed imminent, but this did not happen. Relations between Rwanda and

Uganda continued to be tense, with mutual accusations that the one country was harbouring the other's political dissidents and with troop deployments along their common border. However, there no major incidents.

The slow, but nonetheless considerable progress in the national reconciliation process in **Burundi** was to a large extent the result of the patient exertion of pressure by both regional and international forces. Ever since the 2000 Arusha Peace Accord brought about under the leadership of Nelson Mandela, South Africa (mainly through Vice-President Jacob Zuma) has been the main facilitator in the many difficult rounds of discussions among the various Burundian groups, while a parallel regional grouping of neighbouring countries under the chairmanship of Ugandan President Museveni also made its influence felt through a number of meetings and consultations. An initial AU peace-monitoring force (mainly comprising South African military personnel) was enlarged mid-year and transformed into an official UN operation. The last Hutu rebel group remaining outside the peace process was, however, still able to launch armed attacks from its refuge in the DR Congo. There was a constant danger of regionalising rebel activities by embroiling the DR Congo and Rwanda. The Rwandan leadership was somewhat suspicious of the trend towards an ethnically based power-sharing agreement in Burundi, in contrast to its own approach of negating ethnic differences. Bilateral relations with Tanzania did improve further and were still mainly centred on the fate of the many Burundian refugees in camps in Tanzania.

A large **International Conference on Peace, Security, Democracy and Development in the Great Lakes Region** was held on 19–20 November in Dar es Salaam (Tanzania) after a long diplomatic gestation period (see also the article on Central Africa). Preceded by a meeting of foreign ministers, this first summit of heads of state and government was to deal comprehensively with the interrelated complexities of the various conflicts and to establish an overarching framework for the better coordination of solutions. A joint declaration to promote peace and security in the region was signed by the heads of state of the 11 core countries, witnessed by leaders from another nine African countries as well as UN Secretary-General Kofi Annan and the AU chairman, Nigerian President Obasanjo. The declaration contained a set of principles and policy options in four areas: peace and security; economic development and regional integration; democracy and good governance; and social and humanitarian issues. The declaration was intended to form part of a pact on security, stability and development in the region that is expected to be signed during a second summit to be held in Nairobi in late 2005. However, serious doubts about the political will of all the actors to abide by the declared principles were immediately raised. Only a few days afterwards, for instance, Rwanda threatened to send its troops back into the DR Congo. Almost parallel with the conference, the **UN Security Council** met on 18–19 November in **Nairobi** for an exceptional session away from New York especially devoted to the Somalia and Sudan conflicts.

The belated progress in the **Comoros** to finalise all institutional and legal requirements for the creation of the new Union of Comoros had, as with Burundi, only been achieved through the exertion of considerable pressure by external players (mainly AU, 'Organisa-tion Internationale de la Francophonie', South Africa and France) on recalcitrant local politicians.

Economic Performance

In 2004, the whole of sub-Saharan Africa experienced the highest real GDP growth rate in almost a decade (about 4.6% to 5%, according to slightly varying figures given by ECA and IMF in April 2005), thereby continuing the solid upward trend since the turn of the century. This pattern was also reflected in the generally satisfactory performance of the sub-region, albeit with fairly wide variations, depending on differing country-specific conditions. **Eastern Africa**, in fact, recorded the second-highest **growth rate (around 5.8%)** among the different sub-regions, behind Central Africa, but ahead of West and Southern Africa.

Among the top African performers in 2004, Ethiopia was in fourth place with an impres-sive **growth rate** of 11.6% (largely the result of agricultural recovery in a good year after two disastrous preceding years) and Sudan in eighth place with 7.3% (resulting from the rapid expansion of oil production). At the other end of the scale, Seychelles was the sec-ond-worst performer (behind Zimbabwe) with a GDP contraction of 2% – although still at a far higher absolute level than other countries. Tanzania (6.3%) and Uganda (5.9%) were able to maintain their fairly solid growth patterns of recent years, but these rates were still below the threshold of about 7–8% generally considered necessary to have a noticeable impact on poverty. Both Burundi (5.5%) and Rwanda (4%) showed a good recovery after a climatically difficult preceding year, while Kenya (3.1%), in the second year of the new government, only managed modest improvements after many years of stagnation. Eritrea (1.8%), Comoros (1.9%) and Djibouti (3%) all experienced specific sociopolitical prob-lems, and for conflict-torn Somalia no overall data were available.

By trying to discount volatile annual fluctuations and assessing the **five-year growth performance for 2000–04**, however, a largely similar picture emerges. Judged on the basis of average annual growth rates for this period, Sudan (6.8%), Ethiopia (5.6%), Rwanda (5.5%), Uganda (5.3%) and Tanzania (5%) were among the 14 top performers in Africa (with rates of 5% or above), while Seychelles (–0.1%), Kenya (1.6%) and Comoros (1.7%) appeared among the nine lowest performers (rates of less than 2%).

Continued strides toward macroeconomic stability almost everywhere in Africa reduced the average sub-Saharan **inflation rate** in 2004 to around 9%, the lowest in three decades. In the sub-region, this average was only exceeded by Eritrea (21.4%), Rwanda (12%) and Kenya (11.5%), while all the other countries rather successfully pursued a strategy of mon-etary and fiscal orthodoxy. Efforts towards **local revenue generation** by national govern-ments also presented a very varied picture: against a sub-Saharan average of 23% of GDP, all sub-regional countries (with the outstanding exception of Seychelles, with 49%) remained below this figure, with the noticeably lowest tax bases being in Tanzania (12.2%),

Uganda (12.6%) and Rwanda (13.3%), all highly favoured recipients of external develop-ment aid. Both as a result of increased tax efforts and an influx of aid resources, the **over-all fiscal balance** (including grants) of sub-Saharan Africa generally improved further to a low ratio of –0.8% of GDP. In the sub-region, Ethiopia (–4.5%), Tanzania (–3.0%), Comoros (–2.7%), Uganda (–1.7%) and Kenya (–1.5%), however, exceeded this average, while Burundi, Rwanda and Seychelles were close to it.

Another important measure for general economic performance is the **balance of pay-ments on current account** (expressed as a per cent of GDP). This showed a general improvement for sub-Saharan Africa in 2004 to a ratio of –1.6% (compared to –3.5% two years earlier). Practically all countries in Eastern Africa, however, exceeded this average quite significantly, particularly Burundi (–23.8%), Eritrea (–11.9%) and Djibouti (–10.7%), with the rest being in a range between –1.9% (Uganda) and –6.8% (Sudan), thus indicat-ing above all a persistently weak export basis and heavy reliance on essential imports.

Regional Cooperation and Regional Organisations

The Somalia and Sudan peace processes gave a visible profile to **IGAD**, although they were entirely conducted in Kenya with Kenyan facilitation (under an IGAD mandate), with both material and diplomatic support from the international community and with hardly any role for IGAD's secretariat. A special IGAD summit on 14 October in Nairobi under the chair-manship of Uganda's President Museveni welcomed the outcome of the Somali reconcil-iation conference and recognised with immediate effect the new transitional institutions. An extraordinary meeting of the IGAD council of ministers on 17 November in Nairobi (on the sidelines of the UN Security Council meeting) equally hailed the progress of the peace processes and appealed to both UN and AU for the deployment of peacekeeping forces to Somalia, with Uganda making the first offer of one battalion. On 15–16 December in Nairobi, security personnel of AU and IGAD further discussed the modalities of sending peacekeepers.

All other **regular IGAD activities** received only scant attention. The 23rd session of the council of ministers on 22 March in Djibouti saw the reappointment of the Sudanese Executive Secretary Attala Hamid Bashir for another four-year term; discussion of the con-tinuing grave financial situation of the secretariat (because of membership arrears) and the need for an organisational review; and the decision to locate the secretariat of the IGAD Business Forum in Asmara (Eritrea) – to be supported, it was hoped, by national chambers of commerce. On 20 February, five member states (without Eritrea and Somalia) signed a protocol providing for the establishment of an IGAD inter-parliamentary union to be situ-ated in Addis Ababa and aiming at ensuring peace, mutual trust and cooperation among IGAD members. At the eighth meeting of the IGAD partners' forum (with technical representatives from the secretariat, member states and external partner organisations) on

23 February in Addis Ababa, a new IGAD Strategy Implementation Committee (ISIC) was established for the future discussion of joint programme activities.

Having previously experienced repeated delays and scepticism among observers, **EAC** gained new momentum and a medium-term vision during the year. After several post-ponements in 2003, the protocol for the creation of a **Customs Union** with effect from 1 January 2005 was finally signed at the fifth EAC summit on 2 March in Arusha. Complicated technical discussions over compromise formulae, in view of Tanzanian and Ugandan fears about the likely negative consequences, continued, however, literally until the last day of the year, even after the national parliaments had finally ratified the protocol, which they took until November to do. The Customs Union – creating a potential single market of over 90 million people – established a three-band common external tariff with zero per cent for the import of raw materials, 10% for intermediate goods and 25% for finished products. A five-year transition period was allowed until the full liberalisation of imports from Kenya into Tanzania and Uganda, but the new external tariffs also had uneven effects on the industries of the partner states and the level of customs revenues. An important political step had thus been taken after lengthy four-year deliberations, while full economic integration had still been only partly achieved.

From 27 to 29 August the three presidents met in Nairobi for a special summit to discuss in camera both the progress of and obstacles to EAC since its restart in 1996. It transpired that many decisions and protocols had not actually been ratified and implemented yet and that new vigour was needed to achieve genuine progress on closer cooperation. With this in mind, they set up an expert **committee on fast-tracking EA federation** under the chairmanship of Kenya's attorney-general, Amos Wako. The committee started with a series of wide-ranging consultations throughout East Africa on 21 September and reported to the presidents during the sixth EAC summit on 26 November in Arusha, when the rotating chairmanship was passed from Uganda to Tanzania. The road-map advocated by the committee was positively received by the presidents, with promises to take its ambitious goals into serious account. The key recommendations included the accelerated finalisation of protocols on the free movement of persons and services, the creation of a common market and the introduction of a single currency (by December 2009), as well as the launching of a political federation in 2010, with its consolidation in 2010–12 and common elections in 2013. Burundi's President Ndayizeye and Rwanda's Prime Minister Makuza also attended the summit and were promised that their countries' applications for EAC membership would now be processed diligently.

On the institutional side, the **East African Legislative Assembly (EALA)** on 27 May approved the new 2004–05 budget for all East African institutions for $ 11.8 m ($ 6.2 m for the secretariat). Despite an increase of 40% over the previous year, all EALA members decried the budget and staffing situation as utterly inadequate for the assigned tasks. In March, Kipyego Cheluget (Kenya) was reappointed for a new term as deputy secretary-general and in November, Ahmada Ngemera (Tanzania) replaced Ali Mchumo in the corresponding position. The increasingly close defence cooperation in the EAC context was reinforced by a meeting of the relevant ministers and army chiefs on 29–30 April in Zanzibar, while the **East African Business Council (EABC)** fully endorsed the opportunities for the private sector provided by the impending Customs Union.

COMESA celebrated its tenth anniversary on 8 December in Lusaka (Zambia), the seat of its secretariat, on the margins of the 18th meeting of its council of ministers a day earlier. During the ninth summit meeting on 7–8 June in Kampala, Uganda's President Museveni had assumed the rotating chairmanship, with Djibouti selected to host next year's summit. On 1 January, Burundi and Rwanda joined COMESA's **Free Trade Area (FTA)** arrangement, originally launched in 2000 and now composed of eleven of COMESA's 19 remaining member states. The ambitious goal of turning it into a customs union (still officially foreseen for 2005) and introducing a single currency continued to appear farfetched, as COMESA remained a somewhat heterogeneous organisation with a membership scattered from Northeastern to Southern Africa, without much connectivity. While Namibia's membership formally lapsed on 15 May after its 2003 withdrawal notice, some business quarters in Tanzania started to lobby for a possible return to COMESA (after the country's withdrawal in 2000). Despite its limitations, COMESA had managed to consolidate its role as a primarily trade-oriented organisation and to co-exist with its competitor **SADC**, notwithstanding partial overlaps in membership. Seychelles terminated its SADC membership on 1 July, having been largely inactive since joining in 1997. Among COMESA's affiliate institutions, the **PTA Bank** had still not moved from its temporary premises in Nairobi to Bujumbura (Burundi), despite repeated summit decisions, and the **Trade Insurance Agency (ATI)** had been able to increase its membership to ten, with the addition of Djibouti and Eritrea.

The **Indian Ocean Commission (IOC)**, during its 20th council of ministers meeting on 22 May in Moroni (Comoros), appointed a new secretary-general, Claudine Rasoanirina, a woman from Madagascar, upon the resignation of Wilfrid Bertile to pursue his political career in the French overseas department of Réunion. The rotating IOC chairmanship was routinely passed to France, but a summit of heads of state (including French President Chirac) envisaged for late 2003/early 2004 in accordance with a prescribed four-year cycle did not materialise, owing to French reservations about the shaky Comorian situation, and was re-scheduled for mid-2005. The few IOC technical programmes continued in a low-key fashion. Most notable was a new funding agreement by the EU in January to conserve tuna resources in the maritime region with a view to ensure sustainable fishing of this vital species (particularly for Seychelles).

The **Indian Ocean Rim Association for Regional Cooperation (IORARC)**, with its 18 members covering a vast geographical area in Africa, Asia and Oceania, held its fifth council of ministers meeting on 26–27 August in Colombo (Sri Lanka), with the chairmanship for the next two years going to Iran. Seychelles 2003 notice of withdrawal became effective mid-year. The meeting gave new impetus to the organisation, with a number of technical programmes and general agreement to return to the original charter emphasising the development of economic ties by pursuing the goal of a preferential trade agreement. An official from Sri Lanka was selected as the next executive secretary for the secretariat, which is based in Mauritius.

On the initiative of Belgian Foreign Minister Michel, a meeting was held on 11 July in Brussels with his counterparts from Burundi, Rwanda and DR Congo with the intention of reviving the **'Communauté Economique des Pays des Grands Lacs' (CEPGL)** that had practically collapsed in 1993–94. However, despite some external interest in supporting potential concrete projects, the outcome of this initiative remains uncertain for the time being. This was even more the case for a vague proposal to create a large geographical grouping stretching from the Indian to the Atlantic Ocean by combining the membership of EAC and CEPGL. In October in Nairobi, a new initiative to create a Great Lakes forum of parliamentarians from East Africa and the Horn of Africa was launched, with the first meeting scheduled for March 2005 in Kigali.

In the context of the **Nile Basin Initiative (NBI)**, the water ministers of the ten riparian states met on 18 March in Nairobi for their 12th regular council meeting. With the assistance of various donors, NBI was intended to develop joint use strategies for the water resources of the vast Nile catchment areas, but there have been increasingly strong calls in recent years from upstream countries (Ethiopia and in East Africa) to revise the colonial treaties of 1929 and 1959 that give Egypt the right to veto any use of Nile waters. Concrete conflicts had arisen from plans for large-scale irrigation and power projects in Ethiopia, Kenya and Uganda and from the start of work in Tanzania to divert water from Lake Victoria to inland areas south of the lake. During the council meeting, Egypt declared for the first time its willingness to at least discuss the demands of other countries to exploit the water resources, but general agreement was still a long way off. On 29 May, the first element of the NBI shared vision programme was formally launched in Khartoum, thus opening up the prospect for a joint peaceful approach to the use of the Nile's waters.

The concept of creating an **Eastern Africa Standby Brigade (EASBRIG)** as a regional component of the African Standby Force envisaged by the AU moved a step closer with a council meeting of defence ministers on 9–10 September in Kigali, ending with the signing of a memorandum of understanding and approval of a budget. The IGAD secretariat was designated as the coordinating office for the 3,000-strong brigade, with anticipated contributions from Burundi, Djibouti, Ethiopia, Eritrea, Kenya, Rwanda, Sudan, Tanzania and Uganda. The brigade is to comprise civilian and military components, which will be based in their home countries and ready for rapid deployment on appropriate notice. On 20–21 April, representatives of eleven sub-regional countries met in Nairobi and signed a protocol for the prevention, control and reduction of small arms and light weapons, an endeavour also pursued in the EAC context. An April conference in Kampala reviewed the progress made in implementing the US-East Africa Counter-Terrorism Initiative

(EACTI), launched in 2003 by President Bush, with $ 100 m for Djibouti, Eritrea, Ethiopia, Kenya, Tanzania and Uganda.

None of the sub-regional countries was particularly active in the initial stages of the **NEPAD** initiative and have only belatedly showed growing interest. On the Heads of State and Government Implementation Committee (HSGIC) and the steering committee, Ethiopia, Kenya and Mauritius represented the sub-region, while Rwanda represented Central Africa. An important NEPAD summit deliberated in mid-February in Kigali on the modalities for the crucial **African Peer Review Mechanism (APRM)** intended to produce African self-assessment of general governance performance. Kenya and Rwanda were chosen as two of the first four countries (along with Ghana and Mauritius) to undergo this voluntary process of lengthy monitoring against economic, social and political performance criteria on the basis of wide-ranging consultations with all sections of society.

The concrete negotiations about a new type of **Economic Partnership Agreement (EPA)** between the EU and various sub-groupings of ACP countries envisaged under the 2000 Cotonou Agreement finally started in 2004 (see the article on African European relations). Almost all countries of the sub-region opted to conduct these negotiations under an **Eastern and Southern Africa (ESA)** configuration involving 16 states and coordinated by the COMESA secretariat. The negotiating rounds were officially launched on 7 February in Mauritius and were substantially taken up on 20 October in Madagascar. The only sub-regional country remaining outside the ESA grouping was Tanzania, which opted to negotiate jointly with a (partial) SADC group, thus creating a strange split among the three EAC partner states. Representatives of COMESA, EAC, IGAD and IOC met jointly on 10 February in Nairobi with the EU as an Inter-Regional Coordinating Committee (IRCC) for discussions on the regional indicative programmes under the Cotonou Agreement.

Rolf Hofmeier

Burundi

After ten years of civil war, during 2004 Burundi seemed closer than ever to achieving a negotiated political transition. Despite a great deal of resistance, mainly from 'Tutsi' parties, considerable progress was made in both the political and military fields. A political dispensation was put in place, thus paving the way for elections in 2005. All but one rebel movement entered into ceasefire agreements and a new national army and police force were being established. The regional role in achieving this progress was considerable. Despite these improved prospects, continuing regional instability and the actions of domestic obstructionists, radical Tutsi movements in particular, still represented a danger for the whole transition process.

Domestic Politics

While the 2000 Arusha Accord and subsequent agreements provided for the ending of the transition period on 1 November, this **deadline** was not met. It was decided that the presidential elections, scheduled for the end of October, would be held on 22 April 2005, according to a plan published on 16 October by the national independent electoral commission. Nevertheless, **substantial progress** was made throughout 2004. Under considerable pressure from the region's heads of state and the facilitator, South African

Vice-President Jacob Zuma, several meetings led to the signing of the Pretoria power-sharing agreement on 6 August 2004. This contained the outlines of a post-transition political dispensation, which the transitional government translated into a draft constitution. The interim constitution was adopted by parliament on 20 October, but its approval by referendum was postponed on several occasions, from 20 October to 26 November, then to 22 December, until is was eventually delayed again without a date being set. The divide between mainly 'Hutu' and mainly 'Tutsi' parties was a constant feature, as 'Tutsi' parties opposed both the Pretoria agreement and the draft interim constitution. They feared that Tutsi lined up by 'Hutu' parties would take most or all functions in government and parliament allotted to the Tutsi, and they insisted on taking into account 'political-ethnic' affiliations, i.e., that Tutsi would have to belong to 'Tutsi' parties. This was firmly resisted by the mediation initiative, which eventually, with the support of regional leaders, imposed the power sharing agreement. When its implementation was resisted by interim Vice-President Alphonse-Marie Kadege, a Tutsi hardliner from UPRONA ('Union Pour le Progrès National'), President Domitien Ndayizeye sacked him and replaced him with another Tutsi from UPRONA, Frédéric Ngenzebuhoro, considered more flexible.

The text of the **post-transition constitution** was markedly consociational, attempting to combine majority rule with minority protection. This was to be achieved by classic instruments such as minority over-representation, quotas and a minority veto. The president, likely to be a Hutu, had to be seconded by two vice-presidents: a Hutu from a mainly 'Hutu' party and a Tutsi from a mainly 'Tutsi' party. The government was to be made up of 60% Hutu and 40% Tutsi – while the demographic proportions nationwide were about 85% Hutu, 14% Tutsi and 1% Twa – and 30% of its members would be women. In light of Burundian history, the areas of defence and public order were particularly delicate. Therefore, it was prescribed that the minister responsible for the national defence force would not be from the same ethnic group as the minister responsible for the national police. Moreover, the National Assembly would be composed of 60% Hutu and 40% Tutsi. If this balance were not achieved through election, cooption would ensure it. In addition, a minimum of 30% of MPs would be women and three Twa would be coopted. The senate was to be composed of an equal number of Hutu and Tutsi, as were the defence and security forces. At the local level, a maximum of 67% of mayors would belong to one ethnic (presumably Hutu) group.

It became increasingly clear that **electoral competition** would differ markedly from the 1993 experience, with its dramatic aftermath. The electoral process in 1993 was bipolar in a dual sense, as it involved two main opposing parties (FRODEBU – 'Front pour la Démocratie au Burundi', and UPRONA) as well as Hutu and Tutsi. During 2004, the political landscape had become more multipolar. Thus, for instance, two of the main 'Hutu' parties, CNDD-FDD ('Conseil National pour la Défense de la Démocratie' and its armed wing, the 'Forces pour la Défense de la Démocratie') and FRODEBU started competing for Hutu votes, while several parties were vying for the Tutsi vote, and UPRONA's prominence was challenged by parties like PARENA ('Parti pour le Redressement National'), Inkinzo, RADDES ('Ralliement pour la Démocratie et le Développement Economique et Social') and the MRC ('Mouvement de Réhabilitation du Citoyen').

Two other factors contributed to the more favourable conditions than those in 1993. On one hand, both the **political class and civil society** adopted a more constructive and less radical approach. Although relations between parties were not free of conflict, parties refrained from taking positions likely to result in violent deadlock and they used a language conducive to keeping communication channels open. Civil society and the media more particularly avoided partisan positions. Independent radio stations funded from abroad developed into peace media, as opposed to the hate media so prevalent in 1993–94. On the other, the **army's role** changed considerably. In the past, it was constantly present behind the scenes, always ready to intervene should the interest of Tutsi elites be threatened. Indeed, the coup d'état and the assassination by the military of President Ndadaye in October 1993 laid at the origin of the ten-year civil war. The new situation was different in two respects. The 'Forces Armées Burundaises' (FAB) stayed aloof from politics and most military rejected the return to war and instability. Indeed, the army successfully integrated the main rebel movement CNDD-FDD. Command structures were unified, troops were 'harmonised' and both components conducted joint patrols. The other important new element was the presence of the 5,500-strong United Nations mission (ONUB), under robust South African leadership. In the past, such an international force was always resisted by FAB, but it was imposed by the regional leaders and was now accepted. Its sheer presence rendered coups d'état much less likely.

Although the **human rights** record remained poor, 2004 saw some progress compared to previous years. With one major exception (see below), there were no reports of mass killings of civilians by the army or the remaining rebel group FNL ('Forces Nationales de Libération'), which does not mean civilians were not killed by these forces. On the contrary, FAB and CNDD-FDD killed numerous civilians following the fighting with the FNL, in reprisal for FNL attacks or for suspected collaboration with FNL. The transitional constitution prohibits cruel, inhuman or degrading treatment or punishment, but these practices were continued both by the army and the rebel groups, including the CNDD-FDD, which maintained illegal detention centres across the country. In addition, rape by all fighting forces has remained widespread. Although prison conditions remained extremely harsh (there were over 7,500 inmates, but capacity was under 4,000), the transitional government started providing sufficient food and some medical care to prisoners. Judicial reform was a priority of the Arusha Accord, but little progress was made, in large part because of insufficient financial means.

Press freedom improved considerably. Although the transitional government briefly suspended the operation of an internet newssheet and issued warnings to three other media groups, no journalists were harassed or arrested. Some of the main media (the country's only television station, two radio stations and the country's only daily newspaper) were controlled by the government, but the media landscape has become quite diversified: in 2004, there were six private weeklies, eight private internet and fax-based newssheets, and eight privately owned radio stations. The latter were important in that they reached most of the nation and, as outlined above, played a constructive role in advocating peace and tolerance.

After all but one of the **rebel movements** signed agreements with the government and effectively ceased fighting, the intensity of the civil war considerably abated. During the latter half of 2004, FNL continued attacks in a few municipalities of just one province, Bujumbura rural. However, FNL was substantially weakened militarily, and the fighters it fielded inside Burundi probably numbered well under 1,000. A particularly grave incident occurred on 13 August, when combatants believed to belong to FNL massacred over 150 Congolese refugees, many of them Tutsi Banyamulenge, in Gatumba refugee camp between Bujumbura and the Congolese border. The FNL accepted responsibility for the attack, but claimed it had engaged Banyamulenge combatants who were preparing for a new war in the DR Congo. Accusations, with regional repercussions, were immediately made (see below, foreign affairs), but investigations by the UN and Human Right Watch failed to provide a definite picture. The Gatumba massacre added political weakness to the FNL's military decline, as the organisation was labelled 'terrorist', and both domestic and regional leaders expressed the opinion that it should be marginalised. However, towards the end of 2004, new contacts were being initiated under the auspices of the special representative of the UN Secretary-General. The FNL itself claimed it was interested in a ceasefire and in joining the political dispensation.

Foreign Affairs

Conflicts in the Great Lakes region have been intimately intertwined during the last decade. Domestic wars have linked into **regional conflict**, circumstantial alliances have shifted wildly, and conflicts have been fought out on neighbours' territories. During the second Congo war, Burundian rebel movements sided with Kinshasa against the 'Tutsi-Hima' invaders from Rwanda, Uganda and Burundi. The CNDD-FDD, until its integration into the political system, and FNL operated from bases for attack and retreat in the DR Congo's South Kivu province, where they also concluded local alliances with Congolese Mai Mai and even with Banyamulenge fighters. Although much less intensely than the Rwandan army, FAB occasionally operated across the border into the DR Congo, particularly along Lake Tanganyika.

The potential for continuing regional instability to impact the Burundian political process became very clear in the wake of the Gatumba massacre, as attempts were immediately made to regionalise the incident. The Rwanda-supported RCD-Goma ('Rassemblement Congolais pour la Démocratie') claimed that elements of the Congolese army and Mai Mai militia were involved, while Kigali insisted that the Rwandan rebel FDLR

('Forces Démocratiques pour la Libération du Rwanda'), operating in eastern DR Congo, had a hand in the attack. RCD-Goma thus attempted to disturb the Congolese political transition and Rwanda sought a pretext for renewed intervention in DR Congo.

The current transition was viewed with great concern in **Rwanda**. Indeed, the Burundian 'anti-model' – an expression used by the RPF's (the ruling Rwandan Patriotic Front) spokesman – based on power-sharing and the acknowledgment of ethnicity challenged the Rwandan dispensation based on concentration of power and ethnic amnesia. The Rwandan army has operated on Burundian territory in the past, and unconfirmed rumours claimed that Kigali was attempting to set up a 'Tutsi rebellion' in Burundi.

On the positive side, the Burundian case showed that the **international community** can exercise leverage to achieve political solutions. The **regional leaders** and South Africa played a major role in forcing the Burundian political and military players into finding an accommodation that could not have been achieved without considerable pressure. Indeed, on several occasions, the region put Burundi under de facto trusteeship and imposed solutions. This began with the adoption of the Arusha peace accord in 2000, when Nelson Mandela forced the hand of the very reluctant Tutsi parties. Despite strong resistance from the same Tutsi parties and the Burundian army, an African Union force under South African leadership was deployed. Attempts to reject the draft interim constitution by the Tutsi parties and, subsequently, to amend the text by President Ndayizeye were resisted by regional leaders, who also rejected calls for the postponement of the electoral process. In addition to the International Conference on Peace, Security, Democracy and Development in the Great Lakes Region, held in Dar es Salaam on 19–20 November (which dealt with wider regional issues and not just Burundi), regional summits on Burundi specifically took place in Dar es Salaam on 3–5 June, 18 August and 15 October. The number of meetings showed the willingness of the regional leaders to spend considerable political time on the Burundian issue. Several other meetings organised with South African facilitation took place in Pretoria, and South African Vice-President Jacob Zuma paid several visits to Bujumbura.

The wider international community supported the regional Burundi peace initiative, e.g., by offering financial and diplomatic backing and by turning the AU force into a UN one (ONUB, United Nations Operation in Burundi, which was deployed after 1 June), but consistently subcontracted leadership to the region. Nevertheless, after the UN Secretary-General's special representative Carolyn McAskie took up her duties in Bujumbura on 25 June, she became actively involved in moving the process forward, but did so working closely with South African facilitation and the Burundian parties.

Socioeconomic Developments

In socioeconomic terms, too, Burundi's situation was **more promising** compared to the depressing image of some years ago. The peace dividend was slowly paying off in terms of macroeconomic progress. However, the over-optimism was misplaced. After some economic growth in 2001 and 2002 (2.1% and 4.5% respectively), Burundi's economy suffered from a contraction of 1% in real terms in 2003. Economic growth was expected to pick up from 2004 onwards with growth figures around 5%, but in general the economic performance remained vulnerable.

GDP largely depended upon the performances in the **primary sector** – which accounted for 40% of total GDP – or even more narrowly on food production. Due to the limited availability of technology, this means that the production of food hinged on the climatic conditions, a volatile, uncertain and non-manipulable factor. The lack of infrastructure aggravated this problem as price distortions cannot be neutralised through international or national commerce and exchange. As a result, there exists a strong correlation between GDP growth figures, inflation rates and weather conditions: clearly it will take more than a peace dividend for Burundi to escape economic uncertainty.

Burundi's export sector remained dependent on coffee. Although the coffee harvest of 2002–03 was exceptionally large, the performance of this sector was disappointing mainly due to unfavorable prices on the world market. The prospects for 2004 were even worse, implying a strong contraction in exports, with an important increase in the commercial balance deficit and the current account deficit as a result.

On the other hand, reintegration of Burundi into the **international aid system** was a major positive evolution. While Burundi received aid levels considerably above sub-Saharan standards until 1995, it became an international pariah from 1996 onwards as a consequence of Buyoya's putsch, followed by an international embargo that lasted from 1996 until 1999. Even after the end of the embargo, aid levels increased only marginally and remained far below sub-Saharan African standards. However, in 2004 international financial institutions approved the interim Poverty Reduction Strategy Paper. This was followed by the first disbursement of the three-year IMF Poverty Reduction and Growth Facility (PRGF) (2004–06). Also, bilateral donors such as Belgium, France and the EU increased their assistance considerably. Moreover, Burundi hoped to obtain Paris Club debt relief and also be incorporated into the Enhanced Initiative for Heavily Indebted Poor Countries. These programmes should help Burundi to considerably decrease its debt rate, which was estimated at over 200% of GDP.

Burundi remained one of the poorest countries in the world and one of the **five most deprived countries** in the Human Development Report. Life expectancy was a mere 40.8 years. Around 58.4% of the population lived below the poverty line of $ 1 a day; a staggering 89.2% survived on less than $ 2 a day. Although literacy rates were still considerable, with 50.4% of the population over 15 able to read and write, the conflict has had a perverse impact on education. Further, health conditions were poor: around 45% of children under 5 were underweight, among the worst rates in sub-Saharan Africa. Poor sanitation and housing conditions and a lack of improved water sources strongly contributed to generalised impoverishment. HIV/AIDS has become a serious problem, with estimates of more than 18% in urban areas and over 7% in the countryside being infected. Moreover, population figures were expected to grow by an average 3.1% between 2002 and 2015. Around 10% of the total population was still displaced, either internally or in neighbouring countries.

The **challenges** for Burundi's economy were clear. First, given the structural constraints its economy confronted, would Burundi be able to increase and secure its productive capacity? In its interim PRSP, the agricultural sector was considered to be the motor for growth in the short and medium terms. With a large majority of the population making a living in this sector, it was not only desirable but also necessary to concentrate on agriculture in the fight against poverty. However, it remained uncertain how to translate this ambition into a real development strategy that transcends the actual structural limitations. Second, Burundi faced a major challenge in the distribution of its resources. With a Gini coefficient of 0.33 in 1998, the richest 20% accounted for almost half of total consumption. The challenge ahead was to offer improved living conditions to the poorest layers of its ever-expanding population.

Filip Reyntjens

Comoros

After years of political turmoil arising from the Anjouan secession of 1997 and a bloodless military coup in 1999, this small island state made considerable progress towards completing its transitional phase and setting up all the institutions of the new federal 'Union des Comores' (Comorian Union), whose foundations had been laid by a constitutional referendum in December 2001. Deep-seated conflicts between the key actors of the four distinct state entities about their respective competencies, and scepticism about the functionality of the highly complex and costly new government structures, however, persisted and were not fully resolved by year's end.

Domestic Politics

On 20 December 2003, the combined efforts of a range of international players led to a last-minute **compromise framework** for holding the crucial **parliamentary elections** that were two years overdue. They also resulted in certain interim administrative arrangements (under international tutelage), mainly on budget and security issues, that allowed state institutions to function after being almost paralysed by the feuding between the union president Azali Assoumani and the presidents of the three semi-autonomous islands Ngazidja/Grande Comore (Abdou Soule Elbak), Anjouan (Mohamed Bacar) and Mohéli (Mohamed Said

Fazul). All four presidents had been directly elected in 2002, but their infighting had prevented elections for the island and union parliaments from taking place.

These **elections** were now scheduled for 14 and 21 March for the **three island assemblies** and for 18 and 25 April for the **union parliament**, the two rounds of elections being modelled on the French system. Despite continued mistrust and rivalry, the political actors by and large followed established regulations and the elections were held without major irregularity, and were monitored by observers from the AU and other international bodies. The main dividing line was between the **pro-union forces** of Assoumani, supported by his party, 'Convention pour la Renaissance des Comores' (CRC), and the **pro-island followers of the island presidents**, who were loosely united in an alliance against Assoumani, but strongly presented their respective island identities. In this setting, the former plethora of small political parties had become almost obsolete. The overall result of the elections was a clear **defeat for the adherents of the union** and an expression of support for the centrifugal tendencies inherent in the autonomous island ambitions. In the elections for the island assemblies, the CRC managed to win only 11 seats of a total of 55 (7 of 20 on the main island Ngazidja, 3 of 25 on Anjouan, 1 of 10 on Mohéli), while the rest were won by different groups linked to the island presidents. The new union parliament was to comprise 15 members delegated by the island assemblies (5 per island) and 18 directly elected members. Despite nominating heavyweights and cabinet ministers, CRC again lost heavily in this federal parliamentary contest, winning 6 of 9 seats on Ngazidja, but none on Anjouan (7) and Mohéli (2). The defeat of Defence Minister Hamada Madi Bolero on his home island of Mohéli was seen as a particular blow. CRC candidates also lost both elections in the capital, Moroni. The majorities in the island assemblies subsequently named only pro-island representatives to the federal parliament. A conflict about this procedure of excluding all CRC representatives led to the embarrassing last-minute postponement of the opening of parliament (to 4 June), in which 26 MPs representing the island forces were in clear control, as against six CRC members and one independent (from the traditional Chuma party). The three island presidents practically decided on the allocation of the top parliamentary positions and committees in accordance with the numerical strength of the islands.

On 9 June, Assoumani's union government, which had been severely criticised by the international monitoring committee for non-compliance with agreed arrangements for the interim period, was dissolved and negotiations were started with all the political actors on the formation of a **new national government**. This took much longer than expected after the initial agreement to form an inclusive government with representatives of all major players. The main disputes centred on the size of the government (Assoumani wanting a large cabinet of 13, the island presidents a much smaller one) and even more on the areas of competence, given that the crucial constitutional laws for regulating the division of responsibilities between federal and island authorities remained to be discussed and settled by the new parliament. A new **union government** was eventually formed on 15 July, but without any representatives of the Ngazidja authorities, since Elbak chose to stay away. In addition to Assoumani as president, the government consisted of two deputy presidents from Anjouan and Mohéli (in charge of coordinating state affairs on their respective islands, in addition to their regular ministerial responsibilities) and of eight ministers. In the sharing of political responsibilities, five ministries came to be controlled by the CRC. The formation of the new government was an important step, but potential blockages in crucial areas remained unresolved. The main **battleground for the rivals** was Ngazidja (with the parallel presence of union and island authorities), while the rulers on Anjouan and Mohéli were generally in undisputed control of their own affairs. Nevertheless, the traditional celebrations on national day (6 June) in Moroni were, for the first time since 1997, held in a spirit of national unity and attended by all leading national figures. The last of the new union structures to be put in place was the **constitutional court**, whose seven members (individually nominated by the four presidents, two vice-presidents and the speaker) took their oaths in September and elected their president on 28 October.

In the federal parliament, a **new power struggle** arose almost immediately during the debate and passage of the **organic laws respecting the division of powers between the union and island authorities** in relation to key matters such as finance, security, the judiciary, public institutions, etc. While Assoumani defended the interests of a strong union, and the military leadership – who saw themselves as part of an indivisible national entity – expressed anxiety about an intended transfer of control of the gendarmerie to the island authorities, the majority of MPs, with their pro-island orientation, tried to introduce numerous amendments to the draft legislation that ran contrary to the constitution approved by referendum in 2001. The union government found this unacceptable and in October referred the issue to the constitutional court while also asking for outside technical support and mediation from the EU and the 'Organisation Internationale de la Francophonie' (OIF). In early November, the court declared itself not competent to hear the matter and referred it back to parliament, and the impasse over the organic laws and the linked 2005 budget remained unresolved until the end of the year. It was clear that the new institutions had come far in 2004 and the overall situation was better than for years, but also that full trust in the new situation had yet to be achieved.

A reshuffle of the **Anjouan government** on 17 October (affecting four of the nine ministers in the 2002 cabinet) indicated continuing **political unrest** on this island, where socioeconomic conditions remained particularly precarious after the years of secession and isolation. Demonstrators in September accused Bacar of being a traitor and made new calls for assistance from France, even though Bacar had himself been one of the leaders of the secessionists in 1997. The Islamic party 'Front National pour la Justice' (FNJ) protested in an open letter on 15 September against the authorities' persistent **harassment of Islamic NGOs**. This was in response to a government report warning of terrorist dangers from groups that had funding from Saudi Arabia and other foreign sources.

Foreign Affairs

A range of **external actors** remained **strongly involved in efforts to stabilise the domestic political situation** and to find a lasting national solution. In the forefront, were the AU, EU, OIF, Arab League, IMF, World Bank as well as South Africa and France. Different representatives of these agencies supervised arrangements for the interim period in the early months of the year, monitored the elections and provided assistance and applied pressure in the pursuit of a compromise on the key constitutional issues and the 2005 budget later in the year. An early donor meeting in January in Paris led to promises to resume international aid if there was satisfactory internal political progress. On the whole, the patient, combined efforts of these actors seemed to have finally succeeded in saving the country from complete collapse.

The year saw notable renewed **intensification of relations with France** with the resumption of French aid programmes (suspended after the 1999 putsch) and a clearly expressed desire by Assoumani to re-engage with France as the leading donor. In early September, a French delegation visited the Comoros to prepare the agenda for a meeting of the Franco-Comorian commission that had last met in 1991, but this meeting was eventually postponed to 2005. Detailed plans were also under way for the first-ever official visit by a Comorian head of state to France, scheduled for January 2005. The large Comorian diaspora in France (approx. 150,000 persons) and their estimated annual remittances of € 45 m (about 16% of GDP) strongly influenced the well-being of the country, particularly of Ngazidja. The delicate issue of Mayotte was downplayed for fear of disturbing the rapprochement. The international status of this fourth island of the archipelago remained in dispute, as the government still claimed it as an integral part of the Comoros, while in fact it had become increasingly integrated into the French state since the referendum of 1975. At the 20th ministerial council meeting on 22 May in Moroni, France took over the rotating chairmanship of the IOC after Comoros had held it for one year.

Increased **US interest** in the country and several visits by US agencies were clearly related to the fight against international terrorism, to fears about a potential hiding place for Islamic fundamentalists, and specifically to the activities of some Saudi foundations. The union government for its part was keen to cooperate in the security field as a way to suppress internal Islamist opposition. **China** also maintained a relatively high profile as an aid donor for prestigious projects such as the upgrading of Moroni airport.

Socioeconomic Developments

Owing to the ongoing political uncertainties, the **economy continued to be depressed.** All expectations for recovery had to be further postponed until the following year. Several macroeconomic indicators, however, provided a somewhat ambiguous picture. Overall

GDP growth in 2004 was estimated to be 1.9%, the lowest rate in the current decade and per capita GDP declined for the sixth successive year. Inflation remained moderate at around 5%, largely due to the stabilising effect of membership in the French-controlled Franc zone. Very poor export performance of the few traditional export crops in combination with unrestrained import needs led to a record current account deficit of around $ 30 m, while the external debt of $ 290 m at year's end ($ 107 m of this in arrears) was absolutely unsustainable, with a theoretical debt-service ratio of around 500%. Without substantial economic and financial reform, no debt relief and resumption of significant international aid was in sight. Despite this ominous situation, foreign reserves grew to $ 94 m (about eleven months of import coverage) in the third quarter, and the Comoros remained at 11th position among sub-Saharan African countries in the **UNDP HDI ranking** (on the basis of 2002 figures). One partial explanation for this surprising situation seemed to be the heavy reliance on remittances from the Comorian diaspora.

The most serious problem throughout the year was the continuing extremely **precarious public finance situation**, arising from the unresolved political disagreements over the competencies of the different island authorities and their share of financial resources. The decentralised fiscal management proved to be extremely cumbersome and ineffective. The agreed interim arrangement for the first half of the year supervised by an international harmonisation team had produced a transitional budget (divided into four parts) with drastic expenditure cuts and the establishment of a new customs service. However, in the prevailing climate of the election campaigns, actual budget control remained very poor. Monitors and a subsequent external audit were particularly critical of the union and Ngazidja governments for diverting customs revenue and for major overspending, while the Anjouan administration was judged relatively favourably. In the second half of the year, attention shifted to the crucial organic laws and the related issue of **state budgets** for 2005 and beyond. IMF missions in April (for regular Article IV consultations) and in November, as well as a World Bank mission in October, continued to press for resolution of the political impasse by offering an official IMF staff-monitored programme in 2005 and future funding in the event of agreement on the budget by all political actors. This was not achieved before year's end, but seemed within reach with a **new compromise formula for sharing tax and customs revenue** among the four governments (union 33.8%, Ngazidja 30.7%, Anjouan 26.8%, Mohéli 8.8%).

Given the precarious public finances, and not uncommon in the Comoros, there were persistent long **delays in paying civil service salaries**. This provoked **repeated strikes**, e.g., by primary school teachers for four months after mid-April. Very poor exam results were blamed on the frequent and lengthy closure of schools. Several senior officials imprisoned in late 2003 for embezzlement of public funds were released in February prior to the elections, and despite allegations of many more improprieties there were no further prosecutions of high-ranking personalities during the year. Disputes remained about the scope and pace of the **privatisation of public enterprises**, such as the 'Societé Nationale des Postes et Télécommunications' (SNPT), which was split into two units in August in anticipation of a sale to foreign investors, but was still kept under political control. The future of the parastatal electricity and water utility 'MaMwe' was also not clear: Arab/Egyptian assistance was expected to improve the very grave power situation. The biggest remaining challenge was, however, the complete overhaul and downsizing of **the bloated civil service** both at union and individual island levels.

Rolf Hofmeier

Djibouti

All political activities in Djibouti 2004 were focused on the presidential elections that were to take place in April 2005, after the parliamentary elections held in January 2003. There was little uncertainty about the result in the camp of the president, Ismaël Omar Guelleh, locally nicknamed IOG. Fairly positive economic developments mainly benefited a small circle around the president.

Domestic Politics

Nephew of the previous president, Hassan Gouled Aptidon (1977–99), and his chief of staff and head of security for two decades, IOG was elected in 1999 without any difficulty (with 74% of the votes) after neutralising his most dangerous opponents, Ismaël Guedi Hared, a long-time ally at the presidency, and Moumin Bahdon Farah, a veteran minister of foreign affairs who became an opponent only in 1996. After the tragic events of 11 September 2001, IOG sided with the Americans, Djibouti providing the only permanent US military base in Africa. Thanks to this decision, economic hardships diminished; civil servants could be paid and – above all – the elites profited materially. On 10 January 2003, all 65 seats in parliament were obtained by the ruling party, the 'Rassemblement Populaire pour le Progrès' (RPP), which was founded in March 1979 and was the sole authorised party until the out-

break of the war in November 1991 forced it to adopt a new constitution recognising a multiparty system. Full control of the legislative and executive national bodies – despite an
opposition that represented about 40% of the votes in 2003 – meant that the next elections
would not be difficult to win, but the **participation rate** is an unknown and would show
the degree of popular endorsement of the regime.

On the side of the **opposition**, the situation was indeed not clear-cut and confidence
was lacking. Ten years after the vote on the new constitution in September 1992, political
parties were set up without any restriction and their numbers indicated the **factional
dimension** of Djibouti politics. The oldest organisations were the 'Parti du Renouveau
Démocratique' (PRD) led by Abdullahi Hamareiteh Guelleh and the 'Parti National
Démocratique' (PND) led by Aden Robleh Awaleh, both established in 1992. A partial
peace settlement in December 1994 led to the recognition of the legality of the 'Front pour
la Restauration de l'Unité et de la Démocratie' (FRUD), now led by Ali Mohamed Daoud,
which had sided in the 1999 and 2003 elections with RPP. In 2002, after all restrictions were
lifted and a final peace agreement had been concluded in 2001 with a separate wing of
FRUD, the armed faction led by Ahmed Dini Ahmed, the 'Alliance Républicaine pour la
Démocratie' (ARD) was set up. But other parties had also emerged: the 'Parti Djiboutien
pour le Développement' (PDD) led by Mohamed Daoud Chehem, the 'Parti Populaire
Social Démocratique' (PPSD) led by Moumin Bahdon Farah, the 'Union pour la Justice et
la Démocratie' (UDJ) chaired by Ismaël Guedi Hared and the 'Mouvement pour le
Renouveau Démocratique et le Développement' (MRDD) chaired by Suleiman Farah
Lodon.

This list demonstrates that one of the main challenges facing the opposition was to unite,
or at least not to split further. Before the parliamentary elections, Ahmed Dini, the first
prime minister after independence in June 1977 and a figure in Djiboutian nationalism, was
able to build an alliance, the 'Union pour une Alternance Démocratique' (UAD) comprising ARD, MRDD, UDJ and PDD, and to keep it united despite its defeat in January 2003
by the alliance between RPP and FRUD – called (as in France, curiously) the 'Union pour
une Majorité Présidentielle' (UMP). But Dini died in September, and his death prompted
UAD to unite in boycotting the next presidential elections in 2005. Despite this decision,
the leader of PDD and brother of a long-time adviser to Ahmed Dini, Mohamed Daoud
Chehem, twice declared himself a presidential candidate. PDD was eventually expelled
from the UAD, in December, though it was doubtful that its chairman would be able to
muster the $ 30,000 deposit to the treasury for his candidacy.

The **boycott decision** was not uncommon in Djiboutian politics. From the very beginning, opposition parties claimed (with hard evidence) that, despite its commitments to
reform in 1992, 1994 and 2001, government had never agreed to update and clean up the
electoral list; to offer guarantees regarding the conduct of the election (for example, allowing observers from opposition parties to be present in polling stations); to establish an independent electoral commission and to allow fair access by the opposition to state radio and

TV, the only broadcast entities allowed in the country and highly uncritical of government leaders and policies. All these grievances were cited again and again and were accepted as legitimate by the government under international pressure, yet no improvement in actual practice was ever made on the ground.

Indeed, the government's **human rights record** remained poor and it continued to commit serious abuses. Security forces continued to detain persons arbitrarily and prisoners were often physically abused, and the forces were not held accountable for these acts. Government also restricted freedom of the press and freedom of assembly and association. Yet, unlike in September 2003 when 80,000 migrants were expelled, there were no reports of death in connection with the expulsion of undocumented foreigners, and 4,000 refugees were repatriated under international monitoring, mainly to Ethiopia.

Many Djiboutian people felt that IOG was central to all affairs as head of state, head of cabinet, chief of security and chief of the army. Moreover, the state was far and away the main economic actor: when it provided room for the private sector, all contracts were awarded to IOG's closest associates, such as Abdirahaman Mohamoud Boreh. This perception of IOG's centrality was also frequently reinforced by the clan affiliations of those in power. Among the MPs, the Mamassan clan (IOG's own Issa sub-clan) was over-represented while minorities held only nine seats. This explains the adoption of an alternative name for RPP – 'Rien Pour le Peuple' (Nothing for the People).

Foreign Affairs

One of the main explanations for government's indifference towards political (or human) rights, was the new role Djibouti played in the war against terror. In 2004, as in the previous year, IOG was very confident of broad political and economic support by the **US**, despite the latter's vague reluctance regarding his debatable human rights record. Djibouti was the sole US military base in Africa and Camp Lemonier was the HQ of the Combined Joint Task Force – Horn of Africa with a mandate covering Yemen and all the countries of East Africa. The 1,800 US personnel at the camp were charged with coordinating military training, humanitarian aid, intelligence operations to strengthen local security forces in that part of Africa and Yemen and keeping terrorist groups from operating in this predominantly Muslim region. Washington paid an annual average of $ 30 m to Djibouti for the use of these facilities.

However, this new privileged relationship between Djibouti and Washington raised concerns in Paris that **French influence** would be minimised. This fear was particularly instrumental in generating benefits for the government of Djibouti. The main result of the inexplicit competition between Paris and Washington was a new fiscal agreement signed in June between France and Djibouti for the military base Paris maintained in the small republic. Until the mid-1990s, France had up to 5,000 troops there, often with their families. In 2004, this number stood at only 2,850. There were two main reasons for this decline.

First, conscription for the French army ended in 1996 and caused budget rationalisation and, thus, the reduction of the number of troops based in Djibouti: from the late 1990s, only about 1,800 soldiers were based in Djibouti for two or three years, while others (less than 1,000) were stationed there on a rotational basis for less than six months. Second, before 11 September 2001, the most enlightened elements in French military and diplomatic circles were arguing over the need to pay a few million US dollars for what was the most important French military base outside the country: The cold war was over and Djibouti was not an aircraft carrier (an island does not move!). Of course, the base in Djibouti could be used to train special forces and test new ammunition and could serve to reward soldiers whose salaries in France were as low as other civil servants. In the end, the only strategic motive for retaining the Djibouti base was the existence of defence agreements between France and the UAE: Djibouti could ease the logistical problems posed by these accords, though not eliminate them. The tragic events of 11 September 2001 completely reframed this assessment. After months of heated debate between Djibouti and Paris, a deal was struck by which France would pay € 30 m annually, over a nine-year period, for the presence of its soldiers.

Yet relations between Paris and Djibouti were far from normalised. On 6 April, the French ministry of defence had to release secret documents linked to the **death of Bernard Borrel** in October 1995 to the judge leading the investigation. After years of procrastination on both the French and Djiboutian sides, experts eventually concluded that this French adviser to the Djiboutian minister of justice was killed and did not commit suicide, contrary to the theory supported by Paris and Djibouti. Borrel's family argued that Djiboutian secret services linked to IOG assassinated him because he had evidence on the organisers of the Café de Paris bombing in December 1990, as well as about trafficking by IOG. No evidence, except statements of Djiboutians in exile, supported this thesis but the French investigators eventually raised questions about the alleged dubious past activities of the Djiboutian president and requested testimony from some of his closest associates. French officials' statements about the independence of the judiciary angered the president.

Djibouti maintained its paradoxical position in regional politics. Although most Ethiopian imports and exports transited through its port and the president was known to have huge economic interests in **Ethiopia** (his family lived close to Dire-Dawa before he migrated to Djibouti as a young man), relationships with Ethiopia were not as warm as expected. The main bone of political contention was, of course, the different visions the two capitals had on the resolution of the **Somali crisis**. Since IOG and Abdirahman Mohamoud Boreh were the key architects of the 'Arta conference, Djibouti wanted the Transitional National Government (TNG) to play a central role in the conference in Kenya, or at least to be treated fairly: this was far from the case. As a consequence, and beyond the many incidents that erupted over the management of the Kenya conference, Djibouti offered new facilities to Somaliland, welcomed officials and reauthorised the circulation of the main newspapers that were prohibited in 2000 when the Somaliland media were highly critical of the 'Arta conference. This was a way to highlight the weakness of a national process that Somaliland was not part of, and to antagonise the future president by siding with Hargeysa on the issue of Sool and Sanag (see article on Somalia).

Moreover, Djibouti kept its channels of discussion open with **Eritrea** as a way to counterbalance the influence of the regional alliance between Addis Ababa, Khartoum and Sana'a to corner Asmara. Djibouti did not want to face a too powerful neighbour that was not known to be a flexible partner in regional politics or on economic issues.

The main novelty in Djibouti's foreign relations was to 'look East', which meant building relations with Dubai and Asian countries such as China.

Socioeconomic Developments

If IOG did not challenge his uncle's authoritarian way of ruling the country, he did develop a drastically new economic policy to diminish French influence in the Djiboutian economy (about 40% of GDP) and to attract new economic partners. He proved successful, thanks to the war between Eritrea and Ethiopia (1998–2000) and the plans made by the Dubai port authority to reorganise its international activities by betting on the development of Jeddah, Djibouti and Vasakhapatman. These two events led to contracts with Dubai Port International (DPI) to manage **Djibouti port** and airport, and to be the main shareholder in the development of a new deep-water port, including an oil terminal – with Emirates National Oil Company (ENOC) as a second partner – and a duty free zone, in Doraleh, ten kilometres from Djibouti. Unsurprisingly, the president of the zone and port authority was Abdirahaman Mohamoud Boreh.

One of the paradoxes of this situation was that most of the port activity was linked to re-exports to Ethiopia, generating little revenue for Djibouti, since Ethiopia, through the Ethiopian Shipping Lines, got a near monopoly over those operations and kept very tight control over prices. Ethiopia and Djibouti were to link up their power generation capacity in a bid to boost access to electricity in both countries using loans worth $ 32 m and $ 27 m respectively (allocated by the African Development Fund in December).

Generally, port activity was sharply reduced in 2004. First, in 2003, the port's growth was linked to the delivery of food aid to Ethiopia and the re-export of containers. In 2004, the former terminated and the latter diminished. Due to delivery delays, one of the main companies for container re-export, PIL, chose to move to Aden in October 2003, a move that indeed reduced the container traffic for Djibouti. Although investments were certainly significant, they came mostly from foreign aid and foreign direct investment through ENOC and DPI, with very little local financing.

From a macroeconomic point of view, GDP **growth** reached 4.2% and inflation was kept under control, at 2%. Yet the IMF was far from enthusiastic. Public expenditures continued to rise and reached about 36% of GDP in 2004, while the state was not able to control current expenditures, which increased by more than 10% in the lead up to a new electoral year. Moreover, there were new delays in adopting structural reforms agreed upon with IMF, such as a new labour code and investment code.

A key question remained: who was benefiting from these opportunities? Despite a good number of projects in health and education funded by foreign aid, the expansion of the civil service, and the slow but real demobilisation – by 411 people – of the overmanned army, the very uneven distribution of revenue among the population became more marked. Heavy rains in April killed 48 people and made more than 1,800 people homeless, and emergency measures were necessary because many people lived precariously close to the river. Later in the year, a study commissioned by an international agency made it clear that malnutrition was still a fact of life for the poorest sector of the population.

Roland Marchal

Eritrea

Ten years after formal independence, the government continued to be of a provisional nature. There were no indications that parliamentary or presidential elections were to take place soon. At the close of the elections for regional assemblies in April, the chairman of the electoral commission stated, without giving a specific time frame, that the next election would be for the national parliament. So far the People's Front for Democracy and Justice (PFDJ) is the sole active party. The drought, coupled with post-war effects, has created severe food shortages. The dearth of foreign currency seriously curbed government purchasing capacity, resulting in a general shortage of basic goods.

Domestic Politics

PFDJ, the successor of the armed liberation movement, Eritrean People's Liberation Front (EPLF) continued to dominate the Eritrean polity without allowing political space for competing political parties. No political opposition was allowed to operate inside the country, with the result that all political opposition emanates from outside the country. The blanket prohibition on organised opposition also affected political or civil society associations with views opposed to the government. Minority Christian religious groups were persecuted, many ending up in jails while others went underground. Human rights groups have repeatedly expressed concern about the plight of these minority religious groups. It was reported that in February, 50 members of Hallelujah Church were arrested and that on 31 December, 60 members of the Rema Charismatic Church were arrested.

The **opposition groups**, including the Eritrean National Alliance (ENA), Eritrean Democratic Party (EDP), Eritrean Liberation Front-Revolutionary Council (ELF-RC) and Eritrean People's Movement (EPM), under pressure from Ethiopia and Sudan, held a meeting on 28 December in Khartoum, Sudan, and pledged to form an umbrella organisation. The meeting was held at the same time as the meeting of the **Sana'a Axis** (Ethiopia, Yemen and Sudan), once forged in order to isolate Eritrea (see below). At the end of the Sana'a meeting, President Omar Bashir of Sudan and Prime Minister Meles Zenawi of Ethiopia (two countries involved in a bitter conflict with Eritrea) met the leaders of the Eritrean opposition. While the latter were interested in eliciting the support of these two countries in their fight against the regime in Asmara, the two heads of state stressed the importance of unity within the Eritrean opposition as a precondition for that support. The direct connection of the opposition groups to neighbouring countries, particularly Ethiopia, proved problematic domestically, as it was perceived as tantamount to betraying Eritrean interests, and thereby deprived the opposition of popular support. The interference of Ethiopia in particular in the internal affairs of Eritrea, with its fresh memories of the recent war and Ethiopia's rejection of an international court ruling on the common border, is something most Eritreans loathe.

Members of opposition groups determined to topple the regime in Asmara operated from Ethiopia and the Sudan and committed intermittent **acts of terror** during the entire year. The victims were mainly civilian. Individuals who claimed to be agents of Islamic movements carried out a series of such acts in the Gash-Barka region. On 24 May, during celebration of Independence Day, a bomb was placed under a bus parked where crowds of celebrating people were gathered, leaving half a dozen dead and more than 80 wounded.

The rampant rounding-up of people suspected of avoiding national service invoked rage against the security forces. An incident on 4 November led to the death of a dozen people, including four members of the security forces, and injuries to more than 100 people, causing strong condemnation from all over the world by the Eritrean diaspora, Amnesty International, EU, etc. Several thousands of people were rounded up by the security forces for not having the legal papers to be in the capital city. They were transported to the **Adi-Abeyto military detention centre** outside Asmara. When the alleged national service dodgers attempted to flee, the security forces opened fire indiscriminately, leading to the aforementioned casualties.

Thousands fled the country to escape national service, the majority passing through Sudan on their way to Europe through Libya. Many of them faced harsh asylum policies. In August, about 76 Eritrean deportees from Libya hijacked and forced a Libyan military aircraft meant to return them to Eritrea to land in Sudan. Eventually, 15 of these deportees were brought to justice in Sudan while the rest were permitted to live there, in spite of strong opposition from the Eritrean government, which wanted them to face charges for fleeing the country illegally. In July, the Libyan government deported more than 100 asylum seekers to Eritrea. Many others fled to Ethiopia. Those caught while trying to flee were imprisoned.

The government continued to resist the call to introduce democracy – more precisely, and as core premises of meaningful reform, to implement the ratified constitution (ratified on 24 May 1997), hold a multiparty election, release political prisoners and admit independent mass media. In spite of considerable pressure both from Eritreans and the international community, the government stood firm on all these issues by pointing out that the country was still in a state of war because of Ethiopia's rejection of the boundary commission's decision. Indeed, there existed an undeclared state of emergency.

On 19 May, elections for **regional assemblies** in all six zobatat (regions) were held. This was a culmination of the local elections that began with **village and municipality** elections in 2002. The chairman of the electoral commission stated then, without giving a specific date, that the next election would be for the national assembly. So far there has been no sign that the indicated national election would be held in the foreseeable future. Generally, the regional elections failed to draw interest from outside the country, presumably because they were viewed as being held under a one-party system that lacked competitive democratic content.

Relations between the government and the peacekeeping forces of the **United Nations Mission for Eritrea and Ethiopia** (UNMEE) were strained. In March, the government closed the Asmara-Keren-Barentu supply line to the UNMEE after accusing it of illegal and immoral activities – monitoring Eritrean troops, illegal trafficking in people, making pornographic films. This generated strong opposition from UNMEE and UN headquarters in New York. The Security Council pleaded with the Eritrean government to honour its commitment and facilitate the smooth operation of UNMEE's mission. In August, the route was reopened in conjunction with the installation of the new UNMEE commander, Maj. General Rajender Singh of India, but some weeks later, in September, the ban was reimposed.

The precarious relationship between UNMEE and the Eritrean government was viewed as a sign of Eritrea's frustration at the lack of progress in implementing the Eritrean Ethiopian Boundary Commission's (EEBC) ruling. On 11 November, a junior commander, Colonel Zekarias Uqbagaber, replaced the senior officer responsible for coordination with the UNMEE, Brig. General Abrahaley Kifle. The obvious intention of this move was to mark the Eritrean government's dissatisfaction with UNMEE. In a further sign of frustration, the Eritrean president was quoted as commenting that UNMEE has outlived its mission since it was unable to discharge its mandate of demarcating the border.

On 16 November, the president convened a **special executive session** in Barentu (Gash-Barka region). The conveners of this special session were the cabinet of ministers, governors of the six Zobatat, and military commanders of the five military-operation Zobatat. The session was unprecedented for two reasons. First, it was probably the first time that the cabinet of ministers convened outside the capital. Second, the categories of attendees made it unique (cabinet of ministers, generals and regional governors). Further, because the meeting took place in the aftermath of the Adi-Abeyto incident, it immediately gave rise to speculation that the move had been caused by possible security fears about holding important meetings in the capital.

The cabinet of ministers next met on 28–29 December in Massawa, thereby giving currency to the belief that meetings outside the capital might become a recurrent event.

Foreign Affairs

The border issue, economic aid and political and human rights challenges dominated Eritrea's foreign relations. The country's relations with its neighbours continued to be unstable. The single most important source of tension, which impeded normalisation of Eritrea-Ethiopia relationships, was Ethiopia's continued rejection of the EEBC verdict on the delimitation and demarcation of the border between the two countries.

After **Ethiopia formally rejected the EEBC verdict** on 19 September 2003, there was a total halt in the peace process. With the commencement of the new year, intensive diplomatic activities aimed at resolving the border stalemate were seen. Both German Chancellor Schröder and British Prime Minister Blair travelled to Addis and appealed to the government to accept and implement the EEBC ruling. The former began his visit to Addis Ababa on 18 January, while the later arrived on 7 October. Lloyd Axworthy, the UN Secretary-General's newly appointed special envoy for Eritrea and Ethiopia, was dispatched to the region to try to breathe life into the stalled peace process. The veteran Canadian diplomat visited Addis Ababa in February and had discussions with the Ethiopian leadership. He left the region without visiting Eritrea because he was not welcome: Asmara opposed the appointment of a special envoy, and the devising of an alternative mechanism to the EEBC, and instead pressed for the immediate implementation of the EEBC ruling. US Deputy Assistant Secretary of State for African Affairs Donald Yamamoto also visited the two countries to boost the intense diplomatic efforts to break the deadlock.

Chris Muller, UK's foreign minister for Africa, visited Eritrea and Ethiopia in January and urged the leaders of the two countries to implement the EEBC ruling. Muller, turning particularly to Ethiopia, said it would take "an act of statesmanship" on the part of Prime Minister Meles Zenawi to break the stalemate. He further asserted that Ethiopia should "accept in principle" the boundary commission's decision and engage in dialogue. He told the two governments to compromise and resolve their problem and warned that the West had not ruled out sanctions to ensure the implementation of the peace deal.

On 25 November, Ethiopia issued a statement containing a **five-point proposal** to resolve the stalemate. Although it was dubbed a new initiative, there was no change of heart.

Ethiopia said it accepted the EEBC verdict in principle, but added there should be readiness to give and take. In a further discussion with diplomats, the Ethiopian prime minister made it clear that unless an alteration is made, Ethiopia would not accept the ruling. Reiterating what it has demanded all along, Ethiopia insisted that there be a change made with regard to the 15% of the disputed territory that it believed was illegally and unjustly awarded to Eritrea. In reality, Ethiopia was asking that what an international court had awarded Eritrea should be given back to it through bilateral dialogue.

Eritrea's official response came on 12 December. The proposal was rejected outright, and Eritrea urged the international community, particularly the **guarantors of the Algiers Peace Agreement** (AU, EU, UN and US), to put pressure on Ethiopia to unconditionally accept and implement the final binding verdict. Eritrea remained immoveable in its position of no dialogue before demarcation. Asmara insisted that the EEBC verdict was "closed and hermetically sealed" and that any form of 'dialogue' would lead to an endless talking circus. Hence, the deadlock continued. The Eritrea-Ethiopia border remained closed, and high tension persisted between both countries. The two governments kept on exchanging accusations about mass troop movements along the border and the committing of hostile acts. The delay in implementing the EEBC verdict was taking a heavy toll on Eritrea because its active labour force remained mobilised in defence of the nation.

The **Eritrea-Sudan** relationship was mainly influenced by the internal political situations in each country. Eritrean opposition groups received sanctuary in Sudan, while the Sudanese opposition was provided the same hospitality in Eritrea. In June, several Eritrean opposition groups assembled in Khartoum where Taha Awad, head of Africa section of the **National Congress Party** (NCP), the Sudanese ruling party, delivered a speech in which he called for the Eritrean opposition to unite against the regime in Asmara. This hostility was further entrenched when Eritrea issued a statement in October accusing Sudan of deploying terrorists to attack civilian targets and assassinate President Isaias Afwerki. The relationships between **Eritrea and Yemen** developed in a positive direction over the year. From 8–10 December, the Eritrean president visited Yemen at the invitation of his counterpart. The two presidents discussed bilateral matters such as economic exchange and security. In regard to the crucial issue of fishing in their common territorial waters, they signed a **partnership agreement**. And beyond bilateral relations, President Ali Abdullah Saleh took the initiative to offer to mediate between Eritrea on one side, and Sudan and Ethiopia on the other. In the meeting of the Sana'a Axis in Khartoum (27 December), a call was issued for Eritrea, Djibouti and Somalia to join the Axis. President Saleh received a positive response from the Sudanese regime regarding his initiative to broker a peace agreement between Eritrea and Sudan. Another auspicious development was the peace agreement between the Khartoum regime and the Sudan People's Liberation Movement/Army (SPLM/A). The **National Democratic Alliance** (NDA), based in Asmara, of which the SPLM/A and the Darfur-based movements are part, was also engaged in peace negotiations with Khartoum. The success of these negotiations would certainly have a very positive impact on the relationships between the two countries. So far, the Eritrea-Sudan border has remained closed, except for the UNHCR-sponsored repatriation of Eritrean refugees.

Serious human rights violations (continued imprisonment of senior government and party officials and journalists; closure of private newspapers; persecution of religious minority groups; mistreatment of national service dodgers) severely strained Eritrea's diplomatic relations with the rest of the world, in particular the West. As a consequence, official state visits by the head of state to **Western countries** were rare. Official visits were confined to the ministerial level (mostly the minister of foreign affairs) or to officials of the ruling party PFDJ. Besides Yemen (see above) the president visited **Libya, Kuwait, the United Arab Emirates, Qatar and Yemen**. On 3 November, Isaias left for Libya on a two-day working visit, and from there he went to the United Arab Emirates to convey his condolences to the family of the late Sheikh Zaid Bin Sultan Alnahyan: the UAE has funded various development projects in Eritrea. The purpose of the visit to Kuwait and Qatar was to strengthen existing close relations and seek more cooperation. Both countries have supported projects in Eritrea.

The US interest in the region is dominated by the **war against terrorism**. Following the 11 September attack, the US has resumed an active presence in the southern Red Sea region. Eritrea is, therefore, part of the coalition that includes Sudan, Djibouti, Ethiopia, Somalia and Kenya on the African side of the Red Sea. The US considers Eritrea as one of its important allies in the war on terrorism in the region. Due to its proximity to the Middle East and its demographic configuration, the region is seen by the US as a potential safe haven for al-Qaida operatives. On several occasions, American military commanders visited Eritrea. The commander of the joint task force in the Horn of Africa, Brig. General Samuel Heland visited Eritrea in November and held talks with General Sebhat Efrem, Eritrea's defence minister, and with President Afwerki.

The issue of security and terrorism in the Horn of Africa also drew in France. On 11 November, the commander of the French Indian Ocean maritime zone, Vice-Admiral Xavier Rolin, visited Eritrea and met senior military and civilian officials.

Socioeconomic Developments

The consequences of the **war** with Ethiopia, coupled with recurrent **drought**, made 2004 extremely precarious in terms of socioeconomic development. The total failure or low amount of rainfall of the previous year resulted in the inability to produce enough food for the country's population, thereby dashing the government's ambition to ensure food security. According to the Catholic charity Caritas International, 66% of the population was presumed to live below the **poverty level**, with extreme poverty afflicting 37%. According to the Famine Early Warning System Network (FEWS NET), between March and September inflation for all foods was 78%, for cereals 112%, and for pulses 178%. Real economic development (GDP growth) was estimated to be 1.8%.

In early January, Simon Nhongo, the UN Humanitarian Coordinator in Eritrea announced that 1.9 million people needed **humanitarian assistance** for the year. Nhongo and other UN officials who met donors in Geneva appealed for $ 147 m to meet Eritrea's food needs. Of 600,000 metric tons of cereals and grains that make up annual consumption needs, Eritrea produced only 84,984 metric tons (17%). The deficiency of 515,000 metric tons had to be imported either in the form of commercial imports or food aid. Foreign currency reserves were at all times low, thus constraining the country's import capacity.

The problem was compounded by the reality that about 70,000 people were still living as **internally displaced persons (IDPs)** in makeshift locations and were unable to return to their original areas either because they were littered with landmines or were insecure because of the presence of Ethiopian forces. There were still three million **landmines** and other forms of unexploded ordinance in the country. IDPs were consistently dependent on external help. In addition, almost a quarter of the country's most productive land remained unoccupied because of the **unresolved border dispute** with Ethiopia. This had a considerable impact on food production and the self-reliance of the country. This deadlock had another severe impact on socioeconomic development because of the numbers of the labour force mobilised to defend the nation. It was estimated that more than 10% of the active population was mobilised and on active military duty.

The severe effect of drought and the consequences of war also had a critical bearing on the **social sphere**. The welfare of children was impacted adversely. UNICEF, in its annual report on the state of children in the world in December, expressed concern at the level of child malnutrition. At 16%, child malnutrition in Eritrea was the highest in Africa, according to UNICEF.

The government claimed it was doing its utmost to alleviate poverty and improve social conditions. In an interview with local mass media the president stated that 25% of the budget was allocated for social security (while half of the budget remained allocated for defence). Since no national annual **budget** was issued, it is impossible to verify how much is destined for the social sectors.

Overall macroeconomic policy focused on reinforcing **infrastructure**, the main beneficiaries being road construction and maintenance, rural and urban electrification, and water and housing capacity. In an effort to address the acute rainfall and potable water problems caused by prolonged drought, the government, through its **Warsay-Yekaalo programme**, gave priority to constructing dams, terraces, catchments, etc. to preserve every drop of rain water for the coming growing season. In July, Eritrea received $ 50 m from the Word Bank group for power distribution and rural electrification. The International Development Association (IDA) fund was divided into a $ 29 m credit and a $ 21 m grant.

The acute shortage of foreign currency had a visible impact on the infrastructure projects that are dependent on imported construction material. There were also shortages of basic goods because of the dearth of foreign exchange. Commodities like sugar, wheat flour and fuel became scarce. Since September, **fuel** has been rationed, causing severe transportation problems. The price of fuel was raised by 40% mainly to discourage unnecessary consumption, but consumption behaviour could not be quickly altered and instead a black market and corruption flourished. The fuel reservoir of the country remained extremely low for the year, affecting other socioeconomic sectors as well.

There was no significant **foreign investment** in the country. There were three sites of mineral (gold, silver and copper) exploration – in Gash-Barka (Barentu), Southern Region (Debarwa) and Central Region (Asmara). Nevsum (a Canadian mining firm) undertook the Gash-Barka exploration; the prospecting at Debarwa was carried out by another Canadian firm, Sunridge Gold Corp.; while Northern Mining (a Montreal-based Canadian exploration company) prospected in the Asmara area. However, these explorations suffered a setback in September when the government suddenly, without giving any reason, ordered the companies to halt their activities. Sunridge and Sub-Sahara Resources NL had announced on 14 July significant results from 10 diamond drill holes and one reverse-circulation/diamond drill hole at the Debarwa high-grade copper and gold project. Afterwards, it became clear that the government's reason for ordering the companies to halt work was to raise its stake in the projects. Originally the Eritrean share was set at 10%. This amount had risen to 20–30% before the companies were told to resume prospecting.

Some key indicators succinctly describe the overall socioeconomic development situation for the year: Eritrea ranked 156 (of 177) on the **Human Development Index**. The per capita GDP shrunk to $ 130 compared with $ 170 in previous years. More than half the population lived on less than $ 1 per day.

Redie Bereketeab

Ethiopia

With a population of about 72 million people and a relatively strong state, Ethiopia remains one of Africa's most important countries. Its position, however, continued to be weak due to chronic food insecurity, massive poverty, lack of productive capacity beyond agriculture, an ambiguous democratisation process and unresolved issues as to national identity and policy. There was also continued internal dissent, partly emerging from politicised ethnic differences, with opposition parties and civil society organisations struggling to gain a voice in national politics dominated by a ruling party that came to power through force of arms in 1991. Scattered rebel groups and occasional revolts necessitated a close watch on the security situation. There was also a growing challenge from religious revivalism and several instances of radicalisation among some Muslim youth groups.

Ethiopia's relations with neighbouring countries (Djibouti, Sudan, Kenya and Somaliland) were fairly good, but not with Eritrea and southern Somalia. The unresolved border problem with Eritrea remained in the headlines in 2004, and the insistence by the UN and Western donor countries that the conflict be brought to an end and on the recognition of the border determined in 2002 by the Ethiopia-Eritrea Boundary Commission (EEBC) of the Permanent Court of Arbitration was not productive. GDP growth in 2004 was significant, but the 2.8% annual population increase slowed down overall development. Ethiopia remained a relatively large recipient of donor aid, and continued to be, with Djibouti, a strategic partner of the US and other countries in the 'global war on terror'.

Domestic Politics

Ethiopia's **domestic politics** in 2004 remained firmly under the control of the Ethiopian People's Revolutionary Democratic Front (EPRDF), especially of its core group, the Tigray People's Liberation Front (TPLF) of Prime Minister Meles Zenawi. The state apparatus, the army, the security service and the growing civil service, whose personnel were trained in the government-founded civil service college, were the bulwarks of support. EPRDF control did not preclude frequent elite rivalry and internal political tensions during the year, but this was less prevalent than in previous years. In view of these tensions – partly a result of lingering disagreements over policy towards Eritrea, which in 2001 had led to a major split in the TPLF and declining support for Meles in his own TPLF because of an Eritrea policy seen as too lenient – the prime minister sought to reform the EPRDF and seek more support among the other three 'ethnic' constituents of the coalition, the Amhara National Democratic Movement (ANDM), the Oromo Peoples Democratic Organisation (OPDO) and the Southern Ethiopian Peoples Democratic Front (SEPDF). The current leadership also opened up a little to opposition parties by holding several meetings on procedures for the 2005 elections and on campaigning.

Local conflicts in some regions were frequent, e.g., in Somali, Afar and Gambela (see below), three of the nine 'regional national states' (in Amharic 'killiloch', singular, 'killil') roughly based on ethno-linguistic criteria. Numerous unresolved disputes persisted regarding border demarcation, and, by implication, 'ethnic belonging' which has become the idiom through which 'resources', e.g., rights to land and budget, are secured. In 2004, there were dozens of boundary disagreements between communities (zones and peasant associations or 'qebeles') in Oromiya and Somali over 'who is an Oromo' and 'who is a Somali', a choice often difficult for people to make. The Somali region (the Ogaden) was unstable because of numerous changes in the regional government and a shaky security situation, with deadly ambushes by bandits and insurgent units on Ethiopian troops and garrison outposts. Ethiopian military action in the Ogaden was directed at eliminating armed activities, but human rights violations against non-combatants were a frequent result.

During the year, campaigning started for the May 2005 general elections for the House of People's Representatives (the national parliament, with 548 seats), with public debates in the state media (mass newspapers, television and radio controlled by the government) and the private, free press, and negotiations with opposition groups about 'levelling the playing field' for campaigning, especially in the countryside. But the government controls the National Electoral Board of Ethiopia (NEBE) that will supervise the electoral process and the registration of candidates and parties and handle complaints. A demand formulated by the main opposition party coalition (UEDF) in October 2004 to reform NEBE was not taken up by government.

In 2004, some 55 **political parties** were registered, among them the four parties in the EPRDF coalition. The EPRDF maintained its satellite ethnic parties in rural minority areas all across Ethiopia. The political opposition remained enormously fragmented, but gained public voice. The major opposition coalition, the United Ethiopian Democratic Front (UEDF), formed by 15 parties, the most important of which being the Coalition of Alternative Forces for Peace and Democracy in Ethiopia (CAFPDE) and the Oromo National Congress (ONC). CAFPDE, led by Dr. Beyene Petros, an MP and university lecturer in biology, reflected the southerners, and the Oromo National Congress, led by political scientist Dr. Merera Gudina, had its main support in western Oromiya. Many smaller parties, as well as the new four-party Coalition for Unity and Democracy (CUD), remained outside the broad opposition coalition.

CUD was formed in February 2004 from three existing parties: the All-Ethiopian Unity Party (AEUP), the United Ethiopian Democratic Party (UEDP) and the Ethiopian Democratic League (EDL), and a new one, The Rainbow Ethiopia Movement. This was founded by a number of influential intellectuals and opinion makers in Addis Ababa, e.g., former Ethiopian human rights council head Prof. Mesfin Wolde-Mariam and Dr. Berhanu Nega, the director of an important economic think-tank, the Ethiopian Economists' Association. In September 2004, a new Oromo party was founded: the Oromo Federalist Democratic Movement (OFDM) led by Bulcha Demeqsa, a former World Bank official and banker. Apart from the need to forge a united challenge to the ruling party, the opposition faced the problem of building a support base in the countryside. In 2004, this process was actively 'discouraged' by the ruling party and its supporters in the rural areas. Opposition parties were the regular targets of attacks by government-related forces. For example, an AEUP member (Dessalegn Simegn) was killed in Ibnet district (Gondar area); on 29 April an AEUP member (Hailu Zelleke) was shot dead in Gishe Rabel; and on 15 May government militia killed the AEUP Youth League leader Getiye Alagaw.

Other opposition groups remained illegal and unregistered because they opted for armed struggle: for instance, the Oromo Liberation Front (OLF), a group aiming for the secession of an Oromo state; the Ogaden National Liberation Front (ONLF), a movement claiming autonomy for Somali-inhabited eastern Ethiopia; and various smaller groups. The OLF, a previous partner in government (1991–92), had made itself unpopular by siding with the Eritreans in the 1998–2002 war and accepting arms and training from them. In 2004, it kept its office in Asmara and had significant nuisance value for the Ethiopian army, with several raids and small-scale attacks, but was not a military threat.

Governance in Ethiopia remained marred by a lack of trained and qualified personnel, especially in the regions, by a lack of transparency, by personalism, and by tendencies to abuse public funds for personal gain, i.e., corruption. Democratisation was occurring and was rhetorically promoted, but an authoritarian style of politics often prevailed in practice, with parliament showing little independence from the executive led by the prime minister, a strong federal government hand in local and regional politics and in security matters and ongoing harassment and intimidation of opposition party members. The judicial system remained weak and overburdened, especially at the lower levels, but the slow development towards more autonomy by the judiciary could be discerned. In 2004, the issue of corruption of public officials and EPRDF-associated business people was a continuing point of debate and accusation. A government-installed federal ethics and anti-corruption commission dating from 2001 waged public campaigns against graft. Its activities were initially directed against political opponents and former TPLF central committee members like Siye Abraha, Bitew Belay and others who had opposed the Eritrea and economic policy of the Meles group in 2000–01. Its activities, like monitoring complaints by the public, providing information and education and suing people, had some effect in making people conscious of the problem and of the need to tread with caution, but corruption did not notably diminish.

Muslim and Pentecostal-Evangelical religious adherence continued to grow, and both groups showed revivalist, and, in the case of some Muslim groups, militant tendencies, with a potential to disturb the relatively amicable relations between believers. Muslim leaders like the chairman of the Ethiopian Islamic Affairs Supreme Council, perceived their religion to be the majority religion in Ethiopia, and Muslims started to demand a greater public role for it in the law and politics. In many towns, disputes occurred about the choice of locations for new mosques. In 2004, Wahhabist Islam remained prominent in the form of NGOs and of huge private, often foreign and informal, investments in mosque-building, Islamic schools, social programmes, and the training of religious teachers and leaders in Muslim countries (Saudi Arabia, Pakistan and the Gulf States). This brand of Islam continued to build support at the grassroots against the Muslim establishment (Islamic Affairs Supreme Council and its local branches). In the Alaba region in southern Ethiopia, where Wahhabist Islam is strong, a violent incident occurred on 1 February between Orthodox people and Muslims. A Christian student was killed and a convert to Christianity seriously beaten and his house ransacked. In nearby Besheno village, Muslims chased out 32 Christians. There was also a report about an Ethiopian Orthodox teacher who forbade Muslim pupils to use his (public) school as a place for prayer being beaten and his family being harassed. Elsewhere in Ethiopia, some similar incidents occurred. The presence of 'Takfir-wal-Hijjra'-like groups was reported in some Ethiopian towns.

Pentecostalism continued to grow across the country, especially in the south, with about 6 to 8 million adherents. They had some trans-national material support and were disliked by both Muslims and the Orthodox. Disputes about burial places, mosque or church building sites, the loud playing of religious music and conversion efforts were frequent. The Ethiopian Orthodox church was publicly less prominent and remained internally divided because of the controversial patriarch 'Abune' Paulos (Gebre-Yohannis). Youth movements, however, were active in the church, pleading for revival and renewal and a response to the Islamic and Pentecostal expansion.

The **domestic political debate** in Ethiopia in 2004 was dominated by the perennial development issues (agriculture, health, infrastructure, capacity building) and by the stalemate over the 2002 border decision by the EEBC of the Permanent Court of Arbitration (PCA) in The Hague, handed down at the request of both countries after the conclusion of the 1998–2000 war. Domestic legitimacy of the government depended in large part on the perception among the wider public of how this disadvantageous decision for Ethiopia would be handled and diplomatically dealt with in the face of international pressure from donor countries, which insisted on unconditional acceptance of the PCA decision and even threatened the country with sanctions. A core issue remained the status of Badme town, where the war had started in 1998. In view of the national consensus in Ethiopia, it appeared even more unthinkable in 2004 that Ethiopia would yield this Ethiopian-founded town to Eritrea. Domestic public opinion in Ethiopia moved towards a more uncompromising stand on the border issue, following the perceived intransigence of Eritrea's government. The issue of Ethiopian access to the sea (Assab port) was also rekindled and was set to gain prominence as the dispute lingered on. Prime Minister Meles Zenawi also appeared to seek more support for his position outside his home base of Tigray, where more people showed dissatisfaction with his Eritrea policy, with the aftermath of the split in the dominant TPLF coalition party, and with the lack of improvement in living conditions. For instance, notable protest actions by citizens occurred in the Tigrayan town of Abi Addiy in March.

Ethiopia's 'experiment' in **ethnic democratisation** proceeded in 2004, but the federal authorities dominated by EPRDF kept all significant control of political power. Local-level conflicts were left to be tackled by the regional governments. There were credible reports of abuse of human rights, disappearances, torture and executions (planned or 'by mistake') by police and army, and usually carried out in an unpredictable manner and with impunity. Dozens of people in Oromiya, Somali and Amhara regions, many of them members of opposition parties were the victims. Thousands of people were also forced out of a job for non-economic reasons, evicted from homes or land without compensation and illegally detained without charge. Prison conditions remained very poor, without proper sanitation, food or medical facilities. On 21 January, an Oromo students' demonstration at Addis Ababa University, held after a riot during a contested Oromo cultural event on campus, was beaten up by campus police and 330 students were arrested and later expelled for the rest of the year. Students in several high schools and colleges in Oromiya region subsequently protested this incident, eliciting repression from government forces. On 18 May, another 18 Oromo students were arrested following an investigation into a grenade attack on 29 April in one of the university's dormitories, during which one student had died. Other incidents reported by human rights organisations were arbitrary arrests, beatings and humiliating treatment in southern Ethiopia (in Konso, Sidama, Wolayta). The 2004 US state department report on human rights was quite critical of Ethiopia, and in turn provoked a quite irritated denial from the Ethiopian authorities.

While Ethiopia saw significant improvement in **press freedom** after the fall of the Mengistu regime, many private, independent news magazines were subjected to harassment, pressure and arrest because of articles critical of government and the dominant party. Dozens of journalists were legally persecuted. A tendency to self-censor developed.

However, this year, while several journalists were arrested, awaiting formal charges, in prison or were on trial, killings were, in contrast to some previous years, not reported. At least one journalist, from the 'Tobbiya' weekly, was beaten by police. As a result of harassment, beatings or threats, ten journalists fled the country or went missing in 2004. During the entire year, the Ethiopian Free Journalists' Association (EFJA) remained banned by the government, following an accusation in November 2003 that it had "failed to meet its legal obligations regarding registration" with the ministry of justice. This ban, likely proclaimed in view of the EFJA's criticism of the new draft press law, met with widespread protests, also internationally. The International Federation of Journalists (IFJ) urged government to reassess the move. The new draft press law brought forward by government to parliament in 2004 was seen as draconian and drew a wave of (inter)national criticism because of its proposed restriction of press freedoms. There were still no private television or radio stations, except Radio Fana, which is EPRDF-affiliated, but in June the licensing of private radio stations was announced.

Apart from the tension on the Eritrea border, the **security situation** in Ethiopia was marred by frequent local violent clashes, mainly between 'ethnic groups' and the state military, or among various ethno-regional groups, with hundreds of people killed. The worst example was in January and February in the western region of Gambela, where Anyuwa, Nuer, Majangir and highlanders were at odds. The tension escalated after killings in December 2003 and the renewed fighting in January-February resulted in the massacre of at least 200 to 300 people and widespread destruction of property. These 'ethnic clashes' emerged out of the deeply politicised antagonism – according to many, government-fuelled – of two dominant ethnic groups in the region, the Nuer and the Anyuwa, who already historically had a tense competitive relationship. The Anyuwa were the main victims of these killings, and thousands of them fled to Sudan. Elsewhere in the country, small-scale but repeated violent clashes occurred between pastoralists and cultivators, such as Mursi and Aari, Suri and Nyangatom, Oromo and Somali, Hamar and Boran.

No religiously inspired violence was reported, but there were a number of unresolved killings that might be related to religious beliefs. There were some apparently politically motivated incidents of grenade throwing at Addis Ababa University (29 April, during which one Tigrayan student died), in a business location in the town of Debre Zeit (on 3 May, one person killed), in the town of Ambo (15 April, 30 students injured), and violence in some other places (army beatings of students and protesters in Nekemte and Dembi Dolo towns in March). Violence by police or militia units was usually not prosecuted. Often, cases were delayed and then dismissed. This impunity impacted negatively on the domestic security situation.

The country has remained relatively free from international **terrorism** perpetrated by groups associated with al-Qaida. The government routinely accused OLF and ONLF of terrorism, as in several of the incidents mentioned above, but a relationship to Islamist terror groups was not clear. The radical Somali Islamist group 'Al Ittihad al Islami', previously operating in the Somali-Ethiopian border area ('Luuq'), was defeated in an Ethiopian military action some years ago and did not resurface, at least not in Ethiopia.

Foreign Affairs

There were hardly any interest groups or parties that could influence EPRDF policy. The party's position was strong due to a combination of entrenched political and economic power and a lack of alternative political forces. Only the internal dissent rumbling in the dominant party could lead to power shifts and foreign policy changes in the long run. The position of Meles Zenawi was, however, more closely tied to the proper handling of the **border conflict with Eritrea**. Ethiopia remained adamant in its insistence on a review of the 'illegal and unjust' basis of the EEBC's boundary decision of April 2002, but on 25 November Meles Zenawi presented a new peace initiative, the '5 Point Peace Plan' (5PPP), which proposed to address the underlying issues in the conflict and aimed at long-term normalisation between the two countries. Reversing Ethiopia's formal rejection in 2003, he declared Ethiopia's acceptance 'in principle' of the 2002 decision, despite its still being considered 'illegal and unjust'. The payment of dues to the commission was resumed, and a plea was made for starting the demarcation process. The general thrust was to break the stalemate that had emerged after the Eritrean government refused any dialogue or negotiations whatsoever on the modalities of border demarcation and subsequent peace, insisting the decision be implemented to the letter. Ethiopia saw in this an underlying attitude refusing any normalisation of relations between the two states. While the 5PPP relieved some of the international pressure on Ethiopia (including threats of divestment and sanctions), few people in the country itself, or Ethiopians in the diaspora, supported Meles's about-face: the caving in to pressure by an international community ignorant of the facts on the ground was widely rejected.

Relations with Kenya were generally good but showed signs of strain after several Ethiopian troop incursions on Kenyan territory in March and April in pursuit of OLF rebels, which resulted in a number of Kenyan deaths. Kenya in the same month also deported four Ethiopians accused of harassing or torturing Ethiopian political exiles in Nairobi.

Ethiopia, Sudan and Yemen strengthened their cooperation under the Sana'a Forum for Cooperation, aimed at creating a free trade zone and a common front towards Eritrea. In Somalia, Ethiopia supported the formation of a new Somali unity government within the IGAD context, but in March was also accused of providing arms to allied factions.

During 2004, the **Nile River** issue came under public discussion again because of Ethiopia's plans to harness more water from the tributary Blue Nile, which originates in Ethiopia's Lake Tana. In the context of the Nile Basin Initiative, a meeting was held in March of the ten riparian countries in Entebbe, Uganda, and a week later in Nairobi. Ethiopia announced it would plead for a more equitable sharing of the Nile waters, of which 86 % flows from Ethiopian sources (Lake Tana and the Blue Nile). A reconsideration, supported by Kenya and Uganda, of the 1929 and 1959 Nile Treaties thus looked increasingly likely.

On the northern border with Eritrea, the **United Nations Mission in Ethiopia and Eritrea** (UNMEE) kept a peacekeeping force in place near the Temporary Security Zone, a strip of demilitarised territory on Eritrean soil promulgated after the December 2000 'peace accord' (cessation of hostilities agreement). Despite the mounting tension in 2004, no serious incidents were reported. Minefields created during the war posed a great security threat and claimed the lives of dozens of people. In December 2004, the UNMEE force was reduced from 4,200 to 3,889 men. Direct traffic between the two countries across the zone was still not possible.

During the year, Ethiopia had **peacekeeping troops** under the UN flag in Burundi and Liberia. In November, Ethiopia offered troops for the UN-sponsored stabilisation force to support the newly elected government in Somalia, whose new president, Abdullahi Yusuf, an old friend of Ethiopia, had asked for 25,000 UN peacekeepers.

Many aid and development cooperation agreements were signed in 2004 between Ethiopia and donor countries, especially EU countries, Japan, the US and China (the latter in construction and infrastructure). In January an $ 11 m development aid agreement was signed with the UNDP. In April, a contract was signed with the Jordanian company SI Tech International to exploit the huge natural gasfields in the Ogaden region, with proven reserves of 12.5 bn cubic metres.

Ethiopian **diplomacy** centred on the Eritrean-Ethiopian border issue and regional Horn of Africa politics. In January, the UN appointed a special mediator, former Canadian Minister of Foreign Affairs Lloyd Axworthy, to push for progress on the border issue. He had consultations with the Ethiopian leadership but Eritrea refused to meet with him. British Prime Minister Tony Blair visited Ethiopia in October for talks on the same issue and for furthering his initiative for the 'Commission for Africa', a major plan for a partnership between Western donor and African countries to speed-up Africa's development. In January, German Chancellor Schröder also paid a visit to Ethiopia. UN Secretary-General Kofi Annan was in Addis Ababa from 3–6 July to address the African Union summit on the UN's Millennium Development Goals and also to have bilateral meetings with the Ethiopian leadership on the border conflict with Eritrea .

Cross-border migrations in Ethiopia were limited to refugee movements in western Ethiopia (related to the Sudan conflict) and in the Somali region, where instability increased. In Dima town, southwest Ethiopia, about 19,000 Sudanese refugees were located. Following the Gambela 'ethnic clashes' in early 2004, a reported 4–5,000 (some sources said 10,000) Ethiopian Anyuwa fled to the Pochalla area in Sudan. The numbers of cross-border migrants in 2004 declined compared to previous years, and tensions between local people and incoming refugees were largely absent. More trouble was generated in resettlement areas within Ethiopia between locals and re-settlers. In Tigray region a small but regular influx of Eritrean refugees or deserters was registered, on top of those already displaced by war. In some inaccessible border areas, there were cross-border raids by local people, mainly pastoralists, e.g., Sudanese Toposa attacked villages and cattle herds of the Suri people in southwest Ethiopia at least three times in 2004, and the Ethiopian Dassanetch attacked Turkana people in northern Kenya on 16 and 20 October, with several people killed and cattle stolen. Such incidents caused no diplomatic ripples.

Socioeconomic Developments

Due to the good rains and the resulting higher **agricultural output** in 2004, a GDP growth rate of some 7% (according to IMF; government claim 10%) was reported, up from –4% in 2003. Industrial production and services were slightly up as well. However, the long-run GDP growth trend tends to equal national population increase. Furthermore, the GDP growth figure only applies to the registered economy and excludes the large informal sector.

There was continued massive poverty in Ethiopia, with an estimated 48% living below the poverty line of $ 1 per day. Annual income per capita remained around $ 110. The number of street children increased, as did that of prostitutes. Poverty reduction plans and debt relief schemes were signed with several countries, e.g., Germany in December and with Sweden in May, with the ostensible aim of enhancing Ethiopia's effort to reach the UN Millennium Development Goals in 2015.

EPRDF-affiliated business conglomerates such as Mega-Net, Africa Insurance, Ambassel, Guna, Biftu PLC, Sur Construction, etc. increased their hold on the national economy, drawing frequent complaints from private business people. The other major economic player growing in importance was Saudi-Ethiopian billionaire-tycoon Mohammed al-Amoudi, chairman of the MIDROC Corporation and owner of dozens of enterprises, including the Addis Ababa Sheraton Hotel. The country's largest salt factory in the Afar region was opened in October, built by an EPRDF-affiliated share company.

The overall **economic and food security situation** of Ethiopia remained very precarious: the country could not feed itself. While the harvest of 2004 was good, significantly reducing the number of food-needy people, in December the government again announced a donor appeal for 387,482 metric tons of food aid for about 2.2 m people, valued at some $ 159 m. This was down from the 2004 aid appeal for 14 m people, but again shows the chronic food deficit of the country even in the best of times. Ethiopia also asked for $ 112 m of non-food assistance for urgent humanitarian needs.

The **public health** situation in Ethiopia remained highly problematic. Malaria epidemics were recorded in several areas, as the spread of the parasite-carrying mosquitoes widened. Incidence of TB and other infectious diseases did not diminish. Economy and society were also seriously burdened by the HIV/AIDS pandemic, which in 2004 affected about 3 to 5% of the total population, some 1.5 to 2 m people, one of the highest absolute figures in Africa. There were about 750,000 AIDS orphans who had lost one parent or both. In 2004, AIDS-related deaths reached about 100,000 to 120,000. The reach of treatment was very low: as of June only about 4,500 people received anti-retroviral drugs. HIV-AIDS patients occupy some 40% of hospital beds. The health infrastructure, with 119 hospitals and 412 health centres, is stable but under-funded and understaffed, with a high turnover.

Costs for **education** took about 6% of the national budget ($ 509 m) and the sector's coverage and enrolment expanded significantly. Quality improvement, however, was a point of concern. In 2004, about 60% of eligible children went to primary school. High school attendance was 13%, university attendance 5–6%. The new regional universities (Jimma, Bahir Dar, Meqelle, Awasa) were consolidated, and new ones were built in Soddo-Wolayta, Dilla and some other towns in the south. The teaching load of university staff was doubled because of the requirement by the government that universities, especially Addis Ababa University which produces most of the MA graduates, treble the output of students, in line with the government's 'capacity building' programme. The research time of scientists was thus severely reduced, and salaries remained stagnant. State universities also had to continue the widely unpopular and demotivating evaluation system ('gimgema') that gives students a very big say in the performance assessments of individual staff. Private university colleges served about 15–20,000 students, but had no all-round academic profile.

The World Bank and IMF maintained a close working relationship with Ethiopia, e.g., in the framework of nicely worded plans like the Poverty Reduction and Growth Facility (PRGF), the Sustainable Development and Poverty Reduction Programme (SDPRP) and the Poverty Reduction Support Credit (PRSC). Despite the failure of several phases of these plans, worth hundreds of millions of US dollars, all were extended according to schedule. The government also drew up a PRSP that found acceptance among the donor community, due to the country's meeting the benchmarks, and this allowed Ethiopia to receive additional funds from IMF. Disagreement arose, however, on the 'slow pace' of privatisation, on financial system reform and on government reluctance to open up the financial sector (banks, insurance) to foreign capital, where the government fears dominance and exploitation by foreigners. This, and the many bureaucratic hurdles in the legal and administrative system, probably accounted for Ethiopia's ranking in 2004, despite improvements, as a 'mostly unfree' economy on the US Heritage Foundation index. Notable in 2004 was the continued expansion of Chinese businesses in Ethiopia, e.g., the telecommunications companies Huawei (to set up a switch telephone network) and ZTE (to develop the cell phone system earlier awarded to the Swedish company Ericsson), as well as road construction contracts (April). EU firms repeatedly complained to the Ethiopian government about being excluded and about the aggressive business policies of Chinese firms on the Ethiopian market.

The approved **national budget** in 2003/2004 (the budget year runs from 1 July to 1 July) was estimated at $ 2.24 bn, with capital expenditures of $ 628 m (1 $ was ca. 8.60 Ethiopian birr in December 2004) and $ 919 m of recurrent expenditures. The budget deficit was some 7% and inflation was about 5.5%. The national debt in 2004 was an estimated

$ 6.8 bn (not taking into account the proposed debt cancellations). Military spending was about 5–7% of the budget, education and health 7.5%.

Due to its prudent macroeconomic and monetary policies, its regular debt-service payments, the – relative to other African countries – low rate of corruption and the positive developments in selected sectors of the economy, Ethiopia received a comparatively large share of international and donor country aid, amounting to about 6% of GDP in 2004 (down from 8% in 2003). Still, the absorptive capacity of the country for aid was limited, and many programmes did not have the full desired effect because of a lack of facilities, employment, institutional support or skilled manpower.

Ethiopia was also eligible for the HIPC initiative, and in 2004 had benefited, via the IMF and the World Bank's IDA, from cumulative **debt relief** to the tune of $ 1.3 bn, as well as a larger number of grants-in-aid instead of loans. Another privileged area of donor support was capacity building in higher education, communication technology, the rural economy and administrative reform (decentralisation, local capacity building).

Ethiopia's economy continued to be marked by reliance on **agricultural production**, most of it in the smallholder sector, and showed little growth. While the weather in 2004 was favourable and more fertiliser was used, contributing to a 24% higher agricultural output, there was no marked structural improvement in the sector. Despite renewed extension services and peasant training programmes, investment remained low and poverty rampant. About 80% of the population worked in agriculture. Agriculture generated some 46% of GDP, and constituted 60% of export earnings through coffee, hides and skins, leather products, oilseeds, livestock and the stimulant ch'at (catha edulis). The service sector share in GDP was about 49%, that of industry 12%.

The government still followed the 1993 'Agricultural Development-Led Industrialisation' policy (ADLI), which places agricultural producers at the centre of the economy and sees them as the engine of growth. In view of the unpredictable, weather-dependent and smallholder-based nature of Ethiopian agriculture, this model has not worked well. There were signs in 2004 that the government started thinking about independent urban industrialisation to generate growth and serve the domestic market. In this respect, the example of China's economic development made a great impression on the Ethiopian leadership. The land tenure system of Ethiopia was again hotly debated among experts. The government, however, did not budge from its ideological principle of all land as state property: in its view, liberalising the land market would generate great inequality, drive many people off the land to the cities and create land-based power groups. At the same time, the government in 2004 moved to make the 'registration' of land rights possible, in terms of which parents can transfer their use of land to their children. Customary land rights and practices were not legally respected, although in certain areas they made a comeback in practice. There was investment in the rural sector by private agrarian entrepreneurs and also by party-linked business people, who started commercial farms (flowers, vegetables for export, dairy production, etc.), but in 2004 these comprised only 5% of agricultural production.

Compared to other African countries, Ethiopia has long been marked by a low rate of **migration** of rural people to the cities. The urban population in Ethiopia in 2004 stood at 16%. The new ethno-federal political order in Ethiopia, urging people to remain in 'their own' region, has tended to discourage internal migration. While this was still the case, more people were moving to the towns and cities. There was also a constant outflow of more educated but un- or under-employed or dismissed people to foreign countries (US, Canada, Gulf States, Saudi Arabia). Remittances from overseas were estimated to have reached about $ 220 m in 2004 and represented a vital part of the Ethiopian economy.

In the rural sector, Ethiopia embarked on the implementation of a large-scale, $ 220 m **resettlement programme** to meet problems of overpopulation, soil erosion, drought and recurring famine in the northern and central parts of the country. This programme, designed in 2003, envisaged the move to lower density areas by 440,000 households (or some 2.2 m people) 'on a voluntary basis'. The effort resembled the schemes instigated by the previous Marxist government, but the measure of coercion was less and site preparation seemed better. Still, success was limited: participation was less than expected, facilities were lacking, disease was rampant and some resettled people had already returned to their places of origin (where they kept their rights to land for three years). In some locations, tensions emerged between newcomers and indigenous populations, who used the land for extensive purposes like livestock herding, hunting, beekeeping, etc. and also as ritual or burial sites. The other solution to relieve pressure on the land and on resources – birth control policies – made only slow progress. The fertility rate was an estimated 5.44 children born per woman, which was down from seven 15 years ago. The government prepared a population policy document in 1996, but continued opposition against family planning and population reduction expressed by the Muslim community, the Ethiopian Orthodox church and other religious groups made implementation difficult. Popular opinion was also reluctant. In the countryside, however, many clinics now offered contraceptives and these were in high demand, especially among married women, who carry the largest burden of daily work and childcare.

In 2004, Ethiopia also had a population of **internally displaced persons (IDPs) and refugees** of some 275,000 people, down 29% from 2003. They were located chiefly in the Tigray and Somali regions.

Ecological problems persisted in Ethiopia, such as deforestation, massive topsoil erosion and overuse of resources in many places. A contributory background factor was the pattern of steadily declining rainfall connected to global warming and microclimate change. Related factors are continued high population growth and policy failures in agriculture. There was no significant growth in the agricultural sector, and most peasants perform additional non-agrarian activities to survive. Land remained state property but could be leased and given in use to peasants and urban dwellers. However, it was often unpredictably redistributed at will by state agents on criteria other than economic. An average holding was less than one hectare, too small for proper sustenance and growth. The lack of a land market and legislation to provide security of tenure for rural producers contributed to the lack of investment in agriculture and upkeep of the commons.

The pastoral sector in the lowland areas covers a large land surface and is the domain of several ethnic groups, such as the Afar, Somali, Boran, Guji and smaller groups in the southwest, like the Mursi, Nyangatom, Hamar and Suri. In 2004, they continued to be marginalised, and earlier government plans to assist the sector with education, securing their grazing lands, credit schemes and improving security had not materialised. A World Bank- and government-supported 'Pastoral Community Initiative' was launched in 2004 to address the issue. The government agenda, however, was to move towards settling the pastoralists, regardless of the ecological consequences for fragile ecosystems.

Jon Abbink

Kenya

On the political front, 2004 started in as stormy a manner as 2003, albeit in a diametrically different mood. The early months of 2003 had witnessed the much-welcomed coming to power of President Kibaki and the National Rainbow Coalition (NARC) and the ending of the uninterrupted rule of the Kenya African National Union (KANU) since independence in 1963. In 2004, tensions increased within the NARC coalition, a grouping of 13 parties and two civil-society organisations, negatively impacting the initially hopeful start.

Domestic Politics

In an attempt to stop internal wrangling among coalition members, President Kibaki announced in late December 2003 that **NARC**-affiliated parties would cease to exist and would be dissolved into a single political party. The announcement met with opposition from some of the coalition partners, in particular the Liberal Democratic Party (LDP) and the Forum for the Restoration of Democracy-Kenya (FORD-Kenya). LDP claimed that NARC was a coalition of the National Alliance (Party) of Kenya (NAK) and LDP, thereby indicating that the dissolution of LDP could not be ordained by the political leader of NAK. On 5–6 February, NARC politicians met in Nanyuki to discuss the Memorandum of Understanding (MoU) signed between NAK and LDP when they formed NARC and the dissolution of the 15 coalition parties. A membership committee was instructed to produce a proposal. In April, though, it became clear that unification was still a long way off. LDP, FORD-Kenya and the Labour Party of Kenya (LPK) indicated they preferred membership in NARC by each of the parties as corporate entities. The other parties either allowed for a mix of membership by individuals and corporate membership by parties in the long run (Democratic Party, FORD-Asili and United Democratic Movement) or only in the short run (Mazingira Green Party, Social Party for Advancement and Reforms-Kenya (SPARK), Saba Saba Asili and the National Convention Executive Council (NCEC), while the Social Democratic Party (SDP), National Party of Kenya (NPK) and the Progressive People's Forum wanted NARC to become a single party exclusively composed of individual members. The committee also advised NAK and LDP to stop fighting over the MoU and the allocation of political positions. Some of these, such as the post of prime minister, would need first and foremost the overhaul of the **Kenyan constitution**, an overhaul that had been under discussion since the 1990s. However, the national constitutional conference had only got under way on 28 April 2003 at Bomas of Kenya, a hall used to perform traditional Kenyan dances for tourists. The venue's name became associated with the process through which 629 representatives from different sections of Kenyan society, including parliamentarians and legal experts, gathered to discuss the draft constitutional proposal.

The key issue at stake was the position of prime minister. Raila Odinga's LDP strongly favoured the creation of a parliamentary system of government with an executive prime minister and ceremonial president, as opposed to the current presidential system, which has no position of prime minister. The unicameral National Assembly, encompassing a total of 224 seats (210 elected, 12 nominated and 2 ex-officio, namely the attorney-general and the speaker) is supposed to control the government. Those close to President Kibaki supported a hybrid system in which the country would have both an executive president and an executive prime minister. NAK politicians saw the preference for a strong prime minister and a ceremonial president as an internal coup by the LDP. Justice and Constitutional Affairs Minister Kiraitu Murungi and Internal Security Minister Chris Murungaru were singled out for deliberately frustrating the review process and watering down clauses reducing the powers of the president. In response, they claimed that the composition of the Bomas delegations was the scheming handiwork of former President Daniel arap Moi and KANU. A war of words erupted between those who favoured the process to be in the hands of a team of experts and those wanting to stick to the people-driven debate. On 6 June 2003, the conference was adjourned for two months. On 17 August 2003, Bomas II started but also failed to reach finality. On 12 January 2004, Bomas III made another try. In the Bomas III proposal, the president appoints the prime minister, who subsequently appoints and chairs the cabinet. The president would remain head of the armed forces. The draft constitution, passed on 16 March, led to the walk out of a faction close to Kibaki, including Vice-President Moody Awori (LDP) and threats to block approval of the draft in parliament. Cabinet minister Raila Odinga stayed behind and added a clause that the prime minister's position would be established after the next elections, thus guaranteeing that Kibaki would stay in power until 2007 at least. In the following weeks, several groups aired their support for or discomfort with the review process. President Kibaki addressed the nation on 25 March and appealed for calm. He also stressed the need for 'consensus-building', but at the same time the government officially withdrew from the conference. Other groups, in particular the faith-based Ufungamano group, rejected the Bomas draft constitution and instead offered their own constitutional variants. Several groups sought legal redress, resulting in a high court ruling that the Constitution of Kenya Review Commission (CKRC) was not to finalise its report and the draft bill. In another case, it was stated that the entire draft constitution should be subjected to a mandatory referendum by the people of Kenya. In response, legislative steps were taken by the Kibaki camp, i.e., the 'Constitution of Kenya Review (Amendment) Bill' and the 'Constitution of Kenya (Amendment) Bill', which would have made it possible for MPs to alter the Bomas draft. Separately, an inter-party initiative involving some 44 MPs, called the Constitution Consensus Group, attempted to bridge the differences. In April, Paul Muite (Safina) quit as chairman of the Parliamentary Select Committee on the Review (PSCR) and was replaced by KANU MP William Ruto, a strong supporter of parliamentary government. He got backing from LDP and KANU, among others. On 14 April, Ruto became the first MP to face criminal charges since NARC took power. The case, involving falsely obtaining about Ksh 77 m, was later dropped on a 'technicality'.

NAK-related parliamentarians also discussed the situation at length and criticised the selection of the members of the PSCR. Observers saw these moves merely as attempts to frustrate the efforts of the 'People's Constitution' initiative to deliver a draft proposal in time for the 30 June deadline.

On 28 June, President Kibaki endorsed a bill prepared by the Consensus Group and directed Murungi to drop the two pending government bills on the review process. UN Secretary-General Kofi Annan, after meeting Kibaki in July, expressed his hope that Kenya would soon have a new constitution, and in a peaceful matter. The statement was made one day after police fired on demonstrators in Kisumu, Raila Odinga's home area, demanding swifter change. In November, PSCR members met in Naivasha. After the retreat, a breakthrough was announced in which the position of prime minister was agreed upon, although the president would be the head of both the state and the government. Only a few days later, Minister Murungi refused to publish the 'Consensus Bill' because it stipulated a 65% majority in parliament. Finally, by 11 December the bill had been reviewed and it was agreed that a simple majority would suffice, although most LDP and KANU MPs boycotted the vote. On 14 December, Murungi announced that the constitution would be ready by September 2005 and, once the attorney-general had amended the draft constitution based on the recommendations of parliament, Kenyans would be asked to vote in a referendum on the new constitution (planned for October 2005).

Kibaki reshuffled his **cabinet**, bringing in leading opposition politicians. The new government of 'national unity' included KANU's Njenga Karume (the special programmes portfolio) – during the 1990s a strong supporter of Kibaki – John Koech (East African coop-eration), Abdi Mohammed (regional development) and the leader of FORD-People, Simeon Nyachae (energy). No minister lost his seat, but LDP ministers – in particular Minister of Foreign Affairs Kalonzo Musyoka – were demoted to less important ministries (in his case, environment). This display of power politics did not sit well with LDP supporters and the Kenyan public at large. Protests were aired in Nairobi (3 July) and Mombasa (24 July) by civil society groups, such as Katiba Watch and the Front for Popular Change, some of which ended in violent clashes with the police. In Kisumu on 7 July, police used teargas and bul-lets, killing one person, to quell Saba Saba demonstrations. That same month, LDP helped defeat the government's forest bill in parliament by voting along with the opposition. In July, Professor Yash Pal Ghai resigned as chairman of the CKRC and was replaced by one of his women deputies, Abida Ali-Aroni.

In July, Lena Moi, wife of former President Arap Moi, died. On 26 August, Karisa Maitha, minister for tourism, also passed away. On 16 December, Ananiah Mwaboza (National Labour Party) defeated the LDP candidate in the Kisauni by-election, which was marred by violence and a low voter turnout, to fill the seat left by Maitha. Earlier that year, on 21 April, Rev. Ken Nyagudi (LDP) had won the Kisumu Town West parliamentary by-election, succeeding the late Joab Omino (former LDP chairman). In September, KANU acting chairman Uhuru Kenyatta asked Kenyans to forgive his party for its errors in the past. The request was clearly made to garner support in his battle with rival Nicholas Biwott over KANU's chairmanship. In December, Biwott was mentioned in the Ouko inquiry as one of the suspects who may have participated in the killing of the former minister of foreign affairs in February 1990. In December, Biwott was also barred from the US owing to alle-gations of corruption. Wrangles in FORD-People continued until 10 December, when nom-inated MP Kipkalia Kones, whose presence in parliament had been contested by the party's chairman, Kimani wa Nyoike, was elected unopposed as FORD-People's new chair-person. Following her 20 June promise to Kenyans that they would get free health treat-ment, Health Minister Charity Ngilu unveiled the national social health insurance fund in October. Criticism of the plan came from employers, private hospitals and health insurance providers. By mid-December, Ngilu received the go ahead from the president to submit the bill to parliament, but on 29 December, the Law Society of Kenya claimed the bill was unconstitutional and the Kenya Private Sector Foundation moved to court to block it. The following day, President Kibaki referred the bill back to parliament.

Amnesty International made a number of visits to Kenya in 2004 and claimed that **tor-ture** still occurred in Kenya, despite its prohibition under the constitution of Kenya and despite the enactment of the 'Criminal Law Amendment Act' in July 2003. Likewise, Amnesty International acknowledged that access to prisoners has improved, but expressed its concern about the very poor conditions in Kenyan prisons. For example, on 24 May, it recorded 3,385 prisoners in Kamithi Maximum Security Prison, which has a holding capacity of 1,500 only. And on 27 September, six inmates died and 20 were injured in a reportedly overcrowded cell in the Meru prison. Local human rights organisations have alleged that some inmates had been tortured by prison warders, not only in Meru district, but also in other parts of the country.

The claims of torture were also made in relation to terror suspects. A total of seven detainees, Kenyans of Arab origin, were standing trial for the bombing of the Israeli-owned Paradise hotel in Kikambala on 28 November 2002. **Al-Qaida** claimed responsibility for this suicide bombing as well as for the simultaneous (unsuccessful) attempt to down an Israeli aircraft as it took off from Mombasa airport. In early 2003, Kenya had joined a group of six countries identified by the US to work in a coalition to fight terrorism in the Horn of Africa. In January 2004, the national counter-terrorism centre was established in Nairobi with the aim of providing 'timely' and 'factual' intelligence. That same month, Muslim leaders called for the withdrawal of the 'Terrorism Bill'. In May, an MP wrote a letter in local newspapers citing several cases of arbitrary arrest and deportation of Muslims. The Kenyan government has been dragging its feet on the 'Terrorism Bill', which has been in abeyance since it was first drafted two years ago.

The **Mungiki** sect, a quasi-religious group, emerged once again when over 20 people were brutally murdered or disappeared, particularly in the surroundings of Nairobi and Nakuru. On 14 December, however, there was great jubilation in Nakuru after former MP David Manyara and 12 suspected Mungiki members were set free, owing to lack of evidence. They had been in detention for 23 months on charges of murdering 10 persons in January 2003.

In May, members of the Seventh Day Adventist Church claimed that they were among hundreds of workers fired by private companies operating in Nairobi's Export Processing Zone (EPZ) for refusing to work on Saturdays. The Kenya Human Rights Commission also expressed its concern about conditions in the EPZ.

Acts of **communal violence** reappeared. In August, a clash over land occurred between the Maasai and ranch owners in the Laikipia region. The Maasai claimed the treaty signed in 1904 that took away their grazing areas for the benefit of white settlers had expired after 99 years, but government insisted the treaty was for 999 years. Protest, both in Laikipia and Nairobi, became increasingly violent, resulting in demonstrators being tear-gassed and two Maasai being shot in the Laikipia area. In an attempt to end the hostilities, some Laikipia landowners allowed Maasai livestock on to their ranches at the end of the drought period. In Narok, two people were killed after violence erupted between two neighbouring communities. Another controversial settlement, the Likia Forest, was also rocked by violence, after which government decided to allow some 1,600 acres to revert to forest and cancelled 471 title deeds.

The land question was dealt with in the Ndung'u report released in December 2004. The report mentioned the families of former presidents Jomo Kenyatta and Daniel arap Moi, among other high-ranking Kenyans, as having grabbed public land now recommended for repossession. Parastatals and churches were also among the beneficiaries of corrupt land deals. President Kibaki received the report in July, but it took until the end of the year before the report was released to the public. A further list of people who allegedly got money from the proceeds of the **Goldenberg** scam – ranging from President Moi, to MPs, lawyers and ministers – was released by the Goldenberg commission of inquiry that same month. Kamlesh Pattni, Goldenberg International's founder, had testified during the hearings that he secured Moi's cooperation by paying the former president an initial cash bribe of just over $ 65,000. However, Moi – who refused to testify at the hearings – denied being party to the fraud. Constable Naftali Lagat and David Munyakei, a former clerk at the central bank of Kenya, helped to expose the Goldenberg scandal, one of the largest and most complex financial scandals in Kenyan history, centred on fake exports of gold and diamonds and resulting in a loss of between $ 600 m and $ 1.3 bn. The two men were awarded the Transparency International 2004 Integrity Award.

In 2004, several incidents indicated that the **press** was less free under the Kibaki government than it was considered to be. In January, police arrested 20 vendors and confiscated so-called gutter newspapers, including 'The Independent', 'Kenya Confidential', 'Weekly Citizen', 'News Post' and 'Summit'. The Kenyan union of journalists condemned the raid as an attack on press freedom. Peter Makori, a freelance journalist, investigating corrupt officials in Kisii, was arrested, charged with murdering two local chiefs, and detained from July 2003 to May 2004 without trial. In September, offices of 'The Independent' and the 'Weekly Citizen' were visited by masked men and computers and printing equipment were taken away once again.

In April, Information Minister Raphael Tuju appointed a team to investigate the KISS FM Radio station, associated with KANU, after complaints filed by Water Resources Minister Martha Karua about defamation. However, prominent media people rejected their appointments, and the high court ruled on 31 July that the panel had no basis in law. In May, Minister Kiraitu Murungi said that the 'Books and Newspapers Act', a controversial press law enacted just before the 2002 elections, would soon be repealed. However, the Kenyan government also announced a bill that would ban companies from owning more than one type of media outlet, but shelved it after protests from media owners and local journalists.

Foreign Affairs

Since November 2003, **relations with major donors** have improved considerably following the release of development funds. However, serious hiccups in these relations also cropped up during the year. Coffee was at the centre of the debate with foreign donors when, in April, Co-operative Development Minister Njeru Ndwiga reported that the Kenyan government had rejected Stabex funding from the EU because of its unfavourable conditions.

Ndwiga accused the EU of opposing the purchase of finished coffee products, unlike the US. The EU was quick to deny the claim. More damaging was the clash between the British high commissioner and the Kenyan authorities. In mid-July, during a luncheon of the British business association, Sir Edward Clay accused the NARC government of negotiating a total of $ 187 m in corrupt deals over 18 months. Support for this view came from the US and Norway. Soon after, the EU, referring to the Anglo leasing affair, a shady tender deal to produce new Kenyan passports, delayed the disbursement of budgetary support to the tune of $ 59 m.

At a regional level, Kenya's relationships fared much better. On 2 March in Arusha, Presidents Mkapa (**Tanzania**), Museveni (**Uganda**) and Kibaki signed the treaty for the EAC customs union. EAC will become a free trade area by 2010.

Relationships with other neighbours, notably **Ethiopia** and **Somalia**, were less cordial. On 15 April, Ethiopian militiamen raided three villages near Moyale. The same month, Kenya banned entry to anyone travelling on a Somali passport. This impacted the Somali peace talks when, in mid-May, the head of the Somalia's transitional government refused to continue the process unless he was admitted into Kenya on a Somali passport. These problems did not prevent the conclusion of the Somali peace talks. On 14 October, newly elected Somali President 'Abdullaahi Yuusuf was sworn in at Nairobi's Kasarani sports complex, an event witnessed by Kibaki, Museveni and Obasanjo (Nigeria). The new Somali government would, for security reasons, remain based in Nairobi for the time being. Nairobi was also the scene of an historic UN Security Council meeting in November, which resulted in an agreement ending the 21-year war in southern **Sudan**.

Kenyans were also making headlines abroad. In July, three Kenyan truck drivers were captured in Iraq, but were released in September after 42 days in captivity. In November, a Kenyan firm was mentioned as being at the centre of a multibillion-shilling illegal weapons trade in the Ukraine. A more positive event was the Nobel Peace Prize award to Professor Wangari Maathai on 9 October for her contributions to democracy and sustainable development. Maathai had founded the Green Belt Movement, an organisation that promotes the planting of trees, and entered the NARC government as assistant minister of the environment.

Socioeconomic Developments

On Madaraka Day 2003, President Kibaki called upon all Kenyans to turn Kenya into a 'working nation'. To guide this plan, the government published the ambitious **Economic Recovery Strategy** for Wealth and Employment Creation 2003–07. However, the economy grew by only 1.8% in 2003. For 2004, the economic performance stood at 2.6%, still below the 3% target. Economic activity increased during the first four months of 2004 before slackening between May through September as a result of drought and rising oil prices. The economy, however, picked up momentum in the last quarter. Growth in tourism, horticulture, tea, manufacturing, transport and telecommunications services underpinned overall GDP growth in the last quarter.

By December, overall inflation stood at 16.5%, adding to the average annual inflation of 12.1%, far above the target rate of 5%. Especially against the euro the shilling lost ground, from 95.6 at the beginning of 2004 to 105.3 at the end. For the corresponding period, the US dollar stood at 76.1 and 77.3 respectively.

The **budget deficit** decreased significantly to 0.4% of GDP in fiscal year 2003–04. The good performance was attributed to improved administration resulting in higher tax revenue collection. The increased inflow of external financial means was an outcome of the resumption of IMF and World Bank programme support, although the Kenyan government had aimed for a higher target. The shortfall was due to a tightening of donor funds pending ongoing reviews. In August, Justice Aaron Ringera became director of the reconstituted Kenya anti- corruption authority. During 2004, a number of corruption cases came to light in the housing, transport, electricity, forests and AIDS-prevention sectors. In August, director Margarat Gachara of the national AIDS control council was jailed for one year for theft of Ksh 27 m, but was released four months later, along with 7,000 other 'petty offenders', through presidential clemency.

The **public debt** stood at $ 9.3 bn at the beginning of 2004. This was equivalent to 70% of GDP. The government registered a major breakthrough on 16 January when the Paris Club of creditors agreed to reschedule Kenya's $ 350 m debt with it. At year's end total public debt, however, had increased to $ 9.4 bn. The increase was mainly due to a growth of external debt to $ 5.6 bn, which more than offset the decrease in gross domestic debt to $ 3.8 bn in the same period. Interest rates on borrowings declined from highs of 19% to an average of 12%.

During the period January to October, the value of Kenya's **domestic exports** grew by 12.8%, while re-exports grew by 16.6%. This growth is mainly attributed to the export of horticultural products (flowers, fruits and vegetables) and manufactured goods (iron, steel and textiles). Commercial imports grew by 23.2% to Ksh 285.8 bn for the period January to October 2004. Overall, the trade balance deficit widened from Ksh 81.5 bn to Ksh 116.5 bn.

Coffee and tea exports increased by 5.3% and 5.1% from January to October 2004 and stood at Ksh 6 bn and Ksh 29.3 bn respectively. The leading importers of Kenyan tea were Egypt (26%), Pakistan (23.1%), UK (15.3%), Afghanistan (12.2%) and Sudan (4.8%).

Horticultural exports increased by 22.1% to Ksh 31.2 bn. Europe continued to absorb the bulk of the produce, though the Middle East (particularly the United Arab Emirates and Saudi Arabia) and South Africa were emerging export markets. The growth of export earnings was mainly the result of improved prices, as a drop in quantity was recorded, especially for coffee and horticulture. Chemical products (6%), pyrethrum (3.1%) and soda ash (3%) were other major export products.

Exports to African countries, notably Uganda, stood at 46.6% of the total exports, while the EU, especially the UK (10.4%) and the Netherlands (8.2%) came second. Several

Kenyan goods gained access to the European market through preferential trade agreements under the ACP-EU Cotonou Agreement. On 14 January, the EU lifted a four-year ban relating to compliance with health conditions on Kenya's fish exports. Kenya produces approx. 200,000 metric tonnes of fish annually, worth Ksh 6.5 bn. Almost 30% was exported to fish processing countries.

Agriculture remained the most important economic sector and was responsible for some 24% of Kenya's GDP. Output of tea, sugar cane, coffee, horticulture and pyrethrum grew by 16.8%, 6.6%, 4.5%, 9% and 13.2%, respectively. The improvement mainly reflected the favourable weather conditions and enhanced investor confidence. In the coffee sector, deliveries rose by 4.5% to 58,800 tonnes in the financial year 2003–04. But in early 2004, the biggest producer, Socfinaf, announced that the company would scale down its coffee operations by more than half in the next two years to concentrate on horticulture. Second producer, Kakuzi Ltd, even announced its complete withdrawal from coffee in favour of horticulture, forestry and livestock farming. By late-December, the coffee board of Kenya and the government clashed over the contentious appointment of Tetu Coffee Incorporated as marketing agent. The government, however, denied the claim, stating that three companies had been issued interim marketing licences.

Production of horticultural exports increased by 9% in the financial year 2003–04 to 147,799 tonnes. This remarkable growth was largely in flowers and vegetables, whose export volumes grew by 28.3% and 31.8% respectively. Fruit, however, declined by 14.2%. Early in 2004, worries cropped up that new EU quality control measures to prevent new pests and diseases would threaten Kenya's horticultural industry and its 500,000 employees.

The need to improve resilience in the face of pests and droughts once again became clear towards the end of 2004, when Kenya pleaded for donor aid to feed an estimated 3.3 m people facing starvation in 26 districts across the country. Earlier in the year, some 80 people had died from food poisoning from contaminated grains.

In **manufacturing**, production of cigarettes, beer, processed sugar and soda ash increased by 32.3%, 19.7%, 13.1% and 7% respectively in the second half of the financial year 2003–04. Growth was supported by the AGOA treaty. The companies operating in the Export Processing Zones increased to 70 by June from 54 in the previous year, while private investment shot up from Ksh 2.7 bn to Ksh 15.7 bn. Kenya approved the signing of a 21-year mining lease for Tiomin Resources Inc's proposed titanium mine at Kwale. Protests over environmental and landownership issues had delayed the signing since 2000. The $ 120 m project is projected to produce 330,000 tonnes per year of imenite, 77,000 tonnes per year of rutile and 37,000 tonnes per year of zircon over the first six years of operation. Tiomin has identified three further deposits of heavy minerals in the vicinity of Kwale. Domestic supply of electricity rose by 7.9% during the financial year 2003–04. In January, the World Bank gave Ksh 3.5 bn to strengthen power transmission and distribution, and on 17 February, Japan announced it would release Ksh 8.5 bn needed to complete the

Sondu Mirui hydro-power project, which had stalled two years earlier. Funds released by Germany for the Olkaria geothermal project were also expected to boost Kenya's energy provision. Despite the increase in domestic power generation, the energy sector continued to be plagued by the high cost of power and unreliability of supply.

Since liberalisation, **telecommunications** has become the fastest growing sector in the economy. By the end of June, active subscriptions with mobile service providers totalled more than 2.5 million, representing a remarkable annual growth of over 57.9%. Kencell and Safaricom extended their telecommunications services to parts of the country that had long been neglected. In June, the debt-ridden French operator Vivendi sold its 60% stake in Kencell to Celtel for $ 250 m. This led to the addition of 1.2 million subscribers and made Celtel the leading telephone company in Africa (excluding South Africa) and East Africa's only regional operator covering Kenya, Tanzania and Uganda. In the fixed lines sub-sector, total subscriptions declined by 8.9% to less than 300,000 lines.

Cargo handled by Kenya Ports Authority (KPA) increased by 7.7% to 12.1 m tonnes from 11.2 m tonnes in the previous financial year. Most of the inland transport was by road, rail being second. Cargo handled by Kenya Railways declined by 7.9% in the 2003–04 financial year. In April, Kenya and Uganda launched a plan to jointly lease **Kenya Railways** and Uganda Railways Corporation. The World Bank granted $ 270 m to rehabilitate the Mombasa-Malaba railway. There were also plans to extend the railway line to southern Sudan. In December 2004, a German company, Thormaehlen, announced it would construct a new railway linking Kenya and Sudan via Lokichoggio. Rwanda and Ethiopia indicated an interest in joining the improved network. The company entered a 25-year build. operate and transfer deal with the Sudan Peoples' Liberation Movement (SPLM), with the firm being given a mineral concession in return.

In addition to railway improvements, a **major road project**, the northern corridor project, was taking shape. The World Bank released $ 218 m to make a dual carriageway from Mombasa-Nairobi-Busia through Kisumu and through Eldoret to Malaba. Another important development in Kenya's transport system was the introduction of new safety measures on 31 January. This resulted in over 44,000 public service vehicles temporarily suspended business as efforts were made to comply with the new regulations, which reduced the number of passengers from 18 to 14 and required the installation of seat belts, among other things. About 3,000 Kenyans are killed and 11,000 injured on the roads every year.

Kenya's major **airports**, Nairobi, Mombasa and Eldoret, also received World Bank and US funding to upgrade and improve security. On 3 March, President Kibaki announced an end to the ban on cargo flights from Eldoret airport imposed in 2003. Kenya Airways, one of the few profitable African airline companies, continued to report increasing net profits, Ksh 1.3 bn in 2004, up from Ksh 400 m the previous year. On the other hand, East African Safari Air, the second largest international Kenyan operator, was grounded in early September over $ 1.5 m in fuel debts. As a result of an emergency landing on 29 July in Rome, it was thrown out of IATA. The company had about a quarter of the UK market to

East Africa and over 60% of the southern European markets of Italy, Spain and France.

In spite of this set back as well as adverse global events, in particular negative travel advisories and terrorist threats, Kenyan **tourism** picked up in 2004. During the financial year 2003–04, arrivals increased by 5.5% to 573,254 tourists. During this period, earnings were estimated to have reached $ 376 m from $ 288 m in the financial year 2002–03.

Marcel Rutten

Rwanda

Rwanda's social, economic, political and security situation was deeply influenced by the earlier genocide and by regional issues. The transition period formally ended in 2003 with the referendum on the new constitution and the first 'democratic' presidential and parliamentary elections in the history of Rwanda. Positive economic developments were interrupted in 2003 and 2004 by lack of rain as well as lack of institutional, financial and human resources for the implementation of reforms, falling coffee prices (in 2003) and a severe energy crisis. All of these circumstances proved challenging to the government's precarious efforts to strike a balance between reconciliation and rehabilitation, state and nation building and legitimacy. The role of Rwanda in the region was much contested and the country teetered on the brink of war in the latter half of 2004.

Domestic Politics

Key political developments were the establishment of the newly elected political structures, the tenth anniversary of the genocide, the regional security situation, and the ongoing discussion of 'divisionism'.

The **new institutions** set up in 2003 struggled to find a role and consolidate their functions. Among these where the ombudsman, the two-chamber parliament and the political parties' forum. The National Assembly was criticised for being weak in comparison with the outgoing parliament, not least in relation to the executive, despite the re-election of a large number of former MPs. The political parties outside the governing Rwandan Patriotic Front (RPF) were also weak.

Parliament reviewed a large number of laws, many related to **legal sector reform**. The most important of these were the fundamental laws on the functioning of the supreme court; the prosecution services; the functioning and jurisdiction of other courts; and the mediation committees. In practice, the legal sector was at a standstill for the whole year. The new structures started to be implemented at the end of the year.

The mid-term review in June of the **decentralisation** and **good governance** programmes concluded that important reforms had been implemented to strengthen governance and financial administration. However, poor skills, weak institutional capacity, inadequate remuneration and lack of coordination between donors as well as governmental agencies had hindered public service delivery at the local level. The cabinet approved a five-year decentralisation implementation programme in March.

The third phase of the **civil service reform programme** commenced on 7 June with the objective of achieving a small but effective civil service with fewer, more qualified and better paid civil servants. The reforms started at central government level, and were latter pursued at provincial and district levels. About 1,000 government workers, out of 14,000, were retrenched. The 'Centrale des Syndicats des Travailleurs du Rwanda' (CESTRAR), representing civil servants in the absence of an effective trade union, criticised the government for making 'hasty' decisions. Implementation was largely concluded by the end of the year.

The tenth **anniversary of the genocide, during which**, according to official estimates, 937,000 were killed, pervaded the political atmosphere. On 7 April, 15 foreign delegations attended the commemoration, fewer then expected. The most notable absentee was Kofi Annan. France was represented by its assistant foreign minister, to the disappointment of many Rwandans. Belgium apologised for its role in the genocide, South Africa and Annan, from Geneva, did likewise for not intervening more forcefully.

A **cabinet reshuffle** occurred on 28 September: three ministers were sacked on performance-related grounds; Christhope Bazivamo was transferred from the ministry of local government to the interior ministry; and Protais Musoni, former state secretary for good governance, replaced him.

The new **land law** was passed by the lower chamber and was set to be adopted by the senate in January 2005. The most contentious issue was the 'consolidation' of smaller landholdings in order to improve productivity. The bill prohibited the division of land into plots smaller than one hectare, and was criticised for not clearly stating whether consolidation would result in smallholders' losing access to land and, if so, what would be done to accommodate them. Land shortage had been one of the causes of the conflict that led to genocide. A mechanism for resolving land-related and other disputes was established through the legal reforms.

According to the government, the **human rights situation** had to be understood in the context of the internal and external security situation in a post-genocide/conflict era. Domestic and international human rights institutions, such as Amnesty International (AI) and Human Rights Watch (HRW), however, continued to criticise the government for cracking down on political opposition and limiting debate. On 7 June, for example, former President Pasteur Bizimungu (who resigned in 2000) was sentenced to 15 years in prison for inciting civil disobedience, associating with criminal elements (forming a militia) and embezzling state funds, after an attempt to launch a new political party in 2001 in contravention of the laws of Rwanda's transitional period. The party was allegedly aiming to "fuel ethnic tension". The seven co-defendants got five to ten years of imprisonment. AI and HRW condemned the trial and conviction as falling far short of international standards of fairness. The trial was, however, held in public and Bizimungu had legal representation. He denied the charges and will appeal.

Civil society organisations were, according to AI (June), coming under increasing pressure from government, to the point where at times they had to curtail their activities to avoid being shut down.

The **parliamentary commission** of inquiry set up to investigate murders of genocide survivors and witnesses, concluded on 28 June that "the ideology of genocide was alive in all provinces, especially within religious congregations, schools and NGOs." The National Assembly recommended, among other things, closing down four NGOs for promoting genocidal ideology and 'divisionism', which was explicitly prohibited in the 2003 constitution. Singled out for criticism were the Rwandan League for Promotion and Defence of Human Rights (**LIPRODHOR**), one of the strongest human rights organisations, as well as a few international NGOs, including Trócaire (the overseas development agency of the Catholic church in Ireland) and the Dutch government for supporting the local NGOs in question. The government did not, however, ban these organisations, but called on the attorney-general to investigate and to prepare to prosecute them. LIPRODHOR held an internal inquiry, acknowledged the legitimacy of some of the criticism, denounced a number of its members, asked the Rwandan people for forgiveness and reorganised in December. It also toned down its criticisms of government. Eight senior staff fled the country. International human rights organisations and donors criticised the commission and the government for using the concept of **'divisionism'** to suppress expressions of dissent.

The **press** started to report on corruption and the abuse of power. Five new private radio stations were opened during the year, starting with Radio 10 (25 March). The quality of the media was hampered by the lack of well-educated journalists, in combination with (self-)censorship. It was at times debated whether the authorities' heavy-handedness was sanctioned from the top or was the work of hardliners at a lower level. One example of the possible new openness was when Charles Kabonero, the editor of 'Umuseso', the main independent paper in Kinyarwanda, wrote that the deputy-speaker of the National Assembly, Denis Polisi, was organising a clique working to overthrow the president

(August). Polisi was also accused of corruption. The government did not intervene but Polisi brought 'Umuseso' before the courts in his individual capacity on charges of divisionism and defamation. This was the first press case to go to court since 1999. Kabonero appeared in court on 26 November but was found guilty only of defamation and was fined $ 15 and had to pay Polisi symbolic compensation of Rwfr 1. Polisi appealed. This episode may indicate that press freedom has slightly increased and that the reformed justice system is more independent.

In several speeches, President Paul Kagame took a tough stand on the fight against **corruption**, to keep it at current low levels. In March, the auditor-general's report for 2002 forwarded 44 cases of embezzlement – most in connection with tenders – to the justice system. In June, a review on local government performance was undertaken. As a result, 48 of 106 mayors were sacked for inefficiency, corruption or sickness. The minister for energy, Sam Nkusi, was forced to resign by the cabinet on 24 December on charges of corruption in connection with the extraction of methane gas from Lake Kivu and power generation.

On 24 June, the final phase of **'gacaca'** (traditional justice) for genocide cases was launched. In an amendment to the gacaca law in June, the number of judges was reduced from 212,000 to 169,400. The large number of judges stems from the fact that there is a gacaca court in every village as well as on district level. In addition, the number of judges in each courtroom was reduced from 19 to nine. Restorative justice was supposed to be achieved through public hearings, bringing out the truth, breaking the culture of impunity, as well as confessions and trial. The sentences would be a combination of imprisonment and community service. The trials were postponed for logistical reasons as well as widespread concern about the process, not least among genocide survivors, who argued that it was too lenient to the perpetrators and unsafe for the witnesses. Six witnesses were killed in late 2003. This has raised the concern that survivors may withhold testimony during the trials. Human rights organisations criticised the gacaca courts for lacking the independence, objectivity, impartiality and equity of judicial processes provided for in international human rights conventions. Another critical issue was the ongoing involvement of victims in the processes and the handling of their reawakened traumas. By the end of 2004, 56,500 gacaca cases had been prepared. The trials were expected to begin in March 2005. The number of genocide suspects was expected to grow to 700,000 or more over the coming year, including leaders at different levels.

Relations with the **International Criminal Tribunal for Rwanda** (ICTR) improved. Forty-five cases involving key genocide planners were transferred to Rwanda for trial and punishment. In September, the president of the tribunal, Judge Erik Møse of Norway, warned the UN that lack of funds could prevent the tribunal from completing its mandate within the Security Council timeframe, namely 2008. ICTR has been criticised for being less than efficient and for not being sufficiently in touch with Rwandan history and society. It has found 20 guilty and acquitted 3 people since November 1994. Twenty-five suspects were on trial, while another 17 were waiting to appear. Another controversy was whether ICTR should eventually try RPF/RPA (Rwandan Patriotic Army) war crimes committed during the civil war and, later, in DR Congo when RPA tried to extinguish pro-genocide militias. The Rwandan government argued that it had prosecuted soldiers accused of war crimes in the Rwandan justice system. ICTR's annual budget was more than ten times larger than that of the whole judiciary in Rwanda, including the gacaca courts.

Foreign Affairs

The year started with appeasement and the exchange of ambassadors between **Rwanda and DR Congo** (25 January). From early 2004, however, the Rwandan government claimed that 'Forces Démocratiques de Libération du Rwanda' (FDLR) planned incursions into Rwanda to disturb the 10-year commemoration of the genocide. Several minor attacks were carried out from North Kivu. The regrouping of FDLR forces, in combination with increased fighting between FDLR groups and other militias in DR Congo and the inconclusive integration of military forces, increased instability close to the borders of Rwanda. AI among others claimed that the Rwanda Defence Forces (RDF) re-entered North Kivu in February. MONUC, the United Nations peacekeeping mission in the DR Congo, was unable to verify the claims until late April, when the presence of RDF in the border areas in DR Congo was observed.

The **Bukavu crisis**, starting in February as part of the power struggle between DR Congo's transitional government and RCD ('Rassemblement Congolais pour la Démocratie')-Goma over control of the two Kivu provinces, culminated in early June when pro-Rwanda rebel groups led by General Laurent Nkunda and Colonel Jules Mutebutsi captured Bukavu. Nkunda argued that he attacked in order to protect civilians of Tutsi origin from genocide by pro-government forces. Tensions rose sharply both between governments in the region and between different groups within DR Congo. Persons linked linguistically or culturally with Rwanda were targeted as being associated with activities of the Rwandan authorities in the DR Congo. Following strong international pressure, Mutebutsi and Nkunda withdrew their forces. Mutebutsi was disarmed and detained in Rwanda. Kabila sent 10,000–20,000 further troops to the Kivus. Rwanda accused DR Congo of amassing troops on the border in preparation for an invasion and closed the border on 6 June. Paradoxically, the crisis enhanced FDLR's position, as other forces within the 10th military region (South Kivu) reinvested in FDLR's military prowess by forming new alignments with the group and by supplying it with military hardware, intelligence and logistical support. The DR Congo government was convinced that Rwanda supported the Mutebutsi and Nkunda groups, who were mainly of Congolese Kinyarwanda-speaking origin, and continued to provide military assistance to dissident groups. International Crisis Group (ICG) reports in June and December claimed that Rwanda maintained military positions in North Kivu. Rwanda strongly refuted the accusations, and was later supported by an AU verification mission report in early July.

In late June, the presidents of Rwanda and DR Congo agreed to set up a Joint Verification Mechanism (JVM) committee to ensure border security, after a mediation initiative under the auspices of President Obasanjo of Nigeria. The massacre at **Gatumba**, Burundi on 13 August, of 162 Congolese, mainly Banyamulenge refugees who had escaped Bukavu in June, severely increased tensions. Rwanda threatened to invade the DR Congo to punish the supposed perpetrators. 'Forces Nationales de Liberation' (FNL), a Hutu rebel group from Burundi, claimed responsibility for the massacre, while the FDLR was allegedly also involved.

Parallel mediation efforts where made by the UK, US, Belgium, UN, AU and regional actors, including South Africa. The **JVM** was signed on 22 September after the personal intervention of Kofi Annan. Security Council Resolution 1565 of 30 September authorised the increase of MONUC's strength by 5,900 personnel (to 16,700, less than the requested 23,900), extended its mandate to 31 March 2005 and authorised it "to use all necessary means, within its capacity and in the areas where its armed units are deployed, to carry out the tasks". The US brokered a **tripartite agreement** to monitor border security and resolve disputes, signed on 25 October by Rwanda, DR Congo and Uganda. The International Conference on Peace, Security, Democracy and Development in the Great Lakes Region, Dar es Salaam, 19–20 November, was co-organised by the UN and AU. Eleven heads of government as well as civil society and international actors participated. A regional framework for a stability, security and development pact was adopted.

Tensions continued to escalate. Rwanda claimed at the end of the year that the FDLR had carried out eleven attacks since August in a large coordinated operation, dubbed 'La Fronde', from bases in both North and South Kivu. These were supported by allied groups like the Mai Mai and by simultaneously activated 'divisionist' and 'genocidaire' forces within Rwanda, the whole undertaking being coordinated by the political leadership of the diaspora in Western Europe, North America and Africa. The attacks were well planned, according to Richard Sezibera, Rwanda's special envoy for the Great Lakes: even if small-scale in terms of soldiers and equipment, they targeted the densely populated Gisenyi and Ruhengeri provinces, where Rwanda's main and most sensitive economic interests and industries are, including tourism, hydroelectric power stations and agricultural production. The domestic Rwandan political situation was delicate, with the upcoming traumatic gacaca trials, which would reactivate the tensions between perpetrators and victims. The psychological import of FDLR's attacks was that no witnesses were secure, either in the gacaca process or at the ICTR.

The Rwandan government grew more impatient. Immediately after the Dar es Salaam conference and during the UN Security Council's visit to the region on 20–26 November, Kagame stated in a letter to the AU that if the ex-FAR (Forces Armées Rwandaises)/ Interahamwe/FDLR were not disarmed, Rwanda would have make a 'surgical' intervention to disarm FDLR on its own (25 November), an operation that might already have begun. This position was reiterated in a letter to the Security Council on 30 November.

Charles Muligande, Rwanda's minister of foreign affairs, explained in an interview on 15 December that the threat was meant to awaken the international community and the UN to give MONUC an adequate mandate to disarm the force. The region again appeared to be on the brink of war.

The Security Council reacted on 7 December with deep concern at the multiple reports of military operations by the Rwandan army in the eastern part of DR Congo, but recognised that the presence of ex-FAR and Interahamwe elements in the area was a source of instability and an impediment to good neighbourly relations between DR Congo and Rwanda. It considered the armed presence and activities of ex-FAR and Interahamwe elements to be unacceptable and demanded that they be disarmed and disbanded without delay.

In late December, a détente appeared to be reached. Rwanda pledged on 20 December not to intervene in DR Congo, while DR Congo, MONUC and the international community made firm statements acknowledging that the presence of Ex-FAR/ Interahamwe forces constituted a legitimate concern for Rwanda. The Security Council and the AU respectively acknowledged on 7 and 8 December that a comprehensive solution would have to be found to disarming and reintegrating ex FAR/Interahamwe forces. Mutual mistrust persisted, not least on the ground in the Kivus.

Relations with **Uganda** deteriorated during the second half of the year, when tension increased in DR Congo after mutual allegations of support to proxy forces there. In December, Uganda expelled a Rwandan diplomat allegedly for espionage, and Rwanda retaliated by expelling a Ugandan diplomat. The incident may have been fuelled by the rapprochement between the governments of DR Congo and Uganda. London continued to mediate between Kigali and Kampala. There were also skirmishes on the borders between the Ugandan army and an unidentified force suspected to comprise members of the Rwandan army that was were crossing into eastern Congo.

Rwanda successfully cultivated relations with **AU**, NEPAD and the regional frameworks. The **NEPAD** heads of state meeting on governance in-mid February in Kigali was a triumph for Rwanda as an international actor. Rwanda was one of the first countries to sign up to be assessed under the African Peer Review Mechanism. It was also the first country to contribute troops to the AU operation in Darfur, which probably earned Rwanda goodwill within the AU. The country underscored this commitment with further troops in November.

Relations with South Africa continued to be cordial. In July, Pretoria and Kigali signed a defence agreement. In late November, South Africa expressed understanding of the need to shift from voluntary to forced disarmament of ex-FAR/Interahamwe forces in DR Congo.

Rwanda joined **COMESA** on 1 January. On 14 September, the **EAC** council of ministers approved a programme to process applications for membership by Rwanda and Burundi. The **US** played an active role and facilitated several rounds of talks among the parties on ministerial as well as head of state levels in the region, resulting in the tripartite agreement in October. Rwanda was declared eligible to access **AGOA** on 30 December 2003. The Rwandan government gave full support to the US-led efforts to combat terrorism.

The EU, UK, Netherlands, Belgium and Sweden gave the greatest **bilateral support** to Rwanda. Total EU support stood at $ 43.6 m for 2004. The UK pledged $ 139.7 m in support of Rwanda's Poverty Reduction Strategy (PRS) until 2006. **UK** continued to play a very active role in mediating at various levels in the regional conflict, not the least between Uganda and Rwanda.

Relations with France deteriorated in the spring. In March, 'Le Monde' published articles arguing that Kagame had ordered President Habyarimana's plane to be shot down in April 1994. As noted earlier, France's sending of an assistant foreign minister to represent it at the tenth anniversary of the genocide was viewed with bitterness by Rwanda. In his speech, President Kagame accused France of having knowingly trained and armed the government troops and the Hutu militia that perpetrated the genocide. At this, the French representative left the event. France, through the Security Council, sought to press ICTR to take up the war crimes committed by the RPF, and Paris advocated for the presence of FDLR at the Dar es Salaam conference.

On 30 July, the government formed a special commission to delve into France's role in the genocide. The new French ambassador to Rwanda, Dominique Decherf, called on both governments to engage in "unreserved political dialogue" and declared France's readiness to cooperate with an independent Rwandan commission of inquiry into France's role. Foreign Minister Muligande stated that this would improve relationships between Rwanda and France and Rwanda participated in the Francophone summit in Ouagadougou 26–27 November.

Socioeconomic Developments

Despite efforts to rebuild the collapsed economy after the war, it was only in 2002 that GDP got back to its 1992 levels, and it may take until 2020 for the level of income per capita to regain the level of 1990. GNI per capita was $ 220 in 2004. Aid dependency, at $ 44 per capita, was slightly lower than before the genocide. Population density on arable land was high, even if urbanisation (12.5%) has slightly reduced population per km² in rural areas to 756 in 2003. The population of 8.5 m was growing at a rate of 2.5–2.9% per year. Productivity was low in all sectors, not least agriculture, the main economic activity of 90% of the population. For 85% of farming households, the average size of farms was 0,7 hectares. Many were too small to satisfy subsistence needs, let alone improved productivity.

The 2002–05 **PRS** aimed at halving poverty by 2015 through a private sector and rural-led growth strategy. It required resources far beyond Rwanda's own, particularly given the costly processes of reconciliation and justice. A number of reforms were undertaken to expand the collection and management of taxes. Sectoral strategies for education and health were decided on in late 2003 and early 2004. Patrick Habamenshi, minister of agriculture, was strongly criticised for not concluding the necessary rural development and agricultural strategy. Work continued on the other strategies.

Lack of rain led to a fall of real GDP to 3.5% in 2003, the lowest level since 1994, and an energy crisis. The **budget for 2004** was presented on 4 December 2003 by minister of finance, Donald Kaberuka, as an expansionary budget, as "economic conditions militate against austerity". Public expenditures increased by 34%, resulting in a fiscal deficit of 12.6% of GDP. About 50% of the budget was funded by donors. The budget provided for increased social-sector spending, including the introduction of free primary education; military demobilisation packages; administrative decentralisation; the cost of the new senate; the new ombudsman and the settlement of domestic arrears. However, it provided less for agricultural development than in previous budgets. Donors and civil society organisations criticised the budget process for not being sufficiently consultative. The **2005 budget** was presented on 6 December. The budget aimed at real GDP growth for 2005 of 6%, compared with the 5.1% real GDP growth in 2004. The 2005 inflation target was 4%, compared with 12% inflation in 2004. Total expenditure was scheduled to rise by 12% to $ 630 m. Much of the increase was to finance improvements to the electricity supply. The education budget was increased by 16%. The budget projected a 13% increase in revenue and grants. Donors financed roughly 50% of the budget. Rwanda's role in DR Congo and the expected upcoming elections in that country made the disbursements from external sources uncertain. The IMF was concerned that the overall fiscal deficit, excluding grants, would reach 16% of GDP in 2005, considerably higher than the 12.5% level government and the IMF had agreed, thus testing PRGF benchmarks once more.

Loose fiscal policies, related to increased expenditures on the elections and the construction of two large hotels, led **IMF to unofficially suspend Rwanda's Poverty and Growth Facility** (PRGF) in late 2003. After firm budgetary commitments from key donors and progress on financial management issues, the IMF position softened. The hotels were constructed as a strategy to promote 'high end' tourism and make Rwanda a regional centre for commerce, including conferences. Donors were critical of the investment, as the link to PRS objectives was unclear. South Africa's Southern Sun group was managing both hotels on a fifteen-year contract.

Reforms to the public sector, including financial management, intensified (see above). The **first public financial management review** was held on 30 March and a final draft of a new fundamental budget law was passed by parliament.

On 10 June, the IMF completed the second and third reviews of Rwanda's economic performance under the **PRGF** arrangement. Rwanda became eligible to draw $ 1.68 m. The board reviewed Rwanda's PRS annual progress report and concluded it provided a sound basis for continued access to concessionary financial assistance, and approved interim assistance under the HIPC initiative of $ 6.6 m through 8 June 2005. France's representative on the IMF board, supported by Italy and Germany, tried to have the PRGF review postponed. The proposal failed after interventions from the UK and US.

On 15 June, the World Bank announced a $ 20 m grant to assist the government's decentralisation programme, and in late October, it approved a $ 65 m Poverty Reduction Structural Credit (PRSC).

The **privatisation process** continued. Of 69 enterprises to be privatised, 36 were effectively sold to private entrepreneurs by June. A free trade zone was established in Kigali in June, with the aim of establishing it as an investment hub for businesses servicing the region.

The **energy crisis** deepened during the year, with frequent blackouts, which interrupted production. A **supplementary budget** was passed in August, authorising increased expenditure mainly to cover unanticipated energy costs.

The **annual PRS evaluation**, with participation by civil society, private sector and donors was launched on 21 March. The report, released in October, provided a forward-looking and critical review pointing, among other things, to an increase of poverty in rural areas. The report on the **IMF Article IV consultations** (30 November) concluded that key elements of a market economy had been established and progress made in restoring macroeconomic stability. The government was criticised for not implementing a growth strategy, improving economic productivity, generating employment and strengthening export performance. The IMF warned that if aid disbursements were curtailed, it would be impossible to implement the government's economic programme.

At a **donor conference** on 8–10 December in Kigali, the government expected new commitments to help ease the energy and food crisis. Rwanda needed $ 200 m of additional financing each year to meet its expenditure requirements in order to implement the PRS and be able to fulfil the Millennium Development Goals. However, political events in the DR Congo dominated the discussions. Donors pressured government to withdraw its threat to send troops into the DR Congo, and threatened to withhold aid until it did so. Several donors, including Sweden, withheld budget support and other grants from December. From the Rwandan government's point of view, predictability and timing of external grants, as well as weak donor coordination, impacted financial deficit management and future planning.

The real **GDP growth rate of 5.1%** in 2004 was mainly due to growth in construction, tourism and coffee exports. Except for construction, production fell in the industrial sector, partly as a result of the energy crisis. The unfavourable climatic conditions hampered **agricultural production**, which registered a growth rate of only 0.7%. Total **food crop production decreased** a further 1% in 2004. Food prices increased 16.1%, contributing to the increased vulnerability of poor households, food insecurity and inflation, as well as threatening the reconciliation process as the frustration of the poor increased. Rwanda's export promotion strategy was fairly successful in 2004. **Export earnings increased** by 40% to $ 89.5 m. The coffee export volume went up 73% and the value 83%, to $ 27.5 m. Tea exports increased by 13.8% in value to $ 25.6 m. The value of cassiterite exports increased 277% to $ 12.9 m, owing to a 60% annual increase in the international price and a 135.4% increase in export volumes. Coltan export volumes increased by a modest 14%, but with the international price climbing 60% in the year, export value rose by 90% to $ 10.6 m. Historically, Rwanda has re-exported much of its cassiterite and coltan from illegally operated mines in the DR Congo, but much of the recent increase has resulted from enhanced Rwandan production.

Jonas Ewald

Seychelles

France Albert René, one of the longest serving presidents in Africa, relinquished his post and handed over power to his vice-president, James Michel, thus preserving the political dominance of the **ruling Seychelles People's Progressive Front (SPPF)**. Michel gave clear signals that he would continue with the economic reforms introduced in 2003 and pursue more market-friendly policies with the intention of overcoming the stagnation that has hampered the country for several years.

Domestic Politics

René (68 years old) had been **president** since staging a coup in 1977 and had for some time shown signs of willingness to retire (mainly for age and health reasons) before the expiry of his presidential mandate in August 2006. On 31 March, he finally submitted a letter of resignation and on 14 April **Michel** was formally installed as the **new president**. Michel (59 years old), the only old comrade remaining from the post-independence putsch, had held various ministerial posts and had been largely responsible for the day-to-day management of government affairs in recent years. The constitution allowed for such a handover without fresh elections, although the presidency is otherwise contested in direct elections. The main **opposition Seychelles National Party (SNP)** at first vehemently protested against this procedure and demanded new elections, but then accepted the fact that Michel would serve out the rest of René's presidential term. René did, however, retain his position as SPPF chairman (now in a full-time capacity) and it was clear that he intended to continue exercising some control, since all important government decisions had to be vetted by the SPPF central committee. René's continued influence was also meant to sustain popular support for the SPPF, since Michel's personal appeal came nowhere near to matching that of René.

The change in the top position did not otherwise have major political repercussions. Michel actually retained all his previous responsibilities, was now in charge of seven of a total of 17 government portfolios (including finance, defence, internal affairs) and was thus formally even more powerful than his predecessor. Joseph Belmont, a rising star among the younger SPPF generation, was promoted as vice-president, while keeping ministerial responsibility for tourism and transport. On 1 January, a minor reshuffle in the expectation of René's retirement had already brought two new younger faces into the 9-member **cabinet**, which Michel retained **practically unchanged** throughout the year (except for some restructuring of ministerial responsibilities in July). Michel was quick to demonstrate a more open and team-oriented style than René, who had always appeared very aloof, and he was eager to build a new public profile for himself. This he did through several rounds of meetings with the leadership of the SNP opposition and with representatives of the business community, but above all by installing a new group of advisers in state house and by creating a new 8-person economic team in late May.

The **SNP opposition**, with its eleven parliamentarians (out of a total of 34), and with undisputable sympathy among a strong minority of the population, still found it very difficult to make its dissenting voice heard and to have an impact on the deliberations in parliament. In view of the impending presidential change, the SPPF had in a tactical move in March strengthened the position of the leader of government business in parliament. In May, the SNP publicly voiced its frustration at the continued delaying tactics adopted by the SPPF on issues raised by the opposition. In mid-November, this frustration escalated into a symbolic walkout by all SNP deputies when the speaker disallowed a debate on a certain topic in the full house and relegated it to a committee. **SNP leader Wavel Ramkalawan** was still considered to be a strong adversary for Michel in the next presidential elections due in mid-2006. In August, he used a visit in Belgium to drum up support for the SNP cause among business circles and among liberal political contacts in Europe.

Michel used the opportunity of his **first National Day speech** on 18 June to outline the core elements of his intended economic policy reforms. These were reducing the role of the public sector in the economy and encouraging a more dynamic private sector, but, at the same time, maintaining the traditional SPPF focus on social welfare programmes. In the speech, Michel made a strong appeal for national unity, thereby insinuating that the SNP, which had recently become such a strong and popular opposition, was not in his view acting in the national interest. Despite this veiled attack, **cautious liberalisation of most**

aspects of public life was nevertheless more generally noticeable than in the last few years. There was greater tolerance regarding political liberties and freedom of the media and there was no further discernible harassment of political opponents. On the corruption perception index of the international NGO Transparency International, the country was third-best in Africa, and in the press freedom ranking of Reporters without Borders it moved up by ten places to rank 83, although in December the opposition weekly 'Regar' was, following a court decision, once again threatened with potentially costly litigation expenses.

The sudden dismissal of ten high-ranking police officers in January without explanation came as a shock to the general public, provoked an SNP protest and drew attention to a hitherto unknown increase in criminality. The **reappointment of foreign judges** by the government in January provoked equal criticism from the opposition and a legal challenge on procedural grounds from the bar association, which remained unsettled even after a ruling by a specially convened court of three foreign (African) judges. For the first time, however, one local judge was permanently appointed.

Foreign Affairs

The **withdrawal of membership in the regional organisations** IORARC and SADC that had been announced in mid-2003 became effective in 2004. This move had been justified by the need to save the membership fees (assessed on the basis of the relatively high Seychelles GDP), but the practical benefits of membership had also been very limited. As a result, the government maintained its membership only in COMESA and IOC. Due to the accumulated arrears in membership fees both for the AU and the UN, the Seychelles temporarily lost voting and other membership rights in these organisations. There were also unresolved problems with the non-repayment of old loans from France, while the visit of a Commonwealth mission in November raised some hope of finding a solution for regularising obligations to the Commonwealth Development Corporation, dating back to old loans from 1990 and 1993.

Throughout the year, **renewed strategic-military interest by the US** in the Seychelles became very noticeable for the first time since the closure of the satellite tracking station in 1996. There were a number of American visitors (including General John Abizaid, Chief of the US Central Command in September) to investigate and discuss the utility of the Victoria port facilities for the US navy, given their strategic mid-Indian Ocean location.

Socioeconomic Developments

The **economy** continued to be **in serious trouble** (although still at a very high absolute level by African standards), and it had been stagnating since the late 1990s. GDP was actually estimated to have contracted in 2004 by about 2% for the second consecutive year (by 5% in 2003). Despite clearly visible structural weaknesses and obvious limits on the continuation of the earlier socialist welfare orientation, the country still occupied the top rank for all African countries on UNDP's Human Development Index. The drastic **Macroeconomic Reform Programme (MERP)** introduced by government on 1 July 2003 did begin to show some positive effects and Michel seemed determined to pursue a course of gradual economic liberalisation, although rather cautiously and without antagonising either his predecessor or the general SPPF clientele. The **chronic shortage of foreign exchange** continued to represent a serious bottleneck for many economic activities and was a nuisance for most citizens. For fear of uncontrollable inflationary effects in the highly import-dependent economy, the government continued to resist demands to allow the depreciation of the heavily overvalued currency, thus necessitating continuation of unpopular exchange control measures. The exchange rate of the Rupee (SR) was kept fixed (at SR 5.50 to $ 1), thus allowing at least some noticeable depreciation against the euro. Inflation was successfully kept low at an average of around 4% for the year. The **foreign reserves** experienced a sharp slump in early 2004 and were down to $ 29 m (only three weeks of import coverage) in the third quarter as compared to $ 66 m in 2003. With practically stable export earnings and slightly increased imports (despite general controls largely due to higher oil costs) the current account deficit for 2004 was estimated to have risen noticeably to about 3.3% of GDP (compared to an exceptional low 0.8% in 2003, but still much lower than in previous years).

The main effect of the MERP was visible in the **fiscal management** of the government and in the **budget figures**. The introduction of a 12% goods and services tax (GST) in mid-2003 and stringent expenditure cuts (for recurrent services as well as investments) had brought about a substantial budget surplus of 7% of GDP in 2003 after years of massive deficits (17% in 2002), thus enabling net repayments by the government to the central bank and to commercial banks for the first time in several years. When Michel outlined the new 2005 budget to parliament on 1 December, the preliminary estimates for 2004 showed a continuation of this healthy trend although on a somewhat reduced scale: compared to the original 2004 budget the budget surplus was estimated to reach 4.7% of GDP instead of a super ambitious target of 15.5%, due to less than expected revenue and cost overruns. Moreover, total government credit from commercial banks had fallen significantly (but not from the central bank). The 2005 budget foresaw only a slight revenue increase (due to new tax cuts), very strict controls on current spending and a doubling of public investments, thus aiming at an overall budget surplus of 7.1% of GDP.

Throughout the year, Michel expressed his intention to **move away from the previous tradition of fairly tight state control** and to open up more cooperation with the private sector, but the implementation of these promises proved slow and half-hearted, thus provoking the Seychelles Chamber of Commerce and Industry (SCCI) to deplore the lack of progress. A number of institutional changes did, however, indicate a clearly changed economic and business climate. Michel's core team for economic policymaking (announced on 25 May) was an expression of continuity through well-known personalities, but stressed the team approach and reduced the singular role of Mukesh Valabhji, director of the Seychelles Marketing Board (SMB) and previously influential with René. In June, a new Joint Economic Council (JEC) with nine government and 11 private-sector representatives was created as an advisory forum for all economic policy issues, and had its first full meeting in September. A crucial promise was the long-demanded start to **privatising parastatal enterprises**, and particularly to **cutting back the SMB** to its original regulatory function: it had over the years strongly expanded and enjoyed a near-monopoly as importer and producer of a wide range of products. This was to the obvious detriment of private-sector operators, who were even harassed for overcharging and contravening control regulations. As a first step, SMB's import monopoly was reduced in July to a narrower list of essential goods, with a subsequent introduction of noticeable price cuts, all of this being a clear signal of a changing business climate. In May, a new Small Enterprise Promotion Agency (SEPA) was created, while a new Seychelles Investment Bureau (SIB) became operational later in the year with a mandate to prepare a new investment code and to create a more business-friendly investment climate. The country, nevertheless, continued to see a sizeable influx of direct foreign investments (accounting for about a quarter of total gross capital formation), but mostly for luxury hotels and with only limited impact on the rest of the economy. Changes to top leadership positions in key institutions (such as the important Seychelles fisheries authority and the Seychelles port authority) were also indicative of Michel's seriousness about pursuing a new style.

The crucial high-class and high-cost **tourism sector** continued to experience serious difficulties. The 2003 tourist figures (122,000 arrivals) were the lowest since 1995 and down by 7.7% against 2002, and the first nine months of 2004 showed a further decline by 4.6% (although an increase of earnings of almost 15%). A new tourist influx from Eastern Europe could not compensate for the losses from other traditional countries of origin. There were also problems with regular **air connections** after British Airways stopped its flights in June, just as other airlines had previously done, in reaction to the restrictions on transmitting funds out of the country. Improvement was, however, expected with the opening of new services by Emirates and Air Qatar at the end of the year. A new 6-year **fisheries agreement with the EU** signed in September offered prospects for higher licence payments by mainly French and Spanish vessels, but Victoria encountered increasing competition from other ports around the Indian Ocean as the main tuna trans-shipment port. The production of canned tuna during the first three-quarters of 2004 slumped 5.3% compared to 2003, with a record annual total of 36.400 tonnes.

The Southeast Asian tsunami on 26 December caused considerable material damage on several islands. Direct losses were estimated by government to be around $ 30 million (more than 4% of GDP). In addition to some expected external assistance, government subsequently opted to accept an offer from the Paris Club for temporarily rescheduling its debt obligations. This came as welcome relief since the **foreign debt burden** had reached more than $ 400 million by mid-2004 and had become unserviceable, what with the accumulation of more arrears and the absence of regular aid receipts. Consultations with visiting IMF missions in August and October resulted in continued disagreement, since the IMF demanded much more far-reaching economic reform (particularly depreciation of the SR) and noted on the plus side only the significant improvement of the budget and the proposal for greater independence of the **central bank** from government interference, which was eventually granted in December.

Rolf Hofmeier

Somalia

The election of 'Abdullaahi Yuusuf as president of the Transitional Federal Government of Somalia (TFG) in October 2004 was the much-desired outcome of a long diplomatic exercise that started on 12 October 2002 and was mostly framed by the '9/11' context in the Horn of Africa. As such, this election should be analysed as both the failure of the Transitional National Government (TNG) set up in 'Arta (Djibouti) in summer 2000 and the result of a limited political process that took place in Kenya with the mediation of both a regional organisation (IGAD) and the international community. Both the expected appointment of a cabinet in early January 2005 and the divisions that arose over its resettlement in Somalia raised concerns about TFG's future. Furthermore, among the many challenges TFG had to address was a real reconciliation process among Somalis themselves, as well as negotiations with the self-proclaimed independent Somaliland.

Domestic Politics

When Uganda became IGAD chair in October 2003, many diplomats expected the **Somali peace conference** to make a new start. They were right and wrong. After months of mismanagement by the two Kenyan special envoys, Elijah Mwangale and Bethwel Kiplagat, Ugandan involvement led to a decisive breakthrough in late January. The number of MPs

(275), the manner of allocating seats (the '4.5 formula', see below) and the duration of the transition (five years) were agreed by all major faction leaders. All these points were consigned to the transitional Charter, but major problems remained. Ethiopia wanted at all costs to promote its supporters among the Somali factions, namely those allied within the Somali Reconciliation and Restoration Council (SRRC) that was established as a proxy as against the TNG on 26 March 2001. This situation strained Ethiopia's relationship with Djibouti, which was very supportive of TNG. Moreover, there were no rules of procedure, so that, at different times, faction leaders rightly felt manipulated and temporarily abandoned the conference. It took until May to settle most of the controversies and to start discussion of the selection of MPs. Each of Somalia's four major clans was allocated 61 seats in parliament, while an alliance of minority clans was awarded 31 seats (the 4.5 formula). One question remained: who would have the last word, the clan elders or the faction leaders? This painful process continued until 22 August, when most of the MPs were sworn in. After the election of the speaker on 15 September, a quick campaign for the presidential elections took place and, a couple of weeks later, 'Abdullaahi Yuusuf was elected president of TFG.

Ali Mohamed Geedi was appointed prime minister on 3 November. While 'Abdullaahi Yuusuf was a Majeerteen from Puntland, 'Ali Mohamed Geedi was an Abgaal from Mogadishu and was very close to Mohamed Habib Dheere, a faction leader who controls the town of Jowhar, north of Mogadishu. The first cabinet was announced on 1 December but faced the opposition of parliament and was dissolved on 11 December because constitutional procedures were not respected. A new cabinet was eventually appointed and approved only in January 2005.

Although the **cabinet** respected the 4.5 formula, its selection was not seen as an inclusive process by many Somalis. The international community celebrated the fact that all warlords were now ministers and therefore part of the process. Yet a close look at the appointees and their political backgrounds revealed without doubt that the cabinet was mostly made up of members of the pro-Ethiopian SRRC. The few other appointees had little influence, if any. Moreover, the most important ministries went to people very close to the president, to the extent that the prime minister was likely to have little authority over them. This situation fed rumours and bitterness in south Somalia and in Mogadishu, even among the supporters of the prime minister. In Somaliland, there was both great criticism and relief. Neither the conference nor the cabinet included prominent Somaliland politicians, although Somalilanders were better represented in Nairobi than in 'Arta. Somaliland public opinion was very sceptical about the viability of the cabinet, since many ministers were known to be unable to deliver.

The situation inside Somalia over the year illustrated some of the major flaws of the conference in Kenya. Despite the length of the negotiations there, there was no real reconciliation. Faction leaders met in Nairobi while their troops were often fighting on the ground.

Of course, lip service to peace and reconstruction was paid by all, but no effort was made to address any outstanding issue that undermined them. Lay people inside Somalia were often disappointed by the cabinet, and they could not understand how those who had failed to bring peace over the last 13 years would now succeed. This cynicism was tempered by expectations that, as in 1993–95, donors would pour huge amounts of money into Somalia. In Puntland, the mood was quite different and very optimistic: the population expected its former leader to channel important projects to their region.

Sool and Sanag constituted a contested area between Puntland and Somaliland. These two regions had been part of the British colony of Somaliland but were populated mostly by the same Harti clan as in Puntland. Under the orders of 'Abdullaahi Yuusuf, then president of Puntland, militias occupied the town of Laas 'Aanod in late 2003 and, after months of tension and minor skirmishes, serious fighting broke out in October. This was to become a fixation in regional tensions. Elsewhere in northern Somalia, the situation was quiet and peaceful. This, however, was not the case in the central region, where conflicts erupted between different clans: first between Dir and Mareexaan, and later between Sa'ad and Saleebaan, two sub-clans of the Haber Gidir that belong to Hawiye. With hindsight, many believed that the latter conflict was likely fuelled from the outside. The historical irony was that mediation in the latest feud was conducted by a key figure of al-Ittihaad (a radical Islamist group), Daahir Hasan Aways, and not by any of the delegates attending the peace conference in Nairobi.

The **security situation in Mogadishu** was ambiguous. On the one hand the kidnap industry that boomed in 2003 was seriously impacted by the shariah courts that brought an end to a number of the gangs and thugs involved in it. These courts, which were not as powerful as their predecessors in the late 1990s, tried to build a stronger constituency before the new government settled into the capital city. Radical Islam developed throughout the year, abetted by events in Nairobi and the Arab world. Even the closure of Al-Haramain, an important Islamic foundation, had a doubtful effect. This Islamic charity stopped its operations in Mogadishu, abandoning thousands of children in the orphanages it funded. No alternative was provided to the children and employees. To an extent, the radical Islamic trend took deeper root than ever in some parts of the population, since some of its leaders became more flexible and allowed more room for social relationships framed by clan identity than previously.

Mogadishu also had to cope with a major confrontation of an intensity and duration not seen since 1992. This fighting opposed the then most powerful faction leader, Muuse Suudi Yalahow, and the manager of the 'Eel Ma'aan port that supplied Mogadishu, Bashir Ragge. Ironically enough for those who stress clan explanations of the Somali crisis, both were Abgaal. Again, the conference in Nairobi hardly reacted to stop the battle. A shorter and much less intense version of this kind of incident also occurred in Lower Shabeelle. In Lower Jubba, Gedo and Bay, low-intensity factional fighting or skirmishes recurred as the year advanced. To an extent, some of these conflicts were proxies for the political struggle among would-be cabinet members and their international supporters.

Even more disturbingly, **political assassinations** multiplied in Mogadishu. While they were seen in Nairobi as the revival of radical Islamic groups and proof that foreign troops were needed to secure the capital, many in Mogadishu took quite the opposite view. For them, the Islamists were ideal scapegoats, while some killings were allegedly perpetrated in clan vendettas or even by people close to the new TFG.

Somaliland was in a strange position. After years of experiencing disdain, it had become the focal point of international involvement in Somalia in the late 1990s: peace at least had dividends. The new president, Daahir Rayaale Kaahin, who took over upon the death of Mohamed Ibraahim 'Igaal and was formally elected in April 2003, made it clear that Somaliland would not participate in the talks in Kenya and refused the federal structure as a framework for settling differences with Mogadishu. Yet neither the international community nor IGAD tried to define a framework for negotiations between the newly formed TFG and the Somaliland administration, which only underscored the need for a peaceful resolution. Following the killing of four foreigners in 2003, a new incident occurred in May: an aid worker was killed and another seriously wounded. As always after 11 September, Islamists were said to be responsible. This incident, plus the declining ability of the administration to deliver basic services, may explain why the **conflict with Puntland** became a rallying point. After a referendum on the constitution in May 2001, local elections in December 2002 and presidential elections in April 2003, the political debate in 2004 focused on the parliamentary elections that were planned for 2005. This prospect represented a double challenge. On the one hand, it meant that Somaliland politics were finally shifting from pure clan politics to party politics. On the other, it raised questions about the ability of the party system to survive in an environment where the presidential party used all the resources of the state without limitation.

Puntland closely followed the peace conference in Kenya, first and foremost because all the resources of the administration were mobilised by 'Abdullaahi Yuusuf to get elected. His election as president of Somalia initiated a new electoral process in Puntland, which equally set the elections for early 2005.

Foreign Affairs

The main and possibly only question framing relationships between Somali actors and the outside world was the latter's perception of the Islamic threat. From August 1996 onwards, **Ethiopia** used this argument to justify its diverse interventions in Somalia and Somaliland. However, Ethiopia had a broader agenda than just fighting armed Islamic movements: Addis Ababa wanted its clients to rule Somalia, not simply a secular (or non-Islamist) regime. This created tensions that lasted for months between conference delegates and among IGAD members, to the extent that donors had to pressure Ethiopia to adopt a lower profile. 'Abdullaahi Yuusuf's election was therefore a great success for Ethiopia, and was reinforced by the appointment of his prime minister: 'Ali Mohamed Geedi, while working in Addis Ababa from 1998, was the one who convinced Mohamed Dheere to side with Ethiopia against the TNG.

After the election of 'Abdullaahi Yuusuf, and beyond the appointment of the cabinet, the real issue became the relocation of the cabinet and the debated need for **foreign peace-keepers**. On 24 October, the newly elected president requested the AU to send 20,000 peacekeepers to Somalia to secure southern Somalia and help in the disarmament and demobilisation of the militias. Ethiopia, of course, responded enthusiastically This request was the most controversial for many in southern Somalia. The latter thought that 'Abdullaahi Yuusuf did not want true reconciliation but rather needed foreign troops to fight for a victory that he would otherwise never be able to secure. They pointed to the last 40 years of strained relationships with Ethiopia as the basis for denouncing an alleged new colonial policy. Supporters of 'Abdullaahi Yuusuf pointed to the continuing insecurity in southern Somalia (and especially in Mogadishu, as exemplified by many army officers being murdered in the last two months of the year) and to the reluctance of faction leaders to be reconciled. This disagreement contributed to the eviction of the first cabinet and raised tensions between most of the southern Somali leaders and the Somali president.

Kenya was mandated by IGAD to organise and chair the Somali peace conference. Nairobi successfully managed the long Naivasha process to get a peace settlement in Sudan (albeit undertaken in a radically different manner). Kenya worked hard to get a result, and wanted to do so in a manner most useful to its interests. Disregarding the allegations related to the misuse of mediation money, Kenya needed a government in Somalia to at least allow it to manage the Somali migrants on its territory: a government in Mogadishu would make possible the closing of refugee camps and the expulsion of migrants. Nairobi also needed to maintain warm relationships with Addis Ababa in order to control its border with Ethiopia (because of the Oromo troubles) and parts of its border with Somalia, since Ethiopia was involved in Gedo on a recurrent basis.

This conference (as well as the one on Sudan) left the **Arab League** in disbelief. In both cases, the regional African organisation, IGAD, was preeminent in settling a member state's internal crises. **Egypt** was concerned that the newly formed TFG would increase the influence of Ethiopia in the region. **Yemen** was ambivalent. Like Ethiopia, Yemen was supplying weapons and ammunition to Somalia in disregard of the UN arms embargo. Yet Sana'a, an ally of the US, was part of a regional alliance with Addis Ababa to isolate Eritrea and enjoyed warm relations with 'Abdullaahi Yuusuf, as well as with Mogadishu faction leaders (now ministers) who disagreed with their president. **Djibouti** fought as long as possible in the conference to support the TNG that it had helped to set up, and tried to thwart Ethiopian involvement in the daily management of the peace conference. However, TNG split at different times and Djibouti no longer had a cause to defend. Nevertheless, in defiance of the Kenyan conference, in 2004 (in contrast to 2001 and 2002) Djibouti gave increasing room to Somaliland and supported Hargeysa on the issue of Sool and Sanag. Like Egypt (but for different reasons), Djibouti did not welcome the idea of a too powerful neighbour.

The **US** attitude towards Somalia in 2004 was not as energetic as many expected. In November and December 2001, when the war was practically won in Afghanistan, the US government thought for a few weeks that Somalia should be the next target, since allegations of a strong presence of al-Qaida were being spread in Kenya. However, realism prevailed and a new policy developed. As in Afghanistan, the US made deals with local warlords to kidnap alleged terrorists and transfer them to Ethiopia or Kenya. Leaders like 'Abdullaahi Yuusuf, Mohamed Dheere and Mohamed Qanyere, or businessmen like Bashir Ragge were the most prominent beneficiaries of this policy, since these services were not free. Yet this policy created a number of problems that reached beyond the most radical Islamists. In April, there was an attempt to kidnap a leading member of al-Ittihaad in Mogadishu, but the wrong persons were targeted and killed. Subsequently, people who did not sympathise with this organisation sided with it in opposition to these practices. Despite recurrent mistakes that alienated popular support, the US government did not alter its policy, which, in its view, was very efficient and cheap: in particular, there was no need to argue with a government and to address such niceties as sovereignty. Although the US embassy in Nairobi closely followed the numerous peripeteia of the Somali conference, the lack of US enthusiasm was visible: when the US diplomat in charge departed in May, he publicly expressed his doubts about the whole exercise and questioned the viability of any government that would emerge at the end of it. He had to retract this statement, but off-the-record discussions with US officials confirmed this cautiousness even after the election of 'Abdullaahi Yuusuf.

Other Western states, including **EU** members, and the European Commission, did play a major role in the conference. First, they funded the entire exercise throughout the two years of its existence, despite frequent mismanagement of their money. They also informally advised on crucial issues, for the best and the worst. At different times, they foresaw the collapse of the conference due to strident disagreements between Djibouti and Ethiopia. They opportunely realised that Ethiopia was constantly violating the 1992 UN arms embargo and used this to wring more flexibility out of Addis Ababa. Their behaviour after October 2004 showed how ambivalent they were about the outcome of their efforts. Italy was the only European state to celebrate the warm relations that Berlusconi and his allies had enjoyed in the 1980s with some key figures in 'Abdullaahi Yuusuf's inner circle. Others took a more neutral stance, since they already knew how difficult it would be to make this parliament and cabinet working institutions and how uncertain would be the relocation of these entities to Somalia. Some even questioned the incremental approach that was endorsed over the last year of the conference. In late 2004, it was still unclear what would be the financial commitment of the donors beyond the EC, which already had its money allocated.

Socioeconomic Developments

As far as exchange rates were concerned, 2004 was not a bad year in Somalia and Somaliland, for different reasons. In Somaliland, the currency appreciated slightly since there was a lack of liquidity to sustain economic activity. Since September 2000, Somaliland has been subject to a ban on its **livestock** by Saudi Arabia, far and away its first export market. The livestock sector traditionally comprised 60–65% of Somaliland's GDP and played a major role in the economy as a source of employment, income, foreign exchange, government revenues and food imports. However, the resilience of the economy was considerable: exports to secondary markets such as Yemen and Dubai increased; the diaspora remitted more money; and peace allowed Somaliland a greater share of international aid directed to Somalia. In southern Somalia and Puntland, different factors contributed to the **revaluation of the Somali shilling**. First, the re-export economy (as in Somaliland) was doing well: sugar, building materials, textiles and electronic items formed the bulk of commodities re-exported from Kismaayo, 'Eel Ma'aan and Boosaaso to Ethiopia and Kenya. Second, in 2004, two shipments of bananas were exported to Iran, generating a fair amount of hard currency for the exchange market. Third, diaspora members invested in industrial plants and new services, especially in Mogadishu. For instance, in 2004, a Coca Cola factory worth a few million dollars was inaugurated in July. Many more modest plants started as well: mineral water plants, plastic bag factories, foam factories, tanneries and slaughterhouses were operating in various towns (Beled Weyne, Boosaaso, Hargeysa, Burco and Mogadishu). Fourth, there were some incidental benefits from the conference in Kenya. Delegates got per diems and later, MPs' salaries were paid by the EC. Significant amounts of money circulated, some of which got back to Somalia. Last but not least, counterfeit banknotes were not issued in significant quantity.

Two important trends took shape in the **telecommunications** sector. For years, the main telecommunications companies refused to interconnect their networks: this meant that a call to a neighbour might need to be an international call, unless one subscribed for service with the same company. In January, after several attempts, the three main companies in Mogadishu were interconnected. This was a very positive development since it ended the duplication of investments (three landlines to the same house) and allowed the networks to invest the saved money to extend services beyond major urban centres. Moreover, interconnection appeared to be very profitable, since local calls to another company were charged (they were free within the same network). This meant interconnection was a realistic and feasible solution elsewhere in the country, in Somaliland and Puntland: other telecommunications companies could repeat the exercise. The year 2004 was also the year of the internet café in Somalia. From 2000, internet was only accessible through landlines at very low speed. Internet cafés were therefore barely profitable. In 2004, cheap satellite broad-band connections became available and internet cafés mushroomed in Mogadishu and Hargeysa. This technological change brought new challenges to telecom companies, since telephony through the internet was now a possibility.

The **air traffic sector** had to cope with several setbacks. In May, two negative events occurred for Somali airlines. Kenya and UAE decided to no longer recognise Somali passports, mostly for security reasons: passports had become a commodity to be bought wherever there was a Somali community. Many people had to stop traveling to these two major destinations, which drastically reduced Somali airline profits. Another problem arose. The previous month, an Ilyushin 18 propeller aircraft crashed in the UAE en route back from the Iranian free zone of Kish. UAE decided to prohibit passengers on these aircraft, which were used by all airlines flying to Somalia. The latter then had to rely on jet aircraft, which implied higher costs: only three companies were flying passengers at the end of the year. Freight transportation was not affected.

However resilient the Somali economy was, many people had to cope with a serious predicament in 2004. Insecurity and armed incidents in the countryside meant that displaced people fled to towns where employment opportunities were, unfortunately, minimal. **Drought and desertification** were also a major priority for various donors. Despite rhetorical commitments by warlords, **charcoal** was still exported from Puntland and southern Somalia, a trade that had a devastating impact on the ecosystem. Drought in different places, especially in Sool and Sanag, was a concern for aid agencies. Somalia was once again a place of many conflicting trends: urban development and the birth of a small industrial sector on one hand, and the impoverishment of a larger section of the population on the other.

Roland Marchal

Sudan

The escalation of conflict in Darfur overshadowed all other developments in 2004. As in 1998, the country was described by the UN as the scene of the "world's worst humanitarian crisis". Despite much international attention and diplomatic pressure, the security and humanitarian situation continued to deteriorate throughout the year. This dampened international delight over the success of peace negotiations between the Government of the Sudan (GoS) and the armed opposition in the south, the Sudan Peoples' Liberation Movement/Army (SPLM/A), that helped to end the world's longest civil war. On the economic level, increasing oil production and high prices boosted revenue, and prospects for peace in the south helped raise the level of international investment. Western powers, however, made stronger engagement conditional on settlement of the Darfur crisis.

Domestic Politics

The armed conflict in **Darfur** between non-Arab rebel movements and GoS had already built up for a year when, in early 2004, GoS began to more actively support bands of 'Janjaweed', armed militias drawn from semi-nomadic Arab tribes, and use them as a proxy to crush the rebellion. Janjaweed attacks on villages and farms caused massive civilian destruction and attracted growing international criticism. In December 2003, UN Under-

Secretary-General for Humanitarian Affairs Jan Egeland, described events in Darfur as "**the world's worst humanitarian crisis**", an assessment taken up frequently throughout the year, among others by UN Secretary-General Kofi Annan. International attention had some effect in that negotiations between the warring parties commenced, fighting decreased and humanitarian access improved from mid-year. But ceasefires were never really observed and the humanitarian situation steadily deteriorated. By year's end, negotiations had broken down, fighting flared up, and bureaucratic obstacles to humanitarian relief increased again.

It was difficult to **measure the devastation** caused to civilian life in Darfur. Hundreds of villages were destroyed – by October, aerial surveys revealed 574 completely destroyed villages and 157 damaged, that is, at least half of the non-Arab villages. Fields and crops were burned, over two million livestock looted, women raped, people killed. This led to large-scale and growing displacement. In January, the UN estimated that over 600,000 people had been displaced by the conflict. By February, they spoke of 135,000 refugees to neighbouring Chad and reported that "[h]alf of Darfur's six million people are directly affected by the conflict", but that UN aid reached only 15% of people in need. Estimates of displaced persons were revised steadily upwards, reaching 1.2 m IDPs by July and between 1.65 m and 2.4 m IDPs by year's end: refugees to Chad were estimated at a quarter million by December. Mortality estimates proved more difficult: WHO estimated 70,000 deaths from disease and malnutrition among the displaced between March and September, but this was criticised for underestimating deaths outside official IDP camps. Two independent activists, Eric Reeves and Jan Coebergh, compiled available data to project the total death toll during 2003–04 at 300,000–400,000. Egeland acknowledged that the overall death rate in Darfur since the beginning of the war was "several times the number of 70,000" provided by WHO.

The year began with continued **efforts by GoS to achieve military victory**, refusing 'internationalisation' of what they claimed was an internal problem. In January, daily bombing raids by the Sudanese air force on villages in Darfur killed hundreds of civilians and caused thousands more to flee into neighbouring Chad. Janjaweed followed them even there, and Sudanese bombs fell on the Chadian border town of Tiné, killing three Chadian civilians. Consequently, UNHCR began moving Sudanese refugees to safer areas further inside Chad. On 9 February, President Omar al-Bashir formally declared victory over the rebels, offering them amnesty and promising safe humanitarian passage to the region. The main armed opposition groups, the secular **Sudan Liberation Movement/Army** (SLM/A) and the smaller, Islamist-leaning **Justice and Equality Movement** (JEM) immediately dismissed this, refused to attend proposed peace talks and launched new offensives. SLM sought to strengthen its position by joining the opposition National Democratic Alliance on 13 February and announcing, on 25 February, an agreement with the eastern Beja Congress to launch joint operations. On 18 May, it further declared that it had joined forces with the

Sudan Federal Democratic Alliance. Several times during the year, however, internal tensions surfaced within SLM, partly linked to disputes between field commanders and the political negotiators in N'Djaména. The reliability of SLM's command-and-control hierarchy was also questioned by observers. JEM suffered a split in April when the National Movement for Reform and Development (NMRD, also known by its Arabic acronym, 'Hawat') claimed to have broken away because it disagreed with the influence of Hasan al-Turabi over JEM. While JEM dismissed the group as a 'stooge' of GoS, others cautioned that it appeared to enjoy credibility among many of JEM's military forces.

Following Bashir's promise to grant humanitarian access, the UN began planning needs-assessment missions and the pre-positioning of aid. However, humanitarian access remained limited, and in March a total **breakdown of law and order** was reported, with UN sources reporting that Janjaweed roamed "the region in gangs of hundreds, attacking one village after another." A (probably conservative) estimate of Janjaweed strength of over 20,000 has been circulating, while in February a JEM spokesman claimed that JEM and SLM/A combined had 27,000 troops. Outside estimates spoke of around 10,000 fighters.

International attention finally, on 31 March, brought the warring parties to the negotiation table in N'Djaména under the auspices of Chad, the AU, the US and the EU. On 8 April, GoS, SLA and JEM signed a 45-day, renewable **Humanitarian Ceasefire Agreement on the Conflict in Darfur**. An AU-led joint ceasefire commission was instituted to monitor compliance with the agreement. A major criticism of the agreement was that it failed to explicitly address the problem of Janjaweed militias, regarded as among the main perpetrators of crimes against humanity in Darfur, let alone to include them in the accord. Foreign Minister Mustafa Osman Ismail said the Janjaweed, a "spontaneous tribal response to predominantly Zaghawa rebels", could only be disarmed after rebels had laid down their weapons. To solve the crisis, GoS advocated a general conference of all representatives of Darfur without international participation. This idea was endorsed in a second N'Djaména accord dated 25 April, which also called on GoS to neutralise and disarm militias. The agreement was stillborn, however: GoS did not sign it and JEM and SLA forces on the ground repudiated it, explaining that their representatives in N'Djaména were not mandated to negotiate political issues. They reiterated their commitment to the ceasefire, but this proved ineffective since both sides increased their attacks on military and civilian targets and even on humanitarian aid workers (for example, in June and December). This insecurity, along with problems of cross-line relief (with rebels fearing infiltration and GoS frequently creating administrative hurdles) greatly exacerbated the humanitarian crisis.

The **Ceasefire Commission** (CFC) provided for in the 8 April agreement took several months to become operational, but proved more outspoken than many critics predicted. On 28 May, the **AU** reached an agreement with the Sudanese parties on the modalities to establish CFC and deploy observers. A **monitoring mission** was set up as the operational arm of CFC, to be protected by a small armed force. The mandate of this force was soon interpreted by AU to include protection, within its capacity, of the civilian population. The first contingent (154 Rwandan troops) arrived in al-Fashir on 15 August, followed on 30 August by 30 Nigerians. On 20 October, the AU peace and security council decided to expand the size of the African Mission in the Sudan (AMIS) to 3,320 personnel and explicitly to include in its mandate the protection of civilians "under imminent threat and in the immediate vicinity." Deployment was hampered, however, by financial and logistical problems. By December, less than a third of the force had arrived, and while observers admitted their deployment helped to improve security in some areas, large parts of the countryside where civilians were most threatened remained beyond reach.

The UN became more closely involved in April when **UNHCHR** sent a **fact-finding committee** to Chad and the Sudan. In its 7 May report, it clearly identified "a reign of terror in Darfur" (attacks against civilians, rape, pillage, forced displacements, etc.). It recommended the establishment of an international commission of inquiry (ICI), and called in particular on GoS to immediately disarm the militias, guarantee unimpeded humanitarian access and ensure the rule of law. GoS responded on 8 May by creating its own investigation committee, which had reported by year's end. The Arab League (AL) also sent a fact-finding mission, whose 19 May report was not made public, since GoS vigorously protested its conclusion that massive violations of human rights had been committed by pro-government militias. An emergency AL meeting on 8 August largely supported GoS's political position.

A flurry of high-ranking UN and Western official visitors (most prominently US Secretary of State Powell and Kofi Annan) began in June to prod GoS to change its stance. Annan's visit concluded with a joint communiqué in which GoS committed itself to permit freedom of movement for aid workers throughout Darfur, ensure that there were no militias present in areas surrounding IDP camps, and to start disarming the Janjaweed. A Joint Implementation Mechanism (JIM) was established to monitor this agreement. Although GoS immediately (5 July) announced it had begun disarming the Janjaweed, the UN could see no indications of this, and on 30 July the demand was repeated in **UN Security Council Resolution 1556 that** GoS "bring to justice Janjaweed leaders and their associates". The Secretary-General reported 30 days later on the progress or otherwise by GoS on this matter, and Khartoum was implicitly threatened with sanctions in the event of non-compliance. All parties were urged to respect the ceasefire and to conclude a political agreement – the rebels' precondition to lay down arms – without delay. The resolution also committed states to prevent the flow of arms and provisions to all non-governmental entities and individuals operating in Darfur. Following this resolution, the Secretary-General's special representative to the Sudan, Jan Pronk, on 5 August negotiated a plan of action with GoS that committed it to securing, within 30 days, safe areas for IDPs in Darfur, cease offensive military operations in those areas, declare the militias over whom it had influence and restrain their activities. The latter commitment was reiterated on 19 August to JIM when GoS promised to present names and numbers in the very near future. On 30 August, with the passing of the UN deadline, the Secretary-General presented a report that noted the discrepancy between GoS's announcement of measures and their implementation. The impact on the ground remained uneven, he noted, most critically the reining in the militias, the vast majority of which had not been disarmed. Instead, many were simply integrated into the paramilitary Popular Defence Forces. Annan also criticised the lack of steps to bring militia leaders to justice, thus allowing human rights violations to continue with impunity. He called for an expanded AU mission with a protection element to promote security and facilitate humanitarian assistance.

Meanwhile, pressure built in the US to be more outspoken about the links between GoS and Janjaweed and declare the situation in Darfur **genocide**. On 22 July, Congress adopted a resolution to this effect, urging the US government to consider intervention to prevent genocide should the Security Council fail to act. US Secretary of State Powell, who previously maintained there was not enough evidence to call the violence genocide, changed his position in testimony to the senate foreign relations committee on 9 September. Seized for the first time under the Genocide Convention, the **Security Council** on 18 September passed **Resolution 1564** which called for an international commission of inquiry (which began its work on 25 October). Expressing grave concern that GoS had not complied with Resolution 1556, the Security Council reiterated its call for GoS to stop all violence and atrocities, to improve the security of the civilian population and to identify by name militiamen disarmed or arrested for abuses of human rights and international humanitarian law, so as to end the climate of impunity in Darfur. The resolution encouraged a reinforced AMIS to begin proactive monitoring. In the case of non-compliance, the Council announced it would consider additional measures, including sanctions against the petroleum sector, the government or its individual members. However, when the Security Council met in Nairobi on 19 November, its Resolution 1574 repeated earlier demands but no longer mentioned 'further measures'. The effective removal of the threat of sanctions, at least until the international commission of inquiry presented its report, apparently arose from the wish to push through peace in the south and not to endanger the minimum of cooperation with the international community that GoS had shown. On the ground in Darfur, however, this led to an upsurge in violence towards the end of the year.

The third round of AU-sponsored inter-Sudanese peace talks on Darfur began in **Abuja** on 21 October and resulted on 9 November in the signing of two security and humanitarian **protocols**. These reiterated the demands of the 8 April N'Djaména ceasefire agreement, and called on Khartoum to refrain "from hostile military flights" (interpreted by GoS not to apply to defensive flights). Again, Khartoum agreed to disarm the Janjaweed. On 17 December, GoS signed a separate ceasefire with NMRD, which had remained excluded from the N'Djaména negotiations. None of these held, however; further negotiations stalled; and the year ended with fighting as it had begun. For the people of Darfur, negotiations over the year brought some improvement in the supply of aid to IDPs in the camps, but elsewhere food security deteriorated and violence against civilians was not curbed. By year's end, three to four times as many Darfurians were displaced as at the beginning.

In much of the **south** and adjacent transitional zone, the **ceasefire** agreed in October 2002 was observed throughout the year. Some areas, however, witnessed fighting, mostly related to the defection to SPLA of militia groups formerly allied to GoS. In March and April, pro-government militias and government troops conducted a major offensive in the Shilluk kingdom north of Malakal, with severe consequences for the civilian population (large-scale destruction of villages, looting of cattle, displacement of 70,000–100,000 people, many civilian deaths). Sporadic fighting was also reported from this area later in the year. Other repeated clashes occurred in the oil-producing areas of Western Upper Nile and around Akobo. Both GoS and SPLA also continued to move troops around the south in vio-lation of the ceasefire agreement.

Still, negotiations made continued progress. The year began with a major breakthrough when GoS and SPLM settled the contentious issue of economic resource-sharing, provid-ing the second important building block towards a comprehensive peace accord after the agreement on security arrangements of 25 September 2003. On 7 January 2004, both sides signed the **Agreement on Wealth Sharing** during the Pre-Interim and Interim Period in Naivasha, Kenya. In it, the parties agreed that 50% of net oil revenue from southern states (after the allocation of 2% to the producing state) would be allocated to the Government of Southern Sudan (GOSS) from the beginning of the pre-interim period, and the remaining 50% to the national government and northern states. The oil sector would be managed by a national petroleum commission staffed equally by the national government and GOSS. Existing contracts would be honoured. GOSS would receive 50% of national non-oil rev-enue raised in the south and could levy its own taxes, while national government expendi-ture in the south would be financed from the national pool. A dual banking system would operate during the interim period: an Islamic one in the north and a conventional one in the south, but a single monetary policy would be pursued, with a single central bank. The agree-ment committed the interim administration to raise the war-affected areas to the same aver-age level of socioeconomic and public services as in the northern states

On 5 March, the **Equatoria Defence Force** (EDF), hitherto one of the strongest GoS-aligned southern militias, signed the **Nairobi Declaration of Unity with the SPLM/A**. For SPLA, this was a clear success in the ongoing south-south dialogue. Former EDF fighters were subsequently used in attempts to drive the Ugandan opposition Lord's Resistance Army (LRA) from its bases in Equatoria.

GoS and SPLA solved outstanding political differences on 26 May when they signed three protocols to share political power and on disputed areas within the administrative boundaries of northern states. The **Protocol on Power Sharing** regulated the establishment of a government of national unity, the appointment of the SPLM chairman as first vice-pres-ident, and elections by the end of the third year of the interim period. Prior to these, seats on government bodies at national, regional and state levels would be allocated as follows: in the National Assembly and the national council of ministers, the ruling National

Congress Party (NCP) 52%, SPLM 28%, other northern political forces 14% and other southern political forces 6%. In the south, defined "as per the borders of 1/1/56", the regional GOSS would be established, with SPLM holding 70% of legislative and executive seats, while NCP and the other southern forces would hold 15% each. In state governments in the north, NCP would hold 70% of executive and legislative seats, the SPLM 10% and other northern political forces 20%. In southern state governments, the proportions were inverted. The respective powers of national, regional and state governments were specified in detail. The power-sharing protocol also contained provisions on general principles of government, human rights, elections, the national capital, civil service, national security, judiciary, language (establishing both Arabic and English as official languages of national administration and higher education) and foreign policy. With regard to the application of Islamic law to non-Muslims, the principle of not subjecting non-Muslims to shariah penalties was underscored.

The **Protocol on the Resolution of Conflict in Southern Kordofan/Nuba Mountains and Blue Nile States** stated that prior to elections, 55% of seats in the executive and the legislature in the two states would be allocated to the NCP and 45% to the SPLM. Rotational governorship was agreed, with each party holding office for half the pre-election period, but not in both states simultaneously. Key provisions in the **Protocol on the Resolution of Abyei Conflict** were as follows. Residents of Abyei would be represented in the legislatures of both Western Kordofan (north) and Bahr el Ghazal (south). Net oil revenues from Abyei were to be divided six ways: the national government receiving 50%; GOSS 42%; Bahr el-Ghazal 2%; Western Kordofan 2%; the local Ngok Dinka and Misseriya 2% each. At the end of the interim period, Abyei would vote on whether to retain its special administrative status in the north or become part of Bahr el Ghazal.

These protocols were the last of six texts constituting the core of the peace accord that were reconfirmed in the **Nairobi Declaration on the Final Phase of Peace in the Sudan** on 5 June. Finalisation, however, was hampered by the escalation of the Darfur crisis. Meanwhile, discontent surfaced in the SPLM/A, chiefly among field commanders, not all of whom embraced the priorities of SPLA's political leadership. In October, negotiations in Kenya resumed, and on 31 December, the **Agreement on Permanent Ceasefire and Security Arrangements Implementation Modalities** during the Pre-Interim and Interim Periods was signed. Under this agreement, the Sudanese Armed Forces (SAF) and SPLA were gradually to disengage and redeploy to the north and south of the 1956 border respectively. Joint/Integrated Units (JIU), totalling about 40,000 men, would be stationed throughout the south and in Abyei, Southern Blue Nile, the Nuba Mountains and the capital, and a UN peace mission was called for to support the ceasefire. The state of emergency imposed in 1989 would be lifted "except in areas where conditions do not permit." Upon conclusion of the accord, the parties agreed to sign the comprehensive peace agreement in Nairobi on 9 January 2005. Observers generally welcomed the agreement, though many pointed out that implementing it might prove even more difficult than negotiating it. Human rights groups deplored the lack of provision for holding accountable those responsible for abuses during the war and for ensuring compliance with international rights standards in future administrations.

Political dynamics among **northern factions** were largely determined by each group's struggle to attain the best strategic position in relation to the political arrangements that would follow the signing of the comprehensive peace agreement for the south.

GoS continued its attempt to integrate most northern opposition parties into the existing political system without granting them a real share of power. The largest traditional forces, the Umma Party and the Democratic Unionist Party (DUP), as well as several smaller factions of the **National Democratic Alliance** (NDA), the umbrella organisation of mainly northern opposition parties and the SPLM, remained split into those factions seeking accommodation with GoS and those aiming to maximise the advantages of opposition from abroad. On 15 February, NDA approved the Jeddah Framework Agreement signed with GoS on 3 December 2003, which supported the peace negotiations in Kenya. Several NDA parties criticised the agreement as glossing over serious issues such as accountability for past human rights abuses, and as accepting the overall political and economic set-up in the north without reforming the security apparatus and curbing presidential power. Its endorsement in the end reflected the NDA's wish to enlarge the bilateral basis of the peace negotiations and be accepted as a separate partner, a wish that guided NDA policy throughout the year. Meanwhile, GoS froze the Jeddah Agreement in protest at NDA's admitting the Darfurian SLM/A as a new member on 13 February. For its part, NDA took some time before publicly declaring support for the peace protocols signed in Naivasha on 26 May. Its call to subject them to a conference of all political forces before the signing of the comprehensive peace accord, however, went unheard, and further talks with GoS in September/October remained inconclusive.

Disputes over the attitudes to take vis-à-vis the SPLM and GoS, respectively, **crippled** the northern opposition's hitherto strongest military force, the **Sudan Alliance Forces**. This left that faction of the Beja Congress that had disowned the December 2003 move to Khartoum by its former leaders, and the Free Lions (a militia recruited among the eastern Rashayda tribe) as the major armed opposition groups in the east. Their relations with NDA became strained over the year and they distanced themselves from the Cairo negotiations and, instead, sought links to the Darfur rebels and tried – unsuccessfully – to talk separately to GoS.

The government's **most serious rival** in the political arena remained the Islamist opposition **Popular National Congress** (PNC) led by Hasan al-Turabi. Several times during 2004 it was subjected to arrest campaigns over alleged collaboration with the Darfur rebels. In late March/early April, police arrested 40 people linked to PNC, including Turabi and ten army officers, over an alleged plan (denied by PNC) to overthrow the government. Turabi was not formally charged, but GoS accused him of instigating tribal and regional sedition. The party's offices and its semi-official newspaper 'al-Alwan' were closed. While some of the detainees were soon freed, further arrests followed. By May, 69 followers of

Turabi were detained (18 of them were put on trial in September). An unknown number of army officers and soldiers linked to PNC and/or from Darfur were discharged over the following months. For the rest of the year, restrictions on the party and its paper were repeatedly lifted and reimposed. Beginning on 7–8 September, over 30 PNC members and scores of activists (believed to be over 60 by mid-September) were arrested for conspiracy to carry out sabotage in relation to the Darfur conflict. Turabi was moved from house arrest to jail again. Arrests continued, and on 25 September, authorities imposed a security clampdown around the capital to round up suspects. A day later, President Omar al-Bashir announced the PNC would be allowed to resume political activities if it denounced Turabi. On 24 November, 92 persons, including 18 military personnel, went on trial in connection with the alleged September coup attempt. On 3 December, authorities dropped their charge against Turabi for involvement in a coup plot, but announced he would be detained until a political decree was issued to release him.

The **Umma Party for Reform and Renewal** (UPRR, the faction led by Mubarak al-Fadil al-Mahdi that had joined the government in 2002) went through a crisis with the ruling NCP in October when President Omar al-Bashir dismissed Mubarak al-Fadil from his post as presidential aide. No reason was given, but analysts interpreted the move as an attempt to improve NCP's relations with the Umma Party (UP) of Sadiq al-Mahdi, from which UPRR had broken away. In the end, UPRR's other ministers stayed in government until 13 December when they resigned, protesting that the NCP had not honoured its promise to let them participate in real decision making. Sadiq's UP, meanwhile, remained largely a bystander throughout the year, although on 22 May it signed an agreement with NCP on the Darfur problem, stressing – in the face of growing international concern – that this was an internal issue best solved through a comprehensive national conference.

The Sudanese **media struggled against restrictions** and the imposition of a new law replacing the 1999 Press Act. On 14 January, police arrested Mahjoub Mohammed Saleh, co-founder and editor-in-chief of 'al-Ayyam', Sudan's oldest independent daily. He was charged with tax evasion, but the arrest was widely regarded as part of a campaign to subdue the paper, which had been suspended since November 2003. Mahjoub was released the following day on payment of the tax, and 'al-Ayyam' resumed publication at the end of February. Other papers continued to be suspended at various points during the year. On the other hand, the justice ministry on 16 March announced restrictions on the suspension of newspapers without court order, and on 22 March the independent English-language daily 'Khartoum Monitor' resumed publication after a four-month ban. The Khartoum bureau chief of al-Jazeera satellite TV, who had been arrested in December 2003 for reporting false information, was released in April, but the station's Sudan office remained closed. Over 100 Sudanese intellectuals petitioned government in April to cancel legal provisions restricting freedom of publication. But on 5 June, parliament approved a new **Press and Printed Materials Act** (replacing the 1999 Press Act) that was described by the international freedom-of-expression group ARTICLE 19 as making critical journalism impossible. On

11 September, **pre-censorship** (lifted in August 2003) was reimposed and papers were instructed to publish only government-cleared information on Darfur or PNC.

The Sudan's **human rights record remained poor**, although the US state department noted improvement in some areas. Apart from countless abuses in connection with the armed conflicts, including large-scale civilian destruction and extra-judicial killings in Darfur, arbitrary arrests and ill-treatment in detention were frequently reported, as in previous years. There were, however, fewer reports of police brutality, and arrests of civil society activists decreased. Probably due to the ceasefire in the south, there were no confirmed reports of abductions of women and children (though most old cases remained unsolved), and oil areas in Upper Nile were spared the scorched-earth policy of previous years.

Foreign Affairs

During the first half of the year, the **US** appeared reluctant to exert pressure on Khartoum regarding Darfur for fear of endangering the peace process in the south. Thus, in April no additional unilateral sanctions were imposed under the 2002 Sudan Peace Act, and on 18 May Sudan was removed from a list of countries deemed 'uncooperative' in US efforts to combat terrorism. Once the core agreements with SPLM were signed, however, Washington's tone became harsher, and several political factions there called for sanctioning GoS for committing 'genocide'. In the UN, however, this position was counterbalanced by **China**, which by threat of veto steered the Security Council away from more decisive action. China, which bought 70% of the Sudan's oil, feared that sanctions might endanger its investments there. Russia and France were also reluctant to support sanctions, partly because of their own commercial involvement.

Russia remained of particular interest as a supplier of **arms**. In May, GoS signed a new military cooperation agreement with Russia, and in late July – as the Security Council debate on sanctions against Sudan raged – Moscow announced the final delivery of 12 MiG-29 jet fighters to Khartoum, to conclude a 2001 deal (four other MiGs had been delivered in December and January). In September, Russia's state arms export agency 'Rosoboronexport' openly stated it was seeking to boost sales to Sudan. In reaction to Security Council Resolution 1556, President Putin on 25 October banned the export of weapons to non-governmental bodies in the Sudan. A visit to Russia by President Omar al-Bashir was in preparation by year's end. GoS also approached Ukraine and Belarus for arms and police training: both countries denied they were supplying military equipment. In February, Sudan signed a defence cooperation agreement with Malaysia, and GoS evaluated an Indian offer for military platforms and training.

Chadian President Idris Déby, while trying to mediate between GoS and the Darfur rebels, maintained good relations with GoS, but this stirred up internal rivalries, since many of his Zaghawa power base felt solidarity with the rebels (there was a coup attempt in May). Déby also encouraged **Libya** to mediate in the conflict in coordination with the AU. GoS, which earlier claimed that the rebels were benefiting from 'Libyan channels', welcomed this initiative, while the rebels subsequently rejected it, since Libya's main concern appeared to be to avert Western intervention (affirmed at the Tripoli summit between Libya, Sudan, Egypt, Chad and Nigeria on 17 October). In July, Libya signed agreements with the UN to allow the transit of relief to Darfur through the Libyan desert.

Uganda's cooperation with GoS improved to the point where Khartoum in July effectively ended its tacit support of LRA and allowed the Ugandan army (UPDF) to pursue LRA fighters beyond the 'red line' (the Torit-Nisitu-Juba road) that had marked the permitted limit of Ugandan operations in Sudan since 2002. LRA leader Joseph Kony only narrowly escaped capture, and by the end of the year UPDF had destroyed most of the LRA's infrastructure in southern Sudan. This led to increasing LRA attacks on Sudanese villages for supplies. Economic cooperation was furthered by framework agreements signed in April concerning agriculture, fisheries, animal resources and the voluntary repatriation of refugees. In December, a Ugandan delegation visited Khartoum to explore investment opportunities, especially in the south. Uganda also expressed interest in buying Sudanese oil.

GoS continued to collaborate with **Ethiopia** in containing the Oromo Liberation Front, permitting Ethiopian troops to cross the border in pursuit of OLF fugitives. Relations were marred, however, by a dispute over the demarcation of the border that dragged on throughout the summer.

Tensions with **Eritrea** escalated further. Eritrea, long accused of supporting rebels in the eastern Sudan, was now accused by GoS **of extending this support to rebels in Darfur**, a charge Eritrea denied. When in August, a Libyan plane forcibly repatriating 84 Eritreans was forced to land in Khartoum, Sudan refused to extradite the hijackers unless Eritrea agreed to "hand over Sudanese rebels in Eritrean camps". Eritrea accused Sudan of "encouraging terrorism", and in October claimed GoS was plotting to assassinate President Afeworki.

The Sudan steadily sought to strengthen relations with **Egypt**, which the Sudanese president visited regularly. GoS was interested in securing Egypt's support for its position in the south and in Darfur, while Egypt eyed investment opportunities, including in the reconstruction of the south. Egypt therefore maintained its opposition to sanctions against the Sudan. Bilateral relations took a big step forward with the signing and ratification of an **Agreement on the Four Freedoms** (of movement, residence, work and ownership). Put on track during a January summit, it came into force on 8 September after final endorsement by the Egyptian parliament. Visas for Egyptians were immediately waived, but not the reverse, and overall implementation proved rocky (by December, six memorandums worked out by a joint technical committee were under discussion).

In June, Egypt, Sudan and Ethiopia agreed to a variety of joint **Nile water** projects, especially in irrigation, agricultural development, electricity and drinking water supply.

The **UAE** became the largest source of Arab capital to Sudan, with investments especially in agriculture (April: memorandum of understanding on cooperation in agriculture and animal production), power generation (Merowe dam) and real estate. Bilateral cooperation also intensified with **Saudi Arabia**, the second biggest Arab investor (February: agreement on political cooperation; March: agreements on agricultural cooperation, drug trafficking, smuggling and security; June: memorandum on financing a new international airport in Khartoum). On 4–6 October, **Iranian** President Khatami paid Khartoum his first visit since 1997 to enhance economic, political and cultural cooperation. **Turkey** also sought to expand its presence in the Sudan and to participate in the oil boom. In December, protocols on commercial relations, transportation, technical and economic cooperation, education, culture, health and tourism were signed, and the two sides agreed to start talks on a free trade agreement.

The **re-election of the Sudan to the UN Commission on Human Rights** on 4 May was regarded by experts as the result of an African 'rebellion' against US policies. On 31 October, the Sudan was the sixth Arab country to ratify the two UN optional protocols to the Convention on the Rights of the Child adopted in 2000 to protect children from recruitment into the armed forces and from sexual exploitation.

Socioeconomic Developments

Sudan's **economy** continued to **expand** rapidly, mainly **driven by** the **oil** sector. A 27% increase in production coincided with soaring international prices (highest ever annual average) and growing demand by expanding economies especially in Asia. Profitability was enhanced by the fact that more earnings were left in Sudanese hands after foreign companies had recovered initial costs. Oil receipts were estimated to have risen almost 60% in 2004, with export revenue growth of all goods estimated at 65%. Average daily production grew, as optimists had predicted, to an annual average of 343,000 b/d. In early June, the Sudan's second pipeline linking Block 6 to the Jeili refinery north of Khartoum was completed. Output began in November at 10,000 b/d, signalling the first major extension to the country's oil industry since the start in 1999 of production in Blocks 1 and 2. Contracts for infrastructure development for Blocks 3 and 7, including building a third pipeline, were allocated over the summer (mainly to Malaysian companies, including MMC Corporation, Ranhill and Lankhurst). Russian 'Stroitransgaz' won the tender for one of the four pipeline sections and started work in August. In October, Malaysian Peremba began building a terminal near Port Sudan for the export of crude from Blocks 3 and 7. Tenders were announced for the final work in Block 5a where production is planned to start in 2006. Following the 2003 suggestion of potential reserves all over the country, exploration work was undertaken for the first time outside the south and the transitional zone. Pakistani Zafer began drilling in its allocated Block 9 in June (Jazirah) and November (al-Damer). French Total refused an advance by Indian Oil and Natural Gas Company (ONGC) to take its equity in Block 5, and in December updated its contract to be ready to resume activities once peace takes hold.

Refining capacity also **grew**, and in August, the state-owned ONGC, seeking to secure more supplies for the Indian sub-continent, agreed to oversee construction of a new refined products pipeline from Khartoum to Port Sudan, due for completion in October 2005. ONGC also emerged as a key partner in plans to upgrade the Khartoum and Port Sudan refineries to a capacity of 100,000 b/d each.

On 15 November, the export pipeline was sabotaged near Shendi, but with minimal loss to throughput. Excepting a thwarted attack near Port Sudan in October, this was the first **oil security** incident in over a year. The Beja Congress, which had previously launched such attacks, denounced the Shendi act as criminal.

The **IMF Staff Monitored Programme** followed since 1997 continued to guide economic policy, with privatisation of parastatals and civil service reforms. IMF remained satisfied with economic performance. The Sudanese dinar showed only minimal movement against the US dollar, and consumer price inflation remained relatively stable at around 9% (though exceeding the IMF/government target of 5%). Real GDP growth, driven largely by oil exports and foreign investment, continued to accelerate to 6.5% and reached $ 19 bn, exceeding the IMF/government target. Tax-take growth was estimated at 11%. Central bank foreign-exchange reserves reached record levels ($ 1.2 bn by August). Sudan's efforts to accede to WTO intensified.

By the end of 2003, total **external debt** had **grown by 2.5%** to $ 24.2 bn, according to Bank of Sudan figures: over half of this consisted of interest arrears. In April, the Arab Monetary Fund was the first creditor to write off some of this debt: $ 60 m of the $ 340 m Sudan owed the fund. Several other creditors indicated willingness to renounce claims once a peace accord was signed.

Foreign direct investment (FDI, mostly in the oil sector) had seen record growth in 2003, when it reached $ 1.3 bn, almost twice as much as in 2002, which had itself been the highest to date. Official data for 2004 (just over $ 700 m for the first six months) suggest that FDI **continued to grow**, albeit at a reduced rate. At 7% of GDP (on an annualised basis), this remains one of the highest ratios in the region, and highlighted both the attractiveness of the new oil economy and the dependency of the country's development on foreign financing (primarily from China, Malaysia and India), which accounted for 80% of gross fixed capital formation in 2003.

In May, fixed-line telephone monopoly Sudatel was the first **private-sector** Sudanese company to raise a foreign syndicated loan – $ 40 m from the Arabian Investment Company, which operates under Islamic financial rules. In November (earlier than envisaged), a second fixed-line licence was awarded to Karnatel, a consortium led by UAE's Etisalat, to compete with Sudatel. Commencement of operations by a second mobile phone service, licensed in 2003, was apparently delayed beyond the end of 2004. In what was the first deal to award a private company a central role in municipal services, EBD Lebanon was contracted to enhance Khartoum's sewage network. In the banking sector, al-Salam, a new private Islamic bank dominated by UAE investors, obtained an operating licence. It raised $ 31 m in its initial public offering, twice as much as expected, and with a total capital of $ 88 m was set to become Sudan's biggest bank. In August, GoS invited foreign investors to buy 49% of shares in a new firm to replace the ailing Sudan Airways and announced that all the 2,000 staff would be laid off – their job security had deterred previous investors. FDI played a decisive role in improving the country's **electricity** supply, whose total capacity grew by 80% in 2004. In June, two power stations north of Khartoum went online with a combined capacity of 330 MW. In November, the Sudan's first-ever private power station was inaugurated, at 257 MW the world's largest diesel plant, built by Siemens and owned by the Malaysian company DIT power Kilo-X.

Import levels continued to grow by over 30% as they have since early 2001, driven mainly by the expanding oil sector and infrastructure projects, but also by steadily increasing consumer demand (reflected also in a lending surge to local private retail and wholesale trade). Still, oil (80% of total exports) brought Sudan its first **trade surplus** in years (an estimated $ 667 m). Total export revenue during 2004 rose to an estimated $ 3.3 bn, at 35% markedly higher than the previous record of 2003.

Non-oil export earnings also did well, growing by 75% in the year prior to 30 June 2004. Favourable rains in 2003 produced a **bumper harvest**, nearly 50% above the previous five-year average. Sesame production trebled and earnings quadrupled; exports of sheep almost doubled; and recovering cotton prices helped increase revenue by 30% despite a 9% decline in export volume. Almost 90% of all non-oil exports went to Saudi-Arabia, but exports to Egypt began to grow as political relations improved.

Food security initially improved across the south, helped by favourable weather and the ceasefire. In March, however, IDPs began to return home, and by year's end 300–400,000 of the over four million southern displaced had already gone back. This movement occurred largely spontaneously, and, because support systems were not in place, placed a strain on food supplies and infrastructure. The UN formed a '**sustainable return team**' in the summer to coordinate aid to returnees. Preliminary assessments of the 2004–05 harvest pointed to lower production levels as rains were late and often below average. In the south, the ceasefire and good agency cooperation offset the negative effects of this, but in violence-plagued Darfur crop loss was estimated at 80%, and food shortages were also reported from the east.

The war in Darfur caused a setback to the international anti-**polio** campaign. Sudan had been polio-free for three years, but a new case was reported in Darfur in May (traced to Nigeria). Conflict hampered vaccination campaigns, and by December, 79 reported cases across the country meant the disease had become endemic again.

Activists voiced concern over large-scale environmental **pollution in oil exploration areas** and the wholesale destruction of the homes of 50,000 villagers by the Merowe dam project, but GoS maintained tight control over news regarding such issues.

Albrecht Hofheinz

Tanzania

As in previous years, political developments remained generally calm in the mainland territory and were mainly centred on preparations for the 2005 national elections, especially the establishment of a permanent voter's register. However, local elections saw a limited outbreak of violence on the mainland as well as in Zanzibar, where political tension remained high throughout the year. External relations continued to be cordial with neighbouring countries and with donor countries and institutions. Economic performance was characterised by satisfactory continuity of initiated reforms, albeit without significant further improvements.

Domestic Politics

Preparations for the next presidential and parliamentary elections, due in October 2005, got under way. Despite the formation of a coalition of 13 opposition parties in 2003, the opposition camp remained weak and divided, since the most important parties, Tanzania Labour Party (TLP), 'Chama cha Demokrasia na Maendeleo' (CHADEMA, Party for Democracy and Progress) and Civic United Front (CUF), did not join the alliance. The only potential threat to an overwhelming victory by the ruling 'Chama cha Mapinduzi' (CCM, Party of the Revolution) appeared to be a rather unlikely split in the party, possibly between a pro-reform faction wanting to pursue the politics of **President Benjamin William Mkapa** further and an influential group of elderly politicians more sceptical of the benefits of the present reforms for the country and its people – a quite popular view within Tanzanian society. Since Mkapa's second term was due to end in 2005 and he was constitutionally barred from a third term, the selection of his **successor** as **CCM candidate** was crucial for all further developments in the country. Manoeuvring for the official nomination process scheduled to begin in March 2005 had already started within CCM's inner circles, and allegations of corruption against **Prime Minister Frederick Sumaye** at the end of the year could possibly be seen in this context. In September, a special party committee was established to prepare the CCM election manifesto and a development programme for the party for 2005–10. No cabinet changes took place during the year – another sign of stability and confidence. A parliamentary by-election in Bariadi on 30 May ended with the return to CCM of a former opposition MP who had fallen out with his United Democratic Party (UDP).

The opposition parties' nomination processes were much more predictable. Since it was highly unlikely that the major opposition parties would agree on a common candidate, each of the few more important parties would be likely to nominate its own chairman. Of the several **Zanzibar-based political parties** founded in 2003, only 'Jahaza Asilia' (chaired by a brother of former Zanzibar President Salmin Amour) obtained full registration in 2004. The temporarily registered 'Safina' (founded by the same brother) was struck off the registrar's list after internal squabbles, while the Solidarity of Factual Theories ('Soft') obtained temporary registration in February. Tanzania thus had 17 fully registered political parties at the end of 2004, and several others with temporary or preliminary registration. The registrar of political parties announced plans for a new law that would allow for the deregistration of small parties that had no elected members in any of the country's representative public bodies. It remained unclear whether and how the apparent splits in Zanzibar's political society would find expression in the party system. **Zanzibar President Amani Abeid Karume** undertook the first major reshuffle of his cabinet on 10 September, followed later by a minor reshuffle of district commissioners and heads of administration. The **cabinet reshuffle** was interpreted as a move to strengthen his position within CCM Zanzibar in light of the 2005 elections and the threat of internal splits. CUF did write to Amnesty International and Human Rights Watch to protest against the installation of Ahmed Hassan Diria as the new minister of state for constitutional affairs and good governance, since they accused him of being responsible for human rights violations following the 1964 revolution.

Two aspects of the **pre-electoral process** proved to be very controversial: the role of the **National Electoral Commission (NEC)** and the process for establishing a permanent voter's register. Opposition parties voiced criticism of the fact that NEC members – unlike their colleagues in Zanzibar – were still appointed by the president without the opposition being consulted. In mid-May, opposition parties demanded the dissolution of NEC and even appealed at the end of June to the international community to support their demands. The Union government admitted it was time to change the composition of NEC, but no concrete action resulted.

In June, the Union parliament passed an amendment to the 'Elections Act' of 1985 to authorise NEC to create a **permanent voter's register**, and also approved the funds to finance this project. Both steps were supported by the opposition. The registration process started on 8 October on the mainland, where it proceeded smoothly. After several postponements due to lack of funds and equipment, the process started in **Zanzibar** on 1 November. There, the **registration process** was more controversial and reflected the generally tense political atmosphere on the islands. In mid-February, the two major parties – the ruling CCM and CUF – began to accuse one another of planning to manipulate the voter's register for their own benefit. The permanent register was a crucial aspect of the **2001 peace accord** (known as '**Muafaka**') agreed upon by both parties after violent clashes between supporters of CUF and the police in January 2001. Since support for both parties was considered almost equal and adjacent to respective clear strongholds of each party there were some heavily disputed constituencies, manipulation of registration was obviously regarded as a fruitful strategy for increasing one's votes in a disputed constituency. Alleged manipulation of the registration has been a major source of conflict since the first multiparty elections in 1995. CUF accused the CCM government of transferring mainlanders and soldiers (both perceived as pro-CCM) to Zanzibar, while CCM officials accused CUF of intimidating people from the mainland. In October, leaflets appeared in the CUF-stronghold **Pemba** telling mainlanders to leave and not to register there. In December, leaflets were found on the main island of **Unguja** threatening Pembans in case they did not leave Unguja before the registration. The regulations for the voter's register stated that to be eligible to vote, people must have lived in Zanzibar for three consecutive years if they were born there, and for ten years if they originated on the mainland. The opposition criticised the regulations for allowing security and defence force personnel to be registered anywhere upon job transfer, whereas Zanzibaris must live in their constituency for three consecutive years. Furthermore, CUF felt uneasy about the location of registration centres, since these were allegedly located too close to CCM party offices and even army camps. CUF also complained that the majority of the 20 officers appointed by the Zanzibar Electoral Commission (ZEC) to supervise the registration were CCM-members. In Pemba, a dispute about the registration of coastguard members based in Unguja but transferred to do service in Pemba and a National Service group led to an **escalation of violence**. CUF supporters tried to prevent the registration but were stopped by police. The ensuing clashes left a pupil dead and several people injured. The commander of the Zanzibar volunteer force was killed some days later – an incident widely perceived as an act of revenge for the death of the CUF supporter. In several registration centres, officers were attacked, and violence between officers, supporters of political parties and security forces occurred. At least 50 people were arrested and nine registration centres had to be closed temporarily. The problems were ascribed both to poor administration and the high political tension prevailing on the islands. Additional tension was caused by discussions about redrawing constituency borders following the 2002 census. The opposition accused ZEC of misusing the census by changing boundaries of contested constituencies to benefit CCM. The ZEC chairman received death threats after the announcement.

Voter registration also led to tension in the mainland region of Ruvuma. Catholic nuns and Muslim women refused to take off their headgear to be photographed for the ID cards that were part of the process of establishing the permanent voter's register. Muslim groups announced they would demonstrate against the requirement.

Local elections at neighbourhood and village level were held at the end of November (whereas local council elections were to take place in 2005). On 21 November, chairpersons of the lowest grassroots institutions ('vitongoji') were elected, followed one week later by elections of the chairpersons of 'mitaa' (next higher level). The government promised to conduct these elections using the new register, which predictably was not completed in time. An alliance of 15 opposition parties, therefore, filed a petition to the high court in early October to postpone the elections until the permanent voter's register was ready for use. However, the court ruled that the local elections should be conducted according to the timetable by using the old voter registration. The opposition refrained from launching public demonstrations against the court's decision after consultations with government, in deference to the International Conference on the Great Lakes Region to be held in Dar es Salaam on the same date. As a countermove, Mkapa promised to conduct consultations with opposition leaders. The 'vitongoji' elections did proceed peacefully, and all political parties declared themselves satisfied with the way they were conducted. In clear contrast, however, the 'mitaa' elections were beset by massive organisational (and political) problems. In some cases, electoral materials were delivered too late or were stolen and voter registration lists were often problematic. Violence erupted at several polling stations throughout the country as political activists from different parties clashed with each other and the police. About 150 polling stations had to be closed and the whole exercise had to be repeated in Dar es Salaam and other urban centres one week later. No nationwide election results were made public, but CCM claimed to have obtained about 90% of the popular mandate. In Dar es Salaam, they won 308 of 395 seats, while CUF won 70 and all the other parties had hardly any impact.

Despite the confrontation in Zanzibar, the **agreements forming part of the 2001 peace accord** were by and large implemented in a slow, steady process. However, some issues still needed to be discussed, especially those which could threaten CCM's power in Zanzibar. It appeared at least questionable whether CCM would allow CUF to obtain a share of power in Zanzibar. The general secretaries of the two parties nevertheless started discussions in April about the possibility of a **coalition government**, and a prominent CUF leader declared in May that his party intended to form a coalition government with CCM in the event they won the 2005 elections.

The apparent cooperation between the two parties – despite no clear promise of a predictable and satisfactory solution – seems to have strengthened other, more radical, forces, which intended to challenge Zanzibar's secular constitution. Since the 2001 clashes between CUF supporters and the police, open **violence had become a permanent feature of Zanzibar politics**. CCM and CUF continued to accuse each other of being responsible for these incidents, but at the same time declared themselves free of any responsibility. It seemed that discontent with both major players led sections of Zanzibar's society to opt for different approaches. Increasing confrontations between state and Muslim groups were apparently the upshot of growing anger among parts of the society at the state's interference in what was seen as Muslim affairs. In February, disputes over the date for celebrating the Muslim festival Eid al-Fitr led to confrontations with the police, who fired teargas and plastic bullets into a mosque to stop the prayers. After a demonstration planned by a group known as '**Uamsho**' or JUMIKA ('Jumuya ya Uamsho na Mihadhara ya Kiislamu'/Association of Revival and Propagation of the Islamic Faith in Zanzibar) was banned by the authorities, a spontaneous demonstration on 5 March became violent. About 300 people, including women and children, were demonstrating against Western influence in Zanzibar and the government's tourism policies, which were seen as a source of the perceived increase of alcoholism and prostitution on the predominantly Muslim islands. Protest was also aimed at the position of Zanzibar's highest-ranking Islamic cleric. Since the mufti's appointment, 'Uamsho' had criticised his position and demanded the election of the religious leader instead of his appointment by government. The police forcefully broke up the demonstration with teargas. At least four demonstrators were injured and over 30 people were arrested. Nobody accepted responsibility for the demonstration, but most observers saw 'Uamsho' behind it, despite the organisation's denials. CUF was also suspected by the Zanzibar government of being responsible, an accusation that was strongly denied. A **series of bomb blasts** subsequently shook the islands in March and April. One day after the violent dispersal of the demonstration, three electricity transformers were destroyed by petrol bombs, and a few days later a Catholic primary school bus was blown up. This fate was shared by a police vehicle and a beer depot. The weekend of 19/20 March saw bomb attacks on the residences of the mufti and of Zanzibar's transport minister, a Christian seen by some as anti-Muslim. A hand grenade was thrown into a popular restaurant in Stone Town, where several foreigners were dining, including two Western diplomats. The grenade did not explode and the other bombs caused only material damage. The bomb attacks could have been related to the visit by Germany's President Johannes Rau on 22 March, since this provided a good opportunity to draw international attention to the situation in Zanzibar. The **Union government took immediate action** to bring the situation under control – and to indicate to the international community that the tourist islands were not in the hands of terrorists. However, the steps taken appeared to be somewhat haphazard and precipitate. A team of **anti-terror investigators** was sent to Zanzibar and security personnel were increased. About 40 suspects were arrested. The police were, however, accused of arresting people arbitrarily. On 13 April, 'Uamsho' leader Sheikh Khalid Azan was charged with sedition, but six weeks later was released through lack of evidence. The ministry of the interior **banned the para-military training** of the political parties' youth wings on 1 April. This step was primarily aimed at CUF's Blue and White Guards. CUF refused to stop the military training of their youth and claimed that this was part of the party's organisation that had been accepted by the registrar of political parties. CUF also accused CCM of having a military youth wing.

The Zanzibar government as well as CUF tried to regain the attention of the discontented populace, and both sides embarked on more **nationalist and islamist strategies**. On 13 April, the Zanzibar parliament passed a law stipulating **penalties for homosexual activities** of up to 25 years in jail. Travel agencies specialising in tours for gays and lesbians threatened to boycott Zanzibar, and even groups within Zanzibar criticised the new law. On 11 November, Zanzibar adopted a new flag. Since the creation of the Union with the mainland in 1964, Zanzibar had not had its own state symbols. The **new flag** was an attempt to gain ground on the nationalist forces pursuing the goal of Zanzibar's independence. The government stressed, however, that the flag was not meant as a step in that direction: it was not to be used in an international context, only internally. CUF supported the move, but only after demanding the removal of the Union flag displayed in one corner of Zanzibar's new flag. The introduction of the new flag did not cause any disagreement with the Union government. In similar vein, Zanzibar's football teams were admitted to Pan-African football competitions separate from the mainland.

But neither the symbolic measures nor the heavy-handed reactions of state organs eased the situation, given the general atmosphere of fierce political fighting, mutual distrust and increasing radicalism. On 10 July, a peaceful CUF procession turned riotous when the demonstrators passed the CCM Zanzibar head office and attacked it. On the other hand, several CUF offices had also been attacked during the year. On 5 December, police raided the Zanzibar residence of CUF chairman Ibrahim Lipumba in his absence, claiming to be searching for smuggled cloves. Great concern was caused in October by **fire attacks on three Christian churches** in Zanzibar. Primary suspicion was directed at Muslim extremists, but the possibility that this was also an attempt to menace mainlanders into leaving the islands before the 2005 elections could not been ruled out.

The introduction of a new bill aiming to regulate the conditions for student loans led to **student protests** at the **University of Dar es Salaam**. After protests started on 20 April, members of the Field Force Unit (FFU) dispersed the demonstration with teargas. When protests continued, FFU again reacted with teargas and arrested about 60 students, some of whom were beaten by the police. All students were suspended from the university and had to apply to re-register. Two weeks later all but 17 students were re-registered, and later these 17 were allowed to return. Several organisations, Amnesty International, lecturers and opposition parties condemned FFU's harsh reaction. Mkapa, however, congratulated the university leadership for the peaceful resolution of the crisis. A student demonstration from eleven universities against the 'Higher Learning Bill' proceeded peacefully on 2 May. Other **student protests at the University of Zanzibar** over demands for improved learning conditions turned riotous when police in civilian clothes entered the dormitories to arrest the strike leaders. Police overreaction has become a frequent feature in recent years. The police were generally feared by the population and were widely considered as corrupt.

Some parts of Tanzania witnessed **violent clashes between members of different ethnic groups**. In December, two villagers died as a result of tension between two Kurya clans in Tarime district. A long dispute over land between Sonjo and Maasai in Ngorongoro district led to clashes that left one person dead. Peace talks involving both sides, the minister of lands, the local MP and the regional commissioner eventually eased the tension.

Foreign Affairs

Tanzania's relations with **Western donor countries generally remained excellent**, despite some smaller disputes. Some donors withheld subsidies to the Joint Presidential Supervisory Commission (JPSC) that had been installed to oversee the implementation of the 2001 Zanzibar peace process. The JPSC was accused of misuse of funds, particularly to buy luxury cars for its members. Donors also expressed concern over government's alleged **lack of commitment to combat corruption**, especially in respect to delays in preparing a new anti-corruption bill. The government, however, justified its pace and the issue did not seriously jeopardise its generally good standing among the donor community. The ranking in the corruption perception index of Transparency International has somewhat improved in recent years: in 2004 Tanzania was ranked 90th (equal with India and Russia) among 145 countries.

Relations with neighbouring countries were conducted equally cordially, without serious problems. The integration process of the **East African Community (EAC)** with Kenya and Uganda took a big step forward when the protocol to establish a **customs union** was finally signed on 2 March. The three countries agreed to introduce a common external tariff on imports from other countries with effect from January 2005. The presence of the Burundi president and the Rwandan prime minister at the ceremony underlined the interest in including their two states in EAC at a later time.

In mid-December, the presidents of Malawi, Mozambique, Zambia and Tanzania met in Lilongwe to sign a treaty on cooperation in the **Mtwara development corridor**. Several specific projects, such as the building of a 'unity bridge' over the Ruvuma River between Tanzania and Mozambique, a road from Mtwara to Lake Nyasa and the extension of the port of Mtwara were agreed upon. Minor problems occurred along the **Tanzanian-Zambian border**, when Tanzanian citizens entered Zambia, illegally occupied land there and resisted appeals to return home. **Relations with Burundi remained somewhat strained**. After a massacre in a refugee camp near Bujumbura in August, the Tanzanian government seemed to shift its traditional support for the main Hutu party FRODEBU to a different Hutu-dominated party. Pierre Nkurunziza, the leader of CNDD-FDD with relatively good chances of winning the Burundian presidency in elections in 2005, was received in Dar es Salaam.

The government quite firmly pursued the **repatriation of refugees**, mainly from Burundi, despite numerous problems in their home countries. As in previous years, UNHCR cooperated closely with Tanzanian authorities to facilitate repatriation, but the number of returning refugees remained small owing to the continued insecurity in Burundi. While almost all refugees from Rwanda had left Tanzania, Congolese refugees continued to hesitate about returning. Food shortages due to lack of funding were again a lamentable feature. About 400,000 refugees from Burundi and Congo were still in camps in the west of Tanzania by year's end. British Prime Minister Tony Blair confirmed negotiations on a proposed plan to assist Tanzania in undertaking clearance arrangements on its territory for Somali refugees applying to go to Britain.

In mid-November, a large **International Conference on Peace, Security, Democracy and Development in the Great Lakes Region** was held in Dar es Salaam. Preceded by a meeting of foreign ministers, the First Summit of Heads of State and Government took place on 19 and 20 November. Eighteen African Presidents, UN Secretary-General Kofi Annan and the AU Commission Chairman Alpha Oumar Konare signed a common declaration to promote peace and security in the Great Lakes Region.

A seven-day state visit took Mkapa to **China** in May/June, and in early December he went to Vietnam. The traditionally good relations with China were confirmed by agreements on economic cooperation and projects in various areas. In September, Tanzania was elected to the **UN Security Council** for a two-year term (2005–06). It was the first time in 30 years that the country was elected as a non-permanent member of the highest international body. Early in the year, Mkapa was privileged to become one of the few African leaders selected as a member of the **Commission for Africa** initiated by the British government. The parliamentarian and former minister Gertrude Mongella was elected the first president of the newly constituted **Pan-African Parliament** of the AU in March.

Socioeconomic Developments

The **economy** continued to perform fairly satisfactorily within the general African context, but still had too sluggish a growth rate to bring about really significant structural changes. While the key **macroeconomic indicators** proved healthy as a result of the determined pursuit of market-oriented reform policies, the effect on the material and social well-being of the vast majority of the population was still hardly noticeable. According to preliminary IMF estimates, the **GDP growth rate** for 2004 appeared to be 6.3% (compared to revised rates of 7.2% and 7.1% for the preceding years). This positive outlook was quite surprising in view of the considerable problems in the agricultural sector resulting from widespread drought in 2003 and early 2004. The mining and tourism sectors again contributed most to the strong overall growth performance. The inflation rate was contained at an average of around 5% and the currency remained remarkably stable against the US dollar, while depreciating against the euro. Foreign reserves showed a small increase to $ 2003 m at the end of the 3rd quarter and allowed for a full year's import coverage. The trade balance remained almost unchanged, with estimated export receipts of $ 1,235 m, covering about 62% of the $ 1973 m import bill. The current account deficit of about $ 343 m also remained stable at a ratio of 3.5% of GDP. In the 2004 UNDP **Human Development Index** (based on 2002 figures) Tanzania was listed ahead of 15 other sub-Saharan African countries, but its index rating slipped somewhat compared with 1990, and in respect to per capita GDP for 2002 (in PPP terms) it was the second poorest, at $ 580 – equal with Malawi and just ahead of Sierra Leone. This was proof of the entrenched **structural poverty problem** even after years of relatively positive economic reforms.

The government's **fiscal management** saw a continuation of its cautious strategy of tight expenditure control and gradual improvement of the revenue side. In February, parliament was asked to approve a **supplementary budget** (after many years of not needing such a step) for the current financial year (2003–04). The extra sum of TSh 87 bn (4.8% increase of recurrent expenditures) was primarily needed to cater for the effects of the drought (grain imports and more oil for power generation). The final outcome of the **2003–04 budget** (July to June) showed a largely satisfactory picture. The domestic tax and non-tax revenue of TSh 1,459 bn was about 6% above the budgeted target and 20% higher than in the previous financial year. As a result of better tax administration and less VAT evasion, a **revenue ratio** of 13.3% of GDP was achieved for the first time, which was, however, still far below the African average. Even the total expenditures of TSh 2,550 bn were slightly below budget estimates, with some moderate overspending on recurrent expenditures but a critical shortfall of 15.6% on budgeted development expenditures, resulting from deficient implementation capacity for intended investment projects. About 45% of the total budget was still financed from **external sources** (compared to 47% in 2002–03). Grants and loans received from donors were slightly lower than expected in the budget, but an increasing share was given in the form of budget support and actually disbursed in time for the needs of the Tanzanian budget cycle. The overall situation, with grants included, did allow for an **almost balanced budget** (deficit about 0.9% of GDP) without recourse to untargeted borrowing. Without grants, the budget deficit would have reached about 6% of GDP.

The new **2004–05 budget** introduced in parliament on 10 June envisaged a further increase in domestic revenue by about 20% to TSh 1,739 bn (target ratio 13.8% of GDP) and total expenditures of TSh 2,867 bn (TSh 1,975 bn for recurrent and TSh 892 bn for development expenditures). Of all expenditures, 51% were allocated for the seven **priority sectors** under the **Poverty Reduction Strategy (PRS)**, i.e., education, health, water, agriculture, roads, judiciary, HIV/AIDS. Despite the focus on priority sectors, it was pointed out clearly that available resources were still utterly inadequate and would hardly have a noticeable impact. The new budget was by and large positively received by the public. In April, a new income tax act was passed by parliament and took effect in July. There was some repeated criticism, based on a widely perceived feeling, that international mining companies were not sufficiently taxed and were treated too generously. Other controversies revolved around suitable forms of **financing for the activities of local government**. While the government had in 2003, to widespread public approval, decreed the abolition of many so-called nuisance taxes, several city and district councils continued to enforce different levies as an essential source of local revenue. Under the policy of **decentralisation**, increasing sums were also transferred from central government to local councils, but the right balance between central control and local autonomy was still in dispute.

In March, government published its third progress review of the **PRS process.** Surprisingly self-critical, it pointed out good results in respect of macroeconomic reforms and indicators, but admitted to insufficient translation of these achievements to the micro level and severe capacity constraints for programme implementation. Results of new household budget surveys (with data from 2000–01) showed that 36% of all households still lived below the 'basic needs **poverty level**' (compared to 39% in 1992) and that 19% of households were living on less than $ 1 per day; 90% of all poor people were located in rural areas. In September, an IMF assessment of the PRS also confirmed the good progress to date, while again stressing the remaining challenge, the better implementation of concrete sectoral programmes. This was to be the main focus of a **new PRS document** under preparation by government for the period 2005–08. Earlier in the year, the IMF gave a positive verdict on the progress of its current PRGF (Poverty Reduction and Growth Facility), despite insisting on the need for deeper structural reforms (particularly in the energy sector). Later, IMF raised concerns about planned expenditures on two prestige projects (new stadium and parliament building) perceived as politically motivated, in light of the 2005 elections. Although Tanzania was one of the first countries to benefit recently from considerable **debt relief** under the HIPC II initiative, its **external debt** again started to rise ($ 7.5 bn in mid-2004) as a result of new loans from multilateral agencies. Domestic debt, however, remained relatively low in comparison with similar countries (about 15% of GDP in 2002–03) as an effect of the strict fiscal policy.

Already effective debt relief to the tune of $ 860 m (as part of an envisaged debt cancellation of $ 3.1 bn over 20 years) was used for **additional government programmes** in the priority sectors under the **PRS**. Progress had been made particularly with the achievement of an 85% primary school enrolment rate, and the focus now shifted to the expansion of secondary schools and to a more vigorous campaign against HIV/AIDS. In October, a programme for the free distribution of anti-retroviral drugs was started. The main remaining challenge was the badly needed modernisation of the lagging agricultural sector. The government's newly formulated **agricultural sector development strategy** focused, *inter alia*, on further liberalised marketing facilities for export crops and on enabling farmers to use their land as collateral for obtaining credits (following the ideas of the Peruvian economist de Soto). An effect of the widespread 2003 **drought** was that about 3.5 m people needed

food aid during the first half of the year, while further poor rains and crop failures in the northern regions left some 180,000 people needing food aid towards the end of the year. To cater for the emergency, the government's strategic grain reserve was depleted to its lowest level in years and had to be rebuilt through costly additional imports.

The **privatisation policy** the government had pursued since the early 1990s encountered increasing difficulties and delays in respect of the last remaining parastatals. The intended partial privatisation of the Tanzania Railways Corporation (TRC) was again delayed, but three interested foreign consortia had pre-qualified for the final process by year's end. Plans for privatising the National Insurance Corporation (NIC) and the National Microfinance Bank (NMB), with its unique countrywide network of bank facilities in district centres, were in hand, but had not reached a decisive stage. The management contract for the power company TANESCO with consultants from South Africa was extended by two years, despite public complaints about continuing problems. The foreign management of the urban water authority in Dar es Salaam also encountered major problems and was not able to meet all the high expectations, while the port operations were generally credited with having achieved remarkable improvements (although customs clearance remained a major problem). The sugar industry showed an impressive turnaround after privatisation, and it was hoped that similar results would eventually be obtained by disposing of the loss-making cashew-nut factories and some remaining parastatal textile factories. Generally, the **manufacturing sector** has shown modest recovery in recent years (2003 growth rate 8.6%) after a period of contraction and the closure of many former parastatal firms that were no longer viable. Progress in setting up special export processing zones (EPZ) was, however, disappointingly slow: only two were operating by year's end in Dar es Salaam. For local entrepreneurs, access to affordable credits continued to be a major limiting factor, but the Bank of Tanzania was at least partly successful in bringing down the lending rate in the banking sector to around 13% (from a prohibitive 20%). A joint credit bureau for all commercial banks was to share important information and thus lower the risks of providing business credits.

The government actively continued with efforts to attract **foreign investors**, for instance by holding its fourth international investors conference on 23 November in London. New FDI had slightly increased in 2003 to $ 248 m (after a peak of $ 517 m in 1999 for major gold mining investments) and was still primarily going into the mining sector, and only to a much lesser extent into tourism and manufacturing. Some new gold mines were opened by large multinational mining houses. Because of a long historical build-up, the stock of FDI was, however, still dominated by owners from Britain and Kenya, but since the mid-1990s **South African business interests** have become a new and seemingly dominating force, partly by grabbing at opportunities offered by privatisation. This pervasive South African presence was increasingly perceived as somewhat double-edged: officially welcomed as investors and managers, there was also a growing sentiment among the local business community that it was being sidelined and overrun by South Africans. Local business groups were also still hesitant about the feared negative impact of more competition resulting from the coming **EAC Customs Union**, while others now regretted the Tanzanian withdrawal from **COMESA**.

Despite significant improvements in the management of TANESCO, the **power sector** faced serious problems as a result of the drought and low water levels in dams for hydro-power generation, thus necessitating frequent power cuts, with negative effects for industrial production. An important new stage was reached in June with the start of electricity generation (two generators of 112 MW) from natural gas at the long-delayed Songo Songo project, with expectations of a further doubling of capacity in 2005. The rural electrification scheme made good progress. It was expected that in the following year only three district centres would remain without electricity supplies. **Tourism** recorded a new peak in 2004 with around 600,000 visitors, but the earnings of about $ 730 m remained almost unchanged from 2003.

Separate information on developments in **Zanzibar** continued to be very scarce. After the 2001 peace accord, some renewed aid support by donors had again been forthcoming on a limited scale and GDP growth in 2003 was estimated at about 5%. The year under review proved to be difficult for the island economy because of the negative repercussions on tourism of the political unrest and violence and depressed world market prices for cloves, the traditional main export crop.

Kurt Hirschler & Rolf Hofmeier

Uganda

The country was gripped by debate over issues of constitutional change, namely the return to a multiparty system of government and the removal of the two-term limit on the presidency, and strengthened attempts to end the conflict in the north. In view of the upcoming presidential and parliamentary elections in 2006, the opposition intended to organise into a coalition. While relations with Sudan were improving, relations with Rwanda and the DR Congo remained tense. The donor community put great pressure on the country to find a peaceful solution to the northern conflict, to carry through with political reforms and to improve budgetary performance.

Domestic Politics

The **recommendations of the Constitutional Review Commission (CRC)** on a number of issues requiring constitutional amendment were made public during the first months of the year. They were based on the report submitted by the CRC to Minister of Justice and Constitutional Affairs Janet Mukwaya in December 2003, after two years of review. The recommendations basically set the political agenda for the entire year. Among many other issues, the CRC proposed that the issue of lifting the two-term presidential limit should be decided by referendum, and the transition from the de facto one-party 'Movement' system to a multiparty system by parliamentary approval. Both these possible amendments to the constitution had been raised by President Yoweri Museveni in the preceding year and have since been the subject of discussion and controversy. With regard to a multiparty system, the question was not so much whether it should be instituted, since both government and opposition agreed in principle on the desirability and timeliness of changing the political system. The debate was rather about how the change should be brought about. The preferred procedure envisaged in the constitution is through a referendum. Concerning presidential term limits, the constitution provided that these could be amended by a two-thirds major-ity of parliament in a secret ballot. Hence, the CRC recommendations were diametrically opposed to the constitutional provisions. The issue of removing presidential term limits was contentious not only with regard to the **modus operandi** but also, and perhaps more impor-tantly, with regard to the question itself. Factions in parliament, in the opposition, and even in the Movement system saw the move as a ploy to give Museveni another term, since according to the constitution he could not stand again in the 2006 presidential elections. He remained silent about his intentions throughout the year, although many observers believed he would stand again, given a constitutional amendment.

On the basis of the CRC recommendations, cabinet drafted a **white paper** and submit-ted it to parliament in July. This paper was to accompany the 'Constitution Amendment Bill', which was to come forward for parliamentary approval. It determined that the return to a multiparty system and the lifting of presidential term limits were to be effected through an amendment to the constitution in parliament before being endorsed in a national referendum. Together with this paper, cabinet released a 'political roadmap to 2006', which was a plan, complete with timeframe and action items, leading to the upcoming presiden-tial and parliamentary elections: Parliament was to decide on the 'Constitution Amendment Bill' between September and December. The referendum to approve the bill and its ratification by district councils was to take place in February 2005. Campaigns for the pres-idential and parliamentary polls were scheduled for November 2005 to February 2006. The final elections were to be held in March 2006, and, to save time and money, elections for district council chairs were to be held on the same day. As became clear from the white paper, cabinet did not accept many of CRC's other recommendations, such as reducing the number of members of parliament from 305 to 120, phasing out the ten Uganda People's Defence Forces (UPDF) representatives in parliament, or forcing MPs to give up their par-liamentary seats once they become ministers. Cabinet also did not support the introduction of federalism and decided instead that districts could form regional governments through a tiered system. This decision attracted sharp criticism from the Buganda kingdom, which had long pressed for federal status. A number of high-level meetings between government and Buganda representatives were held but collapsed in August because their positions were irreconcilable.

Upon the release of the roadmap, it became clear that government was already about three months behind schedule. This delay dragged on over the year and parliament did not even receive the draft 'Constitution Amendment Bill', and hence made no final decisions, before the end of December. The delay was partly due to the decision of the constitutional court on 17 November, which **nullified some restrictive sections of the Political Parties and Organisations Act** (PPOA). For example, parties were now free to hold delegates' conferences and choose as their leader a Ugandan who had lived outside the country for three years. Some traditional parties, which had thus far refused to register, now indicated their willingness to do so soon. However, government filed an appeal against the decision, and while this was pending, parliament could not proceed with some essential work on the political roadmap. Due to the apparently inadequate timeframe, some MPs suggested unsuccessfully that elections should be postponed immediately as this would be inevitable in any case. There was considerable concern about potential political and constitutional confusion, based on the negative example of the 2000 Referendum Act, which had been passed in a hurry. In response to a complaint by a group of opposition politicians, the constitutional court ruled on 25 June that the 2000 national referendum, in which Ugandans had voted for the continuation of the Movement system, was unconstitutional because it did not comply with legislative procedures. A widespread debate about the consequences of this ruling ensued. While Museveni clearly rejected the ruling, the opposition claimed that it nullified the government and made it illegal. In consequence, the government launched a successful appeal in the supreme court (2 September): the court held that the 2000 referendum was valid although the act under which it was held was null and void.

The 25-member government delegation under the national political commissar, Dr. Crispus Kiyonga, appointed in October 2003 to talk with different opposition groups in order to achieve agreement on the country's return to a multiparty system, took up its mandate early in the year and met several times with the new **opposition alliance, G7**. This alliance was formed in February by the seven traditional opposition parties – Conservative Party (CP), Democratic Party (DP), Justice Forum (JEEMA), National Democrats Forum (NDF), Reform Agenda (RA), The Free Movement (TFM), and Uganda People's Congress (UPC). In addition to having dialogue with government, G7's aim was to defeat Museveni's National Resistance Movement Organisation (NRMO) in the 2006 elections. The member parties recognised the need for unity based on the success of the Rainbow Coalition in Kenya that ousted former President Daniel arap Moi in 2002. They signed a memorandum of understanding on 18 March in which they agreed to cooperate in undertaking joint rallies, demonstrations, seminars, workshops, lobbying and civic awareness campaigns as well as in issuing joint statements on agreed political matters. In early April, G7 quit the transition talks with the government on the basis of government's alleged refusal to accede to the alliance's demands for meaningful dialogue. It also accused government of promoting the creation of artificial pro-government political groups, an apparent reference to newly formed or registered parties to whom government was talking.

Despite their expressed inclination to join forces in the run-up to the elections, most G7 members apparently neither seriously considered forming a single coalition party nor selecting a joint presidential candidate. Instead, each party held internal discussions about its own candidate. The DP leader Paul Ssemogerere decided to retire after 22 years in office and was thus ineligible to stand for the 2006 elections. Nasser Ssebagala, former Kampala mayor, openly declared his intention in early August to run on a DP ticket, and he was the most likely to be the final choice among several alternatives. UPC did not have an obvious candidate, because Milton Obote, 80 years of age and living in exile in Zambia, was still the formal leader. However, in July, James Rwanyarare, UPC presidential policy commission chair, hinted about his plans for the contest. Instead of selecting a separate presidential candidate at its delegates' conference in late July, RA opted for a joint opposition coalition. It merged with two other opposition groups, the Parliamentary Advocacy Forum (Pafo), a group of MPs opposed to lifting the presidential term limits, and NDF, to form the **Forum for Democratic Change (FDC)**. Due to its nationwide appeal, FDC had the potential to seriously challenge NRMO. Consequently, the future FDC candidate, possibly exiled RA leader Col. Kizza Besigye, was likely to become Museveni's main rival in the 2006 elections. The government apparently recognised this danger and there were reports that it set up a task force up by the end of the year to observe the FDC and devise and implement an election strategy for NRMO. Allegedly, authorities even attempted to delay or prevent FDC's registration as a political party under PPOA, but the party finally succeeded in being registered on 17 December. It was said that the FDC wanted to hold discussions with the remaining G7 members to form one large coalition fielding one candidate. Indeed, on 29 December the newly formed G6, comprising FDC, UPC, DP, CP, TFM and JEEMA, declared that they planned to field a single presidential candidate.

The 18–year-long **conflict in northern Uganda**, which has resulted in 100,000 deaths, 1.6 million displaced people and 20,000 abducted children, assumed a new shape in the course of the year. On the one hand, internal and external actors continued to put great pressure on government to speed up its efforts to resolve the matter finally. Most importantly, they called for peace talks with the rebels of the Lord's Resistance Army (LRA) and appealed to Museveni not to persist with a military approach. On the other hand, LRA was severely weakened in the second half of the year, when a considerable number of rebels surrendered to the UPDF. In the first half, the rebels had continued their atrocities and repeatedly attacked villages and camps for internally displaced persons. The worst of these attacks took place on 21 February at Barlonyo camp, about 25 km north of Lira, which left more than 200 people dead. According to local leaders, as many as 337 people were killed. This incident was not only a humanitarian disaster, but it also attracted widespread criticism of the UPDF, which had not been present at the camp it was supposed to protect. The local militia posted there were easily overwhelmed by the rebels. Since this lack of security had basically made the attack possible, the government apologised officially and stepped-up the UPDF presence. Museveni also blamed the donor community for the escalation because they had insisted on a cap on the defence budget of 2% of GDP.

The government's strategy of increasing military pressure on the LRA paid off by the middle of the year. Between May and August, **an increasing number of rebels, including rebel commanders, surrendered** to government forces. Simultaneously, UPDF operations finally proved successful. According to military statistics, the army captured 215 rebels and senior commanders and killed some 800 between January and July, while about 1,800 former abductees, mainly children, were rescued. This success was also partly due to strengthened cooperation between UPDF and the Sudanese army (see below). The latter allowed the Ugandan forces to advance temporarily beyond the red line, the last point inside Sudan up to which they could pursue LRA fighters. In the hope of killing LRA leader Joseph Kony, UPDF attacked his camp in Bilinyiang and killed more than 120 rebels on 28 July. Kony survived the attack and escaped. These developments represented a flicker of hope to most observers. After mid-June, there were hardly any abductions, and while there were a few ambushes and killings, these were not as devastating as before. Consequently, plans for the rehabilitation of the north were spurred on.

On 30 August, at the first meeting between three rebel commanders and Uganda's ambassador to the AU, Joseph Ocwet, in Gulu, the former indicated they were ready for peace talks. A second meeting was scheduled for 6 September and some persons called for third party mediation. Museveni rejected this but stated that the rebels could talk to Betty Bigombe, former minister for pacification of the north, who had credibility with both sides. In 1994, Bigombe almost succeeded in bringing the rebels out of the bush, but as the talks progressed, the government gave the insurgents seven days to surrender or face the wrath of the army. The rebels chose the latter and war continued. In the current efforts, **Bigombe again became chief negotiator**. The second meeting had to be cancelled because UPDF attacked an LRA camp on 4 September and killed one of the commanders present at the first meeting. Understandably, this seriously undermined the trust of the others.

However, it did not destroy the hopes of ending the conflict soon. On 2 November, LRA Brigadier Sam Kolo told the BBC that the LRA was keen to have talks with the government. On 14 November, Museveni responded and declared a **7-day unilateral ceasefire** in a limited area in the north to allow a group of LRA members to meet with government representatives. This followed a period of considerable uncertainty as both government and LRA waited to see how the other would react. Yet, as expected, the UPDF withdrew from the safe area, large groups of rebels gathered there and Bigombe's team was able to meet with a rebel delegation. The main source of remaining uncertainty was Kony's whereabouts. There were reports that he was in Sudan and had ordered his units to follow him, but the LRA commanders involved in the negotiations confirmed their commitment to the peace process. After intense preparation and three extensions of the ceasefire, the first face-to-face meeting between LRA commanders and high-level government representatives, including Minister for Internal Affairs Ruhakana Rugunda and Minister for Security Betty Akech, took place on 28 December. The negotiating team agreed on the immediate cessation of hostilities and the signing of a ceasefire agreement on 30 December. Thereafter, further meetings would address specific issues raised by both sides. Contrary to most expectations, the rebels delayed signing the ceasefire as they were reportedly still involved in internal consultations. Nevertheless, the year ended with strong optimism that a peaceful resolution to the conflict was within reach.

At the end of January, Museveni asked the **International Criminal Court (ICC)** to open a probe into the human rights abuses of the LRA. Several national and international peace and human rights groups strongly opposed this move, claiming that treating the rebels as criminals made peaceful resolution of the conflict impossible. At the same time, they urged the ICC to investigate crimes committed by all sides of the conflict, i.e., LRA and UPDF, if a probe was to be launched. By the end of July, the ICC officially began its investigations, and in August, a nine-member team arrived in Uganda to prepare for the inquiries.

Foreign Affairs

In the course of the year, a further **improvement of Uganda's relations with her neighbour Sudan** was shaping up. Diplomatic ties between the two countries had been strained throughout the past decade as Uganda repeatedly accused Sudan of supporting the LRA and Sudan counterclaimed that Uganda backed the Sudan People's Liberation Movement/Army (SPLM/A). Following a two-day joint ministerial commission in mid-April, the two countries signed a framework cooperation agreement in order to normalise their bilateral relations. In addition, they signed agreements on foreign affairs cooperation, agriculture and animal resources, and considered future accords on security, immigration, refugees, water and air transport and other issues. This meeting represented a milestone but it was not the only positive development. Different factions in Sudan showed willingness to support Ugandan efforts against the LRA after several villages in southern Sudan suffered atrocities at the hands of the rebels. Two Sudanese rebel groups, the Equatoria Defence Force (EDF) and the SPLM/A, indicated they would retaliate against the LRA for their attacks on civilians inside Sudan. They offered to assist the Ugandan troops but were turned down as the official 'Operation Iron Fist' strictly forbade the UPDF from fighting alongside Sudanese rebels. This prohibition could, of course, be superseded once the southern Sudan peace agreement is signed, which would make the SPLM/A part of the government. Operation Iron Fist, agreed by Uganda and Sudan in March 2002, authorised UPDF to enter, search and destroy LRA bases within Sudan up to the red line. Beyond that line, the Sudanese army was to take over. At the end of June, Uganda asked Khartoum for help to locate Kony, saying he was hiding beyond the line. Subsequently, and for the first time, the Sudanese army demonstrated its full commitment to the campaign against the LRA by blocking the rebels' escape route northwards, providing additional intelligence and even tolerating the advance of UPDF beyond the red line. Furthermore, surrendered LRA fighters reported that after January LRA received no military supplies from Sudan's armed forces.

As the year drew to a close, signs of a comprehensive peace agreement between the Sudanese government and the SPLM/A became more and more apparent. This in turn raised hopes that a resolution to the conflict in northern Uganda was within reach, since it would be harder henceforth for LRA to retreat to its bases in southern Sudan.

At the beginning of the year, it seemed that Uganda was improving **relations with the DR Congo and Rwanda** as well. Once Ugandan and Rwandan troops had withdrawn from the DR Congo in 2003, regional tension began to diminish. Museveni and Rwanda's president Paul Kagame repeatedly hailed the change for the better in January and February. According to the UN mission in the DR Congo, in May Uganda and the DR Congo agreed to set up a system to monitor and eliminate border violations with two mixed verification teams. However, tension flared up when fighting broke out between Banyamulenge (Congolese Tutsi) rebels and loyalist government troops in the South Kivu region in the DR Congo on 26 May. Because of strong concerns that this conflict could spread and jeopardise the DR Congo peace process, the UN Security Council issued a statement on 23 June warning Uganda, Rwanda and Burundi to stay out of the crisis and refrain from supporting any of the fighting groups. In response, the Ugandan government gave the assurance it would not intervene in any form, and asked the AU to investigate the fighting. The situation remained relatively quiet until 13 August, when more than 150 Congolese (mainly Banyamulenge) refugees were massacred at a Burundian refugee camp, an event that dramatically increased the risk of war in the Great Lakes region.

It appeared that this incident jolted neighbouring countries into action. At the end of August, Uganda, Rwanda and the DR Congo agreed to disarm all rebel and militia groups operating in their respective territories within one year. They determined to establish a permanent commission to implement the process, which would include measures for disarmament, demobilisation, reintegration and resettlement. In the same vein, the three countries signed a tripartite security agreement on 25 October, which would lead to the creation of a commission for dealing with numerous diplomatic and security issues in the region. Additionally, they participated in the International Conference on Peace, Security, Democracy and Development in the Great Lakes region, which took place on 19–20 November in Dar es Salaam. Eleven heads of state signed a declaration of **commitment to end conflict in the Great Lakes region** but the protocols for implementing this declaration were still to be worked out. However, at the end of November the situation changed for the worse when Rwanda and Uganda expelled each other's diplomats for alleged espionage and support of rebel groups. Only a week later, Kagame renewed his threat to invade the DR Congo to hunt down Rwandan Hutu rebels who were supposedly advancing on his country. The DR Congo asked the UN Security Council to impose sanctions on Rwanda. The UN subsequently warned Rwanda not to use military force, saying such a move could undermine international efforts to stabilise the region, but it did not opt for sanctions. Reports of Rwandan troops having entered the DR Congo and of UPDF troops having deployed along the DR Congo border remained unconfirmed by the end of the year.

Following these developments, the DR Congo effectively cancelled a high-level inter-government meeting scheduled for 9 December with Uganda and Rwanda. This meeting, mediated by the US, was aimed at developing mechanisms by which the countries could peacefully work out their differences and ensure the security of their respective borders. Another meeting was planned for January 2005.

Uganda's **relations with the US** remained friendly and supportive. In April, the choice of Entebbe for a meeting of representatives from countries that receive US aid under the East Africa Counter-Terrorism Initiative showed the importance that Washington attached to the role of Uganda in fighting terrorism in Africa. Although unconfirmed, there were reports that the US supported the UPDF by providing aerial and other electronic surveillance data to assist in the hunt for the LRA. In 2000, the US had suspended its military aid programmes to Uganda as a result of Uganda's incursion into the DR Congo. However, following the Ugandan withdrawal last year, US officials announced the resumption of what they described as a limited programme of non-lethal military assistance. In March, General Charles Wald, responsible for African operations at the US Central Command, visited Museveni and explained that US aid against the LRA had to be more than moral support. The US ambassador to Uganda, Jimmy Kolker, added that there must be humanitarian and diplomatic as well as military elements in dealing with the conflict. However, it turned out that US support was not unlimited. Kolker said in December that Uganda risked its preferred status under the African Growth and Opportunity Act (AGOA) if political reforms were not carried through satisfactorily. Other bilateral and multilateral donors issued similar warnings and urged the government to adhere to the political roadmap. Moreover, Uganda lost out in a competition for US aid under the Millennium Challenge Account because of serious concerns about governance and corruption.

Socioeconomic Developments

After a three-month delay, the governments of Uganda, Kenya and Tanzania, as members of the **East African Community (EAC)**, signed a protocol on 2 March that, when ratified, would formally establish a **customs union**. It provided for the establishment of a three-band common external tariff structure and the elimination of internal tariffs, which would ultimately lead to a common market. The signing had been postponed twice because of the illness of the Tanzanian president, Benjamin Mkapa, and, perhaps more importantly, because of disagreement on the details of the treaty. Ugandan and Tanzanian manufacturers had always been concerned that they could suffer severe losses from a customs union because they would face stiff competition from the generally advanced Kenyan manufacturing industry. In response to these concerns, a five-year transition period was agreed, during which a number of Kenyan imports into Uganda and Tanzania would attract minimal duties. The protocol was ratified by the three states in December and the customs union was to come into effect in January 2005. This development carried much symbolic weight, as previous attempts at regional integration had collapsed in 1977 when ideological differences, Idi Amin's tyranny in Uganda and fears that Kenya's more developed economy would dominate had led to the break-up of the EAC. However, the success of current efforts depended on the resolution of potential conflicts within other regional trading blocks, since Tanzania is also a member of SADC and Uganda and Kenya of COMESA.

The **budget for financial year 2004/05**, which began on 1 July, was presented on 10 June. According to Finance Minister Gerald Ssendaula, it aimed at promoting economic growth and reducing poverty through development of and competitiveness in the private sector as well as the efficiency and effectiveness of public expenditures. The budget reflected the priorities set out in the Poverty Eradication Action Plan (PEAP), which had just been revised for a second time since its elaboration in 1997. Total domestic revenue in 2004/05 amounted to 54% of total public expenditures, and the budget deficit, projected at 11% of GDP, was to be financed by external grants and concessional loans. MPs, business people and the donor community generally welcomed the budget, saying it reflected the overall concerns of the population, but they criticised it for not addressing the insufficiency of domestic revenues and the need to maintain adequate positions in defence and public administration. Low revenues had always been an issue but became more pressing in the face of losses from entering the EAC costums union. Yet the budget maintained most existing tax measures and did not introduce new taxes: it only raised the excise duty on cigarettes and spirits and proposed further measures to restrict importation of used commodities. High expenditures on defence and public administration, including regular supplementary spending, had long been cause for criticism, in particular from donors. Even though they recognised the country's security problems, they were not convinced that additional defence resources would be spent effectively. Additionally, they rejected the budget proposal of earmarking USh 30 bn ($ 16.6 m) for the upcoming referendum. This position was later revised and adjusted to USh 22 bn ($ 12.1 m).

Preliminary data indicated that **real GDP growth** amounted to 5.7% in 2003/04. The construction and communications sectors were the driving forces behind this growth, but a rebound in agriculture due to good weather also played a role. Non-coffee cash crops, i.e., maize, cotton, tea, flowers and fish, performed particularly well, and strong growth in export volumes together with improved terms of trade helped to narrow the current account deficit. Annual headline inflation declined from 10.2% in June 2003 to 1.4% in May 2004 as food crop prices fell sharply. Underlying inflation, which excludes food crops, declined from 5.4% to 4.8% over the same period. For 2004/05, real GDP growth was projected at 6% and underlying inflation was expected to be around 4%. There were indications that headline inflation was likely to increase again, owing to unevenly distributed rainfall during the first half of the year and a resulting poor harvest.

Under the second and third reviews of the Poverty Reduction Growth Facility (PRGF) conducted in February and September, the IMF praised the country for its sound macro-economic policies. However, it emphasised that the country faced a number of challenges in the near future, most notably reversing the recent setback in poverty reduction, strengthening budget execution and the quality of government spending, and achieving a more sustainable external debt position. The IMF further indicated that corruption remained a severe problem, and this was confirmed by several other institutions throughout the year. A World Economic Forum survey among 21 African countries found Uganda to be the seventh most corrupt. The Anti-Corruption Coalition of Uganda published its report in October claiming that government had created a class of people who could profit from corruption with impunity. According to the 2003 report on graft and abuse of public office presented by Inspector General of Government (IGG) Jotham Tumwesigye, the police force was the most corrupt institution, followed by local government, the judiciary and public hospitals. It was indicative of the government's position on the issue when the IGG's contract was not renewed in November despite his good performance.

The government attempted to revive plans for the construction of the **Bujagali hydroelectric dam**, which had been suspended last year after the US-based AES corporation withdrew from the project. Out of 16 companies that responded to the call for tenders, five were short-listed in May and the final winner was likely to be announced by mid-2005. Yet, it is already conceivable that Wakiso Hydro Consortium, which included the South African Eskom, is the favourite to gain the contract. Norpak Power, a Norwegian consortium, pressed the authorities for permission to go ahead with plans for another hydroelectric dam at Karuma. The Norwegian state company SNPI announced an interest in becoming involved in this project, given that the Ugandan government gave it priority over Bujagali. Museveni had always preferred the latter, but realising the country's future power needs may cause him to change his mind. Access to the Nile's water resources was controversial as the upstream countries were trying to renegotiate the 1929 Nile Water Treaty, which gave Egypt exclusive rights over the resource. In April, Museveni became the first head of state to enter the debate publicly by calling on Egypt not to monopolise this water.

Susan Steiner

VI. Southern Africa

The relative stability of the sub-region during the year signalled positive trends, and these were enhanced in most countries by modest socioeconomic progress. A series of elections resulted in limited political changes, partly in terms of replacing individual office bearers but more so in the consolidation of governments in power. Sub-regional collaboration remained unspectacular but on track, and underlined the existence of a concept of a Southern African community of states. However, the hegemonic role of South Africa as the sub-regional powerhouse both economically and politically remained a challenge for closer mutual ties among SADC countries. Natural disasters, such as drought and floods, were less spectacular than in past years and produced fewer emergencies. The devastating effects of the HIV/AIDS scourge, however, continued unabated and further undermined development prospects.

Sub-regional Organisations and International Networks

Southern African countries acted within a **multiplicity of overlapping sub-regional integration initiatives**, which involve five different organisations. Swaziland is the only country that is a member of all of them. Together with South Africa, Namibia and Lesotho, it constitutes the Common Monetary Area (CMA). The CMA plus Botswana (which has the pula as an independent currency not pegged to the rand) make up the South African Customs Union (SACU). Together with nine other countries (including the DR Congo and Tanzania, which are not part of this sub-regional chapter) they made up SADC at the beginning of the year. In addition to these three core bodies for substantive sub-regional integration, eight Southern African countries were also members of COMESA (see the chapter on Eastern Africa for more details) and seven were active in the Cross Border Initiative (CBI). Sponsored by the EU, the World Bank and the IMF, the CBI has since 1990 aimed not only at removing barriers to internal trade, but also at lowering and harmonising member countries' external tariffs, so as to minimise the trade-diverting impact of a preferential trade area. Parallel processes and initiatives within and between these different sub-regional configurations do not necessarily conflict, but an ECA report during the year underscored that "the presence of so many communities spreads limited resources thin, complicates the overall continental integration process, and puts enormous strains on governments' ability and resources to cope with diverse agendas and exigencies." The report considered it imperative "to move rapidly to rationalize the regional economic communities."

In 2004, **SADC** had a total of 34 legal instruments in place. These comprised 23 protocols, four declarations, three memorandums of understanding, two charters, one agreement and one defence pact. They covered the following distinct core areas: trade, industry, finance and investment; infrastructure and services; food, agriculture and natural resources; social and human development and special programmes; politics, defence and security; and dispute settlement and other legal means. The SADC community of states was reduced to 13 members when the **Seychelles** officially ceased its membership in June, having hardly ever paid its annual membership fees since its admittance in September 1997. The main reasons for the withdrawal were that SADC was not considered central to the country's economic, political or security interests. The small island state felt neither able to afford the frequent travel to meetings nor willing to contribute the requisite 2% of its GDP to the organisation. Compliance with payment obligations to SADC was, however, generally high and could be taken as renewed political commitment to the body: all but one of the member states paid their 2004–05 contributions.

In contrast to the smallest African country's decision to opt out, **Madagascar**, one of the world's largest islands, officially applied for membership at SADC's annual summit of heads of state in Grand Baie, Mauritius (16–17 August). The meeting established new criteria and decided to accord the island the status for one year as a candidate member, to provide it an opportunity to demonstrate how it would meet its obligations to implement various SADC legal instruments. A visit by an SADC troika from Tanzania, Mauritius and Botswana (14–17 December) for further consultations with the government and a wide spectrum of stakeholders paved the way for the country to submit a detailed timeframe and action plan for meeting its obligations as a further step towards full membership of SADC. This situation represented a significant strategic and geopolitical shift for Madagascar, hitherto much more oriented towards the former French colonial power than towards closer links with the Southern African sub-continent. It also underlined growing economic ties with South Africa, which in January opened an embassy in Antananarivo.

During the year, SADC intensified its collaboration with **NEPAD**, which was instituted during 2001 mainly as a result of initiatives pursued by South Africa's President Thabo Mbeki. The NEPAD secretariat was established at the Development Bank of Southern Africa in Midrand. Mbeki's economic advisor, Wiseman Nkhulu, became its executive secretary. Details of NEPAD's continental and other sub-regional activities are presented elsewhere in this volume. The Southern African dimensions of NEPAD became more visible with a high level SADC-NEPAD ministerial meeting in Tanzania (15–18 May). Meetings between senior officials from both organisations as well as another high level NEPAD meeting with SADC followed on 7–8 and 12 August respectively in Mauritius, to precede the sub-regional body's annual summit. This closer collaboration represented acknowledgement by NEPAD of the growing relevance of regional economic communities. As a result, SADC submitted to NEPAD 23 projects with a sub-regional dimension under a short-term action plan. The summit also mandated sub-regional representatives on the NEPAD steering committee and on the heads of state and government implementation committee – Angola, Botswana, Mozambique and South Africa plus Mauritius (4+1 Group) – to enhance their interaction with the region as SADC's representatives on NEPAD, with South Africa as the spokesperson of the group. A **NEPAD stakeholder dialogue** was held on 22–23 October on the occasion of the initiative's third anniversary in Johannesburg. The results of the preliminary stocktaking were mixed. South Africa's President Mbeki noted that "the lack of capacity at regional levels [is] such that even when we have mobilised the necessary resources, we are held back by the fact that we cannot translate some of the good and visionary ideas into concrete, implementable programmes." The continued operation of the NEPAD secretariat from South Africa caused increased discomfort among other African stakeholders in the initiative, who saw this as a sign of the continued dominance of South African interests, especially since NEPAD reports demonstrated the preponderance of South African institutions and companies in investment in and the implementation of NEPAD-related projects.

On 15 July, **SACU** states, representing one of the oldest sub-regional bodies, in existence for more than a century, replaced the agreement of 1969. As the preamble to the new agreement states, this was necessitated by new developments in international trade relations at the beginning of the 21st century. The agreement provided for the joint exercise of responsibility over decisions affecting tariff setting and created a common revenue pool, thus replacing South Africa's formerly rather exclusive role in the administration of and decision-making in the customs union. For some member countries (Lesotho, Namibia and Swaziland), SACU had in previous years been the single most important source of state revenue. The first meetings of the newly created SACU council of ministers and the customs union commission took place in Windhoek from 20 to 22 September. SACU entered into a number of negotiations to conclude free trade agreements during the year. In the negotiation process, the body is considered a single legal entity and, hence, requires unity of purpose. A fifth round of negotiations for a **SACU-US FTA** opened in Maseru on 4 April. However, during the year it became clear that the FTA would not be concluded as originally intended by year's end. After the cancellation of two negotiating sessions, the South African chief trade negotiator announced publicly in late October that because of problems on both sides with some of the basic issues, the deadline would not be met. Part of the problem was the lack of harmonised trade policies among the five SACU countries, which hampered the negotiation process, as did certain demands advanced by the US. Consequently, entry into the first FTA ever between the US and any sub-Saharan African country was delayed.

US trade policy continued to offer privileged trade relations in select areas to several Southern African economies through preferential access to the US market under **AGOA**. Tariff reductions primarily on exports of textiles and apparel to the US had resulted in recent years in the establishment of a textile industry or its significant expansion, especially in Lesotho, Mauritius, Madagascar, Namibia and Swaziland. This had an associated impact on employment creation in these countries, although working conditions were appalling and were tantamount to extreme exploitation of the cheap and abundant labour force. Profit maximisation from these 'sweat shops' also benefited from the maximum subsidisation of operations and investments by the host countries and tax exemptions on surpluses. Notwithstanding these favourable conditions for attracting foreign direct investment in the sector over the past few years, the comparative advantages of the textile producing companies (mainly operated by foreign – in particular East Asian – capital) declined when the Multi Fibre Agreement expired at the end of the year. As a result, exports from other countries are faced with fewer tariff handicaps and the degree of competition, mainly from the vast number of specialised Chinese producers, increased considerably. Several textile manufacturers (especially in Swaziland and Lesotho) had therefore closed or reduced operations by the end of the year and had retrenched thousands of workers. This placed more pressure on the already precarious socioeconomic conditions and provoked a range of labour disputes and strikes.

New and potentially controversial trade negotiations began during the year between the European Commission (EC) of the EU and several Southern African countries over an **Economic Partnership Agreement** (EPA). SADC members had to choose whether to negotiate within either the East and Southern African (ESA) bloc (see the Eastern Africa chapter) or as the SADC group. Angola, Botswana, Lesotho, Mozambique, Namibia, Swaziland and Tanzania opted to negotiate with the EC under the SADC configuration. South Africa – which had already entered a FTA with the EU in 1999 in the form of its Trade, Development and Cooperation Agreement, since it was not considered to be an ACP member country because of its more advanced emerging economy – participated as an observer and in a supportive capacity. EPA negotiations between SADC and the EC were officially launched on 8 July in Windhoek in the presence of EC Commissioners Danuta Hübner and Poul Nielson. Botswana's trade minister acted as SADC coordinator. A joint road-map was adopted, but criticism of the divisive EC approach (subdividing the countries of the sub-region into different SADC and ESA blocs) and of efforts to eliminate the preferential trade clauses that existed under the Cotonou Agreement for Least Developed Countries subsequently mounted. South Africa's Minister of Finance Trevor Manuel summarised the scepticism among Southern African countries when he stated in a lecture at the University of Sussex on 2 December: "Greater transparency of intentions would also be helpful – the EU's request for Africa to divide into groups to negotiate . . . does little to help Africa coordinate its trade policies – thereby reinforcing the legacy of our colonial economic relationships."

Socioeconomic Developments

The sub-regional economy had been estimated to grow during the year by an average of 3.5% (3.2% in 2003). **Growth rates** were expected to be above 5% in Angola, Botswana, Mauritius and Mozambique. Seven of the SADC countries remained below the 10% **inflation rate**. South Africa achieved by far the lowest rate over the year, with a record low of less than 0.2% in January and the highest rate of 3.4% in December. In contrast, Zimbabwe's inflation rate (at some 350% for the year) escalated to a monthly maximum of 622.8% in January and ended the year with a monthly minimum of 132% in December. Angola (with monthly inflation rates between 70% and 31%) ranked second, with an annual average above 55%, followed by Zambia, Mozambique and Malawi, each with an annual rate of close to 20%. **Budget deficits** remained below 5% in Botswana, Lesotho, Mauritius, Mozambique, Namibia, South Africa and Swaziland. Despite modest average progress in socioeconomic terms, however, the region was not on track for meeting the **MDGs**. This was partly the result of a mix of internal structural factors, humanitarian crises and a shortfall in external support. The 'African Economic Outlook' for 2004–05, submitted by the ADB in collaboration with the OECD Development Centre, contained an overview of the extent to which African countries had either achieved or were on track to achieve seven defined sectoral targets. Mauritius was the only African country that scored 7 out of 7, Botswana and Namibia showed remarkable progress (5 of 7), followed by Lesotho, Malawi, and South Africa (4 of 7), Madagascar, Swaziland and Zimbabwe (3 of 7), Angola and Zambia (2 of 7) and Mozambique (0).

After many years of chronic food shortages, there was a partial recovery in the **agricultural sector**. In order to address the issue of food security in a more coordinated manner, SADC member states committed themselves on 10 April, during an extraordinary summit on agriculture and food security in Tanzania, to revamp the agricultural sector. Food supply assessments indicated a regional maize surplus of 1.27 m tonnes for the 2004–05 marketing year. A mid-season review of rainfall during October to December concluded that the rainy season had started in the northern half of the sub-region in time for normal planting. The actual food situation continued, however, to vary considerably. **Food security** conditions remained critical in those countries that had experienced a poor productive season in 2003–04. According to the FAO, external food assistance was required in March by Angola, Lesotho, Malawi, Mozambique, Swaziland and Zimbabwe. The World Food Programme warned in a press release (22 December) that in response to an appeal for $ 404 m over a three-year-period, only about $ 10 m (some 2.5%) had been received. Relief agencies seemed to be more eager to respond with offers of humanitarian emergency support to tsunami victims at the turn of the year than to persist with necessary aid commitments for feeding the most vulnerable people in Southern African countries, who continued for the most part to be in Lesotho, Malawi, Swaziland and Zimbabwe. SADC has not yet conceptualised a comprehensive common **land policy** or integrated land reform within a wider rural development strategy. Given the sensitivity of this issue and ongoing or looming land disputes, particularly in Zimbabwe, Namibia and South Africa, this is a priority that ought to be addressed without delay.

SADC's development agenda was embodied in the **Regional Indicative Strategy Development Plan** (RISDP), approved by heads of state in 2003 and officially launched on 12 March. The plan is closely linked to the NEPAD initiatives summarised above, and is aimed at deepening sub-regional integration through a comprehensive programme of long-term economic and social policies and the provision of strategic direction. The RISDP is implemented on a national basis, with SADC playing the coordinating role through its Gaborone-based secretariat. The sub-region's **energy sector** was tested by ever-growing consumption demands (annual growth over the last six years being estimated at 3%) and will be challenged by supply constraints in the near future. In its final communiqué, the SADC summit expressed concerns about the power supply situation and encouraged immediate action to address the problem. Projects to overcome the looming shortfall were identified within the Southern African Power Pool (SAPP). They include the interconnection of Malawi to SAPP via Mozambique, of Tanzania to SAPP via Zambia, an upgrading of the Zambia-DR Congo link, the interconnection of Angola via the proposed Western Power Corridor Project (WESTCOR) and the establishment of a Zambia-Namibia link. SADC energy ministers met in Johannesburg (22 October) to discuss strategies for coping with the diminishing generation capacity. The way was paved for the formation of the WESTCOR joint venture company when five participating countries (Angola, Botswana, the DR Congo, Namibia and South Africa) and their national power utilities respectively signed an intergovernmental memorandum of understanding and an inter-utility memo-randum of understanding. SADC also identified a need for further efforts towards facili-tating the development and implementation of integrated **water infrastructure** policies, especially through the establishment of trans-border integrated water basin management. Given the crucial significance of water to human existence, failure by the parties to achieve full sub-regional coordination to date has been a major shortcoming.

SADC ministers with responsibilities for **social development** met in Cape Town on 27 November. Poverty eradication, combating HIV/AIDS, reduction of unemployment and underemployment as well as recognition of the 50% target set by the AU summit on gen-der were the priorities discussed. According to the SADC executive secretary, there had been remarkable advancement of **women in politics**: the level of 17.9% for female repre-sentation in parliaments was surpassed by only the Nordic countries (if they were broken out of the European average). South Africa exceeded the internationally set 30% benchmark for female representation in parliament and cabinet, thereby setting an example to most other countries in the world. With regard to **human resource** development, the first phase of the policy support initiative for capacity building in education, started in 2000, was com-pleted in June. National news agencies met in Maputo (20–23 September) to draft a char-ter to strengthen and guide the operations of the pool of SADC news agencies.

In 2004, the average **HIV prevalence** rate among adults in sub-Saharan Africa was esti-mated by UNAIDS at 7.4%, but the rate in Southern African countries is considerably higher. With about 14 m HIV-positive people, the pandemic represents the region's most serious development problem. The most affected countries were Swaziland, with an adult infection rate estimated at 38.8% (190,000 people), Botswana with 37.3% (330,000 peo-ple), Lesotho with 28.9% (300,000 people), Zimbabwe with 24.6% (1.6 m people), South Africa with 21.5% (5.1 m people), and Namibia with 21.3% (200,000 people), according to UNAIDS and WHO data for 2003–04. AIDS is now the leading cause of death and in some of these countries, the **average life expectancy** rate has dropped dramatically to below 40 years of age. Unless the trend is curbed, in the near future the population of some of Southern African countries will decline in absolute numbers due to the high mortality rates from AIDS.

The highest infection rates prevailed among the most productive age groups within these societies. These included young mothers as well as highly skilled and professionally qualified members of the workforce. The **socioeconomic impacts** of this demographic sit-uation are devastating and lasting and represent further, considerable development con-straints. The dramatically escalating number of HIV/AIDS orphans added to the burden. The budgetary implications for the most affected countries (in terms of health expenditure and other necessary interventions) posed increasingly – and almost impossibly – difficult choices.

Botswana made substantial progress in increasing access to **treatment**. An estimated 50% of those in need received anti-retroviral drugs, mainly due to an earlier government decision to provide free medication through the public health system. The South African government, after long debate and mass protests led by the Treatment Action Campaign (TAC), decided to approve a national HIV/AIDS treatment plan, but its implementation failed to reach expected targets.

HIV/AIDS has become a major contributory factor to long-term livelihood decline by reducing the workforce in families, and has significantly increased household **food insecurity**, especially among the most vulnerable rural and urban groups in Lesotho, Malawi, Mozambique, Swaziland, Zambia and Zimbabwe.

Conflict and Security

With the exception of the ongoing, even escalating crisis in Zimbabwe, and the increasingly worrying signs of an emerging crisis in Swaziland, the sub-region enjoyed a comparatively peaceful year with fairly stable conditions and limited unrest. Intra-state hostilities and armed conflicts in Angola and Mozambique had largely come to an end and no new violent clashes within or between countries in the sub-region occurred. Lesotho's prime minister, in his capacity as the chairperson of the **organ on politics, defence and security cooperation**, submitted to the Mauritius summit a Strategic Indicative Plan for the Organ (SIPO) as part of the process of effectively operationalising the body's protocol. SIPO is considered to be an enabling and complementary instrument for the implementation of the SADC development agenda embodied in the RISDP, which has as its core objective the creation of a peaceful and stable political and security environment. South Africa, the chair of the SADC organ since the Mauritius summit, made the establishment of a sub-regional **early warning system** and an SADC peacekeeping standby brigade a priority. However, progress on both remained undisclosed, indeed shrouded in secrecy. The interstate politics and diplomacy committee established in 2002 under the organ, approved at its June meeting in Maseru the principles on which the early warning system is to be based, and at its 25th meeting during July mandated a team of experts from the SADC and organ troikas (representing the previous, current and incoming chairpersons of the bodies) to initiate the establishment of such a system. From 11 to 17 October, a South African team visited ECOWAS, IGAD and the AU as part of a fact-finding process. The first SADC conference on defence and security cooperation was held in Maputo (6–7 December). While political tensions within the sub-region affected bilateral relations, in particular between Zimbabwe and its neighbours (especially Botswana), overall collaboration was characterised by a high degree of consensus on substantive matters and produced no serious security risks or potential for conflict among sub-regional partners.

Elections, democracy and human rights

The year was characterised by an unusually high number of local and, more importantly, **parliamentary and presidential elections**. Polls in Botswana, Malawi, Mozambique, Namibia and South Africa offered the ruling parties reason to celebrate. Not only did they retain political power, but in some cases (particularly South Africa and Namibia, but also Mozambique and Botswana) they also delivered victories substantial enough to result in what could be termed 'elected one-party states'. In the cases of Malawi, Mozambique and Namibia, the dominant parties were also able to usher in elected successors to veteran leaders Bakili Muluzi, Joaquim Chissano and Sam Nujoma respectively (in the latter case the newly elected MPs and the president took office only in March 2005). While the elections fell short of being 'free and fair' in more than a formal sense (if at all), in most of the countries, except possibly South Africa, the manipulations seemed to be less blatant than they had often been before, although in Namibia for the first time since independence the election results were successfully challenged in court by some opposition parties, resulting just before Christmas in a high court order for a vote recount (without subsequent changes in the results).

Parliamentary elections in **South Africa** (14 April) led to the consolidation of the African National Congress's majority. For the first time, the ANC achieved a two-thirds majority in parliament and hence the power to adopt constitutional changes without having to count on the cooperation of other parties. Instead of characterising the holding of a free multiparty election as a positive sign of the further consolidation of democracy 10 years after the end of apartheid, some commentators stressed the perils posed by the overwhelming dominance of one party. Thabo Mbeki was re-elected as president for a second term. One newer phenomenon was the increasing acceptance of constitutional limitations on the number of terms an individual could serve as president (usually two consecutive terms), even though this was often only as a result of internal party pressure on the incumbents to step down. The presidential and parliamentary elections in **Malawi** (20 May) ended with a slight shift in power. After a constitutional change proposed by his own party failed, President Bakili Muluzi was not permitted to run for office again. Because the opposition was not able to agree upon a single candidate, his successor was Bingu wa Mutharika, the candidate from Muluzi's United Democratic Front, while the established tripartite political landscape remained undisturbed by the parliamentary elections. In **Namibia**, President Sam Nujoma, in office since independence, opted not to stand again. In the parliamentary and presidential elections (15–16 November) his personally selected successor Hifikepunye Pohamba obtained over 76% of votes, a vote of confidence similar to what Nujoma had achieved before. Their South West African People's Organisation once again secured more than 75% of the votes and won 55 of the 72 seats in parliament. The third parliamentary and presidential elections since the end of the civil war in **Mozambique** (1–2 December) proceeded along similar lines, but were heavily criticised by international observers for the irregularities and intimidation. The US-based Carter Center spoke of a "shadow over Mozambique's democracy." President Joaquim Chissano was prevented from standing a third time as the presidential candidate for the Frente de Libertação de Moçambique. No major changes occurred in the course of parliamentary elections in **Botswana** (30 October), one of the oldest democracies on the continent. The Botswana Democratic Party gained 44 of 57 seats with 51.7% of the votes, the result of a clever (though dubious) redefinition of electoral districts and voting procedures based on the principle of 'winner takes all'.

The ongoing deterioration of fundamental human rights in Zimbabwe and the continued brutal repression of the opposition and its suspected supporters was the subject of the first-ever official criticism within the African Union. Despite the undiminished Zimbabwean crisis and further repressive trends in a number of other SADC countries (not least Swaziland, but also Angola), the overall human rights situation in the sub-region, including democratic minimum standards, compared favourably with most other parts of the continent. The **Freedom House Index** released during the year assigned to a total of 192 countries a ranking of between 1 (free) and 7 (un-free) for political rights and civil liberties, which it treated as separate categories. Within the sub-region, Zimbabwe (6/6), Swaziland (7/5) and Angola (6/5) competed with other pariahs in the world for the status of 'rogue systems', while South Africa (1/2), Botswana (2/2), Namibia and Lesotho (both 2/3) scored top marks or at least featured more positively. Along similar lines, the **Bertelsmann Transformation Index** compiled related data over the period 1998–2003 from 116 so-called transformation countries (excluding OECD states, but also Swaziland). They were ranked in a status and a management index. Again, Zimbabwe (ranked 108 and 110) and Angola (105 and 84) performed dismally, and Malawi (84 and 88) did not feature much more positively. The success stories were again Botswana (14 and 4), South Africa (16 and 14) and Namibia (20 and 47). However, the Bertelsmann Transformation Index is more oriented to socioeconomic and formal political criteria and is less concerned with substantive issues such as human rights and media freedom, which to some extent explains the disproportionately favourable ratings accorded to Botswana.

Generally, the trend in SADC towards more systematic efforts to introduce the notion of 'good governance' and consideration of related criteria as an accepted official point of reference in its affairs became visible during the year, when all 13 heads of state adopted a new **SADC Regional Charter** at their annual summit in Mauritius. It contains procedures to be followed by SADC observer teams and sets minimum standards to be met for elections to be declared free and fair. The charter calls for full participation of citizens in the political process, political tolerance, free association, regular elections, voter education, equal opportunity to stand for elections and to vote, equal access to state media, independent judiciaries and autonomous, neutral electoral authorities to control the process. According to a summit communiqué, the electoral guidelines aim at enhancing the transparency and credibility of elections and democratic governance as well as ensuring the acceptance of election results by all competing parties. However, there were internal disagreements over the role of Western and other international election observer teams. While a minority of SADC states believed such monitoring would be crucial to establishing credibility, most SADC leaders disagreed. This underscores the risk that the **guidelines and principles governing democratic elections** might be viewed as merely cosmetic, as lip service, since the lofty values espoused do not yet reflect a practical convergence among SADC members on the meaning of democracy and good governance. However, the document created a formal point of reference, despite a lack of enforcement mechanisms, for putting pressure on errant members who openly fail to comply. Thabo Mbeki, as the new head of the SADC organ on politics, defence and security cooperation, pointed out that the SADC treaty allowed for the exclusion of members from the sub-regional body if they are found to be in violation of the treaty, although in the absence of any enforcement mechanism, this remains a vague declaration of intent. The new SADC chairperson, who has a one-year term of office, is Paul Bérenger, prime minister of Mauritius, who took over from Tanzania's President Benjamin Mkapa. In his summit speech, he asked his fellow office bearers to honour democratic reforms. According to him, the new approach is not just about independent electoral commissions but also about allowing the opposition to operate without harassment by the police or anybody else. It is about freedom of assembly, freedom of the press, access to the media and credible observation of the whole electoral process. Bérenger's successor will be Botswana's President Festus Mogae, who takes over at the summit in 2005 and will have to prove if he is up to the mark. As an analyst at the Centre for International Political Studies (CIPS) at the University of Pretoria remarked: "The Summit in Mauritius and the unanimous approval of the electoral guidelines gives SADC a sharper mandate and a focus on the key elements of good governance and democracy. Of course, these adjustments could be simply another facelift. Lacking the capacity or willpower to translate these reforms into practice – arguing for democracy in principle without demanding it in practice – will only make the critics right and the population of southern Africa a loser."

Henning Melber

Angola

Angola in its second full year of peace continued to face a triple transition: from war to peace, from central planning to a market economy and from devastation to reconstruction. War had precipitated urban flight and the collapse of agricultural systems and internal trade. The challenges remained a fragmented national economy, a history of financial embezzlement and misappropriation of funds, a lack of international confidence and donor coordination, poor administrative capacity, a large child population at risk from disease, and weak opposition and civil society that were unable to affect social and political developments.

There were some improvements in human rights, with the exceptions of the Cabinda enclave and the Lunda provinces, and a greater commitment to infrastructural reconstruction. There were no attempts to end impunity and effect national reconciliation. Promised parliamentary and presidential elections were postponed, with no local elections proposed either. Angola, under greater US patronage and with hegemonic regional aspirations, played a less destructive role and joined the APRM of NEPAD. Increasing transparency in the Angolan government's revenues (although not yet expenditures) did not lead to either a formal agreement with the IMF or to a donors' conference.

Domestic Politics

Angola is an example of the use of 'disorder as a political instrument' whereby non-transparency, non-accountable authority and a weak legal framework provide dynamics for **elite accumulation**. Despite some cosmetic changes, little was done to close the massive gap between the political class and citizens during the year. A personal presidential style of rule with patronage networks and political cooptation of opposition parties under conditions in which the latter received state funding continued. A **cabinet reshuffle** in December (which followed an earlier reshuffle in October), in line with the provisions of the 1994 Lusaka Agreement that established the government of national unity and reconciliation under the direction of Movimento Popular de Libertação de Angola (MPLA) saw new União Nacional para a Independência Total de Angola (UNITA) members. UNITA leader Isaías Samakuva realigned its representation with the consolidation of its three former factions.

The **MPLA leadership** failed to open out to civil society and opposition parties, or transform itself from a classic national liberation movement, seeing itself as the only legitimate expression of all Angolans, rather than as being one of several parties in a pluralist system. Juliao Mateus Paulo 'Dino Mattross' – elected at the MPLA congress in December 2003 as secretary-general of the party instead of the younger João Lourenço – pointed to the MPLA 'old guard' retaining power amid suspicions regarding the ambitions of Lourenco. President Dos Santos thus kept his options open and strengthened control over his party, with the strong possibility that he will stand as the party's presidential candidate, despite earlier denials. The MPLA undertook a recruiting drive especially among ex-UNITA fighters – forcibly, UNITA alleged. The MPLA, despite a lack of agreement with the opposition on many aspects of the forthcoming elections, such as the dates, plus the composition and independent status of an electoral commission, appointed a party secretary for organisation and mobilisation: Faustino Muteka, a senior party member and former minister for territorial administration will coordinate the party's electoral strategy.

UNITA, as a now unified party, and in line with other parties' attempts to move beyond previous ethno-regional loyalties, made some tentative links with civil society initiatives on combating the 'insider-outsider' divide in Angolan politics. UNITA initially called for early elections, but subsequently appeared to accept, or even want, delays till 2006. On 6 December, UNITA called for the creation of an independent electoral commission representing government, civil society, churches and opposition parties. On 21 October, Frente Nacional de Libertação de Angola (**FNLA**) reappointed its veteran leader Holden Roberto as party leader for a ten-month period after lengthy faction fighting with followers of his challenger Lucas Ngonda. The second day of July saw the **assassination of Mfulumpinga Lando Victor**, leader of the Democratic Party for Progress and National Alliance (PDP-ANA) and member of the council of ministers, an advisory body that brings together all the parties represented in parliament. Victor was a longstanding and vocal critic of government and his party blamed the state, pointing to previous assassinations of government opponents.

Promised **parliamentary and presidential elections**, for neither of which conditions are yet in place, were proposed (but not finalised) for September 2006 and 2007 respectively, with Luanda estimating their cost at $ 430 m – a sum to which the EU said it would contribute if there was "a proper and conducive environment." UNITA and other opposition parties boycotted the **constitutional commission**. In September, President Dos Santos set a provisional election date. There was disagreement over whether the constitution should be redrafted before or after elections. The opposition parties put forward electoral proposals on 29 September, with the National Assembly inconclusively debating the constitutional commission in October. An Intersectoral Commission for the Electoral Process was set up in early December under the minister of territorial administration, Virgilio Fontes Pereira.

One necessary precondition for free and fair elections, the handing in of an estimated 5–10 m small arms, with an estimated one-third of Angolans being armed, was only addressed by civil society initiatives, despite a government announcement on planned **civilian disarmament** in March. Fears of widespread banditry after incomplete disarmament and demobilisation did not materialise. By January, the government had spent $ 187 m on the processes and by early 2004 the majority of the demobilised (mostly UNITA, but some IDPs) had left the quartering areas and returned home or to other destinations. The Angola Demobilisation and Reintegration Programme (ADRP) for 105,000 UNITA (excluding female ex-combatants until mid-2004) and 33,000 government soldiers was launched in April. Despite some disbursed funds, few promised vocational or economic support programmes were set up. The World Bank in January looked to provide 50,000 demobilisation kits for ex-UNITA soldiers as part of an ongoing project. There were few instances of social conflict involving returnees, according to the UN Office for Humanitarian Affairs (OCHA).

UNDP launched its 2004 **Mine Action Programme** in December 2003, after reaching only 7% of the appeal total of $ 9 m the previous year. Leonardo Sapalo, the Director-General of the National Demining Institute (INAD), said there were likely to be less than 5 m landmines, rather than the 10 m that many in the international community thought. The process of **returning refugees** was not completed, although UNHCR expect to finish in 2005. UNHCR managed to transport home 51,000 of its target 90,000, citing a late start, poor road conditions and rehabilitation after de-mining, and lack of onward transport. It helped another 12,000, who returned on their own, leaving an estimated 54,000 outside the country. Most refugees and IDPs returned home under their own auspices. The government announced in September that remaining IDP centres would be closed by the end of the year. 80% of IDPs were women and children, suffering high levels of mortality, malnutrition, illiteracy, poverty and HIV/AIDS. Angola submitted its first consolidated report to the Convention on the Elimination of all forms of Discrimination Against Women (CEDAW). This outlined the high representation of women in central government. In mid-July, at a CEDAW conference on women's rights in Johannesburg, the Angolan vice-minister for the family outlined the need for special resources to promote **gender equality** in a situation of structural, legal and traditional discrimination against women in the areas of property, inheritance and sexual violence.

The year saw some improvements in the observance of **human rights**, despite a Human Rights Watch report in July pointing to a substantial gap between freedoms promised constitutionally and their realisation, which is largely confined to Luanda and coastal regions. Among the three major exceptions to this improvement was the situation in **Cabinda** enclave, where fighting for independence has persisted since 1963. According to Human Rights Watch, security forces killed, arbitrarily detained and tortured civilians with impunity, and denied civilians access to agricultural areas, rivers and hunting grounds. After the virtual destruction of the liberation movement, Frente para a Libertação do Enclave de Cabinda (FLEC) in the previous year, there was little evidence of it abusing human rights. The Cabindan civic association, Mpalabanda, was finally allowed to take form under Catholic Church auspices in March, and a peace march went ahead in July. There were allegations of torture, harassment of journalists and opposition activists and lack of **freedom of expression** elsewhere in Angola. Media continued to be characterised by small audiences, low literacy rates and a government monopoly of television and controls over radio. There was continuing refusal to allow independent radio stations, such as the Catholic Radio Ecclésia, to operate outside Luanda. Hopes for a community radio station in Mbanza Congo ended when its putative premises were sacked. The mass expulsion of 62,000 Congolese and West Africans for alleged illegal diamond trading led to human rights abuses, according to different sources. Thirdly, there were allegations that UNITA was the victim of **political violence** by the MPLA in Kalima, near Huambo City, and Cazombo, near the Zambian border. The MPLA viewed the latter incident as being the spontaneous reaction by the local population to a disliked former UNITA general who was returning home. This may be true, although it has been used as a pretext before.

There seemed little progress in the **judicial arena**, such as a constitutional court, to ensure international obligations are fulfilled in any new constitution, or ending problems for *habeas corpus* linked to a scarcity of judges. Despite parliamentarians calling for widespread consultation in December over the appointment of an ombudsman, the government unilaterally appointed a former justice minister Paolo Tjipilica. **Civil society**, including churches and NGOs, remained relatively weak and unable to affect policy, despite several initiatives. Such organisations in Luanda continued to argue that yet another bilateral accord between the government and UNITA is not enough. Instead, it called for deeper political change. There were occasional protest demonstrations, including by opposition parties, despite the ever-present police forces. More newspapers were launched, although largely in the urban and coastal regions. The Inter-Ecclesiastical Committee for Peace (COIEPA) announced plans for a major conference in 2005. On 30 March, civil society organisations under the leadership of the Open Society set up the 'Campaign for a Democratic Angola' and called for elections in 2005.

Foreign Affairs

Angola appeared more concerned about its image internationally and within the continent, although without necessarily giving up **hegemonic notions in Central Africa** to rival or complement South Africa's further south. Foreign policy continued its turn away from often-violent attempts to stamp out UNITA rear bases in neighbouring countries. Luanda remained acutely aware that its fortunes were linked to international oil consumers, although its military and economic assets continued to give it bargaining power.

The growing **geo-strategic interest of the US** in the Gulf of Guinea – 'the American lake' – and Angola in particular as alternative sources of supply to the Middle East was illustrated in its better relations with Angola. The country gained a growing share of the US market and the latter has become Angola's chief trading partner, political patron and major aid donor – although not yet its chief arms supplier. In January, and contrary to its 2001 decision in relation to human rights and corruption, the US awarded Angola preferential AGOA treatment. This usually rewards countries that show progress towards market-based economies and embracing democratic principles (or, cynics would allege, which have oil that the US wants). Some saw Angola's lack of opposition to the invasion of Iraq as being rewarded by AGOA access. The US administration spoke positively about Angola's cooperation in combating terrorist links to conflict diamonds. A new US ambassador, Cynthia Efird, was appointed in early July. As well as building a large new embassy in Luanda, the US discussed military training for Angola's armed forces and improving security at airports. However, Angola showed awareness of the new balances of world power in the 21st century by entering into a loan agreement with China in March and by its increasingly close relationship with the Chinese, who are busy extending their influence in Africa.

Angola's term as non-permanent member of the UN Security Council came to an end. During its period in office, the government had agreed on a number of joint positions with **Brazil**, a long-time ally. The year saw **further UN withdrawal** as OCHA closed in June and UNDP and the Transitional Coordination Unit (TCU) were due to be taken over in 2005 by the UN Development Assistance Framework (UNDAF). In July, Angola became the 19th African country to join NEPAD's APRM signalling its **commitment to a more collective African agenda**. NEPAD secretariat staff doubted whether Angola would meet many of its conditions. In March, Franca van Dunem, MP, was elected a first vice-president of the new Pan-African parliament.

Reflecting moves towards a more united SADC, Angola, which had been its chair during 2004, continued to draw closer to **South Africa**, with whom it previously had difficult relations. It signed agreements with Pretoria on repatriating refugees, and in February the Development Bank of Southern Africa made the first South African investment loans to Angola. There was also cooperation in mining, with joint diamond mining projects, and between the intelligence services, shown by the visit of the South African Minister of Intelligence Ronnie Kasrils to Luanda in September.

A regional power agreement (WESTCOR) was signed in October with Botswana, the Democratic Republic of the Congo (DR Congo), Namibia and South Africa on using the Inga hydroelectric plant in DR Congo. Close links with **Namibia** were underscored by the president's visit there on 21 March. Reflecting its historic ties to West and Central Africa, Angola took part in the International Conference on the **Great Lakes Region** on 19–20 November 2004, a UN initiative to tackle problems facing Central Africa. The Secretary-General of the Community of Central African States is an Angolan, and the FAA, the Angolan army, is training the new integrated army of the DR Congo in Bas-Congo. Angola agreed to send 6,240 soldiers to the **UN peacekeeping mission in Côte d'Ivoire** (UNOCI), but after objections because of Luanda's closeness to Abidjan – paradoxically, given previous UNITA links with the government there – it withdrew. It is said Angola played a role in preventing the attempted coup in Equatorial Guinea .

There were marginally better relations with **France and Switzerland**. Following a three-year investigation, in December, the Swiss attorney-general dropped charges against French/Angolan Pierre Falcone, who had allegedly diverted millions of dollars of Angolan government money during complex renegotiations over its $ 2.9 bn debt to Russia ('**Falconegate**'). Abandoning prosecution (although there were still charges against him in French courts and an international arrest warrant) resulted in an estimated $ 17 m being released to Angola for humanitarian purposes. Luanda pledged to honour its agreement with the Swiss government that the money released from a frozen Swiss bank account by the ending of 'Falconegate' would be used for landmine clearance and development.

Socioeconomic Developments

Angola, like many oil-producing countries, has the paradoxical link between the exploitation of oil, gas and minerals and **high rates of poverty indicators**, such as child malnutrition, low healthcare spending, low school enrolment rates and poor adult literacy (and war). As an oil enclave economy with few forward and backward linkages, the industry employs only 10,000. Over one million Angolan people remained dependent on UN-funded food aid, and one child died every three minutes of preventable causes – 480 per day. Oil accounted for 90% of exports and 80% of tax revenues and economic diversification to combat such indicators was still awaited. The effect of oil wealth is to cause economic contraction and inflation through high local prices, expensive exchange rates and depressed levels of manufacturing in other sectors, plus lack of national accountability, especially with increased world demand, tightening supply and, in 2004, extremely high prices. Angola is also the fourth or fifth largest diamond producer – another enclave sector with little regulation or accountability. Two reports in October from Global Witness and Partnership Africa Canada questioned Angola's compliance with the Kimberley process on controlling conflict ('blood') diamonds.

The uncertain economic situation was compounded by crackdowns on the **informal sector**, where most Angolans make their living. Allegations are that such crackdowns, rather than being on claimed public health or traffic circulation grounds, serve the interests of politically connected larger traders, who object to being undercut by smaller ones. The **public sector** remained large, at three-quarters of all formal sector employment, but poor in quality and coverage, in part due to war and the collapse of infrastructure. Employees remained poorly and spasmodically paid and trained, under-resourced and under-motivated. There has been very little trickle down, given the problems of a two or three tier society – the capital and coastal regions benefited to some extent from oil, but the hinterland struggled. The government has budgeted for 16% growth, although economist José Cerqueira said that real wages have been diminishing every year.

Minister for Public Works Higino Carneiro said in Lisbon in March that it would cost $ 4 bn to rebuild **infrastructure**. Many bridges were repaired throughout the year using Luanda's own money, with money for the second phase due to come from a Chinese loan. The mayor of Luanda was sacked after a Luanda management commission under Carneiro was set up in January in response to the deterioration of infrastructure in the city as well as refuse collection. There were controversial proposals and forced relocations in connection with a multi-lane thoroughfare for Luanda to relieve congestion. A new mayor has since been appointed after Carneiro was sacked in October, possibly to prevent him from controlling the Chinese infrastructural projects, which will now come under a new 'reconstruction cabinet'.

Angola earned $ 9 bn from **oil, diamonds and granite**. It pumped over 1 m barrels of oil per day with new major projects coming on-stream to increase this considerably next year. Diamonds were expected to increase to 150,000 carats through the doubling of the capacity of the Catoca diamond mine from $ 50 m to $ 100 m. In April, the diamond-purchasing company Sodiam opened an office in Luanda, after an agreement with Lazare Kaplan International. Increases in coffee production were expected in the year, although low world prices and possible overproduction might affect progress. Little diversification occurred elsewhere.

Allegations of **unaccountability**, lack of transparency and siphoned-off oil revenues continued in the year. Hundreds of millions of dollars supposedly continued to vanish into a 'black hole' between state oil company Sonangol, the treasury and the presidency: Global Witness alleged that dos Santos had $ 37 m in Luxemburg banks and was due to benefit personally from Russian debt negotiations. The government admitted that high-ranking government personnel had deposited money in private foreign bank accounts. It stated, however, that this was a precaution undertaken during the civil war and was to protect the Angolan treasury. Deputy Prime Minister Jaime said in March in the US that massive discrepancies were due to bad accounting practices and different revenue conversions between kwanza and dollars by different agents. IMF figures for 2003–04 were that of an annual

$ 5 bn earned from oil, more than $ 1 bn had gone into private bank accounts – three times the UN Consolidated Appeal for Angola in 2003. The missing billions were uncovered in the KPMG Oil Diagnostic Programme, which is comparing revenue reported as paid by the oil companies operating in the country – currently, mainly Total and ChevronTexaco – with the money that actually appeared on the government's books. International oil companies were, as usual, contractually not allowed (even had they wished to) to publish what they pay to the state, meaning that ordinary Angolan citizens had no information with which to call their government to account over use or misuse of state funds. In September, ChevronTexaco, the largest oil producer in Angola, announced investment of $ 11 bn in Angola between 2003–08.

In the absence of multilateral debt relief and lending to reduce its debt burden, the Angolan government preferred to seek more expensive but less onerous **private loans**. Despite oil prices reaching over $ 50 per barrel, the government preferred to repay its $ 12 bn debt rather than spend on development. Oil production is set up so that foreign oil companies can recoup their enormous investment outlay by taking an increased share of production revenues until costs are paid. Government can use this investment as collateral, however, to fund reconstruction or pay debts off. There have been steps towards **fiscal and financial transparency** in revenues and as yet unfulfilled promises on addressing the vast off-budget and unrecorded expenditure. Inflation came down and government claimed they expected it to be 30% by the end of the year, through the government selling dollars and thereby using up foreign exchange. The floating exchange rate was maintained and there were the beginnings of privatisation. Jaime told the South African journal 'Business Report' in March that government accounts would soon be audited by the International Finance Corporation arm of the World Bank.

In May, government followed up publication of the executive summary by publishing KPMG's full Oil Diagnostic Report on how much of Angola's **oil revenues** are deposited in the central bank. The cabinet/council of ministers announced agreement with its main findings and the 'road map' for implementation, although not with the proposal for a new agency to manage the oil industry, despite discussions with oil companies on how to manage their relationship. The government also disclosed a bonus payment of $ 300 m from the ChevronTexaco Block 0 deal and promised further disclosures. It also set up a reserve fund to hold higher than expected oil receipts, although there were few indications on how this would be spent. In October, the government announced the first-ever audit of Sonangol, although nothing has yet been made public. Some action was taken against **corruption**, perhaps with an eye to elections. Although this was mostly against lower level officials, the former governor of Bengo Province was fined for irregularities in awarding contracts, and a local director in Zaire Province was sacked and charged with embezzlement.

The 'Publish What You Pay' campaign on **transparency of payments** continued to target oil companies in relation to Angola and other countries. The Angolan government negotiated with George Soros's Open Society Initiative. The plan, by which transparency would be rewarded through Soros by means of increased investment in Angola, appeared to have foundered after April as oil prices rose. Angola also appeared to be a long way away from signing up to the Extractive Industries Transparency Initiative (EITI), despite some promising statements earlier in the year. Even with its enormous wealth and without corruption, Angola would find reconstruction, de-mining and rehabilitation a daunting problem. Although many see the role of the international community as crucial in both humanitarian and good governance terms, that community did not engage significantly, looking instead for an agreement between the government and the IMF that would signal IMF's belief that Angola's finances were transparently managed.

Few seemed keen on a **donor conference** called for by President Dos Santos in January, although Belgium offered to play host if it occurred. But insufficient confidence in the government's capacity and commitment to the development process prompted a wait-and-see attitude. Indications were that the international community was keen to invest in infrastructure but less interested in investment in the social sectors. After the government outlined its timetable for its relationship with the IMF in February, Michael Baxter, the World Bank representative for Angola, stated in November that he expected a donor conference in 2005. This followed World Bank Angolan director Lawrence Clark's statement in August that Luanda needed three stages: firstly to produce a PRSP, secondly to implement an IMF Staff Monitored Programme (SMP) leading to full agreement between the IMF and Luanda. There would then be international aid for rebuilding, including a World Bank emergency reconstruction plan – a position seemingly agreed by most international donors.

There were three **IMF missions**. A preliminary visit in April assessed improvements in the government's handling of macroeconomic data and transparency in oil revenue flows. A second, from 7 to 21 July, while praising the progress of Angola towards macroeconomic stability, worried about rising foreign debt levels and high-interest oil-backed loans from commercial banks. Angola joined the IMF's general data dissemination system to "enhance accountability and transparency." The visit by its deputy managing director, Takatoshi Kato, who arrived on 31 October, saw praise for progress in transparency over oil revenues and external debt plus Sonangol transactions and macroeconomic management, including publishing of the Oil Diagnostic, despite deficiencies in fiscal information, monitoring and control of public expenditure. The IMF wanted cuts in subsidies, civilian and military expenditure, cuts in ghost workers on the government payroll and for energy, water and food prices to be brought into line with costs. Luanda worried that this 'shock therapy' would, by ending subsidies, affect political stability and electoral support. Although Angolan economists expected a growth rate of 10% thanks to increased oil prices, they queried this orthodox formula's suitability for a country combining great needs with poor capacity, and saw it leading to the stifling of domestic recovery by crippling small business and farmers with high interest loans. The government opted rather to increase the fiscal deficit through an expansionist state-funded reconstruction backed by outside loans. The loan agreements, high oil prices with increased oil production and bilateral lending appeared to give Angola greater leverage in its dealings with IMF.

The **draft budget** for 2005 was announced in October with a proposed $ 1.89 bn deficit, 8.9% of GDP, which is forecast to grow by 11.6%, a figure the government thinks will fall through rising oil taxes and greater lending. The **World Bank** was due to lend money from its $ 25 m trust fund, which supports reform in low-income countries under stress, calling Angola "policy poor but resource rich." The fund is for those ineligible for IDA funding due to previous defaulting. The bank also continued its assistance to Angola with an 18-month $ 200 m credit facility from the Emergency Multisectoral Reconstruction Programme to replace the $ 125 m programme that was ending. USAID and the IMF funded a special unit in the ministry of finance to oversee financial flows.

A **concessionary oil-backed loan** of $ 2 bn from the Chinese Eximbank was signed in March. China needs oil for its all-out industrialisation and export strategy (it currently imports around 30% of Angola's production, just behind the US at 40%), and Angola has both oil and the need for reconstruction. The agreement between them revolved around China's providing infrastructural development, cars and transmission line equipment; helping rebuild Luanda's government buildings; a local rail network; improving the electricity supply and providing agricultural equipment. Local civil society and economists expressed concerns that the deal sought to contract only 30% with local firms, which meant that the Chinese were largely without competition. There were also questions about whether it would be elite-linked firms that got the 30% non-Chinese component. Questions were asked about future capacity to maintain rebuilt infrastructure. The opaque nature of the deal runs counter to the Angolan government's opening up its books to scrutiny, and restricts the IMF's leverage over Luanda. Rows over corruption linked to the Chinese deal led to the sacking of former Cabinet Secretary António Pereria Mendes de Campos van Dunem in December. There was also a syndicate oil-backed loan through Standard Chartered estimated at $ 2.5 bn, aimed, like the Chinese loans, at financing the public investment programme, but also paying off debts to Portugal.

Problems due to **lack of international donor response** to the WFP appeal for $ 3.2 m for food for returnees until the end of the year led to vulnerable groups having their rations halved. WFP needed $ 55 m over the year for 88,000 tonnes but raised only $ 47.5 m, with Luanda donating $ 4 m. Lack of funding impacted the transition from emergency to recovery. According to the WFP Vulnerability Assessment for 2004–05, 1.5 m people still faced food insecurity, with most of the population of 13.5 m living in dire poverty. Lack of donor response meant slow distribution of seeds and tools and delays in de-mining for returnee areas. Less than 60% of the UN Consolidated Inter-Agency Appeal for Angola (the last) of $ 262 m ($ 116 m) was received by the end of the year, despite donations from the EC and France. WFP was still feeding a million people at the end of the year, despite cuts. Major NGOs had no funding from the Appeal for, for instance, basic sanitation in a situation where

Luanda, a city built for 500,000 people, was growing rapidly towards a population of 4 m, the majority without access to clean drinking water.

The Luanda government announced a **Poverty Reduction Strategy Paper** (PRSP), entitled 'Estratégia de Desenvolvimento de Angola até 2025'. It identifies as a long-term project water, sanitation, education and health infrastructures. As with the rest of the PRSP process that began in 2000, there was very little consultation with civil society and the latter described it as a shopping list rather than a plan of action and planned an 'observatorio' in 2005 to monitor progress. Against the background of more than one million **children** estimated to be outside the formal education sector, the 'education for all' programme calling for free compulsory and quality education by 2015 and full gender equality was launched in January with Japanese funding through UNESCO. Building began on a number of schools. Angola reported for the first time to UNCHR on the treatment of children. Deputy Prime Minster Aguinaldo Jaime promised in November that there would be a dramatic rise in the 2005 budget for social, health and education spending.

The year saw greater recognition of the need to prepare for an expected rise in **HIV/AIDS**, with its proven correlation to poverty and conflict. Statistics had indicated a prevalence rate of 5.5%, rising in urban areas to 10%, although these are likely underestimates, with increased movement of population likely to speed the pandemic's effect. A United Nations resolution of 21 December noted the lack of reliable statistics and urged Angola to improve data collection. In December, the World Bank approved a grant of $ 21 m for an HIV/AIDS-, malaria- and TB-control project, which together account for 75% of deaths in Angola. **Rural security** was not helped by 'fazendeiros' (large-scale landowners, often linked to the elite) fencing off rural land in places where the system of traditional land rights determined by elders was either under threat or had collapsed during the war. The application of the new land law was uncertain, although unlikely to help poor rural Angolans. The government still needed to address HIV/AIDS and associated vulnerabilities in rural areas where access is difficult. The country as a whole saw better (if patchy) harvests than its neighbours (except Zambia). In line with other SADC countries, the government confirmed its ban on GM foods, including unmilled US food aid, despite reports of local farmers sowing GM seeds.

Little happened in terms of growth beyond the capital-intensive oil sector to create the conditions for labour-intensive poverty-reduction and to allow a genuine private sector to develop. This would generate revenues available for social investment and for the increased **delivery of social services**. Despite rhetoric on increased transparency, accountability and democratisation, little was accomplished in the year to overcome the gap between rulers and ruled. Nor was there much to overcome the needs or instability in rural areas or 'musseques' (shanty towns). Given the interest of key members of the elite in not changing the **patronage system** (often called the parallel state), Luanda moved slowly in seizing the opportunities presented by peace and rising oil prices. There remained a need to end corruption and tackle poverty, allow for the development of an independent private sector with an open and transparent tendering process and to transform the political system into a pluralist democracy, including addressing the exclusion of the poor and marginalised, especially women. The underlying unresolved problem was the 'resource curse' of oil-based economic enclaves with greater external than internal linkages, meaning a lack of reciprocity between domestic rulers and ruled in all spheres. Despite being the second largest oil producer in sub-Saharan Africa, the country ranked 166 of 177 in the UNDP's Human Development Index.

Steve Kibble

Botswana

The Botswana Democratic Party (BDP) once again secured a sound victory in the eighth post-independence elections in October. Foreign affairs were marked by apparently growing tensions with neighbouring Zimbabwe. Notwithstanding relative macroeconomic stability, the economy remained heavily dependent on diamonds, and HIV/AIDS continued to pose a formidable challenge to the country's future.

Domestic Politics

The aftermath of the stormy primaries in late 2003 dominated the political parties' **pre-electoral activities**. In particular, factionalism within the ruling BDP continued. The newly introduced electoral system in the primaries, 'bulela ditswe', which for the first time allowed all party members to participate, was accompanied by major irregularities and mud-slinging. On 9 March, the BDP central committee ruled that four primary elections lost by supporters of Vice-President Ian Khama's faction (among them, two cabinet ministers) be rerun. Although all but one of the original results were confirmed in the reruns, this did not signify a comeback for former party chairman Ponatshego Kedikilwe, the other faction's predominant figure, who had been replaced by Khama at a party congress in 2003. Enjoying the support of the Khama faction, on 3 April President Festus Mogae was elected unopposed as the party's nominee for state president at a BDP **special congress**. Although Khama and Kedikilwe publicly declared their warm personal relationships, Mogae appealed in his congress speech for party unity and warned against underestimating the opposition.

The major opposition party, Botswana National Front (BNF), faced similar problems. Candidates who lost their primaries, especially in opposition strongholds in Gaborone, continued to contest the results. Robert Molefhabangwe, sitting MP for Gaborone West, successfully appealed for a rerun, which, after he had taken the party to court, resulted in a clear victory on 23 May over his opponent, Gaborone mayor Harry Mothei. However, primary results for Gaborone North, Central and North West were upheld. The **tripartite opposition electoral pact** among the BNF and two small opposition parties, the Botswana People's Party (BPP) and the Botswana Alliance Movement (BAM), gained momentum when the pact's electoral manifesto was launched on 31 May. To avoid vote splitting, the pact provided for exclusive contestation of constituencies by only one of the three member parties, giving the BNF 42 constituencies, BAM seven and BPP five constituencies. Any prospect of ousting BDP, however, was compromised by the exclusion of two BNF breakaways, the Botswana Congress Party (BCP) and the National Democratic Front (NDF).

The opposition pact's manifesto advocated interventionist economic policies and a more proactive programme of economic empowerment for citizens, in mild contrast to the BDP's manifesto, which, while pledging to maintain fiscal prudence, set out rather ambitious medium-term goals, such as the eradication of absolute poverty, halting the spread of HIV/AIDS and fighting violent crime. However, the opposition **election campaign** centred on narrower issues such as high-handed behaviour by the government, an unlevelled playing field and allegations of malpractice, involving four cabinet ministers, in the allocation of state land in Gaborone by government officials. Since BDP continued to exploit the direct and indirect advantages of incumbency, in particular in terms of financial resources (there is no public funding for parties) and access to state media, the main opposition parties chose to boycott the special session of the **all-party conference** scheduled for July in order to nominate members of the Independent Electoral Commission (IEC), as provided in the constitution. The boycott also mirrored opposition dissatisfaction with BDP's routine rejection of conference proposals, such as the introduction of proportional representation. On 27 July, the conference was held without the major opposition parties. Although the move received a mixed public reaction, the opposition kept criticising the electoral regime, especially the composition of the IEC.

In late May, the government was forced to establish a commission of inquiry led by high court Judge Isaac Lesetedi regarding **irregularities in the allocation of state land in Gaborone**. The resulting report was presented to the president on 28 July and published on 13 August. Contrary to public expectation, no evidence of widespread corruption was uncovered. The opposition suggested that the report covered up major irregularities, but

President Mogae countered these allegations by immediately ordering a full review of the findings, including by the directorate of corruption and economic crime.

Mogae dissolved the National Assembly on 3 September and issued an election writ on 17 September. On polling day, 30 October, a total of 178 candidates contested the 57 constituencies, which had increased from 40 in 1999. Four parties, BDP, BCP, BNF – its leader, Otsweletse Moupo, representing the 'pact' – and NDF nominated a presidential candidate (under the constitution, the president is not directly elected, but nominated by the members of parliament). At the same time, 1,360 candidates contested local elections for city, town and local councils.

According to international observers and the IEC, the **elections were conducted smoothly** without noteworthy incident. Fears of voter apathy proved overstated. After a final registration exercise between 22 March and 4 July, 421,272 of 552,849 registered voters participated in the elections (76%). Unsurprisingly, it quickly emerged that **BDP**, with 44 seats (77.2%), **had secured a resounding victory** over the BNF, with 12 (21%) and the BCP with one (1.8%). Because of his enormous popularity and position as a paramount chief of the Bamangwato, Vice-President Ian Khama won his constituency in Serowe North West unopposed. BCP's Dumelang Saleshando defeated cabinet minister Margaret Nasha in a close race in Gaborone Central by a margin of less than 100 votes. The tripartite electoral pact members BAM and BPP failed to win a seat, likewise the NDF, which received less than 1% of the vote. Local elections also confirmed the dominance of BDP, which won 333 of 487 council seats (68.8%). Upon closer examination, **BDP's landslide proved less impressive**. Its large share of the seats on the basis of 50.6% of the vote was mainly due to the British-style first-past-the-post system and the split opposition vote (amounting to more than 49%). A united opposition could have won at least 10 more seats. The failure to include the BCP in the pact proved to be a particular obstacle and prompted renewed calls for opposition unity.

After more than 50% of elected MPs asserted their support for Mogae and the final results were announced on 1 November, the chief justice declared him duly elected as president. Mogae took his oath on 2 November and moved quickly to **reshuffle the cabinet** extensively (10 November). Only three key ministers, including Baledzi Gaolathe and Mompati Merafhe, the minister of finance and the foreign secretary respectively, were maintained, whereas ten of 14 ministers (and five deputy ministers) were new faces. Apparently, the new cabinet excluded supporters of former party chairman Kedikilwe, whereas the presence of five ex-soldiers in the cabinet indicated the **dominance of the faction led by Vice-President Ian Khama**, the former chief of staff of the Botswana Defence Force (BDF). He was again chosen as vice-president and there is little doubt that he will be Mogae's successor after the latter's second and last term. The major loser in the reshuffle was BDP General Secretary Daniel Kwelagobe (ex-presidential affairs). Almost continuously in cabinet since the early 1990s, he was said to be the last minister close to Kedikilwe. Given the scarcity of women in parliament, five of the seven female MPs received cabinet posts (plus one assistant minister).

The **controversial relocation of the Basarwa** (also called San or Bushmen) did not play a major role in the election campaign but attracted negative international publicity (see below). The Basarwa are the earliest known culturally distinct inhabitants of the country (approximately 3% of the population, up to 65,000), and the government had started to remove some 1,000 of them from their ancestral lands in Central Kalahari Game Reserve (CKGR) in 2001, claiming that hunter-gathering practices were incompatible with wildlife preservation in CKGR. In 2002, government terminated services (healthcare and drinking water) to the Basarwa's settlement on the grounds that such provision was economically unsustainable. In April the same year, government resettled the remaining several hundred Basarwa in government-created settlements in Kaudwane, New Xade and Xere outside CKGR (about 100 remained or returned). The Botswana Centre for Human Rights ('Ditshwanelo') continued to urge government to review its position and to engage in a more participatory process with the Basarwa. It supported Basarwa activists in taking government to court. On 12 July hearings began before three high court judges in New Xade (later moved to Ghanzi). The 243 former residents claimed that the termination of services to the CKGR was unlawful and unconstitutional, whereas government lawyers argued for the dismissal of the case. After a break in late July to allow the applicants to raise further funds, hearings resumed on 3 November. The court case was adjourned once again on 30 November, to January 2005.

Foreign Affairs

The **bitter dispute with the London-based lobby group Survival International (SI)** continued throughout 2004. SI accused government of relocating the Basarwa in order to mine diamonds in CKGR. On 14 February, SI called for a boycott of diamond multinational De Beers (which holds a 50% stake in the Debswana mining company) for its opposition to recognising indigenous peoples' rights on the grounds that doing so would lead to 'apartheid'. SI organised promotional tours featuring Basarwa activists to the US (August) and the UK (September). The court case received extensive coverage by the advocacy group. However, government continued to dismiss SI's allegations. On 17 February, Foreign Secretary Merafhe denounced its 'misguided campaign' and accused the advocacy group of touching the 'very nerve' of the country by targeting diamonds as the alleged reason for the relocation. Because of the 'abrasive' style of SI's campaign, even Ditshwanelo dissociated itself from SI in previous years. Likewise, government dismissed rumours of negotiations with SI in connection with the CIVICUS World Assembly on 21–25 March in Gaborone in which SI participated as one of 400 NGOs. In early November, four British MPs toured the country to get first-hand information, including on the relocation of Basarwa, but could not find evidence of serious human rights abuses.

The **ongoing crisis in neighbouring Zimbabwe**, particularly the influx of illegal immigrants, contributed indirectly to **growing tensions** and fuelled xenophobic tendencies. In

April, a confrontation with Zimbabweans at a Gaborone bus station turned violent. The government reacted angrily to allegations in the Zimbabwean media that Zimbabweans were routinely mistreated in Botswana. On 29 April, the ministry of foreign affairs defended the justice system and released statistics linking the upsurge in crime to the presence of illegal immigrants from Zimbabwe. Contrary to the suspicions aired in the Zimbabwean public media, it was noted that 'cordial relations' with both the UK and the US did not 'in any way imply hostility' towards Zimbabwe. Crackdowns on illegal immigrants continued throughout the year, including the extension of the controversial border fence and numerous deportations. By the end of the year, Botswana's immigration authorities complained that repatriating an estimated 2,500 Zimbabweans per month was a drain on the country's resources. Though government remained keen not to openly criticise Robert Mugabe, Gaborone's increasingly critical view became apparent when Zimbabwean opposition leader Morgan Tsvangirai held talks with Foreign Secretary Merafhe on 22 October in Gaborone.

During a state visit to Ethiopia in early March, Mogae urged the **African Union** to include the issue of refugees on the agenda of the July heads of state summit. Mogae paid another state visit to Lesotho in mid-April, during which Botswana and Lesotho signed an economic and technical cooperation agreement. The **SADC** summit in mid-August chose Botswana as the next host. Earlier, SADC appointed Botswana to coordinate the first phase of negotiations for an Economic Partnership Agreement (EPA) with the **EU** (Botswana had already led the delegation to the WTO negotiations in Mexico in September 2003). On 6 and 7 March, trade ministers from the ACP countries and the EU met in Gaborone in advance of meetings between the EU and SADC that are expected to continue until 2007. In July both these parties agreed on a joint roadmap.

Socioeconomic Developments

On 9 February, Minister of Finance Gaolathe presented the **state budget** for the fiscal year 2004–05 to parliament. As in the previous year, the budget projected a small surplus of 0.2% of GDP, partly from a 46% boost in payments from the SACU revenue pool. A surprise **devaluation** of the pula by 7.5% only four days earlier provoked some confusion and concern about higher inflation rates. In fact, **inflation** remained only just within the target range (4–7%) and was estimated at 6.9% by the Economist Intelligence Unit (EIU). By the end of 2004, figures published by the Bank of Botswana made it clear that the 2004–05 budget will have a small **deficit**. However, EIU estimates pointed to 4.2% real **GDP growth** in 2004 (2003: 4%).

As in previous years, Botswana's traditionally prudent fiscal policy was awarded **relatively positive international credit ratings**. Botswana retained Standard & Poor's A investment rating and Moody's A-2 rating. On the Corruption Perception Index of Transparency International, published on 20 October, Botswana remained the top African scorer (ranking above Italy). Yet, **IMF painted a less optimistic picture** when it released its 2003 Article IV Consultation with the government on 30 July. The report pointed to fiscal problems in connection with slowing GDP growth, the dependence on diamonds and the effects of the HIV/AIDS pandemic. The IMF urged government to strengthen tax administration, to embark on a more ambitious inflation target and to incorporate HIV-related expenditures in the budget.

Botswana remained **heavily dependent on mining**, especially diamonds (minerals accounted for 44% of revenues in the budget for 2004–05). Notwithstanding sluggish diversification and pressures to find new diamond resources, the mining sector continued to be the engine of economic growth. Debswana recorded an all-time high output of 31 m carats in 2004 (an increase of 500,000 carats). Given an average 15% increase in prices, diamond sales totalled nearly $ 3 bn. **Strike activities** did not hinder production. On 22 August, approximately 1,500 members of the Botswana Mine Workers Union (BMWU) went on strike to protest the use of expatriate labour, the treatment of BMWU officials by management and to demand higher wages. Because of the severely restrictive legal framework for strikes (which are possible only after an exhaustive arbitration process), the industrial court ruled the strike illegal. Although most of the union members returned to work on 6 September, tensions continued to simmer during September.

In his state of the nation address on 8 November, President Mogae admitted that **HIV/AIDS** was the most formidable challenge to the country's future. According to UNAIDS, Botswana remained one of the hardest hit countries in the world with a HIV prevalence rate of 37.3% at the end of 2003 among adults between 15 and 49. Mogae pledged to turn back the virus and expand the provision of anti-retroviral drugs to infected citizens. He conceded that weak performance of the non-mining sector had resulted in the **growth of unemployment** to over 20% of the total labour force. To boost diversification and socioeconomic development, Mogae stressed government's commitment to **create a skilled labour force**. He pledged to provide universal access to senior secondary education in keeping with the provisions of the tenth National Development Plan.

Matthias Basedau

Lesotho

Lesotho has achieved remarkable political stability, much credit for which must go to the adoption of the mixed member proportional (MMP) electoral system that provides fair representation for opposition parties in parliament. Civil peace has been underpinned by tight fiscal policies and steady economic growth, although present gains are threatened by a recent reduction in employment in the textile sector and by long-term threats such as HIV/AIDS.

Domestic Politics

Much of the credit for the unaccustomed period of civil peace must go to the MMP electoral system, which, in replacing the formerly used Westminster-style First Past the Post (FPTP) system, has provided for the proportional representation (PR) of opposition parties in parliament. After years of recurrent strife, MMP is almost universally accepted, although a conference on **electoral reform** conducted under the auspices of the Lesotho council of non-governmental organisations in Maseru (13–15 October), worried that improved representation did not automatically translate into accountability and efficiency. Members of parliament elected from PR lists are widely regarded as less worthy than those elected for constituencies; the shift to PR has done little to improve democracy within political parties;

and there remains a need for continuing civic education among both parliamentarians and the electorate about the advantages and workings of the new model. Some of these concerns were subsequently listed as falling under the purview of a 30-member parliamentary reform committee, which, according to the speaker, Ms. Ntlhoi Motsemai, would look at ways of increasing legislative efficiency and public participation in parliamentary affairs.

Local elections were repeatedly delayed, principally because of the complexities of the reformed system of local government that the act envisaged. Essentially, these will introduce four types of authority: community councils (serving approximately 10,000 people each); district councils, which will serve the populations of the ten administrative districts except for those that live in urban areas; urban councils, which will serve smaller towns; and municipal councils, which serve the larger areas (notably the capital Maseru). The reformed system will constitute a massive reorganisation of service delivery, with functions being coordinated at district level through committees that will be composed of centrally appointed bureaucrats and councillors. Hitherto, except in the case of Maseru, local government was in the hands of village development committees with few resources and little authority, alongside a parallel system of chieftaincy, which has provided a framework for such activities as the local management of land and conflict resolution. The new system is seen by many of the government's opponents as a politically motivated attack on the chiefs, who historically have overwhelmingly supported the Basotho National Party (which ruled the country from 1966 until overthrown by the military in 1986).

The government has responded to such criticisms through a **Local Government (Amendment) Act of 2004**, gazetted on 17 May, by providing for chiefs to elect a limited number of their own to sit on district councils. However, this provision is unlikely to be enough to satisfy the chiefs, who continue to wield considerable power, while opposition parties have reacted with howls of protest to the act's further provision that not less than one-third of seats on any council shall be reserved for women. Whilst welcomed by women's groups as a victory, various civic groups and lawyers have questioned the constitutionality of the move, while at least one opposition party (the Basutoland African Congress/BAC) has indicated that it may refer what it has denounced as 'sexual apartheid' to the courts. While the opposition political parties, which are almost entirely dominated by men, may be less enthusiastic about the concept of proportionality if it is extended to include more appropriate representation for women, the more pressing concern may be that the new local government system will not be based upon MMP, with councillors being exclusively elected to represent electoral divisions. As it is not clear how one-third of seats on councils can be reserved for women without some introduction of a PR list system, it is clear that the independent electoral commission (which will supervise the elections) will have its work cut out to convince the opposition parties that they are being fairly treated.

The envisaged changes in local government are in line with other aspects of the government's programme, which Prime Minister Mosisili has worked hard to render more professional and proficient. His growing mastery of the political scene was indicated on 18 November by his implementation of a **cabinet reshuffle**, which saw five senior ministers being allocated to new portfolios and the promotion of two junior ministers to senior positions to fill vacant posts. Another sign that he demands results was the publication of the acting auditor general's report on public accounts for the year ending 31 March 2003. Although dated 30 July and published only at the end of November, this was a marked improvement on recent years, and indicated the government's commitment to combating corruption and inefficiency.

Lacking ideas about how to challenge a government that is as confident as it is dominant, the **opposition parties** appear as fractious and divided as ever. Only two minor parties, the MaremaTlou Freedom Party and the Patriotic Front for Democracy put up candidates against the Lesotho Congress for Democracy (LCD) in a by-election in Qhoali on 16 October. LCD candidate 'Matanki Mokhabi trounced her opponents in what was anyway a very low poll (with a turnout of 26.7%). For its part, the BAC, which has just three MPs, split in two following a struggle between its leader Molapo Qhobela, and its former deputy-leader, Dr. Khauhelo Deborah Raditapole. The latter had been elected as leader of the party at its special conference in November 2003; Qhobela's appeal to the high court that the conference had been improperly constituted was upheld; but Raditapole was re-elected by the party's annual conference on 28 February, subsequent to which Qhobela went ahead with his own annual conference the following weekend. This duly claimed to have suspended Raditapole and displaced her chosen executive committee with its own.

Foreign Affairs

Prior to 1994, Lesotho had served as a strategic site for the diplomatic struggle against apartheid. However, since the advent of democracy in South Africa its international profile has declined. Many countries, which were previously directly represented in Maseru, now covered the country from Pretoria. The latest and most hurtful of all these withdrawals was that made by Britain. Following a downsizing of its representation in Maseru from January, the former colonial power subsequently announced the closing of its high commission, leaving the United States and South Africa as the most significant countries with a direct presence. This merely confirms what has become increasingly evident since the South African military intervention in Lesotho to quell the post-election disorder in 1998. Although remaining a formally sovereign state, Lesotho has now become a de facto South African protectorate, with Pretoria's principal interests lying in the maintenance of political stability and its continuing access to water from the **Lesotho Highlands Water Project (LHWP)**.

The strong ties between **Lesotho and South Africa** were confirmed on 16 March when South African President Thabo Mbeki officiated with King Letsie III at the inauguration of Phase IB of the LHWP, namely the completion of Mohale dam and tunnel. This represents the next major step in the project following the completion of the Katse dam in 1996 and its first release of water to South Africa in 1998. Mbeki used the occasion to praise Lesotho for the way in which it had dealt with **corruption** around the LHWP. **President Festus Mogae of Botswana** joined Mbeki in praising Lesotho for its stand against corruption when he paid a state visit on 15 April, citing the country as a beacon of peace and democracy in Africa. Similar sentiments were expressed by retiring **Mozambican President Joaquim Chissano** when he paid a farewell visit to Maseru on 2–3 November.

Socioeconomic Developments

The **anti-corruption initiatives** praised by the foreign heads of state referred to the prosecution of multinational corporations for their involvement in bribing leading officials, notably Masupha Sole, chief executive of the highlands development authority, in order to gain contracts. Mbeki stated during his state visit that the prosecutions had promoted greater investor confidence in involvement in major development projects throughout the whole region. However, the **cost of the corruption saga** has been far greater than any recompense it may have led to from the payment of fines. Sole's acceptance of bribes led to costly delays in the construction of the 'Muela power station, resulting in a M (maloti) 40 m bypass having to be constructed so that SA could receive its water from the project on time; caused international bodies granting concessionary loans for the hydropower component to distance themselves from the project, forcing the government to obtain commercial loans at much higher interest rates; and although the 'Muela hydropower project had been planned to provide Lesotho with electricity, the cost of the latter had become more expensive than that obtainable from South Africa's Eskom, forcing Lesotho to inject several further hundred million Maloti into the project so that the Lesotho electricity corporation could afford to buy its power from within the country. Furthermore, the cost of the trials themselves amounted in excess of M 28 m. In short, the total cost of corruption appears to have been in excess of M 300 m.

Finance Minister Timothy Thahane presented his **budget** for the 2004/05 financial year on 16 February. Overall, the total budget allocation was M 4,337 m, of which M 483 m would be financed by loans and grants and the remaining M 3,854 m by the government. The economy was estimated to have grown by 3.7% in 2002 but only by 3.4% in 2003, because the strong loti/rand had reduced the profitability of the textile sector. However, projections for 2004, 2005 and 2006 were 3.6%, 3.9% and 4% respectively. The 2003/04 budget had anticipated a fiscal deficit of 5.2% of GDP, although this was likely to be reduced to 3%. For 2004/05, a budget surplus of M 251 m or 2.7% of GDP was anticipated and would be used to repay maturing loans and treasury bills, this made possible by a windfall in SACU revenue. For the first time, it was proposed that people aged 70 or more would receive a pension of M 150 per month, M 45 m being set aside for this purpose. Lesotho's annual inflation rate, which had reached a 34-year low of 4.6% in July 2004, continued to remain low for the rest of the year, buoyed by the rise in the value of the loti against the US dollar.

A major threat to the country's economic performance is the end to the quota system (from January 2005) under which AGOA limited exports of textiles and clothing to the United States from countries such as cheap producers China, India and Pakistan to the marked advantage of Lesotho and other countries in sub-Saharan Africa. Mpho Malie, minister of trade and industry, noted on 13 December that AGOA had provided for a massive increase in jobs in the country's textile and clothing sector, from 20,000 in 2002 to 50,000 in 2004, while facilitating an expansion of the value of exports to the US from $ 120 to $ 400 m and an inflow of foreign direct investment over the period to over $ 150 m. It was for this reason that Lesotho joined with other countries within SACU to invite US trade representative Robert Zoellick to visit the region to discuss the implications of the ending of quotas, which by the end of June 2004 had already resulted in an alarming loss of 12,276 jobs in Lesotho alone, due to the **closure of factories** moving to cheaper production sites elsewhere in anticipation of their ending. The Factory Workers' Union complained that three of the six companies that had left Lesotho by the end of 2004 had done so without paying workers their wages.

To deal with the crisis, the government formed a special task force to prepare for a high-level visit to the US in 2005 in a bid to persuade US politicians and importers to maintain their markets for Lesotho's exports. However, during his visit to Lesotho on 13 December, Zoellick made no such commitments, and, rather, encouraged African cotton producers such as Somalia, Benin and Senegal to forge integrated production linkages with textile manufacturing countries such as Mauritius and Lesotho, thereby increasing their global competitiveness.

A longer-term threat to Lesotho is presented by a decline in its population, as younger people look for opportunities in South Africa next door. Population growth for 2001–05 is estimated at a mere 0.1% **per annum**, and the United Nations Population Fund has recently suggested that Lesotho's present population of around 1.8 m will fall to 1.4 m in 2050. Such statistics reflect a grim deterioration in the health status of Basotho, including an alarmingly high HIV/AIDS infection rate. If such predictions are correct, Lesotho's future may fulfil prophecies that see the country as unable to escape its historic role as an exporter of skills and labour to South Africa, and as a reservoir of the very young, the old and the physically unable.

Roger Southall

Madagascar

President Marc Ravalomanana came into office in 2002 with high expectations at home and massive goodwill from abroad. In 2004, he worked on expending that goodwill in an effort to meet the expectations. A large anti-corruption programme under way got a boost in October with the appointment of the director of Ravalomanana's military cabinet to director general. The World Bank and several major bilateral donors agreed to write off a significant portion of Madagascar's debt. Public companies were sold off as part of a major privatisation programme, and foreign corporations have once again taken interest in the country. Political accountability measures increased while the economy showed significant gains for the second year. The two worrisome factors were that an active, radicalising opposition has been undermining efforts at democratic consolidation, and the uncomfortably close relationship between the president's corporate holdings, his associates and his political position has become stronger.

Domestic Politics

Malagasy politics continued to be shaped by the electoral dispute and resultant melee in 2002 that ultimately brought **Marc Ravalomanana** to office. Ravalomanana's mode of ascension, his youth and personality and the significant improvement in the quality of governance that he represented bought him an unusually long political honeymoon. Also assisting him was the broad popular sentiment that he is not like his predecessor Ratsiraka. Ravalomanana fully used his relative freedom to implement massive reforms in the public sector.

Ravalomanana is founder of **Tiko**, originally a milk products company, and one of the wealthiest men in the country. In many ways, he was the prodigal son of the emergent business class long before he began his political career as mayor of Antananarivo. Once in power as president, he rapidly implemented a programme to rationalise the state bureaucracy. On 18 November, the World Bank announced that these **public sector reforms** would receive $ 30 m in assistance. The public perception is that the public sector is leaner, more efficient and more accountable.

Ravalomanana set up an **Independent Anti-Corruption Bureau** (BIANCO). This was a popular move both at home and abroad. President Ravalomanana appointed General Rene Ramarozatovo director general of BIANCO by decree 944 of 11 October. As director of the president's military cabinet, Ramarozatovo had the president's confidence. Many looked to his success as leader of the investigation into former President Ratsiraka's violent crackdown on demonstrators on 10 August 1991 as a sign of his experience. Detractors pointed to the fact that Ramarozatovo sided with Ravalomanana early in the 2002 conflict and became the head of the presidential security group (a militia). This hardly made him a dispassionate ombudsman or assured his neutrality.

Other public sector reforms were not bureaucratic but rather political. In 1998, Ratsiraka led a successful constitutional referendum that created six autonomous provinces ('faritany mizaka tena'). These were further divided into 111 sub-prefectures ('fivondronana'). On 3 September, Ravalomanana created **22 regions** as secondary administrative divisions. The fivondronana now fall under the regions and have been changed into departments. This was a more significant reform than it may seem. The autonomous provinces were part of Ratsiraka's federalist decentralisation programme but in reality were a tool for enhancing his power base while marginalising his competition in the capital. The new regions undermined both the spirit of those earlier reforms and many of the individuals who profited from them. At the same time, the new regions created new political positions to the benefit of Ravalomanana supporters. His close friend Odette Rahaingosoa became chief of the Sofia region. Hanta Rabetaliana, a friend of Ravalomanana's advisors, became chief of the Haute Matsiatra region. Pijulas Jonah Justin became chief of the Melaky region with the support of the president's party, '**Tiako i Madagasikara**' (TIM), as did Barnest Andriamiarantsoa, chief of the Atsinanana region and Jerome Nosy Hariony, chief of the Diana region. Friends of the Deputy Prime Minister Zaza Ramandimbiarisoa also became chiefs of regions.

Party politics was a smouldering threat to Ravalomanana's reforms and his tenure. Madagascar's political parties are created to serve the candidate rather than the reverse, the norm in more mature democracies. '**Andry sy Riana Enti-Manavotra an'i Mada-**

gasikara' (AREMA), the party of former President Ratsiraka, did not disappear with his flight, but lost most of its bark and nearly all its bite. The legislative elections of December 2002 gave 103 of the National Assembly's 160 seats to TIM and another 22 seats to the Firaisankinam-Pirenena coalition, which supports TIM. AREMA won an anaemic three seats.

The legislative uniformity wreaked havoc on the party system while radicalising political factions. Following the 2002 social upheaval, former President **Zafy Albert** transformed his AFFA party into the '**Comité de Reconciliation Nationale**' (CRN). In 2003, CRN started taking on a more tribalist flavour. President Ravalomanana is of Merina ethnicity. The Merina were historically dominant over the 17 other ethnic groups in Madagascar. This ethnic divide has long formed the country's deepest socio-political divide. Ratisraka, ethnically Betsimisiraka, attempted to use this to his advantage throughout much of his career. With the CRN, Zafy Albert, ethnically Antakarana, has taken the same path. On 27 March, Zafy Albert joined his former nemesis, the AREMA party, and several other small parties in Barikadimy stadium in the eastern port of Toamasina (Ratsiraka's hometown and former stronghold) to form an alliance. They resolved to create a single national conference around the idea of the establishment of a Fourth Republic. By the end of the year, there was not enough unanimity of purpose for a single conference but the groups did agree on certain issues. Nominally, the call was for 'reconciliation' in the aftermath of 2002. In practice, the goal was to unseat TIM officials and push for early elections. The CRN platform sought to reverse the unchallenged victory of Ravalomanana and the TIM and to move to a transitional government. In October, CRN began to build support for the ouster of the current government through various means. The primary goal was to obtain 'millions' of citizen signatures advocating a national reconciliation conference, though at this they failed. Zafy still did not recognise Ravalomanana as president and encouraged his supporters to do the same. The basic questions of reconciliation – Did Madagascar indeed have a civil war that requires reconciliation? What is the meaning of national reconciliation for the CRN? What is a non-Merina cause? Is this the same as reconciliation? – have not been addressed by CRN.

October also saw the formation of the '**Club des 17**'. The name refers to the 17 ethnic groups other than the Merina. Several members of the political old guard, including Zafy Albert and **Herizo Razafimahaleo**, leader of the Ratsiraka-supporting Leader-Fanilo party, are founding members. The basic belief of the Club of 17 was that Merina should not hold significant political positions. They openly used tribalism to discredit the current regime. Ethnic groups tend to fall within provincial boundaries, so tribalism neatly follows provincial lines: Antananarivo province is predominantly Merina and the other five provinces predominantly comprise other ethnic groups. This situation accounts for the fervour of the 2002 divide and Ratsiraka's attempted strategy.

The other major challenge to the dominance of Ravalomanana and TIM came from the coalition of opposition members of parliament called 'Solidarité Parlementaire pour la

Défense de l'Unité Nationale' (SPDUN). SPDUN shared some of the goals and members of CRN. However, it was seen as a more moderate organisation focused on improving governance by alternative means to those posed by Ravalomanana. Its membership was split between Ravalomanana supporters and detractors. SPDUN sought to reform the political party system and the laws that govern it, and the members wanted a universal amnesty for all agitators in 2002, most of whom were associated with Didier Ratsiraka Most importantly, they wanted to see an end to Prime Minister Jacques Sylla's government. In June, several SPDUN leaders, such as Norbert Ratsirahonana (Avi Party leader and a Ratsiraka advisor), Richard Andriamanjato (AKFM-Renouveau Party leader and former speaker of the National Assembly), and Alain Ramaroson (Master's Party leader and supporter of Ravalomanana) voiced support for Ny Hasina Andriamanjato, son of Richard Andriamanjato, as the next prime minister.

Ny Hasina Andriamanjato is also an attractive prime ministerial candidate for Ravalomanana detractors, as the position could serve as a stepping-stone to the presidency. Andriamanjato is the former minister of telecommunications (under Ratsiraka), a leader in the AKFM Fanavaozana party, and sympathetic to the reconciliation cause of CRN. Zafy Albert made clear his intentions to run for the presidency in 2007, though given his age (77) and the fact that he was still tainted by his 1996 impeachment it was hard to imagine how his candidacy could materialise. There are those who hoped to see the return of Didier Ratsiraka: AREMA politicians in self-imposed exile such as former Deputy Prime Minister Pierrot Rajaonarivelo (himself a potential presidential candidate); AREMA leaders in Madagascar such as Senator Adolphe Ramasy; Victor Wong, president of the Association for Families of Prisoners (Ofpacpa), and too many CRN delegates for Zafy Albert's comfort. But as Ratsiraka, at 68, sat in France writing his memoirs, his candidacy seemed equally unlikely. By the end of of the year, only Prime Minister **Jacques Sylla** was a potentially serious challenger.

That CRN, the Club des 17 and SPDUN could be as vocal as they were was a sign of how far Madagascar has come in expanding civil liberties. Freedom House gave Madagascar a score of 4 for civil liberties (with 1 as the highest 7 as the lowest) throughout the 1990s until, when it was raised to a 3. There was reason for concern, however. For even as the public voice grew, public access to media outlets declined. **The Malagasy Broadcasting Service** (MBS) is owned not by the state but by President Ravalomanana and is run by his daughter Sarah. Since 2003, MBS has significantly expanded its holdings, buying up small stations and potential opposition outlets throughout the country. In 2004, the printing division cornered the market for printing product labels. This is of interest because Ravalomanana himself set the tone in 2001 by carefully expanding his name recognition through the use of his Tiko brand name.

Another controversy faced by Ravalomanana was his religiosity. From 18 to 27 August the president sponsored the 15th synodal session of the **Church of Jesus Christ in Madagascar** ('Fiangonan'i Jesoa Kristy eto Madagasikara' or FJKM). He successfully sought reappointment as vice-president of FJKM, a post he held before becoming president of the republic. Madagascar is divided between Catholicism and Protestantism and FJKM is Protestant. It has also long been one of the most important actors in civil society. The president insisted on high levels of religiosity from members of his government, including prayer sessions. He has been accused of showing favouritism to Protestant causes at the expense of Catholics in particular, including, the expenditure of more than $ 11 m in public funds on FJKM security and his personal involvement in building the country's largest cathedral in the Protestant stronghold of Fianarantsoa's Sofia area. The constitutionality of his role in FJKM has been challenged.

Foreign Affairs

Ravalomanana is an unapologetic capitalist whose liberal worldview is consistent with that of the **US**. For this reason, the US made it clear that Ravalomanana had its support even before he won the presidency. The US Agency for International Development drew up a plan for 2003–08 that prioritised 1) good governance 2) economic growth, and 3) social welfare. For the US this translated into three programmes: Democracy, Conflict and Humanitarian Assistance (DCHA); Growth, Agriculture and Trade (EGAT); and Economic Global Health (GH). **France** similarly touted Ravalomanana's democratic credentials, announcing it would bestow one of its highest honours on him, the **Louise Michel Prize**, "for his action in the defence and promotion of democracy, human rights and peace."

It was a boom year for Madagascar's entry into the global economy. A mission of eleven Japanese companies was in the country from 5 to 15 April. The United States Trade and Development Agency (USTDA) hosted several economic reconnaissance missions, starting with the Econergy International Corporation in January. Mauritius, France and Spain all sent economic missions in May. Germany signalled its interest by sending a dozen public works firms on a mission to Madagascar from 8 to 12 March, building on an existing role in that sector. On 19 May, the Overseas Private Investment Corporation (OPIC) announced that it had signed two memorandums of understanding, one with the minister of industry and the private sector and the other with the minister of energy and mining, pledging cooperation in attracting US investment to key sectors of Madagascar's economy. American companies were, for the first time, showing keen interest in the country. **Verizon Wireless** vowed to develop broadband access and **Paul C. Rizzo Associates** signed a contract to upgrade facilities at the Electricity and Water of Madagascar (JIRAMA) Corporation. The Malagasy government began work on a donor-supported **$ 1 bn transportation infrastructure enhancement project** (primarily roads), declared a two-year tax holiday on imports of investment and some consumer goods, and controversially opened up land sales to foreign investors. Madagascar was one of 16 countries that qualified for the **US Millennium Challenge Account** (MCA) assistance, a $ 1 bn programme in 2004. [Ravalomanana was invited to Washington by US President Bush.] On 15 October, James

D. McGee took over as US ambassador to Madagascar from Wanda L. Nesbitt and Stephen Haykin was appointed director of the US Agency for International Development mission in Antananarivo.

Multilateral lending also increased. President Ravalomanana met with **IMF Managing Director Rodrigo de Rato** and **World Bank President James Wolfensohn** in Washington in July. Wolfensohn then led a delegation to Antananarivo in October. Both de Rato and Wolfensohn showered praise on Ravalomanana for stabilising the exchange rate and safeguarding macroeconomic stability. In May, the World Bank signed the largest donor-sponsored environmental project in history – $ 49 m for the third phase of Madagascar's environmental programme (primarily focused on habitat protection). Endemism rates in Madagascar are around 80% making it one of the most biologically important places on earth. Madagascar has been labelled a 'biodiversity hotspot' and there were significant international efforts, supported by Ravalomanana, to invest in its protection. In July, the World Bank approved the **First Poverty Reduction Support Credit and Grant** worth $ 125 m. By the end of 2004, 26 World Bank projects worth $ 964.1 m were ongoing with $ 495 m yet to be disbursed.

For his part, President Ravalomanana worked to increase his global profile. On 21 September he spoke on the floor of the **United Nations** of his achievements as he saw them, including the stabilisation of democracy, the improvement in governance, the evolution of administrative functions and responsibilities and the encouragement of international investment. More interestingly, he spoke like a pan-Africanist leader in support of COMESA, SADC and AU (which was loathe to recognise Ravalomanana). He boldly asked for a **Marshall Plan for Africa**, and criticised the objectives of NEPAD as being just an emergency measure that fell far short of an appropriate plan to promote African development.

The reward for Madagascar's entry into the global economy was the **cancellation of a significant portion of its debt**. In October, the Paris Club cancelled 91% of Madagascar's pre-1983 bilateral debt. Ten of 14 countries cancelled 100% of debt. The largest bilateral debts were to France ($ 421 m), Japan ($ 345 m), Russia ($ 193 m), Spain ($ 169 m) and Italy ($ 164 m), all of which cancelled their debts. The US cancelled only $ 4.5 m of its $ 36.8 m while Britain cancelled all of its £ 27 m. Most critically, Madagascar qualified for debt reduction under the **World Bank/IMF HIPC** and $ 1.9 bn (42%) of its multilateral debt was cancelled in October.

Socioeconomic Developments

The cornerstone of Madagascar's recent economic changes was the massive **privatisation** efforts of President Ravalomanana. For example, 2004 saw one of the worst rice shortages in recent memory and prices skyrocketed to nearly MGA (ariary) 1000 ($ 0.57) per kilo –

an unmanageable sum for the average Malagasy and several times higher than usual. Ravalomanana adopted Ratsiraka's one-time call to arms, 'Fahavitantena ara Tsakafo' (food self-sufficiency). But where Ratsiraka failed was in trying to use the government as a sector guarantor. For Ravalomanana, this was a call to market promotion. Until the advent of Ratsiraka's white elephants of the late 1970s, Madagascar was a net rice exporter. With a rationalised rice market, a more efficient bureaucracy and a prioritised export-led trade sector, Ravalomanana hoped to bring back Madagascar's rice economy.

The government's approach in the water and power sector was similar. When it came to bringing about sustainable development, Ravalomanana was fond of saying 'Mino Fotsiny Ihany' (Just believe in God): what he seemed to mean was 'just believe in the market'. The public water and electricity corporation, **JIRAMA**, was formed in 1975 by the newly appointed Didier Ratsiraka to meet the government's objective of drinking water, sanitation and electrification for all. Unfortunately, it was run as a loss-leading social enterprise and fell far short of meeting its goals. It was put up for auction in June and Vivendi SA (a French conglomerate on the Fortune 100 list) and Lahmeyer International (a large German engineering company) were the two leading bids. On 30 September, the government introduced a modest MGA 1 per litre ($ 0.0006) fee for water at the public fountains where the majority of Malagasy urbanites fetch their water. This was met by claims of water fraud, popular protest, and a water strike, since water has to date been a free good at public installations.

There were some reasons for concern about Madagascar's privatisation programme. Ravalomanana's **Tiko** company has gone through a massive expansion. For instance, the Hiridjee family long held the government contract for rice importation. In October, the contract was voided. A new contract was signed with an association of rice growers headed by Alphonse Ralison (former minister of trade) and Magro, a Tiko subsidiary owned by President Ravalomanana. Magro then received an import tax exemption. It also served as the provincial offices for the TIM party. The Malagasy Broadcasting Corporation, Ravalomanana's company that has eclipsed both state media and all private media, became involved with audiovisual media and went from start-up to market standard for the product-label printing industry overnight. The Ravalomanana family partnered with the South African company Shoprite, which purchased the leading supermarket chain of Madagascar. Tiko bought a stake in Phoenix, the company that replaced the state oil company Solima and has been looking to create Tiko Petroleum. Tiko oil is the sole beneficiary in its sector of a 0% tax incentive. **Asa Lalana Malagasy** (Alma), a Tiko subsidiary, gained a monopoly on government contracts for urban street paving and other public works in Antananarivo and Tulear. The list goes on.

In a further worrying sign of the confluence between the public and private sector, the individuals involved shared a significant overlap. **Heriniaina Razafimahefa** was managing director of Tiko, chairman of Air Madagascar and treasurer of the TIM party. Gedeon

Rajaonson, the president's former chief of staff, was technical advisor to Tiko's Alma company. Patrick Ramiaramanana ran TIM ANALAMANGA, was chairman of the board of directors of JIRAMA, advisor to Mayor Ravalomanana and then himself became mayor of Antananarivo. Tiko was afforded substantial urban privileges (such as sole rights to large advertising space in the municipal stadium). Mamy Rakotoarivelo became the National Assembly vice-president (he was deputy speaker): he was also owner (and former director) of the leading newspaper, 'Midi Madagasikara', and a TIM member. Other former Tiko executives served TIM, including General Andrianafidisoa, Lala Rahamaefy, and Harisetra Raelojaonina. **Solofonantenaina Razoharimihaja**, former logistics director of Tiko and current vice president of the National Assembly, was elected president of the TIM party at the December conference (the party's first conference). In fact, the majority of TIM's leadership was comprised of Tiko executives or other close associates of the president, even as TIM dominated the political sphere.

All of this personal overlap did not seem to hurt the Malagasy economy. The 2002 conflict was devastating for Madagascar. The GDP dropped 12.7% that year as foreign trade came to a standstill. GNI dropped from $ 250 per capita to $ 230. The next year saw a rocketing 9.6 % GDP growth and a commensurate GNI per capita growth to $ 290. The vanilla industry estimated 2004 would bring 1,200–1,600 tonnes of vanilla (a primary export), up from 500 tonnes in 2003. Most other industries were up, services were up, exports were up, imports were up, and gross capital formation was up. The question was, how much of this was a post-conflict bounce and how much real growth? The World Bank projected GDP growth for 2004 at a healthy 5.3%. Yet this statistic, released in September, did not include the massive debt relief which was certain to buoy Madagascar's annual economic standing. However, it was not yet clear whether the government's reform course would create sustainable economic growth, and how it would be distributed. In September, the World Bank estimated that Madagascar would continue to see GDP growth averaging 6.7% through 2007.

Richard R. Marcus

Malawi

Although Kamuzu Banda's dictatorship ended ten years ago, it is only in the past two years that Malawi has rapidly changed into a totally different society in which leaders have to reckon with voices from below. This was evident in the 2004 general election. Bakili Muluzi, the incumbent state president for ten years, was prevented by a mass movement from pursuing a third term. His handpicked successor, Bingu wa Mutharika – popularly known as Bingu – won the election, but by a small simple majority. The political landscape was no longer framed by a dominant party: parties fragmented and coalitions were essential in the political game. Parliament had been the stumbling block for Muluzi in getting his third term, and it has become more and more vocal through its committee system. Not only politicians but also civil society at large, and in particular the media, have as a result secured more space to operate. The economic situation continues to be problematic. Food security remains fragile. The tobacco industry is still the backbone of the economy but is no longer as stable a money-earner as before. Relations with international financial institutions and the donor community have improved because of Bingu's initiatives to fight corruption and assure prudent financial management. However, the donor community is still hesitant. The international profile of Malawi under Bingu is still unclear, but he gave great prominence to a trip to China, Taiwan and Singapore.

Domestic Politics

When Muluzi failed to get parliamentary support for a change in the constitution to enable him to stand for a third five-year term, the ruling United Democratic Front (UDF) fragmented further. There had already been two splinter groups before that: the National Democratic Alliance (NDA) and the Forum for the Defence of the Constitution (FDC). Muluzi imposed Bingu wa Mutharika as **presidential candidate** at a national executive meeting of UDF already in April 2003, and a national convention merely endorsed his choice. He bypassed his vice-presidential lieutenants of the previous ten years, Aleke Banda and Justin Malewezi. Aleke Banda was the first to leave, and joined the People's Progressive Movement (PPM). Malewezi left UDF very late and joined PPM, but he also contested the leadership of another party, Malawi Forum for Unity and Development (MAFUNDE). In the end, Malewezi stood for president as an independent.

Other parties were also splitting. The Malawi Congress Party (MCP), the party that ruled Malawi from 1964–94, could not resolve its leadership struggles. John Tembo, the most prominent politician after Kamuzu Banda when MCP ruled, stood as the presidential candidate. However, this led to the departure of Gwanda Chakuamba, the presidential candidate in the 1999 elections. Hetherwick Ntaba, another ambitious MCP politician, also left after Tembo became the candidate. He formed the National Congress for Democracy (NCD), but he backed out of the presidential race. The Alliance for Democracy (Aford) split as well. Chakufwa Chihana had supported Bakili Muluzi in his bid for a third term, and this was unacceptable to a large number of Aford's MPs. These Aford members started a new party called Movement for Genuine Democracy (MGODE). The result of this **party fragmentation** was that the presidency was contested by five candidates: Bingu wa Mutharika (UDF), John Tembo (MCP), Brown Mpinganjira (NDA), Justin Malawezi (independent) and Gwanda Chakuamba (Mgwirizano Coalition). This coalition was composed of Gwanda's Republican Party (RP), PPM, MAFUNDE and various small parties.

Bingu wa Mutharika won the **elections** (20 May) with 36% of the votes cast. This was a good result for somebody who got 0.4% in the 1999 elections, when he stood against Muluzi. Bingu won because the opposition vote was too fragmented: John Tembo got 27% and Gwanda Chakuamba 26%. Parliamentary elections showed even more fragmentation: MCP was the largest party with 58 seats, UDF got 49 and independents 38. Ten parties are now represented in parliament. The election results necessitated **coalition politics**: the president's party was only a small minority in a parliament comprising 193 seats. None of the pre-existing coalitions secured a strong minority position either.

However, nobody was prepared for the **coalition making** that actually emerged. It was to be expected that Chikufwa Chihana, who had supported Bingu's bid for the presidency, would bring in six seats from Aford. However, although Gwanda Chakuamba's political career in the previous ten years had been in opposition to the UDF, the 16 RP members sided with UDF. MGODE, the rebels from Aford, joined UDF with three seats. About 25 independents, who stood mainly because the UDF hierarchy had not selected them, joined as well. The rest of the necessary support in parliament had to be mobilised from time to time. It took six weeks until 13 June to form a cabinet, because all party leaders in the coalition had to be consulted before anybody could be selected. Muluzi remained chairman of UDF and was thus also a major player in addition to the president. In fact, Muluzi had negotiated a veto over cabinet appointments as party chairman of UDF. Bingu, the state president, was not even an ex-officio member of UDF's national executive committee.

The political pattern of three regional blocks (Aford, north; MCP, centre; UDF, south) that emerged after democratisation in 1994 had become much more complicated. In the early years of democratisation, UDF had managed to succeed MCP as the dominant party in the political system. After the 2004 elections, however, there was no longer a dominant party. This has created more space for **divergent political opinions**. The major newspapers used to follow a much stronger party political line, but that is much less the case now. The courts have proved themselves as guarantors of constitutional freedoms in the struggle over the third term. Parliament is becoming a much stronger institution with respect to oversight as well as policy-making. Committees are critical about appointments, and instigate enquiries into corruption. The queries about the MK (Malawian kwacha) 1 bn loan scheme initiated by the president show the emergence of genuine checks and balances. The parliamentary committees receive considerable donor support.

Bingu also needs to have space to move against forces in the previous government if he wants to regain the favour of the international financial institutions as well as the donor community. Good governance and a good human rights record are essential to re-establish donor confidence. One of Bingu's first initiatives was to send a letter to the Danish government apologising for the governance issues that had made Danish donors leave Malawi.

These intentions are laudable, but it is doubtful whether they will produce tangible results. The **Anti Corruption Bureau** (ACB) has since its inception in 1996 produced only one conviction: the manager of the Petroleum Control Commission (PCC) pocketed bribes in awarding transport contracts. Bingu has appointed a high profile lawyer – Gustave Kaliwo – as head of ACB (20 September). The powers of ACB are limited, however. ACB can give the Director of Public Prosecutions (DPP) material to prosecute, but DPP needs presidential permission to proceed. It is thus very possible that political expediency may conflict with anti-corruption prosecutions. It is highly unlikely, for example, that the accusations against Cassim Chilumpha in relation to massive corruption in the primary schools building programme will be revived. Chilumpha was selected by Muluzi as running mate for Bingu and currently Chilumpha is vice-president.

Malawian politics has changed drastically, but the political arena remains dominated by people that have been around for a long time and are quite old. For example: Bingu is 71, John Tembo is 73, Gwanda Chakuamba is 72, Aleke Banda is about 70. Malawian politics is dominated by a **gerontocracy**. A lively culture of local politics would be conducive to widening the pool of political leadership. However, the **local government elections** that were due in 2004 were postponed indefinitely. The new government has not shown any initiative in promoting decentralisation.

Foreign Affairs

Because of the end of the Cold War and the liberation of Southern Africa, Malawi has reverted to being an **unimportant country in international relations**. It has lost its geopolitical significance as a pro-Western country that was open to dialogue with white minority regimes in Southern Africa. Muluzi used his Muslim identity to create openings to the Arab and Islamic world. Bingu is a Catholic and has shown no inclination to continue this. Malawi remains active as a member of SADC, COMESA and AU.

The Malawian army is trained by US advisors in **peacekeeping operations**. There is a Malawian contingent of peacekeepers in Darfur as part of the AU peacekeeping initiatives. Within Southern Africa, there were no striking new developments. Bingu opened the trade fair in Harare and appears therefore unwilling to follow the attempts to isolate Robert Mugabe. A **visit to Singapore, China and Taiwan** is Bingu's most striking initiative. This can be seen in relation to grassroots development: in the past five years, Chinese traders have established themselves in all district centres in Malawi. Unlike other Southern African countries, Malawi has no resources that would make it attractive to larger Asian direct investments.

Socioeconomic Developments

The Malawian economy suffers from persistent imbalances. **Budget deficits** are persistent and have been dealt with by domestic borrowing at high interest rates, especially in cases where donors have suspended disbursements. The average deficit on the budget on a cash basis including grants was 9.1% of GDP in the period 2001–03. The **trade balance** is also persistently in deficit. In the period 2001–03, the deficit on the current account was on average 9.2% of GDP. Malawi has no sources of foreign exchange other than donor support. Malawi is thus **donor dependent**. Delayed donor support arises from concerns about corruption and governance, but an agreement with the IMF would also restore confidence in the donor community at large.

The **IMF** has sent missions to Malawi under the new dispensation, but this has not yet resulted in a new agreement. IMF Article IV consultations for 2004 considered Malawi to be in a "precarious macroeconomic and social situation. Above budget spending and delays in donor assistance over much of the past two years have left Malawi with an unsustainable level of domestic debt, high interest rates and low private sector investment." The Malawian government is, however, desperate to have access to a new Poverty Reduction and Growth Facility (PRGF). A new government that has nothing to spend cannot fulfil any campaign promises.

Yet, **macroeconomic stability** is not completely elusive. The exchange rate remained stable in the past year at around MK 110 to the dollar. Inflation rose to 11.4% from 9.3% in 2003, but that was still much lower than the 40% inflation recorded in 2000. Interest rates showed a similar pattern: they remained very high but have declined. The reserve bank lending rate is now pegged at 25% from an all time high of 47% in 2000. The interest rates charged by commercial banks fluctuated between 27% and 30%. This relative stability might have been due to Ngalande Banda, governor of the Malawi reserve bank from 2000. The new minister of finance, Goodall Gondwe, is also trusted as a professional. He was on the IMF staff in Washington.

Food plays a major role in the macroeconomic stability of Malawi. Importing large amounts of food for famine relief, unless donor financed, puts pressure on foreign exchange reserves and the government budget. A good harvest means low maize prices, and this in turn lowers inflation. The general consumer price index is heavily influenced by food prices and will not rise much in years with good harvests. The inflation rate for non-food items was higher than the general inflation figure: 15% as compared to 11.4%.

Production figures for **maize** are to a considerable extent influenced by the distribution of free fertiliser and improved seeds to poor households (Targeted Input Programme, TIP). In the 2003–04 season, the government combined this with a fertiliser subsidy targeted at the poor. However, the logistics involved in bringing the required inputs into Malawi were very inefficient and caused the programme to fail. Those who wanted to buy fertiliser on the open market also faced supply difficulties, and fertiliser prices rocketed. The outlook for food production in the 2004–05 season is therefore bleak. A dry spell that occurred at the crucial period when maize cobs were maturing leads to an even more pessimistic prognosis.

Tobacco is the backbone of the Malawian economy. It provides cash income to many smallholders, and it is the major contributor to Malawian exports (61.9% in 2004). Most tobacco (about 87%) in Malawi is of the burley type that is dried in the open air under sheds. Malawi is the third largest producer of burley tobacco in the world after Brazil and the US. Burley production recovered from a drastically reduced output of 10,200 tonnes in 2003 to an all-time high of 14,800 tonnes. Malawi also grows flue-cured Virginia tobacco that is cured in barns by hot air streaming through pipes (flues). Zimbabwe used to be the major producer of flue-cured tobacco in the region, but this production has collapsed since the land invasions started. The Zimbabwean collapse should have opened a market for Malawi, but flue-cured production remained problematic. It dropped to an all time low of 830 tonnes and recovered to 2,300 tonnes. While export prices for burley recovered from a low average of $ 2.02 per kg in the 2002–03 season to $ 2.40 in 2003–04, this was far below the all-time high of $ 2.89 in 1997–98. Prices for flue-cured tobacco showed a similar pattern. Volumes of tobacco production as well as tobacco prices have turned from a downward to an upward trend.

The Malawian tobacco industry, which used to be highly regulated, has been considerably liberalised in the past ten years. This has led to a restructuring in the industry: for example, burley used to be grown on large estates by sharecroppers and is now grown by smallholders. This **restructuring of the tobacco industry** continues. The tobacco-buying companies are campaigning vigorously against obligatory marketing through an auction floor. They are increasingly engaged in direct production on estates as well as in direct marketing from smallholder farms. These forms of production are much more difficult to tax and can have grave consequences for government finances.

Liberalisation of the tobacco industry has led to a great infusion of cash into peasant households. However, tobacco growers are a minority among Malawian smallholders and represent richer households. Malawi remains primarily an agricultural country, with **agriculture** contributing 39.1% to GDP. This figure has fluctuated, but there is no change in the trend over the past ten years. Many households, even in urban areas, attempt to provide for their own maize supply. This increasingly requires inputs, such as fertiliser and improved seeds, as the soil is exhausted and seed degenerates. Those who cannot mobilise the cash for inputs will harvest little. They have to work for others at the start of the new agricultural season to obtain food. Because they undertake outside work at a time when they should be working on their own farms, they are in a poverty trap. There has always been much poverty in Malawi, but an underclass of people who cannot afford to feed themselves is growing fast. The **HIV/AIDS** pandemic continued to rage in Malawi and hit the poor harder than the rich, as they have less resistance to disease. Although anti-retroviral therapy is becoming available for HIV positive patients, this will benefit only the well off.

The **stagnation** in the Malawian economy is thus structural, and this is reinforced by the operation of financial markets in Malawi. The governor of the reserve bank of Malawi analysed this clearly when opening the new headquarters of a Malawian Finance Bank on 26 November: "Government efforts are geared toward reducing its domestic debt stock. Unfortunately, government securities are lucrative investment instruments for most institutions. It is high time, however, that banks resorted to more traditional roles of intermediation. . . . I am talking about making loans to the private sector, which is touted as the engine for economic growth."

Jan-Kees van Donge

Mauritius

Mauritius continued to be an African model case with respect to economic growth, social stability and modernisation. Based on the principles of democratic governance, globalisation and rapid technological innovation, Mauritius has leaped from being a least-developed country at independence (1968) to a middle-income country in the new millennium. Forward-looking government, regional integration and an open market approach to foreign investment and trade proved their effectiveness again in 2004. Some important changes in the political arena dominated domestic politics, including a change in the leadership, but electoral reform made no significant progress. The active foreign policy approach was reinforced and macroeconomic indicators improved.

Domestic Politics

As part of the so-called **2000 reform agenda** negotiated between the Mauritius Socialist Movement (MSM) and the 'Mouvement Militant Mauricien' (MMM), significant **operational and portfolio changes took place** in Mauritius's government. The electoral platform of these two political parties was the basis of their landslide victory in the general elections in 2000. In a carefully premeditated move spanning three years, Paul Raymond Bérenger, leader of the MMM and erstwhile minister of finance and deputy prime minister, became prime minister on 30 September 2003, while in parallel Sir Anerood Jugnauth, leader of the MSM and prime minister since 2000, moved to the honorary post of the president of the republic on 7 October 2003. Thus, for the first time in Mauritius's post-independence history, a member of the white French-speaking minority, Bérenger, took over executive power (the majority of the population and of government ministers is Hindu).

Bérenger introduced a new style of government by switching the locus of decision taking from the typical cabinet sessions to inter-ministerial working groups, over which he regularly presided. In order to accelerate economic and social decisions, bogged down by paper work and administrative lethargy when made under the classical ministerial system, he intervened directly in minister's affairs, without neglecting to secure the affected minister's consent. This approach reduced the autonomy of the minister; but acknowledged and valued administrative and technical expertise in the various ministries. Every minister was to a certain extent forced to adopt this new style ('méthode Bérenger').

Vice-Premier and Minister of Finance Pravind Jugnauth, who took over leadership of MSM from his charismatic father, Sir Anerood, appeared less experienced politically, because of his age. However, he already showed solid expertise in some key government portfolios (agriculture and finance) and was set to build a **bridge** between the generation that assumed leadership after independence in the late 1960s and the younger generation.

In public, this executive duo – the old hand (transformed from a revolutionary in the late 1960s to an honoured elder statesman) and the young technocrat were complementary and strongly appealed to a large public. On 16 December, Bérenger reshuffled his cabinet. By appointing a woman of Indian origin, Leela Devi Dookun-Luchoomun, as minister for art and culture, he appeased the majority of the population of Indian origin. She replaced Sylvio Michel, leader of 'Les Verts/Fraternels', who quit government over the controversial issue of compensation to slave descendants. This action was interpreted as a pre-electoral tactic to seduce the largest (and relatively coherent) block of voters for the next general election in the second half of 2005.

Opinion polls suggested a very close result in the upcoming election. The Mauritius Labour Party (MLP), led by Dr Navind Ramgoolam (son of the father of Mauritian independence, Sir Seewassegoor Ramgoolam) commanded 35–40% of support, while MSM could expect 15–20% and its coalition partner MMM 35%.

Since 2000, constitutional, and more specifically electoral reforms were on the political agenda. Agreement on them was supposed to occur simultaneously with the major government reshuffle of 2003. These reforms, however, stalled. As a result, neither a permanent electoral authority nor a **higher degree of proportionality**, advocated by some political parties for the next elections, was achieved: The so-called Sachs Commission had proposed the addition of 30 parliamentary seats (to 100) to be apportioned through a proportional system, provided the respective parties won at least 10% of the national vote. This proposal was supported by MMM and MLP. MSM feared, however, that this system would favour the larger parties to its own detriment. Hence, it proposed a limited enlargement of parliament by only 14 seats, which would indeed be elected proportionally.

At the same time, the Sachs Commission recommended a scheme for the **public funding of political parties**, but no concrete proposal was tabled. It was evident that the reforms would not pass through parliament before the next elections. However, some technical progress was envisaged: the government announced that Mauritius would introduce **Indian-type electronic voting machines** in order to improve the transparency, accuracy and pace of the electoral process.

Decentralisation was another reform project high on the agenda. After the introduction of regional autonomy for the island of Rodrigues in 2002–03, parliament voted in a Local Government Act in July that established five regional municipalities and made provision for seven additional communes in 2005. By this move, government wanted to promote **public services closer to the citizenry**, provide greater transparency and reconcile the public at large with the state.

Foreign Affairs

With the change in government and the accession of Bérenger as prime minister, Jaya Cutteree (MMM) was promoted to the post of foreign minister, and the foreign ministry was made more competent by being integrated with the ministry of foreign trade and regional integration, all under one minister. Jaya Cutteree, of Indian origin, was now second to Bérenger and handled all important issues related to the WTO Doha Round; negotiations between the EU and the ACP states on the implementation of the Cotonou Treaty; the US AGOA; and regional integration within the framework of SADC and NEPAD. Thus, government acted deliberately on its analysis that Mauritius, as a small island state, was highly affected by globalisation processes by **merging the classical aspects of a foreign policy with new trade challenges**. Cutteree himself was put forward as a candidate for the post of Secretary-General of WTO and was backed by ACP and African states. As negotiation leader within ACP on the sugar protocol, multi-fibres agreement and economic partnership agreements in the sub-regional Cotonou context, he had without doubt acquired the necessary experience for the post.

Mauritius continued to follow a foreign policy based on 'natural orientations': highly dependent on the tourist trade from Europe, good relations with **France** in particular were important. As Mauritius depended on apparel exports to the US under the AGOA II initiative, the government took a **US-friendly** stand on the Iraq issue. Close relations with **India**, influenced not least by ethnic considerations, were further expanded through cooperation in the information technology sector and through joint ventures on the African continent, mainly in Mozambique. Sonia Ghandi, leader of the Indian Congress Party, visited Mauritius in November.

Bérenger visited **Mozambique** from 26–29 May and restored good neighbourly relations with Madagascar. The political climate between Mauritius and **Madagascar** indeed improved considerably, but remained **strained by commercial incidents**. Malagasy President Ravalomanana had visited Mauritius in 2002, significantly his first diplomatic trip as new president, and Bérenger travelled to Antananarivo (4–7 April) with a large ministerial and business delegation. Joint tourism enterprises, a pool arrangement between Air Mauritius and Air Madagascar, the reform and privatisation of the ailing Malagasy sugar industry, export processing zones and agro-industrial projects were on the agenda. Since both countries were complementary in outlook and structure, trade was supposed to create a win-win situation for both. However, because of supply-side constraints, commercial disorganisation and speculation, at least two trade agreements were broken by Madagascar: a potato supply scheme for Mauritius, initially planned to supply 300 tonnes, delivered only nine tonnes, with 40 tonnes of seed potatoes initially provided by Mauritius being sold somewhere on the speculative market in Madagascar. A second incident involved the withholding of delivery of crude oil to Mauritius by the private Malagasy firm, Galana, when Malagasy authorities detained the tanker and charged that Galana had contravened Malagasy ecological regulations. Both cases seemed, however, to be of only temporary significance and did not impede the long-term developments in tourism, transport and sugar.

On 18 August, Mauritius took over **chairmanship of SADC**. Indeed, next to multilateral trade negotiations, Bérenger stressed regional cooperation in SADC and AU. For his chairmanship of SADC he formulated an ambitious political and economic **reform agenda**, including concerted action in multilateral trade negotiations; giving priority to the preferential treatment of the region under the AGOA and Cotonou arrangements; massive efforts by the whole group of countries to reduce supply-side constraints; and coordination of EPA (Economic Partnership Agreements) negotiations due to overlapping membership to SADC and COMESA. Furthermore, Bérenger called for massive improvement in intra-regional trade in the run-up to 2008, in order to safeguard food supplies and attract foreign direct investment. He declared that free and transparent elections would be a condition of political credibility and progress (thus pinpointing Zimbabwe). Externally, SADC should give relations with India and China new economic importance. As a result, Bérenger demanded a massive improvement of the organisational capacity of the SADC secretariat.

In line with continental reform agendas, Bérenger supported the development of a peace and security council as an organ of the AU as a means of fostering an adequate regional security architecture. The government was confident that the **APRM** developed under the NEPAD reform agenda would verify its conviction that good economic governance, democracy and political stability formed a single unity. Mauritius started in June this self-evaluation process in regard to democracy, civil liberties, good governance and the rule of law (along with Ghana, Kenya and Rwanda). In September, the government created an independent National Economic and Social Council (NESC) to undertake the assessment. It was tripartite in character, being composed of people from government, civil society and the economy (capital and labour), and started to collect data on the basis of questionnaires and hearings with all stakeholders and opinion leaders in Mauritian society. These initiatives attempted to provide evidence of the commitment to reform in a partici-patory way with respect to rule of law, transparent decision taking, democracy, civil liber-ties and governance. The government believed that undertaking the APRM process was the only way to demonstrate to donor countries its reliability and to attract aid and direct pri-vate investment.

Socioeconomic Developments

Mauritius continued to be a middle income country that managed to feed her people and provide – in principle – free primary education and health to all, thereby contrasting favourably with many other states of the continent. The main sociopolitical discussions were about the quality of services and upcoming challenges. Given the ambition to become an international **information technology hub**, secondary, professional and university edu-cation had to be reorganised. Post-primary education patterns continued to follow mainly communal/religious lines, creating disparities and inequities. The government and Catholic church negotiated an agreement to provide greater access to all sectors of society. The health and social insurance system was no longer adequate. Mauritius's population began to dis-play the symptoms of industrialised countries: an ageing society with new illness profiles (heart attack, blood pressure syndromes, cancers and others) that called out for structural reform.

Macroeconomically, Mauritius, after two years of low growth (3.9% of GDP 2001–03), regained a **middle growth path** of 4.6% (IMF estimates: 4.4%), brought about by the build-ing industry and transport and supported by a good sugar harvest and a solid tourism indus-try. This growth was, however, accompanied by a **high unemployment rate** of 10%. The inflation rate dropped from 6.4% in 2002 to 3.8% in the budget year 2003. The budget deficit was reduced to 5.4%. GDP per capita rose from $ 3,800 in 2000 to $ 5,000. Foreign currency reserves increased twofold from 2000 to 2004 and amounted to € 1.5 bn. Domestic and foreign investments increased substantially, producing a solid growth outlook for the years to come. In spring, international financial institutions, in particular IMF, testified to Mauritius's excellent results in the implementation of its structural adjustment programme, and declared Mauritius to be an example to and paradigm for other countries.

Despite the encouraging growth rate, the labour market was ailing: in brief, Mauritius faced **unemployment with growth**. Whereas tourism and services were constant, textiles and sugar were affected respectively by the ending of the sugar protocol with the European Union and of the multi-fibres agreement on 31 December. The export processing zones for textiles shrank in terms of numbers of firms and of employment (net -16%). They were partly affected by relocation of establishments to China and elsewhere. Capital-intensive automation, innovation and production for the high-end market were the survival strategy for some large textile firms. The sugar industry was under pressure to downsize and modernise, and is reducing the workforce by 50% through a longer-term process involving early retirement and golden handshake schemes. Energy from sugar cane biomass and chemical derivatives from sugar were innovative developments in this sector.

In order to improve **fiscal efficiency**, parliament passed a 'Mauritius Revenue Authority Bill' on 3 October. Whereas the economic and fiscal logic of this initiative to close loopholes and enlarge the tax base of the fiscal system was evident (in the past a number of specialised institutions had dealt with import duties, income taxes and company duties leading to incoherence and loopholes) and agreed by everyone, employee unrest threatened, since the personnel of the new authority were to be hired on a competitive basis. Public sector trade unions protested massively and prepared to strike. Government finally defused the situation by modifying the recruitment process. Future senior personnel had to go through a competitive screening process, but the rank and file were to be collectively integrated, thereby safeguarding workplace security for the ordinary employee.

Mauritius had preserved, against the odds in the face of structural adjustment programmes, a solid social security safety net comprising two parts, a tax-fed minimum old age pension and a National Pension Fund retirement scheme, financed by workforce contributions (3% labour, 6% capital). In order to concentrate the income effect of the old age pension in the lower income layer, the Mauritius government proposed a reform whereby the tax-based component would only be paid to those who did not reach a certain minimum through their National Pension Fund retirement payments (MRs 20.000, approx, € 240). This proposal was rejected by the general public and the reform was stalled.

In November, the government proposed a new foundation of labour laws in a White Book. Since the labour laws dated back to the late 1970s – when labour unrest led the first post-independence Ramgoolam government to restrict labour organisations and strikes and make government arbitration obligatory – they needed to be adapted to the realities of the 21st century. The ILO explained to the government that the provisions of the **core labour standards** had to be introduced, e.g., Convention No. 87 on the liberty of association. The White Book took up these issues. As to strikes, government stipulated a quorum for a strike decision. This was interpreted by trade unions as an unacceptable setback, and they wanted to see the right to strike guaranteed in the constitution. Government continued to claim a central role in wage setting and collective bargaining and agreements.

The Asian **tsunami** on 26 December did not significantly affect Mauritius, apart from minor damage on Rodrigues Island. Obviously the coral barrier and lagoon around Mauritius protected the coastal areas from flooding. It is thought that due to the destruction of the South Asian tourist infrastructure, part of the tourist influx will be redirected to Mauritius. Nevertheless, due to **over-exploitation of the lagoon and barrier reef**, the marine ecology surrounding Mauritius is in jeopardy. There are some 50 luxury tourist hotels, with their leisure activities, along the coastline. These, along with rapid industrialisation and urbanisation have created extreme problems of waste and water management.

Mauritius has drawn funds from the European Development Fund in order to develop comprehensive sewage and wastewater treatment processes as a matter of top priority, in order to protect the environment.

Klaus-Peter Treydte

Mozambique

The election of a new president dominated Mozambican politics. Frelimo's ('Frente de Libertação de Moçambique') Armando Guebuza won a flawed but convincing victory, suggesting that Mozambique is to be an elected one party state on the model of Botswana and South Africa. Guebuza takes over as president from Joaquim Chissano, whose attempt to stand again as candidate for election was blocked by Frelimo. GDP growth continues at more than 8% per year and there was considerable further expansion of the mineral and energy sector, but more than half the population live in extreme poverty and unemployment is rising. Growth seems to benefit only those who are already better off.

Domestic Politics

The **presidential and parliamentary elections** on 1–2 December gave an overwhelming victory to Frelimo, which has governed Mozambique since independence in 1975. This was the third national multiparty election since the end of the war of destabilisation in 1992. Although support for Frelimo has been declining slowly, in the 2004 election support for the opposition collapsed completely, with Renamo ('Resistência nacional Moçambicana') president Afonso Dhlakama losing more than one million votes. Turnout was 3.3 m (about 43% of registered voters) compared to 5.3 m in 1999 and 1994. Frelimo won 160 seats in parliament compared to only 90 for Renamo. Nearly all observers, including Frelimo, predicted a close race similar to 1999, and the low turnout and **collapse of the opposition** came as a complete surprise. Equally unexpected was the poor showing of the first serious third party, 'Partido da Paz, Democracia e Desenvolvimento' (Party of Peace, Democracy and Development/PDD) and its leader Raul Domingos. He and Guebuza had been the two lead negotiators in the 1990–92 Rome peace talks, but Domingos was expelled from Renamo in 2000. He ran a well-funded and properly organised campaign but gained less than 3% of the vote and PDD only 2%, which was not enough for a parliamentary seat (which requires at least 5% of the national vote).

Frelimo's declining vote is linked to **public discontent** with widespread corruption and what is widely described as the 'deixa andar' ('don't bother, let it go') attitude of the Chissano government: both are contrasted with the integrity, lack of corruption and activism of the Samora Machel era. Grassroots resentment at the rise of corruption and a new self-serving elite was widely reported by Frelimo organisers to be behind the close election in 1999. Under the constitution, Chissano could have stood for one more term, but his bid was rejected at the 2002 Frelimo party congress. Guebuza was chosen instead, with the backing of the Frelimo old guard. This is not a generation change, since both had senior positions in the 1964–74 liberation war and Guebuza, at 62, is only three years younger than Chissano. But Guebuza is an activist on the Samora model, and he spent the year after the congress travelling extensively throughout the country, rebuilding the party base to ensure its loyalty and to ensure that it encouraged the loyalists to vote, which did occur.

Over the past 35 years, **Frelimo** has put party unity above all other goals: there have been no splits and, in recent years, no expulsions. Chissano remains on the 15-member political commission and campaigned for Guebuza. Frelimo has been careful to bring into the party and into government posts political figures who might be considered threats. For example, Luisa Diogo was clearly a rising star, and only joined the party in the late 1990s when she was already deputy finance minister. She became finance minister in 2000 and was named prime minister on 17 February, to replace Pascoal Mocumbi (who moved to the Netherlands to head the European-Developing Countries Clinical Trial Partnership).

Renamo, originally created by Rhodesian security services and promoted by the South African apartheid military, gained a local base of sorts during the 1976–92 destabilisation war. As part of the peace accord, and with substantial help from donors, it became the main opposition political party. But guerrilla leader Afonso Dhlakama kept extremely tight personal control and failed to build an effective party, and good organisers who were seen as a threat, such as Raul Domingos, were expelled. Furthermore, he ran a very negative campaign, stressing his claim that the 1994 and 1999 elections had been stolen from him by fraud, and ignored advice from sister parties such as the British Conservative Party to mount a more positive campaign stressing what he would do as president. The result was that many who voted for the opposition in the past saw no point in voting, since Dhlakama himself was saying it was pointless. Dhlakama was also hurt by a lack of money. Influential backers, such as the US, had decided that he had no chance of creating a real party that could win an election, and funding dried up.

Discontented electors did not opt for any of the 19 other parties on the ballot paper, none of which won parliamentary seats. The low vote for Raul Domingos, a known figure with a well-financed campaign, surprised most observers. One factor in the **low turnout and low support for the opposition** was that none of the parties presented serious alternative policies – and there is, indeed, little that they could do, with development policies and the budget largely set by the World Bank and the IMF. Indeed, Guebuza, who ran on a platform promising 'change' and often seemed to be running against Chissano rather than Dhlakama, seemed to be the only candidate to indicate a break with donor orthodoxy, when he suggested the need for a development bank. It would appear that Mozambicans have accepted Frelimo as the 'natural' party of government, rather like the ANC in neighbouring South Africa. There seems to be no serious political opposition on the horizon, and Mozambique appears to have become an **elected one-party state**.

Although the victory of Guebuza was clear and convincing, the election itself was widely condemned by international observers from the EU, Carter Center and the Commonwealth for **fraud, misconduct and incompetence**. The electoral register was a combination of 1999, 2003 and 2004 registrations and contained more than 11 m names (compared to a voting age population of 9.1 m), while computerisation of the register had been extremely sloppy (an example of the 'deixa andar' attitude that pervaded government) with many errors, omissions and duplications. After the 2003 local elections, the constitutional council ordered a clean-up, but only a rushed partial one was undertaken in the four months before the elections. The July registration update started late and missed many potential voters (especially in Renamo majority areas) because of lack of film for voters' photo cards and fuel for mobile brigades in rural areas.

The whole process was overshadowed by **the obsessive secrecy** of the National Election Commission (CNE). Former US President Jimmy Carter, who observed the election, said he had never seen anything like it in any election he had observed. Computer software for tabulating the results was written by CNE staff and kept secret. At the last minute, CNE ordered an audit of the software, which revealed major security lapses, including uncontrolled access to the database by senior election officials. The same thing had occurred in 1999, and no detailed results were ever published. In meetings with the press during the 2004 election, Carter raised questions about the 1999 results, and, in private, election staff admitted to using their computer access to tamper with results in that year. Discussions during 2004 made it clear that the actual results in 1999 must have been much closer than the official 200,000 votes victory margin for Chissano.

The **chaos in the voters' role** and the confusion caused by the hasty rewriting of the tabulation software meant that an official list of polling stations was never published (CNE said it was 'a state secret') and the computer database contained at least 600 nonexistent polling stations. The counting system is complex. Each polling station has no more than

1,000 voters and the count is done in the polling station in the presence of party agents and observers. Results sheets are then posted at each polling station and sent to the provincial and national levels for tabulation. At national level, CNE then makes 'corrections' entirely in secret and with no explanation. Computer chaos meant hundreds of results sheets were rejected by the computers and had to be tabulated by hand. In addition, the constitutional council revealed that 699 presidential results sheets and 731 parliamentary results sheets – nearly 6% of all polling stations – were not counted in the final tally because the results sheets had simply been stolen or had ink poured over them.

Nor had the **voting process** gone smoothly. The 'Mozambique Political Process Bulletin' estimated that people at more than 700 polling stations were unable to vote because polling stations did not open or opened very late, because they were in the wrong place, or because they had the wrong register books. This seems to have particularly affected areas that had voted for Renamo in the past. Election commissions at provincial and local level also proved as partisan in many areas. More than 100 independent domestic observers were refused credentials and hundreds of Renamo party delegates were refused credentials or expelled from polling stations and often from entire districts by force. This allowed ballot box stuffing in at least 300 polling stations and probably accounted for at least 100,000 of the votes for Guebuza. In some of the polling stations there were turnouts of over 100% and nearly everyone voted for Guebuza. The ballot box stuffing did not change the presidential result, but cost Renamo at least three parliamentary seats.

The fraud and misconduct did not provoke a public response because two **parallel counts** based on results sheets posted at individual polling stations confirmed the landslide victory. The domestic Electoral Observatory did a simple sample count from every 16th polling station (as best as could be located without a full list of polling stations) and 200 Radio Mozambique reporters read out results from individual polling stations live on the air for two days, eventually covering half of all polling stations. By early on the first day after voting, Radio Mozambique had confirmed the low turnout and huge Frelimo majority.

Armando Guebuza promised **sweeping changes**, including an end to 'deixa andar' and curbs on corruption. The government had to be agreed upon with the Frelimo political commission and there was extensive negotiation between factions, as well as a need to protect some allegedly corrupt Chissano cronies. The two top posts went to women – Luisa Diogo remained as prime minister and political commission member Alcinda Abreu became foreign minister.

The new government is much less Maputo-focused. Guebuza in early speeches stressed the need to **prioritise development** outside the Maputo area, and he created a new development and planning ministry. All ten governors in the previous administration were given posts as ministers or deputy ministers, and several other ministers have strong grassroots links in either party or provincial government. The new government has the style of Samora Machel, with ministers making unannounced visits and expecting civil servants to arrive at work on time, at 7.30, and with public meetings in which people are encouraged to speak out and criticise and complain. Guebuza and Diogo also immediately challenged the IMF by ordering the hiring of 6,000 more teachers and presenting to parliament a budget that breaks spending limits. The biggest question remained over the justice system and the willingness of the new government to deal with corrupt members of the Frelimo elite.

On other political matters, **mayors and local assemblies** took office between 5 and 10 February, following elections the previous November. For the first time, the opposition Renamo party controlled four of 33 municipalities, including the port cities of Beira and Nacala. A **revised constitution** was approved at a special parliamentary session on 16 November. It makes no fundamental changes but slightly increases individual rights, allows dual nationality and changes contested wording to confirm that a president can serve only two five-year terms. The **justice** sector remains one of the biggest problems, with widespread corruption and inefficiency. For example, Supreme Court President Mario Mangaze reported that at the end of 2004 the supreme court had a backlog of 107,047 cases. At current rates, this will take more than four years to clear, but new cases are arising faster than old ones are dealt with. Corruption, combined with the huge backlog, make it very difficult to enforce contracts, and this is now seen as a major constraint on investment.

The **looting of two privatised state banks** in the late 1990s continues to cause ripples. It is widely believed that the main beneficiaries were people close to then President Joaquim Chissano. Two people who tried to investigate the matter, editor Carlos Cardoso and the head of banking supervision at the central bank, Siba-Siba Macuacua, were both assassinated. With the informal agreement of most of the donor community, Siba-Siba's murder was never investigated. Cardoso, however, had many friends abroad, and in 2003 six people who carried out the murder were convicted. The alleged leader of the hit squad, Anibal dos Santos Junior ('Anibalzinho') was twice allowed to escape from the high security prison: on 1 September 2002 (after which he was tried *in absentia* and then caught in South Africa in 2003 by a team from the public prosecutor's office operating without the knowledge of the interior ministry) and again on 9 May. He was caught on 24 May in Canada and deported back to Mozambique on 21 January 2005, after the supreme court unexpectedly and without clear explanation granted him a new trial. Meanwhile, on 15 June seven people were sentenced for fraud for taking $ 14 m from one of the banks in 1996: the investigation and trial had been repeatedly delayed, amid rumours that higher level people were involved.

Foreign Affairs

Mozambique remains highly fashionable with the **international donor community**, which continues to increase aid. It has become an important stop for foreign visitors. Mozambique is one of 16 countries eligible for the US Millennium Challenge Account: it has applied for $ 150 m but no decision had been reached. However, corruption continues to be an issue.

Most donors were prepared to turn a blind eye, but the Nordic states were not. After an audit, **Sweden** demanded that the ministry of education repay $ 400,000 that had been misused, allegedly in part for scholarships for friends and family of the minister, and for failure to use proper tendering procedures.

The then Portuguese Prime Minister José Manuel Durão Barroso visited Mozambique on 28 March, but relations with **Portugal** were somewhat tense, in part because changes in the Portuguese government meant the breaking off of the long-running negotiations over the Cahora Bassa dam, which is still 82% owned by Portugal. Brazilian President Luis Inacio Lula da Silva had promised closer cooperation during a visit in late 2003, including plans to build a factory to produce anti-retroviral drugs. Chissano then visited **Brazil** from 31 August to 4 September. No progress was made on the ARV factory, but the Brazilian mining company Companhia do Vale do Rio Doce won a contract on 12 November to take over the Moatize coal mines, which have been largely inactive for more than 20 years. In return, it paid Mozambique $ 123 m and plans to export 13 m tonnes of coal a year to Brazil. **China** continues to build links with Mozambique. The Chinese constructed the headquarters for the foreign ministry, which were completed in 2004, and a Chinese company won the contract to expand the Maputo water system.

Mozambique's President Joaquim Chissano completed his one-year term as president of the **African Union** on 6 July. Because of his position, Mozambique hosted a series of international meetings. The NEPAD implementation committee met in Maputo on 23 May. Chissano was a speaker at the World Economic Forum at Davos, Switzerland on 23 January and on 2–4 June Maputo hosted the African Economic Summit, which is part of the World Economic Forum. The heads of state summit of the ACP partners of the EU took place in Maputo from 23 to 25 June. The summit's final statement was highly critical of the EU on a number of trade issues. And Prime Minister Luisa Diogo, in an opening speech, accused industrialised countries of "a lack of political will to attend to the genuine problems of the developing countries."

Mozambique had a contingent of 200 soldiers with UN forces in Burundi and sent observers to Darfur in Sudan. Mozambique has good relations with all its neighbouring states. **South Africa** has become an important investor and the South African presence is increasingly notable in the south of the country. President Joaquim Chissano and the government have backed Zimbabwean President **Robert Mugabe**, but have not said a great deal in public: Mozambique's leaders do not want to set a precedent for the overthrow of a long-standing leader. Privately, many in the Mozambican elite are fed up with kowtowing to donors and they respect Mugabe for standing up to Britain and the US.

Socioeconomic Developments

Economic growth was again expected to be over 8%, with inflation at 11%, according to the governor of the Bank of Mozambique, Adriano Maleiane. But commercial bank interest rates remained very high at 24%, which limited investment by those without access to credit outside Mozambique. The devaluation of the dollar (down 16% against the metical) helped keep inflation down, but caused problems for those export commodities priced in dollars, particularly cashew nuts and cotton.

Foreign investment remains high primarily in the minerals and energy sector, which generates income for Mozambique but, because of its largely enclave character, contributed little to development and employment creation. The **Mozal aluminium smelter**, one of the largest single private investment projects in Africa, is owned by the Australian company Billiton. It was located in Mozambique because of the port and access to cheap electricity from South Africa (actually imported at low prices from Cahora Bassa). Currently, the Mozal smelter produces 550,000 tonnes of aluminium per year, following the doubling of capacity that came on line in late 2003, but a second planned expansion project will raise this to 750,000 tonnes per year. Natural gas from an offshore field began to flow through a pipeline to South Africa on 26 March.

In October, the Irish Kenmare Resources began construction on a $ 450 m **titanium mine** in Moma: the mine could add 2% to Mozambique's GDP but will create no more than 2,000 jobs. The Australian mining company WMC has rights to titanium in Chibuto, but the project has been delayed by the inability to negotiate a low enough electricity price with South Africa's Eskom.

Management of the central **railway** system from Beira port was won on 5 October by a company which is 51% an Indian consortium and 49% the Mozambican railways company CFM. It will operate the line to Beira and take control of the line to the Moatize coalmines and Malawi, which was destroyed by South African and Renamo forces during the war of destabilisation in the 1980s. On 16 December, the World Bank signed an agreement for a loan to provide $ 104 m of the $ 165 m needed to rehabilitate the railway to the Moatize coalmines, and the Indian partners will provide the rest of the rehabilitation money. Agreement has also been reached on management of the northern railway system linking the port of Nacala to Malawi. The consortium has Malawian, Mozambican, US, Portuguese and South African partners.

Sugar is the only productive sector to be protected by import tariffs, and one of the other two sectors to show substantial growth. Four sugar mills have been rehabilitated with investment from Mauritius and South Africa, and employment exceeds 20,000. But the industry is threatened by changed EU import policies, which may cut the high fixed import price and make the industry unprofitable. **Tobacco** production has jumped from 2,000 tonnes in 2000 to 45,000 tonnes, making it the sixth largest export (after aluminium, gas, prawns and fish, timber and sugar). Tobacco producers are mainly peasant out-growers, but also include a group of farmers expelled from land in Zimbabwe who moved across the border to Manica province.

Unemployment continues to rise. According to the National Statistics Institute Workforce Bulletin, formal sector employment is said to have been 301,000 in 2002, more than half in small enterprises. However, registered unemployment has risen steadily, from 109,000 at the end of 2000 to 140,000 at the end of 2004. **Telecommunications** is slowly being opened to competition. The first private mobile phone company, Vodacom, began operations and had by the end of the year 195,000 subscribers compared to 550,000 with the state-owned M-Cel (although many of those are pre-paid and relatively low use). This compares to 80,000 fixed lines with the state owned TDM. For the first time, there is serious private competition for the state-owned airline, LAM. Air Corridor, based in the northern city of Nampula, now links most major cities. All 128 district-capitals now have electricity, and the power line from Cahora Bassa is being extended and is expected to reach the two northern provincial capitals of Pemba and Lichinga in early 2005. Pemba's oil-fired power station suffered a disastrous fire on 26 December, resulting in serious power cuts.

An estimated 14.9% of Mozambicans between 15 and 49 years old are believed to be HIV positive and **AIDS** now accounts for 23% of all deaths, and an estimated 400,000 Mozambicans have died of the disease. The ministry of health estimates that 1.5 m Mozambicans are HIV positive and at least 200,000 with sufficiently advanced AIDS could benefit from anti-retroviral therapy. By contrast, only 6,500 people were receiving anti-retroviral drugs by the end of the year and the number was planned to rise to only 20,000 during 2005. Spending on HIV/AIDS now exceeds $ 50 m per year. **Malaria** remains the other big disease problem, the ministry of health reported in April. There were 4.5 m cases in 2003, leading to 3,212 deaths in hospital and many more who died without being counted in rural areas.

Confusion remains about whether ordinary Mozambicans are better off and have gained from the high GDP growth rates. Data published in 2004 by the National Statistics Institute cover only through 2002, and show that, despite rapid rises in GDP, **per capita consumption** is actually falling from a high of $ 199 in 1998 to $ 146 in 2002 – the same level as at the end of the war of destabilisation in 1992. On 30 March, the government published its 2002–03 household survey, which showed that Mozambicans living below the local extreme poverty lines fell from 69% in 1997 to 54% in 2003. Income gaps are huge: the bottom 10% of the population accounts for only 2% of expenditure and the bottom 50% accounts for only 21%, while at the top the richest 20% accounts for 53% of expenditure and the top 10% spends 39%.

On 21 May, the national statistics institute and UNICEF jointly released new data based on a **demographics and health** survey. These show 41% of all children under five suffer from chronic malnutrition. Under-five mortality has improved substantially, falling from 263 per 1,000 live births in 1997 to 178 in 2003. Maputo city has the lowest poverty and under-five mortality, while Cabo Delgado in the north is worst. Access to safe drinking water remains low, increasing from 36% to 40% of the population over the last four years, according to Deputy Water Minister Jenrique Cossa. Adult (aged 15 and above) illiteracy fell from over 90% at independence in 1975 to 60% in the 1997 census to 54% in the

2002–03 family survey but education remains only a dream for many children – there are one million children between 6 and 13 who cannot get a place in primary school.

On 16 April, the government increased the **minimum wage** by 14% to meticais 1,120,297 (then $ 46.7) per month. The minimum wage has increased steadily, and faster than inflation, since 1996, when it was $ 23.7. The agricultural minimum wage was increased to $ 33.6. Removing **landmines** planted during the 1964–74 liberation war and the 1976–92 war of destabilisation continues: it was announced on 2 November that 220 m square metres had been cleared since 1996, at a cost of $ 189 m. However, corruption in the de-mining programme caused delays. Over 177,000 weapons have been destroyed over a nine-year period in joint Mozambican-South African police operations. Mozambique retains one of the smallest armies in the region and there is a strong bias against military service. Registration is compulsory for all 18 year-olds, but in January fewer than 10% actually registered.

A new **family law** was approved by parliament on 24 August, which in general improves the status of women. In addition to civil marriages, the law recognises traditional and religious marriages and de facto unions, which in particular means that a man is responsible for paying maintenance for his children and former partner. **Radio** remains the main source of information in the country, predominantly the government-owned Radio Moçambique (RM) and 'Televisão Moçambique' (TVM), which broadcast in all languages and from all provincial capitals, although there are now a number of private television and radio stations. The family survey published during the year showed that 50% of households had access to a radio, compared to 27% in the 1997 census. The Mozambican **print media** remains small but lively, competitive and free. The state-owned daily, 'Notícias', prints 13,000 copies per day, and it owns the Sunday newspaper 'Domingo' (circulation 10,000) as well as the sports weekly 'Desáfio' (4,000), so that the company is profitable. The private Beira-based daily 'Diário de Moçambique' has a circulation of 5,000. There are four private weeklies: 'Savana' (14,000), 'Zabeze' (6,000), 'Demos' (2,000) and 'Embondeiro'. In addition, there were several Maputo-based faxed dailies and various local newspapers and community radios, largely supported by donor funds.

Joseph Hanlon

Namibia

As a result of the parliamentary, presidential and regional elections, the South West African Peoples' Organisation (SWAPO) of Namibia further consolidated its dominance. The nomination of SWAPO's presidential candidate – succeeding the country's first head of state and president of the former liberation movement since its foundation in 1960 – resulted in fierce intra-party competition and the sidelining of longstanding political office bearers. The land issue became further politicised and initiatives to expropriate land contributed to growing insecurity among commercial farmers. Overall macroeconomic performance suffered through export losses due to the strong currency. Public expenditure came under pressure as debts accumulated further, and state finances face a critical degree of constraint.

Domestic Politics

The biggest shifts in the domestic political power structure – maybe since independence in 1990 – took place as a prelude to this year's parliamentary and presidential elections. Due to internal party opposition, Namibia's head of state Sam Nujoma – along with Robert Mugabe, the only remaining independence-era president still in office – decided against pursuing a fourth term. He suggested Hifikepunye Pohamba, the party's vice-president and his closest confidante, to the central committee as his successor. The committee met on

2 and 3 April to prepare submissions to an extraordinary SWAPO congress on the **presidential candidate**, but denied Pohamba the status of sole candidate and nominated three potential successors. Delegates to the extraordinary SWAPO congress, held from 28 to 30 May, were tasked with making a final choice. During the internal campaign, the factional fights revealed disunity to an extent hitherto unseen.

Nujoma used his executive powers as head of state to **dismiss Foreign Minister** Hidipo Hamutenya, Pohamba's strongest contender and rival, from his cabinet post on 25 May, just ahead of the congress. Hamutenya's deputy, Kaire Mbuende (former SADC executive secretary), considered a supporter of his minister, also had to vacate office with immediate effect. Notwithstanding such drastic harassment, almost one-third of the more than 500 congress delegates voted for Hamutenya in the first round, which, however, failed to produce a candidate with an absolute majority. Snatching all but one vote from the third candidate, Nahas Angula, minister of higher education and employment creation (allegedly a "fallback candidate" for Nujoma in case his favourite did not make it), Pohamba finally emerged as clear winner.

The result of the subsequent **electoral convention** held by the party's central committee from 1 to 3 October was the rigorous implementation of the Nujoma line and the strict exclusion of the so-called Hamutenya camp from the party's medium-term political future. The number of votes candidates received decided their ranking on the party list, which was headed by 12 candidates nominated by the president. The party held 55 of 72 parliamentary seats, having won 75% of all votes in the 1999 elections. Hamutenya ended in the 57th position – an obvious indication that he would be prevented from returning as a legislator and cabinet member (ministers have to be members of parliament). The same fate befell those considered to be his supporters, including several ministers as well as the speaker of parliament. They were ranked even lower on the list. The minister of agriculture, another of the victims, drew his own conclusions and tendered his resignation on 7 December. Seemingly with the blessing of Nujoma, former Prime Minister Hage Geingob made his return to Namibian politics. Ousted from office by the president halfway through the third legislature, Geingob had joined a World Bank agency for Africa in Washington DC. He attended the convention, made himself available as a candidate and was ranked sufficiently favourably to ensure safe re-election as a member of the next parliament.

The **parliamentary and presidential elections** on 15 and 16 November were initially beset by minor organisational flaws, mainly in remote rural areas, due to computer problems and the weather conditions. According to all observer missions, the voting process was free and fair. Of a record number of 838,447 ballots (some 85% of close to one million registered voters), SWAPO again secured more than 75% of the valid votes and 55 of the 72 seats in the **National Assembly** with effect from March 2005. In the fourth parliament, parliamentarians will represent seven different parties (previously five), with six of them sharing 17 seats.

Opposition parties were more divided than ever before both internally and among themselves, while the different party platforms represented few if any substantive policy alternatives. The Congress of Democrats (CoD) maintained its second rank in the party political landscape, despite a decline from seven to five seats. Its members had been partly recruited from the ranks of dissenting SWAPO activists prior to the parliamentary elections in 1999. The Democratic Turnhalle Alliance (DTA), the official opposition at independence, has been in steady decline and retained four of its previous seven seats. The Herero-based National Unity Democratic Organisation (NUDO) separated from the ranks of the DTA and obtained three seats of its own. The United Democratic Front (UDF) – another ethnically oriented interest group, rooted in the Damara communities – consolidated its position by increasing its seats from two to three. Like NUDO, the Republican Party (RP), supported mainly by members of the white minority, campaigned for the first time outside the DTA and gained one seat. Surprisingly, the Monitor Action Group (MAG), representing the most conservative white element in postcolonial Namibia, managed to keep its one seat.

Voters expressed unexpectedly high confidence in SWAPO's new **presidential candidate**, Hifikepunye Pohamba, who was elected in parallel through separate ballot papers. Like his predecessor, he obtained more votes than the party (76.4%). Given the preceding conflict around his nomination, this was a surprising victory and an impressive sign of party unity, despite internal differences. As Nujoma remains in office as SWAPO president until the next ordinary party congress in 2007, close collaboration between the comrades of almost fifty years and continuity in SWAPO politics (and, hence, Namibian politics) seems likely.

Numerous minor irregularities and inconsistencies in electoral procedures, however, provoked **legal intervention** by the CoD and RP. They filed a court case to be able to view documents the Electoral Commission of Namibia (ECN) had refused to disclose. The high court ruled on 16 December in favour of the application. On the basis of the evidence collected, CoD and RP contested the election results in the high court on 21 December. They claimed they had discovered an array of failures to comply with the Electoral Act, and discrepancies between voting figures and results, as well as a series of other irregularities. The court was expected to pass judgment in early February 2005.

Regional elections took place on 29 and 30 November and SWAPO enjoyed another landslide victory, thereby confirming its overwhelming dominance. The turnout of more than half (53.5%) of the almost one million registered voters was markedly lower than in the national elections. The party garnered 96 of the 107 constituencies and increased its seats in the 13 regional councils (which also appoint the members to the National Council) from 80% to 90%. Another series of intrigues and power struggles accompanied the nomination of the party's candidates. The most prominent victim was the previous chairperson of the National Council, whose career came to an end.

The **local authority elections** held on 14 May were already characterised by local feuds in numerous urban centres, as party members plotted over the candidate list. Party headquarters interfered in several cases, imposing its own views and even appointed councillors other than those elected. Protests in a variety of municipal constituencies revealed anything but unity on the ground. This tempted President Nujoma to use election rallies on 8 and 9 May to warn against the invasive forces of imperialism and capitalism, forces that would divide even SWAPO's leadership. All told, the various elections during the year consolidated SWAPO's hegemony, but also exposed a degree of internal tension and division hitherto unseen.

Anti-imperialist rhetoric was also deployed in mid-June by government spokespersons to dismiss critical references in Amnesty International's (AI) annual report for 2003 on **human rights** in Namibia. The report was criticised as the "usual garbage", lacking in substance. AI had expressed concern about arbitrary detentions and excessive use of force by police and special units, and about undue delay in the **Caprivi high treason trial**. The latter had dragged on since the failed secessionist plot in August 1999, in the aftermath of which more than 120 suspects were arrested and continue to be held in custody. The trial only started during 2003, and numerous technicalities and legal disputes have since prolonged the deliberations, and there is no end in sight. In the meantime, more of the arrested suspects have died than people were killed during the original skirmishes.

The year 2004 brought reminders of one of the darkest chapters in the country's **colonial history**. However, no senior government official attended the ceremonies, which marked the hundredth anniversary of the beginning of the Herero war against German colonial occupation on 11 January 1904. This conflict resulted in what is considered to be the first genocide of the 20th century. The government commemorated the centenary by issuing a special stamp on the theme of reconciliation on 21 March (Independence Day). Nujoma's designated successor as head of state, however, did attend the ceremony, in which a German minister also participated (see below).

Foreign Affairs

In his new year's message, the president pledged that Namibia would continue to pursue what he termed "**principles of economic diplomacy**" as the core of its foreign policy. The country's international engagement was indeed largely confined to trade and economic negotiations and agreements. The good relations with East Asian countries continued to feature prominently. These operate with companies and contractors in Namibia and employ their own citizens in large-scale projects – much to the dismay of local stakeholders, such as industry and trade unions. **China** honoured Nujoma with the publication of a Chinese version of his autobiography, handed to him on 20 July on occasion of his 12th visit. The Chinese-Namibian trade volume increased by 52% between 2002 and 2003 to reach almost $ 75 m. It was announced during his visit that the five members of the Southern

African Customs Union (SACU) would negotiate a free trade agreement with China. Nujoma then travelled to **Malaysia**. Several thousand workers are employed in a textile factory in Windhoek established by a Malaysian company under the AGOA and with considerable material support from Namibian authorities. This project is considered a success by both governments, notwithstanding massive criticism of environmental damage, appalling employment conditions and numerous violations of labour standards and practices, including the illegal employment of several hundred unqualified contract workers from Bangladesh, a scandal that made local headlines during September.

The Asian trip was part of a round of farewell visits by the president. He had already underlined the good relations to **Brazil** by meeting President Lula da Silva on 21 June, mainly to discuss trade matters and defence cooperation. Brazil seeks to strike a deal worth $ 35 m for supplying ships to the nascent Namibian navy. Nujoma also met President Castro while visiting **Cuba** from 22 to 24 June. Between his overseas journeys, and in connection with them, he stopped in several **African countries** (Zambia, Ghana, Kenya, Tanzania, Angola) and attended the summit of the AU in Addis Ababa on 8 July. President Chissano from Mozambique, was in Windhoek on 6 and 7 December on his own farewell visit.

Due to the dismissal of both the minister of foreign affairs and his deputy in May (see above), Namibia's international policy was hardly visible except for the president's activities. The new foreign minister had no track record in diplomatic affairs and displayed no ambitions in this regard before the end of the legislative session. In the campaign to marginalise those considered to be in the Hamutenya camp, five officials previously nominated for postings abroad were instructed in December that their appointments had been revoked. The minister of trade and industry, originally supposed to sign a trade agreement with Mercosur ('Mercado Común del Cono Sur') in Brazil on behalf of a SACU delegation in mid-December, was replaced without notice upon Nujoma's intervention by the minister of fisheries. The Brazilian government told the trade and industry minister upon his arrival that he was no longer expected and had no role to play.

A century after the **colonial genocide**, the government agreed with the official German position. This is that no apology will be offered, which might have implications for compensation claims being pursued by a group of Herero in a US court. Chancellor Gerhard Schröder, during his first visit to African countries at the end of January, did not include the former colony in his travel plans. However, the German minister for economic cooperation and development attended the commemoration of the battle at Ohamakari near the Waterberg on 11 August. She acknowledged the German warfare as genocide from a modern perspective. Asked for an apology (the word did not appear in the text she read), she explained that her whole statement was an apology. There was, however, no visible change of policy on the issue of compensation for particular groups. If, how, and to what extent the descendants of the victims (mainly Herero and Nama) will be compensated for the historical injustices and their consequences remains to be seen. During her visit on 19 November, the parliamentary secretary of state at the German ministry for economic cooperation and development indicated that Germany would increase its financial support for the redistribution of land. Germany is Namibia's biggest single donor country. Namibians receive more German development funds per capita than anyone else.

Zimbabwe's minister of information, Jonathan Moyo, commented on the land issue (see more below) during an official five-day visit in the last week of February. He expressed satisfaction with the historical moment he could attend when government expressed its determination to pursue expropriation of land from commercial farmers, but dismissed speculation that there was anything more than coincidence between his presence and the announcement. Shortly after, and following the signing of a memorandum of understanding by the two governments, a team of six **experts from Zimbabwe** assisted Namibian authorities with advice in the area of land evaluation and surveying. Minister Moyo's visit served to establish a common **newspaper for the Southern African region** published jointly by the two governments, on the basis of a memorandum of understanding signed with his Namibian counterpart. The two information ministers launched the first issue of 'The Southern Times' on 3 September at Victoria Falls. A further plan foresees the establishment of a 24-hour satellite television news channel, Africa World, to be set up through a joint venture involving the two state broadcasting companies.

These **close Namibian-Zimbabwean ties** were further underlined by President Nujoma in his opening speech at Zimbabwe's international trade fair in Bulawayo on 29 April, during which he stressed that Namibia supported Zimbabwe "openly, whether imperialists like it or not." He assured his hosts at a banquet that Namibia would, in the event of an attack, send its army to the rescue within 24 hours and praised the president and people of Zimbabwe for being "a shining example of resisting imperialism and colonialism."

Socioeconomic Developments

The country's new president-elect served during 2004 as minister of lands, resettlement and rehabilitation. He signalled his hitherto unsuspected determination to pursue an increasingly proactive **land policy**. In a televised statement on 25 February, Prime Minister Theo Ben Gurirab announced that government would, in addition to its policy of willing seller-willing buyer, now also expropriate land within the constitutionally defined framework. He said more than 240,000 people were registered and waiting to be resettled. Minister Pohamba confirmed in parliament on 2 March the intention to implement land redistribution more aggressively. In his May Day speech, President Nujoma emphasised that **expropriation of farms** would not only target under-utilised land, but also serve as a punitive measure. He warned "minority racist farmers" that "steps will be taken and we can drive them out of this land . . . as an answer to the insult to my Government."

A letter of 10 May by Pohamba was sent to some 15 farmers expressing "interest in acquiring their property." In response, a minority of white farmers embarked on a confrontational course. At a meeting on 9 June, they polarised the issue by expressing open defiance of government policy and accusing the commercial farmers' Namibia Agricultural Union (NAU) of pursuing a sell-out strategy. This drew strong reactions from the trade unions and SWAPO representatives. By mid-year the land issue was being widely canvassed in public debate. This matter was also reported and commented on, mainly critically in the international (particularly German) media, which often drew (so far largely unfounded) parallels with Zimbabwe.

The initial provisional valuation role for the 12,509 registered commercial farms in the country, mainly owned by around 3,800 white farmers, was closed on 29 September, after a month for inspection. This was a clear step towards implementing the long-announced plans to introduce a **land tax**, which aims to raise some N$ 20 m annually. At the end of October, Minister Pohamba stated that government had since independence purchased 137 farms, totalling close to 875,000 hectares, on which over 1,500 families had been resettled.

Finance Minister Saara Kuugongelwa-Amadhila tabled the **annual budget for 2004/2005** on 24 March in parliament. Considered to be conservative and typical for an election year, government spending was projected to increase by 3.6% to N$ 12.7 bn. The budget deficit, at N$ 589 m, was estimated to be 1.6% of Namibia's GDP and supposedly well below the 3% target government had earlier set (but failed to meet in most years). The finance minister repeated appeals for **fiscal discipline** from previous years. Government debt by the end of the fiscal year (31 March) had reached 30.3% and was projected to reach 32% a year later. National debts had ballooned by 30% from N$ 7.9 to 10.2 bn between the 2002/3 and the 2003/4 financial years. As the budget allocations revealed, government now spends approximately the same proportion of the budget (about 9%) on each of defence, public order, health and debt servicing.

An **analysis of the past 15 budgets** by the local Institute for Public Policy Research (IPPR) in July, saw "little reason to believe that public spending is becoming more equitable and more focused on the poor", but found evidence of "a strong suspicion that public spending is increasingly being channelled to more privileged groups in society employed in activities that bring little in the way of returns through higher economic growth, such as in defence, paramilitary security, intelligence and poorly performing parastatals." It concluded that "it is quite possible that poverty and inequality have worsened and that the national budget has done little to offset this trend."

Several factors contributed to **negative economic performance**. Fisheries suffered from the high exchange rate and a low fishing quota. The industry was additionally hampered by labour unrest and strikes. The chamber of mines recorded positive new developments and investments in the mining sector, but also myriad problems. Government finance suffered from a lack of taxes not only as a result of sluggish economic performance but also due to decreased revenue from a revised SACU agreement. Some N$ 270 m less income was anticipated, increasing the budget deficit to 2.7%. As a result, and in combination with the growing debt services, the finance minister announced in parliament on 1 December that for the first time there will be no **additional budget**. Instead, the remaining N$ 148 m in **contingency funds** were distributed without parliamentary approval on a variety of items, none of which (except one previously released disbursement to support flood victims in the Caprivi) qualified as unexpected expenditure. Among the biggest payments was an advance to meet contractual obligations in the building of the new state house (N$ 52 m). This is a controversial monument, constructed – like Heroes' Acre a few years earlier – by North Korean contractors. Its costs are now estimated to exceed N$ 750 m.

Against the background of these sobering realities, the country's long-term national development policy, **Vision 2030**, was officially launched on 2 June – six years after President Nujoma had initiated the blueprint. Complementing and guiding the five-yearly national development plans, Vision 2030 aims to place the quality of life of all Namibians on a par with people in the developed world by 2030. It assumes that by then the country will have a population of no less than three million people (currently below two million) and an unemployment rate of less than 5% of the work force (currently estimated between 30% to 40%, depending on the criteria).

On 1 July, the **World Bank** approved a Global Environment Facility (GEF) grant of $ 7.1 m. This signals a deviation from the government's previous refusal to deal with international financial institutions. During the year, Namibia's ranking in the Human Development Index (HDI) dropped by 2 positions and the ILO report presented at the Bangkok AIDS conference on 14 July estimated that more than 150,000 people among the country's labour force were HIV positive. It further projected that **life expectancy** (in previous years well above 60 years) had been reduced to 44 years. Fifteen years after independence, the average lifespan of the Namibian people had dropped below the level prior to decolonisation.

Henning Melber

South Africa

In the third democratic election since the end of apartheid, the African National Congress (ANC) consolidated its hold on power with an even larger majority. South Africa confirmed its role as the leading economic, political and military power in sub-Saharan Africa and as Africa's interlocutor with major foreign powers. While President Thabo Mbeki set out on his second term in office, debate on his succession opened up. Vice-President Jacob Zuma, the most likely candidate for the presidency, became entangled in a drawn-out court case in which one of his business associates faced charges of fraud and corruption.

Criticism of government performance focused on its ineffective HIV/AIDS policies, its policy of 'constructive engagement' with President Robert Mugabe of Zimbabwe and the widening gap between rich and poor in South Africa itself. Economic growth, at 3.7%, exceeded expectations but with little effect on high unemployment figures. In his state of the nation address, Mbeki announced a swing in socioeconomic policies from neo-liberalism towards the concept of the developmental state.

Domestic Politics

Unemployment emerged as the biggest single issue in the election **campaign for the national and provincial elections** on 14 April. The main opposition parties, the

Democratic Alliance (DA) and the Inkatha Freedom Party (IFP) had concluded an electoral alliance on a platform of free market policies, extending to deregulation of the labour market. The alliance blamed the continuing high unemployment on over-regulation and over-protection of workers in the formal economy, whose hard-won rights are being jealously protected by the trade unions. The liberal alternative is a two-tier labour market, with the 'third world' at the bottom effectively unregulated. The DA has also suggested export-processing zones, where South Africa's labour laws would not apply. The DA did not succeed in its attempts to shed its image of being a party of white liberals protecting white privilege, in spite of ongoing efforts to attract prominent black faces into the party. For its part, IFP did not manage to extend its electoral base beyond its core constituency of Zulus and a section of white voters in KwaZulu-Natal. The alliance with the IFP enabled the DA, however, to present a more balanced racial profile on platforms and in local government. The political alternative advocated by this opposition alliance is unacceptable to the Congress of South African Trade Unions (COSATU), the main trade union movement that makes up part of the **tripartite alliance** with the ANC and the South African Communist Party (SACP). In the electoral campaign, the ANC benefited from the celebration of 'Ten Years of Freedom' by underscoring the hard-won liberties and rights in the ten years of democratic rule, which it equated with ten years of ANC government. Among the achievements are vast improvements in access to water and electricity, the building of 1.4 m new houses, an increase in adult literacy from 83% to 89%, an increase in welfare benefits and the beginnings of a more equitable distribution of land. The election campaign passed uneventfully, with none of the campaign-related violence that marked earlier elections. Despite fears of a revival of tensions in KwaZulu-Natal, there were few incidents.

Turnout was 76.7% of registered voters, compared with 89.3% in 1999. Of 27.4 m eligible voters, about 75% had registered. The ANC achieved its largest majority yet. For the first time, the ANC also became the majority party in all nine provinces, including the hotly contested Western Cape and KwaZulu-Natal. With 69.6% of the national vote, the ANC polled well above a **two-third majority**. The official opposition DA came second again, with 12.3%, while the IFP polled only 6.9%, compared to 8.6% in 1999. The **New National Party** (NNP) was virtually annihilated, with 1.8% (seven seats in parliament).

Of a total of 400 seats, 279 went to the ANC, 50 to the DA and 28 to the IFP. Next was the United Democratic Movement (UDM) with nine seats. Patricia de Lille's Independent Democrats, like the NNP, won seven seats; the African Christian Democratic Party six seats; the Freedom Front Plus four seats; and the Pan Africanist Congress (PAC) and the United Christian Democratic Party three seats each. AZAPO (Azanian People's Organisation) obtained two seats, as did the (largely Indian) Minority Front. As in previous elections, most South Africans voted along racial lines, although the ANC made substantial inroads into the Indian working class neighbourhoods of Durban and the Coloured working class areas of the Western Cape.

Mbeki retained a strong women's presence in the **cabinet**. Jacob Zuma was returned as vice-president, in spite of his involvement in a complex case of alleged fraud and corruption (see below). Zuma has been hailed for his conciliatory role in defusing the potentially explosive conflict in KwaZulu-Natal, where IFP-ANC rivalry has claimed hundreds of lives since the mid-1980s. With Mangosuthu Buthelezi sidelined, the Zulu presence in the cabinet was significantly diminished. The reappointment of Zuma, one of the most prominent Zulus in the ANC leadership, may be prompted by the imperative to maintain some kind of ethnic balance in the cabinet. Pallo Jordan, known as an outspoken voice with an independent mind, returned to the limelight with his appointment as minister of culture. Ronnie Kasrils switched from water affairs back to being minister of intelligence services. Alec Erwin moved from the department of trade to public enterprises. Trevor Manuel stayed on as minister of finance. A surprise was the appointment of AZAPO's Mosibudi Mangena as minister of the newly created portfolio of science and technology. The IFP no longer figured in Thabo Mbeki's new cabinet. IFP leader Mangosuthu Buthelezi, who served as minister of home affairs previously, was not appointed to any cabinet position. Two IFP candidates for junior cabinet posts withdrew. After the elections, IFP said it would continue its cooperation with the DA.

The **NNP**, having been deserted by its historical constituency (the white Afrikaans-speaking minority), failed to attract black votes. It decided to dissolve itself as a party after its 90th anniversary in August and invited its followers to join the ANC. NNP leader Marthinus van Schalkwyk himself joined the ANC and was rewarded with the portfolio of environmental affairs and tourism. Former President F.W. de Klerk, however, resigned from the party in protest against the recommendation to join the ANC. Even in the Western Cape, where the NNP succeeded in building a coloured constituency, the party obtained only five seats in the provincial legislature. Afrikaners had either withdrawn from politics or joined forces with the DA or the conservative Freedom Front (Plus). In the 2004 elections, Afrikaners became the largest group of non-voters. It was agreed that local NNP councillors who crossed the floor to the ANC would retain their seats. As a consequence of the floor-crossing option, the ANC also became the majority party in the Cape Town metropolitan council. Thus, the architects of apartheid have been swallowed by their historical foes.

In the **Western Cape**, Ebrahim Rasool took over the premiership from Van Schalkwyk, again heading an ANC-NNP coalition, but with a diminished NNP component. In the **KwaZulu-Natal (KZN)** legislature, the ANC won 38 seats, the IFP 30 and the DA seven. The IFP lodged 42 complaints of irregularities in the election process, but shortly after the independent electoral commission declared the election to be free and fair, the IFP withdrew its legal challenges. Party leader Mangosuthu Buthelezi said that he did not want to spoil the celebrations for the first decade of democracy. In the new ANC-led provincial government, the IFP retained three ministers, but party President Buthelezi said at Inkatha's July conference in Ulundi that the IFP nonetheless considered itself as an opposition party. The new ANC premier S'bu Ndebele declared the city of Pietermaritzburg both the legislative and administrative capital of the province. Under IFP rule, the provincial govern-ment had shuttled back and forth between Pietermaritzburg and Ulundi, the former capital of the KwaZulu Bantustan. In the **North West Province**, Popo Molefe, one of the leading figures in the anti-apartheid United Democratic Front in the 1980s, resigned from politics to pursue a career in business.

The **funding of political parties** became a contentious issue, with both the DA and the ANC refusing to accede to requests to open their books. Some large companies, such as the mining giant Anglo-American, AngloVaal Mining, AngloGold, and the communications giant MTN stated that they contributed to the campaigning costs of all parties represented in parliament. Some black business consortia emerging from black empowerment deals (see below) donated substantial amounts to the ANC. At the request of former presidents De Klerk and Mandela, who made a joint appeal for funds for political parties, the insurance firm Sanlam gave R 1 m each to the ANC and the NNP.

A judicial inquiry, the **Hefer Commission**, named after its head, cleared the Public Prosecutor Bulelani Ngcuka of allegations that he had worked as a secret agent for the apartheid regime. Retired Judge Joos Hefer stated that the allegations were "ill-conceived and entirely unsubstantiated." Rumours about Ngcuka having betrayed his comrades in the anti-apartheid struggle started circulating after his announcement in 2003 that he had *prima facie* evidence that Vice-President Jacob Zuma had been involved in soliciting bribes. Ngcuka added, however, that prosecution would have no prospect of success. President Mbeki acted quickly by setting up a judicial inquiry into the allegations against Ngcuka. During the judicial hearings, the origins of the rumours were traced to former Minister of Transport Mac Maharaj and Mo Shaik, an advisor to the foreign ministry. Maharaj had also been questioned about payments from Schabir Shaik (brother of Mo Shaik) into his wife's bank account. The previous year, in July 2003, Ngcuka had called a confidential press briefing with black editors, which resulted in a wave of unfavourable publicity about the vice-president. Zuma laid a complaint with the Public Protector Lawrence Mushwana, who concluded that the public prosecutor was to be blamed for improper conduct. **Ngcuka resigned** in July, after ten years as national director of public prosecutions. Ngcuka also headed the elite investigative unit, the Scorpions, modelled on the FBI. On 8 November, he was appointed executive chairperson of black empowerment company Amabubesi Investments.

Because of this judicial inquiry, public attention was temporarily diverted away from the original **corruption case** against Zuma and Schabir Shaik. Vice-President Zuma is alleged to have solicited a yearly bribe of R 500,000 from the French arms company Thomson CSF (now Thales) to shield the company from being investigated for improper dealings in the controversial multibillion **arms deal** concluded by the South African government in 2000. On 11 October, the trial against Zuma's financial advisor Schabir Shaik opened in the high court in Durban, amid intense media speculation that a conviction of Shaik would also put an end to Zuma's ambitions for the presidency. Shaik faced charges of corruption and fraud.

Both Zuma and Shaik have a long history in the anti-apartheid struggle, during which Shaik acted as a money smuggler for the ANC. He later became a businessman and acted as financial advisor to his long-time friend Zuma. Shaik owns one of the arms companies under investigation. According to the charge sheet, Shaik's company, Nkobi Holdings, has since 1995 paid substantial amounts to Zuma in cash, bonds, loan repayments, school-fees for his children, etc. in return for Zuma's help in obtaining government contracts. Zuma has not been charged, but he did send legal representatives to the court case, which continued into 2005. Zuma hinted that the charges are inspired by political motives.

Winnie Madikizela-Mandela's appeal against her conviction on numerous charges of fraud and theft was partially successful (5 July). The Pretoria high court changed her four-year sentence to a wholly suspended sentence. The judge dismissed 25 charges of theft against the former president of the ANC's Women's League, but upheld the conviction on 43 charges of fraud. The charges related to a scam involving bank loans, with letters signed by Madikezela-Mandela stating falsely that the applicant was employed by the Women's League. The ANC welcomed the ruling and stated that Madikizela-Mandela still has a valuable role to play in South African society.

Dozens of **parliamentarians** came under scrutiny in a probe launched in 2003 into the **misuse of travel vouchers**. The names of MPs accused of cashing expenses for trips that were never made have not been disclosed. In September, when the Nigerian-owned but Johannesburg-based newspaper 'ThisDay' listed 92 present and former ANC MPs as being involved in the travel scam, the ANC demanded retraction of the article and a written apology to all those named in the article.

Rifts in the Tripartite Alliance were temporarily plastered over during elections times, but flared into the open again in the second half of the year. The SACP was unhappy with the pact with the NNP. A massive strike by public servants, organised by unions in the education, health and security sectors in September, was resolved through a deal with five of the eight public sector unions. They accepted a three-year agreement with slightly higher wages than previously offered by the government. A remarkable feature of the strike was that for the first time large numbers of whites turned out to demonstrate alongside their black colleagues. In November, a meeting of the Alliance was postponed indefinitely because of differences over Mbeki's policy on Zimbabwe and over Black Economic Empowerment (BEE) policies (see below). COSATU voiced unprecedentedly harsh criticism of Mbeki's stance on Zimbabwe, which was seen as supportive of President Mugabe. On 26 October, a 14-member COSATU delegation was deported from Zimbabwe shortly after arrival in Harare, and was severely censured by Mbeki, who accused the COSATU leaders of showing contempt for a sovereign government. Mbeki questioned the motives of the COSATU leaders, whom he accused of adventurism and grandstanding while the South African government was seeking to bring about a negotiated settlement in Zimbabwe.

Archbishop emeritus **Desmond Tutu** added his voice to the mounting critique when he questioned BEE policies in an address on 23 November at the Nelson Mandela Foundation in Houghton. He said that BEE seemed to benefit only a small "recycled" elite and did little for poverty alleviation. He begged his audience to keep the "struggle values" in mind and to strive for a caring, compassionate society. Tutu also raised the issue of Basic Income Grants (BIG) of R 100 to R 200 a month for all South Africans. The government discarded the scheme as unaffordable and undesirable. It also argued that a 'hand-out' would not encourage people to look after themselves. The Nobel laureate branded this response as "extremely cynical" in a society where some people become rich overnight by the stroke of a pen. Tutu praised the many achievements of ten years of democracy, but also voiced concern over freedom of expression and the lack of open debate within the ANC, pointing out the dangers of "uncritical, sycophantic, obsequious conformity." President Mbeki hit back on his ANC website, accusing the archbishop of inadequate knowledge of the facts and a lack of "respect for the truth."

Shortly before the elections, the government announced a national **HIV/AIDS** treatment programme, involving the provision of antiretroviral drugs in all provinces. Treatment became more widely available, with 103 clinics now accredited by government to provide antiretroviral therapy and counselling facilities. Minister of Health Mantombazana Tshabalala-Msimang was reinstated after the April elections, in spite of her unpopularity with AIDS activists. Shortly after her reinstatement, the director of the government's programme on AIDS resigned. More than 20% of people between the age of 15 and 49 are believed to be HIV positive. By 2010, life expectancy will be 43 years, 17 years less than South Africa would have had without AIDS. The South African government remained reluctant to provide statistics. However, the start of the treatment programme did not silence the acrimonious public debate on the AIDS issue, which increasingly unfolds along racial lines. President Mbeki launched a scathing attack on "white bigots" during a parliamentary debate on HIV/AIDS in October. When asked about his silence on a pandemic, which has infected some 5.6 m people in South Africa, causing at least 600 deaths a day, Mbeki replied that some white people regard blacks as "rampant sexual beasts, unable to control our urges." The DA said Mbeki's comments were a disgrace, and that he had made false accusations of racism.

White reactionary minorities remained in the headlines. In Pretoria, the trial began of 22 rightwing whites of the Boeremag (Boer Force) who stand accused of conspiracy to topple the government. Giving evidence, one of the accused stated in May that he believed at the time that a coup d'état was the only way of ensuring the survival of white South Africans. The plotters had planned to take over military bases and police stations. In another case, 60-year-old Eugene Terre'Blanche, leader of the Afrikaner Weerstandsbeweging, was released from jail on 11 June after serving three years of a five-year sentence for attempted murder of a black security guard in 1996.

A scandal involving South African-based **mercenaries** intent on staging a coup in Equatorial Guinea caused much publicity when it turned out that local resident Mark Thatcher, the son of former British Prime Minister Margaret Thatcher, was among the suspected British financiers. In Zimbabwe, 70 men allegedly on their way in March to stage a coup in Equatorial Guinea were arrested on charges of gunrunning and espionage. They were all travelling on South African passports. Zimbabwean authorities said they were on their way to join 15 other suspected mercenaries, including eight South Africans, who had been arrested in Equatorial Guinea. They were accused of plotting the overthrow of President Teodoro Obiang and to install opposition leader Severo Moto as head of state. Initial reports indicated that both South Africa and Zimbabwe wanted the mercenaries extradited to Equatorial Guinea to stand trial in Malabo. Zimbabwe was apparently offered a highly favourable deal involving the delivery of oil. The recently discovered rich oil fields of Equatorial Guinea also attracted South African interest, but both countries changed their mind after damning reports by Amnesty International about human rights abuses and extra-judicial executions in Equatorial Guinea. Between 12 and 16 local plotters had reportedly been summarily executed. The alleged plotters could face the death penalty in Equatorial Guinea. Lawyers acting for the families of the mercenaries took their case to the constitutional court, demanding that the South African government act to protect the men against human rights abuses and to ask for them to be extradited to South Africa to stand trial under the anti-mercenary acts. Counsel for the states argued that respect for the sovereignty of other African states made it impossible for South Africa to intervene, even by diplomatic means. Judge Albie Sachs (himself a previously exiled ANC activist) argued that it is increasingly accepted that human rights conventions supersede issues of sovereignty. Alleged coup leader Nick du Toit stated on 23 August in the court in Malabo that he had been hired by Briton Simon Mann, who had assured him that the coup attempt was supported by Spain, where opposition leader Severo Moto lives in exile. In Harare, Simon Mann, a former British army officer, pleaded guilty to attempts to purchase arms for a coup in Equatorial Guinea. According to their lawyers, both men had been tortured into making confessions. Mann was sentenced to seven years imprisonment, which were later reduced to four years. The two pilots were sentenced to 16 months, while 62 men were sentenced to one year. Two were acquitted, two more freed for medical reasons and one died in jail. After a hearing in Cape Town, Mark Thatcher was released on bail and later fined R 3 m after pleading guilty to contravening South Africa's anti-mercenary law. The affair was considered beneficial for the credibility of South Africa's intelligence services, as it turned out that they had prior knowledge of the plot. They had, however, not prevented the men from boarding a plane to Harare. Most of the alleged conspirators had served in the apartheid defence force.

Many former apartheid soldiers have not been successfully integrated into civilian society. A substantial number of ex-soldiers and ex-policemen are reported to be active in private security firms in Iraq, where very attractive salaries are paid. Some are employed in the burgeoning private security industry in South Africa itself, which also provides employment to veterans from the anti-apartheid struggle. However, two-thirds of former **liberation fighters** are reported to be unemployed. Since the integration process started in 1994,

17,000 MK veterans (the armed wing of the ANC) and 6,000 APLA members (the Azanian People's Liberation Army was the armed wing of the PAC) were inducted into the new South African National Defence Force (SANDF). Once demobilisation began, many found they lacked the qualifications, such as a high school diploma, to find a civilian job.

South Africa's vibrant **print media** sector underwent some interesting changes during the year. 'ThisDay', the newspaper launched only a year earlier by Nigerian media magnate Nduka Obaigbena, closed on 1 November. It had lost about € 1.5 m, with a circulation of less than 20,000. By contrast, the 'Daily Sun', modelled on the UK tabloid, reported a growth in circulation to over 400,000 copies, a record in sub-Saharan Africa.

South Africa mourned the death of three stalwarts of the anti-apartheid struggle. Former Minister of Justice **Dullah Omar** died on 13 March. The death of the prominent anti-apartheid clergyman Christiaan Frederick **Beyers Naudé** (1915–2004) on 7 September was mourned by a broad spectrum of South Africans. Five days later, trade union leader **Ray Alexander** (1913–2004) died at the age of 91. Born in Latvia, she achieved fame through her pioneering work in organising the rural poor in the Western Cape in the Food and Canning Workers Union.

A few weeks before his 86th birthday in July, **Nelson Mandela** announced his partial withdrawal from public life. He said he now needed some time to read and reflect and to be with his family. However, he would still be available for selective occasions: "The appeal is: don't call me, I will call you."

Foreign Affairs

South Africa's dominant role on the continent was further strengthened by the election of Foreign Minister Nkosazana Dlamini-Zuma as chair of the newly created Peace and Security Council of the AU. The council should have some muscle, as the EU has agreed to provide it with $ 320 m for the next two years. African defence ministers reached agreement in January on an African peacekeeping force that may grow to up to 10,000 military and police personnel. At the AU summit, it was agreed that the pan-African parliament would be located in South Africa. Some African states, however, are beginning to display growing resentment towards what they perceive as **South African domination of African affairs**.

To counterbalance growing South African domination, the AU moved to firmly place **NEPAD** under its wings. Thus far it has had a semi-autonomous status, which probably helped to attract donor funds. NEPAD is one of Mbeki's pet projects, the programme to underpin his vision of an African Renaissance. It has a socioeconomic as well as a political dimension. The socioeconomic programme, although criticised as basically representing a neoliberal agenda, has been widely embraced by AU members. The political dimension, focusing on good governance, has met with less enthusiasm. The panel appointed to conduct peer reviews of member states has been stacked with personalities representing the political elite, with a notable absence of social activists. The crisis in Zimbabwe is widely considered as the litmus test for NEPAD's and South Africa's sincerity in the pursuit of good governance, but Mbeki has generally been supportive of Mugabe. In June, Mbeki was invited as one of Africa's spokesmen to the **G8 summit** in Georgia, USA. The G8 has previously committed itself to support NEPAD in exchange for African commitments on good governance and peer reviews.

South Africa took over the chairmanship of the security organ of SADC. One of its priorities is to build African potential for conflict management and **peacekeeping** on the African continent. South Africa favours the formation of a regional SADC brigade, which by the end of 2005 should be ready to undertake peace missions. South Africa itself has peacekeeping forces stationed in two longstanding conflicts: a full battalion and support staff stationed in the DR Congo and just less than two battalions in Burundi. Mbeki also committed 200 men to the AU mission in Darfur. Peacekeeping missions in Africa became more central to South Africa's foreign policy and defence policy. The department of defence budgeted R (rand) 700 m for peacekeeping operations in Africa. The new defence policy no longer lists the defence of the national borders as the primary function of the armed forces, but defines national defence and peacekeeping in Africa as equal priorities. Defence procurements reflected the **shift in strategy**. The government stated its intention to participate in a new type of Airbus, the A400M, which is being developed in a joint project with seven European countries. Pretoria ordered fourteen European Airbus military cargo haulers at a price of R 11 bn to facilitate airlifts for peace missions. Delivery of the new Airbus would take place between 2010 and 2014. South Africa currently charters private planes flown by Russian pilots for haulage flights to other African destinations. The order was additional to previous military procurements, which caused considerable controversy when the spin-off for local contractors proved less than advertised.

On 18 June, South Africa signed **military agreements** with the **DR Congo** and **Rwanda**. The agreements provide for the delivery of military equipment and training from South Africa, and for joint peacekeeping operations. In response to criticism about arms deals with a conflict zone, Minister of Defence Lekota stated that the agreements were signed for defensive purposes only. In the DR Congo, South Africans will also assist with the integration of the various armed forces into one national army. In August, a draft power-sharing deal for **Burundi** was signed in Pretoria. Vice-President Zuma, the South African envoy for Burundi, has been putting pressure on Burundi President Domitien Ndayizeye to speed up the transition process. However, the deal was opposed by the main Tutsi party, 'Union Pour le Progrès National' (UPRONA). South African troops in Burundi now operate under UN command, as the UN took over from the AU on 1 June.

In July, South Africa concluded an **agreement with the US** for the training and equipping of two infantry battalions for peacekeeping missions. Pretoria had thus far been reluctant to accept American involvement in security matters on the African continent. Washington had been offering military training – first through the Africa Crisis Response

Initiative and now through the African Contingency Operations Training and Assistance programme – for the past eight years. In spite of their historical rivalry, the UK, the US and France have become more involved in joint planning and coordination of military interventions in Africa. South Africa also signed two defence pacts with the UK, aimed at boosting South Africa's capacity for peacekeeping missions.

Mbeki's ambitious Africa policy contrasts with the limited capacity of the (SANDF), which is considered over-age and largely unfit for active duty. As a consequence of the merger of the armed wings of the liberation movements with the former defence force, the armed forces could afford little fresh recruitment. With an average age of 34 years, the army is out of tune with most other armies. Moreover, as the incidence of HIV/AIDS in the SANDF is believed to be alarmingly high, many military personnel are unfit for deployment on peacekeeping missions. SANDF told parliament that 23% of the army is HIV/AIDS infected, but unofficial reports have come up with higher estimates.

A substantial increase in the budget for the **intelligence services** reflected the expansion of the presence of the South African secret service on the African continent. Plans were also announced for a more effective system of border control. The choice for South Africa as host for the 2010 Soccer World Cup served as an obvious impetus for a more strict surveillance, as did the decision to locate the pan African parliament in South Africa. According to the Commissioner of Police Jackie Selebi, police foiled a terrorist attack linked to al-Qaida shortly before the April elections, but offered few further details.

South Africa's **diplomatic efforts in the DR Congo** have paved the way for a large-scale expansion of South African **mining interests** into Congo's copper and gold concessions. Black-owned companies are the main beneficiaries, such as the mining corporation Mvelaphanda, headed by ANC veteran Tokyo Sexwale. During a visit to Kinshasa (13–14 January), Mbeki reached agreement on a series of deals totalling more than $ 10 bn. Among the deals is an agreement that South Africa will assist in the rehabilitation of the main state mining company, Gecamines. Talks are also under way on the rehabilitation and expansion of the giant **power generating plants** at the Inga dam on the Congo River, a project with strategic importance for the provision of electricity and water to large tracts of Southern Africa. If implemented, these agreements will integrate the DR Congo more firmly in SADC and tie the country to South Africa's economy. The importance of the DR Congo to South Africa was underlined by the heavyweight delegation, with no less than eight cabinet ministers and prominent business leaders from a variety of sectors, ranging from mining to banking, telecommunications and security. Kabila's government has welcomed South African investors, who could partly replace Belgian and American interests linked to the Mobutu regime. South Africa also agreed to modernise Kinshasa airport and to build a new motorway from the airport to the city.

With **Zimbabwe** heading for an election in March 2005, the South African government began to exert slightly more pressure towards the end of 2004 on its northern neighbour to adhere to international standards for fair elections. When Harare committed itself to the

SADC protocol for free and fair elections, Pretoria hailed this as a victory for Mbeki's constructive engagement policies. The SADC protocol, signed in August, sets rules for freedom of association and expression, and unobstructed participation in election campaigning, with all registered political parties having access to public media. Pretoria has consistently ruled out the use of sanctions against Zimbabwe. At the beginning of the year, Pretoria claimed that its mediation efforts in Zimbabwe were successful, as both Mugabe's ZANU-PF and the opposition Movement for Democratic Change (MDC) had agreed to start informal talks. In contrast, both parties in Zimbabwe denied that talks had been initiated.

Mbeki's visit to the **EU** on 15–17 November highlighted the emerging role of South Africa as a strategic partner on the continent, at least for developments in central and southern Africa. Congo and Côte d'Ivoire figured high on the agenda of Mbeki's talks. His mediation efforts in Abidjan (9 November), where he met with President Laurent Gbagbo but not with his political opponents, brought no visible results. South Africa and Belgium agreed to train several brigades of the future integrated Congolese army before the elections in Congo, scheduled for June 2005. The South African police are also involved in training the Congolese police force.

In May, South Africa granted political asylum to the deposed president of **Haiti**, Jean-Bertrand Aristide. At the beginning of the year, Mbeki had given generous support worth R 25 m for Haiti's celebration of 200 years of independence. Mbeki himself attended the anniversary celebrations in January in Port-au-Prince. Shortly afterwards, when President Aristide was beleaguered by his opponents who were closing in on Port-au-Prince, South Africa sent an air force Boeing with arms in support of Aristide's government. The move came too late to stem the tide of the rebel movement and the Boeing landed instead in Jamaica, because Aristide had already left the country. After an initial stay in the Central African Republic, the deposed Haitian president headed for South Africa. Mbeki's stance on Haiti has wider political ramifications, as it is the **first South African intervention in the Western hemisphere**.

Socioeconomic Developments

On 19 February, Finance Minister Trevor Manuel tabled a mildly expansionary **annual budget**, after years of economic restructuring to limit the budget deficit. Manuel allowed the deficit to rise to 3.1% for 2004–05, as compared to 2.6% in the previous year. The state debt, as a percentage of GDP, was reduced from 43.3% in 2000 to 36.8% in 2004. Expenditure in 2004–05 is budgeted at R 369 bn, from R 332 bn in 2003–04. Projected economic growth for the fiscal year 2004–05 was 2.9% compared with a growth in GDP of 1.9% in 2003. Manuel announced a R 20 bn public works programme designed to create a million jobs over five years. Although South Africa has millions of unemployed, the country suffers from a lack of skilled labour. Skills improvement will be one of the new spearheads of government policy. The education budget was increased by 10%. The relaxation of exchange controls is likely to attract more foreign investors. Most money for social services, poverty relief and social development is spent by the provincial and local governments. Improving the capacity at provincial and local levels is therefore crucial to the success of the delivery of 'a better life for all', the ANC's election slogan. The central state intends to take a more active hands-on approach in dealings with the provinces. The budget was welcomed by COSATU, because of its explicit commitment to job creation.

A UNDP report that indicated continuing **massive poverty** and **growing inequality** within all racial groups caused much political controversy. The report stated that almost half of South Africa's population (21.9 m) continue to live below the national poverty line of R 354 a month. However, there has been visible improvement since 1995, when 51.1% of the people were living below the poverty line. According to UNDP's statistics, this percentage had fallen to 48.5% in 2002. In reaction, the government complained that UNDP had given insufficient attention to the legacy of apartheid. The democratic government, installed in 1994, first needed to focus on building a new constitutional and legislative framework before it could move towards implementation. Now, in this third term, the institutional changes were firmly in place, enabling rapid progress towards delivery.

In its **economic transformation audit**, the Institute for Justice and Reconciliation also argued that the poor have not yet benefited from the improved growth figures, that BEE has not contributed to job creation, that the education system is failing the majority of black youths and that poverty and inequality have deepened. Though 1.7 m jobs were created between 1995 and 2002, the number of job seekers swelled by 5.3 m over the same period. For the first time since 1994, official data suggested a slight decrease in the **unemployment** rate from 28.4% in September 2003 to 27.8% in March. 4.6 m South Africans were unemployed, using the official definition. According to unofficial figures, as used by COSATU, unemployment hovers around 40%, or 8.4 m people. This figure includes the unemployed who are no longer actively engaged in job seeking, but excludes those employed in the informal sector. In the official definition, every person who has worked at least one hour in the previous week is counted as employed. The gap between the new, racially mixed middle class and the millions of largely black South Africans who continue to live in poverty is causing increasing tensions. Trevor Manuel, speaking at the annual convention of black accountants, stated that the top 20% of earners in South Africa earn almost half of all the income in the country, while the bottom 20% earn just 4% of income. In August, the government introduced an ambitious **job creation scheme**, the Expanded Public Works Programme (EPWP), destined to create 200,000 temporary jobs annually in infrastructure development. At the same time, EPWP is meant to improve service delivery, notably in the informal settlements around the big cities. Several isolated incidents indicated that patience in underprivileged communities is running thin. The City of Johannesburg presented ambitious plans to provide proper infrastructure to informal settlements by 2007. According to a 2003 report by the city's department of housing, an estimated 418,000 people are living in backyard shacks, 4,500 people are living on the streets and 170,000 families were being accommodated in dozens of informal settlements across Greater Johannesburg.

Ten years after the formal end of apartheid, **black students** still face a formidable backlog, in spite of the substantial increases in resource allocation to previously disadvantaged schools. In 2003, only 0.5% of matriculation-aged Africans and 3.9% of so-called Coloureds obtained a higher-grade maths pass good enough to gain entry to most natural science, engineering or commerce faculties at universities. Given the low-skills profile of the unemployed, the current skills-intensive growth path for the economy offers no hope for the country's poor. On the other hand, a Merrill Lynch research report noted a spectacular increase in the purchasing power of the **black middle class**, resulting in much increased demand in the consumer market, notably for clothing, furniture, motor vehicles, media, housing and cell phones. Clothing retailers experienced a growth in volume of 15% to 20% over the year. Domestic vehicle sales went up by 5% in 2003. The cell phone market also reported spectacular growth, with an estimated 15 m active cell phone users by the end of 2003. The consumer boom has been encouraged by a sharp fall in interest rates since 2002 and by tax cuts. The reserve bank announced a further cut in interest rates in August, slashing the rate from 8% to 7.5%.

Economic growth picked up in the third quarter. With a growth of 5.6% of the GDP, the South African economy had its best performance in eight years. The first quarter registered 4% growth. Finance Minister Manuel, who has been closely associated with neoliberal economic policies, cited the figures as evidence that government policy is working and that the discipline of the past years has paid off. Critics in COSATU believed that the upward trend was caused by the strength of the rand and the high prices on the world market for gold and platinum, rather than an improvement in productivity. The **local currency** strengthened against the dollar and was expected to maintain its new position well into 2005. From 1988 to 2001, the rand declined each year at an average rate of 14%. Since its lowest point in December 2001, when the currency hit R 13.80, the rand has appreciated by 52%. During 2004, the rate of exchange averaged R 6–7 per dollar, or about R 8 to the euro.

Land reform lagged behind the stated targets. The **land restitution** programme involves land expropriated since the 1913 'Land Act'. Before the 1998 cut-off date, a total of 79,694 claims had been lodged. The processing of claims has been simplified, and by early 2004, 43,205 claims had been settled, often with an offer of monetary compensation. The restitution process is therefore unlikely to make a significant dent in the very uneven racial pattern of land distribution. The vast majority of the claims, some 80%, relate to urban claims. To speed up the restitution process, scheduled to come to an end in 2005, R 1.6 bn was reserved in the 2004–05 budget. Apart from restitution, a programme of land **redistribution** on the basis of willing seller-willing buyer principles aims to achieve a less racialised pattern of landownership. The government promised that 30% of white-owned land will be redistributed by 2015, a substantial departure from previously stated more ambitious goals. Since 1994, about 3.5 m hectares of land has been redistributed. To meet the 30% goal, the government needs to redistribute 1.87 m hectares a year, a fivefold increase on the current transfer rate of 350,000 hectares a year. Total farmland in South Africa is about 122 m hectares, of which 82% is white-owned. The costs for this redistribution programme are estimated at R 17 bn, or about R 1.5 bn per year.

South Africa sought to dispel apprehension on the part of foreign investors about the consequences of its **BEE** programme. Mbeki assured investors that his government has no intention of seizing assets for BEE purposes. Earlier, government officials had stressed that foreign companies were not exempt from meeting empowerment targets. Similar assurances were aimed at China, where Pretoria also hopes to attract investment. Thus far, South African investment in China far outstrips Chinese investment in South Africa. Trade between China and South Africa has expanded considerably, causing massive shutdowns in the South African textile and shoe industry. BEE remained a central tenet of Mbeki's agenda. In order to enlarge Black ownership in the still largely white-owned business sector, the government has set targets for the transfer of shares to black business. By 2014, some 25% to 30% of South African companies should be transferred to black entrepreneurs. BEE has proven unpopular with the ANC's trade union allies. Thus far, most empowerment deals have served a small black elite closely aligned with the ruling ANC. The unions are pressing for worker participation in the share-out.

Top ANC officials acquired 15.1% of the telecommunications giant Telkom, which is destined for partial privatisation. The consortium that bought the black empowerment stake includes the former director-general of the department of communication, Andile Ngcabe, and Mbeki's spokesman Smuts Ngonyama. COSATU proposed a cooling off period for politicians and public servants to avoid suspicions that they had used their official positions as stepping-stones towards a career in business. The trade union leadership branded the deal as the "very worst form of so-called economic empowerment – which benefits only a tiny elite." Other high-profile ANC cadres who have benefited from black empowerment deals over the past years include Bulelani Ngcuka, former Minister of Justice Penuell Maduna and former Minister of Defence Joe Modise. Black empowerment has come under fire not only for enriching a tiny elite, but also for perpetuating the **racial categories** of apartheid. Its advocates claim that unless decisive action is taken to correct the imbalances in wealth and ownership, South Africa will forever be faced with calls to impose quotas in order to achieve proportionally acceptable representation. However, influential voices within the ANC have joined the chorus of critics. Most outspoken was Kgalema Motlanthe, the ANC's secretary-general, who complained that too few people benefit when large white firms hand over minority stakes to black partners. Minister of Defence Mosiuoa Lekota questioned the wisdom of affirmative action policies in recruitment for the army. Minister of Finance Trevor Manuel was even more outspoken in his criticism when addressing black businessmen and accountants, whom he accused of accumulating undeserved riches on the basis of their skin colour.

In the banking sector, Standard Bank, ABSA, FirstRand and the Liberty Group have each offered about 10% of their shares in **black empowerment deals**. Most of the shares went to business consortia headed by ANC heavyweights Tokyo Sexwale, Saki Macozoma and Cyril Ramaphosa. The SANLAM insurance giant, once a prime example of Afrikaner capital accumulation, signed an empowerment deal with Patrice Motsepe, the chairman of mining company ARMgold. In the wine sector, plans to implement BEE by transferring shares to a small group of black business leaders encountered fierce opposition from the farmworkers' union, FAWU. In response to leftwing criticism that BEE has thus far only served the interests of a small black elite, government officials have stressed that the programme is aimed at broad-based empowerment. **Empowerment charters** are concluded by sector. On schedule for 2004 were information technology, construction, transport, wine and agriculture. Charters for the oil, gas and mining sectors had already been concluded in previous years. The highly successful automobile industry has thus far been shielded from empowerment deals. South Africa's automotive industry ranked 20th in the world in 2003 and the government regards it as setting the pace for diversifying the industrial economy. South Africa is responsible for 84% of Africa's vehicle output. In the tourism sector, pressure has also been building for a larger black share in the proceeds.

Tourism is the third largest foreign exchange earner and job creator in South Africa, contributing more than R 25 bn to the economy, or 8.2% of the GDP. A study done in 2003 estimated that only 6% of the tourism enterprises listed on the Johannesburg Stock Exchange were black-owned. The new minister of tourism, Marthinus van Schalkwyk, promised to set clear targets for BEE in the tourism sector that would enable regular monitoring of progress. Both township tourism and ecotourism have the potential to generate more income for black participants in the burgeoning tourism industry. The projected liberalisation of the telecom sector is expected to open new opportunities for **outsourcing**, thanks to a stable economy, relatively low costs and the advantage of sharing the same time zone with Western Europe. Ebrahim Rasool, premier of the Western Cape province, claimed South Africa would be a 'credible alternative' to India. He said that British financial services were already achieving 40% cost savings. A new trade body, 'Calling the Cape', aims to encourage companies in Britain and elsewhere to transfer jobs to South Africa. Randgold Resources announced an expansion of its **mining operations** in Mali, with new programmes scheduled for Senegal, Tanzania and Burkina Faso and a new joint venture in Ghana. AngloGold took over Ashanti Goldfields for $ 1.55 bn. The merged company, to be known as AngloGold Ashanti, would become the world's largest gold producer, with 26 mines on four continents producing 7.5 m ounces of gold per year. Post-apartheid South Africa has become the biggest source of direct investment on the African continent.

In a series of speeches, Mbeki hinted that South Africa was moving away from neoliberal orthodoxy towards the concept of the '**developmental state**'. He cited various examples, from state-led growth in the East Asian economies to the example of the EU's regional funds, which provide subsidies to stimulate backward regions in member states. The government promised a slowing down of the pace of privatisations: in the next five years there would be no major privatisation. The government announced in August that the defence group Denel, the transport utility Transnet and power group Eskom would remain state-owned as they were regarded as strategic assets. The policy shift was hailed by the ANC's allies on the left, the SACP and COSATU, as a shift from American-style capitalism to the **social democratic models** prevailing in the EU. Policy measures included a substantial increase in housing subsidies and increases in welfare benefits. The 'activist state' will provide more jobs through an ambitious public works programme, adult education and the promotion of small business through a new micro-lending scheme. After more than five years of preparation, the National Empowerment Fund started in June, with an initial capital of R 2 bn. The fund aims to provide cheap capital to small and medium-sized business. Another shift in policy is the new emphasis on an improved skills base as a precondition for economic growth and new jobs. Part of the scheme is a campaign to encourage the homecoming of mainly white South Africans who have emigrated over the past years. The economic impact of the massive numbers of AIDS-related deaths remains unsure, but the deaths of tens of thousands of skilled people in sectors such as education, health and other public sector services is likely to cause havoc in years to come.

Ineke van Kessel

Swaziland

Swaziland is often referred to as 'Africa's last remaining absolute monarchy'. While not an incorrect description, it masks a complexity about the political system that needs to be understood if sense is to be made of events in that country. So, while there is no tradition of democracy in Swazi politics, the regime is not one of straightforward monarchical domination. It is actually diarchic, with two distinct but interrelated sets of institutions. The first are those of the 'Swazi nation' (the monarchy and its key advisory institutions) while the second are those of the 'Swazi government', comprising parliament and the cabinet. A new constitution was unveiled in September 2003. While it contained some provisions that represented advances in human rights terms (such as a limited bill of rights and the removal of some restrictions on the rights of women), it retained the absolute powers of the monarch, including the power to make law by decree, and the ban on political parties.

Domestic Politics

Swazi politics was dominated by two related sets of events. One was the struggle over the **adoption of the draft constitution**, while the other was the ongoing **crisis in the application of the rule of law**, with the monarchy continuing to defy rulings of the superior courts. The public was invited to make representations on the terms of the draft constitution, but only as individuals and not as members of organised groupings. This meant that local organisations critical of the draft, such as the Swazi Federation of Labour and quasi-political groupings like the Swaziland Youth Congress, were unable to make submissions, although individual members could do so. Few bothered.

The most **detailed critique** emanated from abroad in the form of a 98-page document by Amnesty International (AI), which in July argued that the draft constitution failed in four areas. These were: 1) the bill of rights, which despite some positive features, failed to offer protection in regard to a series of rights. These included the right to life (by failing to outlaw the death penalty or the lethal use of force and firearms by law-enforcement officials); the right to a fair trial; the unfettered right to appeal against conviction for any offence; and a range of limitations on the rights of free expression, belief and conscience, assembly and association; 2) the rights of women. Here again the draft offered constitutional protection for women in a range of hitherto unprotected areas relating to marriage, property rights and inheritance, participation in politics in the form of representation quotas, and equal pay. Nonetheless, limitations on some of these rights in terms of 'the availability of resources' was criticised, as was the failure to protect fully the rights of girls against forced and early marriages; 3) the independence of the judiciary. While this was guaranteed, AI pointed to a number of provisions relating to the appointment of judges, including the chief justice, which appeared to give wide powers to the monarchy, without sufficient checks and balances; and 4) the powers and immunities of the head of state and state agents. AI noted the sweeping powers of appointment, without adequate checks, accorded to the king. These included the prime minister, heads of the defence and police forces, the attorney-general, chief justice and other superior court judges. This, AI argued, constituted a potential for abuse, as did the extensive powers of immunity accorded the monarch even for acts committed in his private capacity.

These and other representations notwithstanding, a virtually unchanged draft constitution was introduced into the two chambers of parliament on 4 November. As a result of amendments adopted, the two houses passed different versions of the constitution and referred them to the king for his consideration. As of the end of the year, no final version had come into force. Outside parliament, opposition continued with a coalition of four groupings, the National Constitutional Assembly, applying on 16 June to the then inoperative high court for the draft constitution to be set aside.

In November 2002, all the judges of Swaziland's highest court, the **court of appeal**, resigned in protest at the government's refusal to implement two superior court rulings, one of which declared illegal the forced removal of some 200 followers of Chief Mliba Fakudze who refused to accept Fakudze's dismissal and the king's appointment of his brother, Prince Magugu, as their new chief. Lasting for nearly two years, the appeal court's resignation severely hampered the administration of justice and seriously compromised the rights of numerous individuals whose civil and criminal cases were at the appeal stage and could neither be heard nor concluded.

During September, the Commonwealth Secretariat brokered a settlement in terms of which the government agreed to be bound by and to carry out the orders of the kingdom's courts. On 11 November, Chief Fakudze and his followers were allowed to return to their homes and a day later the appeal court resumed hearing cases. Within 48 hours, the returnees were again forcibly evicted by the police. In a statement, Prime Minister Themba Dlamini declared that cabinet had erred in honouring the appeal court's decision. Despite this reassertion of **monarchical supremacy** and continued flouting of the rule of law, the appeal court continued to sit.

Foreign Affairs

In the context of southern Africa, Swaziland pursues a **low-profile foreign policy**. It is a member of the UN, AU, both the SADC and the COMESA, as well as the SACU and the CMA. It maintains missions in nine foreign capitals and at the UN. This includes Taipei, and Swaziland is one of a handful of African states maintaining ties with **Taiwan**. It consequently benefits greatly from Taiwan's aid largesse.

Swaziland's two most important diplomatic ties are to Pretoria, as **South Africa** is the main source of Swazi imports, including electricity and petroleum, as well as its main export market, and to the **US**, from whom Swaziland receives an important sugar export quota and preferential access in terms of AGOA. Through the **Cotonou Convention**, signed in 2000 between the EU and the ACP, Swaziland qualifies for preferential aid and trade benefits.

Links to the former metropolitan power, the **United Kingdom**, have an important symbolic value. The announcement in December that the British would be closing their high commission in Swaziland in 2006 was a blow to national prestige. This will reduce the number of embassies in the country to four (South Africa, Mozambique, Republic of China and the US).

Socioeconomic Developments

Swaziland was once one of Africa's more prosperous states, but its economy has continued its **downward spiral**. Swaziland's real rate of GDP growth fell to 2.9% and 2.1% in 2003 and 2004 respectively. The minister of finance, Majozi Simelane, acknowledged that poverty was on the increase, with the percentage of Swazis living in poverty rising from 66% to 69%. Nearly seven of every ten Swazis were living on less than $ 1 per day. Of these, 20,000 were entirely dependent on food aid, whilst a further 260,000 were receiving some form of food assistance. In large part, this was a result of a fourth consecutive year of drought.

Minister Simelane also conceded that **unemployment** was on the increase, largely as a result of the continuing withdrawal of foreign companies. This was likely to accelerate with the cessation at the end of 2004 of the WTO Agreement on Textiles and Clothing and the anticipated closing of a number of textile factories. According to the UN's Human Development Report for 2004, the **Gini coefficient** (a measure of income inequality) was one of the highest in the world. It also ranked Swaziland in its human development index as 137th of 177 countries. This represented a continued further fall in its ranking.

The current **fiscal crisis** is a result of a number of factors. According to the Economist Intelligence Unit's country report of October, Swaziland's declining real GDP rate has led to lower corporate tax revenue, which the unit attributes to poor decision making on expenditure and poor budget management. This latter factor was reflected in a serious budget-deficit situation: deficits have risen by 200% in five years. The deficit stood at E 221 m (the local currency, the emalangeni, is equivalent to the South African rand), a figure which the IMF described as dangerously high. Another contributory factor was the extended drought, which led to a drop in sugar output at a time of declining world market prices. Sugar is Swaziland's primary export. Its other major source of revenue is the SACU common tariff pool. Currently, that fund is the source of about half of all Swazi state revenues, but that will decline after the coming into force in December of a revised SACU agreement. Among its provisions is a new formula for calculating the size of the annual disbursements, and this will negatively affect the economies of smaller members.

Other factors contributing to Swaziland's economic decline include the lavish and **uncontrolled levels of public spending** by the king. In April, he invited 10,000 guests to a birthday party at the national stadium at a cost of some R 3.5 m. He also became the only Southern African owner of the world's most expensive motor vehicle, the R 3.1 m Chrysler Maybach 62, supplementing a fleet of palace vehicles estimated to be worth R 5 m. He also announced plans to construct ten new palaces for his then ten wives at a total cost of R 96 m.

HIV/AIDS prevalence rates are among the highest in the world. According to the Swazi ministry of health, the rate for adults aged between 15 and 49 was 38.6% in 2002. For those in the age brackets 20–24 and 25–29, the infection rate was 45.4% and 47.7% respectively. By 2004, it was likely that one Swazi in two in their twenties was infected by the disease. The life expectancy for Swazis has nearly halved in 20 years – from 60 years in 1980–85 to 34 in 2000–05. It is projected to fall to 27 by 2010. By then, some 12% of the population – 120,000 children – will be orphaned. The overall population growth rate of 3.1% in the 1980s had dropped by 2004 to 2%. The 'New York Times' (28 November) reported on the pandemic's impact on the Swazi town of Lavumisa, where a quarter of all households had lost someone to AIDS while one-third had a visibly ill member: "It has the appearance of a biblical cataclysm . . . In fact, it is all too ordinary. Tiny Lavumisa, population 2,000, is the template for a demographic plunge taking place in every corner of southern Africa."

John Daniel

Zambia

Having consolidated his majority in parliament over the last two years, President Mwanawasa was mainly concerned with three issues: first, consolidating his power base within his own party, the Movement for Multi-party Democracy (MMD) in preparation for the next general elections in 2006; second, winning back credibility for his anti-corruption politics; and third, implementing austerity policies in order to regain the trust of international donors for further credits and for participating in the HIPC initiative.

Domestic Politics

After succeeding in gaining majority support in parliament by co-opting opposition MPs into his government, President Mwanawasa started to consolidate his position within his own ruling party. As a result of a number of by-elections, MMD had 75 of the 150 elected MPs in June. Late in 2003, supporters of former President Chiluba had formed the so-called **'true blue' faction** (named after the colour of the party's flag) within MMD, which was allegedly sponsored by Chiluba himself. The faction comprised high-profile as well as rank and file supporters of Chiluba, mainly from the 'Bemba-camp' of Luapula and Northern Province, who had been deprived of patronage and privileges through Mwanawasa's anti-corruption crackdown on his predecessor's administration. Mwanawasa had only been appointed by the party's National Executive Council (NEC) and a national convention to confirm his position was long overdue. This convention would not only elect the party's leaders, but would also nominate the party's presidential candidate for the 2006 elections.

In a series of well-orchestrated **provincial party conferences** during the first half of the year, Mwanawasa managed to fend off the threat from the 'true blue' faction and be endorsed as the sole candidate for the party's presidency at the forthcoming party convention. In only one of nine provincial conferences, in Northern Province, a 'true blue' stronghold, did the delegates not resolve to have Mwanawasa stand unopposed, but no other candidate was nominated. Despite this success in securing a solid power base within the party and numerous announcements that the **national convention** would be held during the year, on 23 June it was postponed until 2005. The reasons given were 'lack of funds', 'to curb illegal campaigns' and the dishing out of money by party members wanting to become NEC office-bearers. Meanwhile, Mwanawasa used his position to appoint a number of Chiluba's former allies to the NEC in order to bolster his quest for the presidency at the national convention. Prominent among these was Vernon Mwaanga, formerly information minister under Chiluba. Being a Tonga, Mwaanga's appointment as the party's national secretary was also aimed at strengthening support from the Southern Province, where the opposition United Party for National Development (UPND) has its stronghold.

In reaction to Mwanawasa's securing control of MMD, a number of prominent Chiluba supporters (among them former junior ministers) left the party and formed the **Party for Unity, Democracy and Development** (PUDD), which was officially launched on 20 September in Lusaka. The true strength of the party remained unclear: an official spokesman and former deputy minister in Chiluba's administration, claimed, without further substantiation, that the party had the support of 40 MPs from different parties. As Michael Sata, president of the small Patriotic Front (PF), revealed, there was an attempt to form an alliance with his party: he also claimed that Chiluba was behind the new party. The PF leader was apparently very worried about the new party, which seemed to draw support from the same areas that his own party claimed to be strong in, such as Copperbelt, Luapula and Northern Province. This was the reason PUDD was swiftly branded as a 'Bemba party'.

At the same time, most of the **opposition parties** continued to struggle with serious internal problems as well, and despite all claims to the contrary, there was little effective cooperation among them of the sort that would be necessary to have a winning chance against MMD and Mwanawasa in the upcoming elections. The former state party, United National Independence Party (UNIP), as well as the much more recent Zambia Republican Party (ZRP), the Forum for Democracy and Development (FDD) and the Heritage Party (HP) remained seriously factionalised or almost dormant.

The **split in UNIP** centred on proposed close cooperation or even a 'merger' with MMD, based on a memorandum of understanding between the two parties that the acting UNIP president, Tilyenji Kaunda, a son of the first president, Kenneth Kaunda, had agreed to.

What was reported as a 'merger' late in January was in fact a very detailed agreement on a sort of coalition government. This cooperation, however, was not accepted within UNIP's central committee and even split the Kaunda family, since another son of the former president, Waza Kaunda, publicly opposed the merger and in June he left his 'family's party' to join the PF. The formal cooperation attempt was part of Mwanawasa's strategy to build a new and broader coalition for his re-election, which, given the uncertainty surrounding the 'true blue' faction, would extend the reach of the current MMD. Against the backdrop of the hostile history of the two parties during the 1990s, with all the humiliation of the Kaunda family – UNIP as the old state party, MMD as the party of the democratisation movement – the very idea of a merger was regarded by many inside and outside the two parties as unthinkable. While some UNIP MPs collaborated with the government, two had accepted cabinet posts and others worked closely with UPND, the major opposition party in parliament. During the by-election campaign in May (see below), UNIP's leadership disassociated itself from the opposition alliance. However, in the background of the factional strife there were also differences over the property (companies, farms, real estate) that UNIP still owns and which allows the party a fully salaried central committee, something no other party in Zambia can afford. While T. Kaunda had already sold, without the proper consent of the central committee, some of the party's assets to finance the election campaign in 2001, the majority of the central committee was opposed to selling off the party's riches. In November, the struggle over the party's leadership culminated again when the vice-president, Simon Mwewa, and the president, T. Kaunda, expelled each other and took the leadership struggle to court.

Like UNIP, some of the **other smaller parties**, direct offshoots of MMD caused by the Chiluba's quest for a third term in 2000–01, remained split over the issue of collaborating with government. Mwanwasa had won over two MPs from HP and three from FDD, a development with which none of the parties has come to terms yet. In addition, FDD was still struggling with a massive debt of about ZK (kwacha) 2 bn ($ 340,000) incurred during the 2001 election campaign. ZRP split into two factions over its leadership struggles and became largely paralysed. Its former president, Benjamin Mwila, seemed to have embezzled party funds obtained from an international donor, but in July he successfully challenged his expulsion from the party, along with three other members of the central executive committee, in court. At the same time, he continued to struggle publicly with other ZRP leaders over the control of the party's members.

UPND suffered the least from floor-crossings to MMD by MPs, but its numbers dropped from 49 to 44 through by-elections precipitated by the expulsion of MPs who had switched to MMD or accepted government posts. The party remained the strongest opposition party, but began to suffer a leadership crisis towards the end of the year. UPND's president Anderson Mazoka, who had long been the undisputed leader, did not recover fully from a severe illness that had paralysed him for many months. By the end of December, the leadership wrangle over his succession became public.

Despite the many problems in the opposition, MMD and Mwanawasa received a serious blow to their popularity when PF won the **Kantanshi by-election** in Mufulira in Copperbelt Province on 26 May. MMD's electoral defeat was bitter, since Mwanawasa, who was born in Mufulira, made a personal effort to campaign for the MMD candidate, together with numerous members of his cabinet. PF's victory, led by the popular Michael Sata, was most likely a reaction to the inability of the ruling party to tackle the social hardships of the people in the mining area. Henceforth, Sata was singled out in Mwanawasa's speeches during his tours of the country as a prelude to the 2006 election campaign, as a major challenger from the opposition to his quest for a second term, even though PF had only two MPs at the time and had only limited support in the 2001 election, when it got little more than 5% in only two provinces, Copperbelt and Northern. However, this was only the second of 16 by-elections that MMD had lost since the last elections in 2001.

The ongoing **constitutional review process** dragged on through the year. On 15 June, Mwanawasa announced that the Constitutional Review Commission (CRC) might not be able to finish the whole process in time for the 2006 elections, while the Oasis Forum – a broad coalition of civil society organisations that had been effective during the campaign against Chiluba's third-term – mounted pressure on government to ensure that CRC does present its report before those elections. The Forum continued to be in dispute with the government over the mode for adopting the new constitution. While it demanded a constituent assembly and a referendum, the president continued to be opposed to such an assembly as being too costly and difficult to control. The tension on this issue eased when government conceded that the constitution should be adopted through a 'popular process', whatever that meant. The Forum accepted this as move away from the earlier rigid position on the constituent assembly and referendum. Accordingly, the Forum submitted its own proposals under protest to the CRC on 28 September. Some of the recommendations were that the excessive powers of the president should be curtailed, cabinet should be recruited from outside parliament and the number of ministries should be restricted to 18.

A reason for government's delaying the constitutional review until after the 2006 elections was that the current constitution made it much easier to remain in power. There was mounting pressure for a 51% quorum for the election of the president, as against the current simple majority. Civil society associations, opposition parties, as well as the Electoral Reform Technical Committee (ERTC) appointed by Mwanawasa, supported such an amendment before the 2006 elections. On 23 December, opposition parties, churches, the Oasis Forum and other civil society organisations – among them the Citizens' Forum organised by some professionals and ex-politicians in March as a pressure group, though it was also suspected of being another party in disguise – formed a coalition called **A People's Constitution 2005** to agitate for the enactment of a new constitution before the elections.

Although in May the supreme court finally heard the defence in the opposition's challenge to the results of the 2001 presidential elections and completed the hearing in September, the situation regarding Mwanawasa's tenure and the next election remained unclear, since a verdict was expected only in March 2005. Witnesses clearly indicated that Chiluba sponsored Mwanawasa's election campaign and that government vehicles were illegally used by him.

Earlier in the year, government was confronted by **protests by the labour movement**. On 18 February, for the first time since democratisation, the Zambia Congress of Trade Unions (ZCTU) and the Federation of Free Trade Unions in Zambia (FFTUZ) jointly organised a nationwide strike and protests in front of parliament against the income tax hike – up to 40% for the country's highest-paid workers – and the wage freeze announced in the austerity budget earlier that month. According to the unions, 90% of workers in the public sector heeded the strike call. The rift between the trade unions, which once co-fathered MMD, became even clearer when the ZCTU leader publicly clashed with Mwanawasa on Labour Day, 1 May. The union leader declared that the labour movement would no longer support MMD in the next elections.

Mwanawasa's **anti-corruption campaign** lost momentum and credibility. While a number of senior officials in Chiluba's administration were arrested and charged with theft in February, two of the major suspects were released on bail and disappeared, including former intelligence chief Xavier Chungu. Together with Chiluba, they were prosecuted for the theft of $ 36 m in public funds. Because of technical problems, charges against some of the suspects were dropped on 12 August, probably partly because of the lack of sufficient evidence, in order to be able to continue with the prosecution of Chiluba and Chungu in a separate corruption trial. Similar problems were common: a number of suspects were arrested, released, rearrested and charged with different offences, but no convictions were secured. Related to these difficulties was a row over the **suspension of the director of public prosecutions**, Mukelabai Mukelabai on 3 January. He had allegedly met with Chungu privately, so that Mwanawasa became sceptical about the DPP's eagerness to charge Chiluba and his former officials. Although the DPP was cleared in a tribunal investigation because of a lack of evidence, Mwanawasa did not reinstate him, but retired him with full benefits. There were three possible reasons for the problems encountered with the prosecution of corruption cases: 1) mishandling by the prosecutor either deliberately or because of incompetence in his office; 2) the great difficulty in finding paper proof, while major witnesses (e.g., Chungu) kept silent; and 3) Mwanawasa was not serious about the anti-corruption drive, but used it only to purge his political predecessor and his supporters.

The president did not make changes to major **cabinet posts**, with one exception: Vice-President Nevers Mumba, the former president of the dissolved National Citizen's Coalition, was dismissed on 4 October "for breach of his oath of allegiance" and for endangering Zambia's diplomatic relations with the DR Congo (see below). He was replaced by Lupando Mwape, MP for Lukashya, Northern Province, for which he was a deputy minister. Until June 2003, he had served as Mwanawasa's transport and communication minister.

Foreign Affairs

Austerity measures in the budget affected foreign policy activities as well. Owing to pressure from the trade unions, President Mwanawasa not only directed ministers and government officials to cut down on foreign travel, but also reduced his own travel fund from ZK 37 bn (2003) to ZK 30 bn ($ 6 m) in the finance minister's budget proposal for 2004. This amount was later, after some public debate and criticism from trade union leaders, further reduced to ZK 18 bn ($ 3.6 m and this also covered domestic travel). Overall, **trade and financial issues** dominated the foreign policy agenda, especially with other countries in the region.

President Mwanawasa and his Namibian counterpart, Sam Nujoma, met on 13 May in Katima Mulilo (Namibia) to open the new Katima Mulilo bridge and Livingstone-Sesheke road, which links not only their two countries but also the landlocked neighbouring countries in the SADC region to Walvis Bay harbour on the Atlantic coast. The improved link was seen as 'epoch-making' for regional trade and tourism. The closer ties between the two countries were manifested during the sixth session of the **Namibia-Zambia Joint Commission** in Windhoek on 21–23 July. The Namibians emphasised that they would facilitate landlocked Zambia's desire for access to the sea and two accords were signed, a memorandum of understanding on an agricultural production and cooperation joint venture and the Zambezi Water Basin Commission agreement. The Zambians underlined that they had responded positively to Namibia's request for improved market access within the SADC trade protocol. Later in the year, both countries signed a memorandum of understanding that would result in a giant agricultural project in the border areas of the two countries.

The trade dispute between Zambia and Kenya was the major subject of the **Zambia-Kenya Joint Permanent Commission of Cooperation** meeting held on 27–28 July in Lusaka. Both ministers of foreign affairs explored possibilities for closer cooperation in a number of fields. Bilateral relations were somewhat strained because Zambia did not allow Kenyan cooking oil on to its market, and the East African country barred the sale of Zambian sugar, despite the membership of both countries in the same free trade area. The conflict could not be resolved at the meeting, but both sides agreed to find a way to bridge trade imbalances and to remain in line with COMESA's free-trade area objectives. They concluded their talks by signing a memorandum of understanding to enhance the two countries' relationship in areas such as trade, industry, transport, agriculture and justice.

At the 24th **SADC heads of state summit** in Mauritius on 18 August, Mwanawasa met with his counterparts from Tanzania, Zimbabwe, Mozambique, Botswana and Malawi to discuss tobacco production and trade among the six countries. Nothing emerged from these discussions apart from the comment that they were fruitful and that another meeting would be held within three months. The same day, Mwanawasa participated in the 22nd Summit of the Great Lakes Peace Initiative on Burundi in Dar es Salaam, which reviewed the progress made since the last summit of 5 June.

Late in September, a **diplomatic row with the DR Congo** erupted when the ambassador to Zambia, Jean-Marie Kazadi, sidestepped diplomatic protocol and told the local media of his government's growing unease with the senior Zambian officials who were accusing the DR Congo of "harbouring enemies of the Zambian government." He was referring to Vice-President Nevers Mumba's remarks at an MMD provincial leadership meeting in Ndola. On this occasion, Mumba had claimed that some opposition parties were teaming up with DR Congo nationals and crossing the DR Congo's borders to bring in money in order to destabilise the Zambian government and frustrate the anti-corruption fight. He also stated that former intelligence chief, Xavier Chungu, was believed to have fled to the DR Congo and to be supplying Zambians with weapons to topple the government. The timing of Mumba's statement caused embarrassment to Mwanawasa, who immediately thereafter had talks with DR Congo's President Joseph Kabila in New York. Above all, diplomatic channels had not been used before the vice-president went public with the allegations. Finally, Mwanawasa apologised for Mumba's statements in order to smooth relations with DR Congo. However, the diplomatic tension caused by Mumba, which led to his dismissal, did not ease completely and the soured diplomatic relations were held responsible for the delay in the tenth meeting of the two countries' joint permanent commission in November.

During an eight-day visit to the **US** late in September, Mwanawasa had talks with US Secretary of State Colin Powell and also met with UN Secretary-General Kofi Annan, whom the president invited to Zambia in 2005. In Washington, Mwanawasa met representatives of the business community and sought investment in Zambia. On 22 September, while addressing the 59th annual session of the **UN General Assembly** in New York, Mwanawasa criticised the HIPC initiative. He noted that since its inception, there had been inherent problems that made it difficult for countries to realise the intended benefits. Consequently, external debt continued to consume the larger portion of the national income of developing countries. While at the UN headquarters, he took the opportunity to meet with presidents of neighbouring African countries, namely Sam Nujoma of Namibia, Joaquim Chissano of Mozambique and Joseph Kabila of DR Congo.

Mwanawasa himself attended the inauguration celebration of President Thabo Mbeki on 27 April, but only the Minister of Foreign Affairs Kalombo Mwansa attended the equivalent ceremony for Malawi's new president, Bingu wa Mutharika, on 24 May, while Vice-President Mumba attended the extraordinary AU summit on employment and poverty alleviation from 3–9 September in Ouagadougou, Burkina Faso. Mwanawasa received President Olusegun Obasanjo of Nigeria in Lusaka (18 June) as well as the outgoing president of Mozambique, Joaquim Chissano, on his farewell tour (13 December). The purpose of Obasanjo's visit remained somewhat mysterious: while an official of Zambia's foreign affairs ministry claimed that Obasanjo aimed to reconcile former President Chiluba, on trial on multimillion dollar corruption charges and Mwanawasa, the Nigerian leader dismissed this as speculation and claimed the talks were about the relationship between the two countries.

Socioeconomic Developments

Financial and economic policy was determined by the government's renewed effort to reach the completion point of the HIPC initiative, which was missed in 2003. The **budget deficit** had grossly exceeded the target largely due to a pay rise in the public sector. This had led the IMF and other donors to suspend the disbursement of funds for budgetary support. Negotiations with the IMF on a new Poverty Reduction and Growth Facility (PRGF) – the last one was terminated in March 2003 – had stalled as well. A new PRGF programme was a precondition for debt relief under the HIPC initiative.

The **annual budget** presented on 6 February by Finance Minister Ng'andu Magande clearly indicated strict austerity policies to comply with the conditions laid down by the IMF and international donors. Major austerity measures were a freeze on public sector pay (public sector wages not more the 8% of GDP) – which caused national labour protests – and a rise in domestic revenue through increased income taxes on higher incomes. Related to this were additional structural reform measures, such as improving public expenditure management and financial accountability (i.e., activity-based budget). In fact, most of the economic and financial targets were successfully achieved by the end of the year. The budget deficit was reduced from 5.1% (2003) to the projected 2% of GDP; real GDP grew by a relatively favourable 4.6% compared to the 3.5% target; and, despite high oil prices, inflation remained at 17.5%, fairly close to the monetary policy objective of 15%. Domestic revenue collection was only 2% below target: in fact, tax revenue was on target (ZK 4,551.5 bn, projected 4,536.6 bn), while non-tax revenue (ZK 89.1 bn) fell short by 35%. The implementation of the PRPs improved as well. While in previous years the government was able to release only 25% (2002) or 50% (2003), in 2005 it effectively managed 100%.

Civil society associations, trade unions and opposition parties criticised the **austerity budget**, particularly the wage freeze and demands were made (and echoed by the IMF) to cut cabinet spending, e.g., reduce the number of cabinet posts and travel. The Catholic Commission for Justice and Peace (CCJP) pointed out that poverty reduction, although ill-defined and food security, were not macroeconomic targets. It acknowledged the more realistic targets in the budget (compared to 2003), but raised doubts about the government's ability to overcome its lack of financial discipline. While commending the tax reform as "pro-poor in nature" and expressing "solidarity of the rich with the poor", it demanded more "pro-poor" tax reforms. It also noted insufficient allocations for the health and education sector (including the lack of funds to hire the additional 8,000–9,000 teachers that were required).

The overall **positive economic development** was due to growth in various sectors. The agricultural sector increased by 4.5% owing to favourable weather conditions and, presumably, supportive government policies (various subsidies on fertiliser and seeds). Growth in the mining sector was substantial, at 13.7%. For the fourth consecutive year copper production, the major foreign currency earner, rose (by 15.7%) to 409,000 tonnes, but was still below the level of the early 1990s. Copper earnings continued to improve as a result of increasing world market prices. Manufacturing, concentrated on food processing, grew by only 5.1% and the building and construction sector registered a 10% growth rate.

External economic relations remained highly problematic. The debt burden increased during the year from $ 6.38 m to $ 6.8 m. This rise was due to positive net flows on existing and new loans, minus amortisation payments and exchange rate variations. However, overall the kwacha remained fairly stable against the dollar, trading at around ZK 4,700–4,800. External trade continued to show the almost traditional deficit. Although high commodity prices on the world market, especially for exported metals such as copper and cobalt, resulted in a 51% increase in export earnings (the first time that export earnings had matched the highs of the 1970s), this rise could not offset the increased import bill (exports, $ 1,588 m; imports, $ 1,845 m). One noteworthy positive trend was that Zambian non-traditional exports (tobacco, cotton, sugar and maize seed) rose by about 23%, thereby also reflecting the increased diversification of exports: their share used to account for only 14%, but now stood at 30.6% of total exports.

Because the IMF was pleased with the government's austerity policy, by mid-June, a new three-year PRGF worth $ 320 m was announced. The **reform policies** agreed upon under the new programme concentrated on improving public expenditure management, strengthening the financial sector and overhauling the tax system (e.g., making the copper sector pay taxes). The **privatisation** policy was slowed considerably. By pointing out that the policy had become unpopular in Zambia, especially among certain outspoken civil society associations concerned with social issues, the government managed to negotiate with the IMF a more cautious and slower pace for the privatisation of the remaining companies. According to the Zambia Privatisation Agency, of the 314 companies to be privatised, only 25 remained by January. No major sale was finalised during the year – apart from one, which had been sealed once before. Negotiations continued on the partial privatisation of the Zambia National Commercial Bank (ZANACO) through a sale of 49% of its shares. Potential buyers were the Amalgamated Bank of South Africa (ABSA), a retail bank, and African International Finance Holdings Zambia Ltd, a consortium of the International Finance Corporation (World Bank), European Investment Bank, Netherlands Development Finance Organisation and the National Bank of Malawi. The commercialisation of the Zambia Electricity Supply Company (ZESCO) was still in preparartion: central and local governments had to settle outstanding electricity bills.

In November, the government finally sold Konkola Copper Mines (KCM), the biggest mining company and export earner in the country (approx. 10,500 employees) to India's Vedanta Resources, a London-listed mining-company with worldwide mining operations. KCM had run into problems because the first privatisation attempt had failed. South Africa's Anglo American Corporation (AAC) had taken over KCM – the former state-controlled Zambia Consolidated Copper Mines (ZCCM) – in 1999, but handed it back in

2002 when AAC concluded that the necessary investments for the rehabilitation and development of the mines would be prohibitive. Increasing world market prices made KCM operations profitable, but an estimated investment of $ 1 bn was required for the development of Konkola Deep Mine, and for this the Zambian government needed a strong financial partner. Vedanta acquired a 51% share of KCM for $ 48.2 m. The ownership of Zambia's most important company broke down as follows: 51% Vedanta Resources; 28.4% Zambia Copper Investments (ZCI, of which private shareholders have 48%, the local Copperbelt Development Foundation 44%, with 8% being held through an employee ownership scheme); 26.6% ZCCM Investment Holdings (87.6% held by the government, the rest by private shareholders). The deal was heavily criticised by some civil society organisations, which felt the price paid was too low and that the partner, initially known locally as Sterlite Industries, a subsidiary of Vedanta, was not large enough.

Gero Erdmann

Zimbabwe

The year was characterised by dramatic swings on the domestic political and economic fronts, and relative stagnation and continuity in foreign affairs. ZANU-PF (Zimbabwe African National Union-Patriotic Front) continued its political dominance. It won some crucial by-elections and enacted some controversial legislation. The opposition Movement for Democratic Change (MDC) stuck to its resolve not to recognise the legitimacy of President Mugabe. The free fall in the economy slowed down considerably, prompting government to proclaim that the worst was over. The economy, intra-party friction within ZANU-PF, inter-party bickering, talks about talks, the anti-corruption blitz and electoral politics joined land, patriotism and the defence of national sovereignty at the top of the national agenda.

Domestic Politics

On 1 January, government announced that it would repossess 400 farms from black owners who had been allocated farms seized from white commercial farmers. The more than 200,000 hectares would be redistributed to people still waiting for land. This became the long-running source of **internal political struggles** within the ZANU-PF political elite and threatened to tear the ruling party apart, after influential politicians were accused of being multiple farm owners. On 14 July, publicly backed by President Mugabe, the minister of special affairs in the president's office, John Nkomo, who is also responsible for managing land redistribution, went on the offensive, ordering multiple farm owners to hand over excess farms in keeping with the government's one-person one-farm policy. The move was condemned and ridiculed by the state-controlled media, allegedly under the orders and guidance of Professor Jonathan Moyo, the information and publicity minister, himself believed to have been a multiple farm owner.

Many Zimbabweans were still stripped of their **citizenship** for having at least one parent born outside Zimbabwe, and having failed to regularise that status as per government legislation. The move was probably motivated by a desire to **disenfranchise** two million people, among them white Zimbabweans who were perceived to be opposition supporters.

The assault on the **independent press** continued. Government defied court orders to allow 'The Daily News' and 'The Daily News on Sunday' to reopen. On 10 June, the Media and Information Commission (MIC) shut down 'The Tribune', a weekly owned by a ZANU-PF parliamentarian, ostensibly for licensing violations. However, many believed that the ban was political, coming as it did after the owner had criticised the state's media laws in parliament. Government continued to strictly enforce the 'Access to Information and Protection of Privacy Act' (AIPPA) and the 'Broadcasting Services Act' (BSA), both of which regulate the media. The Committee to Protect Journalists (CPJ) recorded ten arrests, all from the independent media. All were charged with reporting "malicious falsehoods." Most of the expelled foreign press remained banned, with only a few continuing to operate, but with the mandatory accreditation and registration of their reporters delayed, they did so technically illegally.

Inter-party talks between ZANU-PF and MDC did not go far. President Robert Mugabe's insistence – which he reiterated on Independence Day, 18 April – on repentance and recognition of his legitimacy by MDC as a precondition for the resumption of talks, reinforced the view that the ruling ZANU-PF was not genuinely interested in inter-party dialogue. MDC stuck to its position that it would not accept preconditions for talks. Relations between the parties remained tense, with ZANU-PF maintaining that MDC was a front for Western imperialism, which was seeking to effect regime change in Zimbabwe. MDC stood by its decision to treat the regime as an illegitimate one. South Africa's efforts to facilitate talks by meeting delegations from both parties did not yield much. There were, however reports – dismissed by both parties – of high-level informal talks between the parties.

In **electoral politics**, ZANU-PF's hold on rural areas was emphasised when, in the first week of the year, the party won three rural district council wards in Mt Darwin, Makoni and Buhera unopposed. Critics attributed this to the violence against the opposition. During the course of the year, the party won other seats in **parliamentary by-elections**, even managing to snatch a seat from MDC in its urban stronghold Zengeza in a by-election held on 27 and 28 March. This came after the ruling party retained its Gutu North seat in a 2–3 February by-election. ZANU-PF went on to wrest another seat from MDC in a by-election in Lupane on May 15 and 16. All election results were contested by MDC, citing irregularities and violence, allegations that were collaborated by independent observers, among them the Zimbabwe Election Support Network (ZESN). ZANU-PF took these election victories as evidence that MDC was losing its relevance, even boldly predicting that the opposition would finally be buried in the 2005 general elections.

On 25 August, MDC announced an **election boycott**, indicating that it was not going to participate in further elections under existing rules and conditions. It resolved to continue that boycott of all elections until the government levelled the playing field in keeping with the SADC guidelines on **free and fair elections**. It demanded that the government combine comprehensive reform of Zimbabwe's electoral framework with significant political reforms, in particular, the ending of political violence and the repeal of repressive statutes, top of the list being the 'Public Order and Security Act' (POSA) and AIPPA.

In the last quarter of the year, government began efforts to introduce **electoral reforms** in order to comply with the SADC principles and guidelines governing democratic elections that had been adopted by the regional body at the leaders' summit in Mauritius on 17 August. This was accomplished by passing the '2004 Electoral Act', which transformed the country's electoral landscape. These reforms include the setting up of an independent electoral commission, the Zimbabwe Electoral Commission (ZEC), the holding of elections on one day, and the use of translucent ballot boxes. As part of the reforms, all the contesting parties were to be guaranteed freedom to campaign and access to the public media. The MDC and independent commentators raised concerns about the rushed reforms. Of concern was the independence of ZEC, whose members had to be appointed by the president, himself an interested party.

Information and Publicity Minister **Jonathan Moyo** clashed with senior party colleagues throughout the year. In April, he ridiculed Vice-President Joseph Msika over the acquisition of Kondozi farm. In May, he disagreed with ZANU-PF information chief Nathan Shamuyarira when he ejected a Sky News television crew from the country, despite an arrangement between the broadcaster and Shamuyarira. In July, he poured scorn on party chairman John Nkomo, who had ordered him and others to relinquish extra farms. In these clashes, Moyo used the state media to attack and ridicule his opponents. They in return had to resort to the little-read party paper, 'The People's Voice', and to the independent press, to respond to Moyo's frequent attacks. Many interpreted Moyo's insubordination as an attempt to position himself strategically for the presidency.

After the president announced that he would not be standing for re-election in 2008, a decision repeated on 25 May, party stalwarts started to place themselves strategically for the **presidential candidacy**. The fissures thus created threatened to tear ZANU-PF apart. This may in part explain why it took President Mugabe more than a year to announce a replacement for one of his two vice-presidents, Simon Muzenda, who had died way back in September 2003. Appointing a successor would, according to analysts, clearly indicate who was to be the possible next president. Speculation on different factions in the fractious party was only quashed on 20 November, when President Robert Mugabe announced at the ZANU-PF Women's League congress that he wanted a woman to occupy one of the country's two vice-presidential posts. This was in keeping with the decision by the party's highest decision-making body, the politburo. Up to then, many commentators regarded Emmerson Mnangagwa, the party's secretary for administration and the speaker of parliament, a close associate of President Mugabe, as the frontrunner in the race for the vice-presidency. Even after the announcement, some key party members went ahead to try to engineer the elevation of Mnangagwa. The group met in **Tsholotsho** at a meeting convened by Jonathan Moyo on 18 November. President Mugabe did not take kindly to the unsanctioned meeting. Those attending were regarded in some circles as plotting a coup, since they wanted to change the top structures of the party.

The **retribution** that followed the so-called '**Tsholotsho Declaration**' saw those who attended, including six provincial chairpersons, being suspended from the party. Professor Moyo was dropped from the central committee at the ZANU-PF congress in December. He never made it into the politburo either. Mnangagwa was 'demoted' from the powerful position of secretary for administration down to secretary for legal affairs. Legal and Parliamentary Affairs Minister Patrick Chinamasa was also dropped from the politburo. At the congress, Joyce Mujuru, the minister of rural resources, was elected as the second vice-president of ZANU-PF and, therefore, the country.

In December, President Mugabe announced that he would appoint his cabinet only from elected MPs. The announcement meant that all appointed MPs, among them Moyo, Chinamasa and Joseph Made, whose ministry spearheaded the expropriation of land from white farmers, had to find constituencies to represent if they were to come back after the national poll on 31 March 2005. As usual, all ZANU-PF candidates had first to pass through **primary elections**. New party guidelines requiring a proven track record in the party and reserving a 30% quota for women disqualified newcomers, notably Moyo, whose preferred constituency of Tsholotsho was inexplicably reserved for a female candidate.

Violence against the opposition was reported throughout the year. Graduates of the National Youth Service programme, viewed by opponents as ZANU-PF militias, were implicated in much of the violence. President Mugabe confirmed fears when he addressed the ZANU-PF youth congress on 10 July. He urged the youths to ". . . teach them [the opposition] a lesson across the whole country . . ." Telling them to "go and work," President Mugabe warned that should ZANU-PF lose the 2005 election, he would expect the Youth League "to be answerable." He ordered the youth to "deal with these midgets [the opposition]."

ZANU-PF **propaganda** saturated the state-controlled media. Government spent about Z$ 2 bn on galas and parties to celebrate national holidays and other special events. All these were broadcast live on national television and radio. While government claimed it was cementing unity and building up nationalism and patriotism, MDC and other critics saw these as an attempt to dominate public space by abusing public resources.

There were extensive allegations of collusion and partiality among the **security and uniformed forces**, including the army, the Central Intelligence Organisation (CIO) and the police in the **harassment of the opposition**. Using POSA, which requires the sanctioning by the police of all political gatherings, the law and order section of the Zimbabwe Republic Police (ZRP) banned all but a handful of non-ZANU-PF political meetings. In addition to MDC, a few other organisations, in particular Women of Zimbabwe Arise (WOZA), the National Constitutional Assembly (NCA) and the Zimbabwe Congress of Trade Unions (ZCTU) defied the ban and paid dearly, since those taking part in the meetings or demonstrations were assaulted and/or arrested. In most cases, those arrested were released without charge or after paying 'admission of guilt' fines.

Morgan Tsvangirai, the MDC president, spent a large part of the year grounded in court, undergoing trial for one of the two treason charges levelled against him. After the acquittal of his two co-accused comrades, he alone remained on remand until his predicted acquittal on 15 October. While government hailed the acquittal (which it was latter to appeal) as evidence of the rule of law, many commentators did not agree, pointing out that he should not have been charged in the first place, considering the obvious weakness of the government's case against him.

On 18 March, Roy Bennett, a white MDC MP, floored Patrick Chinamasa, the minister of justice, legal and parliamentary affairs in a **brawl in parliament** after repeated provocation and insults from the latter. On 28 October, a ZANU-PF dominated parliamentary committee set up to probe the brawl recommended that Bennett be punished by an effective 12-month imprisonment with hard labour. He was arrested while trying to leave the country before the parliamentary hearing on his sentence, was immediately jailed and sent to a rural prison in Mutoko. The speaker of the house issued certificates preventing the courts from hearing the jailed MP's appeal. The events surrounding Bennett's imprisonment were taken as persecution. The government had earlier on defied six court orders stipulating that it should vacate the MP's farm in Chimanimani.

Save for politically related violations, there was no reported upsurge in the violation of **civil liberties**. The justice system appeared to be bent on bringing to book people long considered immune from justice. On 10 June, the high court denied bail to two suspects, both of them well known ZANU-PF activists, allegedly involved in the murder of two MDC activists and Tsvangirai aides, Tichaona Chiminya and Talent Mabika, during the 2000 election campaign in Buhera. However, the absence on the list of Joseph Mwale, the alleged mastermind of the murder, a CIO operative who was reputedly on the run, gave rise to adverse speculation. On 7 April, another ZANU-PF activist was arrested in connection with the murder of an MDC activist in a shooting incident during the Zengeza by-election. On 5 August, high court Justice Sandra Mungwira **acquitted six MDC activists** who were charged with the murder of a war veteran and ZANU-PF activist. The same judge had in March upheld claims by three of the accused that their original 'confessions' had been obtained under torture. The two parties interpreted these events differently. While the government flagged these as proving the existence of the rule of law and independence of the judiciary, the MDC looked at the procedural aspects, citing delays in the administration of justice and lack of investigation by the police in cases where the courts had recommended it.

In June, there were reports that the government was to order **fighter aircraft** from China and other military equipment worth an estimated $ 200 m. The defence ministry confirmed it was buying defence equipment that included 12 fighter jets and 100 military vehicles from China. The opposition complained that the move was intended to intimidate Zimbabweans ahead of the March 2005 parliamentary elections. It was also revealed that government had received **anti-riot equipment** ordered from Israel. It was paraded in Harare during a heavy military presence on 15 October – the day of the verdict on the Tsvangirai treason trial – when it was feared a guilty verdict would spark widespread unrest. On 10 August, President Mugabe put the army on permanent alert in order "to safeguard . . . [Zimbabwe's] national sovereignty and territorial integrity." He said that government would always prioritise spending on the military in order to enable Zimbabwe's defence forces to deal with "imperialistic efforts to destabilise the nation."

The year saw government drafting the controversial '**Non-Governmental Organisations Bill**' (the NGO Bill) that sought to regulate the work of NGOs. Its primary target was NGOs that deal with corruption, governance and human rights issues. There were fears that if passed into law, the NGO Bill would be used to shut down the operations of any NGO that ZANU-PF believed to be a challenge to its hold on power. The bill required that NGOs be registered and made it unlawful for any NGO to carry on its business without registration. ZESN, one such organisation that would be affected, echoed the opinions of many when it argued that the bill would make it difficult to comply with the Universal Declaration of Human Rights, the United Nations Charter, the International Covenant on Civil and Political Rights, the African Treaty and other regional and international instruments in terms of full citizen participation in governance issues. The controversial bill proceeded through parliament on 9 December.

Government continued its belligerent attitude towards the opposition-controlled **Harare city council**. On 16 April, President Mugabe fired the executive mayor who had been on suspension since 2003. The deputy mayor, who was to publicly announce her defection to ZANU-PF in August, replaced him. By the end of July, 19 of the 45 councillors had been dismissed. On 25 July, MDC announced that it was pulling its remaining councillors from Town House. On 9 December, government announced a commission to run the city of Harare. The commission was expected to implement the 'turnaround programme' that had been crafted by a team appointed in June, and complete the city's formulation of the 2005 municipal budget. Many agreed with MDC's accusation that unrelenting political interference in council activities demonstrated government's contempt for the councillors' roles as democratically elected representatives of the people. The inclusion of known

ZANU-PF cadres in the commission seems to confirm theses accusations. At the same time, government continued its aggressive stance towards the executive mayors of Bulawayo, Chegutu and Mutare, all of them from MDC.

Foreign Affairs

The government retained its status as a pariah state, shunned by the West. Most vocal among these were the US, the EU, Australia, Canada and New Zealand. These countries, together with Switzerland, maintained their **targeted sanctions**. The EU adopted Council Common Position 2004/161/CFSP on 19 February renewing sanctions against Zimbabwe for another 12 months. The sanctions include a travel ban on senior regime figures, freezing of assets and an arms embargo.

In contrast, except for a few countries (among them Botswana, Senegal, Ghana and the Gambia), governments in Africa, Asia and Latin America endorsed Zimbabwe's policies and record. Zimbabwe continued with its **'look east' policy**, which emphasises the establishment and strengthening of **diplomatic and trade relations** with Asian countries, principally China, North Korea and Malaysia. In keeping with this policy, Air Zimbabwe, the loss-making national flag carrier, introduced two weekly flights between Harare and Beijing. The maiden flight was undertaken between 21 November and 25 November. The 'look east' policy did not bear much fruit in 2004. The expected flood of tourists from China failed to materialise. According to the local industrial body, trade with Asia has yet to pick up. The flooding of the local market with cheap goods (locally nicknamed 'MaZhing-zhong') by Chinese businessmen threatened the viability of local businesses, especially the clothing and textile sector, which could not compete with cheap Chinese imports. Despite these setbacks, President Mugabe made Asia, in particular Malaysia, his favourite destination for private and state visits.

Zimbabwe's most loyal friend was **Namibia** (for further details see the Namibia chapter). **South Africa** maintained its controversial policy of 'quiet diplomacy'. On 12 January, President Mbeki announced that President Mugabe had told him that MDC and ZANU-PF had recently agreed to formal negotiations without mediators. MDC professed ignorance. On 30 June, Dlamini-Zuma, the South African minister of foreign affairs, known for her public support of Zimbabwe, told parliament that South Africa's policy would not change. She said that South Africa was actively engaged in trying to bring ZANU-PF and MDC to the negotiating table. As usual, Zimbabwe hailed the statement as support for the ZANU-PF government.

There was no let-up in **emigration**. The favourite African destinations were South Africa and Botswana, with a few trying Mozambique. **Botswana** was accused of ill-treating illegal immigrants. Zimbabwe continued to publicly condemn the erection by Botswana of the 300-mile electrified fence in 2003 to block **illegal border crossings**. Humanitarian organisations accused South African staff of brutality and blocking asylum for most

Zimbabweans who had fled their country. On 16 November, the UK, the favourite overseas destination for Zimbabweans, announced it was lifting its moratorium on deportations of Zimbabweans who had failed to obtain asylum. Some 10,000 Zimbabweans would be affected. In response to this announcement, contradictory voices could be heard in the ZANU-PF government. While Chinamasa, the minister of justice, legal and parliamentary affairs said the deportees would be welcome, on 17 December Jonathan Moyo, the minister of publicity and information, declared all **UK deportees** "mercenaries of regime change." This prompted refugee groups to warn that anyone deported to Zimbabwe could face persecution.

Zimbabwe continued to be hostile towards the Commonwealth, from which the country had withdrawn in December 2003. President Mugabe, at the **UN General Assembly** on 23 September, blasted American President George Bush for making himself a "political god" and British Prime Minister Blair as "his prophet." Zimbabwean parliamentarians from both MDC and ZANU-PF were among the parliamentarians in the Pan-African parliament of the AU, which had its inaugural session in Johannesburg on 18 March.

In early July, the AU was scheduled to consider a damning human rights abuse report on Zimbabwe. The report was prepared by the **AU's African Commission on Human and People's Rights** (ACHPR). The representative from Zimbabwe objected to the adoption of the report on the grounds that it did not contain the views of government. The adoption of the report was postponed to give Zimbabwe an opportunity to respond. A damaging diplomatic embarrassment for Zimbabwe was thus avoided and government bought a temporary reprieve.

Several developments put to test the government's **relationship with South Africa**. In January, the 'Zimbabwe Independent' reported that Zimbabwe was calling in its war debt from the Democratic Republic of Congo after losing badly to South Africa in the scramble for business opportunities in the mineral-rich state. On 5 May, 64 suspected **mercenaries**, mainly Angolans, South Africans and Namibians, were arrested at Harare International Airport after arriving from South Africa on a Boeing 727. They were accused of plotting to overthrow Equatorial Guinea's government. Senior government officials were quick to accuse Britain and America of aiding the mercenaries. On 26 October, a Congress of South African Trade Unions (**COSATU**) delegation arriving for a fact-finding mission was deported. The South African government backed Zimbabwe, reminding COSATU that Zimbabwe was a sovereign country. In December, the Zimbabwean CIO busted a spy ring run by some insiders in ZANU-PF and government. On 15 December, they arrested a South African, who reportedly admitted to spying on Zimbabwe for the South African government. He was also making attempts to recruit the head of counter-intelligence in the CIO. Apart from admitting that the arrested agent was indeed theirs, the government of South Africa did not comment further, despite speculations among many that the spy case revealed historical tensions between Zimbabwe and South Africa.

On 13 June, the 'Sunday Times' of South Africa reported that there was an **arms race in the region**. The 12 Chinese-made FC-1 planes, a lightweight multipurpose fighter type, ordered by Zimbabwe would reportedly "provide a credible answer to the challenge posed by the 28 JAS-39 Gripen multi-role fighters that the South African government . . . ordered from Saab, the Swedish arms manufacturer." The 'Zimbabwe Independent' of 18 June quoted sources as saying that Botswana and Namibia were also in the rearmament race. The two countries were said to have bought Nanchang F-8 fighter/trainers from China. Botswana had also bought a dozen CF-5 fighter-bombers from Canada. On 18 June, in response to a question on the issue, South Africa's foreign affairs minister indicated that "interaction between the desk and the Military Intelligence (MI)" had revealed there was no arms race among the countries in the region.

Zimbabwe also criticised governments that, according to ZANU-PF, were or had become unfriendly. **Botswana** was constantly attacked not only for ill-treating Zimbabwean immigrants, but also for not supporting Zimbabwe and for allowing a hostile radio station to operate on its territory. On 21 April, Botswana lashed out at Zimbabwe over media reports alleging that Zimbabweans were mistreated in the neighbouring country and that Gaborone was plotting with Britain and the US to topple President Mugabe. The Zimbabwean state media launched a scathing attack on **Nigeria** and the person of President Obasanjo, who was accused of acting in cahoots with Britain. Nigeria was also blamed for welcoming and offering land in Kwara state to white farmers whose land had been seized in Zimbabwe.

On 21 October, Foreign Affairs Minister Stan Mudenge announced that government had uncovered plans by "some western countries and organisations" to discredit the 2005 polls. He alleged that these had produced damning reports and were plotting to influence the composition of the AU and SADC observer teams for the elections. According to Mudenge, their intention was to influence the reports of the observer teams to reflect "their [the West's] preconceived opinions and not the actual facts." He threatened to bar the diplomats from observing the elections. **Yoweri Museveni**, the president of Uganda, Zimbabwe's one time foe, made a state visit to Zimbabwe. On 7 October he teamed up with President Mugabe in condemning the West, partly for opposing Mugabe's rule. On 11 May, President Mugabe met a **Chinese delegation** visiting Zimbabwe. The state media took this as a success for the 'look east' policy.

Socioeconomic Developments

The government acknowledged problems with its **land redistribution programme**, indicating that in some areas 60% of the land allocated to small-scale farmers had not been taken up. In December, government revised its widely publicised figure of more than 300,000 resettled farmers down to 160,000. Despite this, government continued to proclaim its land redistribution programme a success and promised a bumper harvest.

HIV/AIDS continued to ravage Zimbabwe. According to UNAIDS, the crisis in Zimbabwe was a complex one in which the impact of drought, international isolation, land reform leading to substantial migration, and HIV/AIDS all combined to further increase the numbers and size of vulnerable groups. Zimbabwe entered 2004 with an HIV prevalence rate among adults and children (0–49 years) of 24.6%, with 1.8 m living with HIV. Of these 930,000 were women aged between 15 and 49.

Zimbabwe staggered into the New Year with an **inflation rate** of some 620%. For the fourth year running, Zimbabwe registered a negative real GDP growth rate (estimated at –4% to –5%). Thanks to the reserve bank governor's unrelenting enforcement of his monetary policy, inflation came down drastically, closing the year at just over 132%. Major victims of hyperinflation and flagrantly corrupt practices were financial institutions, among them commercial banks, a building society and discount houses.

Service delivery and utilities institutions continued to decline. Two of the country's top referral hospitals, Harare central hospital and the Parirenyatwa group of hospitals, continued to decline in terms of infrastructure, supplies, service delivery and human resources. The Zimbabwe Electricity Supply Authority (ZESA) performed badly throughout the year, with a large domestic (over Z$ 60 bn in February) and external debt ($ 143 m in December). The perennially troubled public transporter, the Zimbabwe United Passenger Company (ZUPCO), did not fare better. Even the national museum was not spared.

Shortages of basic commodities in towns and cities that had plagued the country the previous years eased considerably. For the majority, the problem switched from one of availability to affordability. Only fuel continued to run out sporadically, but the situation was not as bad as in previous years.

Agriculture fared better than in 2003. However, the sector inherited some problems. The newly resettled farmers complained of lack of government support. The **seizure of land**, which had officially ended in 2002, continued, with the most notable acquisition being in June when Kondozi, a highly productive enterprise, was forcibly acquired. Most of the 5,000 farm workers employed at the farm lost their jobs and homes. The national cattle herd continued to decline owing to a combination of factors, including rustling, drought and the land reform programme.

By September, it was reported that more than five million people had been on **food aid** for almost a year because of poor harvests and the disruption of farming activities on commercial land. Previously, on 11 May, Labour and Social Services Minister Paul Mangwana had told international donors that the government of Zimbabwe did not need emergency food aid because it expected a bumper harvest. President Mugabe repeated the claim on 25 May. The opposition cautioned that without international help people would starve. The government was accused of scheming to use food as a political weapon, and it was revealed that government was undertaking massive importation of maize from Zambia and South Africa.

In September, Bulawayo city council records revealed that at least 38 people, most of them children under the age of five, had died from **malnutrition** during the previous two months. Early in the year, 65 people, mainly children under the age of five, had reportedly died of **starvation** in Bulawayo. Government refuted the revelations and threatened the Bulawayo executive mayor with dismissal for spreading falsehoods.

On 25 November, the acting minister of finance unveiled the Z$ 27.5 trillion **national budget for 2005**. The 'election budget' made the biggest allocation to defence, followed by education. It also contained the routine revision of income tax bands to benefit workers. The Zimbabwe National Chamber of Commerce (ZNCC) observed that the budget was too focused on resuscitating distressed individuals of the community, but was not bold enough in reviving the economy. The **domestic debt** increased almost fivefold between June 2003 and August 2004. As at 27 June 2003, the government domestic debt stood at Z$ 542,236 bn and by 27 August 2004 it had grown to Z$ 2,326 trillion.

The beginning of the year saw government in an **anti-corruption drive** mainly inspired by the new reserve bank governor's crusade to revive the economy. Two directors of ENG, an asset management company, appeared in court on 6 January on fraud charges. They were the first legal casualties of the financial sector crisis that saw a run on deposits by investors. The crisis was in part a result of the unrealistic controlled exchange rate on the foreign currency market, which inevitably fuelled a lucrative black market, in which it later emerged even government institutions and top regime officials were actively participating. By the end of the year, seven banks had been forced to close and/or were placed under curatorship.

The anti-corruption crusade led to the arrest of a ZANU-PF MP and provincial party chairman (10 January), a businessman and ZANU-PF central committee member (9 February), and the minister of finance (24 April). A successful businessman was arrested in South Africa (25 May) on similar charges. However, government failed to secure his extradition. Also netted in the crackdown were a prominent ZANU-PF linked farmer and a businesswoman. The anti-corruption blitz was buttressed by the '**Criminal Procedure and Evidence Amendment Bill**', which would allow police to hold suspects accused of corruption and externalisation of foreign currency and those facing security-related charges for three weeks without bail. Widely regarded as unconstitutional, the bill was opposed even by ruling party MPs, who reportedly only voted for it on 30 June after being pressured into doing so. As a result of this law, James Makamba, a businessman and ZANU-PF central committee member and Cyril Muderede, a farmer linked to ZANU-PF were repeatedly rearrested even after securing bail. Dr. Chris Kuruneri, the minister of finance entered the New Year in custody. Citing the act, at least five bankers accused of externalising foreign currency escaped to South Africa and the UK.

Labour unrest continued. The major strikes were those by the state-owned Zimpost, Net*One, Tel*One and the partly state-owned bank, Zimbank. The strikes were a result of disagreements over salaries. In all these, about 3,500 strikers were dismissed. In the case of the Zimpost strike, government brought in the army to man post offices.

On 7 July, the **IMF** board of executive directors gave Zimbabwe another six months to consolidate its economic turnaround strategy before the issue of possible expulsion could be reopened. In December, the IMF deferred its decision on whether to expel Zimbabwe for defaulting on its debt. The IMF board, which had cut balance-of-payments support to Zimbabwe five years previously, had in November closed its Harare office and was widely expected to expel the country from the institution. The decision was deferred to early 2005. The lending programme in Zimbabwe remained inactive due to arrears. The bank's role in the country was now limited to technical assistance and analytical work focusing on macroeconomic policy, food security issues, social sector expenditures, social service delivery mechanisms and HIV/AIDS. In early July, Zimbabwe appealed to the World Bank for millions in aid, especially to its agricultural sector. The World Bank rejected the request, citing Zimbabwe's outstanding debt of $ 280 m.

Amin Y. Kamete

List of Authors

Jon Abbink, Researcher, African Studies Centre, Leiden, Professor of anthropology at the Free University of Amsterdam, The Netherlands

Matthias Basedau, Senior Researcher, Institute of African Affairs, Hamburg, Germany

Rémy Bazenguissa-Ganga, Lecturer, University of Lille, France

Redie Bereketeab, Research Fellow, Nordic Africa Institute, Uppsala, Sweden

Heinrich Bergstresser, Editor, Deutsche Welle, Bonn, Germany

John Daniel, Research Director, Democracy and Governance, Human Sciences Research Council, Durban, South Africa

Mirjam de Bruijn, Researcher, African Studies Centre, Leiden, The Netherlands

Stephen Ellis, Researcher, African Studies Centre, Leiden, The Netherlands

Gero Erdmann, Senior Researcher, Institute of African Affairs, Hamburg, Germany

Jonas Ewald, Director, Centre for Africa Studies, Gothenburg University, Sweden

Martim Faria e Maya, UNDP

Moussa Fofana, Independent Researcher and Consultant, Bamako, Mali

Sven Grimm, Research Fellow, Overseas Development Institute, London, United Kingdom/German Development Institute, Bonn, Germany

Joseph Hanlon, Senior Lecturer, Development Policy and Practice, Open University, Milton Keynes, United Kingdom

Gerti Hesseling, Researcher, African Studies Centre, Leiden, The Netherlands

Kurt Hirschler, Freelance Political Scientist, Hamburg, Germany

Albrecht Hofheinz, Associate Professor, Department of Culture Studies and Oriental Languages, University of Oslo, Norway

Rolf Hofmeier, Former Director, Institute of African Affairs, Hamburg, Germany

Cord Jakobeit, Professor of International Relations, University of Hamburg, Germany

Amin Kamete, Senior Researcher, Nordic Africa Institute, Uppsala, Sweden

Steve Kibble, Advocacy Coordinator Africa/Yemen, Catholic Institute for International Relations, London, United Kingdom

Dirk Kohnert, Deputy Director, Institute of African Affairs, Hamburg, Germany

Piet Konings, Researcher, African Studies Centre, Leiden, The Netherlands

Carlos Lopes, UN-UNDP Representative, United Nations Development Programme, Brazil

Bruno Losch, Senior Economist, Centre de coopération internationale en recherche agronomique pour le développement, Montpellier, France

Roland Marchal, Senior Researcher, Conseil National de Recherche Scientifique/Centre d'Etudes et de Recherches Internationales, Paris, France

Richard Marcus, Assistant Professor, Department of Political Science, University of Alabama, Huntsville, USA

Cedric Mayrargue, Associated Researcher, Centre d'étude d'Afrique noire, Bordeaux, France

Mike McGovern, West Africa Project Director, International Crisis Group, Brussels, Belgium

Andreas Mehler, Director, Institute of African Affairs, Hamburg, Germany

Henning Melber, Research Director, Nordic Africa Institute, Uppsala, Sweden

Paul Nugent, Professor of Comparative African History and Director of the Centre of African Studies, University of Edinburgh, United Kingdom

René Otayek, Director, Centre d'étude d'Afrique noire, Institute of Political Studies, Bordeaux, France

Krijn Peters, Doctoral candidate, Technology and Agrarian Development Group, Wageningen University and Research Centre, The Netherlands

Filip Reyntjens, Professor of Law and Politics and Chairman of the Institute of Development Policy and Management, University of Antwerp, Belgium

Marcel Rutten, Researcher, African Studies Centre, Leiden, The Netherlands

Ebrima Sall, Head of the Department of Research, Council for the Development of Economic and Social Research in Africa (CODESRIA), Dakar, Senegal

Gerhard Seibert, Post-doctorate Fellow at the Instituto de Investigação Científica Tropical (IICT), Lisbon, Portugal

Roger Southall, Distinguished Research Fellow, Democracy and Governance, Human Sciences Research Council, Pretoria, South Africa

Susan Steiner, Research Associate, Institute of African Affairs, Hamburg, Germany

Klaus-Peter Treydte, Freelance writer and Consultant, Country Representative Friedrich-Ebert-Foundation Madagascar and Mauritius 2005

Denis Tull, Research Associate; German Institute for International Affairs, Berlin, Germany

Walter E. A. van Beek, Researcher, African Studies Centre, Leiden and Lecturer in anthropology at the University of Utrecht, The Netherlands

Han van Dijk, Researcher, African Studies Centre, Leiden and Professor of Law and Governance in Africa, chair group Law and Governance, Dept of Social Sciences, Wageningen University and Research Centre, The Netherlands

Jan-Kees van Donge, Senior Lecturer in Public Policy and Development Management at the Institute of Social Studies, The Hague, The Netherlands

Ineke van Kessel, Researcher, African Studies Centre, Leiden, The Netherlands

Klaas van Walraven, Researcher, African Studies Centre, Leiden, The Netherlands

Douglas Yates, Assistant Professor of Political Science in the Department of International Affairs, The American University of Paris, France

Nicolien Zuijdgeest, Freelance Journalist, Amsterdam, The Netherlands

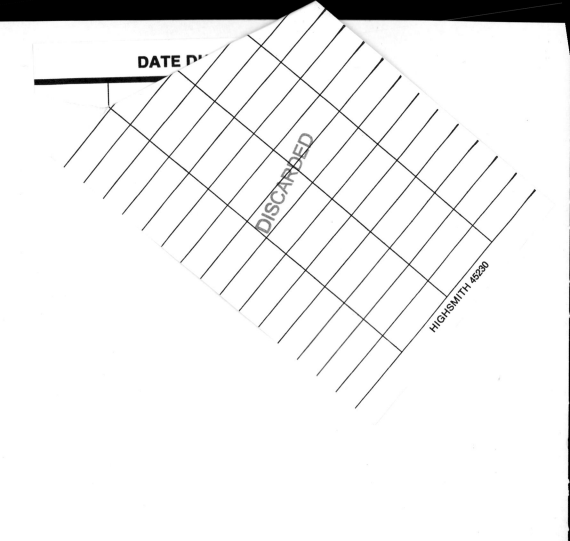

DATE DUE

DISCARDED

HIGHSMITH 45230